1: Paddle Pop
Rainbow ice
cream, 1990s.

PIM REINDERS

Licks, Sticks & Bricks

A World History of Ice Cream

PUBLISHED BY **UNILEVER**

ROTTERDAM 1999

Foreword

Ice cream generates an unparalleled
excitement and enthusiasm across the
world. Witness the children crowding
round South American ice cream carts;
teenagers jostling expectantly in Italian
ice cream parlours; the half-mile queue
for the first Häagen Dazs store in Tokyo;
the avid consumption in Russia as the
temperature hits −30°C; and the universal
rapture as the first lick signals surrender.
• Witness, too, the collectors of ice cream
paraphernalia, as obsessive as
train-spotters, prizing antique ice cream
packaging and merchandising material
as highly as Meissen ice pails, Tiffany silver scoops or glass 'penny licks'.
And the ice cream groupies, who
passionately contest the finer points of
the season's new flavours.
• The last 20 years have seen profound
changes in the global ice cream market.
Product quality has improved, with
gloriously self-indulgent products taking
pleasure to new levels. Manufacturing
ingenuity has created an incredible
spectrum of shapes, constructions and
flavours to delight children; while, for the
health-conscious, ice cream makers are
devising products that are just as delicious, but contain less fat and
sugar. This global market has
grown rapidly as the developing economies (often those without a
native dairy culture) have begun to enjoy
arguably the world's tastiest food.
As we at Unilever looked forward to the
new millennium, we realised that there

2: The Good
Humor Man,
Canada, 1963.

was no comprehensive history of this
fascinating subject, so we commissioned
the cultural historian Pim Reinders to
remedy matters.
• This book has taken just over two years
to complete. I would like to extend our
profound thanks to the scores of people
from dozens of companies, both friendly
and competitive, who have given us their
assistance as well as my personal appreci-
ation to the central team here, who have
worked so hard.
  Paul Jay, Editor

Contents

• = Box stories

Licks, Sticks & Bricks
A WORLD HISTORY OF ICE CREAM

Ice cream memories: an introduction

3: Beach scene at Bergen aan Zee, late 1930s.

4: Long Sunday walks through the dunes from Bergen to Bergen aan Zee in about 1957.

In 1956 there was just one ice cream shop in Bergen aan Zee. The summers in this village, a bathing resort on the west coast of the Netherlands, were invariably short and wet, so the shop was closed from September to May. In my childhood memory the shop was one long, white room, almost entirely filled by the sales counter. The ice cream was eaten standing up, as there was little room to sit.

• The shop was strategically located on a square such that all cyclists or walkers entering or leaving the village had to go past it. The same applied to the passengers who travelled to Bergen aan Zee on the small steam tram, 'Bello', since the tram terminus was in the square. Only the few visitors who came by car missed the shop – but car ownership was still not widespread in the Netherlands of those days.

• Eating an ice cream was a feast and a social activity, usually a treat for whole families or groups. Sometimes it was a reward after a long, Sunday walk from the inland village of Bergen to the seaside. An ice cream cost five, ten or fifteen cents and was scooped onto a small wafer or into a simple cone. As a rule, vanilla was the only flavour available, but every once in a while the shop's owner would produce – using the Italian ice cream machine installed behind the counter – a particular variation. This was called boerenjongens [country boys] and it was vanilla mixed with brandied raisins. One scoop cost fifteen cents and a slightly bigger portion cost twenty-five cents. I shall always remember the occasions when my father treated me to this speciality, not least because they were my childhood introduction to the taste of brandy.

• This youthful memory surfaced again during my research for this book. Scores of studies from dozens of countries showed that for many people eating an ice cream in childhood was predominantly associated with feelings of delight and happiness. Re-living those feelings whilst eating an ice cream as an adult is one of the many reasons why the product is so popular. The bell of the ice cream cart or the jingle played by the ice cream van; the refreshing taste of an ice lolly eaten at the side of a swimming-pool or while lounging in a deck-chair on the beach; the ice cream gâteau as the highlight of a birthday meal – these are all examples of the joy associated with eating ice cream.

Structure of the book

• This book, however, is not a compilation of personal, or even individual, recollections, but an attempt to chart, for the first time, the world history of ice cream. Most books about ices and ice cream are cookery books, but here you will find not a single recipe. The book's primary aim is to outline the cultural history of ice cream and its related business and industrial history. Some attention is devoted to the development of ice cream making techniques, but this is not a work for specialists, nor is it an encyclopaedia that describes all aspects of ice cream in all countries. The book comprises three main sections. The first describes the pre-industrial era of ice cream, which lasted until the end of the nineteenth century; the second mainly deals with the industrial period; and the third brings the story up-to-date and summarises the major themes of ice cream's long history.

• In the first section, the opening chapter describes the evolution from iced water to water-ice, a process that took several hundred years and was completed during the Renaissance. That was the point at which people mastered the freezing process of mixing ice or finely crushed snow with salt, so that they were able to make frozen ices. The first evidence of this dates from the late sixteenth century, which could reasonably be regarded therefore as the starting date for ice cream's history. In chapter two it is argued that the roles in ice cream history attributed in virtually all the literature[1] to Nero, Marco Polo and Catherine de' Medici are based on romantic myth.

• Chapter three describes the introduction and acceptance of ice cream among the nobility and haute bourgeoisie in seventeenth and eighteenth century Europe. It deals with the continuing spread of cookery books containing ice cream recipes and focuses on the production and use of tableware designed for the presentation or eating of ice cream. How ice cream found its way into the eating habits of other social groups in Europe, and its development in North America, are the subject of the fourth chapter, which shows how ice cream came to be sold in coffee houses, restaurants and on the street in the nineteenth century.

• The second and largest section deals principally with developments in the twentieth century, when the industrialisation of ice cream production, and its professionalised selling with the help of advertising and other forms of mass-media communication, turned ice cream into an everyday commodity accessible across societies and universally obtainable. Each chapter forms a self-contained story that ends in recent times and can be read independently of other chapters, to which cross-references have been included where appropriate.

• The first two chapters in this section (5-6) are about the United States, whose ice cream industry grew up in the second half of the nineteenth century. They are followed by a chapter on Australia (7), where an industry based on the American pattern was established in about 1905. Subsequent chapters (8-14) describe developments in the countries of Northern Europe, where mass production of ice cream first started on this continent; and then Southern Europe (15-17), whose colonial links and patterns of migration have left a clear mark on the history of ice cream in Latin America (18). The final chapters of this section (19-20) outline the introduction and advance of ice cream in Asia and Japan.

• In the third and final section, the first chapter (21) outlines the role of Unilever in the history of ice cream, as well as that of Nestlé and Mars. The following chapter (22), the final one of the book, looks at the world history of ice cream in terms of a continuous process of innovation.

Sources and working method

• Research for this book started in October 1996 and writing was completed at the beginning of November 1998. Although the book was commissioned by Unilever, the company histories covered do not relate solely to Unilever ice cream operations. The author was given freedom in the way the book was structured and in the conduct of his research. Artisanal ice cream making in various countries was just as much a subject for research as the history of the ice cream industry. The source material has been compiled in the broadest possible way, limited only by time constraints and the available resources.

• Writing the book was preceded by exploratory studies of the relevant literature, an analysis of potential source materials and an extensive series of interviews with specialists. Following this, it was decided to concentrate the research on Western Europe, the United States and Australia, adding Latin America and Asia at a later stage. With the exception of Russia and Israel, the Eastern Europe and Middle Eastern and African regions were covered to only a limited extent.

• For the first part of the book, covering the period up to the end of the nineteenth century, critical use was made of various written sources - both recent and much earlier. The references in literature, for example in eighteenth century French cookery books, were in many cases tracked down and corroborated. The resultant findings were included in the critical interpretation. In several instances an extensive exchange of views was held with a specialist and the critiques were intensively studied and discussed with other experts. In the case of the story concerning Catherine de' Medici, for example, contact was established with the author of the most recent biography and other leading studies of her life were consulted.

• The classicist Elvira van Eeten studied all original texts on the relevant themes by Greek and Roman authors. Research into the introduction, development and use of dessert services for ice cream was undertaken by the art historian Steven Braat. The commissioning of these studies and the incorporation of

their results are the responsibility of the author.

• For the description of developments in the twentieth century many archives were consulted as well as the relevant literature. Use was made of the central company archives of Unilever in Rotterdam, London and Port Sunlight. Ice cream businesses were also visited in Ireland, the United Kingdom, Sweden, Denmark, Germany, the Netherlands, Belgium, France, Italy, Spain, Israel, the United States and Australia. Nestlé also provided valuable documentation on the history of many ice cream companies. Where available, historical materials were examined on location; the sources included annual reports, company magazines, photographs, anniversary publications and advertising materials.

• An extensive questionnaire was sent out to other ice cream businesses and more than 100 interviews were held all over the world with managers and specialists, past and present, from the ice cream industry and the artisanal sector. The information gleaned from these interviews, although principally used as background information, was an important aid to interpreting archive documents and relevant literature. In a few cases oral information has been used as the sole source.

• Documents from the company archives of Gram, the Danish manufacturer of ice cream machines, were studied, as were those held in the archives of the Dutch Association of Ice Cream Manufacturers and a number of municipal and national archives in the Netherlands and Germany. Conversations were held with staff members, directors and specialists of trade associations in the United States, Japan, France, Spain, Denmark,

5: Ice cream memories from the Good Humor Man on Metropolitan
Avenue in Brooklyn, New York. On a fine afternoon in May 1932 he warns
the two girls to wait safely on the other side of the road while he brings
their ice creams across to them.

the Netherlands and Italy. Dr Christoph Heinz Gödeke was commissioned to undertake research in Japan, and his findings were incorporated by the author.

• French, Italian, Dutch, German, Danish, British and American trade journals were also consulted. The two leading American trade journals, The Ice Cream Trade Journal and The Ice Cream Review were a rich source of information, covering both ice cream history in the US and developments in other countries. On the basis of the initial outline for this book the relevant information from these journals was selected by the American historian Chris Shaffer. The history of ice cream in the Netherlands was researched by students of Dr Thera Wijsenbeek of the Department of Socio-Economic History at the University of Amsterdam, many of whose findings have been incorporated. Igor Bogdanov, a historian living in St. Petersburg, provided valuable information on Russia.

• In addition to written and oral sources, various materials and artifacts were studied to provide historical background. These included photographs, advertising materials, items of pottery, ice cream glasses, cutlery, ice scoops and ice moulds. As well as the publicly accessible collections, a few exceptional and extensive private collections were traced whose owners kindly made items available for more detailed study.

• These materials are not only important as historical sources, they also provide wonderful illustrations for the book. Over 600 illustrations have been included, some from the private archives and collections mentioned above and many others from libraries, museums and photographic archives all over the world.

- Fittingly enough in this age of technology, the final source used for my research was the Internet, including databases of historical filmed documentation.

Acknowledgements

- This book is the result of the cooperation, dedication, generosity and support of many people. The prime mover was Kees van der Graaf, Senior Vice President of Unilever's Ice Cream Category Team, who asked me in 1996 to write this book and gave me every latitude that an author could wish to have. His confidence and enthusiastic support throughout the project served as a great stimulus to me.
- Paul Jay, a member of the Ice Cream Category Team, chaired the working group that monitored the project's progress. Without his decades of experience and expertise in the ice cream industry and his rich international network of contacts, the research would not only have been much more difficult but would also have missed much. He was not only the coordinator of the project but also its editor, a task that he fulfilled with much verve and patience. The quality of the book has benefited immensely from the contribution he made. Jaap Winter, Sue Meeson and Ruth Partridge, as members of the Working Group, all made invaluable contributions, based on their legal, corporate and project management expertise. Dick Newman took over chairmanship of the Group in September 1998, guiding the project to completion with great spirit and professionalism.
- Ton Bannink, the archivist of Unilever's historical company archives in Rotterdam, and also a member of the working group, ensured in his own inimitable way that I could draw on the treasure-house of Unilever's past which he manages with such care and skill. His contribution, however, went much further; he regularly fulfilled the role of adviser and sounding board. Kim Prudon provided considerable help in accessing ice cream archives. René Trommelen, the company archivist of Unilever in Rotterdam, Jeannette Strickland and Tony Cole of the company historical archives in London and Gary Collins of the company historical archives in Port Sunlight kindly allowed me to consult the archives in their custody.
- Were it not for the great dedication shown in the provision of administrative, process and logistics support by Marianne Cool and her colleagues Nathalie Karreman, Nicolette den Haan and Anja van der Klift of the Ice Cream Category Team, this project would have been impossible. In addition, Mariëtte van der Elburg was exemplary in the way she handled the orders and copyright requests for hundreds of photos from all over the world. She also monitored the writing, translation and production process.
- The factor that ultimately decides whether a book like this will be successful is its design. Toni Mulder and Merel van Meurs have used their talent to great effect. As mentioned in the introduction, the art historian Steven Braat, the classicist Elvira van Eeten, the historian Chris Shaffer and the economist Dr Christoph Heinz Gödeke carried out research into particular areas. Their expertise and dedication made it a pleasure to work with them, while their findings ensured that the author achieved the book he had in mind.
- Similarly inspirational was the cooperation

provided by Dr Thera Wijsenbeek, of the Department of Socio-Economic History at the University of Amsterdam. Ten of her students researched various aspects of the history of ice cream in the Netherlands, aided by the courtesy of the Dutch Association of Ice Cream Manufacturers in agreeing to open its archives.

• More than 100 retired and current managers and experts from the ice cream industry, many but not all from Unilever companies, cooperated in providing the information on which this book is based. They gave of their time, openly and freely, in order to pass on their expertise and views and to answer my questions. Andrew T. Bradley, Senior Vice President of the ice cream business unit of Nestlé, kindly saw to it that questionnaires about a number of his group's ice cream businesses were answered. Nestlé also supplied documentation and photographic materials.

• I owe a great debt of gratitude to the London businessman and collector Robin Weir. His contacts and his input enriched the research enormously. He was not only prepared to make materials available from his collection and to share his great knowledge of the subject with me, his contagious enthusiasm was an inspiration. The collectors Herb Engel, Bill Stallings and Martijn Le Coultre also provided the most generous cooperation. As a result, it has been possible to illustrate this book with unique, previously unpublished pictures. Martijn Le Coultre was also the man who persuaded me a number of years ago to take an in-depth look at the history of ice cream.

• I am very grateful to the Sinologist Frances Wood, of London, for her advice on the alleged role played by Marco Polo in the history of ice cream. Professor Ullrich Hellmann of Mainz, Germany, kindly made available his research into the history of 'artificial cold'. I am likewise greatly indebted to Donna Panciera and to the Milanese author Fulco Portiani for their expert help in my research into the history of ice cream in Italy.

In Washington I received every cooperation from Tip Tipton, director of the International Ice Cream Association; and in France from Mme Jouillac, director of the Paris-based Confédération Nationale des Glaciers de France. Without the contribution of Remo Bertorelli in London, I could never have written the history of Kwality Ices in India. The same holds true for Ude Jr. from Hamburg, Werner Warncke from Bremen and Juan Rimblas from Madrid and the information they gave me about their ice cream businesses.

• A special word of thanks goes to Alan Hemingway, who translated the book into English. He completed this herculean task with a great sense of accuracy and dedication. Numerous foreign documents were made accessible to me by the translators Gerrit Delfstra (Spanish), Giulia Gerola (Italian), Gitte Möller (Danish), Andrea Voigt (Danish), Hans de Vries (Spanish), Karin Veldhuizen Wanrooi (Japanese) and Harry Weelinck (Swedish). Dr J.J. Witkamp, curator of the Oriental Collections of the University Library of Leiden, kindly translated an ancient Arabic text.

• For the correction of the Dutch text I was most agreeably assisted by the Dutch linguist Murk Salverda. The proofreading of the English edition was in the immensely capable hands of Tim Blackburn.

Pim Reinders, November 1998

Licks, Sticks & Bricks

A WORLD HISTORY OF ICE CREAM

From ice-water

to water-ice

6: Part of a wall tapestry of 1643 showing an ice harvest in Italy, possibly near Florence. The tapestry, almost six metres square, was commissioned by one of the Medicis and made by the Flemish carpet weaver Peter van Asselt on the basis of a design by Jacopo Vignali. It forms part of a series of four tapestries, each depicting one of the seasons.

Many myths and legends surround the origins of one of the world's best-loved delicacies, ice cream. The Roman emperor Nero (37-68 A.D.), for instance, is said to have eaten a sort of water-ice and there are claims that the Chinese have been making ice cream for centuries. Marco Polo (1254-1324), so the story goes, brought Chinese ice recipes back with him to Venice in 1296. If the tales are true, these recipes were subsequently introduced to the French court by Italian chefs in the retinue of Catherine de' Medici when she married Henri II of France in 1533. None of these stories mentions how the ice was made or what the recipes consisted of, nor is there any historical evidence to corroborate them.

• The early history of ice cream is complex. It is a story filled with etymological pitfalls and a confusing collection of concepts and terminologies (see box on p. 22). Its development involves Arab physicians, alchemists and other scholars who, via southern Spain, passed on to the West the culinary knowledge of antiquity and of the Orient. In Italy the first known treatises on the artificial cooling and freezing of water were published in the sixteenth century.

• The history of ice cream has been an evolution: from drinks cooled with ice and snow to semi-frozen lemonades; from water-ices to dairy ice cream; from ice cellars and snow-pits to the heat-extracting effect of adding salt to water and thence to refrigeration technology based on ammonia gas.

• Today, we can no longer imagine ice cream without refrigerators and freezers. But what was it like many hundreds of years ago,

when ice was eaten but no refrigerators existed? The first indications of the use of cooling techniques stem from ancient Mesopotamia, Egypt and China. In Ur, one of the chief cities of Mesopotamia (present-day Iraq), royal ice cellars were built on the banks of the Euphrates around 2000 B.C.[1] These early cellars took the form of simple pits covered with straw. In the winter months they were filled with ice from rivers and lakes or with snow from the mountains.

7: Exterior of the ice cellar of Courbeton, near the French city of Orléans. Litho by Victor Petit, Paris, 1854.

They were insulated with soil, straw or turf; in later times they were fitted with drainage systems. Until the nineteenth century ice cellars continued to be built almost everywhere in the world where ice was available. They varied from semi-underground huts to specially designed edifices built in classical style.[2] The ice or snow stored in this way was used for cooling wines and lemonades and for preserving foodstuffs.

• The 'harvesting' of ice is described in Chinese writings that date back to the eleventh century B.C. The book Etiquette of Zhou refers, for example, to the function of the iceman ('ling ren') at the Chinese court.

¶ There are any number of different terms for ices and ice cream, each reflecting its origin. Sometimes the same expressions have a different meaning in different languages or have changed meaning with the passage of time. The terms are often related either to various types of cold sweetened drinks or to the dairy world. That the former derivation is older than the latter can immediately be seen from the word sorbet (English, Dutch, German), sorbetto (Italian), sorbette (French) and sorbetes (Spain). The word stems from the Arabic word sharab or sarab, which refers to a cold, sweetened, non-alcoholic drink. After the discovery in the second half of the sixteenth century of the freezing process whereby salt was added to snow or ice, sweetened drinks in a semi-frozen state were sold on the streets. The ice crystals in these sorbets were still not frozen solid; this only happened later when people gained a better mastery of the process of ice preparation. Gradually, a new type of recipe emerged which differed from that of the original sorbets. Milk and cream were added to water that had been sweetened with sugar and fruits. The sorbet became more and more like an ice cream,

8: Sorbet, Dutch-style, 1998.

though it continued to be the term for a chilled sweet drink. In Turkey today, for example, sorbet or serbet (sherbet) is not associated with ice cream, but with ice-cold lemonade. On the other hand, someone who orders a sorbet today in an ice cream parlour in the Netherlands will usually be served a tall glass filled with (tinned) fruit, scoops of ice cream, lemonade and whipped cream, topped with a wafer. And in the United States the customer would give a quizzical glance if, after ordering a sorbet or sherbet, he received a cold lemonade; what he expects is an ice cream (with between 2% and 5% dairy fat, as prescribed by the Food and Drug Administration). In Italy a special word exists for the semi-frozen drink that consists of fruit, sugar and water: granita. It has a 'granular' texture because the crystals of water and sugar have still not frozen together to form a solid whole. The term granita is sometimes also used to describe a substance made of crushed or shaved natural ice over which lemonade syrup has been poured. In Asian countries this is still a popular product and is regarded there as a water-ice. Ice cream in Italy is called gelato. Italian ice creams traditionally had a more custard-like texture, containing more eggs and less cream and air than French ice creams. In America the situation is different again. Original American or Philadelphia ice cream contains cream and sugar, but no eggs and no milk. This makes the ice cream seem colder on the tongue, since it is the eggs which ensure that cream and sugar emulsify better with each other.[1] Anyone in eighteenth century France who ordered a neige (snow) from a waiter in a café would be served a frozen fruit juice. In Spain and Mexico the same applied: nieve meant more than just snow. The eighteenth century Frenchman could also order a fromage glacé.

This would not be a 'frozen cheese' as the literal translation might indicate, but something which we would today describe as an ice cream and which in France has meanwhile become known as a crème glacée (iced cream). Iced creams was also the description used in 1688 in a London newspaper to describe a dessert that was served in Stockholm during a dinner to celebrate the birth of James Francis Edward, Prince of Wales.[2]

9: Italian granita, 1998.

The Netherlands was the only country to refer to the ice cream as an ijsco. This strange word is an abbreviation of ijscompagnie, a typically Dutch expression to describe associations of confectioners who as long ago as 1916 banded together for the joint production and sale of ices. The fact that today some ice cream contains not dairy cream but vegetable fats will certainly have been noticed by anyone who has studied the ingredient lists on modern ice cream wrappers. Ice cream composition has always been subject to change. Only with the industrialisation of ice cream production in the twentieth century was any standardisation introduced.

After the Second World War, the constituent parts of ice cream became more closely regulated, at least in Europe and the USA. National governments stipulated the standards that ice cream or water-ice, and varieties such as milk ice, yoghurt ice cream or sugar-free ice cream, had to meet in order to qualify for such designations.

In the USA, it was not until 1997 that any product with a vegetable fat content was allowed to be called an ice cream. Before this it had to be called 'Mellorine' or designated a 'frozen dessert'.

At the time of the Zhou dynasty (1066-256 B.C.) this government official was in charge of the harvesting of ice from the rivers. Every year in December his subordinates chopped the ice blocks into pieces and stored them in the ice cellar. When spring arrived, bronze ice jars were made ready for use. They might contain any type of food or drink that was to be cooled for the imperial family or for making offerings to the gods. Guests were served small pieces of ice, while on hot summer days the emperor distributed ice to his courtiers. In the autumn the ice cellar was cleaned once more in readiness for the new winter supplies. The iceman had 94 subordinates including two to keep the books, two for other administrative work and eight to make copies of the accounts. The actual harvesting of the ice was done by slaves.

• Another famous source about Zhou culture, the Book of Songs, contains a verse

10: Richly ornamented Chinese bronze pot dating from between 475 B.C. and 221 B.C. The pot is from the grave of Zenghouyi in the Sui district of the southern Chinese province of Hubei and was used for storing food cooled with ice.

referring to the harvesting of ice: 'In the days of the Second they cut the ice with tingling blows. In the days of the Third they bring it in to the cold shed'.[3] (Here, Second means the month of December and Third the month of January.) In other poems, composed between 475 B.C. and 221 B.C., there are references to drinks cooled with ice, such as in the verse entitled Great Requiem:

'Four kinds of matured wine
Won't rasp on your throat fine, eh!
Do not drink to excess with cheer
The fragrant ice-cooled liquor clear, eh!'[4]

• Another centuries-old cooling method is that of evaporation. Water was stored in porous, thin-walled earthenware jugs. The jugs were kept wet on the outside and were exposed to the wind or fanned with air, so that the water would penetrate into the pores of the jug. In an environment with low relative humidity the water would then evaporate through the wall to the outside, thus extracting heat from the jug and cooling down the water inside the jug itself. This method is depicted on an Egyptian fresco dating from around 2500 B.C. showing several slaves busy fanning air at jars of wine.[5] In the second century B.C. the Greek historian Protagorides described how in Egypt jars were placed in the sun during the day and then stored at night in the highest point in the house, where slaves continually wetted them with water throughout the night. 'At dawn they take the jars downstairs, and again drawing off the sediment they thus make the water clear and in every way healthful. They then place the jars in heaps of chaff and thereafter use it without the need of snow or anything else whatever.'[6]

'A divine drink of white snow'

• Protagorides' observation reflects his surprise at how the Egyptians could serve cold water without snow. In the Greek world, people had been used to mixing their drinks with snow since at least the fifth century B.C. (a custom which continued to be widespread, for example in the Mediterranean region, Asia and Mexico, until the beginning of the twentieth century[7]). The poet Theocritus (310-245 B.C.) refers in his poem The Cyclops to 'a divine drink of white snow'.[8] The Greeks regarded snow as a commodity and it was on sale in the market in Athens.[9] It was placed direct into wine

beakers or was used to fill a toadstool-shaped cooling vessel ('psykter'). Double-walled amphoras were also used. Snow or water cooled by snow was put in the outer wall.[10] The use of snow is also evidenced by snow-pits that Alexander the Great (356-323 B.C.) ordered to be dug after his conquest of the Indian city of Petra in 325 B.C. According to the Greek historian and contemporary of Alexander, Chares of Mytilene, there were 30 such pits ('psycheia') dug and filled with snow. For insulation the pits were covered over with oak leaves.[11]

11: Marble head of the Roman philosopher Seneca. In letters to his friend Lucilius, Seneca writes of the use of ice blocks and snow in wine.

• The Romans, too, put snow in their wine. Unlike the Greeks, however, they also used ice. The philosopher Seneca (circa 5 B.C.-65 A.D.) writes in a letter to his friend Lucilius about the lack of appetite of a sick person. 'They say: "Oh, the poor sick man". Why do they say that? Because there is no snow in his wine? Because he has not refreshed his drink with broken pieces of ice?'[12]
• Wine mixed direct with snow in this way was filtered through a linen cloth or a special sieve before it was drunk.[13] In fact this was not the usual Roman method for cooling wine, which was to put the snow in a linen

12: Greek amphora, circa 550 B.C., height 40.2 cm. An amphora could be either single-walled or double-walled. In the latter case, snow or well cooled water could be inserted between the walls to keep the jar's contents cool. This amphora is painted with the figure of Dionysus, the Greek god of wine, surrounded by satyrs.

bag and then place the bag in a wine vessel. In Seneca's time snow was carried down from the Apennines by beasts of burden and stored in shops.[14] According to the Roman historian Pliny the Elder (circa 23-79 A.D.), Nero had come up with the idea that water that had been boiled froze faster and was healthier. Pliny the Elder was of the opinion that water was thus 'given the benefit of freshness without the adverse effects of snow'.[15]

• Nothing more is mentioned by the Roman sources: no mixing of ice or snow with honey, lemons or other fruits, no indication of anything that might resemble any sort of water-ice.[16] The nearest they come is in a letter of Pliny the Younger (circa 61-114 A.D.) that describes 'halica', a sort of porridge made from groats and flavoured with a mixture of wine, honey and snow.[17]

• In one of the few cookery books from antiquity, De Re Coquinaria, written in the first century A.D. by the Roman cook Apicius, there are several recipes for salads and sweet desserts which he recommends sprinkling with snow just before serving.[18] This custom survived for centuries. In 1533, a traveller from Venice reports seeing the inhabitants of Syria sprinkle snow over their dishes.[19]

13: Psykter, a toadstool-shaped cooling vessel developed by the Greeks, circa 520-500 B.C. Originally a rope passed through the handles on both sides of the jar. This could be used to suspend the jar in a barrel of snow so that its contents cooled down. The jar's special shape gave it improved floating properties. This psykter shows men dancing, including one playing a harp. Athenian, height 33 cm.

Ice-cold drinks with rhubarb

• In Persian culture the custom of cold, sweet drinks is centuries-old. According to the Greek physician Galen (130-210), people in his times drank sakanjabin, a syrup made of honey, vinegar and herbs. Also popular were sherbets, a sort of sugar-water cooled with ice or snow, flavoured in various ways. In the vicinity of Nishapur, in north-eastern Persia, these sherbets were commonly mixed with rhubarb, which is very popular in this region.[20] Excavations at Nishapur have brought to light many superbly

14: Roman coin with the head of the emperor Nero (37-68 A.D.). According to Pliny the Elder (circa 23-79 A.D.), Nero came up with the idea that boiled water cooled with snow froze better and was healthier than a glass of cooled unboiled water.

worked drinking glasses and pot-bellied bottles of polished glass with long, narrow necks dating from the tenth century A.D.[21] The shape of these Persian bottles is like that of the tin and copper bottles that were used in India, Afghanistan and Turkey for the cooling of drinks.

15: Ice house near Sirjan in Persia, photographed in 1975 by the English researcher Elisabeth Beazly. Behind the ice house stand the ruins of a wall which shielded the ice house from the sun. In the shadow of walls like these the centuries-long custom in Persia was to dig shallow pits which, filled with water, froze in the cold desert night. The ice was then harvested and stored in the ice house.

• Also in the tenth century, the Persian Daqiqi wrote in his Book of the Kings:

Water and ice, behold within a glass
How candle-bright all three do shine; but see
The twain will fuse, yet one a frozen
mass/Remains.

One hue, one lustre have these three'.[22] Whether the phrase 'yet one a frozen mass/Remains' can be interpreted as meaning that a residuum of ice was somehow

engineered is doubtful. Certainly the Persians of the time made ingenious use of the freezing cold of the desert night to make ice. They built very tall crescent-shaped walls, the concave face of which faced north. In front of them, small, shallow pits were filled with water which froze during the night. In the morning the ice was collected, placed in deep pits and covered with straw. The shadow of the wall ensured that the ice pits were not exposed to full sunlight.

• A similar production method for ice, but without the use of walls, was still in use in the winter months in India in about 1830.[23] As well as methods involving the use of snow, ice cellars, evaporation in porous jugs

16: Engraving from 1850 showing
two ice houses (left) and rows of
small, shallow ice pits near Alla-
habad, India. Men are filling the
pits with water, to freeze overnight.

and shallow pits of water that froze in the desert night, another way of cooling was developed that would ultimately form the basis for the modern-day manufacture of ice. If water is mixed with salt, saltpetre or alum (a double sulphate of aluminium and potassium), a reaction is triggered which reduces the temperature of the water (see box on p. 31). One of the oldest and most famous works of Indian literature, the fourth century epic poem Pancatantra, contains the line 'The water is cold if it contains salt', the first ever reference to this cooling method according to the German physicist and expert in refrigeration technology, Rudolf Plank, in his standard work Handbuch der Kältetechnik (1954)[24].

• Thirteen centuries later, Western trav-

ellers to India were reporting the widespread use of the same practice. In a letter from New Delhi in 1663, for example, the French doctor François Bernier described how the rich used saltpetre to cool their drinks. 'They put their drinks in tin bottles', wrote Bernier, 'and rotate these bottles in a vessel of water to which saltpetre has been added'.[25] The salt water extracts heat from the contents of the bottles and, although the fluid in the bottle does not really freeze in this method, the resulting cold beverage will certainly have been refreshing in the sweltering heat of Delhi.

• The oldest document in which the process involving water and salt is described in detail is an Arabic medical work, Kitab Uyan al-Anba fi Tabqat al-Atibba ('The book of the

I   v ⠀M

¶ If you place ordinary kitchen salt in water, it dissolves. But there are a great many other types of salt: saltpetre, alum, soda, sal-ammoniac and so on. [Alum is itself a mixture of two salts: aluminium sulphate and potassium sulphate.] Not all salts dissolve equally quickly in water; however, as they dissolve, all salts extract heat from the water. The observation that 'the water is cold if it contains salt' – a line from the famous Indian epic poem, Pancatantra – is perfectly true. If heat is extracted from water, its temperature drops. The amount of heat extracted and the resulting water temperature will depend on the type and quantity of salt that is added. For example, a mixture of 5 parts sal-ammoniac, 5 parts saltpetre to 16 parts of water will reduce the temperature from +10°C to -12°C. A bottle of pure water placed in this solution will also cool as the solution extracts heat from the bottle. The water it contains will freeze naturally- when its temperature falls below 0°C.

Water sweetened with sugar and fruit is more difficult to freeze than pure water because it has a lower freezing point. It is there-fore necessary to extract more heat in order to lower the

temperature of the salt solution that much further. If the salt is first mixed with snow, then the starting temperature is already no more than 0°C (or the snow would melt). The temperature of the mixture of snow and kitchen salt can thus be lowered as far as -20°C, enough to freeze a mixture of fruit in a solution of sugar. The cooling effects of salts in water were first noted in an Arab book in the eleventh century. In the experiment 'good Yemenite alum' was used.[1] The cooling effects of salt in snow were only mentioned some 500 years later, in an Italian treatise of 1530.[2] After that came a period during which the freezing effects were further studied by means of trial and error without any proper measuring instruments. The study of the subject became much more accurate when thermometers were developed towards the end of the seventeenth century.

The next advance stemmed from the realisation in the seventeenth century that ice crystals would combine better if eggs were added to the ice mix. Ice (cream) was prepared in tin boxes which were placed in a barrel of snow or ice. Salt was then added to the snow or ice; and as sugar- and ice crystals formed on the inside of the tin, they would be scraped off with a spatula and mixed to form a smooth, cold mass. This means of preparation remained in use for a long time, even after the introduction of mechanisation in the twentieth century.

17: Lithograph, circa 1500, showing a married couple playing cards, by the German artist Israël Meckenhem (1450-1503). In the foreground is a bowl in which a glass and a jug containing drink are being cooled in a saline solution. Louvre, Paris.

information sources of the categories of physicians'), published in 1242 by a doctor named Ibn Abi Usaybi'a. In a paragraph entitled 'Description of the freezing of water' (or: 'Description of making water into ice' [26]) the author cites the work of a certain Ibn Bakhtawayh, who in about 1029 had written Kitab al Muqadditmat ('The Book of Premises'), a work since lost in which he explained his method. He 'took one pound of good Yemenite alum and crushed it thoroughly to powder, then put it in an earthenware jar and added six pounds of water and then placed this in a baking oven and covered it with clay until two-thirds had evaporated and one-third was left over and reduces no further, as it has become hard.

18: Indian man cooling two bottles of water. Holding the bottles by their long necks, he rotates them in a tub filled with water and saltpetre. Illustration by an artist in Mushidabad, Bengal, 1790.

Then it is put in a bottle whose opening is well sealed and if you then want to work with it, you take a new vessel containing clean water. Put into the water ten mithqâl of the water that has been treated with the alum. Leave this to stand for an hour and it becomes snow'.[27] (The mithqâl is a basic unit of Islamic weight measurement, one mithqâl being about 4.5 grams[28]).

• Although Ibn Abi Usaybi'a introduced the text of Ibn Bakhtawayh with the words 'the freezing of water', the end-result is not in fact ice, but snow. The freezing capacity of water containing alum depends very much on the mix ratio. The more alum in the water and the better the heat conductivity of the material from which the bottle is made, the greater the heat-extracting effect. In the experiment described by Ibn Bakhtawayh the water froze to form ice crystals, but still did not constitute solid ice. Knowledge of the process may have reached the Arabs from India. All sorts of contacts existed between the two cultures in the early Middle Ages.

As well as for ice and snow, the salt-and-water process also formed the basis for ice-cold drinks sweetened with sugar and fruits, which the Arabs called sharab and the Turks serbet (sorbet). Dating from about the same time as Ibn Bakhtawayh's text is a manuscript describing such drinks discovered in Spain. An anonymous Arabic text, it is untitled but is referred to as The book of sorbets.[29] It is a work of 115 pages devoted entirely to the preparation of sorbets and sugar confectionery. One of the recipes is for a 'sorbet of fresh roses'. Besides one pound of sugar, the list of ingredients includes one pound of rosebuds. These are to be steeped in warm water and then left to stand for a day and a night until the rosebuds have dissolved. Then the liquid is to be reduced together with the sugar until it acquires 'the texture of sorbet'. The author claims that his recipe makes a good medicine against dropsy, a weak stomach and ailments of the liver and other internal organs.[30] Almost 700 years later, when the first cookery books with ice recipes were published in Paris and Naples, rose water-ice would find a permanent place in the repertoire, albeit without the medical claims (see chapter 3).[31]

Ice cream, a Chinese invention?

In 1242, as Ibn Abi Usaybi'a was publishing his work containing the description of the water-and-salt cooling method, Mongol horsemen were nearing the gates of Vienna, fresh from inflicting a crushing and bloody defeat near Wahlstadt in Saxony on an army of Knights of the Teutonic Order and Polish soldiers. The events shocked the Western Christian world. A papal concilium was held in Lyons to discuss the Mongol threat. In 1245 Pope Innocent IV decided to despatch a diplomatic mission to the Mongol rulers, led by the Franciscan Giovanni Piano Carpini. His mission was to find out as much as possible about the Tartars, as the Mongols were known in the Middle Ages. Carpini succeeded in meeting the Mongol chakan (chieftain), recording his observations in his book Historia Mongolorum of 1247. Subsequently many men of the cloth took the same route; the first bishop arrived in Peking in 1307.

These developments accelerated the contact between the Western world and distant China, providing the context in which the Venetian merchant Marco Polo (1254-1324) started out on his journey to China in 1271. Polo, then seventeen years old, was travelling in the company of his father and uncle. Whether he really got as far as China is seriously doubted by modern experts (see box on p. 35).[32] Nevertheless, most histories of ice cream ascribe a leading role to Marco Polo: on his return to Venice in 1296, he is said to have brought with him the first ice recipes from China and thus to have introduced the eating of ice cream to Europe.

It is this assertion that underlies the assumption that the roots of ice cream lie in China. Yet there is no historical evidence to support this. Marco Polo's report on his travels, Divisament dou Monde (Description of the World), contains not a single word about ice or ice cream; and his name is nowhere associated with the eating of ice cream until late in the nineteenth century. The travel report, noted down in a French dialect in 1298 by the author Rustichello of Pisa and based on the story as told orally by Marco Polo, only mentions kumiss, a drink

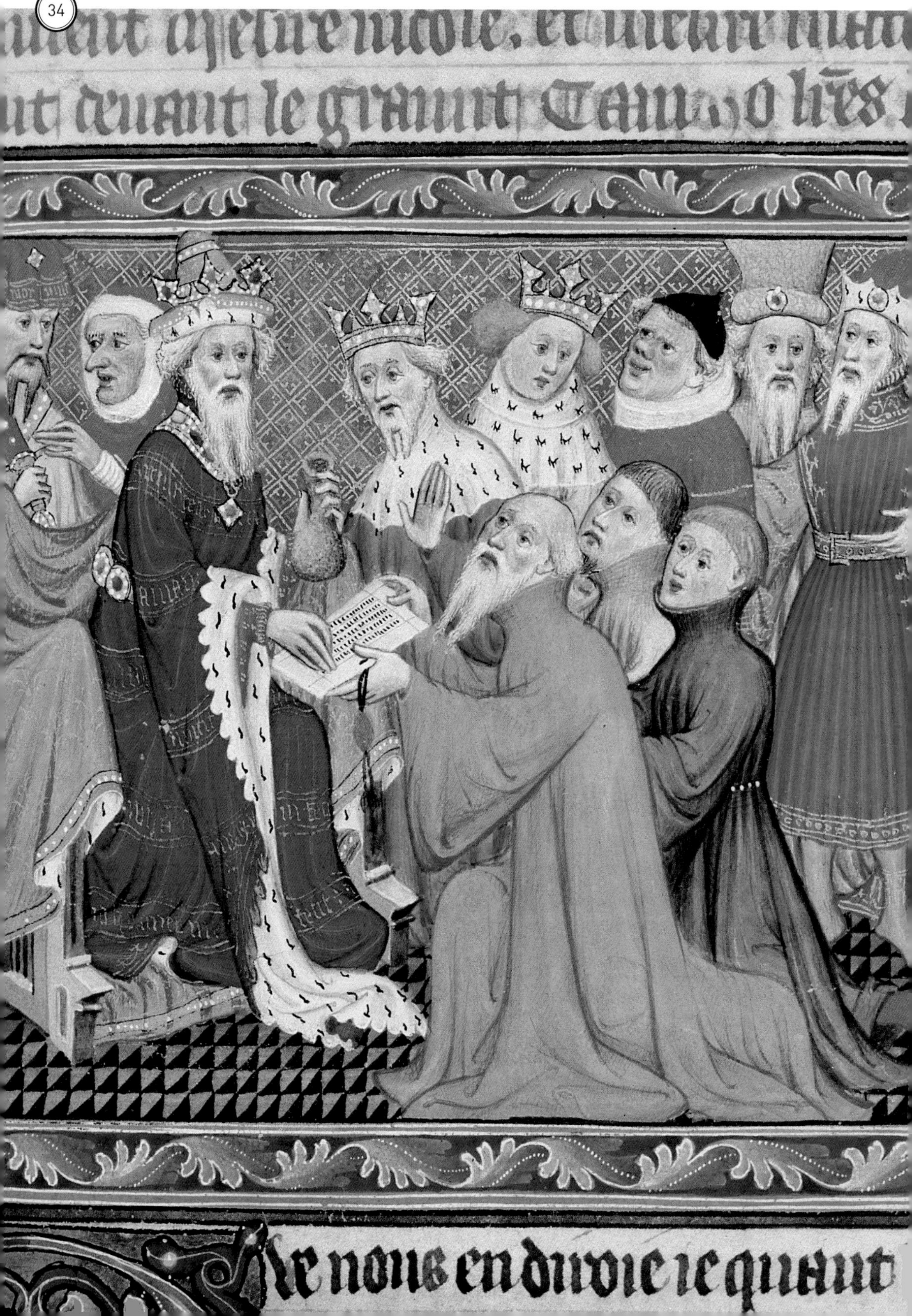

Did Marco Polo bring back ice cream from China?

¶ In 1298 the Venetian merchant Marco Polo (1254-1324) was languishing in a Genoese prison in the company of the writer Rustichello of Pisa. To pass away the time, the one told stories, the other wrote them down. Thus was born one of the most famous travel accounts in Western literature, Description of the World, a report of Marco Polo's travels and his stay in China from 1271 to 1295, which Rustichello noted down in one of the dialects of medieval France. The reliability of this record has been doubted by experts for many centuries.[1] In 1995 all these doubts were examined by the London Sinologist Frances Wood in her book Did Marco Polo go to China?

The original manuscript of Marco Polo's travelogue has been lost. The manuscript that is generally regarded as the oldest is the Bodley manuscript, which dates from around 1400, some 75 years after Marco Polo's death. The story is contained in one volume which together with two other narratives runs to 58 folios, including 38 illustrations. These facts are significant when evaluating whether Marco Polo was dictating from first-hand knowledge or whether he had heard accounts from others and was simply retelling them. If the latter, the authenticity of his story would be considerably impaired, for all the invaluable picture it paints of thirteenth century China.

This issue is an important one for the history of ice cream, since legend has it that Marco Polo brought ice recipes back with him from China, making China the birthplace of ice cream. However, none of the manuscripts of Polo's story makes any mention of ice or ice cream and there are few pointers in China itself to suggest that anything like ice cream was eaten at that time.

There are many other considerations to be taken into account when assessing the authenticity of Polo's account. In his reports, for example, there is no mention of the Great Wall of China, the Chinese art of printing books, eating with chopsticks or the drinking of tea. Moreover, the provenance of each manuscript is of great importance. Some 150 exist, written in a great number of languages. Often, selected editions are taken as a basis for analysis, leading to arguments that lack rigour. The first printed publications date from the end of the fifteenth century. Compared to the Bodley manuscript, most of the later versions contain more pages and have been expanded to include many extra details and new stories. They also mention events which occurred only after Polo's death. Furthermore, though it does give correct Arabic and Persian designations, the oldest Polo manuscript contains few Chinese names. Although the language spoken at the Mongol court where Polo is said to have stayed was not Chinese but Mongolian (as well as Persian), the absence of names in the local language is remarkable from a man claiming to have travelled around China for some twenty years. These and other arguments have led experts to conclude that Marco Polo's book is more likely to be a compilation of Persian and Arabic sources and traditional stories than a report based on personal experience. It appears, sadly, that Marco Polo himself never actually got to China, where ice cream in any case appeared only several hundred years later.

19: Illustration of around 1400 from a French manuscript of Marco Polo's Description of the World. The picture shows the Polos offering a letter from the Pope to the Mongol ruler Kublai Khan. The original manuscript of Marco Polo's story from 1298 has been lost. Whether the Polos actually reached China is disputed.

made from fermented mare's milk. The Franciscan Willem van Roebroek, who visited China between 1253 and 1255 at the behest of the French king Louis IX, describes kumiss as a drink whose appearance was such 'that you would take it for white wine'.[33] Nor do the many eye-witnesses who journeyed to China after Marco Polo make any reference to anything resembling ice cream.[34]

• For a very long time milk, the ingredient that differentiates ice cream from water-ice, did not feature in the popular Chinese diet and even today consumption of dairy products is low. Its introduction took place during the Tang dynasty (618-907). Even then, milk provided by carabaos (domesticated water buffaloes) only became popular among the upper echelons of the population. Dating from the same era is a cake prepared from mare's milk, sago and camphor, which was cooled to a low temperature before being eaten.[35]

• Another milk-based dish was kaymah, a curdled, thick cream mixed with honey. At the time of the Tang dynasty this was a much-loved dish, particularly in the north of China. Just as during the Zhou dynasty (1066-256 B.C.), extensive use was made during the Tang era of ice cellars and ice pails.[36] But this was still not ice cream. A verse by the poet Yang Wanli (1127-1206), which refers to a milk-like substance 'that looks congealed yet still seems to float' and that 'melts like snow in the light of the sun', seems to come closer to ice cream,[37] although it may be only describing kaymah cooled with ice.

• As for the technology required to make ice cream, not one reliable historical source exists to indicate usage of the salt-and-water freezing method. Some six centuries after Yang Wanli, the Jesuit Dominique Parennin (1665-1741) gave a demonstration at the court of Emperor Khang-Hsi of the freezing effect of saltpetre, adding it to a bowl of snow in a dish. The water in the dish froze and his audience – two ministers and ten members of the Han-Lin Academy – was deeply impressed.[38] Parennin had made use of a French dissertation published on this subject in 1716, a thesis that was by no means the first publication on this particular topic in the Western world.[40]

Naples: the cradle of ice cream

• The first book in the Western world to mention the cooling effect of salt in water was published in 1530. Entitled *Problemata Aristoteles*, it was written by the Italian scholar Marco Antonio Zimara, who was affiliated to the University of Padua, one of Europe's oldest universities and the scientific centre of the Renaissance.

• Not long afterwards, in 1550, the Spanish physician Blas Villafranca, who practised in Rome, published his book, *Methodus Refrigerandi ex vocato salnitro vinum acquamque*, which included a much more extensive explanation of the effects of salt in water. He instructed his readers on how they could cool their wine and water using the new method and makes it clear that in Rome this means was already being used by both high-born and ordinary citizens.[40] Similarly, the Dutch physician Levinius Lemnius (1506-1568) explained in his *Occulata Naturae Miracula*, published in 1559, how you could prevent a cask of wine from being spoiled by placing it in a container of cold water 'and then put in Saltpetre, and it will so cool the wine that your teeth can hardly endure it'.[41]

• Of greater importance for the history of ice cream, however, are experiments that were conducted at around the same time in Naples, which since 1442 had formed part of the Spanish empire. These experiments may have made use of scientific knowledge from antiquity, as recorded by the Arabs in Spain, which included a knowledge of cooling techniques. In 1589 the Naples-based natural scientist Giambattista Della Porta (1535-1615) published a new and expanded edition of his principal work, Magia Naturalis. When studying this edition, the English culinary expert Elizabeth David came across a previously unnoticed description of a method for freezing wine in a glass.[42] 'The chief thing desired at Feasts,' says Della Porta as quoted by Elizabeth David, 'is that wine cold as ice may be drunk, especially in Summer.' He achieved this by rotating a bottle of watered-down wine in a tub of snow to which saltpetre had been added. The result was a wine 'that you cannot drink except by sucking and a drawing in of your breath.'[43]

• Even so, a laboratory experiment with diluted (semi-frozen) wine still does not represent a water-ice. To freeze water that has been sweetened with sugar and fruit, a much lower temperature is required than for diluted wine. Della Porta's attempt was however an important step in the right direction, paving the way for further experiments which culminated in the production of real iced desserts during the course of the seventeenth century. The first clue that the new cooling technique had found its way to

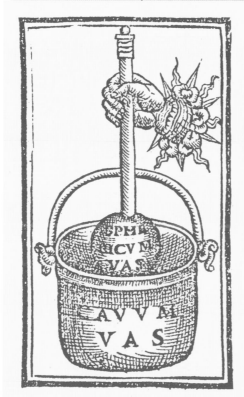

20: Engraving taken from Methodus Refrigerandi, published in 1550 by the Spanish physician Blas Villafranca, who practised in Rome. In his book Villafranca gives a comprehensive description of the cooling effects of saltpetre in water.

the dining-table can be found in a novel, entitled Argenis, that was published in 1621. The book was written by the Scot John Barclay, who at the time of his death that same year was an ambassador to Rome, having also served as secretary to King James I. In his novel Barclay describes a summertime meeting in North Africa between the characters Juba and Arsidas. Juba, the host, serves 'apples encased in shells of clear, shining ice' and says to Arsidas: 'When you entered the Garden, these Apples were hanging on the Tree, and the Water, that now is Ice, came out of the Spring.' After showing the astonished Arsidas metal moulds in which the apples were frozen, Juba tells him exactly how this was done: in a tub filled with snow that had been mixed with saltpetre.[44]

21: Print depicting the Italian physicist Giambattista della Porta. In 1589 della Porta published a book in Naples in which he described how he had frozen a glass of wine using snow mixed with saltpetre.

22: Illustration of an ice cellar from Robert Boyle's New Experiments & Observations touching Cold, London, 1683. In it the physicist who gave us Boyle's Law describes an ice cellar or 'snow pit' based on Italian examples. The pit is more than seven metres wide and fifteen metres deep. and is filled to the top with ice or hard-packed snow. At the bottom of the pit a wooden grating allows melt-water to drain off.

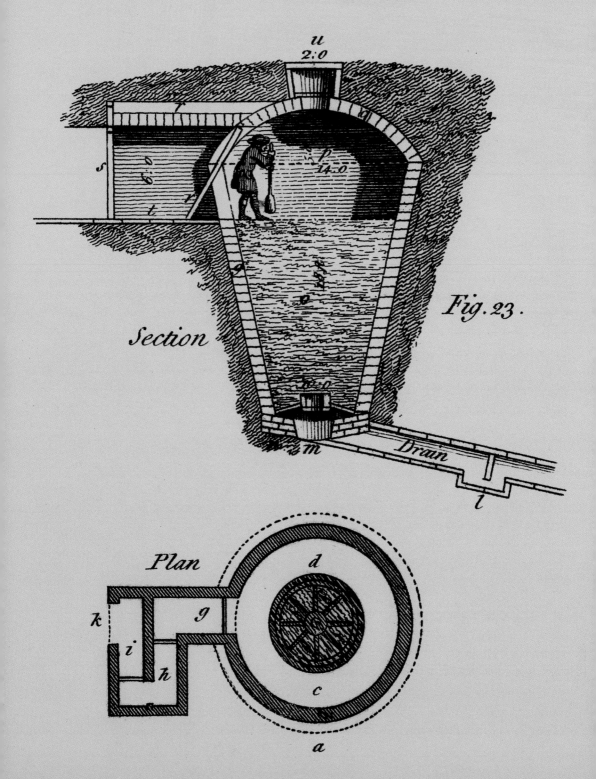

I C E House

Section

Fig. 23.

Plan

23: Cross-section and floor plan of an ice cellar, England, 1819. Just above the drain is a cartwheel, which ensures that the ice does not end up there. The floor plan shows how access to the ice in the cellar was closed off by double inside doors. This 'airlock' served to prevent warm air from entering the cellar.

• Two years after Barclay's novel was published, Antonio Frugoli attended a feast in Rome to celebrate the Assumption of the Virgin Mary. It was the warmest of summer days and the table was decorated with a mountain of ice containing various frozen fruits. (He was served a similar frozen delicacy in 1625 at a dinner in the royal palace in Madrid). Frugoli gives extensive descriptions of these and a whole range of other dinners in his book Pratica e Scalcaria, published in Rome in 1631, which deals with the art and practice of a skilled court steward.[45]

Although only ten of the dinners that Frugoli describes in his book include what was then known as an 'ice banquet', it is clear that by the middle of the seventeenth century artificially frozen fruits and water-ices were beginning to feature in festive evening meals given by the nobility and the court.

• Ice-water had become water-ice and was soon to become ice cream. In 1676 Pierre Barra, a doctor in Lyons, wrote in his treatise L'usage de la glace, de la neige et du froid of the way people in Italy and Spain 'mixed fruit with cream and sugar and put it in glazed earthenware jars or in glasses and then froze it with snow and saltpetre so that they could then eat it in an icy-cold condition'.[46]

1661: a Florentine marriage feast with iced fruit

• During the festivities that took place in Florence in June 1661, ice with fruit was seen as normal, as one of the array of desserts.

The city was excited by the marriage of Prince Cosimo de' Medici to Princess Marguérite-Louise of Orléans, for it held echoes of another Florentine-French marriage, more than a century before. In 1533 Catherine de' Medici had given her marriage vows to Henri, the Duke of Orléans and the second son of King Francis I (1515-1547). Legend has it that her retinue included ice cream makers (see box on p. 42).

• Now, in 1661, the latest Medici-Orléans marriage was being celebrated in Florence. On the afternoon of 10 June Cardinal Carlo de' Medici, the great-uncle of the bridegroom, gave a light dinner, a merenda, in honour of the newly-weds. Only the very best was served: Parma hams, chocolate from the Spanish colonies, oysters, cheeses, pâtés, pigeons, drinks, fruit, fruit compôtes, sugar confectionery, truffles, marzipan, nougats – a total of 35 separate dishes, presented on silver salvers and platters. And following the new fashion, there were also iced fruits, presented in pyramids more than 50 centimetres high.

• Meanwhile, in France, the court was being acquainted with ice preparation through the limonadier and chef, Audiger. He had learnt how to make it in Rome in 1659 (see chapter 3). Not long after, the first ice recipes appeared in print. In 1674 d'Emery, the apothecary of the French king, Louis XIV, published his Recueil de Curiositez Rares et Nouvelles in Paris. In it was a recipe for a water-ice made from strawberries, cherries and other fruits.[47] After centuries ice-water had become water-ice and the latest craze at the French court. The next decades would see water-ice develop into ice cream and become fashionable among aristocracy all over Europe.

¶ The fleet of sixty ships, one with gold-embroidered purple sails, which anchored in the harbour of Marseilles on 12 October 1533 offered a colourful spectacle. The royal ship had carried Catherine de' Medici from Florence to the French port to marry Henri, Duke of Orléans and second son of King Francis I. The city of Marseilles was decked out in its most sumptuous finery. Suspended from the balconies were costly, embroidered velvet tapestries, while the streets were overarched with garlands of deep-pink damask roses and French lilies.

The Florentine guests rode through the city in a splendid cavalcade. The procession was headed by Henri on a white horse with white reins and bridle led by two equerries also dressed in white. This steed, carrying the host who had been consecrated by the Pope, was immediately followed by the Pope himself, Clement VII, seated on a throne borne by lackeys. His Holiness – Catherine's uncle – was escorted by a lengthy train of cardinals and bishops on horseback. At the back of the grand procession rode the bride-to-be, dressed in a gown of gold brocade.

On 28 October, in Marseilles Cathedral, the Pope performed the marriage ceremony between the fifteen year-old Catherine and Henri.[1] For Catherine, this was the start of a lonely period in the shadow of a court which was constantly on the move. Henri was not the Crown Prince, but second in line to the throne. Moreover, Henri was infatuated with Diane de Poitiers, who had been his mistress since 1538, and seldom spent time in the company of his wife.

In 1547 Catherine's position improved when on Francis' death, predeceased by his eldest son, she became Queen of France. Diane de Poitiers continued to be

24: Portrait of Catherine de' Medici (1519-1589) by Corneille de Lyon.

Henri's favourite, however, and it was only after his death in 1559 that Catherine, acting as regent for the young son who was to become Charles IX, gained real influence.

Why dwell in so much detail on the ups and downs of Catherine's life? Because in almost all essays and publications on the history of ice cream, in culinary encyclopaedias and in many historical works, the introduction of ice cream in France is attributed to Catherine. Yet in 1891 Pellegrino Artusi, author of the famous standard work on Italian cuisine, La scienza in cucina e l'arte di mangiar bene, declared himself unable to authenticate the claim, despite making every effort to establish the truth.[2] In addition to ice cream, Catherine is said to have introduced numerous other culinary novelties into France. In her train, it is claimed, came a whole army of cooks and other servants of Lucullus who lay the foundations of French cuisine. Again, however, historical sources provide not a shred of evidence to back these assertions.[3] In her first 26 years at the French court, Catherine's influence was so slight that she would simply not have had the authority within the royal household to replace the French chefs with Italians, as legend would have us believe.[4] And, as far as ice cream is concerned, it should also be noted that the procedure of artificial freezing using ice or snow mixed with salt was in Catherine's day known only to a handful of scholars in Italy. In 1574 another of her sons acceded to the French throne as Henri III (1551-1589). A satirical book about the customs at his court, L'Isle des Hermaphrodites, written by A. Thomas d'Embry, was published in 1605. In this

portrayal of morals and customs the use of ice is mentioned in two places, both relating to the use of ice to cool wine and fruit.[5] To explain the origin of Catherine's alleged position in culinary history, the American historian Barbara Ketcham Wheaton quotes in her study of the history of French cuisine, Savoring the Past, a fragment from the famed Encyclopédie of Diderot and d'Alembert from 1754: 'The Italians were the principal inheritors of the debris of Roman cookery, so it was they who made the French acquainted with the art of dining well, the excesses of which so many of our kings attempted to suppress. But finally it triumphed in the reign of Henry II, when cooks from beyond the mountains came and settled in France, and that is one of the least debts we owe to that crowd of corrupt Italians who served at the court of Catherine de' Medici.'[6] In the nineteenth century this probably inaccurate view of Catherine de' Medici's culinary role was reiterated and popularised by many writers. A romantic fiction thus became entrenched and was subsequently presented as fact in authoritative studies.[7] In 1893 we find the French trade journal for confectioners, Le Journal des Confiseurs, referring to a recipe for apricot ice as 'la glace

Médicis' (the ice of the Medici).[8] Italian ice cream makers, who fanned out all over the world in the latter part of the nineteenth century in particular, carried the ice legend of Catherine with them and so the myth passed as truth. The story may also have gained support from misunderstanding of the word sorbet. At the time of Catherine de' Medici the term was used as a general name for a cold drink. Only after the development during the seventeenth century of the technical ability to freeze lemonades, by using snow and salpetre or natural ice and salt, did the word sorbet come to denote the solid icy dessert rather than a cold liquid drink.

Ices for kings, emperors and admirals

The date is 11 July 1674. We are guests at Versailles on the second evening of a gargantuan feast of the kind that only the French King Louis XIV (1638-1715) can give. Princes, dukes, counts and other members of the French aristocracy, secretaries, ministers, intendants, marshals, generals, cardinals and diplomats from all over Europe, as well as writers, artists and other talents are enjoying the endless series of delicacies prepared for His Majesty and his guests by the hundreds of officers of the Office de Bouche – the 'cold' kitchen. On a gigantic table, a hundred dozen small porcelain bowls and trays, filled with confitures, pastries and fruit, together with an enormous structure of candied sugar, cover almost the entire table. Candles in crystal candlesticks illuminate the dishes, revealing large numbers of crystal glasses filled with coloured water-ice and liqueurs. Violin and woodwind players perform a sweet melody.[1]

• This festive evening – the second in a series of five – was held to celebrate the conquest of the Franche-Comté region by the French army and was at the same time a demonstration of the absolute power and grandeur of the then 36 year-old Sun King. The presence of eau glacée (water-ice) on such festive tables may still have been a luxury at Versailles in 1674, but it was no longer exceptional. During a royal feast in 1668, crystal goblets filled with

26: Engraving by J. le Pautre of a feast at Versailles given in 1668 by Louis XIV (1638-1715). Pictured in the centre is a stand on which all sorts of desserts such as fruit and confitures are displayed.

27: Engraving by J. le Pautre of a banquet held in the 'small park' at Versailles in 1668, part of a large-scale feast given by Louis XIV. Water-ice was served to the guests in crystal and porcelain goblets and dishes and displayed alongside other delicacies such as confitures, gâteaux and fruit. Goblets and dishes filled with desserts can be seen at the end of a tray immediately to the right of the fountain.

25: King Louis XIV, painted in 1701 by Hyacinthe Rigaud. From 1674, water-ice was a regular feature of the sumptuous banquets thrown by the Sun King at Versailles.

water-ice had also been served.[2] To judge by the treatise La maison reglée by the French confiturier and distillateur Audiger, published in 1692, Louis XIV had probably been served water-ices as early as 1662.[3]

• Audiger had learnt how to prepare water-ices during a fourteen-month stay in Rome. In January 1661 he had presented the King with fresh garden peas he had brought with him from Italy. This novelty was much appreciated by the King and provided Audiger with a successful entry to court circles. Thereafter he served a number of prominent members of the nobility and was regularly asked to add lustre to royal feasts and banquets by supplying confitures, liqueurs and ices.[4]

• In his book of 1692 Audiger explains how he got his ices to freeze using a mixture of ice and salt. After a series of recipes for lemonades, he describes the freezing process. 'The manner of freezing each of the above waters is to put three, four or six containers (boîtes), or other vessels according to their size, in a tub, at one finger's distance from each other', writes Audiger. 'Then you take the ice, which you pound well, and salt it when it is pounded, and promptly put it in the tub all round your boxes, until the tub is full and the boxes covered. For a tub of this kind in which there are to be five or six boxes, and to freeze them rapidly and well, two litrons (about 24 ounces)[5] of salt are needed'. After half to three-quarters of an hour, explains Audiger, the mix in the containers must be whisked so that it will freeze like snow. After this, the containers must be placed back in the mixture of ice and salt and left there until serving.[6]

• Audiger also explains in his book how ice can be frozen in metal moulds in the shape of a pyramid. At banquets this creates 'a most beautiful effect'. The ice required for freezing Audiger's eaux glacées was readily available thanks to the construction of ice cellars at Versailles and at other French royal palaces. The first ice cellars at Versailles, built to keep ice harvested from lakes and rivers in the winter, date from 1664[7] (see also chapter 2).

The spread of French culinary culture

• In 1692 another book with recipes for ices was published in Paris: Nouvelles instructions pour les confitures, les liqueurs, et les fruits. Written by François Massialot, it also included a whole range of recipes for ices

28: Pewter ice pot, ice pot in wooden bucket and goblets, one of which is filled with ice, as depicted in L'Art de Bien Faire les Glaces d'Office by Emy (Paris, 1768).

perfumed with floral essences: violets, jasmine, roses, daffodils, carnations, hyacinths. The flowers were soaked in sugar water for six to seven hours. After that the juice was sieved through muslin and put into moulds to be frozen.[8] For the winter months, 'when flowers and fruit are scarce', Massialot had a special recipe: grated chocolate with sugar and water. Massialot's book was revised and reprinted many times in the first half of the eighteenth century and remained the leading cookery book in its field until the 1730s. Massialot had previously published a cookery book, Le Cuisinier Roial et Bourgeois, and in 1702 an English translation of both his books was published under the title The Court and Country Book. Partly because of this publication, English confectioners and chefs also became more familiar with the preparation of water ices. One of Audiger's recipes had been for an ice made with milk and cream instead of water - a crème glacée, as he had called it. In his 1712 edition Massialot added for the first time a recipe including milk, which he referred to as a Fromage à l'Angloise – an ice in the English manner. A comparison of the ice recipes included in English and French cookery books published in the eighteenth century shows that English books at first gave exclusively, and later predominantly, recipes for ices based on

29: Pewter ice pot, early nineteenth century.

cream and sugar, while the French publications mainly gave recipes for water-ice. In the French ice recipes which were based on cream, egg-white is normally used as well.[9]

• Apart from through cookery books, French cuisine – including ice recipes – also spread through descriptions in the newly emerging medium of journals. For example, the monthly magazine Mercure Galant, which was published from 1672 to 1705, contained regular and detailed articles about the banquets held at the court of Louis XIV. Often 300 to 400 pages long, the magazine was read throughout Europe.[10]

• Reports like these of the Sun King's magnificent feasts contributed greatly to the establishment and spread of French fashions and cooking among Europe's élite. Even after the death of Louis XIV in 1715, French style continued to be widely imitated. In most of the palaces of European aristocracy food was served à la service française. A typical meal consisted of three courses. The first two courses were cooked in the cuisine and the final course was prepared by the officers of the Office de Bouche. This 'cold' kitchen was responsible for the desserts and the drinks and was completely separate from the kitchen in which the soups, the hors d'oeuvres and the roast meat (the rôti) were prepared.

¶ No. 13, Rue de l'Ancienne Comédie, in the very heart of Saint-Germain on the left bank of the Seine, used to house one of Paris' oldest and most famous cafés, Le Procope. (Nowadays the premises are home to a renowned restaurant.) In 1686 a certain Francesco Procopio dei Coltelli started a café here. His trade prospered, mainly because Molière's famed theatre company, Les Comédiens du Roi (later known under the name La Comédie Française), was established only a few doors away in 1689. Theatre-goers, actors, directors, authors and philosophers alike flocked to the café, where Procopio served them with coffee, tea, drinking chocolate, liqueurs and ices. The start of Procopio's career was closely linked with a privilege that Louis XIV granted on 28 January 1676 to the newly founded Parisian guild of limonadiers and marchands d'eau de vie. This privilege gave the guild's 250 members the exclusive right to produce and sell all kinds of liqueurs, perfumed essences, lemonades, coffee, tea and chocolate beverages as well as to make 'glaces de fruits et de fleurs' and sell them in the city streets.[1] This privilege – for which the limonadiers had to pay a sizeable sum each year – meant that the popularity of water-ice spread from the court to the general public.

Procopio, born in 1650 in Palermo, had started out as a street vendor of coffee in 1672. By 1676 he had progressed to become the proprietor of three shops in Saint-Germain. During the local annual fair – which lasted from the beginning of February until Easter – he sold coffee, tea, drinking chocolate and lemonades. He had learnt the trade of waiter from an Armenian coffee shop owner, Pascal, who had left for London when business took a turn for the worse.[2] When Procopio opened his café on the Rue de l'Ancienne Comédie, he decorated its interior with big mirrors, crystal candelabras and marble-topped tables. Compared with the dark and cramped establishments in which the Parisians were accustomed to sipping their coffee, Procopio's approach to interior design was revolutionary and came to be much copied. But Le Procope's main claim to fame is the many celebrities who frequented the café in the eighteenth and nineteenth centuries. Great names of the French Enlightenment, such as La Fontaine, Voltaire, Diderot, d'Alembert, Rousseau and d'Holbach, were all regulars at Le Procope. Leading figures of the French Revolution, such as Danton, Marat and Robespierre,

were often to be found there, as were writers including Honoré de Balzac, Victor Hugo, Alfred de Musset, Anatole France and Paul Verlaine. This extraordinary parade of literary and historical figures, allied to centuries of serving coffee and ices, has lent Le Procope near mythical status, swelled by a flood of stories and anecdotes about the café. Coffee, ice cream, the French Age of Reason, the French Revolution – Le Procope has been credited as the birthplace of all of them. The origin of legendary status for Procopio's establishment can be traced to 1779 and the publication of the book L'Art du Distillateur by M. Dubuisson. In this work the Sicilian is for the first time named as the introducer of ice cream to the French capital.[3] Dubuisson makes no mention of the water-ices served by Audiger at the French court in 1661, which the Frenchman had published in detail as early as 1692.

Paris was not the only city where Italians and Armenians set the trend for coffee houses. They also made a name for themselves in London, Amsterdam and elsewhere. There, too, their repertoire was not limited to coffee and liqueurs. In 1698 the City Fathers of Utrecht in the Netherlands granted one Lucius Rosselli permission to sell 'all manners of waters, scents, pastes, chocolateries and other liqueurs' in the city. Rosselli describes himself in his memoirs as 'the unfortunate Neapolitan', saying that he had fled Rome to escape persecution by the clergy. In Utrecht he opened a coffee house in which he almost certainly sold ices; for, underneath the house, an ice cellar was later found and during rebuilding work the stripping of wallpaper from an old door revealed wooden panels carrying the words 'Au..DChoc..Caffe Italien' and 'Glaces'.[4] Subsequently, Rosselli's name also surfaced in Amsterdam and The Hague. In the latter, 'the meeting place of all the Powers in Europe', he ran a coffee house for quite a while.

By around 1700, coffee houses had appeared in almost all Dutch cities. Some ot them sold water-ice or ice cream. For example, one such establishment in Breda, in the south of the Netherlands, had a shop sign-board proclaiming:

> 'Here one can buy Coffee
> and Chocolat,
> Sorbet, Tea and Lemonade,
> The Purest Whey and Good
> Tobacco.
> Come in and taste and you'll
> come back'.[5]

But, even though ice cream had found its way into the coffee houses, it was only as the nineteenth century wore on that its popularity started to rival that of coffee itself. For the time being ice cream remained beyond the reach and pockets of the vast majority of the population who still lived in rural areas. They were happy if they got a square meal a day and did not have to go to bed on an empty stomach.

• Table settings and serving at table were subject to strict rules. Everything was worked out in fine detail, from the symmetrical arrangements of the dishes to the exact placings of the guests at table. Initially the food was served on silver or even gold dishes and plates, but during the course of the eighteenth century, when Europeans learnt how to manufacture porcelain, complete dinner services made of porcelain became more popular. The emergence and growing popularity of tea, coffee and drinking chocolate in the second half of the seventeenth century led to an increased demand for porcelain services particular to these beverages. Water-ices were served both in crystal glasses and in porcelain cups.

• Before about 1740, however, porcelain ware had had to be imported from China or Japan. Following countless trials, the method of making porcelain had been discovered in 1709 in Meissen, Germany, but it was only when the secret became more widely known that porcelain factories began to spring up in Europe, chiefly in France and England. Most of these factories were granted royal patronage, with many sets of porcelain being commissioned by royalty as gifts to express goodwill or gratitude. Nobles at court were thanked for services rendered, marshals and generals for victories won; friendly relations with foreign courts were strengthened and marriage proposals were sealed. The porcelain services attested both to the wealth of the giver and to the artistic skills of the factories.

• As the European porcelain factories flourished, the luxurious culinary culture of the court became increasingly imitated in aristocratic circles and among the emerging haute bourgeoisie. What were generally

substantial first and second courses were followed by a third, often served in a separate room. There, the rich enjoyed numerous small dishes, such as fresh fruit, candied fruits, various types of jam and a choice of puddings, cream and ices.

Porcelain ice pails and ice cream cups

• The Office de Bouche had an extensive collection of porcelain, silver and crystal objects for serving desserts. Special dessert services, often in porcelain, formed part of the inventory of châteaux and country houses. A service might comprise pineapple and chestnut shaped vases, orange beakers, plates and dishes, custard cups, ice pails, ice cream cups – sometimes with a special serving tray – and a whole range of baskets for fruits and flowers. A centrepiece and small sculptures commonly completed the table decoration.

• The ice pails and the ice cream cups were intended to allow fruit and confitures to be eaten cold and to keep the ice cream in good condition. A pail typically consisted of three parts: the pail itself; a liner tray which fitted snugly inside it; and a lid with a raised edge and a handle that protruded above the edge (see box on p. 54). Crushed ice was put in the pail and also in the lid, cooling the container on all sides. Salt may also have been added to the ice to cool it further.[11] The idea of a lid with a raised edge for natural ice may have been copied from stewing pans[12] whose lids held glowing charcoal so that the food could be kept heated from the top as well.

• Before the advent of ice pails there had long been earthenware jars for the cooling of wine. The shape of the container in the most common type of ice pail is derived from these. Ice pails and ice cream cups were used by the wealthy until well into the nineteenth century in almost all European countries and in the United States. Together with cookery books, correspon-

30: Earthenware ice pail, circa 1725. The ice pail was manufactured in the Clérissy factory in Moustiers, one of the oldest pottery facto- ries in France. To keep the ice or fruit cold, natural ice was placed inside the lid with the raised edge. The design for the lid may have been adopted from a partic- ular type of stewing pan, where hot coals were placed in the recess of the lid. The coat of arms on the pail is that of Jean Frédéric Phélyppeaux (1701-1781), Count of Maurepas. The Count was Minister of the Navy in 1723, but subsequently fell out of favour with Madame de Pompadour, the mistress of Louis XV. In 1774, however, Louis XVI appointed him Prime Minister. Musée National de Céramique, Sèvres, total height 17.5 cm, width 28.5 cm, depth 21.5 cm.

dence, diaries, travel journals and other contemporary reports, these ice pails and ice cream cups form a rich source for the early history of ice cream in the eighteenth and early nineteenth century.

Porcelain splendour from Sèvres

• The oldest ice pails that have survived are two French examples made of earthen- ware. One was manufactured in the port of Rouen and the other in the town of Moustiers, in the south of the country. The Rouen ice pail dates from 1700-1725, while the one from Moustiers was manufac- tured in about 1725 in the Clérissy factory.[13] Ceramics had been produced in Rouen since the early sixteenth century, and in Moustiers from about 1670. To make it look like porce- lain, the earthenware was covered with a layer of white glaze. The most famous porce- lain factory in France is undoubtedly that at Sèvres, now a south-western suburb of Paris.

The factory, which still exists today, produced extraordinarily beautiful services, sometimes numbering many hundreds of pieces, for the aristocracy across Europe. French interest in porcelain services had been stimulated by the dowry of Maria Josepha of Saxony on her marriage in 1745 to the French crown prince Louis Ferdinand (1729-1765). The dowry included a complete Meissen service that epitomised the national ability and skills of Saxony, where the Meissen porcelain factory was located. The service made a great impression on the French court and soon resulted in more and more porcelain services being used in place of silver.[14] French facto- ries, notably Sèvres, acquired an internation- al reputation, not least because of the orders placed by the French kings. The Sèvres facto- ry had in fact moved there from Vincennes, where it had been founded in 1738. In 1753 one-third of the factory came into the pos- session of Louis XV (1710-1774), who in 1759 acquired full control of the factory, which thereafter traded under the name Manu- facture Royale de porcelaines de Sèvres.[15]

What's in a name: ice pail, glacière, Kühlgefäss, gelatiere...

54

¶ In the eighteenth and early nineteenth century special ice pails were manufactured all over Europe for cooling fruit and ice cream. Initially they were made of earthenware but later, at least from 1758, also of porcelain. These ice pails consisted of at least three parts: a pot, a bowl or liner which fitted inside the pot, and a lid with a raised edge and a handle that stuck out above the edge. Both the pot and the lid were filled with crushed natural ice, so that the bowl containing the fruit or the ice cream was cooled from all sides. The terminology used for this item differed from country to country. In England the manufacturer Wedgwood invariably referred to pails by the French name glacière. In its 1774 catalogue Wedgwood made it perfectly clear what purpose they served: the inner liner was meant for ice cream. So the customer who ordered crockery in 1784 was not making a mistake when he asked for 'two large ice cream vases'[1]. To the French, however, a glacière more usually means an ice cellar. To denote an ice pail the French will normally use the terms seau à glace, jatte à glace, vase à glace, and some-times even rafraîchissoir.

In England, Wedgwood was the only manufacturer to use the French word glacière. Other manufacturers and authors called it an ice pail. The German language has also developed a

31: Cross-section drawing of an ice pail. The drawing originates from the pattern book of Leeds Pottery, England, circa 1780. At the bottom of the drawing are the words: 'Size and profile of an Ice Cellar'. The three different parts are explained as 'The lower part to put the Ice', 'The false bottom, wherein are put the things that are to be iced', and 'The Ice Cellar Cover or Lid must be open at the top to contain the Ice, so that there can be Ice both below and above'. The drawing had been brought over from France. Victoria & Albert Museum, London.

variety of terms for the ice pail: Kühlgefäss, Eiskühler, Eisgefäss and Eistopfgestell. In Italy the terms gelatiere, recipiente da gelato, recipiente per gelato and rinfrescato per gelato are used.

The pot of the ice pail developed from that of the bottle cooler. In many ice coolers the pot has virtually the same shape as a bottle cooler and can also be used as such. As a result of this, the names used for the 'separate' pot of the ice cream cooler are the same: seau, ice pail or Kühlgefäss. To distinguish an ice cooler from a bottle cooler they are referred to in England as ice pail complete or ice pail with liner. Except at Wedgwood, where an ice pail means a bottle cooler! Of the many ice coolers that have survived the inner liner is often missing. Originally, these were made either of porcelain or of metal, with the metal inner liners probably introduced later. In any event, a number of nineteenth century design drawings show a metal inner liner.

The special ice cream cups – mentioned in accounts dating from as early as the seventeenth century – also have a number of names: tasse à glace, (France), ice cup, cream cup (England), Eisbecher, Geleebecher, Cremebecher (Germany), tazza da gelato, recipiente da gelato (Italy).

Louis stipulated that Sèvres would be the only porcelain factory in France that could use coloured decoration, and it was expected to surpass Meissen in quality and design.

• The first big order that Sèvres received came from Louis XV himself, for an impressive combined dinner and dessert service, delivered between 1753 and 1756 and comprising some 1,747 pieces. It included 150 ice cream cups, but no ice pail. The ice pail appears for the first time in 1758, when a seau à glace, along with 28 ice cream cups, was included in a service that Louis XV gave as a present to the Austrian empress, Maria Theresa. Ice cream had already been known for some time in Vienna. In 1697 a publication compiled by three aristocratic ladies included two recipes for gefrorenes, or water-ice. For freezing the water-ice they recommended a mixture of ice and salt, just as Audiger and Massialot had done five years earlier.[16] In 1716 Lady Mary Wortley Montagu wrote home to England from Vienna: 'The company are entertain'd with ice in several forms, Winter and Summer'.[17]

• The ice pail that was delivered to Empress Maria Theresa is mentioned in the Sèvres factory stock lists of 1 October 1759. Like most Sèvres ice pails it was U-shaped, in the manner of the bottle coolers which had been

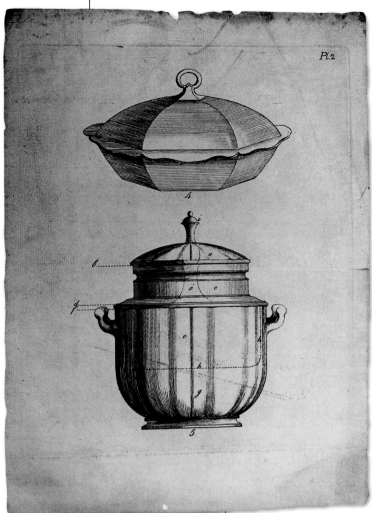

32: Cross-section of a Wedgwood ice pail, from the Wedgwood catalogue of 1774. The various component parts of the pail can be clearly seen. Wedgwood Museum, Barlaston, Stoke-on-Trent, inv. no. M-0328-14.

popular since the end of the seventeenth century.

To this basic shape were added the liner and the characteristic lid with its raised edge. Porcelain factories throughout Europe copied the design. The 1780 pattern book of the English factory Leeds Pottery, for example, contains a cross-section drawing of an ice pail that originated in France. The drawing carries both the French text and an English translation.[18] This imitation was not surprising: in those days French taste set the fashion.

Pl. 4

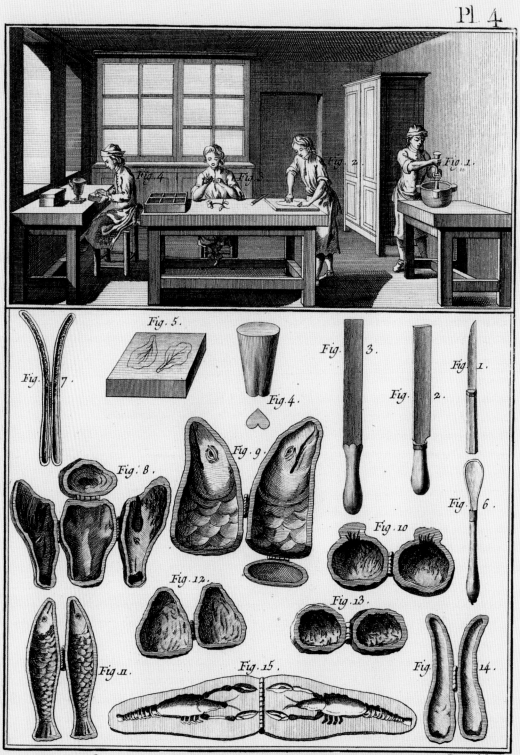

Benard direxit.

Confiseur, Pastillage et Moulles pour les Glaces.

• As Massialot and others had reported in 1692, ice was not only spooned from glasses at that time but also from porcelain cups, known as tasses à glace. In those days the cups were still made from Chinese porcelain. As we have seen, Sèvres started producing cups of this kind several years prior to the introduction of the ice pail in 1758. The Sèvres ice cream cups had one handle and stood on a pedestal base. Saucers, like those for coffee and tea services, were not required. The cups were served on a special porcelain serving tray which came in three different types.[19]The four ice cream cups of Sèvres porcelain that Louis XV had delivered in June 1754 to his mistress Madame de Pompadour at Château Bellevue stood atop a matching triangular serving tray.

• Mme de Pompadour's ice was very different from the ice Audiger had served to Louis XIV in the seventeenth century. The repertoire of ice recipes had been substantially extended to include all sorts of fromages glacés, or ices based on sugar, cream, eggs or egg-whites. The use of eggs changed the taste and texture, making it smoother and rounder in taste. The outcome was not iced creams, but softer, more custard-like ices.[20] French cookery books in the eighteenth century devoted considerable space to these new recipes (see box on p. 58), whilst a whole range of special moulds had become available (see also box story, chapter 4).

33: Metal moulds designed for freezing shaped ices, from the Encyclopédie of Diderot and d'Alembert (Paris, 1754). The picture includes, from left to right, moulds for ices in the shapes of asparagus, a boar's head, a salmon's head, a pomegranate, a salmon trout, figs, truffles, a calf's tongue and a lobster. Next to the pomegranate ice mould is a whisk (Fig. 6) for whipping the ice mix. Pictured at the top is the workplace of a confiseur.

These moulds were depicted in various recipe books as well as in the famous Encyclopédie of Diderot and d'Alembert of 1754, which also included a treatise on the preparation of ices.[21]

Ice pails for the beau monde of the whole of Europe

• In 1763, to cement Franco-English relations, Louis XV presented a Sèvres service to the English Ambassador, the Duchess of Bedford. It included sixteen ice cream cups decorated with floral motifs. Around 1768 the Danish king, Christian VII (1749-1808), received a service with ice cream cups and two ice pails.

• In 1770 Sweden's Crown Prince Gustaf (1746-1792) stayed at the French court. During his stay his father died and he returned post-haste to Stockholm to be crowned King Gustaf III. To mark the coronation Louis XV presented him with a gift of a 586-piece Sèvres service with four ice pails, 56 ice cream cups and four special serving trays. By then the eating of ices had been known at the Swedish court for quite some time. It was introduced soon after 1660, the year when Audiger first served his eaux glacées to Louis XIV. On 30 June 1688 the English Ambassador organised a banquet and a firework display in Stockholm to celebrate the birth of James Francis Edward, Prince of Wales. The London Gazette commented on the meal: 'After the meat was taken off, there was served up a very fine dessert, with many great Pyramids of dry Sweet-meats, between which were placed all such Fruits, Iced Creams, and such other Varieties as the Season afforded'.[22]

¶ In 1692 the first cookery books with ice recipes were published in Paris. These were by Audiger and Massialot and their recipes were for water-ices. Audiger had learnt how to prepare ices in Rome in 1659 and had since 1661 been a distillateur and limonadier who supplied his products to French court circles. Massialot's book was updated and reprinted many times during the first half of the eighteenth century and remained the leading cookery book in its field until the 1730s.

In Naples, the two-part work entitled Scalco alla Moderne (The modern steward) had been published in 1692 and 1694. The author, Antonio Latini, was steward to the prime minister of Naples and Sicily, the Spaniard Don Stefano Carillo y Salcedo. In his book Latini gives several recipes for what he refers to as sorbetti. To judge by his sketchy descriptions, these were half-frozen drinks which differed considerably from the coloured, pyramid-shaped French water-ices of Audiger and Massialot.

Another Italian publication from the same period, a twelve-page booklet entitled Breve e Nuovo Modo da farsi ogni sorte di Sorbette con facilità (A quick and easy new way of making sorbet of all kinds) was devoted entirely to the preparation of sorbetti.[1] This booklet, published anonymously in Naples, contains 23 ice recipes, including some based on milk. The ingredients for one such milk-based recipe include skimmed milk, orange-blossom water, cream, butter, cinnamon and shredded candied pumpkin. Apart from flavours of flowers such as jasmine or fruits like apricots, strawberries and cherries, the booklet also gives a recipe for a water-ice with sugar and vanilla. The vanilla presumably came from Peru, a Spanish colony since 1532. For freezing, the compiler recommends the use of ice moulds modelled in the shape of various types of fruits.

A book translated from a French

L'ART
DE BIEN FAIRE
LES GLACES D'OFFICE;
O U
LES VRAIS PRINCIPES
Pour congeler tous les Rafraîchiffemens.
La maniere de préparer toutes fortes de Compofitions, la façon de les faire prendre, d'en former des Fruits, Cannelons, & toutes fortes de Fromages.
Le tout expliqué avec précifion felon l'ufage actuel.
A V E C
UN TRAITÉ SUR LES MOUSSES,
Ouvrage très-utile à ceux qui font des Glaces ou Fromages glacés.
Orné de Gravures en taille-douce.
Par M. EMY, Officier.

Prix, 2 liv. 10 fols broché ; 3 liv. relié.

A PARIS,
Chez LE CLERC, Libraire, quai des Auguftins, à la Toifon d'or.

M. DCC. LXVIII.
Avec Approbation & Privilege du Roi.

L'Art de bien faire les Glaces

34: Title page of Emy's recipe book, L'Art de Bien Faire les Glaces d'Office, published in Paris in 1768. It was the first cookery book devoted entirely to ice recipes. The title page shows angel-like figures busy preparing ices in tin boxes. Small cups containing ices can be seen on the table. Such goblets were made of either porcelain or glass.

edition and published in Hamburg in 1689 is evidence that water-ices were also known in Germany at the end of the seventeenth century. This anonymous publication - Schatzkammer Rarer und Neuer Curiositäten in den aller-wunderbaresten Würkungen der Natur und Kunst

(A treasury of rare and new curiosities to be found in the most astonishing workings of nature and art) - contains a chapter of recipes and instructions for the preparation of ices made from 'water of strawberries, cherries, apricots or morellos'.[2]

At the beginning of the eighteenth century, further cookery books with ice recipes were published. In many cases they were imitations of Massialot's book, for example The Modern Cook of 1733 by the French chef Vincent La Chapelle. This changed in the middle of the century when three French cookery books full of recipes for ices were published in fairly rapid succession. Unlike the works of Audiger and Massialot, these cookery books gave a whole series of recipes for dairy ice cream, or fromage glacé (frozen cheese) as it was then known. These French recipes also used eggs and egg-white, which changed the flavour and texture of the ice cream. The mixture became smoother and had a fuller taste. The result was not iced creams, but softer, more custard-like ices.

The first of the three books was Menon's La Science du Maître d'Hôtel Confiseur, published in 1750. The second, Le Cannaméliste, appeared in 1751 and was written by Gilliers. The third publication, by Emy, was called L'Art de Bien Faire les Glaces d'Office (1768) and is devoted entirely to ice recipes.

As well as recipes, the authors give descriptions of the freezing process using natural ice and salt. Emy also refers to the experiments in this field by the French physicist René Antoine Ferchault de Réaumur (1683-1757).[3] Réaumur had conducted

35: Ice glass, third quarter of the eighteenth century, England. The shape of the glass is the same as that of an ice glass or gobelet pictured in L'Art de Bien Faire les Glaces d'Office.

extensive research into freezing processes and in a 1734 treatise on physics he discussed the preparation of ice. Ice, he wrote, had to be soft and like snow.[4] Réaumur said this could be achieved if the big ice crystals that were formed during the freezing process were regularly scraped off the wall of the ice tin in which the ingredients were frozen. If the crystals were then whipped, the result would also look rather like 'snow'. Not only would the ice crystals be reduced in size, air would also be introduced into the ice mixture, producing a softer and smoother taste.

For the ice cream recipes that were being developed at this time, Réaumur's recommendations proved very useful. Emy's publication in his book of Réaumur's findings ensured their dissemination in culinary circles. The method is still being used in the twentieth century,[5] since the beginning of which industrially produced ice cream has generally contained between 30% and 50% air.

36: King Gustav III of Sweden (1746-1792) painted by Alexander Roslin. Ice had been eaten at the Swedish court since at least 1688. During Gustav's reign ices became extremely popular with the nobility and haute bourgeoisie. Gustav had a great admiration for the French and his palace employed French chefs who were famous for their bombes glacées.

pails and 72 ice cream cups.[23] This order was perhaps not so surprising, as the Duke of Parma, the Spaniard Philip of Bourbon, was married to Louise Elisabeth, Louis XV's eldest daughter, who played a key role in introducing many French fashions and customs to the court of Parma.

• A much more remarkable order was placed in 1776 by the Russian empress, Catherine II, or Catherine the Great (1729-1796). This was a dinner and dessert service for 60 persons, supplemented by a coffee service and a table decoration of porcelain sculptures. It was the most expensive order in the history of Sèvres, costing 331,317 livres (in 1755 a typesetter in Paris earned around 750 livres a year).[24] More than 800 pieces, in a completely new, classical style and in new shapes, were required. Most pieces bore the monogram of the Empress – the letter E of Ekaterina with a tsar's crown in the centre, under which appeared the Roman figure II. The entire motif was surrounded by a laurel. The background was turquoise, a colour unique to Sèvres. Numerous cameos of famous people from antiquity[25] were applied to the objects. The service contained 10 ice pails and 116 ice cream cups, with two types of serving trays: twelve plateaux for seven ice cream cups and eight for six cups.

• Sèvres services with ice pails were also exported to Italy, supposedly the home of European ice cream. The court of the small state of Parma placed an order with Testard, the Parisian merchant for Sèvres porcelain, for a 434-piece service, including six ice

• Porcelain was also produced in St. Peters-

37: Ice pail forming part of a Sèvres service manufactured for the Russian tsarina, Catherine the Great (1729-1796). Consisting of more than 800 pieces, the service was produced between 1776 and 1779. The relief along the edge of the ice pail's lid carries decorations in the form of a frozen overflow of water. These refer to the cooling function of the pail, as does the knob, which is designed as a frozen fountain. The pail is decorated with cameos depicting figures from antiquity. Wallace Collection, London, height 24 cm.

Sceau a Glace nombre 10

burg. In 1744 an imperial porcelain factory had been founded and this enjoyed great
success during Catherine's
reign. The factory manufactured ice cream cups, as did
another set up near Moscow in
1765 by the Englishman Francis Gardner. Foreign influences
were strong at the Russian court. The eating
of ices was introduced during Catherine's
reign, probably from France, and in 1791 a
two-volume cookery book was published in
Moscow whose title translates as The Newest
and Most Comprehensive Cookbook. According to the preface, the book had been trans-

38: Design in watercolour for an
ice pail that formed part of a
Sèvres service ordered in 1776
by Catherine the Great. This
superb service was destined for
the Russian prince Grigori Poty-
omkin as a token of gratitude
for services rendered. On Poty-
omkin's instructions the service
was designed in classical style.
The service included ten ice
pails, 116 ice cream cups and
twenty special trays for serving
the cups. A photograph of the
finished piece is shown on p.61.

lated from the French. One
chapter was devoted entirely
to the making of ices and gave
recipes for chocolate, strawberry, lemon, cherry, raspberry and cranberry ice creams.
• The Empress maintained an
extensive network of contacts
with artists and scholars
throughout Europe, corresponding with
Voltaire, Diderot and others. Diderot visited
St. Petersburg in 1773 as did many foreign
architects, painters, scientists and soldiers,
sometimes staying at her court for years. In
1789 the Italian count Julius Litta came to
Russia and spent many years serving at

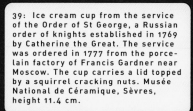

39: Ice cream cup from the service of the Order of St George, a Russian order of knights established in 1769 by Catherine the Great. The service was ordered in 1777 from the porcelain factory of Francis Gardner near Moscow. The cup carries a lid topped by a squirrel cracking nuts. Musée National de Céramique, Sèvres, height 11.4 cm.

40: Two ice cream cups from the service of the Order of Vladimir, one of the four orders of knights at the time of Catherine the Great. The cups were manufactured in the Russian porcelain factory of Francis Gardner near Moscow and were delivered in 1785. The cups carry the insignia of the Order and the colours of the Order's sash. The pot-bellied shape of the cups with the two C-shaped handles bears a strong resemblance to that of the ice glasses depicted in the French cookery book, L'Art de Bien Faire les Glaces d'Office by Emy, which was published in 1768. Musée National de Céramique, Sèvres, height 8.4 cm.

Catherine's court, rising to the rank of admiral. According to the 19th-century Russian chronicler Michael Piljaev, the count was besotted with ice cream. On 24 January 1834, the day he died, he is said to have emptied a silver cup of ice cream to the last spoonful. Piljaev also mentions the names of four confectioners who supplied the count with ice cream, including the Italians Metsanelli and Salvator.[26]

• The Russian nobility often employed French chefs. One of the most famous, Marie-Antoine Carême (1783-1833) served for a while under Tsar Alexander I (1777-1825), maintaining the popularity of ice cream at the Russian court into the nineteenth century. Documents from the reign of Tsar Nicholas I (1796-1855) instructed that the Tsar's wife, Alexandra Feodorovna, be served two portions of ice cream each day.[27]

41: George Washington, portrayed in Princeton by Charles Peale (1779). During his presidency Washington regularly treated his guests to ice cream at official receptions.

Ice pails in the United States for George Washington

• French porcelain was also in demand in the fledgling United States whose first president, George Washington (1732-1799), was a great pottery and porcelain enthusiast. As his first term of office started in 1789 he purchased porcelain services and other costly tableware to ensure that official dinners radiated the appropriate elegance. His model was the banquets and dinners given by the French diplomatic mission, then located in New York. On 14 May 1789 the French Ambassador, Count de Moustier (1751-1817), organised a gala ball for the American President. Congressman Elias Boudinot of New Jersey wrote to his wife: 'Three rooms were filled and the fourth was most elegantly set off as a place for refreshment. A long table crossed this room, in the middle, from wall to wall. The whole wall, inside, was covered with shelves, filled with cakes, oranges, apples, wines of all sorts, ice creams, etc. and highly lighted up. A number of servants from behind the table supplied the guests with everything they wanted, from time to time, as they came to refresh themselves.'[28]

• George Washington and de Moustier continued to correspond after the latter returned to France in October 1789. It comes as no surprise, therefore, that Washington moved into the former French Embassy and purchased all the remaining contents of the house, including a 309-piece Sèvres porcelain service decorated with gold beading. During his presidency Washington regularly served ice cream at official receptions and by 1784 had his own 'machine' for making ice cream.[29]

• However, the earliest mention of the eating of ice cream in the United States dates from 1744, when a Scottish colonist recorded in his diary that in Annapolis, during a visit to Thomas Bladen, the governor of Maryland, he was served ice cream as a dessert which 'with the Strawberries and Milk, eat[s] most Deliciously'[30].

• The author of the American Declaration of Independence and subsequent president, Thomas Jefferson (1743-1826), also served ice cream in the White House. From 1785 until 1798 Jefferson had been the American Envoy in France and brought back an ice-cream recipe from his French cook. The ingredients were '2 bottles of good cream, 6 yolks of eggs, 0,5 lb. sugar' and a 'stick of vanilla'. To freeze the ice cream Jefferson used a sabottière and an ice mould.[31] Sabottière (variant spellings such as sarbotière and sorbetière also exist) is an eighteenth century French designation for a long tin jug, fitted with a lid and a handle. It was filled with a mixture of cream, sugar and egg-whites, which were then frozen.

The last Sèvres service before the French Revolution

• In 1783, shortly before Jefferson's arrival in Paris, Louis XVI placed an order for the most prestigious Sèvres service ever, destined for use in the dining room of his private chambers at Versailles. It was to comprise 132 pieces for the dinner service and 290 pieces for the dessert service. The cost was estimated at 164,390 livres - this at a time when France's national debt had soared to dizzying heights (in 1785 it stood at 120 million livres). The service had to be ready by 1803 and the King himself had drawn up a production schedule specifying which pieces had to be delivered each year.[32] The dessert service was to include eight ice pails and 32 ice cream cups. But it was not to be. Production was halted in 1792 in the turmoil following the French Revolution, with only 26 ice cream cups and one ice pail complete.

• The planned production time of twenty years resulted from what we would today call the 'supply chain'. The service was to be decorated with some 1,032 scenes from Greek and Roman mythology and history. At Sèvres only a handful of top-quality artists were capable of painting such scenes in all their delicate precision. Moreover, the objects had to be fired at least nine times during the production process, of which three firings were needed for the actual painting. The single ice pail that was completed is the standard model as developed in 1758.

42: Ice cream cups with matching serving tray from a Sèvres service of Louis XVI, circa 1785. The scenes are derived from a Paris edition of Ovid's *Metamorphoses*. The service was not completed owing to the outbreak of the French Revolution. The Royal Collection, Her Majesty Queen Elizabeth II, Windsor.

43: Sèvres porcelain ice pail, 1812. This ice pail formed part of a gift from Napoleon to Emperor Francis II of Austria (1768-1835) to mark his marriage to Francis' daughter, Marie Louise. The special model for these ice pails was designed in 1806 by the artist Brachard. The ice pail is painted on both sides with scenes from Napoleon's life. The picture here shows one of his castles, Château Ecouen. The paintings are the work of Jean François Robert (1778-1832) and were by far the biggest cost item at 350 francs. The British Museum, London.

44: One of two ice pails from a Sèvres service manufactured between 1823 and 1836. The service was presented by the French king Louis Philippe to the Austrian statesman von Metternich, the key player at the Congress of Vienna (1815). Both ice pails were painted by the artist Charles Develly with scenes showing the cultivation and processing of coffee, tea, cocoa and sugar. The ice pail illustrated here depicts the cultivation of coffee. Musée National de Céramique, Sèvres, height 31.2 cm.

The pail is decorated with scenes based on a Parisian edition of the Metamorphoses by the Roman poet Ovid. Louis XVI did not live to enjoy using the service, since in 1793 he was beheaded and the leaders of the new Republic sold it.[33] Staunch Republicans henceforth consumed their food and drink from modified, 'politically correct' Sèvres crockery, bearing such depictions as that of the head of Louis XVI after his death by guillotine![33]

45: Napoleon Bonaparte in his study. The painting is by Jacques Louis David and dates from 1812. As emperor, Napoleon resumed the tradition – interrupted by the French Revolution – of presenting costly Sèvres services to foreign princes, high-ranking subjects and close relatives. Ice pails often formed part of these services.

Sèvres from Napoleon to Von Metternich

• By adapting to the new era Sèvres somehow succeeded in continuing production after the Revolution, despite the loss of its principal patron. In 1799 Napoleon Bonaparte seized power and on 18 May 1804 had himself crowned Emperor, creating a new and important customer for Sèvres. Napoleon soon resumed the tradition of presenting Sèvres services to foreign sovereigns, high-ranking citizens and close relatives. For example, Tsar Alexander I of Russia received a Sèvres service with four ice pails in 1807. The Bavarian prince Maximilian Joseph I delighted in a similar service in 1810; and in May 1812 Napoleon presented his father-in-law, Emperor Francis II of Austria (1768-1835), with a gift of Sèvres porcelain worth 25,000 francs. The gift also included a pair of glacières à gorge à têtes d'éléphant (ice pails with handles in the shape of elephant's heads) then priced at 1,000 francs each. The oval-shaped model of these 'Napoleonic' ice pails differed considerably from the U-shaped containers from the period of Louis XV and Louis XVI.

• After the restoration of the monarchy in 1814, with the coronation of Louis XVIII (1755-1824), the practice of ordering special services from Sèvres continued, but with an important change. Instead of ostentatious designs reflecting the monarch's personal taste, the preference was now for nationalist themes aimed at glorifying France and the French. Services now tended to depict panoramas of French landscapes or illustrations of French professions. An example is the service 'des Départements', manufactured between 1824 and 1829, which included two oval ice pails with handles shaped like the heads of satyrs. The service derives its name from the départements of France. One of the vases à glace, for instance, depicts the Louvre and a view of the Tuileries Palace and Gardens. The Austrian statesman von Metternich (1773-1859) was also the delighted recipient of a Sèvres service, including two handsomely painted, oval ice pails,[34] given to him in 1836 by the 'bourgeois king', Louis Philippe (1773-1850).

Ice recipes from England and glacières by Wedgwood

• The eighteenth century European aristocracy did not eat ice cream solely from French porcelain. German, Danish, Italian and in particular English manufacturers of pottery and porcelain built up a reputation for their own wares. The leading producers in England were Wedgwood, Chelsea, Derby, Worcester and Spode, but factories also operated in Neal, Rockingham, Coalport and Pinxton and, in Wales, Swansea. All manufactured services with ice pails[36] and, by comparison with France, the English factories produced vast quantities of dessert services. Firms like Flight and Chamberlain in Worcester specialised in services of this type.

• There were more customers in England than in France. For one thing, wealth was distributed more evenly than in France. Moreover, the English dessert repertoire already included creamy puddings such as syllabub (milk or cream that is curdled with wine or liqueur and then mixed with whipped egg-whites or gelatine).

• The eating of ice cream started in England during the reign of Charles II (1660-1685). Folklore has it that the French chef Tissain introduced ice cream in England during the reign of Charles' father, Charles I, and that he was subsequently told to keep this recipe a secret. However, no historical evidence survives to corroborate this claim.[37] The earliest mention that is substantiated dates from 1671. On 28 and 29 May of that year, on the Feast of St. George at Windsor, the dishes served at the table of Charles II included not only Chinese oranges, dried fruits, cherries and strawberries, but also an ice cream dessert.[38] From 1646 to 1660 Charles had been in exile at the French court and after his return to England he maintained close contact with the court of Louis XIV. Just like Versailles, the English royal household had its own ice cellars. Immediately after his coronation in 1660 Charles II gave instructions for an ice-house to be built in St. James' Park.

46: Ice pail manufactured between 1800 and 1805 by the Chamberlain pottery factory in Worcester, England. This spectacular ice pail is supported on a base formed by the tails of three dolphins. The knob on the lid is also in the shape of a dolphin. The handles of the pail are in the form of mermaids. Like the other pieces in the service, the ice pail is decorated with scenes from Aesop's Fables. R.H. Williamson Bequest, Tullie House, Carlisle, height 36.3 cm.

• The recipes and methods for making ice cream spread from the court to the nobility, after which they found their way into recipe books. The personal recipe book of Countess Grace Granville contains a handwritten recipe for 'ice creame'. The countess used 'cream, Sugar & 3 Spoonfulls of Orrange flower water'. The recipe was probably written down during the 1690s and may originate from the royal palace of Whitehall.[39]

• The first original English cookery book containing an ice cream recipe appeared in print in 1718 and was compiled by Mrs Mary Eales, who had been confectioner to Queen Anne. The ingredients for her ice cream consisted of 'any Sort of Cream you like, either plain or sweeten'd, or Fruit in it'.[40] Just as in the French recipes, the cream was frozen in tin boxes placed in a barrel of natural ice to which salt had been added. There is no mention of the tins being rotated or of the cream being whipped at intervals so as to prevent the formation of coarse ice crystals.

• Mary Eales' book had been preceded in 1702 by an English translation of the book by the French chef Massialot. In 1703 the English chef Charles Carter published The Complete Practical Cook. Carter had been in the service of generals, ambassadors and envoys abroad. In his introduction he stated that his book contained both English and foreign recipes. His book did indeed give recipes for ice cream in various flavours – raspberry, pistachio, chocolate, lemon – but it is unclear whether the resultant products tasted good: his instructions for the method of prepa-

ration were very vague.[41] In that respect the English were to benefit more from The Modern Cook, which was published in London in 1733 by the French chef Vincent La Chapelle. La Chapelle had worked as Chef de la Cuisine for the Earl of Chesterfield until about 1735 when he entered the employ of the Dutch stadholder William IV (1711-1751). This Prince of Orange had travelled to London in 1734 to marry Anne of Hanover, the daughter of the English King George II.

• By about the middle of the eighteenth century ice cream had become common as a dessert amongst the rich in England. Of the English chinaware factories, Wedgwood soon gained international repute. Established in 1759 by Josiah Wedgwood, the factory developed numerous new types of pottery, new models and also new pieces. One new type of pottery was known as cream ware, china that was glazed in a pale cream colour, light in weight and cheap to produce by comparison with porcelain. In 1765 Wedgwood supplied a cream ware coffee and tea service to Queen Charlotte (1744-1818). Her Royal Highness was so enthusiastic that from then on Wedgwood was given permission to call his invention Queen's ware, and so it appeared in the company's 1774 catalogue. The fifth design in that catalogue was an ice pail consisting of four parts. Wedgwood invariably referred to ice pails by their French name, glacière (see box on p. 54). The Wedgwood ice pail was available in various formats. In shape it very much resembled the U-shaped Sèvres model of 1758, the only difference being that Wedgwood placed an extra lid on top of the lid that contains the ice.[42]

• To develop exports the factory used the services of agents abroad. In St. Petersburg that role was successfully played by the

47: Portrait of Countess Grace Granville (circa 1664-1744), attributed to the painter Johann Kerseboom. A recipe book by the Countess has survived, with a handwritten recipe for 'ice creame'. As ingredients the countess used cream, sugar and '3 Spoonfulls of Orrange flower water'. The recipe was probably written down in about 1690 and may have originated from the royal palace in Whitehall.

48: Wedgwood ice pail, circa 1775. The English Wedgwood porcelain factory produced numerous ice pails between 1775 and 1825. The pail shown here is made of cream ware, pottery with a pale cream-coloured glaze and light in weight. Wedgwood was the first to put this on the market and it proved a great success. The lid and base of the ice pail are decorated in ajour, a technique in which parts of the object have been left open. Decorations of this type were applied using a semi-mechanised technique and were considerably cheaper than hand-painted decorations. Wedgwood Museum, Barlaston, Stoke-on-Trent, height 23.8 cm.

49: Ice pail from the 'Green Frog' service of Catherine the Great (1729-1796). The Russian tsarina had ordered the service in 1773 from the Wedgwood factory in England. It comprised a total of 952 pieces and was decorated with 1,244 different scenes of houses and gardens. Each piece also carried a green coat of arms with a frog. The service was destined for the Kekerekeksinensky Palace. 'Kekerekeksinen' is the Finnish word for frog, a creature found in great numbers in the marshy surroundings of the palace. Hermitage, St. Petersburg, h. 34.5 cm.

50: Ice pail from an 1821 service manufactured by Spode in Stoke-on-Trent. The service may have been presented in 1814 to the King of Oudh, a kingdom in Northern India, since in that year the English appointed the Nawab Ghazi-ud-din-Haidar as king. The ice pail is decorated with the King's family coat of arms, which consisted of a katar, a dagger of Mahratti origin. During an uprising in 1842 the King's palace was plundered. The rebellion was quashed by the Ninth Regiment of Lancers, who returned the ice pail to England. Derby Museum, 9th/12th Royal Lancers Museum, Derby.

51: Ice pail, circa 1820(?), manufactured by Spode, England. The Spode Museum, Stoke-on-Trent, height 29.6 cm.

52: Ice pail made by the Flight, Barr and Barr factory in Worcester, England, circa 1813-1815. The handsome, hemispherical shape of the ice pail is typical of the English style. Both sides of the pail are painted with intricate still-lifes of shells and flowers, attributed to Thomas Baxter. Museum of Worcester Porcelain, Worcester.

53: Glass ice pail manufactured by the English factory Perrin, Seddes & Co., Warrington, England, circa 1815. In the first quarter of the nineteenth century impressive ice pails were made from glass in England where glass-cutting skills were of a high standard.
The ice pail is decorated with various geometrical patterns applied using a mechanically driven grinding-wheel. The high, bell-shaped lid, crowned by an acorn-shaped knob, adds a touch of stately elegance. Victoria & Albert Museum, London.

English Ambassador and his wife, Lord and Lady Cathcart. In 1770 the English factory supplied an extensive cream ware service to Catherine II of Russia.

• Three years later the Tsarina ordered from Wedgwood a combined dinner and dessert service for 50 persons. This 'Green Frog' service consisted of 952 pieces and was decorated with as many as 1,244 different views of houses and gardens. It derived its name from the frog that was depicted on the green coat of arms painted on every single piece. The service was destined for the Kekerekeksinensky Palace, which was built in English neo-gothic style between 1774 and 1777. The palace is situated close to a marsh; the Finnish word Kekerekeksinen means "marsh frog". (It was later renamed Chesmensky Palace.[43]) The service included four glacières and 24 ice cream cups with lids. Noteworthy features are the seated female figures form-ing the crown of the lid and representing Ice, Cold and Winter. Before delivering it in 1774, Wedgwood exhibited the Green Frog service in London, evidence of the porcelain manu-facturer's commercial acumen.[44] A Derby order of 1792 records: 'We wish it [the service] very complete, there is to be like-wise 2 ice pails such as Jos. Wedgwood makes for carrying iced creams, they are very low with a shallow basin at top and to receive ice underneath.'[45]

• Up until the French Revolution of 1789 the English pottery and china factories were

1   2

7

54: Models for ten ice pails and one wine cooler, taken from the pattern book of Spode of 1820. To allow the models to be shown in one illustration, they have been detached from the pattern book and arranged according to shape. Number six is a wine cooler. According to the original annotations in the pattern book, the models were as follows:
1. Porous shape, Antique Double Icepail. One size.
2. New Shape, Beaded, Antique Double Icepail. Two sizes, 'made for London, Feb. 1820'.
3. Flanged Top, Antique Double Icepail. One size.
4. Derby Shape Icepail. One size.
5. Jar Shape Icepail. One size.
6. Single Icepail. 4 in. within top. 'made for London, Jan. 1819'.
7. Dresden Shape Icepail. One size.
8. Upright Double Icepail. Two sizes.
9. Lady Stafford's Icepail. One size.
10. Basket Rim Icepail. One size.
11. Flower Embossed Icepail. One size.

strongly influenced by France. Large quantities of French porcelain were imported and various English factories sent representa-tives to Paris to make purchases and to recruit talented porcelain painters and designers. John Flight (circa 1766-1791), owner of the oldest porcelain factory in Worcester, made various journeys to France in 1788 and 1789, where he bought at least 50,000 livres' worth of porcelain. Flight also hired a new modelmaker, so that he could offer a more fashionable product in his own country.

• After 1789 the influence of France waned and English factories began to develop their

own new models and decorations. A good example is the 1820 pattern book of the Spode factory in Stoke-on-Trent. This contains pictures of as many as eleven different ice pails,[46] including various types of U-shaped jars, and an urn-shaped ice pail, with different lid designs. Spode, founded in 1770, made a name for itself in the first quarter of the nineteenth century when it invented bone china. In addition to feldspar and a special clay, bone china contains a quantity of animal bone ash, resulting in a softer, but cheaper porcelain. Many Spode services with ice pails were exported in the nineteenth century, including to the United States.

Danish flora on an 'ice bell'

• Among the most unusual ice pails in European dessert history are the so-called 'ice bells' which feature in the 'Flora Danica service', one of the most prestigious and sumptuous porcelain services of the eighteenth century. This service was commissioned by the Danish crown prince Frederick – subsequently King Frederick VI (1768-1839) – and produced between circa 1790 and 1802 by the Royal Copenhagen Porcelain Factory. When production was discontinued in 1802 – it was still not fully completed – it numbered

55: Ice bell from the Flora Danica service, Copenhagen. This exceptional service consisted of 1,802 items and was manufactured between 1790 and 1802 by the Royal Copenhagen Porcelain Factory. It was commissioned by the Danish crown prince Frederick, who later became King Frederick VI. The ice bell was probably used to serve stepped, conically shaped bombes glacées. The floral motifs on the ice bell were copied from the Flora Danica, a multi-volume botanical encyclopaedia in which the entire flora of Denmark was recorded in words and pictures, published between 1761 and 1883. Rosenburg Castle, Copenhagen.

56: Ice pail from the Flora Danica service. Rosenburg Castle, Copenhagen.

1,802 objects, of which 1,530 have been preserved. The service included six ice pails, 104 custard cups with lids, plus ten circular serving trays, each for four custard cups and four ice bells. The remarkable ice bells are beehive-shaped, openwork cloches set on a saucer with a raised edge. In the factory's archives they are referred to by various names, including 'Isfad med Klok' (ice barrel with bell). It seems likely that the ice bells were used for presenting bombes glacées, for which the step-shaped conical moulds had been in use since the second half of the eighteenth century[47].

• The striking decorations that give the service its name are copied from the Flora Danica, a botanical encyclopaedia containing 3,000 hand-coloured illustrations in which the entire flora of Denmark was catalogued between 1761 and 1883. The greater part of the service was painted by the German Johann Christoph Bayer (1738-1812) previously an illustrator of a famous Danish botanical work on fungi.[48] This interest in botany and decorative motifs itself derived from the publications of the Swedish botanist Carolus Linnaeus (1707-1778). Linnaeus was one of the first people to own a classical porcelain service with botanical decorations. This was a tea service in Chinese porcelain dating from around 1754, decorated with the pink flowers of the Linnaeus borealis,[49] a plant he had discovered in Lapland in 1732.

• The Flora Danica service was used for the first time on the occasion of the King of Denmark's birthday on 29 January 1803. Subsequently it was used for weddings, birthdays and visits by high-ranking foreign dignitaries. During a New Year's dinner of King Christian VIII (1786-1848) the service was used to serve a dessert of 'ice pudding à la Celestine, cake, 3 kinds of ices with biscuits and meringues.'[50] Pieces of the Flora Danica service are still being produced today by Royal Copenhagen Porcelain, albeit in a slightly modified version. The original Flora Danica service has remained in the possession of the Danish royal family. Part of it is on display in two royal palaces that are open to the public in the Danish capital: Rosenburg Palace and Christiansborg Castle.

The ice pails of Frederick the Great

• Meanwhile, what of Europe's longest-established porcelain factory, Meissen? Ices were already known in Germany at the end of the seventeenth century. A translation of a French book (see box on p. 58) with recipes for water-ices was published in Hamburg in 1689.[50] However, hardly any Meissen ice pails or ice cream cups have been found, perhaps as a result of political developments.

• In eighteenth century Germany, which still consisted of many independent principalities and small kingdoms, a strong man emerged in King Frederick II of Prussia (Frederick the Great, 1712-1786). A great admirer of the French Enlightenment, Frederick conducted a famous correspondence with Voltaire and did his utmost to ensure that Berlin could match French fashions, including the eating of ice cream.

57: Ice pail produced by the Nymphenburg porcelain factory in Munich. The elliptical cooler has four tall lion's paws and stands on a pedestal with saucer. The ice pail forms part of an extensive service decorated with Bavarian landscapes and national costumes. The service, manufactured between 1804 and 1816, also includes nineteen 'cream beakers'. The beakers were also used to serve ice cream. The subjects for the paintings were derived from the art collection of the Elector of Bavaria. Wittelsbacher Ausgleichsfonds, München.

¶ Early on the morning of 30 August 1766 a long cavalcade filed through the countryside of Overijssel Province, a region in the east of the Netherlands. Seated in one of the leading carriages was 'Sijne Doorluchtigste Hoogheid' [His Most Serene Highness] Stadholder William V, Prince of Oranje-Nassau (1748-1806). In his train came coaches and horses carrying the courtiers: his personal chamberlains and gentlemen-in-waiting, along with equerries, grooms, valets, lackeys, surgeons, saddlers, cooks, a hairdresser and sundry other members of the royal household – 121 people in all. Alongside the coaches rode the Stadholder's personal bodyguard, the garde du corps.[1] Their destination was Zwolle, the capital of Overijssel Province. There, on this summer day, the prince would be handsomely received by the town council. A few months earlier William V had attained the age of eighteen, signalling the end of the regency of the Duke of Brunswick and the prince's right to inherit his role as Stadholder. To mark this happy event, the prince travelled to the various regions of the

Republic of the Netherlands for his investiture. In Overijssel Province the ceremony took place in Kampen, once a prominent Hanseatic League city, not far from Zwolle. After that the prince continued his journey to Zwolle itself.

At the city gates the town council had arranged for four marquees to be erected: one for the official reception itself, one for the 'Ladies and other Persons of Rank', one for the déjeuner that was to be offered to the prince, and one for the chef and his assistants.

At half-past-eight in the morning the prince and his retinue arrived in Zwolle. The new Stadholder was welcomed in the marquee, from which he could also watch the parades by the local garrison and enjoy the déjeuner which, served on blue porcelain, was laid out on a long table. The select company feasted on turkey, pheasant, partridge, haunch of venison, pasties, cakes, two 'compotes' of ice cream, grapes, melons, peaches, apricots and pineapples, cheese, smoked meat and tongue. To quench their thirst, wine, lemonade, liqueurs and other drinks had been laid out on three smaller tables. For the 'Ladies and other Persons of Rank' in the other marquee there was only coffee, tea, chocolate and pastries.

After watching the military exercises, the distinguished guests were received at the city hall, attended a reception and an organ concert – both held in the church – and travelled through the town, which was abundantly decorated with triumphal arches. Afterwards they returned to the city hall for what was to be the highlight of the visit: a copious meal consisting of three 'services' or courses. About 40 people were seated at the banqueting table. The local chef, Engelman, had done his very best. For the contracted price of 3,000 guilders he served almost 50 different dishes on a Meissen porcelain service: soups, poultry, game, leg of lamb, oysters, lobsters, 'diverse Sorts of Seafish and River Fish', sweetbread, pasties, vegetables, puddings, cakes and salads. For dessert there was fruit, 'French confitures' and '12 crystalline bowls with Ices of diverse sorts'. The guests were able to refresh themselves with champagne, hock, Bordeaux, Burgundy, Moselle, Cape wine and 'Prince Beer', brewed in Amsterdam. Sixteen musicians ensured that 'a soft melodious tone continued'. By 4 o'clock in the afternoon the meal was finished, bringing an end to the Stadholders visit. It had cost the city of Zwolle the appropriately princely sum of 15,629 guilders.

58: Stadholder William V, Prince of Orange-Nassau (1748-1806). In 1766, on attaining the age of eighteen, the prince took up his duties as Stadholder. For this investiture he toured the various regions of the Republic of the Netherlands. During one such reception in Zwolle, '12 crystalline bowls with Ice of diverse sorts' were served.

In 1761 he had been involved in the establishment of a porcelain factory in Berlin as a competitor of Meissen. When in 1763, at the end of the Seven Years War, Saxony had been forced to cede large areas of its territory to Prussia, Frederick secured control of Meissen. He renamed it Königliche Porzellan Manufaktur and went on to order no less than 21 services from it for his castles. The factory also produced services – of which ice pails were a regular constituent – for the Prussian nobility.[52]

59: Sèvres ice pail from the Egyptian service of the Duke of Wellington, circa 1812. The British general and hero of Waterloo was presented with the service in 1818 by the French king Louis XVIII. The 102-piece service had originally been manufactured for Joséphine, the first wife of Napoleon.
The handles of the ice pail are in the form of Egyptian serpents, while the outside of the container is painted with Pharaohs. Egyptian motifs became popular following Napoleon's expedition to Egypt in 1798. Sèvres sought advice from the diplomat and artist Vivant Denon, who had taken part in the expedition. Victoria & Albert Museum, London, inv. no. C. 128-1979.

• After Frederick's death, the factory continued to produce numerous porcelain services. One manufactured in about 1795 was presented to Catherine the Great's successor, Tsar Paul (1754-1801). Frederick William III (1770-1840) gave a series of services to his leading generals between 1817 and 1820 to thank them for their part in the defeat of Napoleon at Waterloo in 1815. The successes of his generals and marshals were portrayed in their decoration. The most handsome service went to Prince August of Prussia; the King decreed that it depict the towns and cities that the Prince had conquered in the war.'[53] In 1820, the British hero of Waterloo, the Duke of Wellington (1769-1852), received a similar service from the Austrian Emperor Francis I; it included a dessert service of 195 pieces, of which four were ice pails, and depicted eight scenes of Wellington's victories.[54] Earlier, in 1818, the French king Louis XVIII had shown his gratitude to his commander-in-chief by presenting him with an exceptional Sèvres service decorated with Egyptian scenes, including four elegant, ellipse-shaped ice pails and an enormous table centrepiece in the form of an Egyptian temple.

Napoleon's first wife, Empress Joséphine de Beauharnais (1763-1814) had ordered the service in 1810, but when it was ready she decided she did not like it and had it sent back to the factory.[55]

• In other German princedoms, such as Höchst, Fuldau, Frankenthal and Fürstenberg, factories were manufacturing services with U-shaped ice pails between 1770 and 1785.[56] In the south, the Nymphenburg factory produced numerous services for Bavarian nobility, who were already familiar with gefrorenes, or ice cream, for example through the Austrian court. Peter Melchior, the factory's model-maker, designed several ice pails at the beginning of the nineteenth century, describing one in 1804 as 'an ice-jar for ice cream or confitures with four feet and two handles and a matching base.'[57]

60: Ice pail from a service of Joséphine, the first wife of Napoleon. The service was manufactured in Paris in 1811 by Dihl et Guérhard factory. The ice pail is completely gilded, except for two frames which enclose paintings. The painting shown here is a copy of the picture 'Rust van een ruiter' [Horseman at rest] by the Dutchman Philips Wouwerman (1619-1668). Musée de Malmaison, Rueil-Malmaison, height 40 cm.

61: Six ice cream cups with matching serving tray, manufactured circa 1775 at the Fürstenberg porcelain factory, Germany. The cups and the tray are decorated with birds and fruit. Kultur-geschichtliches Museum, Osnabrück, h. 6,5 cm.

Ice for the Duchess of Parma

• Just like Germany, Italy in the eighteenth century was a fragmented country comprising many small city-states. Its southern region (Naples and Sicily) was then controlled by Spain. Its many pottery factories enjoyed less princely patronage than those in Germany or France and experienced much more modest growth. Some of these factories had ice pails in their product range in the second half of the eighteenth century. Ice pails based on the Sèvres model were manufactured in the 1770s at the factory of Pasquale Rubati in Milan.

• A leading Italian porcelain factory was Capodimonte in Naples. This factory was re-established in 1771 by Ferdinand I, King of Naples. Founded in 1743, the original factory had sixteen years later been moved lock, stock and barrel to the Buenretiro resort near Madrid by Ferdinand's father, Charles III, when he acceded to the Spanish throne. This relocation meant Spain had its own porcelain factory from 1759 – yet no ice pails produced by this factory have so far been found.

• Even more than Italy, Spain enjoyed cooled, non-frozen sorbetes, while frozen ice, or garrapina, was for a very long time much less fashionable (see also chapters 2 and 17). Highly cooled drinks like aloja were much more popular than ice cream. Aloja – a mixture of water, honey and spices such as cinnamon – was cooled using snow.[58] In 1786 the cookery book Arte de la Reposteria by Juan de la Mata was published in Madrid. Almost without exception, the ice recipes in the book related to water-ice. By that time recipes in France and England had long been expanded to include ingredients such as cream, milk and egg-white. In a popular book of 1871, the anonymous Libro de las familias, such ice was described as quesitos (literally a portion of cheese), so named because of its shape and because, like fresh cheese, it was served in serviettes.[59] As we saw earlier in this chapter, one of the terms used in France to describe ice cream from the mid-eighteenth century on was fromage glacé, or 'frozen cheese'.

• After its re-establishment in Naples the Capodimonte factory manufactured a number of services with ice pails in the 1790-1805 period. The Duchess of Parma was supplied in 1790 with a service that included eight ice pails decorated with figurative scenes taken from the frescoes at Pompeii, which had been excavated earlier that

century.[60] The low cylindrical model of these Italian ice pails resembles the early eighteenth century French glacières produced in Rouen and Moustiers.

• Several years after supplying the service to the Duchess of Parma, Capodimonte manufactured a large dinner service, possibly commissioned by the Duke of Tuscany, and around 1801 a follow-up order was received for a dessert service with various ice pails. This time Egypt formed the theme for the ornamentation, the knob on the lid of the ice pail, for instance, being formed by an Egyptian figure from the time of the Pharaohs. Following Napoleon's Egyptian campaign in 1796, Egyptian motifs were briefly popular across Europe.

Ice cream becomes more common

• The spread during the eighteenth century of ice pails and cookery books with ice recipes, both in Europe and in the United States, shows how ice cream entered the dining culture of the élite everywhere. In their production and use of ice pails there are clear differences between countries. England, with the largest number of porcelain factories, produced the most dessert services and ice pails owing to the early and widespread prosperity generated by the first industrial revolution. But there is more to it than that. Direct links between the English monarchy and the porcelain manufacturers were rare. The clientele was much wider than the country's own royalty and aristocracy: successful export initiatives meant that the nobility in Continental Europe and well-to-do citizens in the United States also dined from Wedgwood or Spode chinaware. Most of the French, Danish, Russian and German porcelain manufacturers, by contrast, enjoyed royal patronage.

• In the first half of the nineteenth century particularly, decoration for services came to reflect nationalist sentiments. No longer do Greek or Roman classical themes or symmetrical flower patterns adorn the pottery, but each nation's cities, costumes and the heroic deeds of the country's own generals. As far as the design and shape of the ice pail is concerned, however, the Sèvres porcelain factory clearly set the trend for the whole of Europe.

• In their catalogues both English and German manufacturers make it very clear that their ice pails are intended for ice cream. In the Sèvres factory archives no such statements are made about the use for which the glacières were intended. Nomenclature such as ice, ice cream, ice pail and ice cream cups (see box on p. 54) reflects the development of ice and ice cream in Europe, for instance from eau glacée to the subsequent fromage glacée in France (see also box in chapter 2: A brief vocabulary of ice cream). The Spanish had their sorbetes and the Italians their sorbetto, whereas the English spoke of iced creams, a term which had been used in Sweden as early as 1688. The ice recipes in eighteenth century French and English cookery books reflect the same picture.

• As a result, we can see taking shape in Europe the industry terminology that distinguishes between 'warm' and 'cold' ice: in Mediterranean countries 'cold' sorbets or water ices are consumed because of the heat, whereas in more northerly climes the 'warm' and nutritious dairy ice cream was much sought after as a high-calorie dessert to ward off the cold (see chapter 14).

• One of the last Sèvres services that contained pieces for serving an iced dessert was destined for the palaces of Napoleon III (1808-1873). Dating from around 1855, it included special ice cream dishes.[61] Ice pails have disappeared, as by then they had from the product ranges of most manufacturers. For quite some time the eating of ice cream had been spreading from the royal courts and palaces to resplendent dining rooms in hotels, luxuriously appointed restaurants and cafés with waiter service. The culture of dining had also changed. Dinners were no longer served à la française by a small army of lackeys catering to every whim. Now, desserts were served on plates by a small group of servants according to the service à la Russe system. This name derives from a dinner given by the Russian prince Kurakin in 1810 at his residence in Clichy near Paris. No longer were all the courses placed on the table at the same time; they were individually served. The meal started and finished with dishes that were light and easy to digest. A card placed next to the plate showed what the successive courses would be; this was the origin of the menu-card.

• As the nineteenth century progressed, eating ice cream, in both Europe and the United States, became increasingly common (see chapter 4). Consumption was no longer the preserve of kings, emperors and admirals, but was enjoyed by a greatly expanded middle class. However, it was not until the invention of new freezing techniques (see box story, chapter 4) and the mechanisation of ice cream production that the delicacy would become available to the mass-market, starting in the United States.

62: Ice pail from the Italian pottery Capodimonte, near Naples, 1790. The pail formed part of a large service produced for the Duchess of Parma. The service contained a total of eight ice pails and was decorated with figures based on the frescoes found at Pompeii, where excavations had started in 1748. The ice pail has a remarkably low, cylindrical shape and stands on three legs in the shape of a gryphon, a mythical beast with an eagle's head and the body of a lion. Raccolta Enzo Catello, Naples, height 20.5 cm., diameter 20 cm.

63: Chinese porcelain ice pail from a large dessert service, circa 1800-1810. The service, of which 738 objects still survive, was produced in China for an unknown, but presumably Dutch, client. Dessert services of oriental porcelain are very few and far between. Of the vast quantities of porcelain that were imported into Europe during the eighteenth and the early nineteenth century, most of the products related to dinner and coffee and tea services.
The more luxury products like dessert services were ordered by the European royal families from their own factories, especially in the second half of the eighteenth century. Fries Museum, Leeuwarden, height 25 cm.

64: Ice pail, Amstel porcelain, circa 1800. Inside the pail is a separate container. The shapes used for Amstel porcelain, named after the river Amstel in the Netherlands and manufactured between 1784 and circa 1810, were strongly influenced by French styles. Rijksmuseum Amsterdam, height 43.5 cm, diameter 19.5 cm.

Licks, Sticks & Bricks
A WORLD HISTORY OF ICE CREAM

Ices from the dining-table to the street

Les Mangeurs de Glaces.

63.

By about 1800 interest in good food was growing significantly. Characteristic of this were the publication between 1803 and 1813 of the first Almanach des Gourmands in Paris and in 1825 La Physiologie du goût (The physiology of taste), a treatise by the Parisian author Brillat-Savarin. French cooking began to blossom under the leadership of chefs who before the French Revolution had worked for the nobility, but who now found their way into the kitchens of restaurants, which were fast growing in number.

• Until late in the eighteenth century ice cream had been a luxury product mainly eaten at the dining-tables of the European aristocracy. The wealthy middle classes, however, could now increasingly be seen eating ice cream in cafés. The interest in cuisine was also reflected in the publication of numerous cookery books, which included imaginative recipes for desserts like ice cream. These cookery books often enjoyed substantial print-runs, with reprints following in rapid succession.[1]

• Attention to good food was not limited to Paris. Gastronomy also flourished in cities like London, Vienna, Prague, Berlin, New York, Philadelphia and San Francisco. Cookery schools were an emerging phenomenon, while restaurants, hotels and dining clubs experienced a golden age.

65: 'Les mangeurs de glaces' – 'The ice cream eaters', 1825 lithograph by the French artist Louis Boilly (1761-1845). Right from its introduction at the French court in around 1662, ice was served in glasses. That remained so until the advent of wafers and ice cream cones in about 1895.

• The revolution in transport played an important part. From all over the world, steamships and steam locomotives brought in increasing quantities of exotic ingredients like vanilla pods – the raw material for the most popular ice cream flavour. The advent of the railways also made it easier to supply the cities with milk. Other technical

Le Bon Genre. N: 98.

La Belle Limonadière.

66: 'La Belle Limonadière' – 'The beautiful lemonade girl', anonymous lithograph, 1816, from the series 'Le Bon Genre', which illustrates the pleasures of the Parisian bourgeoisie in the nineteenth century. The lady at the table on the right is eating an ice cream. The lemonade girl, seated behind a counter designed in Empire style, is keeping a record of the orders.

advances, such as the development in the second half of the nineteenth century of modern, ammonia-operated freezing machines, accelerated the spread of ice cream throughout the Western world. Using these machines, blocks of ice could be produced artificially, with the result that production no longer depended on the availability of natural ice that had been harvested during the winter months.

Les Glaces.

Le Bon Genre, N° 4.

Rue Montmartre, N° 132.

• Another important innovation was the ice cream making machine of 1843. The introduction of the first refrigerators and ice cream salons in the United States around 1860 also gave a fillip to ice cream's popularity. Until well into the twentieth century, however, refrigerators remained simple, cork-insulated wooden constructions, clad with zinc on the inside and cooled by a block of raw ice.

• At the same time as ice cream production

67: 'Les glaces' – 'The ice creams', 1804 lithograph by the French artist George Jacques Gatine (1773-1841). The ladies, dressed in the fashions of Napoleonic times, are licking away at their ice creams with great gusto, ignoring the spoon available. At the turn of the century, following the terrors of the French Revolution, the new bourgeoisie – particularly in Paris – took an increasing interest in good food and drink.

was being modernised, the income of more and more citizens started to improve. In the final quarter of the nineteenth century factory workers in America and England were given free time and, thanks to the railways, a visit to a bathing resort on a fine summer's day was no longer reserved solely for the well-to-do.

• These developments ran in parallel with the biggest migration in modern-day history. Between around 1850

L'Embarras du Choix.

Le Bon Genre, N.° 44.

68: 'L'Embarras du Choix' – 'Choice a-plenty', anonymous lithograph, 1810, from the series 'Le Bon Genre'. In the many café-restaurants on the Boulevard des Italiens, and in the arcades of the Palais Royal, people gathered to enjoy ice creams and other delicacies.

and 1914 millions of Italians emigrated, fanning out all over the world. Wherever they ended up, they triggered an explosion in ice cream consumption. First in Europe, and later in North and South America, they brought ice cream from the dining-table to the street, enabling the masses to become acquainted with it for the first time.

Ices in the gourmet's paradise: Paris

• At the beginning of the nineteenth century, however, things had not quite reached that stage, although ices were certainly gaining in popularity. 'Ices are strictly necessary', wrote the Parisian journalist Grimod de la Reynière (1758-1837).[2]

• And no-one was better qualified to give that verdict than de la Reynière, compiler of the Almanach des Gourmands. In small booklets,

69: Café Frascati, Paris, 1807, engraving by the French artist Debucourt. This establishment was described by the Parisian journalist Grimod de La Reynière in 1803 in his Almanach des Gourmands as follows: 'We congratulate M. Garchi on the luxury of his splendid palace and on the reputation of his ices.' Situated close to the Opéra, Frascati was a highly popular gathering place. To round off the evening, opera enthusiasts liked to go there for a glass of ice cream.

published at a rate of almost one a year, de la Reynière reported on his strolls through Paris, calling in at dozens of cafés, restaurants, confectioners, chocolate makers, cheese shops, wine merchants, fruiterers and other suppliers of delicacies. In the first almanac of 1803, for example, he saunters down the Boulevard des Italiens and 'perfumes his mouth with chocolate from Monsieur Tortoni, almost as delicious as the chocolate of the King of Spain'.[3] The shop of the Italian Tortoni was also famous for its ice cream, as was the nearby Frascati establishment, which de la Reynière praises with the words: 'We congratulate M. Garchi on the luxury of his splendid palace and on the reputation of his ices.'[4] Frascati was located close to the Opéra and opera enthusiasts loved to go there after the performance to indulge in a glass of ice cream.[5]

• The ices at the most famous restaurant in Paris at the time, Vévy, were also widely acclaimed, as were those of Café Zoppi on the Rue de l'Ancienne Comédie where, according to de la Reynière in 1803, you could eat the very best 'glaces en tasse' (Ice creams in a cup) in Paris. Café Zoppi was the successor to the renowned Café Le Procope, which had been serving ices ever since its establishment in 1686 by Francesco Procopio dei Coltelli (see box story in chapter 3).

• After the gruesome years of the Revolution, going out to eat or simply enjoying an ice cream in the summer held great appeal for the new bourgeoisie. In the numerous cafés under the arcades of the Palais Royal there was ample for them to enjoy. No longer did people eat to live, they lived to eat.

• The emergence of this epicurean lifestyle reflected and reinforced the place that food had begun to occupy in French culture during the eighteenth century. For more and more people eating was becoming an art. The pre-eminent place for indulging the taste buds was the restaurant, a phenomenon which in Napoleonic times became a tremendous success not only in Paris, but also in other great European cities such as Vienna and London. Before the French Revolution, noted Grimod de la Reynière in his Almanach, there were about a hundred restaurants in Paris. By 1803 that number had increased fivefold[6], many of them presided over by famous chefs who in pre-Revolution times had served under princes, dukes, marshals and bishops. Such a man was Marie-Antoine Carême (1783-1833), who in his time had served kings, emperors and ministers. Carême now raised cooking to an art form.

• He had started his career in 1798 as a pupil of Bailly, a famous Parisian confectioner[7], under whom he had learnt not only how to make all sorts of ingeniously constructed cakes and other sweet desserts from flour and sugar, but also how to develop new designs of his own. Carême had a passion for architecture and he regarded cooking as an architectural art. Apart from tasting good, the food also had to look exciting. His dishes were superbly decorated structures, using ingredients in highly sophisticated arrangements. Desserts such as mousses, puddings and gâteaux, including ice cream gâteaux, lent themselves well to enchanting, fairytale presentations.

• Although Paris had an army of inventive chefs to serve its needs, Carême long remained the trend-setter of culinary artistry in the nineteenth century, not least because of his cookery books, such as L'art de la cuisine au XIXème siècle (The art of cooking in the 19th Century). His vision found many imitators. He was followed by chefs like Martin-Jules Gouffé, Émile Bernard, Urbain Dubois and Pierre Lacam whose publications helped to popularise French cuisine. In France, England, Germany and the United States more and more cookery books and specialised journals were being published, including periodicals issued by confectioners which are full of incredible desserts requiring fiendishly complicated preparation, but which offer up a dazzling kaleidoscope of the confectioner's creative talents.

• In the meantime the range of ice cream moulds had been steadily expanded since the seventeenth century. In the final quarter of the nineteenth century in particular, specialist suppliers started putting on the market ice moulds of every conceivable type: fruit, vegetables, mushrooms, eagles, ballet dancers, hearts, lions, horses, elephants, cats, doves, lobsters, sea-shells, trains, cannons, soldiers, lighthouses, windmills,

Tafel **105** u. **106**

Marschall-Bombe.

70: Designs for two bombes glacées from the *Neues illustriertes Konditorei-buch* by Carl Krackhart, Munich 1898. Nineteenth century cooks and confectioners from all over Europe lent their skills to creating festive ice cream dishes. They often named their creations after famous contemporaries. Napoleon, Wellington, Nelson, Washington, Bismarck, Kaiser Wilhelm I, the Austrian empress Marie Louise ('Sissy'), Marshal Radetzky, Madame de Pompadour, the Count of Monte Cristo, Othello, Mozart, Sarah Bernhardt, La Fontaine, Chateaubriand – all had ice cream specialities named after them.

KRACKHARTS KONDITOREIBUCH, Ausgabe A. 11. Auflage.

Radetzky-Bombe

G. Ritzer

Verlag H. Killinger, Nordhausen.

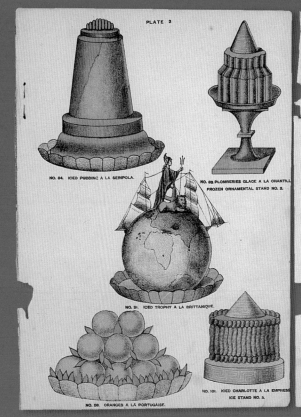

PLATE 2

NO. 84. ICED PUDDING A LA SERIPOLA.

NO. 86 PLOMBRERIES GLACE A LA CHANTILL
FROZEN ORNAMENTAL STAND NO. 2.

NO. 91. ICED TROPHY A LA BRITTANIQUE.

NO. 98. ORANGES A LA PORTUGAISE.

NO. 101. ICED CHARLOTTE A LA EMPRESS
ICE STAND NO. 5.

PLATE 4

NO. 114. ICED SOUFFLE A LA NOYAU.

NO. 94. TROPHY GLACE A L AMOUR.

NO. 118. BISQUET GLACES A LA REINE.

NO. 105. MELON A LA SURPRISE, ICE STAND NO. 4.

NO. 120. ICED CHARTREUSE A LA MADAME FAVART.

gnomes, angels, Eskimos, Red Indians, harps, violins, Japanese fans, skulls, pyramids, clowns, Father Christmases, Easter lambs and floral bouquets. An ice dessert shaped like the Eiffel Tower or the Statue of Liberty? Coming up. A popular shape was the simple large hemisphere known as a bombe glacée or, as the Germans called it, an Eisbombe. Ice cream desserts in the shape of timbals were also referred to as bombes.

• Ice cream desserts took on every conceivable shape and form (see box on p. 146).

71 and 72: Four pages illustrating ice cream gâteaux in Ices, Plain and Decorated by Fred T. Vine, London, 1890. Many of the ice recipes are inspired by French cuisine, as is reflected in their names: Oranges à la Portugaise, Trophy glace à l'amour (an ice with a figure of Cupid on top), Iced pudding à la diplomatique, Ice Trophy à l'automne. There is even an Ice Trophy à la Britannique, topped by the symbol of Britannia ruling the waves.

Often they were named after famous people: princesses, duchesses, statesmen, generals, authors, musicians, actresses and opera divas. Kaiser Wilhelm I, the Austrian empress Marie-Louise, Napoleon, Wellington, Nelson, Washington, Bismarck, Field-Marshal Radetzky, Madame de Pompadour, the Count of Monte Cristo, Othello, Mozart, Sarah Bernhardt, La Fontaine, Chateaubriand – all had ice cream desserts named after them. This diversity was a precursor of what were to become known as a 'novelties' in the ice cream industry terminology of the second

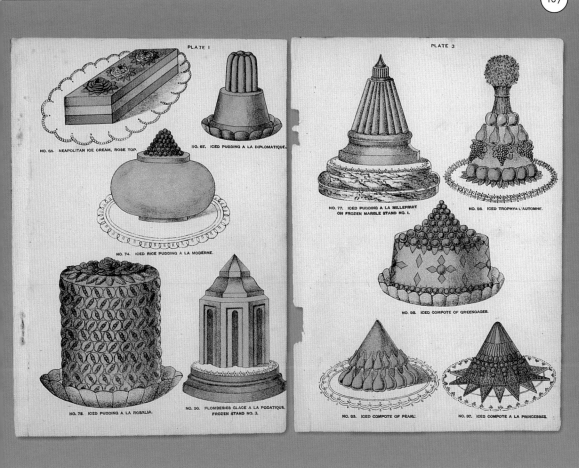

PLATE I

NO. 65. NEAPOLITAN ICE CREAM, ROSE TOP.

NO. 67. ICED PUDDING A LA DIPLOMATIQUE.

NO. 74. ICED RICE PUDDING A LA MODERNE.

NO. 72. ICED PUDDING A LA ROSALIA.

NO. 30. PLOMBERIES GLACE A LA PODATIQUE. FROZEN STAND NO. 3.

PLATE 3

NO. 77. ICED PUDDING A LA MILLEFRUIT ON FROZEN MARBLE STAND NO. I.

NO. 93. ICED TROPHYA L'AUTOMNE.

NO. 96. ICED COMPOTE OF GREENGAGES.

NO. 95. ICED COMPOTE OF PEARL.

NO. 97. ICED COMPOTE A LA PRINCESSES.

half of the twentieth century, with new ice creams included in the range every season.
• Several of these nineteenth century ice cream desserts have stood the test of time: Omelette Norvégienne (also known as Omelette Sibérienne), Poire Belle Hélène, Dame Blanche and Pêche Melba [Peach Melba]. However, only the names remain unchanged. Even during the lifetimes of their creators, the composition and method of preparation of these illustrious ice creams could alter – not always for the better, as the inventor of the Peach Melba, Auguste Escoffier (1846-1935), another famous name in the pantheon of French chefs, complained in his memoirs.

London: eating ices at Gunter's

• It was not only in France that bourgeois cuisine became very popular, with ice cream increasingly taking its place in dessert culture. In England, and above all in London, a gastronomic tradition was developing and restaurants and dining clubs mushroomed. Carême and Escoffier both built a reputation in the British capital for their cooking. It was at the Ritz Hotel in 1896 that Escoffier created his Peach Melba (see box on p. 110).
• Just as in Paris, Vienna, Berlin and New York, the ice cream in London was mainly

produced by confectioners. They advertised their 'ice creams' using the methods of the times. Not much advertising was done in newspapers; instead it took the form of a sort of visiting card. In 1802, for instance, the confectioner J. Hards of No. 57, Houndsditch – near Liverpool Street Station – extolled his ice cream on a card decorated with cherubs. As the customer could read on the card, Mr Hards served his wares 'in the gentlest stile'.[8]

• In London the Italian confectioner Domenico Negri long remained at the top of his profession. In 1769 he opened a confectionery shop in Berkeley Square which soon expanded to become the foremost business of its type. In his shop Negri sold every kind of confectionery: cake, biscuits

73: Portrait of Auguste Escoffier, the renowned French chef who thought up the recipe for Peach Melba in 1893.

and 'all Sorts of Ice, Fruits & Creams [made] in the best Italian manner.'[9] After 1780 James Gunter became a partner in Negri's business. By the beginning of the nineteenth century the name of the shop had been changed to Gunter's and the business was appointed purveyor to the Royal Household; and in 1815 Gunter's son Robert travelled to Paris to take up an apprenticeship with Tortini.

• In 1820 Guglielmo Jarrin, 'Confectioner and Ornament Maker at Mr Gunter's', published his book The Italian Confectioner.[10] Reprinted many times, the book contains a whole series of delicious ice cream recipes devot-

ing much attention to the technical aspects of ice cream preparation. 'In ices that are badly mixed', writes Jarrin, 'the sugar sinks to the bottom, and they have necessarily a sharp, unpleasant taste. Another very general defect in ices is their appearing full of lumps; they are often of a disagreeable, dirty, red colour; and there are few houses in London where ices are to be found entirely free from these faults'.[11] Jarrin had worked in Paris and probably came to London with Robert Gunter. His wealth of experience made a considerable contribution to the growth of the business. Over forty years later this publishing tradition was still going strong, a fact underlined by the appearance in 1861 of Gunter's Modern Confectioner by William Jeanes, 'Chief Confectioner at Messrs Gunter's, Confectioners to Her Majesty'.[12]

• Gunter's continued to be a well-known name in London up until the Second World War. The business could not always keep pace with demand. Sometimes no raw ice was available for freezing the ice cream. On 5 July 1822 Gunter's placed an announcement in The Times to inform their clientele that a batch of ice had arrived from the watersoff Greenland and that 'they are able to supply their cream and fruit ices at their former prices'.[13]

JOHN BULL AND HIS FAMILY AT AN ICE CAFÉ. THE OCCUPATION.

74: John Bull and his family eating ice cream in a London cafeteria. Lithograph by J.J. Chalon, circa 1820. The character is derived from the 1712 novel The History of John Bull by John Arbuthnot and remains a personification of the typical Englishman.

• This announcement emphasised how much ice cream makers of that time were dependent on the availability of natural ice. Artificial cooling other than with ice and salt was still in its infancy and the ice harvested from rivers and lakes and stored in ice cellars (see chapter 2) was no longer sufficient, at least in England, to meet the greatly increased demand. The meat, fish and beer trades also used enormous quantities of ice each day to cool their products.

Frederick Tudor, Ice King

• In the United States, early in the nineteenth century, there sprang up a lively trade in ice based on Boston, where a certain Frederick Tudor established an ice trading empire. Having started in 1805, he soon gained the nickname of 'ice king of the world'. With his wooden three-masters Ice King, Iceberg and Iceland, he began shipping ice all over the world, initially to cities on the eastern seaboard of the United States like New York, Philadelphia, Baltimore,

¶ On 15 May 1893 the Australian opera diva Nellie Melba (real name Helen Porter Mitchell) (1861-1931), who was particularly celebrated in England, gave a performance at Covent Garden in London. The role she played was that of Elsa in the opera Lohengrin by Richard Wagner.[1] As we read in his memoirs, one of the people in her audience that evening was Auguste Escoffier (1846-1935), the founding father of French cuisine and a great admirer of the 'Australian nightingale'. The opera singer came to dine in the Savoy Hotel where Escoffier was then head chef and, inspired by her performance, he created a special dessert: the Pêche Melba (Peach Melba). 'To express my admiration and to thank her for the evening that I spent spellbound by her extraordinary voice, borne by a veritable talent for acting, I wanted to prepare a surprise for her', Escoffier later wrote in his memoirs. 'The day after the performance Madame Melba gave a dinner for several of her friends. That was my opportunity, I felt. I recalled the majestic mythical swan from the first act of Lohengrin and, when the right moment arose, I wanted to present her with a silver tray of peaches on a bed of vanilla ice

cream between the wings of a splendid swan carved from a block of ice and covered with a voile of candy-floss'.[2] Escoffier initially called his new dessert 'Les Pêches au Cygne' – peaches with a swan. The name 'Pêche Melba' only came about

75: Nellie Melba (1861-1931), the stage name of Helen Mitchell, the Australian opera singer after whom the French chef Auguste Escoffier named his 1899 ice-cream creation 'Pêche (Peach) Melba'.

six years later during the opening of the Carlton Hotel in The Haymarket, London, on 1 July 1899.[3] Escoffier had been appointed as chef de cuisine at the Carlton and Nellie Melba attended the inaugural dinner. Escoffier had his waiters serve his special ice cream dessert, now enhanced with a purée of sweetened fresh raspberries

covering the peaches. Nellie Melba was enchanted by the dessert and wanted to know its name. Escoffier asked whether she would do him the honour of allowing him to call it 'Pêche Melba'.

The Peach Melba ice cream soon became a world-wide hit, though its presentation between the wings of a swan carved from ice, perhaps unsurprisingly, remained rare. Before long it was being made using different ingredients. 'Much to my regret I have seen that the real recipe is changed all too often', complains Escoffier in his memoirs. 'The Pêche Melba should be composed of soft, properly ripe peaches, vanilla ice cream and a sugared purée of raspberries.' Modifications or additions, such as flour in the raspberry purée or a topping of cream on the peaches, were altogether wrong. 'They will not satisfy the palate of a connoisseur', sniffs Escoffier. He did like the sprinkling of a few flakes of fresh almond over the peaches. 'But you must never use dried almonds', was the maestro's stern injunction.[4]

76: Ice-sawing machine, as depicted in the Scientific American of 22 July 1882. The machine was invented by Chauncy Sager from Indianapolis. His ingenious device was capable of sawing the ice both lengthwise and breadthwise at the same time and the hefty spikes fitted in its tyres gave it purchase when travelling over the ice floor. In the United States up until about 1915, the volume of natural ice harvested in the winter was greater than that of the artificial ice produced by freezing machines. Well into the twentieth century natural ice continued to be used to cool ice cream.

Washington, Charleston and Savannah, and to New Orleans; and, later, to London, Rio de Janeiro and as far away as Bombay, Colombo, Hong Kong, Tokyo, Shanghai and Sydney.
• In Calcutta, then capital of the British colony of India, the first shipment arrived in 1833. During the voyage only a third of the ice had melted, proof of the quality of the insulation methods that Tudor used.[14] Within Tudor's ice business, a whole range of tools and equipment were developed to improve the yield of the ice harvests: ice

saws, ice hooks, ice scrapers, ice chisels and ice ploughs.
• Around 1837 others began to follow in Tudor's footsteps and gradually ice companies were set up everywhere along the rivers and lakes in the northern United States. One of the best-known was the Knickerbocker Ice Company, which was founded in 1842 in New York. A whole industry now developed, the total investment in the sector being estimated in 1882 at $18,000,000 – an astronomical sum for those days.[15]

SAWING AND PLOUGHING THE ICE ON THE ST. LAWRENCE.

THE ICEHOUSE, NUNS' ISLAND, MONTREAL.

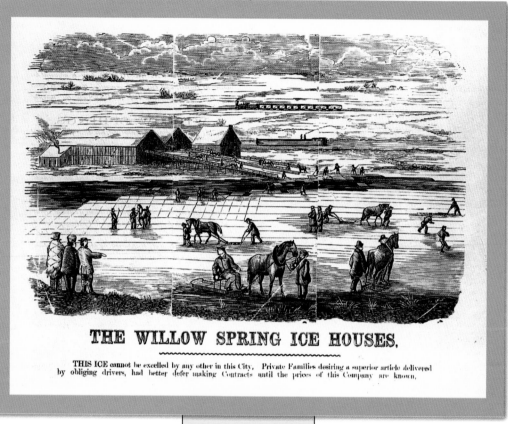

THE WILLOW SPRING ICE HOUSES,

THIS ICE cannot be excelled by any other in this City. Private Families desiring a superior article delivered by obliging drivers, had better defer making Contracts until the prices of this Company are known.

79: Woodcut depicting an ice harvest using horse-drawn ice ploughs at the Willow Springs Ice House near Chicago, circa 1856. In the US tens of thousands of men worked each winter on the harvesting of ice from lakes and rivers.

Every winter tens of thousands of men looked forward eagerly to employment as the waters froze over and harvesting could begin.
• Ice was shipped to European ports not only from America but also from Norway and Sweden. In London the first shipload of ice from Norway arrived in 1822, but it was not until around 1850 that the Norwegian ice trade really got under way.

77: (above left) Engraving from The Illustrated London News of April 1859 showing ice harvesting, both by horses and by hand, on the St. Lawrence River, Canada.

78: Engraving of ice house on Nun's Island, Montreal, circa 1860.

By about 1900 Norwegian ice exports had reached their peak at 300,000 tons.[16] Among Londoners the ice harvested by the American Lake Wenham Ice Company from the lake of that name was very popular because of its translucency. For the English it became a brand name which denoted top quality ice, so much so that the owners of the Lake Wenham Ice Company acquired the right to call the Oppegaard Lake in Norway Lake Wenham, so that ice harvested there could be sold under that name.[17]
• By the beginning of the twentieth century, however, the trade in natural ice was in decline. Since 1870 more and more modern freezing machines had come on to the market and they were increasingly reliable. In 1882 around 40 different types of freezing machine were operational throughout the world, most of them using ammonia[18]

RAPHAEL THOMSON, LITH. 69ª WELLS Sᵀ, OXFORD Sᵀ, W.

MOULDS FOR THESE DESIGNS CAN BE HAD OF A.B. MARSHALL.

80: Designs for ice moulds from Mrs A.B. Marshall's The Book of Ices, published in London in 1885. Her book contains recipes for dairy cream ices, water-ices, sorbets, ice cream soufflés, mousses and 'dressed ices'. By the latter expression she meant bombes glacées and ice cream puddings.

(see box on p. 116). 'Natural ice continues to be sent to the seaports of the south by northern operators', noted Henry Hall in 1882, who himself worked as an agent in the American ice industry, 'but inland in the south, the trade is local and now almost wholly in artificial ice'.[19]

• In London the imported natural ice was used not only by Gunter's and their confectioner colleagues, but also increasingly in the cookery schools which started to emerge in the second half of the nineteenth century. The art of making ice cream was taught in these schools. A pioneer in this field was Agnes Marshall (1855-1905). The books of ice cream recipes by this doughty Victorian cook, and the cookery school that she started in 1883, were of unparalleled quality. In 1885 she published her first book of ice cream recipes, The Book of Ices, and followed it with Mrs. A.B. Marshall's Cookery Book (1888) and Fancy Ices (1894).

• Her ice cream recipes are not only of an exceptionally high standard but also very detailed and accurate. The Book of Ices contains recipes for cream ices, water-ices, sorbets, ice soufflés, mousses and 'dressed ices'. By the latter Mrs Marshall meant

bombes glacées and ice puddings. As ingredients for the cream ices, she used not only many varieties of fruits, nuts, chocolate and vanilla, but also cucumber, tea, rhubarb, rice, white wine and ratafia – a delicate liqueur made from brandy, fermented sugar water and the juice of various fruits or flowers. The recipes for 'dressed ices' are accompanied by illustrations of 41 different ice moulds, mainly for ice puddings. She also gives all sorts of practical tips for the preparation of ice cream: too much sugar means that the ice will not freeze properly; ice with too little sugar becomes as hard as a rock.

• Worthy of special note were the recipes for ice cream in cones that she included in Mrs. A.B. Marshall's Cookery Book. This was published sixteen years before ice cream cones became popular following their introduction at the 1904 World's Fair in St. Louis, USA[20] (see chapter 5).

ICE from ROCKLAND LAKE N° 24

81: Water-colour drawing of a supplier of natural ice from Rockland Lake, New York, produced around 1840 by Nicolino Calyo. The iceman is carrying the ice with ice hooks. After the blocks of ice had been gripped in the hooks, the hinges of the hooks were 'locked' into position. The ice harvested during the winter months was used for various purposes, including the cooling of ice cream.

¶ In the eighteenth and nine-teenth centuries physicists, chemists and engineers came up with a succession of inventions that were to lead to the modern cooling installations, both industrial and domestic, now in use. Without these machines consumption of ice cream on today's scale would be impossible.

If the eighteenth century can be characterised as a time of theory and experimentation in the development of artificial freezing techniques, the nineteenth century was more about putting the physical theories of cooling technology into practice and improving on them. The most effective process was found to be a system of compressing gases and evaporating liquids with a low boiling point, such as propane or ammonia. By this process the gas is first compressed by a pump or a compressor. During this operation the gas becomes very hot. If it is then passed via a condenser – an assembly of tubes – the gas cools down again. Its temperature is reduced to about five degrees above the ambient temperature and it liquefies again. The liquid is then propelled via a capillary tube – a very narrow pipe with a diameter of about one millimetre – into a system of tubes with a much bigger diameter. In these tubes normal atmospheric pressure prevails and the gas starts to boil and evaporate. In so doing it extracts heat from its surroundings, the principle whereby cold is generated in the freezing compartment of a refrigerator. One of the first people to investigate the cooling properties of gases during evaporation was the Scottish chemist William Cullen (1710-1790). In experiments in his Glasgow laboratory in 1748 he found that when ethyl was evaporated, the ambient temperature decreased substantially. In 1755 Cullen constructed the world's first freezing machine, producing a small piece of ice.

But the first successful application on a larger scale was not the work of a physicist, chemist, or engineer, but of an American doctor, John Gorrie. In the hot climate of Apalachicola, Florida, on the Gulf of Mexico where Gorrie lived, the irregular supply of natural ice was problematic, since cooling was urgently needed for the treatment of patients in his hospital. In 1844, on the basis of the theoretical know-how that was available, the doctor managed to develop a cooling machine which, operating using compressed air, was able to produce several kilos of ice per day. However, his invention was not taken seriously and the modest Gorrie could not gather together the capital that was

82: Cover of a 1935 brochure issued by the German firm von Linde and describing cooling equipment sold under the Nordpol name to confectionery bakers. The equipment was intended both for the cooling of glass display cabinets for pastries and cakes and for the preparation of ice cream. The firm was founded by the German engineer Carl von Linde, who in about 1870 had developed a successful cooling machine based on the process of compression and evaporation of ammonia gas within a closed circuit.

required to develop the prototype further.[1]

The French engineer Philippe Edouard Carré (1824-1900) enjoyed more success in this respect. His cooling machine, which operated by ammonia gas absorption, caused a sensation at the 1862 World Fair in Paris. Capable of turning out between 12 and 100 kilos of ice per hour, it became a great commercial success, being soon manufactured in several European countries. In 1863, in the midst of the American Civil War, two of Carré's 'cooling machines for the production of ice' were even smuggled to New Orleans and Texas, where they were used to make ice for the field hospitals of the Confederate armies. The machines were desperately needed, as Union forces had halted the supply of natural ice by their blockade of southern ports. In 1869, three ice-making machines were in operation in the United States, all located in southern states. However, it was much longer before artificially produced ice started to replace

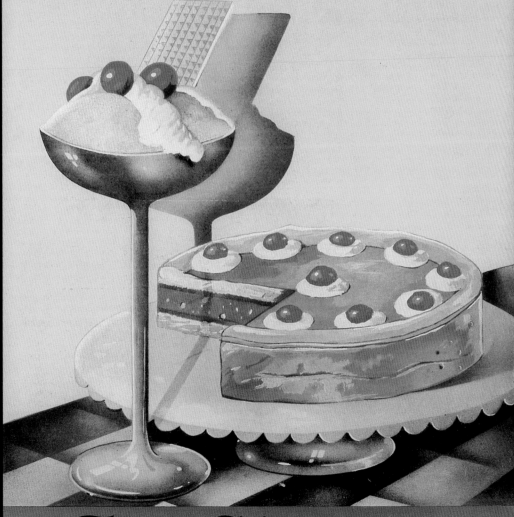

8. MAI 1942
Firmenkataloge

Linde
KÜHLUNG

Für die Konditorei

natural ice in the US. Of the 4.5 million inhabitants of New York in 1908, one-third still used natural ice that had been harvested during the winter. Only in about 1915 did the production of artificial ice come to exceed that of natural ice.[2]

In Europe, the cooling machine's real breakthrough took place after 1870. In that year the German engineer Carl von Linde (1842-1934) presented his own prototype cooling machine which operated through the compression and evaporation of ammonia gas. He found an immediate buyer in the Bavarian brewer George Sedlmayr.

Three years later, von Linde launched a revised design at the World Fair in Vienna; the entire system for the compression and evaporation of ammonia gas was now housed in a closed circuit. This approach was much more efficient and dramatically reduced production costs.

As a consequence von Linde's cooling machine quickly became tremendously popular. In 1879 he established a factory in Wiesbaden and his cooling installations were soon to be found in breweries throughout Western Europe. His invention was also used by meat processing plants, shipping lines, margarine factories, manufacturers of raw ice, chemicals businesses, chocolate factories, sugar refineries and

LES PYRÉNÉES (3ᵉ SÉRIE)

381. - MONTAGNARDS PORTEURS DE GLACE

countless other concerns. In the 1890s sales of Linde's Kältemaschinen **really took off.**[3] Primitive refrigerators for household use had already been in kitchens since the beginning of the nineteenth century. They

83: Picture postcard, 1908, showing two men in the French Pyrenees lugging blocks of ice. Long after the advent of modern cooling installations, the harvesting of ice and snow from the mountains remained customary practice in many countries. Until the 1950s most households in Europe used natural ice to cool their refrigerators; in several Asian and Latin American countries that is still the case today.

were simple wooden boxes, insulated with cork, lined with zinc and cooled by a block of natural ice. With the advent of the electro-motor in the 1880s, initially in the United States, the development of a modern cooling machine for domestic use came much closer, since the compact electro-motor could be used as a simple way of powering the compressor.

The first refrigerator constructed according to this principle was put on the market in America in 1915. Its maker was Alfred Mellowes of Fort Wayne. He called his refrigerator the Frigidaire, a name that later became a generic word in the USA for refrigerators. In 1919 he sold his small factory, the Guardian Refrigerator Company, to General Motors, the automobile giant. Sales of refrigerators rocketed. Whereas in 1921 only 5,000 American households owned a Frigidaire, by 1930 that number had increased to 850,000.[4]

The early refrigerators were involved in a number of accidents. The gases were highly flammable and were used in fairly large quantities. Explosions were common. In the 1930s the industry developed a new, non-flammable refrigerant, called freon – a collective term for fluorocarbons. In the 1970s, however, it was realised that the

84: Advertisement for a Gram refrigerator, circa 1950. Since the 1930s Gram has been manufacturing refrigerators for both industrial and household use.

chlorine present in the refrigerant attacked the ozone layer. Freon has therefore not been used in refrigerators or freezer cabinets since 1995 and refrigerants such as propane or isobutane have reappeared on the scene – except that today, thanks to much better insulation and other improvements, they are used in much smaller quantities.

The dough for Mrs Marshall's ice cream cones consisted of almonds, sugar, flour, eggs, vanilla essence and 'one tablespoonful of orange-flower water'.[21] Although she claimed that none of her recipes had been copied from other books, several of her ice cream recipes have been found to originate from Gunter's Modern Confectioner by William Jeanes (1861).[22] To promote her books Agnes Marshall toured England giving cookery lessons. In the summer of 1888 she travelled to Philadelphia, USA, and returned with recipes for Philadelphia and Chicago doughnuts.

• One thing that certainly did not impress this enterprising lady was the quality of the 'hokey-pokey' ices sold by Italians on the streets of London. 'Besides being variously flavoured, hokey-pokey was dread-

fully sweet, dreadfully cold, and hard as stone', she wrote in 1901 in a column in Across the Table, a magazine she had started. 'Swede turnip, converted to pulp, was known to have formed its base in lieu of more expensive supplies from the cow. Nevertheless, such adulteration is harmless compared to the awful foreign substances, including enormous numbers of sewage bacteria even, that have been found to permeate Italian ice-cream, which is often prepared amidst the most loathsome conditions.'[23]

85: 'Margaret Cornets', recipe from Fancy Ices by the English cook Mrs A. B. Marshall, 1894. As early as 1884 Agnes Marshall had pioneered cornets, or cones, filled with ice cream. The dough mix for her cornets comprised almonds, sugar, flour, eggs, vanilla essence and 'one tablespoonful of orange-flower water'.

The Italian diaspora

• The ice desserts made by confectioners, chefs and pupils of cookery schools were mainly consumed by the well-to-do citizens who could afford this new delicacy. There are instances of ice cream beginning to be sold on the streets early in the nineteenth century. In 1819, for example, the Journal des Dames informed its lady readers about itinerant boys who sold excellent ice cream on the streets of Paris for three sous.[24] But the great mass of the population in the Western world only experienced ice cream for the first time in the final quarter of the nineteenth century.

• This popularisation was largely the work of large groups of Italian émigrés. In summer in the big cities their cheerfully painted ice cream carts were to be seen everywhere, the vendors announcing their presence by tooting their copper horns. Their ices found eager buyers in Vienna, Berlin, London, Paris, New York, and as far afield as Buenos Aires, Lima, Brisbane, Prague, Stockholm, Liège, Glasgow and Dublin.[25] The German Georg Johann Kohl, travelling in Russia, noted in his 1841 report that ice cream was sold on the streets in summer in St. Petersburg, Moscow and Odessa. Not all vendors were Italian. Towards the end of the nineteenth century the street-cry that could be heard in Helsinki was 'haroschi, maroschi' – very cold ice. Clad in blue trousers, blue shirts, a white apron

and a dark-blue cap, these were Russian ice cream vendors selling their wares.[26]

• Of the nearly 100 million Italians in 1990, 40 million lived outside Italy.[27] Half of the 14 million Italian emigrants from the 1876-1915 period crossed the Atlantic. Of those, over 4 million settled in North America and 3 million in South America, principally in Argentina and Brazil. France and Germany were the primary destinations in Europe, with communities of

86: Lithograph of an ice cream seller in Naples, 1820. At the vendor's feet is a barrel. The top part of a tin box containing the ice cream is just visible above the rim of the barrel. The ice cream man has just scooped a portion from it using a very long spoon. The ice is served in unusual ice cream glasses: they have no foot and their conical shape resembles that of the later ice cream cones.

over 1.1 million and just under 700,000 Italians respectively.[28]

• At first the migrants were mainly from the north of Italy. From Piedmont they moved to France, from Lombardy to Switzerland and from the region around Venice they trekked into the Austro-Hungarian Empire. Italians also lived and worked in cities like London, Amsterdam and St. Petersburg. They tended to be artists and craftsmen: barometer and spectacle makers,

87: The Italian couple Paola and Marina Ciprian in their work-shop in Berlin, 27 July 1906. The ice cream is rotated in the barrel on the right. In the fore-ground are several white earthenware ice cream containers in a barrel containing ice and salt. From about 1860 many Italians migrated to Germany and Austria to start small coffee shops and ice cream parlours. In the winter months they usually returned home.

terrazzo workers, pianola- and organ-grinders. Then their numbers were swelled by smallholders and unskilled labourers from the poor mountainous areas, already accustomed to leaving their villages to take on seasonal work. Their arduous livelihoods had started to come under increasing pressure. In the valleys of the Dolomites, for example, the iron ore mines were nearly exhausted. When, for political reasons, the inhabitants of Ticino, an Italian-speaking region of Switzerland just north of Milan, lost their traditional jobs in the ports of Genoa, Pisa and Livorno, they moved to Vienna, into the south of Germany and further afield. The arrival of railways and other avenues of travel (the St. Gotthard Tunnel was opened in 1882) facilitated their movement.

• The Italians maintained close links with the families they had left behind. They helped relatives join them abroad as waiters, cooks, shop assistants, confectioners, ice cream vendors or cleaners in the small businesses they established, which included greengrocery shops, sugar confectionery bakeries, ice cream and coffee parlours, small restaurants and chocolate factories. There emerged a system of padrones

who organised the labour and the supply of ingredients. These padrones often owned both the workshops and the lodging houses where the migrants slept. They were the lords and masters of trade, dividing up the city districts among themselves and arranging for new emigrants to come across from Italy. Almost without exception, these new arrivals came from the same locality as the padrone himself.

• This 'chain migration' came to assume major proportions. With increasing frequency people moved to the other side of the Alps. The unskilled migrants took on all sorts of work to earn a living. They opened up new markets and held jobs that were still not exposed to the influence of the trade unions. The preparation and sale of ice cream – which had already been part of the street scene in Italy for longer than elsewhere in Europe – was certainly one such

88: Italians busy preparing ice cream in Mühlhausen, South Germany, 12 June 1900. In this photograph, which has clearly been stage-managed, the workers are shown (from left to right) crushing crude ice with a hammer; preparing ice cream in a barrel; polishing a copper lid on the ice cream cart; and preparing an ice cream mix with milk, eggs and sugar.

89: Italian ice cream vendor with an ice cream cart in the shape of a Venetian gondola, South Germany, circa 1900.

way to earn a living. In the 1860s, for instance, Antonio Tomea Bareta from Zoldo, a village in the eastern Dolomites, moved to Vienna and started selling ice cream there. In 1865 he received an official licence as a vendor of Gefrorenes in the sparkling Austrian capital.[29] Long before Bareta arrived in Vienna, ice cream was an accepted part of café and restaurant life, as it was in Paris and London. As early as 1785 an eye-witness described how on summer evenings people congregated in the cafés 'to slurp up their cup of ice cream, have fun, laugh, flirt, exchange kisses and relax after the heat of the day'. A wide assortment of ice cream flavours was on offer: Seville orange, lemon, cherry, strawberry, peach, pineapple, almond, vanilla and chocolate.[30]

• By 1890 58 Italian ice cream sellers were active in Vienna. By then Bareta had sold his licence to a fellow-countryman from his own village and moved to Leipzig, where he came to own 24 ice cream carts. In 1915 he transferred his activities to Budapest, where he opened 15 ice cream salons and in the summer had 60 ice cream carts out selling on the streets. All his ice cream vendors came from his native Zoldo and the surrounding area.[31]

Carlo Gatti, London's first ice cream king

• The first reports of Italian ice cream vendors on the streets of London date from 1850. In 1851 Henry Mayhew wrote in his famous study London Labour and the London Poor: 'The sale of ice-creams in the streets was unknown until last summer, and was first introduced, as a matter of speculation, by a man who was acquainted with the confectionery business and who purchased his ices of a confectioner in Holborn. He resold these luxuries daily to street sellers, sometimes to twenty of them, but more frequently to twelve. The sale, however, was not remunerative, and had it not generally been united with other things, such as ginger beer, could not have carried on as a means of subsistence. The supplier of street traders sometimes went himself, and sometimes sent another to sell ice-cream in Greenwich Park on fine summer days, but sale was sometimes insufficient to pay his railway expenses'.[32]

• At that time most of Holborn comprised slums offering the cheapest lodgings in the city. The majority of residents were Irish immigrants, but in the 1820s Holborn had been the cradle of England's first Italian community, which is why so many of the Italian emigrants in the second half of the nineteenth century went first to Holborn. Many of them were en route to America and only stayed in London to earn their fare for the transatlantic crossing. Others decided to stay in Britain for good, spreading to all corners of the island.

• At about the time Mayhew was publishing his observations, Carlo Gatti (1817-1878) began selling ice cream on the streets of Holborn. He was from Ticino in Switzerland, from where he journeyed to England via Paris in 1847.[33] Gatti came to be regarded as the patriarch of Italian ice cream in London. He started out as a seller of roast chestnuts, but within ten years he and his brothers built up a commercial empire that embraced ice cream, confectionery shops, restaurants, music halls and an ice import business. In 1850, in partnership with Battista Bolla, Gatti opened a café-restaurant in Holborn. About three years later Gatti was the owner of four stalls in Hungerford Market where ice cream was sold for one penny a portion. His ice cream carts travelled the streets in the summer

90: Portrait of Carlo Gatti (1817-1878). Gatti is regarded as the patriarch of Italian ice cream in England. After starting as a roast chestnut vendor, he and his brothers built up a whole empire in the 1850s: ice cream businesses, confectionery shops, restaurants, a music hall and an import business for natural ice.

months, while in winter his vendors sold hot potatoes and sweet chestnuts that they roasted on small stoves. To freeze the ice cream mix Gatti had his own storage for ice and he also operated as an independent trader in natural ice. In 1857 he started importing ice on a large scale from Norway, using some for his own business and selling the rest to the meat and fish trades and to breweries.

• The Gatti empire was competed by a music hall that opened in Charing Cross in 1866 and quickly became famous. Gatti's reputation reached such a pitch that Italian immigrants in other English cities cheekily tried to make use of his name. Across southern England

91: Equipped with special pickaxes, men and women collect blocks of frozen snow near Saalfelden, Austria, in the autumn of 1897. Standing behind them is a train waiting to transport the ice.

cafés and restaurants "à la Gatti" sprang up, forcing the Gatti brothers to advertise that only the Adelaide Gallery and Adelphi restaurants were under their management.[34]

• Carlo Gatti's empire was largely a family affair. In 1852 his brothers had come to London and set up a confectionery and chocolate business. In addition to family members, padrone Gatti also recruited other migrants from Ticino. Between 1857 and 1900 a chain of restaurants was established throughout England, all run by Ticino families.[35] By then most of them were no longer working in the ice cream sector. For some time that had been the domain of the 'real' Italians and the Swiss 'Ticinesi' wanted to have nothing to do with it. 'It is more than thirty years since we Ticinesi left this itinerant occupation to the Italians', wrote one of them in 1897 in La Gazetta Italiana di Londra. 'They have rushed into it as if it were a gold-mine and the numbers increase year by year by 30 per cent, making this trade, which was once profitable, an increasingly despised and abhorred occupation, so that 'Ice-cream Jack' has become the most degraded individual in the whole vast itinerant trade in this Metropolis.'[36]

'Hokey pokey'

• The growth of Italian business activities and ice cream sales in England is reflected in the figures from the population censuses held every ten years. From 1861 onwards people's occupations were recorded and although the figures for Italian immigrants are not totally reliable for various reasons, they do give an idea of trends. According to the 1861 census, 4,489 Italians then lived in England and Wales. An occupation was recorded for 1,339 of them with by far the majority, 872, working as organgrinders, while just 33 said that they worked as street vendors, who would mostly be ice cream sellers. Thirty years later, in 1891, the census revealed 9,909 Italians of whom 990 were now street sellers – representing 20% of those with registered occupations.[37] Between 1901 and 1911 the number of registered Italians grew little, partly on account of the restrictions on immigration that England introduced in 1905. However one striking statistic is that the number of ice cream vendors more than halved, from 2,824 in 1901 to 1,281 in 1911, a decrease attributable to the stricter hygiene measures enforced by most city councils.

• Doctors and hospitals had been urging such action for years. The general level of knowledge and practice of hygiene was appalling, not only during preparation but also during the selling of ice cream. It was sold in small, thick glasses of different sizes. Between sales, these so-called

ANTONIO
HOKEY POKE
ICES.

OH ! OH ! ANTONIO.

92: English picture post-card, 1909, showing an Italian ice cream vendor selling 'hokey pokey' ice creams in small, thick-walled glasses known as 'penny-licks'. Two of these glasses are standing on Antonio's ice cream cart. 'Hokey pokey' was an English corruption of the Italian street vendor's cry 'O, c'è un poco' – 'Try a little'. The hugely popular music hall song Oh! Oh! Antonio, sung by Florrie Ford, was all about a being abandoned by an Italian Ice Cream Vendor - 'Oh! Oh! Antonio, He's gone away, Left me alone-i-o, All on my own-i-o.....'.

'penny-licks' (see box on p. 130) were rinsed in none-too-clean water or simply wiped off with a cloth and re-used. Alternatively, ice cream might be served on a piece of paper, itself not always pristine. Children, in particular, fell victim to these practices. Typhus fever and other diseases spread, often with fatal results.

• It was not only the medical profession that was up in arms about this. British confectioners, the traditional suppliers of ice cream, also disapproved of the Italian competition. Their trade journal, The Confectioner's Union, regularly lambasted the opposition. In 1896, for example, the journal published a ballad in seven couplets, in which Lucretia Mary Borgia Brown poisons a rival in love by giving her an ice cream. Lucretia regularly passes a shop in Hampstead where ice cream is sold:

PURE ICES

hot chestnuts 15 a1d

WOT'S IT TO BE, MAUD—'OT OR COLD LUNCH?

93: English picture postcard from around 1900 depicting Italian vendors of ice cream and sweet chestnuts. At the end of the nineteenth century large numbers of Italians emigrated to Great Britain. In the winter months they sold roast chestnuts and in the summer ice cream.

'His den she'd often pass
There lived a man who ice sold
'A ha'penny a glass'
Lucretia saw those ices made
With water foul and black'.[38]

• Reports and newspaper articles about the poor conditions under which ice cream was prepared were published with growing frequency. City councils started to take action. In 1893, the health committee of Glasgow City Council decided to start registering ice cream businesses as places in which milk was handled. Hitherto, Glasgow had not regarded ice cream as a foodstuff and so it went unregulated.[39] In 1902 the City of London introduced requirements for the production, storage and sale of ice cream.

94: Ice harvest in Norway, circa 1905. A group of men fish the enormous ice blocks from the water using ice hooks. The ice was then transported in the holds of ships to London and other British ports. Between 1860 and 1915 Norway exported millions of tons of natural ice.

Henceforth ice cream vendors had to state legibly on their ice cream cart the name and address of the person who had made the ice cream. Regular inspections and medical checks were also established.[40] Slowly things improved.

• The introduction in about 1895 of ice cream wafers and ice cream cones helped considerably. In the world of confectionery bakers wafers and cones had long been in use, but now biscuit factories in England started marketing round, square or triangular wafers to accompany ice cream; and, shortly after the turn of the century, specialist factories began to be set up.

95: Detail from drawing published in The Illustrated London News showing visitors to the Hampstead Heath Holiday Fair on a warm afternoon in May 1872.
The Italian ice cream vendor pictured on the left is doing good business. Using a big iron spoon he scoops the ice cream into the re-usable glasses known as 'penny-licks'.

'Give us a licker, Jack'

¶ 'Who now remembers the old cry: "Give us a licker, Jack"? Where are the little green glasses gone? The modern ice-cream barrow serves the confection either in little wafer cups or as sandwiches between wafers', wrote the English newspaper The Daily Telegraph in July 1918.[1] By 'little green glasses' the newspaper was referring to the ice cream glasses which had been used, mostly by Italian ice cream sellers, throughout Great Britain for decades.

From the time of its introduction as a dessert at the French court in around 1662, ices were served in glasses. At the dining table, in cafés and restaurants and later on the street, ice cream was licked or spooned from glasses. Glasses were specially designed for street sales. An Italian illustration of 1820 shows an ice cream seller serving his ices outdoors in Naples in special, conical glasses with no base, the shape prefiguring that of the ice-cream cone. When Italians started selling ice cream in the streets of London in the second half of the nineteenth century, they served it in the same sort of small, thick-walled, often green-coloured ice-cream glasses. These glasses were well known before 1845, for a **Punch** cartoon of that year features them in the original "penny ice shop". The glasses were known in the vernacular as 'penny-licks' and

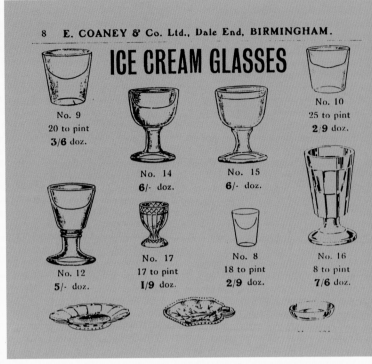

96: Page from catalogue of E. Coaney & Co. Ltd. for ice glasses ('penny-licks'), England, circa 1928.

cost either a halfpenny or a penny. After use the glass was returned to the ice cream vendor, who (if the next customer were lucky) dipped it in a bowl of cold water and wiped it with a cloth before re-use. In 1845 taxes on the production of glass were abolished and, not long after that, technical improvements facilitated the manufacture of cheap glassware. This rapidly resulted in the production of ice cream glasses of all shapes and sizes. Almost all the glasses had thick bases, however; some were so concave that only a tiny piece of ice cream would fit in them, while creating the illusion that they contained more ice than was actually the case. The ice cream

vendor sold the ices with a curl on top, another way of trying to increase the apparent size of the portion.[2]

Ice-cream glasses were used not only in Great Britain, but also in other countries such as America and the Netherlands. The poorly washed glasses were a breeding ground for bacteria, including the dangerous tuberculosis bacilli. It was not until 1926 that their use was banned in London.[3] By that time, however, the 'penny-licks' had largely made way for ice cream served between wafers or in cups and cones.

97: English nursery rhyme, 'The Penny Ice Man', from 1900. The Italian ice cream salesman is serving the children ice cream in glasses, as was the custom until the arrival of wafers and cones. An ice cream could be had for a halfpenny or a penny – hence the title of the rhyme.

The Penny-Ice Man

IN summer when the sun is high,
　　And children's lips are parched and dry,
An ice is just the thing to try.
So this young man who comes, 'tis plain,
　　From Saffron Hill or Leather Lane,
A store of pence will quickly gain.
"A lemon ice for me," says Fred;
　　Cries Sue, "No, have a cream instead."
"A raspberry!" shouts Newsboy Ned.
"What fun! Although we're now in June,
　　It feels"—says Ned—"this afternoon,
Like eating winter with a spoon!"

98: Various 'penny-licks' as used in Great Britain from 1870 until the end of the 1920s for street sales of ice cream, and also in other countries such as the United States and the Netherlands.

• The burgeoning of Italian café-restaurants and ice cream parlours in England was fuelled by the growing purchasing power of the urban working classes, the introduction of paid summer holidays and a greatly improved railway network, all of which enabled large numbers of people to descend on seaside resorts in the summer. In towns like Hastings, Brighton and Blackpool the Italian lemonades and 'hokey pokey' ices were snapped up by the public. 'Hokey pokey' was a corruption of the Italian phrase 'O, c'è un poco' – 'try a little', the

99: Sticker, circa 1880, depicting an Italian ice cream cart in Great Britain. The cart is covered by an elegant awning to protect it from the sun. In about 1850 Italian immigrants introduced ice cream to the streets of London. By that time ice cream had been on sale on the streets of New York, Philadelphia and New Orleans for more than ten years.

street-cry with which ice cream vendors used to attract their customers. It became the name for a hard piece of milk-ice with, in the middle, a streak of raspberry or strawberry ice made from lemonade syrup.[41] The evening before, it was frozen in layers in long moulds so that it could be cut into small pieces the next day and sold in a piece of paper. This was the precursor of the vanilla block, which in the 1920s was to be the first product marketed by the modern ice cream industry in England and Ireland (see chapters 8 and 9). 'Hokey pokey' was cheap and popular, but British confectioners took it seriously, even publishing a recipe for it in their trade journal.[42]

New York: 'I scream, Ice Cream!'

• The Italian influence on ice cream sales in the big cities of the United States developed differently from in England, though there were some similarities. Street selling had gone on in America long before the wave of Italian migrants to the New World broke in the last quarter of the nineteenth century. As early as 1828 The National Advertiser had descibed a group of noisy men in the streets of New York who, kettles in hand, cried out the words 'I scream, Ice Cream'.[43] By the 1840s the ice cream seller was already a feature of other cities like New Orleans and Philadelphia. As with the Italian vendors in London, the ice cream was proffered in glasses which had to be handed back after use. A quick wipe with a cloth and they were ready for the next customer.[44]

• To judge from a cookbook dating from 1892, Italian 'hokey pokey' ice cream also gained wide acceptance in the United States.[45] But the Italians dominated ice cream sales there much less than in Europe. Groups of

100: Cover illustration of Ally Sloper's Half Holiday, September 1899, depicting an ice cream cart from which ice is being sold in 'penny-licks' on the beach at Bournemouth on England's south coast.

ENLARGED TO 12 PAGES. RAILWAY ACCIDENT LIFE POLICY FOR £150.

ally Sloper's Half Holiday

FOUNDED AND CONDUCTED BY GILBERT DALZIEL.

Vol. XVI.—No. 803. SATURDAY, SEPTEMBER 16, 1899. ONE PENNY.

TRY OUR
ICES 1½D
FRESH DAILY
FROM
SAFFRON HILL

A BOURNEMOUTH BEANO.

"*Poor dear Papa's impersonation of Carlo di Strawberrycreamo at Bournemouth fell a bit flat, as he was clean bowled out by some youthful natives who detected the nez Sloperian. Pa's anger found vent in an attack upon one of the spies with his ice spoon, and that kid's head must feel jolly pulpy still, I should say. Aunt Geeser, who is staying with the Menagerie for a day or two, had her spine refrigerated by Jubilee, and gave forth most awful squawks until things became a bit warmer in that direction. Fortunately for a long-suffering public, Pa's Annual Seaside Crawl is drawing to a close.*"—TOOTSIE.*

THE CRIES OF NEW YORK. 29

ICE CREAM MAN.

"Ice Cream! Ice Cream!" *that* fact is very plain—
We *hear* you *scream*—don't tell us so again!

101: Woodcut of an ice cream seller in New York, from *The cries of New York* (1846) by Frances Osgood. By then the ice cream man was a common sight in a number of US cities.

immigrants from other countries were also active as makers and sellers of ice cream. Moreover (and this was a major difference compared to Europe) ice cream saloons and ice bars were every-where and the US consumer could visit them for ice cream, coffee, lemonade or a sandwich. After the end of the Civil War (1861-1865) the development of the ice cream sector picked up speed and the number of outlets exploded. 'No town, village and crossroad settlement throughout the land is without its "ice cream saloon" and this grateful luxury may be found excellent and cheap everywhere', wrote the National Cookery Book in 1876.[46]

102: Picture postcard, 1904. Three ladies in an English seaside resort are enjoying 'penny-licks'.

• The early mechanisation of ice cream production; the extremely fast expansion of the railroad network in the second half of the nineteenth century; the establishment of distribution outlets such as ice cream saloons; and the arrival of modern freezers – these laid the foundation for a tremendous upsurge in ice cream consumption in the United States.

Ingredients, mainly milk but also fruit, sugar and vanilla, could be supplied by rail and, with the advent of the first ice cream making machines, product prepa-ration took less and less time.

• In 1843 Nancy M. Johnson from Philadelphia applied for a patent for the world's first ice cream machine. Her invention was based on the long-estab-lished method of preparing ice cream by placing a tin container with ice cream mix in a barrel filled with ice and salt and then scraping off the ice crystals that formed on the inner wall of the container with a spatula (see also chapter 3). John-son's machine consisted of a long, cylindrical barrel inside which two spatulas, pierced with holes of more than 2.5 cm, fitted exactly.

103: Drawing, circa 1890, published in a New York newspaper, captioned 'Ice for the poor'. Barefoot children in New York's impoverished Five Points borough lick their ice cream from a piece of paper.

The spatulas were fitted on both sides of a shaft which was rotated using a crank. This not only simplified the preparation of ice cream, but ensured a more uniform texture. In her patent specification Johnson wrote that glass containers were preferable to metal ones and that the spatula should be made from ivory or hard wood, materials better able to withstand the effects of the acids in fruit juices.[47]

The tubes were attached to a lid to which a crank could be fitted. The entire assembly was then suspended in a tank of water to which a special salt had been added. The ice cream maker only had to rotate the tubes in the salt solution for twelve minutes by turning the crank and the ice cream was ready, according to Giacomo Perini, who described the invention in his book Der Schweizer-zuckerbäcker (The Swiss Confectioner), which was first published in 1852. In a later edition of 1858 he reported that the Parisian machine was now also much used in Germany and was obtainable in Leipzig.[49]

104: Drawing of the ice cream making machine described in the 1843 patent application by the American Nancy Johnson from Philadelphia. She was the first to design an ice cream machine with a rotating spatula, an invention that heralded the start of mechanised ice cream production.

• It was Nancy Johnson's machine, however, which proved to be the most practical and the most imitated. In the 25 years following its invention the United States Patent Office registered as many as 91 different patents for ice cream machines, almost all of them offering the prospect of faster and better preparation.[50] In Philadelphia the machine patented by the Quaker Eber C. Seamen in 1848 proved highly successful. His invention contributed to a rapid spread of the recipe for Philadelphia ice cream, consisting of pure cream, sugar and vanilla (no eggs). For many decades the Philadelphia recipe was seen as the standard for American ice cream.[51] The American ice cream machines were soon powered by steam or electricity. In 1887 an ice cream machine fitted with an electric motor is recorded as being in use in Chicago.[52]

• While Nancy Johnson was developing her machine in Philadelphia, on the other side of the Atlantic the English confectioners Thomas Masters and William Fuller were devising other ice cream machines. Masters was granted a patent for his invention in 1843; Fuller's followed in 1853.[48] In France, too, there was activity on this front. In June 1845 the Société d'Encourage-ment in Paris demonstrated a new type of machine for ice cream preparation. The ice cream mix was placed in a number of thin tubes that could be sealed by a screw cap.

105: Silver ice cream dish manufactured by Tiffany & Co., New York, in 1878. The dish has a diameter of approximately 30 cm and weighs just over 2.5 kilos. It formed part of an extensive silver dinner and dessert service which John Mackay, one of the wealthiest men in America, ordered from Tiffany's in 1877 for his wife, Marie Louise Hungerford. The service was manufactured under the supervision of Edward Moore, Tiffany's leading silversmith. The decoration of the dish was inspired by motifs from India. Note the legs in the form of elephants' trunks.

106: Soda fountain made by James W. Tuft, shown here at an exhibition held in Philadelphia in 1876 to mark the centenary of the US Declaration of Independence. For the sum of $50,000 Tuft had acquired the exclusive rights to sell soda water during the exhibition. His impressive marble installation could produce many litres of soda water. This soda water was served mixed with syrup and a ball of vanilla ice cream, a combination which became all the rage. The idea for the mix had been thought up two years earlier by the Philadelphian lemonade salesman Robert M. Green.

Mechanisation meant that much bigger volumes could be produced and now the advance of ice cream in America really got under way. In the winter of 1851-52 Jacob Fussell, a dairy farmer from Baltimore, Pennsylvania, built a small ice cream factory in the nearby town of Seven Valleys. His example was soon followed by others and formed the beginnings of the modern ice cream industry (see also chapter 5).

• In the big cities across the USA the dining habit was blossoming. Dinners ended with fresh fruit, nuts, cake or celebratory ice cream dessert[53], which was highly regarded both in restaurants and at home. It was often presented in highly imaginative ice moulds, whose appearance would match the occasion – for example, a heart on Valentine's Day or, on Independence Day, a soldier holding the American flag. Fashionable New York restaurants such as Delmonico's and Sherry's, and prestigious hotels like the Waldorf-Astoria, possessed entire series of (sometimes exclusive) ice moulds (see box on p.146).

• The chefs in the United States were certainly on a par with the great French chefs, regularly inventing new ice cream creations which, as in Europe, they named after celebrities or after important historical events. An example of this is a recipe for an ice cream cake by Charles Ranhofer, the chef at Delmonico's between 1862 and 1894 and a good friend of the French chef Urbain Dubois. He called his recipe 'Baked Alaska', after the territory that had been bought by the United States from Russia in 1887. His ice cream gâteau was conical in shape, one half of it consisting of banana ice cream, the other of vanilla. Its base was formed of a hollowed-out cake filled with apricot jam.

Just before serving, it was topped with a thick layer of whisked egg-white, coated with sugar and then baked in a hot oven for two minutes.[54] In 1893 Ranhofer published a bulky cookery book, The epicurean. A complete treatise of analytical and practical studies of the culinary art, containing nearly 300 ice cream recipes.

• The march of ice cream across American dining tables also had consequences for cutlery. Mass-production of ice cream spoons commenced in the 1860s; some ten years later the use of ice cream knives and forks came into fashion.[55] In 1868 Tiffany, the renowned New York jeweller, began marketing specialised ice cream cutlery, including elegant serving spoons and even an ice cream saw (see p. 142).

Ice through a straw in the soda fountain bar

• As well as at home, in ice cream saloons, restaurants, hotels and cafés, ice cream in America was also eaten at a venue created in that country – the soda fountain bar.

• As the nineteenth century opened, American drugstores were selling carbonated water, a drink regarded as a medicine. From the 1830s onwards, syrup was added to the carbonated water. John Matthews in New York is recorded as having developed the first soda fountain. Matthews produced carbon dioxide gas from a reaction of vitriol oil with marble dust. He purified the mixture in a water reservoir from which the gas was fed into a second reservoir. There the gas was mixed with fresh water with the aid of a rotating mixer or by agitating the reservoir. To keep the drink cold, the reservoir was

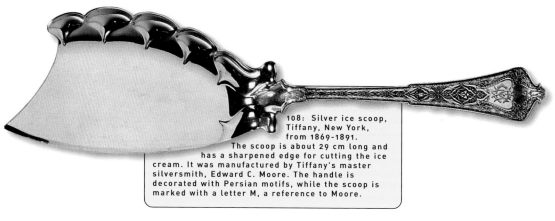

107: Silver ice-cream saw, Tiffany, New York, 1866. Length about 29 cm. The saw was produced for Tiffany by the New York silversmith John Polhemus. In 1868, Tiffany started making silver tableware in its own factory.

108: Silver ice scoop, Tiffany, New York, from 1869-1891. The scoop is about 29 cm long and has a sharpened edge for cutting the ice cream. It was manufactured by Tiffany's master silversmith, Edward C. Moore. The handle is decorated with Persian motifs, while the scoop is marked with a letter M, a reference to Moore.

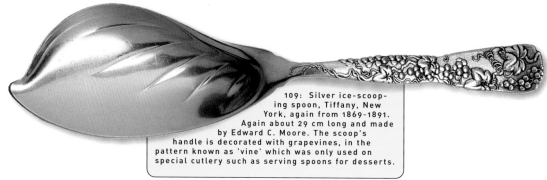

109: Silver ice-scooping spoon, Tiffany, New York, again from 1869-1891. Again about 29 cm long and made by Edward C. Moore. The scoop's handle is decorated with grapevines, in the pattern known as 'vine' which was only used on special cutlery such as serving spoons for desserts.

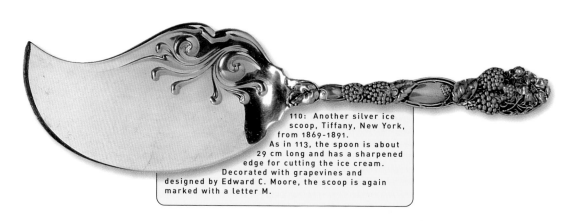

110: Another silver ice scoop, Tiffany, New York, from 1869-1891. As in 113, the spoon is about 29 cm long and has a sharpened edge for cutting the ice cream. Decorated with grapevines and designed by Edward C. Moore, the scoop is again marked with a letter M.

111: Two silver ice cream forks, Tiffany, New York, from 1869-1891.
The handles of the forks, which are some 13 and 14 cm in length, are decorated with a strawberry and a grapevine.

112: Silver ice cream spoon, ice cream fork, sherbet spoon and sorbet spoon, from Tiffany, New York, from the 1884-1891 period, made by Edward C. Moore.
In the United States a sherbet is not exactly the same as a sorbet. A sherbet, for instance, contains milk, whereas a sorbet does not. The items are around 14 cm long.

113: Four ice cream forks each about 14 cm long, Tiffany, New York.
Between 1869 and 1958 Tiffany marketed at least 42 different models of ice cream spoons and forks.
The forks depicted here are, from top to bottom, the models Olympian (1878), Florentine (1900), Renaissance (1905) and Castalian (1929).

encased in blocks of ice or was pumped to
the dispenser tap via a spiral pipe packed in
ice.[56] The use of marble as a raw material
gave Matthews the idea of mounting the
reservoirs, pipes and taps in elegant marble
racks. From this beginning, the soda fountain developed into impressive edifices,
modelled on every conceivable style of
architecture – Egyptian, Roman, Gothic,
Byzantine – and carrying appropriate names
such as Ice Floe or Naxos (a reference to the
Greek island).

• Matthews' invention was a success and
was soon imitated. Fountain bars were
installed on drugstore premises everywhere.
A sales outlet for pills and powders became
a busy meeting place where, seated on high
stools at the marble fountain bar or on
stylish metal chairs at a marble table,
customers could quench their thirst and
have a chat. Fitted out with mirrors and
shiny metal and glass decor, the common
drugstore now boasted a soda fountain as its
centrepiece. The barman would put blocks of
raw ice in the soda water so that he could
serve the drinks cold, drinks which – despite
containing no ice cream – were called ice
cream sodas.

• By the late 1870s, however, ice cream was
increasingly put in the soda water in place of
plain ice. It was served in big, characteristic
glasses which, just like Russian tea glasses,
were fitted with a metal holder. The
customer was expected to sip the drink
through a straw. According to the most widely accepted version of history, this innovation
was first introduced in 1874 by Robert M.
Green, a lemonade salesman from Philadelphia, during the centenary celebrations of
the Franklin Institute. Ice cream soda now
became even more popular, being described

in 1893 by an American
magazine as 'our
national drink.'[57]

• As the years went by,
the soda fountain
generated a language
all of its own. There
were some 250 expres-
sions in circulation that
were understood only
by the customers, wait-
ers, waitresses and the
soda jerk – as the
barman was nicknamed
on account of the jerk-
ing required to pump
the soda from the soda
fountain. 'Virgin ball',
for instance, meant a
cherry ice cream; a
'houseboat' denoted a
banana split; 'high
yellow' was a chocolate
soda with vanilla ice
cream; and a 'whizz
bang' was a waitress
with whom customers
would find it easy to
make a date.[58]

• Although soda foun-
tains were also estab-
lished elsewhere in the
world after the turn of

the century – in England, Australia, the
Netherlands, Denmark, Germany and
Finland – they were largely an American
phenomenon. The marble constructions
disappeared with the passage of time, being
replaced by more modern equipment, but the
soda fountain remained an integral part of
American society for decades.

114: Interior of the soda fountain bar in Collins Pharmacy in Islip, Long Island, circa 1900. The young man on the right wearing the white coat is the soda jerk. His job was to mix the soda water with syrup and to add, if desired, a scoop of ice cream. After its introduction in 1874, ice cream soda was to remain extremely popular in America for decades.

• By the 1930s ice cream had become a central component of popular American culture, as celebrated in the 1932 song When I'm Sippin' a Soda with Susie, in which the young man dreams of a date in the soda fountain with his Susie, 'sweet as vanilla'.[59] Unlike in Europe, ice cream was available to everyone, everywhere, any time.

• By now the word soda had become a generic term for carbonated lemonades and until the late 1950s the soda fountain bar was the place to be in America on a warm summer's evening, enjoying an ice cream soda sipped slowly through a straw.

¶ In 1875, a year before the cele-
bration of the first centennial of
American independence, the
Franco-American Alliance was
established amidst a great
fanfare of publicity. Its aim was to
collect money to erect the Statue
of Liberty, which was ultimately
unveiled on 28 October 1886.
While its sculptor, Bartholdi, was
at work in Paris, fund-raising
activities were organised in both
France and the United States
including auctions, lectures,
lotteries, sports events and
dinners. Sometimes the guests at
the benefit dinners were treated
to an enormous ice cream
confection in the shape of the
future statue. The two-part
pewter mould for this was almost
one metre tall, with a base 26 cm
in diameter. Made in about 1876
by the firm of Eppelsheimer &
Co. in New York, this spectacular
mould required some seventeen
litres of ice cream to fill it.[1]
Eppelsheimer & Co., and the
older firm of Krauss & Co.,
also of New York, were the best-
known American manufacturers
of ice cream moulds.
Pewter moulds for ices in the
shape of fruit had been used in
Europe since the beginning of the
seventeenth century. The first
pictures of them were published
in 1751 in Le Cannaméliste by the
French cook Gilliers (see p. 59).
In America moulds for ice creams
had been in use since the end of

Legend for the moulds

E&Co. = Eppelsheimer & Co., New York
K&Co. = Krauss & Co., New York
S&Co. = Schall & Co., New York
ACM = American Chocolate Mould Co.
All dimensions are given in centimetres in height x breadth x depth, unless otherwise indicated. All moulds are made of pewter and all models are painted and made from plaster or wax.

the eighteenth century. For example, the inventory of the palace of Lord Botetourt, governor of Virginia between 1768 and 1770, lists nineteen different moulds for ices.[2]

Most of the moulds that were used in the eighteenth century – conventional fruit shapes including strawberries, lemons, nuts or asparagus – were reproduced in the nineteenth century by the New York firms, but their repertoire was much more extensive. As well as being shaped into fruits, toys, musical instruments, animal figures, birds, butterflies, mugs, flowers, Santa Claus and the Easter bunny, ice cream could also be moulded into shapes representing American historical events, personalities, comic-book characters and sports stars. There were ice cream moulds in the form of Columbus, Abraham Lincoln, George Washington and Teddy Roosevelt, as well as

Walt Disney characters like Mickey Mouse and Pluto.

To mark the anniversary of the 1898 Spanish-American war, there was the bust of Admiral Dewey or a cannon; to celebrate Independence Day on 4 July, the US flag, the American eagle, the Bell of Liberty or Uncle Sam; for St. Valentine's Day, a heart or Cupid; a turkey for Thanksgiving Day; an aeroplane to celebrate Charles Lindbergh's first transatlantic flight in 1927, and so on. The sizes of the ice cream moulds varied widely. There were small moulds for individual portions, with average contents of 20 cc, and large moulds for a festive meal. The smallest individual moulds made by the firm of Eppelsheimer, such as a tiny apple, would hold a mere 25 cc of ice cream, whereas a large aeroplane held 40 cc. The contents of ice moulds for festive meals ranged from half a litre to more than two-and-a-half litres.

In addition to the ice cream moulds, coloured plaster display models could be ordered. On the basis of the colours the ice cream maker could select the appropriate ice cream flavour (for example, strawberry ice cream for a heart on St. Valentine's Day); or, after the ice cream had been frozen, he could paint it by 'apply-

ing pure food coloring'. The dishes had to have 'eye-appeal', as Krauss & Co. noted in the foreword to one of its catalogues.[3] Ice cream moulds became fashionable in America in the second half of the nineteenth century. The moulds of the first US manufacturer, Schall & Co., appeared on the market in New York in

116: Page from a brochure with ice cream moulds by the firm of Eppelsheimer & Co., circa 1950.

1854; Krauss & Co. was a later name of the same company. Eppelsheimer was founded in the 1870s and remained in existence until the early 1950s. The buyers of the moulds were ice cream manufacturers, bakers, confectioners, hotels and restaurants. In the winter months and for public holidays, the ice cream manufacturers advertised their 'specialities' and 'fancy ices', as

they called them. A Breyers brochure of 1933 gives an overview of 'delicious and fascinating [confections], made of Breyers ice cream!'
Between 1921 and 1925, a boom period for ice cream consumption in the United States, Eppelsheimer & Co. received 5,169 orders for individual ice cream moulds. The orders resulted in

England included Biertumpofel & Hepting and Harton & Sons, whilst in Paris the firms of Cadot, Perrault and Letang competed for the customer's favour. Cadot, like Letang, also made moulds for chocolate and sugar confectionery products; established in 1826, Cadot operated until at least 1932. Perrault was active between 1847 and 1884.

for example, Cadot could supply moulds in the shape of the Eiffel Tower or a Breton fisherman and the 1933 catalogue of Letang Fils offered Puss-in-Boots, based on the character in the seventeenth-century fairytale by the French author Charles Perrault.[5]
In Germany pewter ice cream moulds were made by the firms of Julius Bohmer (Dresden), Johannes Reinohl (Ulm, 1847-1890), Berthold Keinke (Hamburg, 1872-1957), Georg Norman (Nuremberg, 1800-1900) and Georg Lieb (Stuttgart). This last firm commenced production in 1868 and operated until the 1960s.[6]
Nowhere, however, was the variety of moulds as wide as in the United States, where in the early 1950s the production lists of various manufacturers comprised at least 2,000 different designs.[7]

These delicious and fascinating Cakes, Fancy Forms and Special Moulds, are made of Breyers Ice Cream!

"Bon Voyage" Ice Cream Mould

Birthday Ice Cream Cake

Smart hostesses everywhere delight their guests with these delectable colorful ice cream sculptures.

For successful dinners and charming parties serve ice cream in this, its most modern form.

Here are just a few of the many fancy ice cream forms appropriate for every occasion.

Animals, Birds, Novelties — Flowers and Fruits — Wedding and Fraternal Emblems — Holiday Forms

the production of 17,429 ice cream moulds, in 357 different designs.[4] The speciality ice creams were delivered to consumers' homes packed in boxes with a layer of dry ice at the top and bottom to keep them frozen.
Ice cream moulds were also popular in France, Germany and Great Britain. In the second half of the nineteenth century firms producing ice cream moulds in

117: Overview of 'fancy ices' from Breyers catalogue, 1933.

Letang Fils was started in 1832 by Jean Baptiste Letang and the company is still active in France as a supplier of culinary utensils. Between 1855 and 1931 still another firm, founded by Marie Letang, made ice cream moulds under the name Letang.
The French firms included French themes in their ranges. Around the turn of the century,

118: George Washington,
mould and model
(E&Co., 1929: 36.5 x 16 x 11.5).

119: Abraham Lincoln
(S&Co., circa 1887: 11.5 cm high).
In 1887 a party was given in the
famous Delmonico's restaurant in
New York in honour of Lincoln's
birthday. The mould was probably
produced for that occasion.

120: Symbols of Independence Day
on 4 July. From left, the Liberty
Bell, the US shield, the US flag,
Uncle Sam (mould and model),
statue of freedom from the Capitol.
The Liberty Bell (1931: 20 x 25
diameter) is modelled after the
original in Philadelphia. The name
Uncle Sam was first used during
the war between America and
England in 1812. The character only
really came to life after 1870 when
portrayed by cartoonists in numerous newspapers and magazines.

121: Walt Disney creations,
from left: Clara Bell, Mickey
Mouse, Pluto, Minnie Mouse and
Horace Horsecollar.
Maker: unknown, circa 1930-1934.
Pluto: 9 x 12 x 3.5,
all others; 12 x 9 x 3.5;

122: Lobster (S&Co.,
pre-1897; body: 34 x 20 x 10;
claw: 25 x 7.5 x 6).
The claws were separately filled
with ice cream.

123: Skull mould
(E&Co., circa 1876: 17 x 15 x 20).
Designed when the actor
Edwin Booth was enjoying great
success in the role of Hamlet.

124: Sports figures and sports
attributes.
Back row, from left:
American football player
(K&Co., 1897: 13 x 7 x 5.5);
baseball player
(K&Co., pre-1902: 13.5 x 6.5 x 6).
Middle row, from left:
male golfer, mould and model
(E&Co., circa 1896: 13 x 7 x 5.5);
female golfer, mould and model
(E&Co., circa 1896: 12 x 7 x 5).
Foreground, from left: baseball bat
(E&Co., pre-1908: 16.5 x 4 x 3); golf
bag with clubs
(K&Co., 1932: 13 x 7 x 3.5),
American football (K&Co., 1897: 7.5
x 9 x 6) and tennis racquet (E&Co.,
1888: 16 x 8 x 2).

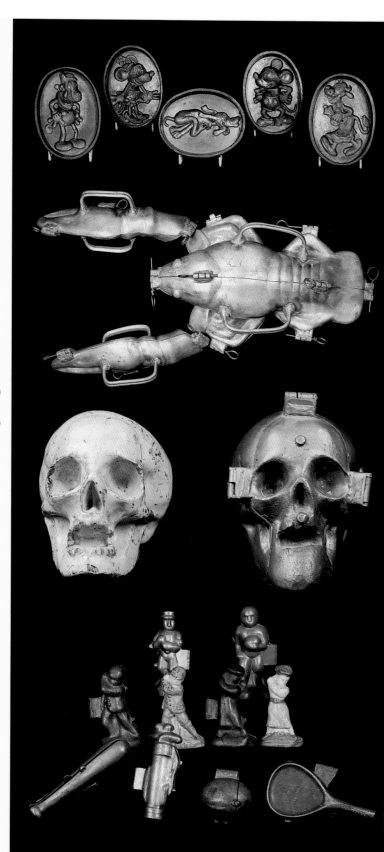

125: Centre: model of flowers and basket (E&Co., no year: 14 x 26 diameter). From left: dahlia (E&Co., pre-1908: 9.5 diameter), passion flower (E&Co., pre-1908: 9.5 diameter), lily, mould and model (S&Co., 1897: 28 x 17.5 diameter).

126: Various fruits. Back row, from left: model of peach (E&Co., pre-1880: 13.5 diameter), mould of fruit baskets with models of various fruits (S&Co., pre-1897: 30 x 19 x 14), model of pineapple (E&Co., pre-1880: 20 x 9 diameter). Front row, from left: strawberry (S&Co., 1897: 17 x 16 x 10), grapes (Gustav Krieg, 1914-1938: 13.5 diameter).

127: Asparagus (all by S&Co., pre-1897; the maker of the longest model is not known). Ice moulds in the shape of asparagus had existed existed since at least the first published picture in Le Cannaméliste (1751) by the French chef Gilliers.

128: Teddy bear (E&Co., circa 1910: 15.5 x 7 x 5). The teddy bear was invented in 1903 by Morris Michtom from Brooklyn, N.Y. He thought up the idea when he saw a newspaper cartoon of Theodore Roosevelt on a hunting trip holding a bear cub in his arms. Michtom received permission to use Roosevelt's name.

129: Heart with Cupid figure
(E&Co., 1929: 25.5 x 22 x 11.5).
Also, from left:
Valentine envelope and model
(K&Co., 1906: 7 x 11 x 2),
Hearts Aflame
(S&Co., pre-1897: 10 x 12 x 3),
small heart with Cupid figure
(E&Co., pre-1913: 9 x 8.5 x 5),
Valentine envelope
(E&Co., circa 1896: 7 x 12 x 2).
Valentine's Day (14 February) was
proclaimed a Christian feast-day
in 496 A.D. by Pope Geliasus in
honour of Saint Valentine.
The custom of sending poetic or
amorous messages began in France
in the fifteenth century.
The first commercial Valentine
cards were marketed in America
in about 1800.

130: Halloween moulds and models
(E&Co. and K&Co.).
Pumpkins, skulls, devils and
witches are traditional on the
evening of 31 October.

131: Father Christmas and
Christmas tree, mould and model
(E&Co., 1894: 31 x 15 x 13; 1929:
15 x 10.5 x 4).

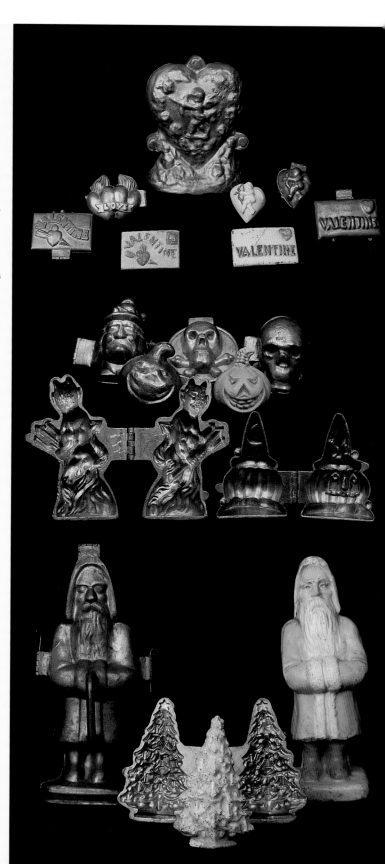

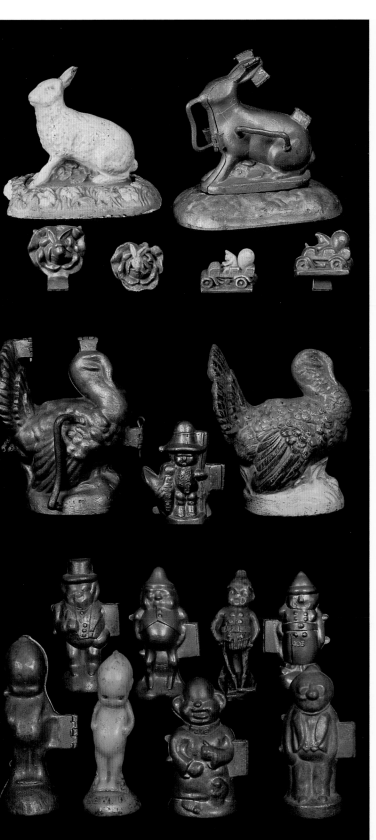

132: Easter bunny,
mould and model
(E&Co., circa 1875: 21.5 x 20 x 9).
In the left foreground an
Easter bunny in a cabbage plant
(E&Co., pre-1908): 7 x 9 x 4) and,
right, a rabbit in a car
(E&Co., pre-1908: 9 diameter).

133: Turkey, ice cream mould
and model (E&Co., circa 1880:
22 x 20 x 12) and Pilgrim Boy
with Blunderbuss
(E&Co., 1935: 13.5 x 10.5 x 4.5).
Turkey is the traditional dish on
Thanksgiving Day, which falls on
the fourth Thursday in November.
It was first celebrated in 1621 when
English colonists in Plymouth, New
England, organised a day of
thanksgiving and prayer after the
harvest. In 1863 the day was
declared a national public holiday
by President Abraham Lincoln.

134: Popular cartoon figures. Back
row: three moulds and one model
of the Brownie figures: the Irish-
man, the Dude, the Soldier and the
Policeman (all: S&Co., 1897: 13 x 7
x 5). The characters were thought
up in 1883 by the artist and journalist Palmer Cox. His Brownie
stories were immensely popular; in
1895 sales of Brownie books had
already exceeded 100,000.
Front row, left, is an ice cream
mould and a model of the Kewpie
doll (E&Co., 1925: 15.5 x 6); centre,
the Yellow Kid; and, right,
Foxy Grandpa (both by S&Co.,
circa 1897: 12.5 x 8 x 5 and 1902:
14 x 7 x 5).
The Kewpie doll was created in
1912, was extremely popular with
children and was depicted on the
packs of ice cream manufacturer
Hendler. The Yellow Kid was a
cartoon by the artist R.F. Outcault
and was created in 1894.
After its publication in The New
York World, the Yellow Kid brought
about a steady climb in that
newspaper's circulation figures.

135: Napoleon
(S&Co., 1894: 13 x 13 x 4).
The ice cream mould was
presumably made to celebrate the
production of the play Napoleon
Bonaparte by Lorimer Stoddard,
which was staged in the Herald
Square Theater in New York City
in 1894.

136: Lady on bicycle
(S&Co. pre-1897: 27.5 x 23 x 8),
man on bicycle
(E&Co., pre-1897: 12 x 11 x 5)
and woman on bicycle
(E&Co., pre-1902: 11.5 x 10.5 x 4).
After the invention of the
inflatable bicycle tyre in 1887
by John Boyd Dunlop, the bicycle
spread beyond select clubs to
become a mass-market product.

137: Means of transport.
At the back: steamship
(E&Co., 1931: 21 x 42 x 6);
just in front of it: mould and model
of the Graf Zeppelin dirigible
(E&Co., 1930: 6 x 15 x 4).
Next row down, from left:
ocean passenger liner
(E&Co., 1939: 6 x 19 x 5),
fire engine
(S&Co., pre-1897: 7 x 12 x 5),
airplane
(E&Co., 1927: 12 x 12.5 x 4).
Front row, from left:
automobile
(E&Co., 1939: 5 x 16.5 x 4),
passenger coach, coal wagon,
locomotive
(S&Co., 1897: 6 x 12.5 x 4, 5 x 10 x
4 and 6 x 14 x 3 respectively).
The ice cream mould for the
aeroplane was put on the market
within one month of Charles Lindbergh's first crossing of the
Atlantic in his Spirit of St. Louis.

138: Ice cream moulds of company logos. On the back row, from left: the logos of General Electric (E&Co., no year: 13.5 x 13.5 x 3.5), RCA (E&Co., 1930: 8 x 14.5 x 3) and Suburban Gas Corporation (ACM, no year: 10 x 10 x 3). Front row, from left: Hoover (E&Co., 1924: 11.5 x 11.5 x 2), Frigidaire (E&Co., 1925-1926: 5 x 8.5 x 3), Mobil Oil with the Trilon and the Perisphere, symbols of the 1939 New York World's Fair (E&Co., circa 1940: 13.5 x 13.5 x 3.5), Swift (ACM, 1955: 9.5 x 11 x 2.5).

139: John Bull locomotive, mould and model (E&Co., between 1874 and 1880: 21 x 21 x 8.5). The John Bull was built in 1831 by Stephenson in England and was in service between 1833 and 1866 on the Camden and Amboy Railroad, USA. The locomotive is now on display in the Smithsonian Institution's National Museum of American History in Washington D.C. In those days the steam locomotive was seen as a symbol of industrial strength and progress and was therefore used as an ice cream mould during festive meals to celebrate Labor Day on the first Monday in September. The day was instituted in 1894 by President Cleveland after trade unionists had demonstrated in the streets of New York for its introduction.

140: Christopher Columbus (E&Co., circa 1892: 14 x 8.5 x 6.5). The ice cream mould was designed at the same time as a mould for Columbus' ship, the Santa Maria, to mark the 400th anniversary of his discovery of America in 1492.

Licks, Sticks & Bricks

A WORLD HISTORY OF ICE CREAM

How ice cream became an American favourite

The
ICE CREAM REVIEW

For decades, Americans have eaten more ice cream per head than any other nation. In 1997 they consumed on average over twenty litres each. Ice cream is enshrined in their everyday eating habits, being seen as convenient, delicious and nutritious. Such is ice cream's status in the US, it has become woven into the fabric of innumerable short stories, songs, comic strips, cartoons, radio programmes and TV shows. Sports heroes, film stars, singers, poets, authors, comedians, cabaret artists and movie-makers have sung its praises in all sorts of ways. Ice-cream memorabilia are passionately collected and displayed in museums. During the 1960 presidential elections consumers could choose between the Kennedy Bar and the Nixon Bar, identical ice creams made by Good Humor and carrying pictures of either candidate. In 1996 the American poet Nellie McClung even called her book containing poems about Marilyn Monroe, including some written by Monroe herself, My sex is ice cream.[1]

• The beginnings of modern American ice cream history date back to the second half of the nineteenth century and the period of rapid industrialisation that followed the end of the Civil War in 1865. However, the real foundation for America's ice cream industry was laid in the first few decades of the twentieth century. In October 1929, the oldest publication of the US ice cream industry, The Ice Cream Trade Journal, published a retrospective of the key developments in the sector over the preceding 20 years. The major milestones

141: Ice cream is also good for your teddy bear. Cover of The Ice Cream Review, December 1922.

highlighted within the industry were the establishment in 1906 of the National Association of Ice Cream Manufacturers; the enactment of regulations governing hygienic preparation; the development of ice cream standards; professionalisation through training and scientific research; and the establishment of a nationwide system of costing.[2]

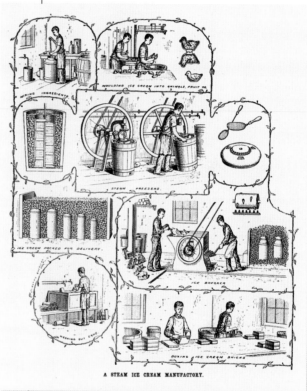

A STEAM ICE CREAM MANUFACTORY.

142: The production process in about 1890 in the ice cream factory of George Schmidt in Jersey City, New Jersey, as depicted in The Scientific American, 21 July 1894. From left to right: the ingredients are mixed; the mix is put into moulds (birds, fruit); cross-section of freezer, and freezers with drive-belts powered by steam engines; ice cream churns in crushed cooling ice, ready for delivery; men busy crushing blocks of ice; boy washing ice cream churns clean; bricks of ice cream being packed in cardboard.

• External factors, however, were equally important. Mechanisation and automation of production; the introduction of processes for homogenisation and pasteurisation; freezing with brine instead of crushed ice and salt; the invention of the horizontal batch ice cream freezer; and the enhanced distribution brought by the advent of the automobile and railroad – all were critical to expansion. Important, too, were the wide-scale introduction of the ice cream cone after 1904; the development of high-speed packaging machines; the standardis- ation of dimensions and pack sizes; Clarence Vogt's 1927 invention of a continu- ous ice cream freezing machine; the installation of electrically powered freezers in shops from 1923 onwards; the use of dry ice during transport; and large-scale adver- tising campaigns using the new mass media of radio and cinema.

143: Advertising leaflet for Jell-O Ice Cream Powder, circa 1905. The introduction of ice cream powder at the end of the nineteenth century gave a tremendous boost to home consumption.

cream consumption plum- meted. However, grocery store chains began selling ice cream in the summer, ice cream saloons and soda fountain bars enjoyed halcyon days, vending machines were installed, ice cream was transported to other cities by air and the first chains of dedi- cated shops were set up. By 1936 ice cream consumption had climbed back to its pre-Crash level and in the years that followed grew by leaps and bounds. Between 1936 and 1946 per capita consumption more than doubled, from 7.5 litres to just under 16 litres per annum.[4]

• In addition, the early 1920s saw a revolu- tion in ice cream with the introduction of the first chocolate-coated ice cream bar under the Eskimo Pie brand name and of water-ices on a stick, such as the Good Humor products branded Ice Cream Sucker and Popsicle. At the same time ice cream became less and less of a seasonal product and more and more something that was eaten the whole year round, acquiring a permanent place in the American way of life. During the First World War the United States authorities did not regard ice cream as a luxury, but deemed it a food whose manufac- ture had to be continued despite the war. Ice cream was a product of national impor- tance and was described as 'the balance wheel of the dairy industry'.[3]

• After the Wall Street Crash of 1929, ice

Jacob Fussell: founding father of the US ice cream industry

• The birthplace of the modern American ice cream industry can be traced to greater Philadelphia, the state capital of Pennsyl- vania. For many people Philadelphia ice cream set the standard for American ice cream (see also chapter 4).

• The conditions for the development of an ice cream industry in Philadelphia were perfect. A large seaport as well as leading commercial centre, its food industries were already flourishing. In south-eastern Penn- sylvania and the adjoining state of New Jersey lay a rich hinterland of dairy farms and orchards. Milk and fresh fruit for ice cream production were therefore in plentiful supply[5] and, thanks to the fast-expanding and increasingly efficient railroad network, could be transported to Philadelphia without difficulty. Other ingredients were shipped in by sea: vanilla from Mexico and cane sugar from Caribbean islands like Cuba. In 1877 the city of Philadelphia was home to no fewer than thirteen sugar refineries.[6] Moreover, the fast-growing populations of Philadelphia and nearby New York, Washington and Baltimore offered vast sales potential.

144: Advertising leaflet for Jell-O Ice Cream Powder, circa 1905.

• Ice cream had in fact been a familiar product in America for some time, but its production and distribution were still small-scale operations (see chapter 4). The first to try to change this was a prosperous dairy trader from Baltimore, Jacob Fussell (1829-1912). In common with many dairy wholesalers, Fussell had regular surpluses of cream in the summer which he could not sell. Milk yield was much higher in spring and summer, but consumers bought less milk during the warmer months. Fussell calculated that he could use the cream surpluses to make ice cream and sell it for 25 cents per US quart (just under a litre), giving a modest profit.[7] Since the usual selling price was 60 cents a quart, this cost calculation gave Fussell the idea of producing ice cream on a bigger

145: Advertising leaflet for Jell-O Ice Cream Powder, circa 1905.

scale; and since milk was much cheaper in rural areas, he decided to build a small ice cream factory and an ice-house close to his suppliers. Accordingly, in the winter of 1851-52 Fussell built his factory in the little Pennsylvanian town of Seven Valleys, north of Baltimore, to which he sent his ice cream by train in metal cans, kept cold in tubs filled with ice and salt.

• Like all later ice cream manufacturers, Fussell soon discovered the chief drawback of an ice cream business: that demand is strongly influenced by the weather and therefore hard to forecast. One day he would have too little ice cream, the next too much. With no modern means of communication, Fussell was unable to send timely instructions regarding changes in production volume to his factory in the countryside – one reason why he relocated his small factory to Baltimore in 1854. In 1856 he handed over its management to a business partner and started a small ice cream factory in Washington. Subsequently, Fussell expanded his business to Boston and New York. Fussell's New York outlet opened in 1863 on Fourth Avenue, close to 23rd Street, and was the first shop in the city to sell ice cream on a large scale. Shortly after the shop had

147: Factory girls in the United States enjoy an ice cream during their break on a summer's day in 1909.

opened Fussell received a visit from a delegation of the Associated Confectioners of New York. The visitors asked him to sign an agreement in which he undertook to sell his ice cream at the fixed price of $1.25 per quart. 'Refusal meant war, and pretty certain annihilation' is how Fussell's son described the incident 42 years later.[8] Fussell refused to sign and was not annihilated. Sales continued as before and an invoice dated

146: 'Ah! so pure'. Advertising leaflet of the Colonial Ice Cream Co. from Philadelphia, circa 1930. Ice cream with fresh peaches from the Alberta Peach Growers Association.

March 1865 shows a quart of ice cream from Fussell's retailing at 70 cents.[9]

• In 1870 Fussell decided to expand his New York business. To raise the necessary capital he joined forces with a number of business partners, one of whom was James Madison Horton. A few years later, in 1874, Horton bought out the other partners, Fussell retired to Washington and the business continued under a new name: the Horton Ice Cream Company. In 1928 Horton was in turn taken over by Borden, the large dairy company.[10]

¶ In February 1809 James Madison (1751-1836) was sworn in as the fourth President of the United States. Madison, one of the founding fathers of the young republic, was married to Dolly Payne Todd. The arrival in the White House of this buxom, vivacious woman who, according to a contemporary, the author Washington Irving, 'has a smile and a pleasant word for everybody', brought new life to the social scene in the seat of government.[1] The crème de la crème of Washington attended her Wednesday **soirées** and discussed the latest political developments, admired and displayed the newest fashions, sang and danced to piano music and enjoyed the many refreshments and delicacies that were served up by the French chef de cuisine, **Pierre Sioussat**.

One of those delicacies was, of course, ice cream. Madison's predecessors in the White House had also regularly treated their guests to ice cream. Back in 1784 George Washington had a machine to make ice cream and Thomas Jefferson, on his return from Paris in 1798, had brought back a recipe for ice cream from his French cook. But these beginnings pale into insignificance when compared to the place that Dolly Madison won for herself in American history books and, no less importantly, in children's literature.[2] Characteristic was the title that one of her biographers gave to her 1928 book: Dolly Madison, the nation's hostess.[3] Three years before that, the trade journal of the American ice cream industry, The Ice Cream Review, had claimed (wrongly) that Dolly had introduced the eating of ice cream into the White House 'and, thereby, won for herself the title "our lady of ice cream"'.[4]

The American ice cream industry helped to maintain this legend. In October 1931 during the annual exhibition of the Dairy and Ice Cream Machinery and Supplies Association, held in Atlantic City, the Association displayed a painting showing Dolly Madison receiving her guests. Pictured in the foreground is the black servant who had made the ice cream. The Association had thousands of reproductions made of this scene, which had been painted by Ernest Hamlin Baker. In a description on the back of the print the reader was told that it was thanks to Dolly that ice cream had become the 'queen of desserts'.

Also linked to this story is the tale of the black cook Augustus Jackson, who worked as a chef at the White House and, according to some sources, was the person who made the ice cream for Dolly Madison[5] – hence Baker's depiction of the servant on his 'artist's impression'. At the end of the 1920s Jackson opened an ice cream shop in Philadelphia. He was the first black American to do so, eventually becoming very prosperous.[6]

And today you can still eat Dolly Madison ice cream. In the State of New York Dolly Madison is a long-established ice cream brand.

148: Reproduction of a painting by Ernest Hamlin Baker, 1931, commissioned by the American Dairy and Ice Cream Machinery and Supplies Association for its annual exhibition in 1931. In it Dolly Madison, the President's wife, is showing her guests the kitchen in about 1810. The painter has depicted an ice cream machine with a spatula which is rotated by use of the handle (also shown). Machines of this kind were only invented in 1843, so this is an anachronism.

149: Frederick W. Breyer (left) and Henry W. Breyer in their office in Philadelphia, circa 1895.

150: One of the first Breyers ice cream shops at 2976 Frankford Avenue, Philadelphia, circa 1895.

151: Production hall in the Breyers ice cream factory at East Somerset in Philadelphia, circa 1890. Second from the right is Henry W. Breyer (1876-1936), the youngest son of founder William Breyer. Until the opening of the new factory with new ice cream freezers at Ninth and Cumberland Street, the ice cream was frozen with cooling ice and salt. However, the scrapers were already powered by electro-motors.

152: Horse and cart selling (or distributing) Breyers ice cream, Philadelphia, circa 1894.

153: Breyers garage for vans, horses and carts, circa 1912. In 1916 Breyers had 31 trucks.

Breyers and innovations in Pennsylvania

• Meanwhile, back in Philadelphia the city's bulky business directory for the year 1892 lists only one ice cream maker, Abraham Enghard. In 1870 Enghard had started a confectionery bakery-cum-ice cream business at 4962 Germantown Avenue in the north-eastern part of the city. By 1892 his business had grown to the point where it employed ten men and had three carts distributing his ice cream.[11] Breyer, founded in 1866 and set to become Philadelphia's most famous ice cream manufacturer, did not yet feature in the directory.

• William Breyer (1828-1882) was born in Württemberg, Germany, and settled in America in 1856.[12] According to the 1870 census his occupation was that of vinegar maker and grocer; but in 1866 he had also started to make ice cream in the summer, just as Enghard would a few years later. Breyer set up production in the back room of his house in the same Germanstown district where Enghard was to locate his business.

• For the first fifteen years of its existence William Breyer's ice cream business remained very small. To cool his ice cream he used ice and he had a horse and cart from which he sold his wares in the surrounding area. Then in 1882, at 2776 Frankford Avenue, Breyer opened the first of what was to become a series of Breyer's ice cream shops. Shortly after that he died, but his widow Louisa continued the business and in 1896 demand for Breyer ice cream had increased so much that the company had outgrown Frankford Avenue's modest capacity. Bigger premises were bought in 1904 on Ninth and Cumberland Street, where a new ice cream factory was established. At the same time Henry W. Breyer (1878-1936), the founder's youngest son and successor, thought up a logo for the business: the Briar Leaf (Breyer is pronounced "briar").[13]

• While Breyer was busy expanding, the entire American ice cream industry was developing apace. Production equipment was being continuously improved; machinery was now powered not by steam but by electric motors. Dairy institutes and universities studied the process of ice cream making and began courses on the subject, the first being given in 1892 by the University of Pennsylvania's dairy department.[14]

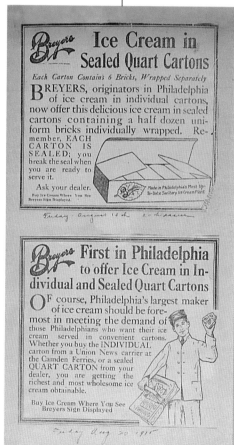

154: Two 1915 advertisements for bricks of Breyers ice cream packed in cardboard boxes.

Centennial Philadelphia, 1876. People from all over the world journeyed here to see this first great international exposition.

Breyers Ice Cream was first made ten years before the Centennial Exposition. Ever since, it has been delicious, pure and wholesome—made from the freshest and finest of materials. Substitutes have never been used in its making. Breyers has always been the good, old-fashioned home-made kind of ice cream. Stop in at our store and try some, or enjoy this treat at home. We gladly deliver when requested and you receive it in perfect condition.

Special orders for parties, picnics, church and club affairs carefully handled. Quantity prices quoted on request.

Phone—Gtn. 4653
Special Deliveries
Quality and Service
Unsurpassed

BAXTER'S
"ORPHEUM PASTRY SHOP"
60 W. Chelten Ave.

All Cakes and Pastry
Our Own Make

"Have You Tried Our
Butter Creams?"

Breyers Ice Cream
"The Old Fashioned Kind"

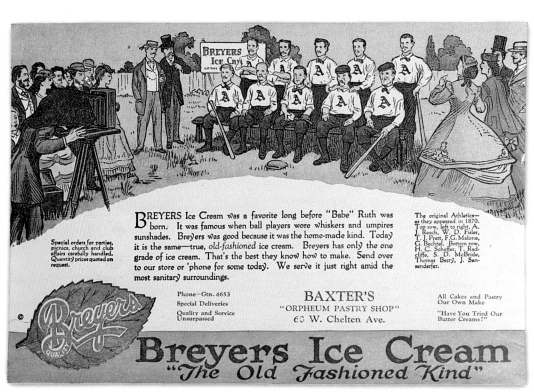

Special orders for parties, picnics, church and club affairs carefully handled. Quantity prices quoted on request.

Breyers Ice Cream was a favorite long before "Babe" Ruth was born. It was famous when ball players wore whiskers and umpires sunshades. Breyers was good because it was the home-made kind. Today it is the same—true, old-fashioned ice cream. Breyers has only the one grade of ice cream. That's the best they know how to make. Send over to our store or 'phone for some today. We serve it just right amid the most sanitary surroundings.

The original Athletics—as they appeared in 1870. Top row, left to right, A. J. Reach, W. D. Fisler, T. J. Pratt, F. G. Malone, G. Bechtel. Bottom row, H. C. Schaffer, T. Radcliffe, S. D. McBride, Thomas Berry, J. Sensenderfer.

Phone—Gtn. 4653
Special Deliveries
Quality and Service
Unsurpassed

BAXTER'S
"ORPHEUM PASTRY SHOP"
60 W. Chelten Ave.

All Cakes and Pastry
Our Own Make

"Have You Tried Our
Butter Creams?"

Breyers Ice Cream
"The Old Fashioned Kind"

• Another major advance in the industry was a change in the method of freezing. Although the refrigeration process using compressed ammonia gas had been adopted all over the world since 1870 (see chapter 4), it was little used in the ice cream industry. That changed after 1900 when an ice cream manufacturer called E. Walker, the owner of IXL Ice Cream Co. in Warren, a small town in the far north-east of Pennsylvania, invented an ice cream freezer that was cooled with liquid brine instead of by ice and salt. Walker's machine consisted of a metal container into which brine supplied by an ammonia compression freezer was pumped through pipes fitted with valves. Inside the container was an ice cream tub with a dasher connected to a drive-belt. The brine refrigerant ensured that the ice cream mix in the tub froze within eight minutes, after which the brine was pumped back to the cooling installation.[15]

155 and 156: Advertisements, circa 1916, for Breyers ice cream by Baxter's 'Orpheum Pastry Shop' at 60 W. Chelten Avenue, Philadelphia. The pictures show that Breyers ice cream was already widely on sale prior to the 1876 centennial of the American Declaration of Independence, long before the introduction of the motion picture and long before the day when 'Babe' Ruth hit his first home run in Baltimore in 1914.

• This circulating brine process was substantially improved in 1905 by Emery Thompson, who hit on the idea of freezing the ice cream mix in a vertical, double-walled container. The brine was pumped through the outer shell of the container, causing the mix in the inside drum to freeze and enabling larger quantities of ice cream to be made in a much shorter time. Thompson succeeded in making about 1,500 litres of ice cream a day using two ice cream freezers.[16] His improved machine revolutionised the ice cream industry as, one by one, ice cream manufacturers switched to a horizontal version which was quickly developed. The first horizontal freezer had been invented in 1904 by the Ohio-based Miller Pasteurizing Machine Co.[17] That prototype, however, was still cooled with crushed ice and salt.

• At the same time as the new type of ice cream freezer came on the market, the homogeniser also found its place in the ice cream factory. A homogeniser breaks up and emulsifies the fat particles in milk by forcing it under high pressure through tiny holes about the size of a pin-head. This machine, originally developed in 1899 by the French businessman and inventor Auguste Gaulin, brought a considerable improvement in the quality of the ice cream mix, giving it a smoother, creamier texture. The homogeniser also made the ice cream industry much less dependent on the supply of fresh cream, since excellent ice cream could now be made using butter-fat, condensed milk or powdered milk – ingredients which could be kept in stock for a longer period without spoiling. 'The homogeniser has stabilised the ice cream business', concluded the trade journal The Ice Cream Review in 1921.[18]

• In the new Breyers factory at Ninth and Cumberland Street, homogenisers and the new type of circulating-brine freezers were soon installed. The same brine was used to cool the coldstores in which the ice cream was stored. The production of ice cream started on the second floor where the milk, once it had been pasteurised, was passed through the homogeniser and stored in ageing tanks before being pumped to ice cream freezers on the ground floor. An electric motor powered a central drive-belt connected to the spatulas (also known as scrapers) inside the freezers. Next to the freezer room was a packaging department and after that came the coldstore. This effi-

157: Drawing of the new Breyers ice cream factory alongside the Pennsylvania Railroad. Opened in 1924, the factory was for many years the world's biggest and most modern ice cream factory.

cient factory layout was praised in 1907 by The Ice Cream Trade Journal, which described it as a model 'well worthy of investigation by ice cream manufacturers contemplating installation of mechanical refrigeration.'[19]

• The refrigeration plant that cooled the brine was also used to produce blocks of ice, each weighing around 100 kilos, which were broken into small pieces by a massive crushing machine. The crushed ice was used to cool the containers of ice cream during transportation to the many sales outlets in Philadelphia and the surrounding area. Increasingly this was done by van rather than horse and cart. In 1916 Breyers had a fleet of 31 trucks and, thanks in part to this improved mobility, Breyers' sales climbed to more than 3.7 million litres of ice cream per year in 1914.[20]

• For the saloons, soda fountain bars and drugstores, where the ice cream was served in dishes, glasses or, after 1904, cones (see box on p. 172), the churn was no longer the only means of supply. By the outbreak of war

in 1914, the quick delivery of pre-packaged, quart-size ice cream bricks was standard and wholesalers and shopkeepers were able to place their orders by telephone.[21] Breyers, as the company was re-named in 1908, regarded the ice cream brick in a carton as one of its specialities and advertised it widely.

• As the owner of a number of dairy factories, Breyers supervised the processing of the milk itself. Upon receipt the milk was subjected to stringent inspection. It was transported by train to the ice cream plant in Philadelphia only after first being pasteurised in the dairies – by no means the practice everywhere. From about 1890 the American dairy industry had gradually started to introduce pasteurisation, but the need for this was much discussed and it was some time before cities and states made pasteurisation obligatory. In 1907 a government committee concluded that pasteurisation could 'prevent much sickness and save lives'.[22] The city authorities in Chicago, the first to take action, ruled in 1909 that dairy products, including ice cream, that had not been tuberculin-tested had to be pasteurised.[23] Only in the 1920s did the pasteurisation of ice cream mix become compulsory in virtually all states, by when most ice cream manufacturers had decided for themselves that pasteurisation was not only essential for public health reasons but also brought them economic benefits. 'By using the process of pasteurisation we are enabled to use sweet butter, milk powder and sweetened condensed milk', argued R.L. Hargrove of The Southern Creameries in Texas in 1923.[24] As a result pasteurisation, just like homogenisation, made the ice cream industry less dependent on the supply of fresh milk. 'Pasteurisation prevents deterioration. [...] As the sales of ice cream are not the same from day to day due to weather changes, we often find it to be necessary to hold a mix over 24 hours. This could not be accomplished unless the mix had been properly pasteurised', wrote Hargrove.

• Hygienic production conditions and the purity of ingredients were qualities that Breyers emphasised very early on in its advertising. The company published a 'pledge of purity', complete with Henry Breyer's signature, assuring its customers that no thickening agents, artificial flavourings or other, non-natural ingredients had been used in making its ice cream. It was made only from 'real cream, granulated sugar and pure flavorings'. In a city like Philadelphia with an extensive flavourings industry, whose products included vanilla essence, this was not superfluous information. 'Specks?' questioned

the headline of an early advertisement referring to the tiny particles of finely ground vanilla beans that could be seen in the ice cream. 'Breyers Vanilla is made only from Vanilla Beans', came the answer.[25]

• At the beginning of the 1920s the factory at Ninth and Cumberland Street proved to be too small. A new ice cream factory, the biggest in the world, was constructed in 1924 alongside the Pennsylvania Railroad. Another ice cream factory opened in 1925 on Long Island near New York City, followed in 1927 by one in Newark, New Jersey. Breyers was now the largest ice cream producer in the United States, with ice cream sales in seven states on the country's eastern seaboard.

Hygiene, standardisation and advertising

• The developing US ice cream industry was not restricted to the area round Philadelphia. All along the east coast, and to a lesser extent on the west coast of the United States, the second half of the nineteenth century saw the establishment of ice cream factories which experienced the same sort of development as Breyers, albeit on a smaller scale.

Damsel Ice Cream in Barnesville, Ohio (1855); Cunningham in Chicago (1856); Cuscaden in

158: Pasteurisation, hygienic production conditions and the purity of the ingredients used were qualities that Breyers underlined at an early stage in its advertisements. In about 1914 the company issued 'a pledge of purity' that carried Henry Breyer's signature.

¶ 'The ice cream cone is the biggest selling idea [there] has ever been in the ice cream business and it is the biggest little thing in the ice cream business', said the American ice cream manufacturer L.J. Schumaker during a speech in 1919 to a meeting of the Association of Ice Cream Manufacturers of Pennsylvania.[1]

Schumaker delivered his speech fifteen years after the birth of the ice cream cone in 1904 during the World's Fair in St. Louis. A Syrian from Damascus, Ernest A. Hamwi, had a stall on which he sold zalabia – sweet Persian waffles. Next to Hamwi another exhibitor was selling ice cream. As the ice cream exhibitor ran out of dishes and was unable to sell any more ice cream, Hamwi had the bright idea of rolling his waffles into the shape of a cone and scooping the ice cream into them.[2] The cones were immediately snapped up by consumers and soon Hamwi was baking them for other ice cream sellers

at the exhibition. The fact that this occurred at a World's Fair attended by tens of thousands of visitors helped ensure that the ice cream cone spread rapidly throughout the whole of America. In 1929 an old hand in the US ice cream industry, John W. Miller, noted down his reminiscences of the preceding 60 years: 'Before

159: 'The biggest little thing in the ice cream business': an ice cream cone.

the advent of the cone, ice cream was sold most exclusively in candy and drugstores. The only way it was sold then was by the dish or in an ice cream soda. Of course, it took several months before the cornucopia got a foothold in the ice cream trade, as very few saw its possibilities. [...] Gradually, one could see an increase in the number of stores where ice cream was

sold. Peanut and candy stands on the streets added ice cream to their stock, ice cream peddlers appeared at schools, the byways and highways had stands and the ice cream trade grew to proportions no one dreamed of, until today it is safe to say that nearly 50 per cent of all ice cream is sold in cones'. Miller concluded that 'nothing has been produced during the past twenty-five years that helped the industry so much as the little five-cent cone.'[3]

Before long manufacturers such as Sayso and Nabisco (National Biscuit Company) had embraced the production of ice cream cones. New types and formats were regularly introduced, a good example being the Jack and Jill cone – with two cups alongside each other – brought out by Nabisco in the early 1930s.

160: Wooden mould for the manufacture of ice cream cones. While still warm, the wafer was wrapped around the mould.

As often happens with successful innovations, there were many others besides Hamwi who laid claim to having invented the ice cream cone.[4] The most serious claim came from Abe Doumar, a Lebanese immigrant and also a trader at the St. Louis World's Fair. According to Doumar, one evening after business had ended he was standing chatting to one of the waffle bakers at the exhibition. Then he rolled a waffle into a cone shape, walked across to a nearby ice-cream seller and put some ice cream in it. He took the cone back to the baker and suggested to him that his sales would increase substantially if he used his waffles in this way. The waffle baker was delighted and at the end of the show presented Doumar with a waffle iron to show his gratitude.

Doumar took the gift with him to New York where, together with his brothers, he started an ice cream stall on the seafront promenade at Coney Island, where their ice creams in cones sold well. His inventiveness extended to new promotional ideas. At moments when business was slack he hired a couple of attractive girls and had them stroll up and down the promenade eating an ice cream.[5] Doumar's example was soon copied all over America.

Initially, however, a lady of good manners was not supposed to eat an ice cream cone in public. 'If the occasion should arise when a Gentlewoman is offered an ice cream cone, she should refrain from eating it in a public place. Exposure of the tongue by using its tip to lick the ice cream from the cone will serve only to mark her as a woman of unsavory and unattractive appetites. The Gentlewoman should take the ice cream cone home, place it upside down in a shallow dish, discard the cone and eat the ice cream with a spoon.'[6]

In fact, the ice cream cone was invented well before the World's Fair in St. Louis. Confectionery bakers in Germany and France regularly sold cones filled with cream and as early as in 1888 the British cook Agnes Marshall published the recipe for 'Margaret Cornets' – cones filled with ice cream – in her book Mrs. A.B. Marshall's Cookery Book (see chapter 4). But it was thanks to the St. Louis World's Fair that the ice cream cone became 'the biggest little thing' in the ice cream business.

161: Waffle iron made from cast iron, Sayso Cone. Waffle irons like this one are still used to bake wafers for ice cream cones.

Louisville, Kentucky (1875); Abbotts Dairy, established in 1851 as a dairy manufacturer in Philadelphia; Hood in Boston (established in 1846 as a dairy business and also operating as an ice cream producer from 1899 onwards); Mansion Ice Cream in Cambridge, Massachusetts (1886); Hendler in Baltimore (1905); Browns Velvet Ice Cream Co. in New Orleans (1904) – these were just a few of the many pioneers. [26] Like Breyers, they soon made use of the new production and distribution methods, encouraged not only by the manufacturers of ice cream machines, but also by their own industry associations which were set up after 1900 in the various states.

• In 1906 the National Association of Ice Cream Manufacturers was founded in Atlantic City, New Jersey. In the following year the organisation held its first annual meeting in Pittsburgh, attended by 100 participants. In 1909 that number reached 800. [27] A major motive for the establishment of the national association was the Federal Department of Agriculture's imposition of a standard butter-fat content of 14% for ice cream. The manufacturers thought this was much too high; they advocated a fat content of between 8% and 10%. Ultimately, the standard varied from state to state, but in most instances it was closer to the level sought by the ice cream manufacturers.

• Apart from fat content, discussions also covered the regulations for hygienic production and supervision of compliance. Standards of hygiene at that time varied widely. In 1898, the Scientific American had reported typhus epidemics in Michigan, Wisconsin and Illinois caused by eating ice cream. The magazine specifically attributed the outbreaks to the conditions under which street sellers, 'the dirtiest of dirty itinerants', made their ice cream. [28] Yet the conditions prevailing in the premises of ice cream manufacturers were often little better. 'Five years ago hygienic methods and sanitary arrangements in the ice cream factory were practically unknown', wrote the Ice Cream Trade Journal in 1910. 'Every man made his product in the easiest and cheapest way possible.' [29] In its first issue, published in January 1905, the journal had advocated a standard for ice cream.

162: One-pint pack of Millikin ice cream, circa 1935, bearing the Sealtest seal, which since 1925 has provided proof that the ice cream is checked in laboratories.

163: Father comes home from work with a box of ice cream. Cover of The Ice Cream Review, April 1923.

164: Cover of The Ice Cream Review, January 1923. Ordering ice cream by telephone was already possible in some places by 1918.

The ICE CREAM REVIEW

Without a standard, it argued, the ice cream industry would be 'at the mercy of less scrupulous competitors who come into the market with a frozen compound that deserves no better name than dope and cannot be prevented from selling it as ice cream.'[30] In the first paragraph of the proposed standard of 1906 the Department of Agriculture stated that 'ice cream should be made of pure fresh cream and derived under sanitary conditions. It should not contain more than 100,000 bacteria per c.c.'[31]

• Although they differed in their views about the desired minimum butter-fat percentage, the state associations of ice cream manufacturers wanted effective regulations to be enacted. They wanted to protect themselves against 'swindlers' who made ice cream from margarine or beef tallow and who, by incorporating all sorts of 'dubious' ingredients such as saccharin, undermined public confidence in the product. Together with the dairy industry, which had to ensure the supply of properly inspected, wholesome milk, they began to draw up their own standards over the years and many of their proposals were adopted by the authorities. By around 1918 most states had legislation governing the manufacture of ice cream, although the legal battle over the level of the butter-fat content was to drag on for decades.

• America's entry into the First World War in 1917 led to shortages, particularly of sugar. Initially the authorities designated ice cream an 'essential' foodstuff and manufacturers were able to continue buying as much sugar as they needed. Only in July 1918

165: Cover of The Ice Cream Review, September 1922. Father holds a tray on which he presents a big bowl of ice cream to his wife, while daughter is already enjoying a cone.

were certain restrictions introduced. The larger producers had to accept a 25% reduction in the amount of cane sugar used; smaller ice cream makers, such as owners of soda fountains, were entitled to use 50% cane sugar. Sugar or sugar syrup obtained from maize was used as a supplement.[32] Rationing did not however stop ice cream consumption growing. In 1920 the US produced more than 560 million litres, from just over 200 million litres in 1906,[33] an increase of 180%. This growth was attributable partly, as we have seen, to better organisation, standardisation and production improvements, but equally important were improvements in distribution and increasingly professional advertising.

• The flourishing automobile industry (by 1912 Ford's assembly lines had already produced half a million of the famed Model T) developed a succession of refrigerated trucks for the transport of ice cream. Manufacturers set up their own garages and began to train drivers. The new means of transport also made it easier to supply freezer cabinets to shops and other retailers, each new delivery of ice cream being accompanied by ice and salt for cooling the cabinets. In 1916 one ice cream manufacturer remarked that 'the cabinet system has doubled, tripled or quadrupled the business.' Even though business was brisk, there was no need for the shopkeeper to be out of stock and telephone calls for costly follow-up deliveries became a thing of the past.[34] The system was improved still further after the installation in 1923 of the first electrically powered freezer cabinets. Since ice cream could now be stored in good condition for much longer, it became practical to keep a wider stock of flavours. That in turn made it

166: Using a straw to 'drink' ice cream
from a soda glass. Cover of
The Ice Cream Review, June 1923.

possible to advertise 'flavours of the week'.

• Advertising played an important role from a very early stage in the United States. Back in 1777 Philip Lenzi, a confectionery baker from London, had placed an advertisement in The New York Gazette announcing that his ice cream was on sale. One hundred and thirty years later US ice cream manufacturers began 'systematic advertising campaigns' featuring special coupons inside the packs, competitions, ice cream recipes and slogans in which celebrities served as an example for the ice cream fan. One of the first personalities to be involved in such advertising was the millionaire oil magnate John D. Rockefeller, the founder of the Standard Oil Company. 'John Rockefeller eats ice cream every day', proclaimed an advertisement in 1907.[35] Cars, theatre programmes, programmes for church services and dance-halls, showcards, shop windows, posters and balloons carried advertising for ice cream and, as early as 1906, illuminated signs drew the public's attention to ice cream shops. By 1909 department stores and big grocery shops were offering ice cream at reduced prices as a 'loss leader' to attract customers, a marketing technique that was also used to promote sales of coffee.[36]

• The latest publicity media were also brought into play. On 11 July 1919 W.H. Irving, director of the ice cream factory of the same name in Houston, Texas, was the first to use an aeroplane to advertise ice cream. His biplane, in pristine white livery, scattered more than 28,000 leaflets in cities over a 200-mile area. One in every twenty leaflets carried a coupon that could be redeemed for a free half-litre of Irving ice cream.[37]

• Another method of advertising was the door-to-door distribution of price lists and circulars containing special offers and descriptions of delectable speciality products. For public holidays and feast-days like Independence Day, Labor Day, Christmas, St. Valentine's Day, Easter, Thanksgiving Day and for birthday celebrations, the manufacturers offered special 'fancy ices'. These ranged from bricks of pre-packed ice cream of various flavours to specially shaped ice cream creations, such as a turkey for Thanksgiving Day, the head of George Washington for the Fourth of July or an ice cream in the form of a steam locomotive for Labor Day (see box on p. 146).

• Ice cream was becoming big business. The First World War was over; the Roaring Twenties arrived; and the advent of radio and motion pictures opened up a new world of possibilities for ice cream advertising. Film stars, singers and sports heroes could now be used to reach all those consumers who did not read newspapers or magazines, but who listened to the radio. This was the age of revolution in the ice cream novelties business – and also of Prohibition, when alcohol consumption was banned in America. Although the ban was circumvented on a large scale, it stimulated the sales of ice cream. Many a business that had hitherto built its livelihood on the sale of alcohol tried to make money in other ways; selling ice cream was one of them.

'Oh my, eat Eskimo Pie'

• If you switched on your radio in America at the end of the 1920s, there was a fair chance that your room would resound to the following lyrics, accompanied by a ukelele:

'Way up in the land of ice and snow, oh, oh,
There's a place you really ought to go, oh, oh.
All explorers could tell,
If they only could tell,
Of a dish made by the Eskimo.
What will ev'rybody eat today,
When they want to keep the 'Doc' away?
There's a melody we sing today:
If you're well and want to keep that way,
Oh my, it's Eskimo Pie,
Oh my, eat Eskimo Pie.'

• So went the first verse of a song written by 'radio's favorite singing song writer', Dale Wimbrow.[38] The subject of his song, Eskimo Pie – a square block of vanilla ice cream covered in chocolate – was the first in a series of 1920s ice cream novelties. It had been invented in 1919 by Christian K. Nelson (1893-1980), a Dane by origin who ran an ice cream parlour in Onowa, Iowa. One day a boy came in who wanted to spend a nickel on sweets but could not decide between an ice cream and a bar of chocolate. This gave Nelson the idea of making an ice cream with a chocolate coating. After a couple of months experimenting he succeeded in making the ice cream he had in mind. He heated cocoa butter to approximately 80°C, dipped a piece of vanilla ice cream in it and then immediately froze it.

• Nelson's 'Temptation I-Scream-Bar', as he initially called his new product, sold well.[39]

168: Nancy Carroll (1904-1965), Paramount Pictures star between 1929 and 1931, dressed in characteristic 'flapper' fashion, advertising Harding Ice Cream from Omaha.

167: Sleeve of gramophone record of the song 'O! My Eskimo Pie' by Dale Wimbrow, 1939. Songwriter and singer Dale Wimbrow first composed his song about Eskimo Pie ice cream in the late 1920s. The 1939 version, however, no longer described the Eskimo Pie ice cream bar covered in chocolate that had originally been launched in 1919, but a chocolate-coated ice on a stick.

In 1920 the 27 year-old Nelson applied for a patent and moved to Omaha, Nebraska, with the intention of making his ice cream into a commercial success. There he met Russell Stover, a supervisor in an ice cream company. Stover thought up the name Eskimo Pie and in the summer of 1921 the first of the new, foil-wrapped ice creams were sold. The ice creams had a content of only about 45 cc – early ice cream sizes were very small by comparison with today's. Customers snapped them up and within 24 hours the entire stock had been sold.[40] The two men moved to Chicago and set up the Russell Stover Co. to sell licences for manufacturing the Eskimo Pie ice cream product. Within a year 1,000 licences had been sold.

• The nation went Eskimo Pie crazy. Machine makers began to market all sorts of equipment for producing Eskimo Pies. Ice cream gave rise to a flood of innovations in the mechanical engineering industry and also brought about the first wave of automation. In next to no time chocolate heaters, cutting machines, packaging machines, conveyor belts and new storage facilities were on the market. In 1921 machine manufacturer Mojonnier Brothers introduced an automatic cutting machine and in 1923 Anderson Brothers Manufacturers Co. developed a fully automatic machine that cut the blocks of vanilla ice cream into small rectangular portions, dipped the bars in chocolate sauce and then wrapped them at the rate of 90 Eskimo Pie products a minute.[41] In 1923 70 million Eskimo Pie ice creams were sold; in 1924 some 169 million.

• Despite the enormous success of Eskimo Pie ice cream, however, the founders of Russell Stover Co. got into financial difficulties owing to the high legal costs they incurred in protecting their patent against infringement. In 1923 the company was spending almost $4,000 a day on this[42] and, to make matters worse, many licensees were not paying the compul-

169: Eating ice cream on the beach. Cover of The Ice Cream Review, August 1923.

sory royalties. In 1924 the business was taken over by the supplier of foil packaging, Reynolds Metal, which continued operations under the name Eskimo Pie Co.

• The introduction of the packaged Eskimo Pie ice cream had another effect: it helped the ice cream industry considerably in its attempts to sell ice cream in the winter months. Unlike scooping ice cream, individually wrapped ice creams could be easily and compactly stacked and kept in retailers' freezer cabinets for a lengthy period. In addition, the Eskimo Pie product was presented less as an ice cream that you ate only in the summer, but rather as confectionery or a snack.

• The Eskimo Pie Co. made every effort to bring these new product features to the attention of licensees, retailers and consumers. A manufacturer in Iowa organised the first Eskimo Pie Balloon Saturday in 1923, just after the end of the summer season. Ice cream sellers received thousands of

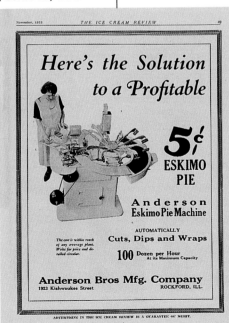

170: Advertisement for the Eskimo Pie machine of Anderson Bros. in The Ice Cream Review, November 1923. The first Eskimo Pie products went on sale in the summer of 1921.

balloons from the Eskimo Pie Co. In newspapers and on leaflets and showcards it was announced well in advance that on Balloon Day every buyer of a five-cent Eskimo Pie product would receive a free Eskimo Pie balloon. 'When you give a balloon free for a 5c purchase', wrote The Ice Cream Review in September 1924 in an article about the campaign, 'you have the perfect premium. Every child wants a balloon. Every child can eat Eskimo Pie. And the final factor of success is the fact that a balloon of equal size and quality would ordinarily sell for 5c without the Pie.'[43] The balloon days became a great success. They signalled the beginning of the winter season. Notice of balloon days therefore became a regular feature of the handbook that the Eskimo Pie Co. compiled each year for its licensees and retailers.[44]

• Not surprisingly, Eskimo Pie ice cream attracted imitations. In June 1922 the Elite Chocolate Coated BaseBall Co. of El Paso, Texas, launched chocolate-coated ice creams in the shape of a baseball. Babe Ruth, baseball's 'home run' king, endorsed the ice cream and took part in the $250,000 campaign that accompanied the launch. He and his team-mates appeared in an advertising film, while the packaging carried his name and signature. The Texan manufacturer claimed that he had been working on the development of the ice cream since 1912,[45] and in 1928 a judge in New York ruled the patent for Eskimo Pie ice cream invalid, noting that a veteran of the ice cream industry, Val Miller, had published a recipe in 1907 for 'Ice Cream Cannonballs' covered with chocolate. Miller's cannonballs were frozen in spherical, metal moulds and then immersed in a mixture of melted sweet chocolate and cocoa butter, after which they were immediately re-frozen.[46] In the end, the Eskimo Pie Co. was not much affected by the court ruling. The brand name had become well established by that time and Eskimo Pie remains to this day a fixture of the American ice cream market. In 1929, the Klondike, a similar square, chunky chocolate covered product and today's victor in the 'bar wars', was launched by the Isaly Dairy Company in Ohio (see chapter 6).

• In 1927 the New York division of Eskimo Pie Co. surprised consumers with a new and very modern selling method. In downtown New York, automatic ice cream vending machines cooled by electrically operated compressors were installed from which you could buy an Eskimo Pie ice cream for a nickel. The tall,

171: Page from a catalogue of ice cream freezers made by White Mountain, circa 1920. The two models at the top are meant for use in the home and are hand-operated; the other two are destined for hotels, restaurants and confectionery bakers and are fitted with a drive-wheel. White Mountain was by far the most important manufacturer of hand-operated freezers in America.

UNDERWOOD & UNDERWOOD

octagonal vending machines could carry 450 Eskimo Pie products.[47] At the time this experiment did not prove commercially that success-ful, but ten years later Eskimo Pie ice cream vending machines were again installed in New York, this time not cooled by electrical machinery but by dry ice.[48]

• In 1930 the New York division of Eskimo Pie Co. launched another innovation. This was a small, cylindrical vacuum container, invented

172: President Calvin Coolidge and his wife eating ice cream during the annual garden party at the White House early in the summer of 1926. Ice cream was Coolidge's favourite dessert, a preference which the ice cream industry used to its advantage by referring to its product as the 'President's Pudding'.

by Christian Nelson, in which the Eskimo Pie ice cream would stay cold, it was claimed, for seven to eight hours. Consumers could obtain the containers, which were painted bright orange, from 'the better grocer' for a deposit of $1.25. The New York Eskimo Pie Co. hoped in this way to stimulate ice cream consumption at home. For house-holds without a refrigerator the flask certainly offered a solution.[49]

'Popsicle Pete'

• Major competitors of the Eskimo Pie ice cream product were two other ice cream novelties, also introduced in the early 1920s, which went under the trademarks Popsicle and Good Humor Bar. The Popsicle product was the brainchild of Frank W. Epperson, of Oakland, California. His product was a 'frozen drink on a stick', a water-ice lolly. According to his own account, he had invented the product in 1905 but only had it patented in 1923. Popular myth has it that Epperson stumbled on his discovery by accident, after leaving a soda with a straw outside on a freezing cold night and waking up the next morning to the world's first ice lolly. He then set up the Epsicle Company of California, basing the name on a combination of the first two letters of his surname and 'icicle', and commenced production of 'the original fruit ice stick'. Shortly afterwards Epperson thought up the name Popsicle, which was to develop into America's biggest selling brand of ice lolly.
• Like the Eskimo Pie Co., Epperson licensed production of his ice lolly and from 1924 onwards special machines for the production

of Popsicle ice lollies came on the market. Around 1925 Epperson sold the rights to this brand name to the Joe Lowe Co., a New York-based business principally involved in bakery wholesaling rather than ice cream. In order to maintain the rights to a product that was simple to make, Joe Lowe Co. required licensees to agree to be exclusively supplied by the company with recipes, lemonade syrups or other flavourings, packs and sticks.[50] Special codes on the packs enabled the company to check whether an ice lolly bearing the name Popsicle had or had not been made by a licensee, thus protecting the brand and permitting quality control.
• At the beginning of the 1930s Joe Lowe Co. introduced an ice lolly under the brand name Twin Popsicle. Like the

173: 'Kewpie on the moon', picture postcard, circa 1920. Until Mickey Mouse appeared on the scene in 1928, Kewpie was America's most popular doll. The character had been designed in 1912 by the American illustrator Rose O'Neill, who based her on drawings she had produced for The Ladies Home Journal in 1909. The name Kewpie is derived from the word Cupid and the little cherub appeared in all sorts of guises: as a musician, gardener, soldier, baker or as an ice cream fan ('Kewpies love ice cream'). In the 1920s ice cream manufacturer Hendler used a picture of Kewpie on its packs.

Popsicle itself, it cost a nickel (5 cents). It had two sticks and so could be split down the middle. In the Depression years this was a bright idea: now you could easily share with a friend. Many shopkeepers themselves split the Twin Popsicle ice lolly into two and sold the halves for a couple of cents apiece.

174: Advertising poster for the Twin Popsicle ice cream product of Joe Lowe Co., 1940.

175: Mould for the manufacture of the Twin Popsicle products, marketed in the early 1930s by Joe Lowe Co. Patented by Joe Lowe, the mould could produce twelve Twin Popsicle ice lollies in one operation.

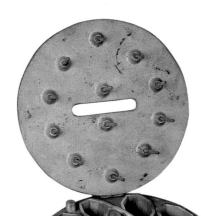

176: Machine for freezing water ices, circa 1925.

• In 1938 Joe Lowe Co. launched another new product, the Creamsicle (a water-ice with some milk solids), supported by specially-written radio adventures of the American cartoon hero Popeye. Backed by the world-famous spinach-eating sailor, sales of the Creamsicle product were further promoted by a large selection of gifts. This new phenomenon was characteristic of the Depression years and still continues in many countries. Consumers of the Creamsicle and the Popsicle ice creams – principally children – could collect the packs or the sticks and save them up for a range of toys and gifts: flashlights, roller skates, hunting knives, school satchels, drums, baseball mitts, watches, dolls, table tennis sets, whistles, model-making kits, etc.

• The range of rewards was constantly extended and updated. In 1939, for example, a Buck Rogers water pistol appeared on the list. Buck Rogers was another of the comic-book heroes with whom popular American culture is so richly endowed and who came to inhabit a parallel universe through the new mass media of cinema cartoons and radio plays. 'On the air! Starting April 1 & May 1. Buck Rogers in the 25th century. Also at the movies and in the comics', announced a 1939 Joe Lowe Co. illustrated catalogue of gift articles. The same brochure introduced a new hero: Popsicle Pete, a smiling boy with a permanent twinkle in his eyes,[51] who during the 1940s was used to recommend Joe Lowe Co.'s Popsicle promotional items. In 1948 he himself became the hero in a proper comic strip, The Adventures of Popsicle Pete.

The 'Good Humor Man'

• Before the owners of the Popsicle brand could begin doing good business, they first had to reach agreement with Harry B. Burt Sr. and Jr., who had introduced a vanilla ice cream with chocolate on a stick in 1920.

• Burt Sr. was the owner of a combined sweet shop and ice cream business in Youngstown, Ohio. In 1910 his range included an ordinary lolly on a stick which he called Good Humor. When the Burts invented the Good Humor Ice Cream Sucker in 1920, they submitted a patent application for the production process. The patent was granted

177: Good Humor ice cream van owned by Burt Jr., Tulsa, Oklahoma, circa 1928. Burt Jr. had thought up Good Humor ice together with his father in 1920.

in October 1923 and, after a few legal skirmishes with Joe Lowe Co., it was agreed that the latter company would restrict itself to water-ices (sold by them under the Popsicle brand name) and milk-ices (sold under the Creamsicle brand name) on a stick and that the Burts would concentrate on ice cream products.[52]

• Just like Eskimo Pie ice cream, the Good

178: Good Humor Man with cool-box, circa 1932, dressed in immaculate white with a white cap and bow tie, carrying a change machine attached to his Sam Browne belt.

179: Good Humor ice cream sellers gather together in the canteen of the ice cream factory in Los Angeles, circa 1928.

Humor product became a success. Convinced that its sales had to be tackled in a special way, Burt Sr. decided to paint one of his refrigerated vans white, put the name Good Humor Ice Cream Sucker on it and equip it with a range of five bells taken from an old family bobsled. Then his son, Burt Jr., put on a white uniform, donned a white cap and attached a money change machine to his Sam Browne belt. The Good Humor Man was born – and quickly became a familiar figure, particularly in the big cities on the east coast. His popularity was based both on large-scale, well thought-out advertising campaigns and on the selling concept of carefully planned routes through the city suburbs. At regular times in each neighbour-

hood, the well trained, immaculately dressed and resolutely cheerful Good Humor Man would make his appearance and, as the bells rang out, children came running. Perhaps this time they would get the one on which the words 'lucky stick' or 'free' were written so that you could have another treat for nothing! And which ice creams were on special offer today?

• The Good Humor Man grew into an American icon. He appeared in more than 100 films. The Marx Brothers made jokes about him, television stars invited him onto their shows, artists drew cartoons of him in daily and weekly papers and in 1950 he was immortalised in a full-length motion picture, The Good Humor Man, starring Jack Carson.

180: Group of children in front of a Good Humor van in New York City, circa 1926. The ice cream with a bite taken out of it was a registered trademark of the company.

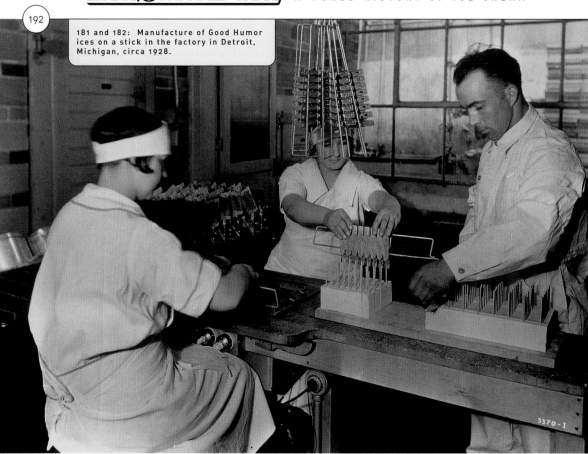

181 and 182: Manufacture of Good Humor
ices on a stick in the factory in Detroit,
Michigan, circa 1928.

• Although Good Humor operated chiefly on the east coast, from 1928 you could also buy its ice cream in Los Angeles on the west coast, after the Good Humor Ice Cream Company of California opened a modern factory in Hollywood. The factory was run by the brothers Paul and Elza C. Hawkins.[53] It had been they who had devised the system of dividing up the sales territories and mapping out efficient routes based on knowledge of the local market. The Californian company made every effort to boost sales. It made sure, for instance, that a Good Humor van was always parked near the film studios so that it was captured 'by chance' on film if shoots were taking place. And in California you had not only Good Humor Men but also Good Humor Girls.

• Upon the death of Burt Sr. the patent rights were sold in 1928 to a group of businessmen from Cleveland. They set up the Good Humor Corp. of America and sold the right to market their ice cream to concessionaires in return for a down payment of $100. One such concessionaire was Tom Brimer, who bought a number of these rights and started selling Good Humor ice cream in Detroit and Chicago. In Chicago Brimer fell foul of the Mafia, who in the spring of 1929 demanded that $5,000 protection money be paid within 24 hours. Brimer did not yield, but he did increase the insurance cover for his vans. A few days later eight Good Humor ice cream vans were blown up at the factory, making front-page news. As publicity, it was certainly original and nothing if not cost-effective, making the whole of Chicago familiar with the Good Humor name.[54]

• In the meantime, to fund his investments in the business, Brimer found himself a financial backer from New York, the busi-nessman Michael J. Meehan. In 1928 Meehan invested $25,000 in the company without even knowing what Good Humor actually did. Because of the good profits that Brimer was able to achieve and the high dividend (25%) that he was thus able to pay out in the Depression years, Meehan decided to acquire the national rights of Good Humor Co., buying 75% of the shares in 1930 for $500,000.[55] The Mehan family remained the owners of Good Humor until 1961, when the business was sold to Unilever's US subsidiary, Thomas J. Lipton Company (see chapter 21).

Sundaes, Dixie-cups and Drumsticks

• Between 1920 and 1930 ice cream production almost doubled from 560 million to 962 million litres.[56] These were the days of 'I Scream, You Scream, We All Scream for Ice Cream, Rah! Rah! Rah!', the popular song composed in 1927 by Howard Johnson, Billy Moll and Robert King. Despite the advent of packaged ice cream novelties, the lion's share of ice cream production was still served in scoops, between wafers or in a cone, and consumed in traditional sales outlets such as drugstores, ice cream parlours, soda fountain bars, hotels and restaurants. A typically American creation like the ice cream sundae had never been so popular. Usually made with vanilla ice cream, lemonade syrup, fresh fruit and nuts, the sundae had been born in the soda fountain bar at the end of the nineteenth century.

• Many of the 1920s crazes did have an influence on scooped ice cream, however. Not only were new flavours, combinations and names created, but also new types of ice cream

scoops or dippers. The first specially developed ice cream scoop had gone into production in 1876. Between then and 1940 patents were granted for around 200 different models in America alone. In the 1920s more new types came on the market than ever before. Of the 69 that were patented, at least nineteen were actually produced.[57] There were scoops, for example, which shaped the ice cream into a heart or as an oval to accompany a banana split. Some of them were ingenious devices for fast, convenient preparation of an ice cream sandwich. One such, marketed around 1924 by the Italian immigrant James Denaro, was very successful. Denaro's IciPy product was a wafer folded to give it three sides and which could easily be filled using the special scoop. It became a popular alterna-

183: In the late 1920s aviation became a sport for the rich. In August 1932 two of these 'ladybirds', Frances Marsalis and Louise Thaden, broke the world flying endurance record for women by three days. During their stopovers Good Humor bars were specially delivered to them at the landing strips.

184: 'IciPy' scoop, German silver (an alloy of copper, nickel and zinc). Automatic Cone Co., Cambridge, Massachusetts, 1914 onwards. 24.5 cm long, it was devised by the Italian immigrant James Denaro. Ici Py was made by pushing ice cream into a flat tray made of pastry.

tive to the ice cream cone.

• At the beginning of the 1920s the ice cream cone and wafer were joined by the ice cream cup, which was now marketed on a large scale for the first time. The Individual Drinking Cup Co. in Easton, Pennsylvania, which had been making cardboard drinking cups since 1908, started production of an ice cream cup in 1923. Named the 'Dixie' after a doll that was popular at the time, its special feature was its thin coating of wax, which prevented the ice cream soaking into the paper. Here again, manufacturers of ice cream machinery responded to the new developments: Mojonnier Brothers became the first engineering firm to market an automatic filling machine for the Dixie-cup, followed by Anderson Brothers Manufacturers Co.[58]

• If the cup introduced a new, individual ice cream pack format that strengthened the position of the manufacturers of ice cream, it also offered good opportunities for advertising. In 1929 Elliot Brewer, who worked in the lithographic industry, came up with the idea of printing pictures on the inside of the lid and protecting them with a thin piece of wax-coated paper. In this way the faces of popular film stars, sports heroes, animals' heads and other collectibles (during the Second World War, for instance, pictures of US battleships) found their way onto the lids. Encouraged by

product. In 1930, together with his brother, Parker set up the Frozen Drumstick Co. and, in co-operation with the Pangburn Candy and Ice Cream Company, began industrial production of the Drumstick cone. Initially the products were filled and packed by hand; but as sales grew, Parker asked Mojonnier Brothers to develop a special filling machine for the product.[60] Later on, special packaging machines also became available and in 1955 the Frozen Drumstick Co. introduced a fully automatic filling machine.

• The pre-packaged cone went on to gain

the radio programme Dixie Circus, children began swapping and trading lids.
If they sent in a complete series, they received a poster of a film star or animal from the series.[59] Such was the Dixie-cup product's success that the Dixie brand ran the danger of becoming a generic name for ice cream cups.
• In 1928 I.C. Parker, an advertising man at the Pangburn Candy and Ice Cream Company in Fort Worth, Texas, invented an ice cream that was to gain a permanent place for itself on the international ice cream market. Parker took a sugar-coated ice cream cone, filled it with vanilla ice cream, dipped it in chocolate, rolled it in a tray of nuts and let it freeze again. Tradition has it that it was his wife who thought up the name Drumstick for the new

185: Placard for Dixie ice cream cups by the Turner Ice Cream Co., circa 1931. The Dixie ice cream cup had been developed by the Individual Drinking Cup Co. in Easton, Pennsylvania, and was first marketed in 1923.

success abroad, starting in Sweden (see chapter 7). However, in most of Europe it was the version without the chocolate and nut dip which became successful. In 1959 Algida launched the Cornetto, today one of the world's known ice cream brands (see chapter 21). The Frozen Drumstick Co. itself was bought in 1991 by Nestlé together with the rights to the Drumstick name in most countries. Nestlé then sold back the franchising part of the Frozen Drumstick Co., including the manufacture of cone filling machines and the cone baking business, to the company's management. For a while Drumstick operated as separate companies in the USA and Europe, only to merge once more as a global operation, now called Norsk Dairy Systems, in 1997.

186: Iron ice cream scoop, V. Clad Co., Philadelphia, 1876. Length 21 cm. Turning the small knob on the top operated a small rod which eased the ice cream off the inside wall. Invented in 1876 by William Clewell, the owner of a soda fountain in Reading, Pennsylvania, this is regarded as the world's first mechanical ice scoop.

187: Nickel ice scoop, Kingerly Mfg. Co., Cincinnati, 1892. Length 21 cm. This was the first scoop that served a portion of ice cream by squeezing the handle with one hand.

188: Scoop made from aluminium, nickel and copper, Mosteller Mfg., Chicago, 1906. Length 25.7 cm. An unusual mechanism involves pressing the small lever on the handle which moves the scoop half a turn up and down past the scraper, depositing the ice cream.

189: Scoop made of bronze, copper and nickel, Erie Specialty Co., Erie, Pennsylvania, 1905. Length 27.5 cm. The inside of the scoop was nickel-plated. It was available in eight different sizes and, according to a 1909 sales catalogue, cost $24 per dozen, regardless of the size.

190: Scoop made from nickel-plated copper, unknown maker, circa 1910. Length approx. 27 cm. The point was used to make a small depression for the cherry on the top of an ice cream sundae.

191: Scoop made from nickel-plated copper, United Products Co., Chelsea, Massachusetts, circa 1930. Length approx. 28 cm. The shape of this type of ice cream scoop, used for making banana splits, was patented in 1928.

192: Scoop, German silver Fisher Motor Co. Ltd., Orilia, Ontario, Canada, 1923. Length 23 cm. 'Warm yourself up with a Cold Dog!' was the slogan used by the Choco-Ice Company of Brooklyn, New York, to advertise its chocolate-dipped, hollow, crunchy wafers wrapped in a piece of paper carrying the words 'Cold Dog'. The scoop pictured here was used to take a curl of ice cream from the tray and then 'shoot' it into the round wafer.

193: Scoop made plated copper, from chromium-Hamilton Wisconsin, Beach Co., Racine, 1930, length 24.5 cm. During the Depression ice cream sellers did everything to keep sales going. A scraper on the scoop ensured that ice cream protruding trough the hole was chopped off, resulting in a saving of 10%-16%.

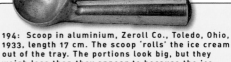

194: Scoop in aluminium, Zeroll Co., Toledo, Ohio, 1933, length 17 cm. The scoop 'rolls' the ice cream out of the tray. The portions look big, but they weigh less than they appear to because the ice cream is not compacted. According to an American dairy industry catalogue of 1936, this produces a saving of 10%-20%. The hollow handle is filled with a liquid that transmits the heat of the user's hand to the scoop, making scooping easier.

195: Ice scoop, aluminium, manufacturer unknown, 1931, length 25 cm. The scoop, invented by Ernest S. Millo from the Bronx, New York City, was designed for serving very small portions.

The 1930s and the New Deal

• During the Great Depression fewer ice cream novelties were devised than in the early 1920s, although major advances did take place in engineering, distribution and selling techniques. One such development was the introduction of a continuous ice cream freezer designed by the engineer Clarence Vogt in 1927. This machine considerably reduced the cost of making ice cream, a welcome benefit in the years of the slump. In Vogt's machine the ice cream mix was fed through pipes and cooled in a reservoir. From there it was transported via a vacuum pump to the drum of the ice cream freezer. Inside the drum were two rotating cylinders filled with brine, past which the ice cream mix was pumped and frozen into a thick mass. At the same time the required quantity of air was pumped into the mass, which was then continuously scraped from the walls of the drum, issuing into churns or other containers.[61] Machine manufacturer Cherry-Burrell acquired the rights to Vogt's invention and was soon selling it all over the world.

• Despite this and other innovations, the ice cream industry could not escape a sharp fall in consumption in the first few years of the Depression. After 1929 production tumbled from 962 million litres to 570 million in 1933,

though subsequently it rose again. 1933 was also the year in which Franklin D. Roosevelt was elected as President for the first time and began the energetic implementation of his New Deal, a system of measures and plans aimed at putting the economy back on its feet. For the dairy industry the New Deal brought the guarantee of a minimum price for milk.

• In the 1930s the distribution structure for ice cream also changed. Whereas the main sales channels in the 1920s had been drugstores, soda fountain bars, candy stores, hotels and restau-

196: Window poster for 'fancy ices' made by Hood's of Boston, Massachusetts, circa 1931. Hood's, founded as a dairy in 1846, started producing ice cream in 1899 and is still popular in New England and New York state today.

rants, a survey conducted in 1933 revealed the advance being made by grocery stores, whose ice cream sales were climbing more quickly than those of any outlet save hotels.[62] One of the first ice cream manufacturers to seek out grocery stores as a sales channel was the Eskimo Pie Co., which supplied the vacuum container to take purchases home in. The A & P grocery chain started providing its customers with insulated carrier bags in 1931.

• Another new development was the advent of chains of ice cream shops-cum-restaurants with their own ice cream manufacturing facilities: Howard Johnson's was one of the first. This trend fitted in with Americans' increased mobility, with soaring car owner-

197: Good Humor ice cream van parked in Hudson Valley, New York State, circa 1928.

198: Window display advertising Harding ice cream, circa 1928. The various showcards emphasise the nutritional value of ice cream and mainly show mothers with children.

199: A father and son standing
beside a shop window displaying
all the items to be won by saving
Popsicle wrappers, about 1940.

201: In the Deep South four boys make ice cream with a hand-operated freezer. Stella Gentry Sharpe published this photograph in her book To Be (1939).

200: Soda fountain. Oil painting by William J. Glackens, 1935, whose son is depicted in the role of soda fountain attendant.

ship – in spite of recession – reflected in the many drive-in restaurants where ice cream was a menu fixture. The emerging airline companies became customers, too; in 1937 United Airlines was the first company to serve ice cream as part of its in-flight meal.[63]

• In parallel with these changes in sales chan-nels, other develop-ments in the 1930s included the growth in the market share of cheap milk-ice, a temporary upsurge of street sellers of ices of dubious quality, a number of mergers and takeovers and the advent of ice cream production by the big dairy businesses Borden (Columbus, Ohio), Carnation (Seattle, Washington) and Beatrice Creamery Co. of Chicago. Mergers and acquisitions had been taking place in the ice cream industry ever since 1912. In 1926, for example, Breyers itself

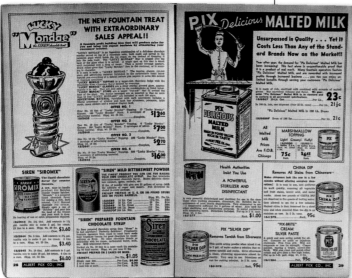

202: Advertisement for the Lucky 'Mondae' ice cream glass, circa 1933. Around the base of the glass was a star-shaped piece of paper, on which might appear a joke or a message that the ice cream was free.

had been taken over by the National Dairy Products Corporation, which comprised numerous dairy manufacturers with ice cream departments operating under the name Sealtest. The name Sealtest was a guarantee of a quality that was regularly checked in laboratories – an affirmation that the ice cream had been sealed in the pack after hygienic testing.

• Ice cream in the US had thus become a fully-fledged industry with efficiently organised distribution channels, continuous product innovation, dynamic improvements in production methods and constant developments in the area of sales and marketing. The American approach became the great exemplar for ice cream indus-

tries abroad. For the US consumer, ice cream was no longer just a summer delicacy or a feast-day treat, but something tasty and convenient for everyday.

• Meanwhile, an America that was prosperous again was heading for the 1940s, heralded by the striking view of the future given at the New York World's Fair of 1939. At this event, which lasted until the autumn of 1940, the biggest national dairy company, Borden, which had been active since 1928 as an ice cream producer selling through hundreds of milk shops, had its own pavilion. There, the public could gaze in admiration at dioramas and a miniature modern dairy factory or see the Borden mascot, Elsie the Cow.[64] Afterwards they could stroll along to one of the snackbars or restaurants on the complex to have an ice cream or listen to a big band. America was swinging again and enjoying ice cream like never before: 1,280 million litres in 1940, eaten on the beach; in the restaurant ice cream saloon, soda bar or drugstore; or simply at home, from the refrigerator that many Americans now had in their kitchen.

203: American ice cream glasses made from pressed glass, early 1930s. On the left a Lucky 'Mondae' ice cream glass and, right, a 'Big Boy' ice cream glass. The recipe for a Lucky 'Mondae' consisted of chocolate-flavoured soda water topped by a scoop of chocolate ice cream and a cherry.

204: Chorus girls cool down during a heatwave in New York City, summer 1939.

205: Sales brochure for Breyers ice cream, early 1930s. The words 'sculptors in ice cream' refer to the many 'fancy ices' that Breyers offered in the brochure.

Licks, Sticks & Bricks
A WORLD HISTORY OF ICE CREAM

Ice cream
in post-war
America

6

In June 1943, eighteen months after the United States had entered the Second World War, the American authorities decreed that ice cream should be included in the official national nutrition pro-gramme 'Eat the Basic 7 Every Day', despite the rationing of ingredients which was soon to be introduced. The decision was a major boost for the American ice cream industry, giving it priority in the allocation of ingre-dients and other materi-als. It also meant that key figures in the sector were granted postponement of their military service.[1]

• Ice cream was becoming an ever more important constituent of the American diet. The context for the authorities' affording the industry preferential treatment was a 45% increase in consumption in three years, to over 1,800 million litres; and before the war was even over, articles began appearing in the trade press on how the industry could grow further afterwards and what needed to be done to make that

207: Page from Joe Lowe Co. gift catalogue, 1941. Apart from advertisements for Popsicle and Fudgicle ices, the catalogue also contains a picture of Uncle Sam urging readers to buy war bonds and stamps.

happen. 'A glorious opportunity stretches out its arms to us from the coming days of peace', wrote the vice-president of Beatrice Creamery Co., A.J. Claxton, in December 1944. 'It is ours to see and know and grasp. It is our magnificent opportu-nity, it is our tremendous obligation. With a pent-up desire for ice cream, a clamoring for our goods, a great unsatis-fied appetite, we can fail miserably at the critical hour if we are unable to meet the challenge'. As Claxton saw it, the main challenge would be distribution. He advocat-ed the production of family packs of ice cream that would fit in a refrigerator's freezer compartment and contain enough ice cream for a family meal. With this in mind he advised his colleagues to keep a close watch on developments in the frozen foods industry.[2]

• Claxton's analysis proved prescient. After 1945 America did indeed have a great 'unsat-isfied appetite' – ice cream consumption in 1946 reached a record 2,826 million litres, equivalent to twenty litres per capita.[3] Although this figure fell slightly in the years that followed, post-war America was easily the world's biggest nation of ice cream eaters. Developments already in bud in the 1930s flowered in the 1940s and 1950s: the emergence of big dairy companies and supermarkets; the increasing use of freezers and refrigerators with freezer compartments;

206: Cover of The Saturday Evening Post of 22 September 1951 by Stevan Dohanos. 'As cops are human beings, Stevan Dohanos easily found one for a model who actually was an incurable ice-cream-cone addict', reads the caption. 'He was also a candy friend. He said that his wife often upbraided him for eating sweets, claiming that his belt was beginning to slip down under his stomach. '"It doesn't, of course", the officer exclaimed. "I just wear it loose to have my muscles free and unhindered. Well, buy me a cone and I'll pose, but if my wife hears about this, I suppose I'll get 'hail Columbia'." 'So Dohanos has painted dark glasses on the chap, hoping that the Mrs. won't recognize him, but will think of him as a typical American policeman, thus mellowing her attitude toward sugar in the diet and bringing peace into her husband's life.'

the growth of chains of ice cream parlours like Baskin-Robbins, Dairy Queen and Carvel; and the use of franchising to sell ice cream. Innovations such as TV advertising

208: 1941 advertisement by Joe Lowe Co. for the Mystery Box of Popsicle Pete, for which you had to save twelve Popsicle wrappers.

and other sophisticated techniques were used to reach consumers and offer them new products to fit their changing lifestyle. There was a wider variety of products and flavours, though vanilla ice cream still remained number one. Soft ice cream and ice cream for diabetics were launched, followed by low-calorie ice cream.

• During the course of the 1950s supermarkets became the most important sales channel, at the expense of the drugstores and soda fountains. Ice cream manufacturers were confronted with intense competition from supermarket chains, which began producing or buying in their own ice cream and selling it under their own label. In the areas of hygiene, packaging, storage, transport and, above all, in automation there were

also major innovations. In the early 1950s came the introduction of 'multipacks' – packs containing several impulse ice creams. Environmental regulations were introduced and in ever-bigger supermarkets the freezer chests were replaced by long rows of vertical freezer cabinets with glass doors.

• The number of ice cream factories, as in Europe, decreased substantially from 3,700 in 1945 to around 500 in 1981.[4] In the 1980s large-scale dairy businesses with ice cream divisions, such as Borden, Beatrice and Carnation, all faced tough times, as did dedicated ice cream brands like Bresler, Breyers, Good Humor and Eskimo Pie. Eventually the ice cream divisions of Borden and Beatrice disappeared from the stage. Others were taken over, Carnation and Breyers being acquired by Nestlé and Unilever respectively, the world's largest ice cream businesses. Against this, however, some regional ice cream producers like Dreyer's, based in Oakland, California, and Blue Bell of Texas flourished, Dreyer's becoming one of the country's two largest manufacturers. New

209: Back cover of a Joe Lowe Co. sales brochure for the retail trade, 1944. Popsicle Pete, with his ever-twinkling eyes, had been introduced by Joe Lowe Co. in 1939.

210: Two pages from a 1944 Joe Lowe Co. sales brochure for the retail trade, showing the special sales campaigns held in the 1938-1941 period: Popeye in 1938, Buck Rogers and Wilma in 1939, the Money Box in 1940 and the Mystery Box in 1941.

players like Häagen Dazs and Ben & Jerry's also entered the market. Their creamy, premium-priced ice cream was sold first through their own shops, and then in all types of outlets, alongside the low-calorie ice cream products also demanded by customers.

• During the 1980s ice cream novelties experienced a major revival. Young, high-earning 'baby boomers' revealed a preference for expensive dairy ice creams enveloped in pure chocolate. Market growth, coupled with the profit margins on such products, led Mars, one of America's two largest chocolate

companies, to enter the ice cream market in 1986. But despite all these changes, one thing remained constant: the consumer's predilection for freshly made ice cream scooped into a fresh, crunchy cone.

The 1940s

• As in the First World War, sugar was the first ingredient to be rationed during the Second World War. This happened in 1942, with honey and sugar syrup or sugar derived from maize again being used to make up the shortfall. Eighteen US states reduced the statutory minimum butter-fat content in ice

211: Popsicle pack with Popsicle Pete: a 'genuine Jo-Lo product'. Jo-Lo is an abbreviation for Joe Lowe.

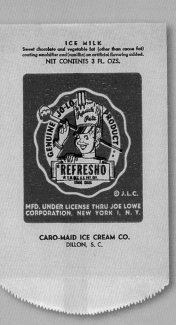

212: Advertisement for ice lollies of the Fruit Products Co., New York, 1953. The packs from Ducky Dubble water ices could be saved and exchanged for all sorts of gifts.

213: Metal advertising sign for Popsicle ice by Joe Lowe Co., 1940s (30 cm x 90.5 cm).

214: Poster for the push-up ice, Polar Pole, 1940s.

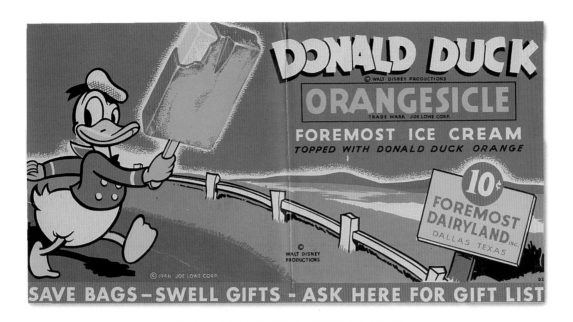

215: Poster for the Donald Duck Orangesicle of Joe Lowe Co., 1946. The comic-book and cartoon heroes introduced in the 1920s were commonly used in advertising campaigns.

216: Poster, 1946, for Joe Lowe Co.'s Popsicle ice, showing Popsicle Pete on a water-ski.

cream to 8%, whilst the consumption of the much cheaper sherbet (with much lower fat content still) climbed from less than 2% in 1937 to almost 11% in 1944.[5]

• In 1942 the authorities imposed restrictions on the marketing of new types of ice cream, introduced a freeze on retail prices and limited the number of permitted flavours. Ingredients such as whey, soyabeans, vegetable fats and flour found their way into new ice cream recipes.[6] Petrol was rationed, the manufacture of special ice

217: Barman at work at a soda fountain in Harlem, New York, circa 1950.

cream trucks was limited and a ban on ice cream deliveries on Sundays followed in June 1943. Ice cream manufacturers responded, improving the loading capacity of trucks and installing freezer cabinets in more and more outlets so as to reduce the frequency of delivery trips. However, the supply of freezer cabinets was restricted because manufacturers gave precedence to the war effort.[7]

• During the Second World War the US army was the biggest single customer for ice cream, consuming between 20 and 25 per cent of total production. Ice cream was good for morale and a welcome variation in the GI's monotonous diet and towards the end of the war the army too was equipped with mobile ice cream making machines, weighing some 600 kilos and turning out 100-litre batches made from ice cream powder and water. Most American warships had their own production facilities on board. The stationing of American troops in Europe and Asia after the war ensured that in many countries the local ice cream industry was re-established. This was the case with Schöller in Germany, Mio and Artic in Belgium and Ortiz in France. In Italy, the US presence gave rise to one of the country's first ice cream factories, Algida. In Thailand and Taiwan, American dairy business Foremost supplied US troops with ice cream, whilst in Japan and the Philippines ice cream factories were re-fitted for their benefit.

• A further development in the 1940s was that more and more ice cream producers set up departments to manufacture frozen foods, which they could then sell in the winter months when ice cream sales slackened off. Good Humor had been the first business to embark on this in 1940.[8]

218: Self-service cabinet at a supermarket with advertisements for Sealtest ice cream, 1954.

219: Interior of soda fountain bar, 1959. During the 1930s the style in furnishing of soda fountain bars began to change. The marble around the counter disappeared; new materials such as chromium-plated steel and aluminium were introduced. The soda fountains themselves had long been gleaming, chromium-plated stainless steel machines.

• In June 1945, shortly before the end of the war, the US ice cream trade association, re-named the International Association of Ice Cream Manufacturers, launched a nation-wide ice cream nutrition programme. The programme was directed at government authorities, legislators, civil servants, scien-tists, doctors, nurses, hospitals, dentists, dieticians and school principals, who were made aware that ice cream was one of the seven basic, everyday foods, as the govern-ment had defined them in June 1943. The programme's aim was to lay the foundations for the post-war growth of ice cream consumption.[9]

• And grow it did. In 1946 a higher percent-age of butter-fat was again permitted, while 1947 brought the end of sugar rationing. With real dairy ice cream available once more, the nation experienced an unpre-cedented boom in ice cream consumption. In 1946 twice as much ice cream was eaten as before the war. Meanwhile, the supply of electricity to most rural areas had been completed, productivity was climbing and people were becoming affluent. Consumers bought television sets, cars and houses with superb kitchens, complete with the latest refrigerators and freezers. 'A supermarket at your finger-tips. Family-size cuts of your favorite meats [...] Fresh in-season berries, vegetables, fruits. Your prize cakes, bakery, soups, game, poultry. Ice cream treats for the children', enthused a refrigerator manufacturer's brochure in 1952.[10] Between 1945 and 1952, 27 million new refrigerators with a freezer compartment and four million freezers were sold.[11]

• In response to this development the ice cream industry began to market cartons containing half a gallon (1.8 litres) of ice cream, a quantity suitable for an average family. From 1952 onwards manufacturers also started selling small tubs (under the Dixie brand name) of ice cream, ice lollies and ice cream sandwiches in packs containing multiples of four or more units each. Initially packed in bags, these 'multipacks' were soon packed in carton boxes, with lower unit prices that stimulated sales.[12] Most of the family packs of ice cream and multipacks were sold in the fast-expanding supermarkets. In 1938 11.4% of the sales of industrially-manufactured ice cream found their way to consumers via supermarkets; in 1952 the figure stood at about 30%; and by 1981 the figure had reached 74%.[13]

• Ice cream manufacturers stimulated their sales not only by advertising, but also by increasing the number of freezer cabinets they provided to retailers, a practice which had been around since 1910. In those days the cabinets had still been cooled with ice and salt, but now the freezers were modern machines, powered by electricity and fitted with transparent lids. The conditions for supply included agreements on prices, profit margins and the exclusive use of the freez-ers by the manufacturer supplying them. In 1954 smaller ice cream manufacturers on the east coast complained about what they saw as unfair competition from the major dairy companies with ice cream factories of their own, such as Borden, Beatrice, Hood, National Dairy Products and Foremost Dairies. The case, which was investigated by the Federal Trade Commission, dragged on for many years and brought no immediate solution. In 1962, Borden turned the issue on its head, arguing that the company's share of the markets that were under investigation had in fact declined because competitors had also installed exclusive freezer cabinets.[14]

• Meanwhile, supermarkets had started making ice cream under their own label. The first supermarket to begin selling own brand ice cream was the Supreme Supermarket in Dorchester, Massachusetts, in January 1942. Four decades later, in 1981, the two largest supermarket chains, Safeway and Kroger, together accounted for an estimated 26% of total ice cream production, exceeding the combined volume then produced by the two largest manufacturers, Borden and Beatrice, which accounted for 12% and 10% of total production respectively.[15] Kroger, which had started life as a grocery store in 1883 in Cincinnati, Ohio, had had its own ice cream factory there since the early 1940s, but in 1960 opened a large new factory in Indianapolis, Indiana, marking their major commitment to the business.[16]

Borden and 'Elsie'

• Borden had begun trading in the nineteenth century as a manufacturer of condensed milk. In 1856 its founder Gail Borden (1801-1874) had patented his invention for boiling milk in a vacuum pan, adding sugar and then canning it. This "condensed" milk proved to have a long shelf life. In partnership with the banker and foods wholesaler Jeremiah Milbank, Borden set up the New York Condensed Milk Company in 1858. In 1899 the name was changed to Borden Condensed Milk Company and in 1919 to Borden Company.

• At the end of the 1920s Borden showed tremendous growth. In 1928 and 1929 more

than 100, mainly small-scale milk operations were bought in the south, west and east of the United States. These purchases did however include two large, well-known ice cream manufacturers, J.M. Horton Ice Cream and Reid Ice Cream Corporation, acquisitions that mark the beginning of Borden's serious investment in the production and sale of ice cream. Ice cream was one of the four separate businesses into which Borden Co. was split in 1929, the other three being foods, milk and cheese.

• Although Borden already had eighteen factories producing ice cream by 1930, the production and distribution of ice cream remained closely linked to its milk activities.[17] Many of Borden's milk distributors also distributed its ice cream. Expansion continued in the 1930s, as hundreds of small milk businesses throughout America were acquired by Borden and began to sell their milk under the Borden brand.[18]

• In 1936 the company mounted an advertising campaign in medical journals in support of its milk sales. The health benefits of milk were dramatised through Elsie the Cow, whose appeal was such that doctors asked for framed copies of the advertisement to display in their waiting-rooms. When the advertisement was published in colour in 1939 in leading US periodicals, Elsie achieved national fame. She was pictured in front of the Borden pavilion at the New York World's Fair, which had then just opened. A reported 60% of the visitors asked "Where's Elsie?"[19], so Borden brought a real cow to the pavilion during the exhibition's second summer. By the time the World's Fair ended in October 1940, eleven million visitors had seen 'Elsie'. She even featured in that summer's Hollywood film production 'Little Men' and, shortly afterwards, a children's book was published telling of her adventures. Other Elsie products included picture postcards, dolls, badges, drinking glasses, playing cards, colouring books and cookery books. Elsie was Borden.

• In 1954 the company mascot became an ice cream brand when Borden launched a series of ice novelties under the Elsie name. There were ice creams on a stick and in tubs, ice lollies, an ice cream cone and if you collected ten Elsie ice cream packs or ten lids from an Elsie tub, you could buy a stand seat for $0.25 instead of $1.25 to see the Dodgers, one of New York's two leading baseball clubs.[20] During its centenary celebrations in 1957, Borden also marketed Elsie ice cream in the form of special packs of Elsie Golden Vanilla Cream. Although Borden did not publish sales figures, business was flourishing. According to a 1951 estimate by the Federal Trade Commission, Borden held approximately 10% of the market.[21] Since 1947 the company had also been selling 'premium' ice cream throughout the US under the Lady Borden name. This high-quality, expensive ice cream was promoted with advertisements in Life, The Saturday Evening Post and Time. Other ice cream producers followed suit. In 1952, Sealtest – which had been operating as part of the National Dairy Products Corporation since the 1930s – introduced their own premium product, Prestige, a 'French Ice Cream'.

• Borden also spread its wings internationally, acquiring food businesses in Latin America, Europe and Asia towards the end of the 1950s. Although ice cream played only a minor role in this foreign expansion, Borden started producing ice cream in Mexico in 1959[22] and opened dairy and ice cream businesses in Colombia, Panama and Costa Rica. In 1971 a joint venture was set up with the Meiji dairy business in Japan for the production of Lady Borden ice cream (see chapter 20). Ultimately, however, ice cream for Borden turned out to be a sideline. Its ice cream products, like those of many other dairies, consisted largely of cartons of ice cream for home and hotel, for restaurants, soda fountains and ice cream parlours.

220: A pack of Borden's ice cream, 1940s, and three sizes of metal holders. The pack carries a picture of 'Elsie the Cow'. 'Elsie' had been introduced by Borden in 1936 to promote the company's dairy and ice cream products.

Despite investing in ten Gram RIA ice lolly machines between 1956 and 1964[23], Borden did little in the way of developing new novelties. Of the more than 100 novelties in Borden's range in 1986, only a few had been developed by the company itself.[24]

• After 1980 Borden was drastically restructured. Numerous subsidiaries were sold off and in seven US states the company discon-

Licks, Sticks & Bricks A WORLD HISTORY OF ICE CREAM

The Elks MAGAZINE

JULY 1954 E

In this issue: DICKSON HARTWELL
WILLIAM BYRON MOWERY
HORACE SUTTON
COMDR. MACBAIN

tinued or consolidated its dairy activities. In 1989 it withdrew entirely from the dairy market in California and in several states in the South-East and Mid-West.[25] Borden was bought in 1995 by the investment company Kohlberg, Kravis Roberts & Co. In 1997 its domestic dairy activities including ice cream were transferred for $435 million to Mid-America Dairy-men Inc., a dairy coop-erative with 17,000 members and establish-ments in 30 states; and in 1998 Borden's new owners sold its remaining ice cream and dairy activities in Latin America to Nestlé. After 140 years Borden's activities as a dairy and ice cream business had come to an end.

name was changed in 1916 to the Carnation Milk Company; then, in 1929, to the Carnation Company.[26] In 1926 the company had taken on the production and sale of fresh milk and ice cream and by 1932 acquired numerous ice cream businesses in California, Oregon, Iowa, Oklahoma and Texas.[27] After 1945 expansion

222: Enjoying after-school vanilla ice cream with Kraft strawberry sauce. Advertisement for Sealtest, circa 1950, portraying prosperity, American-style.

in the same states resumed with the purchase of a series of ice cream and milk distribution and wholesale businesses. In 1974 Carnation opened ice cream restaurants in Dallas, Denver and San Francisco.[28]

• Despite these expansions and innovations, Carnation was unable to build a market for its fresh milk and ice cream on the east coast, so it never became a national business for those products. By contrast, Carnation had long been a household name in condensed milk from coast to coast. In 1985 the business was sold to the European pioneer in this field, Nestlé, which thereby gained a solid footing in the American ice cream market (see chapter 21). In 1988 Nestlé invested $80 million in constructing an impressive new factory at Bakersfield, California. The level of investment reflected the cost of the production lines for Impulse products, an important part of the new

Carnation, Beatrice Foods, Sealtest and others

• In addition to Borden, the major dairy companies Carnation and Beatrice Foods Co. were also active in the ice cream market. Carnation had been established in 1899 by Elbridge Amos Stuart (1856-1944). In September of that year he started a small business named the Pacific Coast Condensed Milk Company in Kent, 25 miles south of Seattle. The

221: Cover of Elks Magazine, July 1954. Father is churning ice cream in the old-fashioned way in a hand-operated freezer. The children look on expectantly, while the dog licks at the ice. No-one seems to be interested in the factory-made ice creams of the Good Humor Man in the background.

factory. The plant had a reported production capacity of over 130 million litres of ice cream a year and it marked the beginning of Nestlé's efforts to capture a larger share of the American ice cream market.[29]

selling ice cream under the Meadow Gold name.[32] After 1956, in spite of strong competition from Breyers in New York City, the Brooklyn factory went on to become the most profitable business in Beatrice's ice cream division, its many prestigious customers including New York's Waldorf Astoria Hotel.

• In the post-war years Beatrice developed into a prominent foods company and one of the top dairy businesses together with Borden and Kraft. Expansion began in 1952 with the purchase of Creameries America, which had branches in California, Texas, New Mexico, Colorado, Utah, Idaho and Hawaii.

• Excellent dairy profits were used by Beatrice to finance other activities.[33]

223:
Valley Farm's Bing Crosby ice cream, sold in the early 1950s as 'the cream of the stars'. Valley Farm was the first firm to sell ice cream named after a famous singer.

• After Borden and Carnation, the third dairy group in the ice cream market was the Beatrice Food Co. Founded in 1894, Beatrice Creamery Co., as it was then called, was producing ice cream on a small scale in Topeka, Kansas[30] by 1907, but was chiefly a producer of butter under the Meadow Gold brand name. In 1928, 83.3% of its turnover stemmed from butter, poultry and eggs and only 2.5% from ice cream.[31] In the 1930s this began to change. 'As President of Beatrice my first goal is to develop a program of diversification with the objective of developing milk and ice cream sales', said its new head, Clinton Haskell, in 1929. Shortly afterwards, despite the Depression, Beatrice opened new ice cream factories in Baltimore, Washington D.C., Pittsburgh and Brooklyn ,

In 1961 a condensed milk factory opened near Kuala Lumpur, Malaysia, and in April of that year Beatrice's president, William G. Karnes, visited many businesses in Europe. There he started negotiations with various manufacturers, including the Belgian ice cream producer Artic (see chapter 13), the greater part of which was acquired by Beatrice in 1967. In the same year it was the turn of Marisa in Spain, followed by the Italian ice cream company Gelati Sanson of Verona, and in 1969 by one of Denmark's oldest ice cream businesses, Premier Is of Esbjerg (see chapter 10).[34]

• Beatrice Foods thus developed manufacturing operations worldwide. The group also became the owner of chains of department stores and chemicals businesses, of Taylor

Freeze (the world's biggest manufacturer of machines for making soft-ice) and of other businesses such as Avis Rent-A-Car, Tropicana and Samsonite. But after its 1984 purchase of the meats and foods group Esmark Inc. for $2.6 billion, Beatrice got into financial difficulties and its management disagreed on future strategy. Within a few years the company had been broken up and sold off to various buyers, including Borden and Borden's eventual nemesis, the investment company Kohlberg, Kravis Roberts & Co.

• Within Sealtest, another national ice cream company that had its roots in the dairy industry, things developed differently. Sealtest's parent, The National Dairy Products Corporation, formed part of the Kraft dairy group, which later merged with General Foods. Ice cream manufacturer Breyers – a subsidiary of National Dairy Products Corporation since 1926 – had in the meantime also been taken over by Kraft.

• While Breyers was the group's premium brand, Sealtest served the cheaper end of the market. In East Coast supermarkets Sealtest built a wide reputation after 1952 thanks to its special offers, focusing on a different flavour each month, often dictated by the fruit that was in season. In June this would be peach

ice cream, in September apple ice cream; and special products were sold for traditional feast-days, such as pumpkin ice cream for Halloween. Large-scale advertising

for your bars- "Sunday Best" every day

Coatings by

224: Ice cream as a feast. Advertisement in The Ice Cream Review of June 1956 for chocolate coatings made by Ambrosia Co.

campaigns and the wide use of point-of-sale materials promoted sales to the housewife. Like Breyers, Sealtest was an ever-present brand in East Coast supermarkets. In 1993, however, operating losses led Kraft-General Foods to sell its Breyers and Sealtest businesses to Unilever, thus creating the Good Humor-Breyers ice cream company.

225: Film star Gina Lollobrigida enjoys an ice during the Monaco Century Ball in Monte Carlo in 1966. In the 1950s 'La Lollo' was the best-known European sex symbol.

Dairy Queen and Baskin-Robbins

• There were two types of ice cream that the consumer would not find on supermarket shelves: Dairy Queen soft-ice and the 31 flavours of Baskin-Robbins. These were available solely in the many ice cream stores that these manufacturers opened throughout America after 1945. The first outlet selling Dairy Queen soft-ice opened its doors in the summer of 1940 in Joliet, Illinois. It was a simple store located on North Chicago Street

and run by J.F. 'Grandpa' McCullough, his son Alex, and Sherb Noble. In 1929, after several years of experimenting in co-operation with the inventor Harry Oltz, the McCulloughs had succeeded in developing a freezer and an ice cream mix that could be used to produce soft ice cream. Through trial and error 'Grandpa' McCullough had discovered that soft-ice was best served at a temperature of approximately -8°C[35] and tasted best if it contained 5-6% butter-fat instead of the 10% that was then customary for ice cream. In many states therefore his recipe was later classified not as ice cream, but as ice milk.

• The store in Joliet was a success. People queued to buy the new soft ice cream and by the end of the first season the initial investment had almost been recouped. The war temporarily prevented the further advance of the new product, as there were no machine parts with which to construct freezers and many ingredients were rationed. After the war, however, the business started to take off. With the aid of an agricultural machinery salesman, Harry Axene, a franchise system was set up. The seventeen Dairy Queen stores at the end of 1945 grew in the space of two years to one hundred.[36]

• In 1948 franchisees established the Dairy Queen National Trade Organisation. Standardised instructions were issued for the manufacturing method, the fittings and furnishings of each store, advertising, the ice cream cone and the maintenance of machines. Milkshakes were added to the range and the Maryland Cup Corporation developed a wafer cup with a flat base for their use. Competition from snackbars, cafeterias and roadside restaurant chains like Howard Johnson's forced Dairy Queen to put hamburgers, hot dogs, French fries and

226: The American president Dwight D. Eisenhower (1890-1969) bites into a Good Humor ice cream, circa 1955. 'Ike' was an ice cream fan. As a boy he had worked in the ice cream factory of the Belle Springs Creamery Co. in Abilene, Kansas, where his father was chief engineer for almost twenty years.

founders of this new firm, who energetically expanded the business. Within a couple of years outlets had been opened in Germany, Italy, the Netherlands and a number of Latin American countries. In Canada Dairy Queen had already had a strong presence for several years. In 1997 'the cone with the curl on top', as the soft-ice was called, was on sale all over the world: from Moscow to Tokyo, from Beijing to Mexico.[37]

• The other great story of ice cream parlours, Baskin-Robbins, started in 1949. On 7 December 1945 Irvine Robbins had opened an ice cream business under the name Snowbird in Glendale, California. In his store he sold 21 different flavours, more than most ice cream fans had ever seen before in one ice cream parlour. A small wooden spoon was used to sample the flavours before buying.[38] When Robbins opened his second store, his brother-in-law Burt Baskin dropped by on a visit. Before the war Baskin had operated a small haberdashery store in Chicago and he was now contemplating setting up a fine clothing store in Beverly Hills. Robbins convinced him that a rich future lay in ice cream, but at first Baskin opened his own parlours and it was only in 1949 that they amalgamated their 43 sales outlets under the name Baskin-Robbins. In 1953 they launched a new formula with the slogan 'We Make People Happy'. From that time onwards, customers in Baskin-Robbins ice cream parlours could choose from 31 different flavours every day. Sixteen flavours were constant while the other fifteen were changed each day. More than 430 different flavours were offered during 1970 alone in Baskin-Robbins ice cream parlours, which by then had grown to 1,000 in number. Nearly two-thirds of the ice cream was sold in cones.[39]

sandwiches on the menu. Dairy Queen also developed new ice creams on sticks, such as the Dilly in 1955, while yoghurt ice cream was produced in their soft-ice machines from the 1970s onwards. Hygiene was greatly enhanced by the fitting of automatic cleaning systems and, as the years went by, freezers were substantially improved, becoming more compact and energy-efficient. The hit product of the 1980s was the Blizzard, a refreshing mix of soft-ice and fruit juice.

• In 1960 the International Dairy Queen company was established. McCullough sold his rights and the brand name to the

227: Supermarket point-of-sale materials for Sealtest peach ice cream, circa 1954.

• This massive expansion, begun in 1959, was made possible by the company's franchise system. In return for a fee, operators could set up an ice cream parlour using the Baskin-Robbins name, formula and approach. Baskin-Robbins gave advice on the location, arranged for supplies, advertising and the timetable of alternating flavours, and guidelines for fitting out the shop. Alongside this direct franchise system Baskin-Robbins also operated an indirect system under which the recipes, name and approach were contracted out to a local ice cream manufacturer, who then set up Baskin-Robbins ice cream saloons in his region. In 1965 shops were opened in New York and Washington. Baskin-Robbins became a national chain, offering flavours such as Pralines 'n' Cream, Minute Man Mint, Mighty Gorilla, West Point Sammy, Lunar Cheesecake, Beatle Nut, Quarterback Crunch and Baked Hawaii.[40] Many of

228: A pack of Sealtest peach ice cream, circa 1954. From the spring of 1952 Sealtest began showcasing a different flavour each month, based on the seasonal fruit available.

229: 'Free Cone Day' at a Dairy Queen store in Albuquerque, New Mexico, 1962. The event was co-sponsored by a local dairy.

the ices had been thought up to commemorate special events or famous people. Lunar Cheesecake, for example, marked the landing of Apollo 11 on the moon in 1969.

• In 1974 Baskin-Robbins opened its first ice cream shop abroad, in Rhode-St. Genèse, on the outskirts of Brussels, home to 500 American families.[41] This was the start of a worldwide expansion, initially in Belgium, the Netherlands, the United Kingdom and Japan. Expansion was helped by the fact that Baskin-Robbins was by that time 83% owned by the British food and ice cream business J. Lyons & Co. Ltd. Subsequently, in 1985, Lyons was sold to Allied Breweries becoming Allied Lyons. The ice cream business was bought by Nestlé (see chapter 8), who in 1994 sold it to Allied-Domecq. With 4,400 establishments in 1997 in 60 countries, covering all continents, Baskin-Robbins is the world's largest chain of ice cream parlours. Three-quarters of these outlets are in the United States and represent 6% of the American ice cream market.[42]

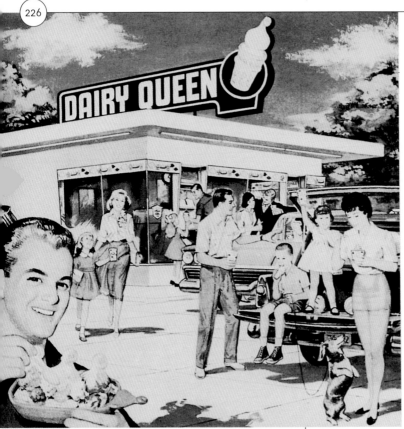

was expressed by weight: one gallon (3.785 litres) of ice cream had to weigh at least 4.5 pounds. A list of permitted artificial colourings, emulsifiers and preservatives was published. Ice cream containing vegetable fat had to carry the designation 'mellorine'.

• These decisions in part reflected technological developments in the dairy and ice cream industry in the post-war years. For butter-fat the ice cream manufacturer could use cream or milk, but also some 25 other dairy ingredients ranging from condensed milk, dried skimmed milk or whey to powdered milk and butter-oil.[43] Ingredients such as these had been in use since about 1905 thanks to the introduction of the homogeniser (see chapter 5). The 1960 standard was therefore a move to codify common practice.

• In the 1970s labelling requirements were also introduced. According to the label, a 1980 family carton of Sealtest strawberry ice cream contained milk-fat, non-fat milk, sugar, strawberries, corn syrup, whey, monoglycerides and diglycerides, citric acid, guar gum, carob bean gum, polysorbate 80, carrageen, dextrose and artificial colour.[44]

The standardisation of recipes

• For many years the ingredients of the ice cream eaten in America were not specified on the pack, nor was the consumer much wiser for studying the price lists or the week's special offers in ice cream parlours. A 45-year battle between the Federal government and the ice cream manufacturers over standardising the composition of ice cream ended in 1960 when the Food, Drug and Cosmetic Act defined the various product categories, from dairy ice cream, ice milk and sherbet to water-ice and soft-ice. For example, the minimum butter-fat content for dairy ice cream was fixed at 10%. The permitted quantity of air in ice cream

231: Advertising poster for the Sealtest Choco Cherry Bar, circa 1959. By sending in the required number of packs, one could obtain a Mr. Cool puppet specially designed for Sealtest ice cream.

Taste the Lemon Twice

LEMON DROP FREEZE

made with

Sealtest
TRADE MARK
SHERBET

¢

EACH

233: Drive-in serving Sealtest ice cream, 1940s.

234: Poster for Seal-test ice cream, circa 1960. In return for the flap from a pack of Sealtest ice cream plus 60 cents, the postman would deliver a superb walking stick, just like the one that Bat Masterson used to disarm his enemies in the popular Western series from 1959-1961.

232: Poster for Sealtest sher-bet. In America a sherbet contains not only water and flavourings, but must also include between 2% and 5% dairy ingredients.

Häagen Dazs

• In 1960 Reuben Mattus from the Bronx in New York City began marketing ice cream that was composed only of natural products: fresh cream, fresh skimmed milk, cane sugar, egg-yolks and natural flavours. It contained 12% butter-fat instead of the customary 10% and only about 20% air instead of the customary 50%. Mattus' wife thought up the name Häagen Dazs, a fantasy name that sounded as if it came from Denmark, a country universally known in the United States as a dairy nation. The first tubs of Häagen Dazs even had a map of Scandinavia printed on them in Danish, with an arrow pointing towards Copenhagen. In fact there is no letter "ä", in Danish nor are the letters "zs" conjoined in this way. The pack was also distinctly different: a tub containing some half a litre instead of the usual half gallon (two litre) carton sold by the supermarkets.

• Reuben Mattus grew up surrounded by ice cream makers. Since 1921 his mother Leah had run an ice cream store in the Bronx, making lemon ices which Reuben delivered to candy stores in the neighbourhood.[45] In 1932, Leah and Reuben Mattus started a small ice cream factory. Their company, Senator Frozen Products Inc., marketed family packs of ice cream and ice cream novelty products under the name Ciro's. By the mid-1950s the battle for a place in supermarket freezer cabinets had hotted up. Major ice cream

235: Advertisement in Life, circa 1952, for Prestige French Ice Cream by Sealtest. The tub of ice cream has been placed in an elegant cooler, recalling the special ice pails made of porcelain or earthenware in the eighteenth century.

manufacturers such as Borden, Sealtest and Breyers concluded pricing agreements with supermarket chains and supplied them with freezer cabinets at substantial discounts. Ice cream prices were falling and there was no great demand for Mattus'. It dawned on him that in a city like New York it ought to be possible to sell high quality, high price ice cream. For the larger manufacturers, his reasoning went, the proposition would not be attractive because the sales volume would be too low.

• The Häagen Dazs story began with only three flavours: vanilla, chocolate and coffee. The chocolate was purchased from the Dutch cocoa producer Droste and the vanilla via Chicago.[46] In 1961 Reuben Mattus registered his new trademark and very slowly his ice cream found its way to discerning consumers in Manhattan. Despite no advertising and a price that was over twice as expensive as regular ice cream, the demand for Häagen Dazs kept climbing. In 1976 Reuben's daughter, Doris, opened the first Häagen Dazs ice cream parlour in Brooklyn and in 1978 production was transferred to a new factory in Woodbridge, New Jersey. A franchising system was established and after some years Häagen Dazs became a familiar name, with outlets on both the east and west coasts.

• About the same time, another ice cream manufacturer started to produce premium ice cream from purely natural ingredients: Ben & Jerry's from Vermont (see box on p. 234). Manufacturers of regular ice cream also sought to reach the connoisseur with premium ice cream. For example, Bresler Co. of Chicago began selling Vala, a premium ice cream with 18% butter-fat; Carnation introduced a product called Elegante; and

236-238: Display posters for supermarkets advertising Sealtest's Banana Split, circa 1957.

Kraft Foods, which by then owned Breyers, launched its premium me-too called Früsen Gladje.[47] However, none of them could match the success of Häagen Dazs.

• In 1983 Reuben sold Häagen Dazs to the Pillsbury food group in Minneapolis, which also owned Burger King. Advertising was stepped up and in the space of four years turnover quadrupled and the brand became a globally known name.[48] This growth accelerated when Pillsbury was acquired by the British Grand Metropolitan group in 1989. With a 4.2% share of the world market, sales of £3.8 billion and over 1,000 parlours in dozens of countries, Häagen Dazs was by 1997 the world's fourth largest ice cream brand.[49] From Tokyo to Paris and from Shanghai to London, people everywhere could now enjoy superb ice cream, made from natural ingredients, in flavours that could be exotic, like Bailey's Original Irish Cream, or simple like Orchard Peach Sorbet.

• In February 1986 Häagen Dazs made an important new move: it launched a large luxury vanilla ice cream on a stick. The ice cream was coated in a thick layer of imported Belgian chocolate made by Callebaut. Although the product was hardly advertised at first, and was both expensive and high-calorie, production struggled to keep pace with demand. Ten months after the launch sales were already 300% higher than had been estimated.[50] 'The First Ice Cream Bar Good Enough to be called Häagen Dazs', boasted the manufacturer's publicity. Its success outstripped that of the original product of this type, the Dove Bar, a brand which had made its national debut in 1984 and was acquired by Mars in 1986. Both ice creams

reflected the emerging demand for superb quality, regardless of price or calorie count. A similar product, the Magnum ice cream, introduced by Unilever in Belgium in 1988, also capitalised on this trend (see chapter 21). An ice cream on a stick was no longer simply for thirsty children on a summer's day; the now adult 'baby boomers' had devel-

oped a taste for 'affordable luxury' and premium ice creams fitted the bill perfectly. Häagen Dazs was the first to identify and satisfy this market, whose consumers became the driving force behind the major growth that the ice cream novelties market was now to experience.

¶ In the summer of 1986 a strange-looking vehicle cruised most of the big cities in the north of the United States. It was a ten year-old bus decorated with pictures of cows and called 'Ben & Jerry's Cowmobile'. The bus was driven in turn by Ben Cohen and Jerry Greenfield, founders and owners of the Ben & Jerry's ice cream business. Since starting an ice cream parlour in Burlington, Vermont less than ten years before, their ice cream business had become known throughout America.

The Cowmobile took them from Burlington to Los Angeles. En route the duo scooped thousands of ice cream samples from the freezer installed in the bus.[1] The trip was typical of the unorthodox way Ben & Jerry's do business. They never employed expensive commercials on TV, but regularly came up with imaginative and original stunts to attract attention to their products. Other factors that established their reputation included their use of natural ingredients, the original design and typography of their packaging, their festivals, ice cream give-aways, letters to consumers, the visitor centre integrated in the new ice cream factory which attracts hundreds of thousands of visitors a year, their foundation that promotes social change (7.5% of their pre-tax profit goes into this foundation) and their great sense of humour and creativity. It was not until 1997, nearly twenty years after setting out, that they advertised on radio. By that time they held a 4% share of the American ice cream market and had branches in Europe and Israel.[2]

It had started in 1977 as the adventure of two childhood friends who decided to set up an ice cream business together. Ben Cohen and Jerry Greenfield each invested $4,000, took a correspondence course on ice cream making and looked for a suitable location. They picked Burlington, a university town located in the northern state of Vermont with 40,000 inhabitants and 12,000 students. They wrote a business plan, securing a bank loan of a further $4,000, and in December 1977 they formed Ben & Jerry's Homemade, Inc. They rented an abandoned filling station, renovated it with the help of friends, fitted it out with second-hand furniture

239: Half-litre tub of Cherry Garcia ice cream, launched in 1987 by Ben & Jerry's and named after the late guitarist/leader of the Grateful Dead rock group, Jerry Garcia.

and equipment they had bought at auctions and asked a friend, Lyn Severance, to create the typography and design style for their ice cream parlour.

On 5 May 1978 they opened their doors, and soon found themselves selling not 100 ice cream cones a day, as they had planned, but 1,000. The students of Burlington formed long queues. Within a year they began selling their ice cream to restaurants and other sales outlets in Vermont. Ben delivered using a second-hand ice cream van, while Jerry constantly prepared new recipes, all from natural ingredients. The first breakthrough came when their ice cream, packed in one-pint cartons (about half a litre), proved a success in supermarkets and small grocery stores in Vermont and beyond. When they wanted to enter the market in Boston in 1984, they were opposed by the Pillsbury foods group, which had owned Häagen Dazs since 1983 and regarded Ben & Jerry's ice cream as a threat. In 1984 Pillsbury banned their distributor from supplying Ben & Jerry's ice cream to the supermarkets. Ben & Jerry's fought the ban with the help of lawyers, but more importantly through a public relations campaign. Stickers on Boston city buses demanded 'What's the Doughboy Afraid of?'

– the doughboy was the symbol of the Pillsbury brand – and they sold T-shirts printed with the message 'Ben & Jerry's Legal Defense Fund – Major Contributor' in their scoop shop. Jerry demonstrated outside Pillsbury's head office in Minneapolis and they appealed for public sympathy with slogans like 'Don't Let Pillsbury's $$$ Strangle Ben & Jerry's'.[3] They won a huge amount of free media coverage before the case was settled out of court in favour of Ben & Jerry's.

In 1983 a start was made on setting up Ben & Jerry's scoop shops elsewhere in the country on a franchise basis. In the meantime a new ice cream factory was planned in Waterbury. To raise the required capital the business was converted in 1984 into a publicly listed company and, with the funds provided by the shareholders plus a bank loan, a new factory was built the following year. Slowly but surely, Ben & Jerry's expanded to become a unique and innovative business with a turnover of millions and a worldwide reputation for superbly imaginative ice creams, delivered with style and a social conscience.

The resurgence of ice novelties

• After the Second World War there was little innovation in the area of ice novelties by comparison with what had taken place before it (see chapter 5). The sale of the classic novelties from the 1920s – Eskimo Pie, Good Humor Bar, Popsicle, Drumstick and Dixie-cup – continued much as before, with the majority of manufacturers producing the ice novelties under licence. The most important change was the arrival of the Danish-made Gram ice lolly machine (see chapter 10). Coupled with packaging machines made by Anderson Manufacturers Co., the Gram RIA revolutionised the production of ices on a stick, turning them out at unheard-of speeds and with unprecedented efficiency. The new machine sold well in America;[51] machine manufacturers like Høyer, Vitaline and Glacier later introduced their own new systems for the production of ices on a stick.

• One of the few ice cream novelties introduced in the immediate post-war period was the creation of Pat Decicco. In 1949 Decicco had been on holiday in Italy, where he saw very small bonbon-like ice creams coated in chocolate. On returning to the United States he approached a machine manufacturer and together they developed the first machine for the industrial production of ice cream nuggets. In 1950 Decicco set up the BonBon Company; his product caught on and between 1951 and 1955 BonBon machines were installed under licence in 22 ice cream factories in America.[52] BonBon enjoyed similar success in Sweden and Germany (where it was marketed by Langnese under the name Pino) and in Italy. One of the first

American ice cream manufacturers to acquire a licence for the product was Carnation; but by about 1965 Carnation was the only firm still making BonBon ices in America and in 1974 it took a majority stake in the BonBon Company.

• The resurgence of the ice novelties market in the 1980s began with the introduction of a completely new type of ice cream sandwich – the Chipwich, launched in 1981. The Chipwich, claimed by the lawyer Richard LaMotta to be the outcome of four years' development work, was a large disc of vanilla ice cream between high quality chocolate chip cookies instead of the customary chocolate-flavoured biscuits. Some 160 cc in size, it retailed for the high price of one dollar.[53] An ingenious campaign gained the Chipwich product widespread media coverage, while colourfully dressed, well-trained vendors pulling small, specially designed ice cream carts attracted consumer attention on the streets and in busy shopping malls.[54]

• The Chipwich ice cream was produced by third parties and offered by wholesalers to supermarkets which stocked it in their freezers. Its success was due to its quality: the ice cream was bigger and better than previous ice cream sandwiches and so consumers were prepared to pay extra for it. In next to no time some 40 imitations appeared on the market and Chipwich Co. became embroiled

240: Cover of The Saturday Evening Post of 31 July 1954 by Stevan Dohanos. 'This is a scientific painting by Professor S. Dohanos, a physiological study in reflex action', reads the caption in the newspaper. 'Observe that each child is involuntarily performing an act because an impulse has been transmitted from a sense organ to a nerve center to a muscle. First, Mr. Impulse, the ice-cream man, enters a child's eye. This agitates a nerve center near the child's stomach, which in turn agitates his muscles hastily in the direction of his mother. The mother automatically opens a pocketbook and agitates the contents until some money turns up. Then Mr. Impulse, feeling silver in his hand, reflexes ice cream, and in time this gives him the impulse to go clean up at another beach. If learned physiologists don't understand this explanation, at least laymen will.'

The Saturday Evening
POST
July 31, 1954 – 15¢

Available for Adoption:
BABIES FOR THE BRAVE

HOW I LEARNED TO WIN
IN THE MAJORS
By Carl Erskine, of the Dodgers

WILL NEW ORLEANS
LOSE ITS RIVER?

in a series of court cases to protect its brand. These legal costs, coupled with over-optimistic investments, led the business to bankruptcy in 1984, although it was later re-established.[55]

• The success of the Chipwich product encouraged other ice cream manufacturers and foods businesses to develop ices for the new market of young adults. Frozfruit Co., Dole, Shamitoff, Chiquita and Fruit-A-Freeze all launched high quality fruit ices, while Coca-Cola introduced Minute Maid water-ices. In 1983 foods giant General Foods launched Jello-O Pudding Pop, a stabilised product that could be distributed through the frozen food distribution systems in the USA, which ran at a higher tempera-ture than the -20°C required for ice cream. Jello-O Pudding Pop was supported by the highest advertising budgets yet seen in the ice cream sector: everyone was familiar with the product from the television commercials featuring comedian Bill Cosby, and the pro-duct experienced record-breaking sales.[56]

• As a result of these developments the market share of traditional brands such as Popsicle, Good Humor and Eskimo Pie came under severe pressure. Innovation at higher quality levels suddenly became even more important. For a business like Popsicle Inc. drastic restructuring became inevitable. This was the major reason why its owner Sara Lee (which had bought Popsicle Inc. from Joe Lowe in 1966) decided in 1986 to sell the business to Gold Bond Ice Cream Co., based in Green Bay, Wisconsin. Gold Bond, founded in 1938 by Tom Lutsey Senior, had for many years been making Popsicle ices for both super-market chains and other

241: Dogs, too, love a tub of Good Humor ice cream (circa 1960). In about 1986, an ice cream for dogs was launched in the USA called Frosty Paws.

customers including Baskin-Robbins and Good Humor. Since 1973 it had also been producing water-ices in the shape of Disney characters, such as the Mickey Mouse Bar, under licence.

The renewal of Good Humor

• Like Popsicle Inc., Good Humor was going through turbulent times. Since 1961 it had been a subsidiary of the US Unilever busi-ness Thomas J. Lipton Ltd. and until the 1970s its turnover was mainly achieved in the big cities on the east coast, through street sales from the Good Humor vans.

• The business was performing poorly. Profits on ice cream products like Straw-berry Shortcakes, Toasted Almonds, Chocolate Eclairs, Strawberry Whammys or Cherry Berry Swirls were insignificant. Repeated attempts had been made since 1963 to find success with multipacks in supermarkets,[57] but competition from big companies like Borden and Breyers was intense, profit margins remained low, and there were many years when the business operated at a loss.

• In 1985 Good Humor closed down its facto-ries and contracted out its production to Gold Bond in Green Bay, which was already manu-facturing some of the Good Humor products. It had become a matter of sink or swim. An analysis drawn up at that time expressed the dilemma very clearly: either Unilever had to sell Good Humor and exit the USA or there had to be a substantial expansion through acquisition.[58] Only through acquisition could the company start to operate on a national scale and therefore negotiate with the

distributors to secure adequate profit margins. There were plenty of candidate ice cream businesses, but which was the most suitable and available at the right price?

242: A fishing trip, on a calm sea on a sunny day in 1960, without Good Humor ice cream? No fear, the Good Humor Man is there in his boat!

• Financially, the purchase of Popsicle Inc. in 1986 had taken a lot out of Gold Bond and in 1989 its owner, Tom Lutsey, was thinking about selling his business after 51 years. The Lipton director and former President of Good Humor Blaine Hess, who knew Lutsey well, got news of this and reached agreement with Lutsey on the main outlines of the deal. At a stroke, Good Humor gained control of the factory that already produced its ices, the national ice cream brand Popsicle and Gold Bond's extensive distribution network. It also acquired a range of licences, including those for Coca-Cola's Minute Maid, the Disney products and Choco Taco ice cream brand. This taco-shaped ice cream with chocolate and nuts had been patented in 1984 by Jack & Jill Ice Cream Co. from Philadelphia and its production and marketing had been contracted out to Gold Bond.[59] A more sophisticated version of this ice cream was rolled out in Europe in 1997 under the name Winner Taco by a number of Unilever ice cream businesses. The Disney licence was however terminated three of four years after Good Humor's acquiring it.

• In 1993 Good Humor purchased Klondike, the brand name of a generously sized, square ice cream dipped in chocolate that had been produced since 1929 by the Isaly Dairy Company. The company had been founded around the turn of the century near Youngstown, Ohio, by the Swiss immigrant William Isaly. His Klondike Bar ice cream became so popular that only two years later he set up a second factory in Pittsburgh, Pennsylvania. For decades the ice cream was largely made by hand, including the slicing of the ice cream, immersing it in chocolate, allowing it to dry on racks and packing it; but in 1963 a specially developed, automatic machine made by Polarmatic Co. was installed, enabling a daily output of 35,000 Klondike Bar products.[60]

• Until the 1970s these ice creams were on sale only in Pennsylvania and Ohio. Then the business was taken over by Clabir International Co. and in 1978 the ice cream, in its very distinctive silver foil pack with a picture of a polar bear, was introduced to Florida, New England and New York. In May 1982 a new factory was inaugurated in Clearwater, Florida, and a nationwide publicity campaign launched. Klondike commercials with the payoff line: 'What would you do for a Klondike Bar?', tempting people to perform ludicrous stunts in exchange for a Klondike Bar ice cream, were carried by 125 television stations. Supporting advertisements were published in hundreds of local newspapers.[61] In 1986 a new factory near Los Angeles ensured that Klondike Bar products were available from coast to coast, including in 92% of supermarkets.

• Good Humor's position, reinforced by the Klondike brand, became even stronger when it took possession of one of the crown jewels of American ice cream. In 1993 Unilever learnt that Kraft-General Foods wanted to dispose of its ice cream divisions. Chief brands were Breyers and Sealtest, while the Californian business Knudsen was also part of the group. Unilever top ice cream executives flew to New York. After a week of negotiation, the companies reached agreement for $265 million[62] and Unilever achieved its objective: a leading position in the world's greatest ice cream nation. Not only did the newly formed Good Humor-Breyers business now hold the number one position in the market for family packs, but its ownership of the Popsicle, Klondike and Good Humor brands also gave it the leading share in the fast-moving market for frozen novelties.

• The Breyers All Natural brand has since grown to become one of the two major ice cream brands in the USA, with a sales volume equivalent to almost 1.5 litre per head average consumption. Henry Breyer's idea, around 1910, to create an ice cream only from "real" cream, sugar and pure flavourings, and his "pledge of purity", had proved an enduring success.

Dreyer's Grand Ice Cream

• While this was happening on the East Coast and in the Mid-West, a revolution had been under way on the west coast. Dreyer's, an ice cream producer headquartered in Oakland, California, had succeeded step-by-step in becoming a national ice cream company. This process had started in the 1970s when the company began to expand outside the San Francisco Bay area, making Dreyer's a familiar name in western states.

• The business had been set up in Oakland in 1928 by a German immigrant, William Dreyer, and Missouri-born Joe Edy, the owner of a candy store. At 3315 Grand Avenue they opened an ice cream parlour called Edy's Grand Ice Cream.[63] Grand Avenue was a popular shopping street and visitors to the nearby Grand Lake Theater liked to drop in at Edy's to enjoy an ice cream sundae after the movie. Notwithstanding the name, it was Dreyer who made the ice cream, having learnt the trade at the National Ice Cream Co. in San Francisco. At Edy's he created new lines such as Rocky Road, a chocolate ice cream with walnut and pieces of marshmallow.

• After the war Edy decided he wanted to concentrate on his candy store business, so in 1947 the partners split up and the company name was changed to Dreyer's Grand Ice Cream. New factory premises at 5929 College Avenue were equipped with modern ice cream equipment.

• In 1953 William Dreyer's son took over the business. He decided to copy the example of Baskin-Robbins and Dairy Queen and set up a chain of small restaurants around San Francisco Bay. This approach failed and by about 1960 Dreyer's was on the verge of bankruptcy. In 1963 Dreyer Jr. sold the business to several of its leading executives and sales director Ken Cook became the new president of Dreyer's Grand Ice Cream.[64] A new business strategy was adopted and by 1976 sales had increased, outstripping the capacity of the factory on College Avenue. As the site offered no possibility for expansion, a new factory would have to be built elsewhere. With an annual turnover of $6 million, Cook did not anticipate problems in raising the required capital, yet the bank

loan did not materialise. As this news reached him, Cook was being visited by Gary Rogers, who ran a restaurant with his friend Rick Cronk. Rogers raised the possibility of buying Dreyer's and in May 1977 the transaction was finalised.

• Under the leadership of Rogers and Cronk the company began to expand eastwards. An ice cream manufacturer in Denver began making ice cream for Dreyer's and in 1981 the company was floated on the stock exchange. An agreement was reached with Breyers that, to avoid confusion between the names, Dreyer's would sell its ice cream in the states in the East and Mid-West under the name Edy's Grand Ice Cream.

• In 1984 Edy's was present in supermarkets in Ohio; by 1986 it had reached New York; and from 1991 it was available in Florida. In 1994 a factory was opened in Houston and Dreyer's went into battle with Blue Bell, the leading manufacturer in Texas. Blue Bell had been selling ice cream in Texas ever since 1911, but had only started to expand the geographical scope of its operations in 1960. The firm quickly grew to become the leading ice cream brand in Texas and by 1988 its sales in terms of dollars ranked in the top five of the US ice cream industry.[65] In 1994 Nestlé bought 25% of the shares in Dreyer's, who began to distribute Nestlé's own ice cream product alongside those of Ben & Jerry, an arrangement which had begun in 1976.[66]

• A crucial factor in the growth of Dreyer's was innovation. After three years of research, the company launched Dreyer's Grand Light Ice Cream in April 1987. This low-calorie product met the growing consumer interest in good-tasting, healthy, non-fattening ice cream. Containing less than 7% butter-fat, it should have been classed as an ice milk. However, Dreyer's chose to label their product as a 'light dairy dessert', as they wanted to avoid ice milk's connotations of poor quality. As spokesperson Diane McIntyre said during the product launch, 'We feel this tastes like ice cream'.[67]

• Although many consumers still sought out the richer, high-calorie ice cream made by Häagen Dazs and others, growing numbers of health-conscious consumers wanted reduced-calorie products. Good Humor-Breyers recognised this trend in the 1990s and introduced 'light' ice cream varieties. But was this trend really all that new? Ever since the early 1950s regular attempts had been made, with varying degrees of success, to market full-flavoured, low-fat ice cream. Since 1951, Beatrice had been marketing special ice cream for diabetics that contained saccharin in place of sugar.[68] In 1952, the Quality Chekd Dairy Products Association launched low-calorie Chekd ice cream and in 1957 an ice cream called Trim appealed to the weight-watching consumer of Dallas. 'The trend to low-calorie eating is pretty universal these days, and we think it's here to stay', said the president of Trim Food Products Co., John D. McEwen, in 1957.[69] Low-calorie eating habits have stayed the course – without quite ever becoming universal.

• The post-war American ice cream industry experienced far-reaching changes. Major ice cream manufacturers which had their roots in the dairy industry, such as Borden, Beatrice and Foremost Dairies, disappeared from the stage. 'Dedicated' ice cream companies large and small, including Good Humor-Breyers, Dreyer's and Blue Bell, remained in business and expanded.

• Post-war improvements in standards of living enabled the mass purchase of freezers or refrigerators with a freezer compartment. This, plus the fact that ice cream had become a cheap, tasty and convenient food, led to an enormous growth in ice cream consumption in family homes in the 1950s. Demographic changes and growing affluence brought more drastic changes in lifestyles and tastes in the 1970s to which Häagen Dazs pioneer Reuben Mattus was the first to respond with his high-quality ice cream.

• Americans love ice cream and are always eager to try new flavours, new combinations, new names and new shapes. Modern-day technology makes it possible to manufacture endless variations on a large scale. In no other country in the world is that skill as far advanced as in America; and if you are not satisfied with the products on offer, you can always surf to the Good Humor-Breyers Internet site and compose your own 'virtual' ice cream.

Licks, Sticks & Bricks
A WORLD HISTORY OF ICE CREAM

Australia: 'health, strength and happiness'

7

'Stir sugar to taste slowly into cream. Mix well. Then strain into tin with close-fitting lid. Set in tub of cracked ice sprinkled generously with salt. Scrape cream down with a spoon as it freezes round edge of tin. While freezing, gradually add lemon juice or mashed strawberries or raspberries. When frozen take out frozen cream and place in glasses'. So ran the instructions for a recipe given in The English and Australian Cookery Book: For the Many, as well as for the "Upper Ten Thousand", a book dating from 1864 and compiled by 'an Australian Artist-ologist'.[1] It was one of the first ice cream recipes published in Australia. At that time Australia, like the United States of America, was a young nation with no culinary traditions of its own – a nation which, from the late seventeenth century, had been primarily built by soldiers and convicts from Great Britain and which, after the Second World War, would gain strength from the arrival of emigrants from all over Europe.

• Many of the eating habits on this vast, almost empty continent originated from Britain. Gradually, however, they took on a character of their own, influenced by the climate and the locally available foods. Whereas Australians had at first paid little attention to the quality of their food, towards the end of the nineteenth century a quality-conscious middle class began to emerge, catered for by more and more cookery books.

• Australia's immense cattle herds yielded dairy products in abundance; much of it was exported to Great Britain, while cheese and ice cream were made from the milk surpluses. In 1902 the state of Victoria was the first place in the world to introduce standards governing ice cream

243: Advertisement for Streets ice cream, circa 1975.

making: one stipulation of its Pure Food Act was that dairy ice cream had to contain at least 10% butter-fat.[2]

• Thanks to the pioneering work of the journalist and inventor James Harrison (1816-1893), the country's refrigeration industry soon acquired a good reputation. Although Harrison's refrigerator, invented in 1856 and operated on ether, did not turn out to be a commercial success, his efforts stimulated both the scientific study of artificial freezing processes and the refrigeration industry.[3] Many of the first ice cream manufacturers also produced ice, for their own purposes but also for farms and homes wanting to prevent their foodstuffs from spoiling[4] in the scorching Australian summers.

• At the beginning of the 1930s electrical refrigerators started to replace the cabinets cooled with blocks of ice and, as in the United States, ice cream manufacturers installed freezer cabinets in retail outlets as long as the shopkeepers used them only to sell their brand of ice cream. In the 1920s and 1930s Australia was increasingly influenced by the US, particularly in the fields of film, music, dance and architecture.[5] American influence extended to ice cream: the soda fountain bar, usually installed in a sweet shop or a confectionery baker's shop, became a common sight in all Australian cities.[6] At the same time a newcomer arrived in town: the milk bar, where – in the days before Coca-Cola reached Australia – you could drink milk, coffee, tea or lemonade, buy newspapers, sweets and other items or sit and eat ice cream in the summer. In the second half of the 1930s leisure time began to increase and a lively beach culture developed, based around surfing.[7] Eating ice cream formed part of this flourishing beach life.

244: Children gather round a seller of 'American Ices' in Sydney in 1914.

• During the Second World War ice cream consumption continued to grow and then to boom in the same way as in the United States and Sweden. The 1950s brought many new immigrants and greater prosperity, with more refrigerators, washing machines and cars, more nights out and more holidays. In 1956 commercial television was launched in Australia. The ice cream industry profited from all these developments.

• In the 1960s the structure of the ice cream market changed. Milk bars and small grocery stores were increasingly superseded by supermarkets and the freezer compartments in household refrigerators began to fill with larger packs of ice cream. Competition compelled the ice cream industry to rationalise. Mergers and acquisitions took place and two local ice cream manufacturers, Streets and Peters, expanded to become nationwide businesses. By 1996, with a per capita consumption of around seventeen litres, the Australians were second only to the United States in ice cream consumption.

J.P. Sennitt: Australia's ice cream pioneer

• At the end of the nineteenth century all the big cities – Brisbane, Sydney, Melbourne, Adelaide and Perth – had factories for the production of ice and, as in the United Kingdom and elsewhere, it was in the refrig-

IF YOU FEEL QUEER
TRY DUNCANS BEER - YOU GET IT HERE
ICE CREAM & CONFECTIONERY

SMITHS CRISPS

245: Children in 1935 pictured in front of Sonny Duncan's mobile shop. The photo was taken in Cobar, a small town in New South Wales, more than 300 miles west of Sydney.

eration industry that the roots of the first Australian ice cream factory lay.

• In 1888 the British refrigeration engineer J.P. Sennitt had settled in Melbourne with his son W.J. Sennitt. The Sennitts had already installed refrigeration plants in the South African seaports of Durban, Cape Town and Port Elizabeth, on commission from the Melbourne-based Victorian Cold Accumulator Ltd., maker of accumulators for the cold storage rooms in butchers' shops. The Sennitts owned shares in the company and in May 1896 they took it over and continued trading under their own name.[8]

• The city of Melbourne was growing. Restaurants were opening and demand for ice cream was on the rise. Around the turn of the century several small ice cream businesses were set up, including the Melbourne Ice Cream Co., founded in 1904 by W.J. Sennitt and T.W. Tatchell. In November 1906 the Sennitts turned their refrigeration business into a limited company, J.P. Sennitt & Son Ltd., a few months later amalgamating with the Melbourne Ice Cream Co. The draymen who delivered ice by horse and cart to the butchers' shops began to sell bricks of Sennitt ice cream for one penny on a commission basis. Competition was keen. The ice cream maker W.B. Thompson also sold bricks of ice cream in Melbourne, under the Snowdrop name, and he invoked the patent that he held for their manufacture, hoping to stop Sennitt's sales.

However, the action failed when it was demonstrated that packaged bricks of ice cream were already on sale in Melbourne before 1905, the date of the patent.

• Sennitt's company was a success. In 1907 a plot of land was bought on which bigger stables were erected to accommodate the growing number of horses and carts. Sennitt's distribution activities became motorised in 1912, when the business bought its first ice cream lorry, a Belgian FN, for £500. For more than 60 years Sennitt's ice cream, identifiable by its polar bear logo, remained part of Melbourne and Victoria life, until in 1961 Sennitt's was taken over by Unilever and became part of Streets. In 1977 the name J.P. Sennitt & Son Ltd. disappeared from the Australian stage.

'Peters Ice Cream, for Youngsters, Young or Old'

• While the Sennitts were building up their ice cream business in Melbourne, Frederick Augustus Bolles Peters began producing ice cream in Paddington, a suburb of Sydney. Peters, who originated from Michigan in the USA and who was known amongst his staff as F.A. or F.A.B., had arrived in Australia in 1883. At the beginning of the 1907 season, in August, Peters churned his first batch of ice cream, which he sold from his horse and cart.[9] The name of his business was Peters American Delicacy Company. He used the term 'American delicacy' instead of ice cream, believing that the association with

247: Van of Peters Ice Cream Ltd. in Sydney, circa 1950. The American Frederick Peters had started making ice cream in Sydney in 1907. His business grew into a nationwide ice cream company.

America would inspire confidence and generate more custom.

• In August 1911, Peters opened what was then an ultra-modern ice cream factory in Sydney's Redfern district, modelled on American principles. The red-brick factory building, measuring 30 metres square, had three storeys and was equipped with an electric lift. For the personnel there was a canteen, a changing room and showers.[10] The American machines could produce 10,000 gallons of ice cream a week.

• Around 1910 the trade journal Dairy and its Products wrote: 'Ice cream has been recognised not only as a palatable diet but also as a desirable food. It has high food value especially when the standard of the butter fat

content of the milk and cream from which it is made is high'.[11] Nonetheless, Australians still regarded ice cream as a treat rather than a food, so shortly after the First World War Peters launched a large-scale advertising campaign in New South Wales to persuade consumers to see ice cream in a different light. American-style billboards and advertisements reiterated the message, year after year, that ice cream was a nutritious dish for every day. As in the United States, the medical profession was enlisted to emphasise the importance of ice cream for good health. Ice cream was 'The Health Food of a Nation'. Posters showed children and adults eating ice cream with the slogan 'Peters Ice Cream, For

248: Advertising sign for Lynam's Ice Cream, circa 1955. Lynam's was founded in 1934 in Parramatta, an eastern district of Sydney. In 1950 the business was taken over by Streets Ice Cream Ltd.

Youngsters, Young or Old', thus challenging the view that eating ice cream was childlike or unseemly.[12]

• By 1912 Peters had set up two independent ice cream businesses in Brisbane and Perth. In Brisbane Peters encountered competition from Arctic Ice Creams Ltd., established in 1923. Arctic enjoyed great success with Eskimo Pie ice cream (see chapter 5), which it manufactured under licence. In 1927 Peters' Brisbane business merged with Arctic to form the Queensland Peters Arctic Delicacy Co. The new company then expanded, opening further ice cream factories in the coastal towns of Rockhampton and Townsville by 1929. In the same year Peters also built a small factory at Meyers Place in Melbourne which, under the management of a young food chemist, Emil Christensen, began to produce ice cream. Five years later the factory at Meyers Place had become too cramped and was relocated to the site of a former shoe factory in the Richmond area. As well as ice cream, this new complex produced 60 tons of ice a day. Peters continued to be successful and the business acquired many exclusive contracts with cinemas, theatres, swimming pools and beachside cafeterias. Peters now bought a manufacturer of freezer cabinets, Nizer Pty. Ltd., and began to supply them to shopkeepers on condition that they sold only Peters ice cream.[13]

Ice cream in Sydney: Lynam's and McNiven Bros.

• In 1937 Frederick Peters died and management passed into the hands of A.E. McCartney. His relationship with Christensen was poor and the two companies grew further and further apart. Not long afterwards they began to operate independently.[1]

• In the 1920s people in the big cities could buy ice cream not only in milk bars, but also in the numerous sweet shops equipped with soda fountains and run by Greek immigrants. According to a report in the August 1928 issue of the American trade journal Sweets Magazine, there were 3,000 or so soda fountains in Australia at that time. In New South Wales alone, three soda fountain manufacturers together sold about 100 fountains per year to sweet shops, confectionery bakers, department stores, cinemas and theatres.[15] To judge from photos from the early 1930s, much ice cream was still sold in the street from horse-drawn ice cream carts,[16] but the advent of dry ice meant ice cream could after 1927 also be served in railway trains. Dry ice was a particular godsend for ice cream distribution over the vast distances in Australia.

• 'In every Australian capital city is now located at least one ice cream manufacturer', wrote Sweets Magazine in 1928. 'In some, as in Sydney and Melbourne, there are several such producers.' From the mid-1930s two other ice cream manufacturers, besides Peters, were active in Sydney. In 1934 Lynam's Ice Cream Co. was established in Parramatta on the eastern side of the city and in 1936 McNiven Bros. was founded in Camperdown, to the south of the city. In Parramatta Edmund Lynam and his son Reginald ran a milk bar which was famous for the quality of its ice cream. Lynam's ice cream was cheaper than that of Peters and he sold most of it in the street from vans cooled by dry ice,[17] though all the grocers in Parramatta also sold his ice cream. In 1941 Lynam's became a limited company, but Peters had floated his business on the stock exchange and that provided him with a more favourable tax position. By 1950 the competition with Peters had become more intense. Ice cream manufacturer Edwin Street, who had been active in Sydney since 1939, therefore proposed to Lynam's that their two businesses should merge, which they did. Lynam's ice cream remained on sale until the end of the 1950s, when the operation was wound down, and in 1962 the Parramatta factory closed for good.[18]

'Streets, the cream of the coast'

• Edwin ('Ted') Street (1891-1975) was a farmer's son from Corrimal, a small town 25 miles south of Sydney on the northern edge of one of Australia's most prosperous dairy farming districts. Between the wars Street, with his wife Daisy Grigg and his brother Daniel, laid the foundations for what would ultimately become Australia's biggest and best-known ice cream manufacturer.[19]

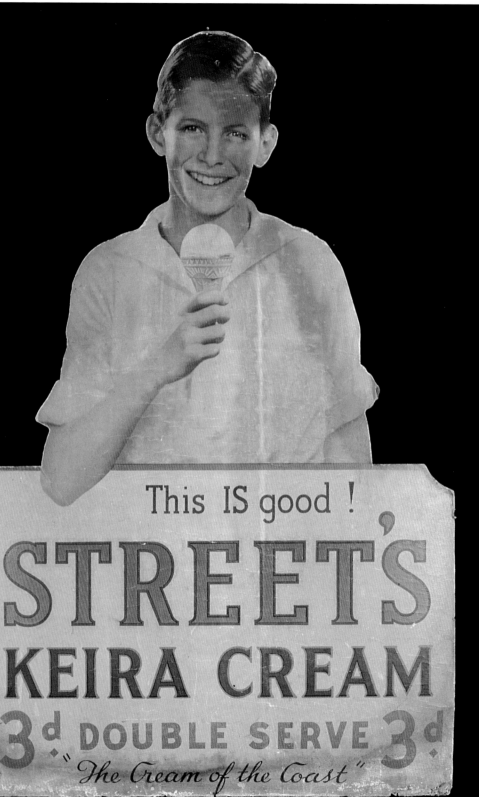

• At first Ted worked on his parents' farm. When the First World War broke out in Europe in 1914 he voluntarily enlisted, together with another of his brothers, in the specially formed Australian and New Zealand Army Corps (ANZAC). On his return to Australia, Ted – then 28 – bought a fruit and vegetable shop in Corrimal, which he ran with the help of his wife. They also sold sweets, cakes, lemonade and ice cream, which he made himself in the back of his shop using a simple machine cooled with ice and salt. The recipe came from his sister-in-law, who had learnt it whilst attending a confectionery course in Sydney during the war.[20] Street's ice cream caught on and a neighbour suggested selling it locally from a cart. Street therefore bought a one horse-power motorbike and coupled it to his ice cream machine.[21]

• Demand grew and Street began looking for the funds to finance an ice cream factory. On 13 December 1923, with his brother Daniel and William Ewart Jones, the director of the local coal mine, he set up The Illawara Delicacies Company. The objectives of the new company were to produce 'ice, ice cream and other delicacies', and its directors invested £1.200 in setting up a small factory.[22] At first the business concentrated on the production of blocks of ice for use in domestic refrigerators. The electricity for the factory's refrigeration plant was supplied from William Jones' mine.[23] Both Corrimal and the nearby town of Wollongong proved to be good sales areas.

• When they started to produce ice cream, one of their most successful products was

249: Showcard for Keira Cream, circa 1935. The product was named after Mount Keira, near Corrimal. It could not be called an ice cream because it contained less than the legally prescribed 10% butter-fat, as well as more air than normal.

'Penny Pinky', a strawberry ice cream in a cone sold for one penny. To counter the effects of the Great Depression in the 1930s, Street invented a product known as 'Keira Cream', named after nearby Mount Keira. It had an 'overrun' of around 135% (i.e. it contained 67.5% air), about 35% higher than was usual, and contained somewhat less than the minimum legal limit for ice cream of 10% butter-fat.[24] 'We were putting out something – not called ice cream – that tasted exactly like ice cream and the customer was getting twice as much value for his money', explained Edwin Street in an interview he gave many years later.[25] According to his wife, it was the Keira Cream product that saved the company from going under.[26]

• Trade progressed so favourably that in 1934 Street wanted to build a new factory. On 4 October The Illawara Delicacies Company was converted into a limited company – Streets Ice Cream Ltd. – with a share capital of £50,000 and seven shareholders: the three original founders, their wives, and Gordon Francis Rider, who worked as a lorry driver for Streets.[27] In 1935 a start was made on the new factory, at a building cost of £1,000, on Main Street in Corrimal. It was equipped with Vogt freezers imported from Cherry-Burrell, each with a capacity of 150 gallons.[28]

• In 1936, the production of ice cream at the new factory really began to take off and in 1939 Edwin Street felt that the time was right to make an entry into Sydney's large ice cream market. A depot was built in Bexley, in the south of the city, and during the season the Streets shuttled between Corrimal and Sydney. Bexley was the first step towards Streets becoming a national ice cream company.

250: The Streets ice cream factory on Main Street in Corrimal. The factory, which began operating in 1936, had been built at a cost of £1,000 by Oscar V. Jeffree. It was fitted with Vogt freezers imported from Cherry-Burrell in the United States, each with a capacity of 150 gallons.

Rosy cheeks thanks to Amscol ice

• It was not only in the big cities of New South Wales, Queensland and Victoria that the ice cream industry prospered.
In Adelaide, the country's second biggest city and capital of South Australia, an ice cream factory was set up at the beginning of the 1920s. In January 1920 P.C. Manuel, a farmer from Enfield, founded a cooperative whose aim was to promote the interests of farmers in negotiations with the milk wholesalers in Adelaide. In 1921 the cooperative had at least 579 members and at the end of that year it purchased a major share in Beauchamp

Bros., Adelaide's largest milk wholesaler. In January 1922 the Adelaide Milk Supply Co-operative Limited (Amscol)[29] began operations. The company also produced ice, which was distributed in lorries bearing the slogan 'Use ice at home and preserve your food'.

• In 1923 one of Amscol's directors visited the US and the United Kingdom to study the latest developments in the dairy industry. On his return, Amscol decided to expand its production facilities in Adelaide: in 1924 a more powerful freezer was installed and a start made on the production of ice cream. Milk, cheese, butter and now ice cream were supplied to dairy shops and milk bars and sold door-to-door by horse and cart.

Amscol thus became a household name, first in Adelaide and later throughout South Australia.

• The driving force behind the business was still the Beauchamp family, particularly the first managing director, Walter J. Beauchamp. In 1927 dairy and ice manufacturing and cold storage warehousing were expanded and new American machines installed. For ice cream distribution Amscol had a fleet of eleven lorries.

In November 1927 the first airborne shipment of ice cream, from Adelaide to Port Pirie, some 300 kilometres to the north-east,[30] attracted widespread public interest.

• In the early 1930s Amscol started selling ice cream in cinemas and theatres. During the intervals uniformed men sold tubs of ice cream from boxes they carried cooled with dry ice. Amscol Ice Cream 'Promotes Rosy Cheeks, Bright Eyes, Health, Strength and Happiness' was the optimistic advertising slogan used in those years.[31] Though the Depression did have some initial effect, ice cream sales began to climb again after 1933. In fact, in the next five years Amscol's sales doubled, from £186,629 to £382,245.[32]

• Growth continued during the Second World War, when some milk bars and grocers began to keep stocks of ice cream in freezer cabinets the whole year round. From 1943 onwards Amscol also supplied ice cream and milk to American troops stationed in Australia's Northern Territories, the Philippines, Indonesia and Papua New Guinea.

After the war: Heart and Paddle Pop

• In the post-war years ice cream consumption boomed, as it did in the United States (see chapter 6). In the 1944-1945 season Australians ate 10 million litres of ice cream; five years later this had risen to 17 million litres.[33] Amscol's sales grew from £652,112 in 1948 to £2,234,599 in 1959; at Streets they climbed from £727,333 in 1952 to £2,117,991 in 1959.[34]

• Streets' sales in Sydney came on so well that the company opened a second

251: Logo of the dairy and ice cream business Adelaide Milk Supply Co-operative Limited (Amscol), circa 1970. Amscol was founded in 1922 and became a household name in the state of South Australia. In 1978 75% of its shares were transferred to Unilever. The remaining 25% of the shares were acquired in 1981 and Amscol was then merged with Streets.

ice cream plant in Turrella on the site of an old farmhouse in 1948. The nearby railway line had influenced the choice of location, but soon the transport of milk and cream by special refrigerated lorries proved more advantageous than by rail. Road transport was faster and, using a fleet of lorries equipped with electrical freezers, the goods could be delivered direct to increasing numbers of depots and sales outlets. Like the British company Wall's Ice Cream (see chapter 8), Streets had the bodywork of its cork-insulated vans assembled in-house.[35]

• At around the time that the new Turrella factory was opened, Streets launched its first novelty ice: a chocolate-coated, heart-shaped, vanilla ice on a stick, sold under

the name Heart. It is said that Edwin Street had picked up the idea from Pauls, an ice cream company set up in Brisbane in 1933 with which Street maintained cordial relations.[36] The Heart was made from rectangular blocks of vanilla ice cream which, in a frozen state, were passed through a 'zippy cutter', a kind of bread-slicing machine which cut the ice cream into heart-shaped pieces. The stick was inserted by hand and the ice cream block was dipped in hot chocolate sauce, packed and frozen. After Streets became part of Unilever in 1960, the Heart product was adopted by many other Unilever ice cream companies, becoming a worldwide success.

• In the meantime Ronald Street, the engineer son of Edwin's brother Daniel who had died before the war, had joined the Streets board as technical director. Early in 1953 he went on a study trip to ice cream factories in the United Kingdom and the United States. In the UK he visited Midland Counties Dairies; in the US he called on the Gold Bond factory in Green Bay, Wisconsin (see chapter 6).

253: Signs for Streets, mid-1950s. The sign at the bottom is advertising Paddle Pop, an ice first marketed in 1953 with which Streets enjoyed tremendous success.

252: Cover of a Streets brochure (1948). In the background, the recently opened factory in Sydney's Turrella district. In its lifetime the factory was expanded and modernised several times. In 1998 an ultra-modern factory was opened in Minto, some 30 miles southwest of Sydney, and the Turrella production unit was closed.

At both he saw 'frozen confections' that were made with children in mind. Back in Australia Ronald experimented with recipes and picked a name that he may have brought back from his visit to Gold Bond in the States: Paddle Pop.[37] It was launched in September 1953 and the name registered as a trademark the following March. As it contained only 3.5% vegetable fat, it could not be called an ice cream, but was sold as a 'frozen confection'. This had the advantage of not attracting the 22.5% sales tax on ice cream, enabling its retail price to be kept very low. The Paddle Pop product proved an unprecedented success: between 1953 and 1988 over 1.5 billion of them were sold and it still features on the Streets price list in various flavours today.

• Shortly after launch, Streets began advertising its Paddle Pop product using a friendly lion figure. Over the years the lion's appearance was updated and he was given more character. In 1982 Unilever introduced the Paddle Pop lion into Europe and gave him a name: Max. Max the Lion became the mascot of a range of children's ices sold by many of Unilever's ice cream businesses (see box story on p 262).

new from Streets

Paddle Pop

beaut
flavours
frozen
on sticks!

vanilla, chocolate, fruit salad
. . . try them all!

SC3/33

1959: Unilever enters the Australian ice cream market

• Unilever's first move into the Australian ice cream market came in 1959 with its purchase of McNiven Bros. of Camperdown, Sydney, for £525,000.[38] The McNiven range comprised family packs of ice cream bricks, ice cream in tubs, water-ices, chocolate-coated vanilla ice lollies, and ice creams in vanilla, strawberry, chocolate and passion fruit flavours. The 'Speciality of the House' had long been the Triple Treat product – vanilla ice cream with chocolate and marshmallow between wafers.

• Apart from ice cream, McNiven also supplied shopkeepers and milk bars with ice cream cones, wafers, drinking straws, ice scoops and freezer cabinets.[39] The various types of ice cream cones (with names such as Single, Double, Square or Little Beauty), along with the wafers, tubs and drinking straws, were produced by McNiven itself in a separate factory in Adelaide. The drinking straws were supplied to a wide range of outlets throughout Australia.[40] McNiven also provided its customers with signboards, parasols, showcards, window posters and stickers. It even had its own signwriters, who visited retailers to paint the company's logo and the words 'McNiven's Ice Cream' on their shop fronts.[41]

254: Advertising poster for the Streets Paddle Pop product featuring the Paddle Pop Lion, circa 1955.
This children's ice came on the market in 1953. It contained only 3.5% fat and was (and still is) sold as a 'frozen confection'. Paddle Pop ice has been a stunning success story. In its first 25 years more than 1.5 billion were sold.

• Similar policies were adopted by Streets, Sennitts, Peters and others. In Parramatta, on the site of Lynam's Ice Cream, Streets had its own bakery for wafers; it, too, employed its own signwriters, who ensured that the lettering on the company's delivery vans and lorries were the same everywhere. The main feature that distinguished Peters from its rivals was its large-scale use of TV advertising. After the introduction of commercial television in 1956, the children's programme Peters Junior News carried advertisements for Peters children's ices, whilst on the Melbourne TV station the comic duo Zig & Zag brought the house down every Saturday night in their programme Peters' Fun Fair, which ran until around 1967.[42]

• The purchase of McNiven Bros. by Unilever was only the start of consolidation in the industry. In 1966 McNiven's share of the New South Wales ice cream market still stood at only about 10%, the biggest manufacturers being Peters with a market share of 50%, followed by Streets with 30%.[43] In the spring of 1960, the opportunity of buying Streets arose. In return for over £3.9 million the 69 year-old Edwin Street saw his lifetime's work pass into the hands of Unilever, who a year later also bought J.P. Sennitt & Son Ltd. of Melbourne.

The 'ice cream war' of the 1960s

• In the 1960s and 1970s the Australian ice cream market was transformed. Instead of buying ice cream from a milk bar or a small grocery store, consumers increasingly bought from supermarkets. Gone too were the days when ice cream companies like Streets made superbly decorated ice cream cakes for Christmas or birthdays and delivered them, packed in foil and cooled by dry ice, to the home.

¶ In 1997 the annual Royal Easter Show in Sydney attracted a record attendance of almost 1.2 million people. Originally an agricultural exhibition held in Australia since the beginning of the nineteenth century, the show has expanded to become one of the biggest events in the southern hemisphere. Over its sixteen days the crowds encountered a familiar figure in a safari suit, strolling around handing out Paddle Pop ices. Where did the Paddle Pop Lion come from, what made him so popular - and what had he got to do with ice cream?

The Lion's history starts in 1953 with the launch of the Paddle Pop, one of Australia's most successful ices. In that year Ronald Street of Streets Ice Cream Ltd. returned to Sydney after a study trip spent visiting ice cream factories in America and Britain. There he had seen the great success of 'frozen confections', cheap ices made from sugar, water, vegetable fat, flavouring and colourings. He suggested to his Uncle Edwin, the founder of Streets, that they should make something similar for the Australian market. Edwin Street was not enthusiastic, but allowed his nephew to give it a try, so Ronald experimented with recipes and decided on the name Paddle Pop.

Paddle Pop ice cream was

255: Advertising poster for the Streets Paddle Pop product, with the Paddle Pop Lion, circa 1956.

launched in September 1953[1] and owed much of its success to the advertising that Streets developed for it. Soon after launch, a friendly lion was incorporated in advertising posters and on the packaging. To begin with the Paddle Pop Lion was not much more than a simple illustration, but by the early 1970s the increasing importance of TV advertising motivated Streets to develop the Paddle Pop Lion further. From a simple cartoon drawing, he was transformed into a brand mascot with

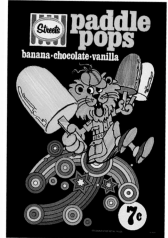

256: (Above) The Streets Paddle Pop Lion, circa 1968.
(Above right) 628 : The Streets Paddle Pop Lion, circa 1980. 627 : (Right) The Streets Paddle Pop Lion, circa 1975.

well developed traits.[2] Nor, with his new look, were his appearances confined to television. Streets kept a number of Paddle Pop Lion costumes ready for use at outdoor festivities, in supermarkets, at sporting events and at children's parties. The character handed out ices and helped build the image of the friendly, humorous and reliable Paddle Pop Lion.

In 1990 the character was further updated and precise rules for the mascot's development were drawn up. His character and his role in sales of Paddle Pop ices were laid down in detail and guidelines were issued for the storylines of the TV commercials in which he was to appear.

He was the 'King of the Jungle' and only he knew the secret trail that led to Paddle Pop ice cream. Time and again he overcame the jungle's perils to guide children to the ice treat.[3]

The Paddle Pop Lion was by now no longer purely Australian; indeed, he had become something of a citizen of the world. Unilever's Asian ice cream businesses employed his services; and in 1985 he arrived in France. Travel had broadened his mind:

in Europe, where he symbolised a wider range of products, he went under a different name, Max, and presented a slightly altered appearance. The Belgian artist Kiko put him into a cartoon strip and so the Lion started a new life in the children's magazines Pif and Mickey. In 1995 Max the Lion had another facelift; and in 1997 he underwent a complete metamorphosis, this time being drawn in the Japanese manga style. The name Max was in fact already in use in Unilever's Portuguese ice cream business, Olá, whose children's ices his cartoon dog character had been promoting very successfully since the mid-1970s. Sales of Super Maxi ices in a season peaked at around 20 million, backed by numerous special campaigns. For example, stickers with pictures of 96 different breeds of dog could be collected and contests were organised in which the participants could win a real pedigree puppy of their choice.[4]

257: The character for Max Ice Cream, 1998.

258: Streets ice cream lorries line up in front of the factory in Turrella, Sydney, in 1957. The advertisement on the back of the lorries refers to the popular film The Shiralee, with Dana Wilson in one of the starring roles. Released in 1957, this was based on the novel of the same name by the Australian author D'Arcy Niland. In 1989 the film was made into a mini-series by Australian television.

• The range of impulse ices was now expanded. In 1962 Streets launched a new ice cream on a stick under the brand name Gaytime. Modelled on a product made by the US manufacturer Good Humor (see chapter 6), it comprised strawberry ice cream enclosed by vanilla ice cream and covered with a layer of chocolate mixed with short-cake crumbs. 'An exciting new ice cream Sundae-on-a-stick!', read the full-page colour advertisement announcing the Gaytime product's arrival – the first time colour had been used in an ice cream advertisement in Australia.[44] Other impulse ices followed: in 1963 a second Gaytime variety, under the brand name 'Devil's Food', went on sale and two years later Streets introduced an ice cream cone under the Cornetto brand.

• Ice cream consumption grew like never before: from 85 million litres in 1960 to 240 million litres in 1970, or from 9.2 litres to almost 20 litres per capita. After the launch of the first Gaytime ice cream in 1962, sales of impulse ices climbed by more than 80% in the space of a few years: from 115.6 million litres in the 1961-1962 season to 208 million litres in 1966-1967. Overall, however, the share of impulse ices in the total ice cream market remained small: in 1984 they accounted for just 18% of the ice cream market, with 70% of ice cream volume still consisting of take-home packs of family ice cream.[45]

• The competition between the expanding ice cream companies of Streets and Peters became increasingly keen; the supermarket chains also made their presence felt. The 'ice cream war', as that period in the 1960s was later described, put heavy pressure on profits. In 1963 Streets responded by marketing a new premium ice cream under the brand name Blue Ribbon, sold in half gallon tubs. The name referred to the blue ribbon that was awarded each year in the 1930s to the passenger liner that made the fastest transatlantic passage. Blue Ribbon ice cream sales helped Streets to emerge successfully from the 'ice cream war'.

259: Family pack of Streets ice cream, circa 1955.

260 : Streets advertising signs, mid-1950s. Streets had its own signwriters to paint the company's logo and advertising on shop fronts. The sign at the bottom is advertising the Heart ice cream, which was launched in 1948. After Streets was acquired by Unilever in 1960, Heart became a success in many countries around the world.

261: Two Streets logos. The top one was in use from 1948 until about 1965, when it was replaced by the one at the bottom. This logo was used by most of Unilever's ice cream businesses until 1997.

262: Logo of Streets. This logo was in use until about 1965.

New concentrations, new competition

• In the 1970s Streets started a telephone sales and ordering service for its customers. The Corrimal factory closed down in 1961, but Turrella was repeatedly modernised and expanded. Streets began selling ice cream in more and more states. After Queensland (a depot was opened in Brisbane in 1962) and Victoria (through the purchase of Sennitts), it was the turn of Adelaide in South Australia in 1971.

• By 1974 Streets had a market share of about 20%. The market leader was Petersville – formerly Peters – of Melbourne with 25%, followed by the Brisbane-based Queensland United Foods (Q.U.F.) with 24%. Petersville and Q.U.F., however, were operating at a loss.[46] The fast growth of the 1960s and early 1970s had come to an end and Unilever now contemplated a joint venture with Petersville. Petersville, however, wanted to retain 50% control, which was of no interest to Unilever. Furthermore, Australia's government of the time was unenthusiastic about foreign investors.[47]

• In 1980 Petersville established Australian United Foods together with Pauls Ice Cream, the ice cream division of Q.U.F. The new company did not prosper: in 1981 Petersville was bought by HC Sleigh Ltd. and three years later the ice cream business was re-named Petersville Sleigh. In 1991 Petersville Sleigh was taken over by the multinational Pacific Dunlop Ltd., becoming Peters Foods. Four years later the company decided to dispose of its foods division and Peters

Foods was sold to Nestlé, after which it traded under the name Nestlé Peters.[48]

• In Adelaide Streets had started to compete in 1971 with the Amscol dairy business, which had by then been operating independently for nearly 50 years. Amscol was finding it increasingly difficult to keep its ice cream department in profit and ultimately it decided in 1978 to sell its ice cream activities for £2.33 million to Unilever (75%), the Southern Farmers Co-operative Ltd. and the Dairy Vale Metro Co-operative Ltd. (each 12.5%).[49] Three years later, Unilever became the 100% owner. Meanwhile, Unilever also acquired Dairy Farmers Ice Cream in New South Wales and in 1983 Streets began selling ice cream via concessionaires in Western Australia, making it the first ice cream company in Australia to operate a nationwide distribution network.

• The 1980s saw newcomers entering the Australian ice cream market. One of them was Norgen Vaasz, a firm set up in 1981, probably in imitation of Häagen Dazs, but which was taken over in 1986 by the confectionery company Rowntree Hoadley Ltd. The American multinational Kraft Foods also started selling ice cream in Australia, through Everest Food Industries which it had acquired in 1984. Competition grew more severe and profits were squeezed; 1986 was a poor ice cream season and Streets' profits fell by 46%. The introduction of a new sales tax of 10% on ice cream, and hefty price increases for dairy products brought about by new regulations in the dairy industry, made business even tighter. Streets set about economising. The number of products was reduced, the workforce in the Sydney and Melbourne factories was slimmed down and ice cream manufacture at Amscol in

263: Window display advertising McNiven Bros. ice cream, circa 1959. Established in Sydney in 1936, McNiven was purchased by Unilever in 1959 and amalgamated with Streets.

264 : Stand of McNiven Bros. at the Sydney Annual Show, 1959. The product being advertised is the Triple Treat, consisting of vanilla ice cream and marshmallow coated in chocolate.

Adelaide was discontinued in June 1989 after more than 60 years. In 1991 it was decided to concentrate all Streets ice cream production in the factory in Turrella, Sydney. The factory in Notting Hill near Melbourne was then also closed.[50]

• In 1992 Streets launched its first Magnum ice cream, with spectacular success. There had been strong local misgivings about launching the product in mid-recession, and the likely effect on their important brand Heart, but ice cream consumption in fact rose, from 309 million litres in 1990 to 325 million litres in 1994.

• In 1996, the same year rival Nestlé bought Peters Foods, it was announced that an ultra-modern factory would be built at Minto, some 40 kilometres south-west of Sydney, meaning the closure of the Turrella factory after more than 50 years. The capacity of the new Minto complex, which involved an investment of more than $70 million, was geared not only to serving the Australian market but also markets in New Zealand – to which Streets had began exporting in 1994[51] – and other Pacific islands. The new factory was officially opened in the spring of 1998, heralding a new era for Streets in its almost 75-year history. The business which had started life as a fruit and vegetable shop had grown to become Australia's biggest ice cream company, with a 1996 market share by volume of 56.7%, followed by Nestlé Peters with 31.3%.

265: Streets semi-trailer, about 1957.

266: Streets semi-trailer, 1961.

Licks, Sticks & Bricks
A WORLD HISTORY OF ICE CREAM

United Kingdom: 'Stop me and buy one!'

In March 1909 a spectacular new department store boasting eight floors, a hundred sales departments and nine lifts opened on London's Oxford Street. This superb white stone edifice, its 250-metre frontage decorated with Ionic columns, was the sensation of the year. Within a week of opening, one million Britons had passed through its revolving doors. The store's creator and proprietor, an American named Harry Gordon Selfridge (1858-1947), had incorporated many of the latest US fashions, including a splendid soda fountain in gleaming marble. Now Londoners too could enjoy that exciting combination of soda water, ice cream and lemonade.

• Until the 1960s Selfridges produced its own ice cream in the basement, to be eaten in the store or taken home.[1] Selfridges' soda fountain signalled the start of a change in the British ice cream market, hitherto chiefly served by Italian street vendors and restaurants (see chapter 4). For the first time the general public was offered a different kind of ice cream. As in other European countries, people in the United Kingdom looked to America for new ideas – including the production of factory-made ice creams. The UK was one of the first European countries to sell manufactured ice cream, following the American example. Soon an innovation was introduced: ices were sold from tricycles.

• In 1922 T. Wall & Sons began making ice cream 'in the American way' in London and their sales slogan, 'Stop

me and buy one', became a popular catchphrase. In March that year Wall's was acquired by Lever Brothers.[2] Lord Leverhulme, who owned Mac Fisheries, had a vision of selling fish through Wall's customers, and ice cream through Mac Fisheries customers.

• In 1929 when the Lever business joined up with Margarine Unie in the Netherlands, Wall's became part of the new Unilever group. After the Second World War the successful working methods of Wall's were to form the foundation for Unilever's worldwide ice cream operations.

268: Stout, ginger ale, lemonade, ice creams and other refreshments were on sale in about 1905 at Sam Earl's in Burton on Trent, Staffordshire. The ices were served between wafers or in glasses for a halfpenny or a penny.

267: The W logo of Wall's, circa 1925. These cards were distributed at the beginning of the season. Displaying the card in the window was a signal to the salesmen to call by.

• Another feature of British ice cream manufacture after the war was the use of vegetable fat. Numerous food ingredients were rationed in those years, including sugar, milk, cream and butter, and there was a ban on using dairy cream in the production of ice cream. As a result, ice cream manufacturers turned to vegetable fats, a practice which continued even after rationing ended in 1953. In 1959 new labelling regulations stipulated that a distinction had to be made between ice cream produced from dairy ingredients and other types of ice cream; but even then, for cost reasons, most ice cream continued to be made from vegetable fats.

• Food rationing had other consequences. Since sweets were rationed and ice cream was not, after the war the British began eating far more ice cream. They were additionally persuaded by the manufacturers' advertising that ice cream was not just a treat on a summer's day, but also a nutritious dessert in the dark days of winter. And so, despite its climate, the UK became one of the major ice cream consuming countries in Europe.

A soda fountain in Weston-super-Mare

• The soda fountain at Selfridges was soon copied by Italian ice cream makers. After the turn of the century, thousands of Italian immigrants had opened ice cream shops in the big cities and coastal resorts, in which they also sold coffee, tea, lemonade, cakes and sandwiches. Many of them now installed soda fountains in their shops. 'The café at Weston-super-Mare, the popular resort near Bristol, was large and imposing, in an excellent position right on the seafront. Its two floors, furnished with hefty Lloyd-loom armchairs, could seat over a hundred people. The shopfront was faced with marble. Called 'The

269: 1910 advertisement for ice cream cones made by A. Valvona & Co.,of Manchester, where the Italian Antonio Valvona had set up a factory in 1898 specifically for wafer production.

Ice Cream Parlour', the café was really an American soda fountain with a kitchenette, where they made sandwiches and prepared snacks, and there was an espresso machine for the coffee'. That was how Charles Forte recalled his Uncle Dominic's business, where as a lad of seventeen he went to work in 1925.[3]

• At that time Forte divided his time between Weston-super-Mare, the town of Alloa in Scotland – where his father ran another ice cream parlour – and Monforte, a mountain village south-east of Rome, where Forte had been born in 1908. His parents moved a couple of years later to Scotland, along with thousands of other Italians unable to find work in the major industrial areas of Manchester, Liverpool and Birmingham, nor in the south of England where there were already numerous Italian ice cream businesses and restaurants. Forte's father was the owner of the Savoy Café in Alloa, which served ice cream as well as cakes, coffee and sandwiches. In 1934, Forte was to open his own milk bar in Upper Regent Street in London based on the Australian model (see chapter 7). It served ice cream, milk shakes and sandwiches[4] and was his first step towards becoming owner of one of Britain's largest hotel groups after the war. By the time Forte opened his milk bar, ice cream had already become an accepted part of British life, due more than anything to sausage manufacturer Thomas Wall & Sons Ltd.

The beginnings of the British ice cream industry

• On 21 June 1922 Wall's sent a mailshot to London's grocers and restaurant owners, inviting them to start selling its factory-made ice cream. 'Do you realise what a healthful, nourishing and sustaining food Ice Cream is? Real Ice Cream of course – not mere cornflour or custard. Wall's Ice Cream is made in precisely the same way that the famous American Ice Cream is made – from pure cream and ripe fruit juices in a hygiene Model Factory. We have made an exclusive study of American methods of Ice Cream manufacture, sending out one of our Directors' sons for that purpose; and the plant we have installed includes all the very latest and the very best American machinery.'[5]

• T. Wall & Sons Ltd. had made sausages since 1786, building a national reputation for its products. In 1913 chairman Thomas Wall had the idea of smoothing out the company's month-on-month turnover by marketing ice cream – principally a summer product – to offset seasonally lower sales of sausages, popular in winter. The First World War delayed his plans, but in 1922 an ice cream department was set up in the sausage factory at Acton, West London. A small vertical ice cream freezer was installed, one manufactured in the USA by Emery Thompson (see chapter 5) which could produce 19 litres of ice cream mix in each production run.[6] The ice cream contained

14% butter-fat and 13% sugar. The butter, from New Zealand, was blended with water, milk powder, gelatine and sugar.

• The ice cream for scooping was packed in tin canisters, while bricks of ice cream to take home were packed in pint and half-pint cartons. Both canisters and cartons were transported in oblong metal containers, carried in large wooden crates lined with cotton-wool and cooled with salted ice. Wall's had assumed that the sausage sellers would be keen to boost their traditionally low sales in summer by selling its ice cream to grocers and restaurants, but this was a miscalculation. The sausage sellers showed little enthusiasm, as the crates were heavy and unwieldy. When filled, they weighed around 250 kilos.[7]

Delicious Cream Ice

Direct from Maker to Customer

270: Page from sales brochure for the retail trade published by T. Walls & Son Ltd., London, 1923. The previous summer, Wall's was one of the first businesses in Europe to start industrial production of ice cream.

• The ice cream was usually first delivered by van or horse-drawn cart to central locations, including such unlikely places as cricket pavilions. This helped mitigate the frustration of salesmen arriving at shops to be told that the ice cream was no longer wanted, as the weather had turned cooler or because delivery was too late. Retailers often had to return deliveries on discovering that the salted ice used to cool the product had pierced the packaging, tainting the ice cream. Another common mishap in these early days stemmed from shopkeepers failing to replenish the crates with fresh ice and salt, with the result that the ice cream melted. 'The prospects were certainly not good', as one of Wall's' future directors, G.A. Stonestreet, recalls in his description of that time. 'Neither the grocer nor the caterer seemed willing.'[8]

• Obstacles like these forced Wall's to look for a different approach to distributing its ice cream. Day-to-day management of the company was in the hands of Thomas Wall, Lionel and Charles Rodd and A.G. Short. The solution – delivery by tricycle, a method long used by bakers and other street vendors – was the brainchild of Lionel Rodd.[9] Crates of ice cream were fitted on rented tricycles and the first ice cream sellers set out to pedal the streets. One of those pioneers was Cecil Warren Rodd (1901-1961), son of Charles, and the 'Director's son' who had been sent to Chicago in 1922 to study American ice cream production. From Chicago he sent back a flow of information to Acton, where the ice cream department was equipped in accordance with his instructions.[10]

• Cecil Rodd was to become a director of Wall's in 1924, and later its Chairman; in the summer of 1922, however, he was still selling ice cream from a tricycle on the streets of London. 'The first few days I was out I was nothing but a 'Tricycle-pusher', that is, I went along the roads hoping that somebody would stop me and buy something', he wrote later in a message to sales personnel published in a Wall's brochure. 'Not many people did, and I could see that unless something was done to get sales I should lose my job, so I mustered up

WALL'S ICE CREAM PUDDING

is obtainable in the following twenty varieties:

1 Vanilla	8 Chocolate & Vanilla	15 Raspberry & Vanilla
2 Strawberry	9 Coffee	16 Tangerine
3 Strawberry & Vanilla	10 Peach	17 Tangerine & Vanilla
4 Banana	11 Pistachio	18 Ginger
5 Cherry	12 Pistachio & Vanilla	19 Coffee and Vanilla
6 Cherry and Vanilla	13 Pineapple & Vanilla	20 Cherry Pie
7 Chocolate	14 Raspberry	

PLEASE ORDER BY NUMBER

Packed in special containers and guaranteed to keep in perfect condition for four hours.

271: Page from Wall's sales brochure, circa 1928. The slogan 'Stop me and buy one', which was painted on all Wall's tricycles, had been thought up in 1922 by Cecil Rodd, who later became the company's Chairman.

all the courage I possessed and decided to go and try and get sales.'[11] Rodd then knocked at doors instead of travelling the streets and, slowly but surely, he managed to sell his ice cream. 'From a Tricycle-pusher I had become a Salesman.' The sales techniques he developed that summer were to prove invaluable to subsequent salesmen: 'Let me give a few "Sales Tips". The door may be opened by a kiddie. [...] If you are a married man and have children of your own, you will know how to deal with the kiddie. Make friends with them: there is no surer way to a Mother's purse than through a

kiddie's appeal.' It was Cecil Rodd who came up with the slogan 'Stop me and buy one'[12], which was painted on the side of the tricycles that became such a feature of the London scene, as well known as the chimes of Big Ben.

> 272: Sellers of Wall's ice cream with their trikes in front of the entrance to the factory in Acton, London, circa 1928. Until shortly after the Second World War Wall's ice cream was mainly sold by tricycle.

Wall's expands and starts advertising

• Using tricycles to deliver to the front door was an immediate success. True, the first season profit figure was not startling – from turnover of around £5,000 had to be deducted the costs of the ice cream, tricycles, equipment, depreciation, selling expenses and sundries amounting to a total of £3,677[13] – but the directors thought the results encouraging enough to warrant substantial investment for the new season. Four new ice cream freezers, each with a capacity of more than 22 litres, were installed to produce American-style vanilla ice cream bricks with a coating of chocolate (Eskimo Pie). Fifty new tricycles were fitted with insulated boxes at a total cost of £1,350. In 1924 the salesmen were issued with uniforms, boots and caps, in dark blue set off with white, and had their tricycles also painted dark blue. Distribution depots were established and in July 1924 the board invested £50,000 in setting up a second ice cream department in the sausage factory at Godley near Manchester.[14] The business flourished. Cecil Rodd concluded a contract with the Aerated Bread Company (ABC), a London business with a large chain of cafés.[15] In 1925 Wall's launched its first advertising campaign; it employed posters, for the Wall's board had doubts about the value of press advertising at a time when so few people read newspapers.[16]

• More Wall's tricycles appeared on the streets and people became familiar with the sound of their bell. Sales increased thirtyfold over five years, from £13,719 in 1924 to £444,000 in 1929.[17] In imitation of the American system, cards printed with a large W were distributed door-to-door at the beginning of the season. By displaying the card in the window, customers could tell the 'Wallsies', as the salesmen had been nicknamed, that they wanted ice cream. Inspectors were employed to ensure that the salesmen did not encroach on each other's sales patches. The ice cream sellers started work at 9.30 a.m., cleaning and loading their tricycles and completing their paperwork; at 10.30 a.m. they hit the road, being expected back by about 8 p.m. The insulation of the ice cream boxes was improved by replacing the cork lining with foam rubber, which was also lighter. Dry ice was introduced for cooling, further reducing payload. In 1927 Wall's decided to produce its own dry ice and the British Oxygen Co. equipped the Acton

273: Girl in a dress covered in Wall's ice cream tubs, circa 1927. This was a far from unusual sight: many women wore Wall's creations they had designed themselves. This specialised form of publicity was not restricted to ice cream or to the UK. In the same period, for instance, women in Germany wore dresses made entirely from newspaper advertisements for Persil soap flakes, while sporting an empty Persil box on their heads.

factory with a plant manufactured by the German company Esslinger.

• The most successful Wall's ice cream in those days was the 'brickette', a slab of vanilla ice cream eaten between two wafers that were supplied and paid for separately. 'Make your wafers pay for your boots', was the slogan, again devised by Cecil Rodd, that the salesman read inside the lid of his carrier box.[18] Initially Wall's bought its wafers from Huntley & Palmers, but later it started making its own wafers on the grounds that they were cheaper and, Wall's believed, of better quality than those of the biscuit manufacturer.

274: Tub of Wall's ice cream, circa 1925.

• In 1926 – alongside the 'brickettes', family-size bricks of ice cream, tubs of vanilla or strawberry ice cream and 'choc bars' – Wall's began making water-ices.[19]

275: Advertising leaflet for the Wall's Snofrute, circa 1948. The Snofrute was Wall's first water-ice, introduced in 1926 at the price of one penny.

This followed a board rejection of a proposal by the American ice cream manufacturer Joe Lowe that Wall's should start making the Popsicle (see chapter 5) under licence.[20] Instead, the Wall's Snofrute, made from pure Sicilian lemon juice and orange and lime juice from Africa and packaged in a cardboard triangle, sold for one penny and for many years proved extremely popular, being the cheapest ice in the range. In 1939 a record 25 million Snofrutes were sold. In 1936 Wall's added to its range the Snocreme, which came in the same triangular shape as the Snofrute but contained much less butter-fat than the customary 14% that Wall's used in its dairy ice cream at that time.[21]

• In about 1931 Wall's experimented by supplying 50 Manchester shops with ice cream that it delivered daily in large vacuum cylinders cooled with dry ice. Before dry ice, the delivery of ice cream to shops had involved costs of £70-£80 for the ice, the salt and the cabinet which the cylinder replaced. The new method cost only £5, with the consequence that whereas back in 1922 it had been very difficult to persuade shopkeepers to sell Wall's ice cream, the business was now overwhelmed with requests. This was a major breakthrough for Wall's on its way to becoming a large-scale ice cream seller.[22]

• Distribution and accounting systems were developed to accompany the growth that ensued. Throughout the length and breadth of the country depots were set up from which small grocery and sweet shops were supplied with ice cream by Ford Model T vans. Many depots were equipped with electric freezer cabinets in which a small buffer stock of 60 canisters of ice cream

276: Wall's Ford Model-T, circa 1928. One of the van's routes was between the Acton factory in London and a depot in Windsor.

could be stored. Coldstores were sub-sequently built in Birmingham and Southampton with a storage capacity of over 40,000 large canisters of ice cream.

• In the second half of the 1930s Wall's began to supply electric freezer cabinets to shopkeepers and restaurants.[23] Wall's also supplied cinemas, theatres, schools, clubs, dance-halls and Marks & Spencer stores. 'Without that account, Godley [the Manchester factory] would have been in very poor shape', wrote Wall's director G.A. Stonestreet;[24] and during a conference of Unilever managing

directors in 1934 Wall's directors described Marks & Spencer as their best customer.[25]

• At about that time Wall's Ice Cream began press advertising, overcoming its previous objections. Between April and August 1931 fortnightly advertisements were published in provincial newspapers with the aim of familiarising the public with Wall's sales tricycles and the price of their products.[26] The advertisements also set out to persuade consumers that ice cream was nutritious and not just a deli-

277: Wall's tricycles were not only used for ice cream sales. In around 1930 they were also used as a design for a doll's pram for children.

278: Horse races, cricket matches and other summer sport festivals, school parties, fêtes, bazaars, open air exhibitions and the like were popular venues for the sellers of Wall's ice cream (circa 1932).

cacy, reinforcing the slogan 'Wall's Ice Cream is a Food as well as a Sweet', which had been running since 1925.

• Hygiene was key. The image of ice cream in the United Kingdom was chiefly determined by the activities of Italian ice cream makers and reports of the conditions in which they worked (see chapter 4). Wall's advertisements therefore played up the certificate awarded by the Institute of Hygiene in 1926, claiming that its factory-made ice cream was risk-free.

In support, Wall's cited the view of the medical profession: 'For good health, the doctors say'; and, since other ice cream manufacturers had started selling ices from trikes, Wall's employed the slogan 'Wall's Ice Cream, only from the Blue Tricycles.'

279: Showcard with Wall's products, late 1930s. The ice cream tub was re-designed in the 1930s.

• The extent to which Wall's' technical ability had developed was demonstrated in 1935, when the company marketed an Ice Cream Pudding in seventeen different flavours.

This 'family treat' was packed in special cardboard containers and kept cold with dry ice. The addition of the word 'pudding' to the name of the product, which actually consisted of 100% ice cream, invoked a long British culinary tradition.

Eldorado and Lyons

• At the end of 1934 Wall's surveyed 250 Londoners of various income groups in order to identify consumer preferences, who ate ice cream and when and where it was bought. Only 12% of the respondents said they never ate it.[27] Most of those who did (49.5%) bought their ice cream from Wall's. A further 38% bought it from Lyons and 7.5% from Eldorado, two companies that had begun producing ice cream in the 1920s. The smaller of them, the Eldorado Ice Cream Company, was set up in 1924 in London by the Pure Ice Company, which since 1898 had been supplying ice to the capital's many daily markets from their premises near Black-friars Bridge. The arrival of electrical refrigeration reduced the demand for ice, leaving several of the Pure Ice Company's freezing machines idle. 'Let's think of something we can produce to keep our machines working', said the company's director, Sir Edmund Vestey, to his employees.[28] So in 1923 the Pure Ice Company began manufacturing ice cream, so successfully that in 1924 £5,000 was invested in setting up Eldorado as a separate ice cream company. Eldorado's 22 workers and two ice cream freezers could turn out 100 litres of ice cream an hour and, slowly but surely, the company grew to be the country's third-largest ice cream

manufacturer. By 1949 it employed 2,000 people and its machines had an hourly output of 27,000 litres. Later, in 1963, Eldorado merged with J. Lyons & Company Ltd., one of the two biggest ice cream manufacturers in the UK.[29]

• Lyons also had its roots in the nineteenth century. In 1894 the enterprising Joseph Lyons opened a tea shop in London serving tea and sandwiches, cakes and jam and simple lunches. The financial backing came from the tobacco company Salmon & Gluck-stein, which wanted to diversify its interests. One of its directors, Montague Gluckstein, had noted the poor quality of food and drink at trade exhibitions and resolved to try and offer a better quality catering service, beginning with the Newcastle Exhibition in 1887. For his experiment he wanted to use a name other than that of himself or his company, so Joseph Lyons, who had had experience of handling the catering at the Liverpool Exhibition[30], agreed to lend his name to the new business.

• After seven years of catering at exhibitions, Lyons opened his first tea shop, in Piccadilly. The intention from the outset was to set up a chain of such shops, to a standard design, favourably located to catch the passing trade and with prompt service provided by attractive, uniformed waitresses known as 'nippies'. The food, though of good quality, was cheap. In the 1920s the profit margin on a standard meal was just one farthing (a quarter of an old penny), for Montague Gluckstein's maxim was: better to have low profits on a high turnover than low turnover at higher profits.[31]

• Commuting office workers and housewives out on shopping trips soon confirmed Gluck-stein's business acumen.

280: Poster for Eldorado ice cream, 'A Pure Joy', early 1930s. London-based Eldorado had commenced production of ice cream in 1923. In 1963 the business merged with J. Lyons & Co. Ltd.

By 1920 Lyons was the biggest caterer in the UK, with 250 shops nationwide,[32] all supplied from the headquarters at Cadby Hall in West London. Around 1923 ice cream started to appear on the menu and in 1926 Lyons opened its own ice cream factory at Cadby Hall.[33] With its chain of tea shops Lyons – unlike Wall's with its sausage shops – had an immediate network of sales outlets for its ice cream. Lyons Pola-Maid Ice Cream was obtainable in two flavours – vanilla and strawberry – and was also sold in take-away packs.

• The Depression of the 1930s meant fewer jobs, and also a reduction in working hours, so there were fewer customers for breakfast or high tea. (Afternoon tea was taken at around 4 p.m.; high tea was more substantial and eaten around 5 p.m. to 6 p.m.). By contrast the company's wholesaling activities were experiencing enormous growth, with trains and vans transporting Lyons products to myriad shops and distributors. In 1939 there were 200,000 agents and distributors selling Lyons tea. The company produced 63,000 tons of bread and cakes and 3.5 million gallons (approximately 16 million litres) of ice cream,[34] slightly ahead of Wall's, which that year made three million gallons and for which 160 depots supplied a fleet of around 8,500 tricycles and bicycles and 15,000 shops.[35] Of the total UK market of some 20 million gallons, the remaining 13.5 million were produced by Eldorado and by an estimated 10,000 smaller ice cream producers like Jeffry's Cornish Ice Cream Ltd., founded in 1933. Many of the smaller businesses were hotels, restaurants and ice cream shops, often operated by Italians.[36]

• The small producers set up their own trade association in the 1920s: The Ice Cream Association. One of the members, Cremier Ice Cream Company, a subsidiary of United Dairies, was acquired in 1938 by Wall's for approximately £20,000.[37] Cremier sold mainly through London restaurants and the purchase gave Wall's a foothold in this market, as well as an insight into the requirements of restaurateurs and chefs. Because of this, Wall's was able after the Second World War to service the market for caterers, restaurants and hotels across the UK.

281: Advertising poster for Pola-Maid ice cream by J. Lyons & Co. Ltd., London, early 1930s.

The war years: 'Keep cool, keep calm'

• For the British, the Second World War began two days after the Nazi invasion of Poland on 1 September 1939, when Britain declared war on Germany. The following week Wall's advertisements appealed: 'Keep cool! Keep calm! You can still buy your Ice Cream from the familiar Blue Tricycle.

282: Wall's Ice Cream depot in Southampton, circa 1948.

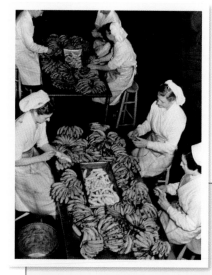

283: Peeling bananas in the Wall's ice cream factory in Acton, London, 1953. Eight years after the end of the Second World War, many products were still rationed, but bananas were now in supply once more, making it possible to produce banana ice cream again.

284: Man tipping a bag of sugar into the ice cream mix at the Wall's factory in Acton, London, 1954, the year sugar rationing ended.

285: Grinding vanilla beans in the Wall's factory in Godley, 1952. At the end of the nineteenth century it became possible to produce vanilla essence via a chemical process. This cheaper product was thereafter used by the foods industry on a wide scale.

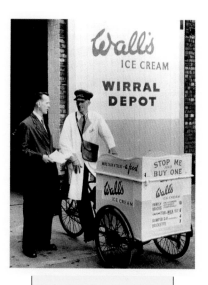

286: A Wall's salesman consulting the Wirral depot manager before setting out on his tricycle, 1953.

The trikes that went to war

¶ 'It may not have been Britain's 'secret weapon' but it was a surprisingly effective machine'. In a 1960 issue of Wall's Magazine Tim Butler, a former lieutenant-commander in the Royal Navy, told the story of 'the trikes that went to war'.

'Have you ever wondered what happened to ice cream trikes during the war? It might surprise you to know that they were called into national service – although they never actually came under fire.

'Most of you will have seen films of fighter aircraft taking off to intercept enemy bombers, and you may have heard the peculiar language used by the ground controllers to direct the pilots. In the Navy, these controllers were trained by directing modified ice cream trikes, "piloted" by Wrens.

'In those war-time days, fighter direction officers were trained at H.M.S. Harrier – a shore establishment near Haverfordwest in Pembroke-shire. Aircraft were needed for more important duties than ground control training, so an 'artificial' method had to be found. An anonymous genius suggested trikes.

'Each trike was fitted with a walkie-talkie radio, a metronome and a compass. A Wren impersonated the pilot – and

287: A 'Wallsie', as the public called the Wall's salesman, on his way to his customers, circa 1932.

the engine! A small range-finder was mounted on the football field to simulate a radar set. The trainee direction officers were accommodated in a nearby hut and equipped with boards on which they plotted the positions of the "aircraft" as reported by the "radar". They also had radio control over their "fighters".

'The fighters, using the trike's compass, were ordered to intercept the enemy. Speed was regulated by pedalling in time with the metronome, which was calibrated in knots. The fighter was not allowed to "sight" the enemy unless within a certain prescribed distance and in a good "attacking" position.

'Needless to say, "air disas-

ters" were not infrequent – often due to the fighter turning too tightly, too fast, overturn-ing or "spinning". Fortunately, heights were imaginary and thus no casualties were ever notified following a mid-air collision.'

Wall's Ice Cream is carrying on!'[38] But this optimism did not last. By early 1940 there were shortages of ingredients for ice cream, petrol for transport, packaging materials, oil for the manufacture of dry ice, and manpower. The distribution trikes came to a virtual standstill.[39] In 1940 the use of milk or dairy products for the manufacture of ice cream was banned. In October 1940 two Wall's ice cream factories were converted, at government behest, to margarine production.[40] In September 1942 the government issued a total ban on the production of ice cream and a few months later the authorities began requisitioning Wall's tricycles to distribute food to canteens at airfields, army camps and munitions factories.[41] The trikes were even used to train fighter direction officers (see box story on p. 286).

• Nonetheless, Wall's continued through 1943 and 1944 to work on improving its ice cream packaging and devoted thought to how it would conduct its production and marketing once the war was over.[42] The extrusion and cutting of blocks of margarine were to prove good preparation for the post-war production of ice cream of the Eskimo Pie type.[43] At the end of 1944 ice cream production was permitted once more and manufacturers began preparations for the 1945 season. On 30 November 1944 the board of Wall's, attending a Unilever Managing Directors Conference, said that the factory in Acton would be capable of producing 10,000 gallons (approximately 45,000 litres) of ice cream per week, to be distributed through shops equipped with Wall's freezer cabinets.[44]

• After the war there were global food shortages, but the UK, which had been accustomed to importing much of its food, was particularly badly hit. Important raw materials for ice cream production, such as butter and sugar, would in normal circumstances have come from the Commonwealth countries of New Zealand and Jamaica. Sugar beet was not cultivated in the UK. Many vessels had been lost during the hostilities, resulting in a shortage of shipping capacity.

• Consequently, many products, including sugar, were rationed. It was forbidden to use cream in the making of ice cream and supplies of milk remained disrupted. This prompted manufacturers to use vegetable fats, often in combination with milk powder. (Unilever, with its margarine technology, was well placed to develop such recipes.) Various types of animal fats were also tried.[45] Imports of 'swephat' ('sweet fat'), a blend of sugar and whale oil, were permitted and were sourced by Wall's through businesses in the Netherlands, Sweden and Norway.[46] Some experiments were unsuccessful. Rapeseed oil, for example, was found not to be suitable, and cod-liver oil was rejected because its characteristic flavour could not be removed. Groundnut oil from tropical regions proved more acceptable and the business later began using palm oil and coconut oil, sourced principally from Asia.

• Even after most of the rationing ended in 1953, Wall's' standard ice cream was still produced using vegetable fat. The British public had grown used to the taste and it was much cheaper than using dairy fat. Until 1959 98% of Wall's ice cream was made with vegetable fats,[48] only changing with the introduction of new labelling regulations that stipulated that a product claiming to be 'dairy ice cream' had to be made with dairy fats. In 1959 Wall's used 5,000 tons of vegetable fat; this figure dropped in 1960 to 3,800 tons

288: Vendors with boxes of Wall's ice cream in the North Devon seaside resort of Barnstaple, winter 1948. Wall's conducted a test in Barnstaple that year to explore ways of sustaining ice cream sales through the winter months.

plus 2,000 tons of butter;[49] but in 1975 almost half of the ice cream Walls produced was still being made with vegetable fat. This pattern was typical of all major UK producers, and even of some in other European countries. In 1960, for instance, 80% of the ice cream production of the Italian manufacturer Algida was also made with vegetable fats (see chapter 15).

After the war: 'Ice cream. More than a Treat, a Food'

• Raw materials for traditional dairy ice cream were rationed but the product itself, now almost always made with vegetable fat, was not. On the other hand, sugar and chocolate confectionery were both still rationed. According to a survey published in 1938, the British were second only to the Danes as the most sweet-toothed nation in the world, with a per capita annual consumption of 110 pounds of sugar.[50] Demand for ice cream as a replacement for sweets or as a sweet dessert therefore grew tremendously. Every restaurant offered ice cream on its menu and taking home a 'brick' of ice cream was a popular treat.[51]

• The post-war period transformed Wall's from a business that had sold about 90% of its ices via tricycles before the war into one that sold 90% of its ices via shops.[52] Sixty-six of the 160 depots had been destroyed by bombs and it became clear that lack of man-power would render large-scale distribution using trikes unsustainable.[53] In October 1947 Wall's sold 3,300 tricycles and early in 1948 invested £40,575 in 750 new Sterne freezer cabinets for installation in shops.[54]

289: Ice cream at a cricket match. Advertisement for Wall's, May 1951.

290: Page from a Wall's sales brochure for the retail trade, circa 1950, part of a campaign to convince the shopkeeper to sell ice cream to 'Mrs. Housewife' in the winter.

291: Design for a small window poster for Wall's, January 1951.

292: Design for a window poster for Wall's, January 1951.

• Wall's now began to contemplate continuous production and sales throughout the year as a way of offsetting seasonal costs. The task was to persuade consumers to eat ice cream between October and March. Before the war, ices had been eaten in the winter in theatres, cinemas, dance-halls, music halls and restaurants, but not at home.[55] To help develop home consumption, market research was needed. Which products, at what prices, might induce consumers to buy ice cream regularly in the winter? How would they react to new advertising and selling techniques? Wall's developed a test campaign together with Ivor Cooper of Lintas, Unilever's advertising agency. The campaign ran in the Devon seaside resort of Barnstaple (population 43,000) between October 1947 and April 1948.[56] An unusual feature of the campaign was that Wall's managed their raw material supplies so as to provide an unlimited supply of their ices, including dairy ice cream. 'The test was designed to provide experience and information that would be of value in planning a

293: Inspection of ageing tanks containing ice cream mix in the Wall's factory at Craigmillar, near Edinburgh, 1951.

national selling campaign once the supply position was sufficiently eased to allow for an intensification in selling plans', said a report from 1947.[57] Like its American counterparts, Wall's emphasised the nutritional value of ice cream in its Barnstaple test and used new advertising slogans: 'Ice cream. More than a Treat, a Food' and 'Take home some Wall's Ice Cream'.

• The Barnstaple experiment proved a mine of information. When rationing was abolished in 1953, Wall's was able to make an immediate start on nationwide advertising campaigns. Although the sun continued to be the ice cream seller's best salesman, the campaigns succeeded in getting 'Mrs. Housewife', as the consumer was described in those days, to serve ice cream in the winter. The 35,000 or so sales outlets selling Wall's ice cream welcomed the additional sales.[58] Apart from grocers, dairies,

I love Mummy, Daddy.. *and* Ice Cream

· ISSUED BY THE ICE CREAM ALLIANCE ·

294: 1952 poster for the Ice Cream Alliance, London, designed by Thompson-Bennett. Silkscreen print (51 cm x 38 cm). The Ice Cream Alliance is the organisation representing the UK's smaller ice cream producers. In the early 1950s the Alliance published a poster at the beginning of each new ice cream season as part of its annual collective advertising campaign.

department stores, cafeterias and restaurants, many of these outlets were the corner shops that sold sweets, tobacco products and newspapers. These CTNs (Confectionery, Tobacco, Newspapers) stocked only one brand of ice cream. That, too, was characteristic of the market. 'This is a unique feature of retailing in this country, and it is on this particular aspect that our policy tends to diverge from what is normal on other sides of the Unilever business', said the chairman of Wall's Ice Cream, J.D.O. Knowles, in 1960. Wall's had gained 6,000 new sales outlets in that year, which he described as 'a very good omen for the future, because it is absolutely vital that we increase availability in order to develop the market for Wall's and not for someone else's ice cream'.[59] Contrary to what might be inferred from Knowles' words, the practice of exclusive ice cream sales via retailers had already been in existence since the 1920s elsewhere in the world, for example in America, Denmark and Switzerland (see chapters 5, 10 and 12).

• When commercial television began in 1955, Wall's seized the opportunity. A cartoon commercial was created by the French puppeteer Yves Joly featuring the amusing adventures of 'The Wallsies'. The spots were broadcast twice a week in the London area, with the message "Take home some ice cream!"[60]

• During the late 1950s TV advertising became increasingly important for Unilever. In 1956 13% of the advertising budget handled by Lintas was spent on television. In 1957 it was 26% and in 1958 around 40%.[61] On television and in cinema, Wall's advertisements ended with the jingle 'You can't help falling for a Wall's'.

Cinemas: eating ices in the dark

• In the meantime, sales of industrial ice cream in Britain had taken off and most ice cream manufacturers were booking good profits. Production capacity was expanded in 1948 when Wall's opened its third factory at Craigmillar near Edinburgh. In 1955, 100 million gallons of ice cream – five times as much as before the war[62] – were being produced by the 3,000 ice cream manufacturers. In 1956 a new manufacturer appeared, soon to capture a substantial market share: Neilsons Ltd., a subsidiary of the Canadian Garfield Weston group.

"It's a cinch!" with these 4 favourites

A smash hit to draw the crowds

WALL'S FRUTIES

WALL'S CHOC BARS

WALL'S TUBS

Wall's ICE CREAM — most people prefer it!

MARKETING HEADQUARTERS

295: Advertisement for Wall's ice cream in a 1955 cinema magazine. The photo is of the then 31 year-old Marlon Brando who, with co-stars Frank Sinatra and Jean Simmons, was currently a big box-office hit in the film comedy Guys and Dolls, directed by Joseph L. Mankiewicz.

Walls *Frutie* – the 15 minute drink 6ᴰ

IT'S A WALL'S PRODUCTION –

ALREADY A PROVED SUCCESS!

EXHAUSTIVE pilot-tests carried out in a number of cinemas have proved that there is a tremendous demand for this new Wall's line. Ice Cream sales which averaged 1½d. per head of admissions before the introduction of Frutie, consistently exceeded 3d. after the introduction of Frutie. In some cases Frutie accounted for half the total ice cream sales.

HERE'S YOUR CHANCE

to make a substantial increase of your all-round ice cream sales. Stock up with Wall's Frutie – your sales per head will soar – and you'll make much more profit!

FRUTIE IS MADE FROM FRESH JUICY ORANGES

WALL'S Frutie is made with fresh juicy oranges. The rich liquid, obtained by crushing whole oranges, is used to make a cool, refreshing, frozen, non-drip drink-on-a-stick. So deliciously different – everyone will love Frutie in its attractive foil pack.

YOUR NEW FROZEN ASSET

296: Page from a Wall's sales brochure for the retail trade, 1955. In that year the ice cream manufacturer launched a new orange-flavoured ice lolly under the name Frutie. The ice was well received and sold unexpectedly well in cinemas.

• Lyons' own efforts to stimulate winter sales of ice cream were helped by a contract with Associated British Cinemas (ABC); and in 1958 Eldorado acquired the exclusive rights to sell ice cream in the Essoldo cinemas, giving it 20% of the cinema market.[63] Wall's also competed in this sector, with such products as the Gaytime, launched in 1952, and the Frutie ice lolly (a 'drink-on-a-stick'), introduced in 1955 as the successor to the pre-war Snofrute. They became best-sellers in cinemas and theatres, with the Frutie being seen as the product that persuaded adults to eat ice lollies. 'Partly as a result of the success of Fruties in the cinemas, where they are eaten in the dark, we have at last begun to over-come adult resistance to this type of product', said the marketing director of Wall's,

J.A.A. Beer, in 1960 during a meeting with Unilever's Special Committee.[64] How-ever, it would be another generation before eating an ice lolly outdoors was seen as acceptable by the majority of adults in the UK. The British were less accus-tomed to eating ice cream in the street than other Europeans, partly perhaps because of the British climate. During a 1978 survey conducted by Wall's in London and Paris, only 51% of Londoners said they would eat an ice cream in the street, compared to 77% of Parisians.[65]

• With the advent of television in the 1950s more and more cinemas closed their doors and their importance for ice cream sales declined rapidly.

297: Advertise-ment for a family pack of Wall's raspberry and vanilla ice cream, May 1960. The slogan 'You can't help falling for a Wall's' was intro-duced at the end of the 1950s.

Of nearly 5,000 cinemas in the UK in 1950, only 1,500 remained in 1977 – by which time attendance figures had plummeted to a mere tenth of their 1956 level.[66]

• The Wall's factory at Acton, meanwhile, was bursting its seams and there was a clear need for a new facility to be built. The chosen site abutted the railway line outside Gloucester; good new roads aided the delivery of supplies and the disappearance of the local aircraft industry meant that skilled personnel were available in numbers. Between 1959 and 1961 a modern factory was built, with a bakery for the production of wafers and cones.

• In 1983 the decision was taken to invest £65 million in a major expansion of the Gloucester factory.[67] Three years later the

298: Poster for Wall's Gaytime choc bar, circa 1954.

299: Poster for Wall's Gayfrute ice lolly, circa 1954.

factory boasted an enormous new production hall with sixteen production lines, plus a new coldstore. Computers guided products to the correct pallets and then transported the pallets to the coldstore, where they were placed automatically in the right rack. The wafer and ice cream cone bakery in Gloucester was also refurbished and extended. (This business was 50% owned by Lyons, and operated independently, producing products for both.) The Acton factory was closed in 1986, the Godley and Craigmillar factories having been shut down in the early 1960s. In concentrating production, Unilever was pursuing in the UK the same course it had already adopted with its margarine and detergents factories in Europe.[68]

The Wall's organisation in the 1950s and 1960s

• Compared with the period that followed, interest in novelty ices was slight in the 1950s, the main emphasis being on family packs of ice cream. This changed in the late 1950s with the advent of the Danish Gram RIA machines (see chapter 10), a number of which were installed in Wall's' Acton factory in 1958.[69]

• Prior to this, the thrust of innovative endeavour is typified by the launch in 1952 of an oblong wafer tray into which a 'brickette' would fit. The tray was invented and patented by Embisco Ltd. (Empire Biscuit Company), owned by the brothers A.A.G. and 'Joe' Marcantonio, and was marketed under the name Headmaster. Wall's took an immediate interest, producing it under licence and selling it under the Wallsie name,[70] and shortly afterwards bought Embisco for £137,000, thus acquiring sole rights to use of the tray's patent.

The Wallsie continued to sell successfully in the UK until the 1970s and was also sold for many years in Belgium, the Netherlands and France by Unilever ice cream firms.

• Soon after the war Wall's was operating an extensive fleet of insulated delivery vans and lorries for the distribution of its products. In

300: Long row of tanks filled with ice cream mix in the Wall's factory in Gloucester, 1962.

1947 experiments began with door-to-door sales by ice cream van.[72] The vans were identified by their chimes, like the Good Humor vans in America and later also in Belgium (see chapter 13). In the summer, vans stationed themselves in seaside resorts, in parks and at swimming-pools, children's playgrounds, sporting fixtures – anywhere, in fact, where there were crowds. The vans were assembled in the company's own workshops on bought-in chassis, an arrangement shared with the Wall's Meat company until 1955 when the two businesses were formally split.

• Maintenance of the freezer cabinets supplied to shops was also handled by Wall's itself from a large workshop in Southall, Middlesex, where teams stood ready to repair faulty appliances.[73] In the early 1960s Wall's, together with Lyons, set up a firm called Total Refrigeration, whose hundred or so fitters handled freezer maintenance for both manufacturers. In 1965 Wall's and Lyons decided to contract out the supply and maintenance activities to Prestcold, a specialist subsidiary of the British company Pressed Steel that manufactured freezer cabinets for the professional market. Wall's and Lyons each took a 25% stake in the venture 'in order to ensure proper priorities in the ice cream season'.[74]

302: 1961: One of the eight fully automated ice lolly machines, made by the Danish engineering firm Gram, in the Wall's factory in Gloucester, which had just been opened. The machine could produce 15,000 ice lollies per hour.

303: Cans of ice cream are loaded onto pallets in 1960 in the coldstore at the Wall's factory in Acton, London.

301: Poster, circa 1956, for the Ice Cream Alliance, designed by Thompson-Bennett (50.5 cm x 38 cm). 'At work or leisure Ice Cream gives pleasure'.

304: Wall's 'Athenian ices sales stand' during a charity fireworks display at Edenbridge, Kent, in 1952. The 'Grecian' columns of the stand were intended to lend a certain air of distinction to the whole structure. The stand was mobile and was fitted with plenty of lights to help promote ice cream sales outside the summer season.

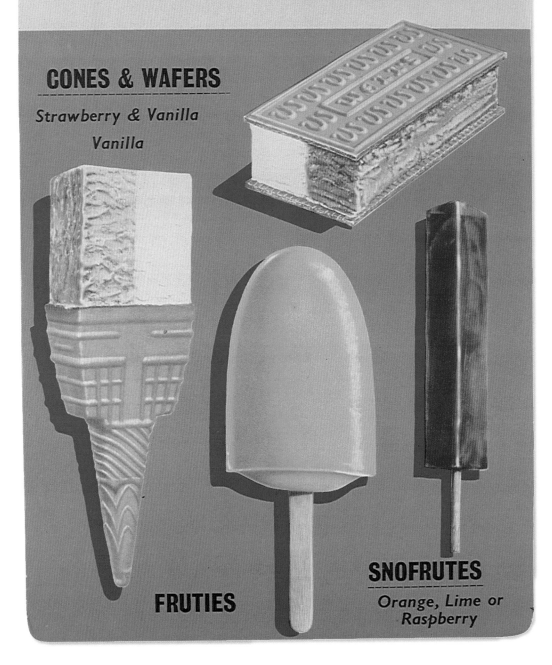

Have a Wall's

CONES & WAFERS

Strawberry & Vanilla

Vanilla

FRUTIES

SNOFRUTES

Orange, Lime or Raspberry

306: Making ice lollies at the Wall's factory in Acton, London, 1960.

307: Poster for the Wallsie', circa 1953. Besides being the name that the public used to describe the Wall's salesmen, 'Wallsie' was also the name for a brick of vanilla ice cream sold in specially designed cones. In 1952 Wall's had bought Embisco Ltd. principally in order to gain access to the square-shaped cones that Embisco had begun marketing, into which a standard brickette of Wall's ice cream fitted exactly.

308: Advertisement for Wall's ice cream in a weekly magazine, 1955.

309: Window poster advertising Wall's, circa 1952. The mother's leather-gloved hand is showing her children a family pack of ice cream: 'It's all goodness!'

305: Showcard for Wall's, 1961.

310: Showcard, circa 1950.
Tommy Wall's makes the W sign of
Wall's outside a confectionery,
tobacco and newspaper shop.
Wall's introduced the Tommy Wall's
figure at the end of the 1940s.

311: Page from the boys' weekly comic, The Eagle, of
23 June 1950 with a Tommy Wall's comic strip. Between
1950 and 1952 there was a new Tommy Wall's adventure
every week. Eating Wall's ice cream enabled Tommy to
perform superhuman feats and pull off amazing rescues.

312: The finishing touches to a Crinoline Lady ice cream gâteau in 1956 in the Gâteau Room of the Wall's factory in Acton, London. Ice cream gâteaux like this one formed part of the Wall's range well into the 1970s.

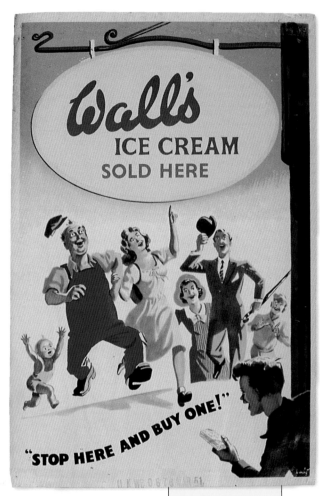

313: Display poster for Wall's, March 1951. After the Second World War shopkeepers took over the selling function from the tricycles.

314: Wall's van supplying The George and Dragon pub in Chipstead, Kent, in 1954.

• For the successful sale of weather-dependent products like ice cream, detailed planning is vitally important and demands the effective co-ordination of numerous information flows and activities in the areas of raw materials purchasing, manufacturing, quality control, transport, storage, marketing, sales and personnel. 'The Planning Office is in reality the nerve centre of the business', declared the Wall's director J.G. Short in 1960.[75]

• Part of that planning process involved keeping weekly records of the average weather conditions in order to calculate the effect on sales. Erroneous interpretations of weather forecasts could mean the difference between profit and loss. The greater accuracy of weather forecasting brought by satellites, the increasing skill at matching production volumes to sales and the longer shelf-life of products all helped, but poor summers still took their toll. As with other Unilever businesses, improving the quality of the planning process at Wall's was the subject of continuous effort, with support from Unilever head office, aimed at optimising manufacturing, transport and selling and marketing activity. After the introduction of the centralised product group co-ordinations in 1966, systems became more and more sophisticated. Unilever's global ice cream activities continued to expand and international knowledge began to supersede local methods, as national and local strategies came to be influenced by expertise gained in other countries (see chapter 21).

Mr. Softee and Mr. Whippy

• In the meantime Lyons was not idle, having taken over various ice cream manufacturers shortly after the war: Walkers Dairies Ltd. in Liverpool in 1947, Glacier Foods Ltd. (mainly a manufacturer of ice lollies) in Maidenhead in 1951 and in 1954 the Dorchester-based Massarellas Supplies Ltd. In 1957 Lyons opened a big, new factory at Bridge Park, Middlesex.[77] The long warm summer of 1959 led to record sales and ice cream continued to ride high until 1962 when the government

315: Mr. Whippy ice cream van, circa 1965. In the 1960s Mr. Whippy and Mr. Softee, subsidiaries of Wall's and J. Lyons & Co. Ltd. respectively, battled doggedly for the market for soft ice cream. Sometimes the specially designed vans with their noisy signature tunes arrived in the same streets within minutes of each other.

decided to introduce a 10% sales tax on ice cream, causing manufacturers difficulties. Lyons attempted to reduce costs by purchasing the ice cream businesses of Neilson and Eldorado in 1962 and 1963 respectively, then closing the Eldorado factory in London and gradually assimilating the successful products of the two acquired companies. In 1965 came the purchase of the London company Bertorelli, which was well known for the high quality of the ice cream it supplied directly to restaurants and hotels.

• By now Lyons was no longer just a business that traded in cakes, tea and ice cream and operated restaurants. Its diversified activities now also included a chain of hamburger restaurants (Wimpy), a frozen foods company, the production of bitter lemon and LEO computers (Lyons Electronic Office). The formation of J. Lyons International Ltd. followed in 1973 and the group expanded abroad.

316: Early in the autumn of 1960, Wall's Ice Cream salesman Arthur Rainbird delights children on the Hangleton Estate in the south coast resort of Hove with a 'Wallsie'.

In Europe, hotels, meat-processing businesses and manufacturers of cakes and biscuits were acquired. In the United States Lyons began selling tea, while the tea shops in its home market were renovated or closed. The dairy and ice cream company Midland Counties Dairy Ltd. was purchased in the early 1970s, meaning Lyons was operating four ice cream factories and 70 depots.[78]

• In 1959 Lyons began to equip some of its vans for the production of the cheaper 'soft' ice cream, a product that had been highly successful in America (see chapter 6). It bought the exclusive rights to

manufacture and distribute Mr. Softee soft-ice mix from the American business Mister Softee International Ltd. In 1969 Lyons acquired Tonibell, a company that sold soft-ice and scooped ice cream from vans. Wall's, too, recognised the popularity of soft-ice and, of the 900 or so Wall's ice cream vans selling ice cream direct to consumers, some 150 also supplied soft-ice.

• In 1962 Wall's introduced special 'mini-vans' to sell soft-ice[79] and the following year entered into talks with the Forte company about acquiring its soft-ice business, Mr. Whippy. This business had been set up in the 1950s by Burton Saunders from Ipswich, but since its acquisition in about 1960 by Charles Forte had been operating at a loss.[80] Wall's became half-owner of Mr. Whippy, with its fleet of 900 vans, and used this stake to rationalise its system of depots. The joint venture was still reporting a loss of over £500,000 in 1965,[81] but Wall's persevered, becoming full owner of Mr. Whippy in 1966.

Lyons Maid | *New* FAMILY BRICK | *New* Eating Pleasure | VANILLA

PULL OFF PERFORATED BAND AND TAKE OUT INNER SLEEVE

PULL HERE

317: Pack from a brick of Lyons vanilla ice cream, 1960.

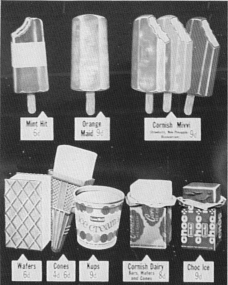

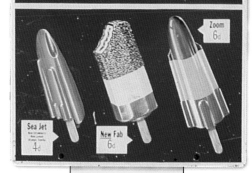

318: Lyons price list from the mid-1960s.

By 1974 the market had altered radically, due principally to the emergence of super-markets, and Wall's moved its Mr. Whippy activities onto a franchise basis. In 1978 there were some 1,200 independent Mr. Whippy vans supplied with their soft-ice mix by Wall's, about the same number as today.[82]

'Just one Cornetto'

• In 1955 Unilever's world-wide co-ordinator for foods, J.P. ('Jamie') van den Bergh, noted – rightly – that there was still 'plenty of scope in the impulse purchase trade'.[83] After the installation of Gram RIA machines in 1958, Wall's began to devote more attention to such products and in 1964 began marketing the Cornetto ice cream cone, a product that originated from its Italian sister-company Spica and had recently been launched in Belgium and Germany. The introduction was not a success – the price was high and the cone had a tendency to sogginess – and further test-marketing in 1970 only confirmed Wall's in its decision not to go through with a full launch.
• In 1976, however, the new chairman of Wall's, Hugo Mossel, felt that the time had come for another try. Before his arrival in the UK, Mossel had been the chairman of Iglo-Ola in Belgium, where the Cornetto had been successful. To start with, therefore, Cornetto was sourced from the Ola factory in Belgium.
• The Wall's sales organisation viewed Mossel's proposal to try again with much scepticism.[84] But partly thanks to an extra-ordinarily warm summer, and to the quality of the Belgian product, the Cornetto this time proved a resounding success and in the years

that followed Cornetto was to benefit from the most successful advertising campaign in the company's history. Italy was the country in which, according to the British consumer, the best ice cream in the world was made, so the TV commercials were shot at famous Italian locations and the melody of the Italian love song 'O Sole Mio' was commandeered to accompany the words of 'Just One Cornetto'.[85] The storylines, which featured people abandoning their usual roles to grab a Cornetto, went down a storm with the British public. One of the original commercials was awarded a Silver Lion at the Cannes Advertising Film Festival of 1977 and the campaign was taken up and re-used by dozens of comics, cartoonists and TV performers. In the four years to 1980, Wall's tripled Cornetto's advertising spend to £1 million and was rewarded with a tenfold increase in sales to £20 million (see box on p.614).

• Cornetto's success was undoubtedly helped by the strong rise in spending power in the UK after 1964. It also led to development of the notion that impulse ice cream, as opposed to family packs, has a high price elasticity. 'This implies that for impulse ice cream, prices may be raised above the rate of inflation without harming volume sales, real revenue or real profits',[86] claimed a 1970 Unilever study.

• The 1970s brought a boom in impulse ices, particularly for children. The production of fantasy shapes derived from the world of children was made more exciting thanks to a technical innovation by Wall's and Iglo-Ola Belgium. In about 1976 the development department began experimenting with ice moulds made from rubber instead of metal. Using rubber moulds it was possible to produce ice lollies in the shape of cartoon

319: Wall's price list, 1965. The price of the Cornetto had been reduced by threepence following its unsuccessful launch the year before. The 1976 relaunch of a greatly improved Cornetto was to be a resounding success, with sales increasing tenfold in just four years.

characters like Spiderman, Tom & Jerry and the Muppets. After research lasting almost two years, the first of the ices manufactured using this process, a cartoon caveman figure called Silex, rolled off the conveyor belt in Baasrode in Belgium. A year later, the Gloucester factory began production[87] of a black Dracula figure designed by the British sculptor Bob Donaldson.[88]

The 1980s: Birds Eye and Wall's join forces

• The increase in prosperity in the 1960s also prompted rapid growth in the number of households with refrigerators, which in the 1970s came to incorporate generously sized freezer compartments. From 13% in 1972, the proportion of UK households with refrigerators had risen by 1979 to 48%.[89] At the same time the number of supermarkets also grew. Cash & Carry stores appeared on the scene, as did the British phenomenon of the home freezer centre, whose long rows of freezer cabinets bulged with a huge variety of frozen foods and ice cream products. When supermarket chains like Sainsbury, Tesco and Safeway started marketing packs of ice cream under their own brand, they became a formidable competitor in the ice cream market. Their commercial clout gave supermarkets the leverage to negotiate lower prices from ice cream manufacturers resulting in pressure on their profits.
• Further efficiency improvements and rationalisation by the manufacturers were essential. One of the biggest cost items in the ice cream business is distribution. In the early 1960s Wall's had started to work with Birds Eye, Unilever's British frozen

foods business.[90] In 1966 an umbrella company, Unifreeze, was set up to handle joint distribution via the company Unilever SPD (Speedy and Prompt Delivery). The chairmen of both companies had a seat on its board of directors. The intention was that the sales representatives of Birds Eye would also sell Wall's ice cream to greengrocers and supermarkets, while the Wall's sales force would sell Birds Eye frozen desserts such as Arctic Roll to traditional Wall's outlets. The joint operation was not an entirely happy one, however, and towards the end of the 1970s, when the profitability of both companies began to decline, the Rotterdam-based team of Johan Erbé, Unilever's co-ordinator for the ice cream and frozen foods product group, reached the conclusion that only a complete merger of the two businesses would achieve the required cost savings, for example through greater negotiating power with the supermarket chains. Unilever had already amalgamated its ice cream and frozen foods operations in Germany, Austria, Belgium, the Netherlands and Italy, but those rationalisations had been less drastic because they affected smaller or newer businesses. For Wall's employees the announcement in 1980 that their company was to be combined with Birds Eye came as a major shock. After almost 60 years, the autonomy of Wall's had come to an end.[91]
• The merger process was energetically tackled by Don Angel, the chairman of Birds Eye Wall's, as the new company was to be called. During the 1980s Birds Eye Wall's, following the example set by Sages, Unilever's ice cream and frozen foods business in Italy, began to switch over to an ice cream distribution system based on the use of

concessionaires. By about 1988 that process was complete, with 42 concessionaires handling distribution of the company's ice cream products.

• The profitability of the ice cream activities of the new business was given a major boost by the successful launch in 1982 of the Viennetta ice cream gâteau. Viennetta had been invented by Kevin Hillman, a development manager at Wall's (see Viennetta box story in chapter 21) and within three years sales climbed from £3 million to £23 million.

Lyons Maid becomes part of Nestlé

• Lyons' many acquisitions and expansions in the 1960s and early 1970s had mainly been financed with borrowed funds.[93] When the world was hit by economic recession following the 1973 oil crisis, Lyons got into financial difficulties. Interest rates were rocketing and it became increasingly difficult to keep up with the repayments on foreign loans. At the end of 1974 Lyons was forced to sell its 50% stake in the UK branch of the Findus frozen foods operation to its co-owner, Nestlé. That was followed in 1976 by the sale of its hotels for £27.6 million to Trust House Forte Group.[94] After more than 80 years, the family business came to an end in 1978 when Lyons' remaining operations, including its ice cream activities, were sold to Allied Breweries Ltd.[95]

• However, Lyons Maid's ice cream activities did not prosper under the new management. More and more market share was lost to Wall's. Between 1983 and 1986, for example, Lyons Maid's share of the take-home ice cream market fell from 12% to 8%. In the same period the share of Wall's went from 22% to 27%, one of the chief reasons being the success of Viennetta.[96] Lyons Maid's loss of share was even more marked in pre-packed impulse ices where, over a period of ten years from 1976, Wall's' share increased from 50% to over 70%, largely on the back of brands like Cornetto and Feast and a vigorous innovation programme for children's products.

• The policy of rationalisation that Allied Breweries implemented at Lyons in the 1980s (two ice cream factories were closed down in 1982), coupled with the low level of investment in new products and high discounts to the trade, did nothing to halt the slide[97] and in December 1991 Allied Breweries decided to sell Lyons Maid to the American businessman Henry Clarke, the owner of Clarke Foods. Clarke had turned the Klondike Bar into a national brand in America and had then sold it to Unilever (see chapter 6). Earlier in 1991 Clarke had already acquired three other, smaller British ice cream businesses (Fiesta Ice Cream Company, Lewis Bros. Ltd. and Mor-Isis Ice Cream Ltd.). Now, in 1992, its first real ice cream season in the UK, Clarke Foods got off to a flying start. Renovation started on the factory in Stourbridge and in the spring, with the backing of a substantial advertising campaign, the company launched a series of new premium ice creams under the Clarke name, including an equivalent of the Klondike Bar. But delays to the factory's renovation impeded supply of products and Lyons Maid customers turned to other ice cream manufacturers such as Wall's. The costly advertising campaign had been in vain. Although Clarke had solved the supply problems by about June, the weather then

HOW ICE CREAM IS MADE

Wall's

RAW MATERIALS
The fine quality of Wall's ice cream begins with the freshness and pureness of the ingredients which come from all parts of the world. To the factory in Gloucester comes:

COFFEE mainly from West Africa

FRUIT from Britain and New Zealand

VANILLA from Madagascar and Tahiti

CACAO (for chocolate) from West Africa

SUGAR from The West Indies

MILK from Britain and New Zealand

VEGETABLE OILS from Ghana and Malaysia

BUTTER from Cornwall, New Zealand and Denmark

ICE CREAM PRODUCTION ENGINEERING WORKSHOP COLD STORE CONES AND WAFERS

VEHICLE REPAIRS OFFICES & LABORATORIES STAFF CANTEENS BOILER HOUSE COLD STORE ASSEMBLY TRAINING CENTRE

LABORATORIES

All ingredients are subjected to analytical testing and physical inspection. The laboratory is also responsible for factory hygiene.

QUALITY CONTROL Testing is carried out at all stages of the production process to ensure absolute purity and high quality.

PRODUCTION

This modern ice cream producing factory, pleasantly situated in 65 acres of Gloucestershire parkland has been designed especially to allow for flexibility in plant layout. 3 miles of internal roads link the various units with the main road at the site entrance. Daily production is approximately 90,000 gallons of ice cream, 2,500,000 lollies, 2,500,000 wafers, 1,000,000 cones, 2,000,000 brick-ettes, and 500,000 family sweets besides many ice cream puddings and desserts for hospitals, restaurants, shops, cinemas, canteens and homes. Manufacture is largely controlled by automation.

1. STORAGE VESSELS Hundreds of tons of liquid raw materials are pumped straight from the delivery tankers into these storage vessels.

2. ELECTRONIC BRAIN Here is the Control panel from which all the mixing processes are controlled.

3. MIXING TANKS Automatically measured ingredients are pumped into these tanks for mixing at the rate of 6,000 gallons per hour.

4. THE PASTEURISER Now the mixture circulates in this machine and is held at a temperature of 91°C (178°F) for 25 seconds. This ensures purity.

5. MORE STORAGE VESSELS After pasteurisation the mixture goes into these huge vats where it is stored at temperatures between 5°C (40°F) and then pumped to the freezers at the rate of 6,000 gallons per hour.

6. THE FREEZER Here the various mixtures are reduced to a temperature of -5°C (23°F) and the finished ice cream goes out for cutting and packing.

7. BRICKETTES Are formed on this machine, frozen and passed on to the packing belt for automatic wrapping.

8. GRAM RIA This machine can make 15,000 ice lollies per hour.

9. COLD STORE Ice cream is stored in pallets each containing 200 gallons which are stacked by fork lift trucks designed to operate in a temperature of -27°C (-18°F)

10. DISTRIBUTION These huge supply vans each carry 20 tons of ice cream to the Wall's depots throughout the country. It is delivered to the customer untouched by hand

11. RETAIL VAN The driver has been specially trained in road safety.

PRESENTED BY WALL'S ICE CREAM

---

took a turn for the worse and a very wet summer followed. This was the death blow for the company. The market share of Clarke Foods/Lyons for impulse ices fell in value, in just that one year, from 18% to 10%.[98] In October a small supplier filed for the bankruptcy of the company; the administrators looked for a buyer, which they found in Nestlé.[99]

• And so, from 1992, the ice cream giants Unilever and Nestlé began competing for the UK consumer's favour. That consumer had

> **320: Poster showing the ice cream production process at the Wall's factory in Gloucester, 1961.**

been able, since 1990, to enjoy a tub of Häagen Dazs or Ben & Jerry's ice cream in London's Leicester Square or a Mars Ice Cream from a vending machine. Someone living in or visiting Devon – a county famed for its clotted cream – might still prefer an ice cream from the Devonshire Farmhouse Ice Cream Co., which in 1992 was one of many successful regional producers. These small businesses, often still bearing Italian names, continued as before to make and supply their ice creams.

Licks, Sticks & Bricks

A WORLD HISTORY OF ICE CREAM

Ireland:

'a brick after

mass'

9

DECEMBER, 1960

Hughes News

Until recently most Irish families looked upon Sunday lunch as the main meal of the week. It was the time when the whole family gathered together for a meal after attending morning mass. A big oven-roast was put on the table and for dessert there was often ice cream, cut from a vanilla 'brick', with fruit sauce sometimes added. It was a real treat, representing for children the highlight of the week: the 'brick after mass'. 'Make every day a Sunday, take home a brick today', went the advertising slogan by the ice cream company, Hughes Brothers, commonly known in Ireland as HB.

• The origin of this Sunday custom is very much linked to the agricultural and Catholic traditions in the Republic of Ireland, traditions that are still strongly embedded in that society today. A large proportion of the population lived in the countryside, in cottages and farmhouses that were often situated in remote areas. In 1926, 61% of the Irish did not live in towns or villages.[1] Sunday was a day of rest and in the morning people went to mass. In 1990, 90% of the Irish in the Republic were Catholics and 82% still went to church regularly.

• In the hard existence of many rural Irish, a visit to church was a welcome break and people would take the opportunity while in town to do some shopping. When

321: Cover of HB's house magazine, Hughes News, December 1960, with a picture of Hazelbrook Dairy. The factory had just been totally renovated and extended.

mass was over, Father headed for the pub with his pals, while Mother took the children grocery-shopping and then went home to prepare Sunday lunch. Where money allowed, those groceries would include a brick of vanilla ice cream packed in a carton and tightly wrapped up in newspaper for extra insulation. Back home it would be placed in cool cellars or in simple refrigerators without a freezer compartment. The vanilla brick has become the ice cream icon of Ireland: in 1969, more than 40 years after its introduction, it was still the most successful product in the HB range.[2]

• Until the beginning of the 1960s people in Ireland lived in some seclusion from the rest of the world. Consequently, the range of products available in the shops was rather limited. A brick of vanilla ice cream, for instance, was one of the few ready-to-eat desserts. In plain Irish cooking there were few alternatives to ice cream as a dessert, unlike in, say, France, Italy or Spain where a meal typically ends with fruit, cake, ice cream or cheese.

• Another reason for ice cream's popularity in Ireland is that it was relatively cheap. It was quite feasible to keep the price low in a country which enjoyed a high level of milk production, low labour costs and an ample availability of sugar from sugar-beet. According to a 1972 estimate, ice cream prices in the Irish Republic in the mid-1960s were some 30-40% lower than in the United Kingdom.[3]

• The Irish origin of many of the raw materials for ice cream also played a role. It fuelled a sense of national pride. A 1968 press release by HB refers with satisfaction to the use of 'Good Irish Sugar and Glucose', adding that '80% of the product is in the form of pure Irish milk and cream from our hills and valleys'.[4] Ice cream also retained its popularity because eating habits changed more slowly in Ireland than elsewhere in Europe.

• These agricultural, economic, social and culinary factors provided fertile ground for ice cream businesses like HB and help to explain the relatively high level of ice cream consumption in Ireland. At 8.3 litres per capita, Ireland is – with Sweden – at the top of the European ice cream consumption charts. But when and how did this come about? How did ice cream find its way onto the Irish menu? And how did HB become Ireland's biggest ice cream company?

Ice houses

• In 1665 Theobald, Earl of Carlingford, acquired the exclusive right to build and operate 'snow houses or ice houses' in Ireland for a period of fourteen years.[5] In this he was following a fashion instigated five years earlier by Charles II, who on his restoration to the throne in 1660 had commissioned the construction of an ice house in London's St. James's Park (for more about ice houses in general, see chapter 2). Charles II had prior to 1660 spent many years in exile at the French court and, perhaps as a consequence, it was during his reign that the English nobility made their acquaintance with ice cream. In any event, ice cream featured on the menu at the Feast of St. George held at Windsor on 28 and 29 May 1671.[6]
• It is not known whether the Earl of Carlingford used snow and ice from his ice houses to freeze his ice cream, but it seems plausible that the customs of the English court found their way to the nobles who lived in Ireland. In fact, there were established in Dublin in the 1680s[7] at least three confectioners, the tradesmen who traditionally prepared ice cream for the nobility in Europe at that time (see chapter 3). By the mid-eighteenth century the popularity of ice

cream had increased to such an extent that there was felt to be a market in Dublin for a cookery book with instructions on how to prepare it. The Compleat Confectioner, by Hannah Glasse, was published in 1742 and was an adaptation of a book published under the same title in London in 1733 by Mary Eales. This 'confectioner to her late Majesty Queen Anne' had been the first person in England to publish an ice cream recipe in a cookery book back in 1718.[8]
• Thus, via England, ice cream gradually started to appear on the menu of the Irish nobility and gentry. The confectioner John Kelly, whose premises were at 40, College Street in Dublin, will no doubt have had such customers in mind when he wrote on an invoice in 1799 that he could supply 'ices of various Sorbets, Italian Ice, fruits and ice fruits of every Denomination [...] which are ready every day from Ten in the Morning Till Twelve at night, and will be sent [....] to any Part of the City'.[9]

The Italian connection

• The vast majority of the Irish population, however, only got to know ice cream at the end of the nineteenth century when Italians started selling it on the streets of Dublin. In his short story More pricks than kicks, published in 1934, the Irish playwright Samuel Beckett gives a description of Pearse Street, 'that is to say, long straight Pearse Street with its two Cervi saloons, ice cream and fried fish'.[10] Beckett was referring to Dublin's oldest ice cream saloon, opened in 1916 by the Italian Lorenzo Cervi. Lorenzo's father, Giuseppe Cervi, originally

322: Italian immigrants pose in front of their ice cream cart, circa 1912. Italians had started selling ice cream on the streets of Dublin at the turn of the century.

from a small village south-west of Rome, had arrived via the port of Cóbh and settled in Dublin in 1882. He started a boarding house in Little Ship Street, close to the city's notorious main police station, the Castle. His customers were mainly Italian seasonal workers and émigrés who, as in other countries, had during the nineteenth century come to comprise a small Italian community (see chapter 4). Like Lorenzo Cervi, many of them had ended up in Dublin via Cóbh. Others had first moved via London to Scot-

land and later settled in Belfast or Dublin.[11]

• In the summer of 1896 Giuseppe Cervi mustered a sizeable number of Italian seasonal workers from his boarding house to make ice cream in his back garden. Cervi bought the raw materials and provided the equipment. His workers prepared the ice cream and sold it on the streets from wooden carts they had knocked together themselves. It was now the turn of Dubliners to become familiar with the street vendor's cry of 'Ecco un poco', (Try some! - see chapter 4).

323: Dublin, 1920: the
Italian ice cream vendor
Antonio pictured in front
of an ice cream van of
the firm of Borza & Son.

• In Ireland ice cream making thus became the main livelihood of many Italians. The 1911 census recorded 417 Italians – men, women and children – of whom around 300 lived in Dublin. The most frequent professions were ice-cream vendor (64) and confectioner (33). In 1988 there were 2,359 Italians in Ireland; 500 of them, or 46% of the Italian working population, stated that their profession was that of ice cream vendor.[12]

• And yet the Italians are not primarily known in Ireland as vendors of ice cream. They are associated much more with 'fish and chips'.[13] Given the rainy Irish climate, this was a sector in which many Italians thought they were more likely to earn a living than by selling ice cream. It was therefore a fish-and-chips shop which Lorenzo Cervi

first opened in Pearse Street, his ice cream saloon following a full decade later. Just as in some parts of the United Kingdom, especially in Wales and Scotland, the Italians ran what in Ireland were known as 'double shops', shops that had two counters: one for fish and chips and one for ice cream.

• In 1922 the fiercely fought-for Irish Republic became fact and one year later, when the Irish civil war had also been settled, the path was clear for further economic development. Three Italians joined forces to set up their own factory for the production of natural ice, The Modern Irish & Cold Storage Company. In Dublin such factories – indispensable to the modern brewing and fish-processing industries – had first been established around 1900.[14]

• Gradually ice cream became more and more a part of daily life. The 1927 edition of the Dublin directory mentioned wholesalers in ice cream for the first time. They were Italians: Bernedetto Forte and a Mr Macari. The directory also contained the address of a firm selling ice cream powder mix, the Twinem Brothers.[15] Lorenzo Cervi modernised his business in 1926 by purchasing electric ice cream making machines, enabling him each day to produce five to ten gallons of ice cream.[16] In the 1930s the Italians Cafolla and Antonio Cervi opened up elegant ice cream saloons in O'Connell Street in the centre of Dublin which soon became very well known.

• It was not uncommon for an artisanal ice cream business to grow into an industrial operation.[17] In 1947 Capaldi, an Italian from Glasgow, opened two ice cream-cum-coffee shops in Dublin and a few years later he founded the ice cream company Palmgrove Ice Cream Ltd. The business was a success, Palmgrove's inexpensive ice lollies proving particularly popular. In 1955, Capaldi was the first person in Ireland to install a Gram RIA machine for the mass-production of his ice lollies.[18] With the purchase of this revolutionary Danish ice cream machine (see chapter 10), Palmgrove automated the previously labour-intensive manufacturing process for ice lollies and increased its production capacity substantially. In 1970 Palmgrove's market share was estimated at 13%.[19]

• Palmgrove was eventually sold in 1981 to Premier Co-op Milk, which closed it two years later. Nowadays the Dubliner who wants to eat Italian ice cream goes to the ice saloon of Forte Gelateria Ltd. on Parnell Square. Influences that have blown over from America are still making themselves felt. Not only can the ice cream fan order a 'Knickerbocker Glory' at Forte, but the shop also proudly bears the title 'Soda Fountain', originally an American phenomenon (see chapter 5). The 'Knickerbocker Glory' was an English variant of the 'Knickerbocker Sundae', an ice cream that came out of New York at the end of the nineteenth century, the name deriving from the wide-bottomed pantaloons worn by Dutch sellers which the Sundae glasses, when upside down, resembled.

Hughes Brothers

• The development of industrial ice cream production in Ireland, however, was dominated not by the Italians but by the Irish themselves. Many of the first small ice cream factories were established in the Dublin area, not long after Irish independence in 1922. They were mainly dairies which sold their products in Dublin and also produced ice cream during the summer season. Near the village of Rathfarnham, in the shadow of the hills south of Dublin, the oldest and today largest Irish ice cream company, Hughes Brothers (HB), began production in 1926. The countryside around Rathfarnham then consisted of extensive grazing pasture, dotted with the occasional farmhouse. Now the farms have made way for housing estates, shops and industries, including HB, and the village has become part of the Dublin conurbation.

• The foundations for HB were laid in 1898. That was the year when William and Margaret Hughes built a big, new farmhouse in Rathfarnham, calling it Hazelbrook. The farm flourished; their herd of Shorthorn

324: Hazelbrook Dairy, the milk and ice cream factory of Hughes Brothers (HB), photographed in 1927. Established in 1924, the factory was located in Rathfarnham, then a village to the south of Dublin. The present HB factory, renovated in 1960, is situated not far from this spot.

cows expanded; and they steadily increased the acreage under pasture. In 1906 William Hughes died and his sons James, George and William took over the reins. These were the men who in 1924 set up Ireland's first dairy factory at Hazelbrook at a cost of almost £4,000.[20] They installed a state-of-the-art Danish-made pasteuriser and bottling machine capable of treating 1,000 gallons of milk a day, representing a revolution in a poor country like Ireland. The brothers financed this substantial investment by selling their herd of 170 Shorthorn cows and two Friesians.

• The Hughes brothers' switch from cattle to milk treatment and distribution had been prompted by a crisis in Irish cattle farming. Foot and mouth disease was rife, the winters of 1923 and 1924 were particularly wet and, to make things worse, a six-month strike of port workers in 1923 slashed farmers' earnings from cattle exports.[21] With their background in cattle, but also because they were the first to operate a dairy factory in Ireland, the Hughes brothers had little difficulty in securing a local milk supply.

• In 1926 the brothers made another momentous decision. They invested money in ice cream machines so that in the spring and the summer, when cows yield more milk, the surpluses could be used to produce ice cream. That seemed much more promising than feeding the milk to the calves or even churning it to make butter.[22] The new ice cream machines were driven by electric motors. The electricity for the machines was supplied by a generator, since Ireland as yet had no electricity grid. In its first ice cream season HB produced 8,000 pints.[23]

325: Hazelbrook House, Rathfarnham, Dublin, circa 1925. William and Margaret Hughes started a farming business here in 1896, which was later expanded by their sons to become Ireland's biggest ice cream company: Hughes Brothers.

at £67,[24] an enormous outlay when the average weekly wage in Ireland was less than £2.50. HB was one of the earliest companies in Europe to place cabinets, free of charge, with their retailers.

• As well as the refrigerator, HB supplied the shopkeeper at cost with a stainless steel knife and a marker. The marker was used to divide up the block of ice cream into eleven portions which were then cut off using the knife. The ice cream was placed between two wafers and sold for tuppence (2d or two old pence). The retail margin was 100%.[25]

• In those days most ice cream was still sold not in shops but by street vendors. In November 1926, however, HB achieved a major commercial breakthrough when it won an exclusive contract to supply ice cream to the Irish branches of F.W. Woolworth, the American store chain. Up until 1922, Woolworth had been supplied by an Italian ice cream maker in Dublin,[26] but now the company started to look around for a new supplier. HB got wind of this and contacted the Woolworth's representative for the British Isles in Liverpool. The upshot was that Woolworth became HB's best customer, selling more ice cream at Christmas time than any other shop in Dublin.[27]

Frigidaire with generator

• Electricity for the few refrigerators to be found in shops and cafeterias was also provided by generators. But then, at the end of the 1920s, HB took the initiative and installed refrigerators (from Frigidaire in the USA), along with the necessary generators, in cafeterias, grocery stores and other outlets so they could sell HB ice cream. For the time this was a remarkable sales technique, especially in view of the investment needed for each refrigerator: one freezing unit plus generator worked out

326: William Hughes (1874-1946), one of the three Hughes Brothers, pictured c.1935.

327: George Hughes (1877-1952) pictured in the late 1920s.

• HB's products were of a high quality. During inspections their milk was usually stamped as 'very good' and 'rich'. Thanks to this quality and the great sense of enterprise that the brothers showed, the business soon built up a good reputation in Dublin and for miles around. Sales of the company's ice cream, which had been advertised since the early 1930s under the slogan 'The Cream of Hospitality', developed favourably. In 1938 ice cream sales were worth £22,000 and the milk turnover was £58,000.[28]

• Gradually, cold storage depots were set up throughout the country. According to a list from 1938, there were depots in Cork, Limerick, Tipperary, Donegal and Wexford. Transport to the depots was by rail or bus, from the depots to the shopkeepers by horse and cart. The ice cream was packed in solid cardboard boxes which were placed in canvas-lined, cork-insulated shippers, each holding 45 bricks, the exact capacity of the original fridge freezer. If there was a heatwave, the result was a shortage of canvas shippers, because shopkeepers did not return them on time.[29]

• In 1933 a continuous Vogt freezer machine was installed which produced an uninterrupted flow of ice cream, in place of the previous batches.

328: Vanilla ice cream 'brick' from the Irish ice cream company Hughes Brothers (HB), dating from about 1960. This type of ice cream had been in HB's range from the very start of its ice cream operations in 1926. Today, it is still one of HB's best-selling products.

This American machine, manufactured by Cherry-Burrell, enabled the ice cream mix to be kept at constant low temperatures and also allowed much better control of the quantity of air added to the ice cream (see also chapter 5). In its first year of operation the new Vogt machine produced half a million bricks of vanilla ice cream.[30]

• At the end of the 1930s HB suffered a major setback. James Hughes, the commercial brains behind HB's success became seriously ill. Financial problems arose,[31] and the company's predicament demanded the active involvement of its bankers. In 1939 representatives of the Royal Bank took a seat on the board and HB's independence as a family business came to an end.

329: Pen and ink drawing of James Hughes (1879-1944), another of the three Hughes Brothers.

HB after the war

• Ireland was one of the few countries in Europe that was not caught up in the Second World War, having adopted a policy of neutrality. Though wartime austerity put the brake on further economic development, the production of milk and ice cream remained largely unaffected.

• Shortly after the war, in 1947, HB modernised its dairy factory. An ultra-modern pasteuriser was installed and the range of ice creams expanded. The following year, HB introduced the Irish to chocolate-coated vanilla ices. These 'choc-bars' soon became just as popular as in other parts of the world.

• In 1952 the Irish Government introduced new regulations stipulating what could and could not be deemed ice cream. Henceforth a product could only be called ice cream in Ireland if it contained at least 10% fat (of which half was to be milk-fat), 9% other solids and 10% sugar by weight. HB decided that it would no longer use 12% milk-fat as it had done since 1924, but the minimum of 5% set under the new regulations. HB also added 5% vegetable fat to its ice cream, so that it contained a total of 10% fat.

• In the 1950s new distribution methods were introduced. The insulated canvas bags were replaced by refrigerated cells, which HB built itself and fitted to the chassis of its delivery vans.

• Between 1952 and 1960 HB doubled its ice cream sales[32] capturing around 40% of the Irish market. By 1959 the company was producing six million bricks of vanilla ice cream per year, an increase of 1,200% in 26 years.[33] (A small proportion of this production was exported to Northern Ireland.) This growth led to the purchase of new machines and expansion of the factory. Eight new coldstores were built, each with a capacity of twenty tonnes of ice cream. A brand-new ice cream production depart-

330: Cover of HB's house magazine, Hughes News, December 1961. At that time the business still had a stable of 60 horses as part of its distribution effort. The horse-and-cart was mainly used to transport milk, but also 'Cream Ices', as can be seen from the sign above the driver's head.

ment was also added to the factory in which HB installed three new Gram RIA machines, each with an output of 1,100 to 1,200 ice creams on sticks per hour.

• From the arrival of the first machine in 1959, HB was able to market new types of ice creams (see also chapter 10). First in this series was a vanilla ice on a stick called the Golly Bar, which retailed at threepence (3d) and is still popular with children today. It owes its name to a children's book published in 1895, The Adventures of Two Dutch Dolls and a 'Golliwogg' (see box on p. 326).

Modernisation and concentration

• In 1959 Séan Lemass became Taoiseach (Prime Minister) of Ireland. He succeeded Éamon de Valera[34], the éminence grise who had controlled Irish politics almost without interruption since 1932. Lemass set about modernising Ireland and broke away from his predecessor's conservative policies. For the first time in its history Ireland sought to attract substantial foreign investment[35] and, with the launch of the TV station Radio Telefís Eirean in 1962, Ireland acquired its own window on the world, its television viewers no longer being obliged to watch BBC transmissions from Britain.

• The new policy towards foreign investors had major consequences for the Irish dairy and ice cream industry. In 1964 the American international group W.R. Grace & Co. bought the crown jewel of the sector, HB, and instantly acquired some 40% of the Irish ice cream market to add to the Irish chocolate factory Urney it had bought the previous year.

• Grace had been founded in 1854 by the Irish emigrant William Russell Grace. Until the early 1960s the company had mainly been active in the chemicals industry. In 1962 the group widened the scope of its operations and started making sizeable investments in the food and consumer goods sectors in both the US and Europe. The purchase of HB formed part of this new strategy and the Americans wasted no time introducing the company to modern management and marketing techniques. Market research was tackled in a professional way; planning and accounting were revamped; and the construction of a completely new factory was announced.

• Grace's arrival on the Irish market was the immediate reason for the merger between the other three main companies producing milk and ice cream: Merville Dairies, Dublin Dairies and Sutton Dairies. In 1966 they amalgamated to form Premier Dairies. Another firm, Lucan Dairies, had already sold its ice cream interests to HB and merged its milk business with its remaining dairy operations. Like HB, Merville Dairies, Sutton Dairies and Lucan Dairies had all been established around the turn of the century, in 1890, 1884 and 1898 respectively. These companies were Protestant; with the support of the Catholic Church, Dublin Dairies had entered the market in 1947,[36] attracting large numbers of religious institutions as customers. Regardless of religious orientation, however, the modernisation which started in the 1960s made it clear that so sparsely populated a country as Ireland could not sustain so many dairies and ice cream factories.

• Two years after the Premier Dairies merger an even more sweeping development

occurred in the Irish dairy and ice cream industry. In 1968 the newly formed Premier and HB concluded what was known as the 'milk for ice cream' deal. HB acquired the ice cream interests of Premier, which in return took over HB's milk activities. This agreement gave HB about 80% of the Irish ice cream market, leaving Palmgrove Ice Cream and Suir Valley as its only competitors in the Republic. The main competition now came from Northern Ireland, where Northern Dairies controlled around 40% of the market.
• On 10 July 1968 the Irish prime minister, Jack Lynch, officially opened the new ice cream factory at Rathfarnham. The complex, covering an area of 56,320 sq. ft., was one of Europe's most modern ice cream plants. Its construction had involved an investment of £1.3 million, including some £300,000 of subsidy from the Irish Government. A substantial part of the investment was spent on an array of new ice cream machines, enabling the production of a whole range of different products. Two Vitaline machines and five Gram RIA machines provided a combined production capacity of 88,000 ice lollies per hour.[37] Five Rose Forgrove machines were together capable of turning out 20,000 bricks of vanilla ice cream per hour, whilst a Flex-E-Fill and a Drumstick handled the production of ice cream tubs and cones. Two Benhill machines produced 7,000 Golly Bars per hour – foil/paper-wrapped plain portions of vanilla ice cream on a stick. The freezing of the ice cream took place using a method that was regarded at the time as the very latest technology: the 'Rollerbed' system (see box on p. 328).
• From the outset it was clear that the new factory, which employed about 150 people,

had a bigger production capacity than was justified by HB's position in the Irish market. Even working only one shift, the new factory had an aggregate capacity of fifteen million litres of ice cream per year. With continuous shiftwork this figure could easily be doubled. Grace therefore planned expansion not only within Ireland, but also into international markets.[38] There were prospects of exports to the neighbouring United Kingdom. Since 1966 Grace had also been the owner of the Danish ice cream company Helerup Is; and it held a majority stake in the share capital of Tanara S.P.A. in Italy.

Unilever

• The developments in Ireland were being closely monitored by Unilever. In a study in 1970 the group's Economic & Statistical Department analysed the potential threat of Grace to the British market.[39] The Lintas advertising agency was forecasting that the next five years would see the number of supermarkets in Britain quadruple. For food manufacturing groups, therefore, it was vital that their products continued to be stocked on the shelves of this sales channel.
• The Unilever study noted how several supermarket chains, including Tesco, were increasingly developing their own, cheaper brands and selling them in their outlets. This could be expected to put pressure on the more expensive, well-known manufacturers' brands. The Unilever report looked into the possibility of HB starting to supply British supermarket chains with own-brand ice cream and concluded that such a co-operation might be highly profitable for both

¶ What do the composer Claude Debussy, the author James Joyce, a jar of Robertson's jam and HB's Golly ice cream have in common? They are all connected by the 'golliwog', a black-faced rag doll that was created at the end of the nineteenth century. The doll was a grotesque figure topped by a shock of black hair and dressed in bright-coloured clothes.

In 1908 Debussy composed the work he called 'Golliwog's cake-walk', part of the 'Children's Corner' suite that he wrote for his little daughter Chouchou; James Joyce immortalised the figure in his novel Ulysses ('Madcap Ciss with her golliwog curls'); Robertson has used the figure on their jam jar labels ever since the 1920s; and HB launched the still-popular 'Golly' vanilla ice cream in 1959.

For decades the Golly was a much-loved figure in children's playrooms in America, England and Ireland. Golly (or 'Golli') was at least as popular as the teddy bear. Both figures were created at about the same time: the teddy bear in 1903, named after the US President Theodore 'Teddy' Roosevelt, the Golly a couple of years before that. The teddy bear was specially designed as a cuddly

toy and only found its way into children's books later. But with Golly the situation was exactly the opposite. This figure started life in a children's book, 'The Adventures of Two Dutch Dolls and a Golliwogg', written by Florence and Bertha Upton of New York and issued for the first time by an English publishing house in 1895. The book was a tremendous

331: Illustration from a 1923 edition of the children's book The Adventures of Two Dutch Dolls and a Golliwogg. Golly, a rag doll and the main character in the book, was a popular figure in children's playrooms for decades. In 1959 that popularity gave HB the idea of using the name 'Golly' for a new vanilla ice cream on a stick.

success and was reprinted many times. The illustrations in the book were by Florence Upton, the story by her mother, Bertha. The Golly figure was inspired by a doll that Florence had played with as a child. Presumably this was a 'minstrel' doll,[1] an easy-to-make imitation of the white actors who, 'blacked up' and colourfully dressed, acted as 'Negroes' in what were known as 'minstrel shows'. These largely song-and-dance shows began around 1820, going out of vogue after victory for the Union in America's Civil War (1860-1865).[2]

There was no copyright on Florence Upton's creation, so her Golly soon became widely used. Toy manufacturers like Steiff, Merrythought, Hermann and Deans put their own versions on the market. 'Golliwog' also became the name of a popular dance. In 1907, for instance, an English newspaper wrote: 'A clever golliwog dance received the enthusiastic applause it deserved'.[3]

And over the past 70 years jam manufacturer Robertson has rewarded the patient collectors of tokens attached to its jam jars with hundreds of thousands of Golly gift articles. In the main, these have been in the form of enamel badges and brooches, but clocks, watches, aprons, knitting patterns, porcelain figurines, dolls, pens and erasers have also been issued.

In dozens of children's books Golly started to lead his own life, often a completely different life from the one his creators had in mind for him. Whereas in the Uptons' book Golly was loveable and courteous, in later books he turned into a gawky, ugly Negro figure

HB ICE CREAM LIMITED, WHITEHALL ROAD, RATHFARNHAM, DUBLIN 14, IRELAND.

MIN. CONTENTS: 3.33 fl. oz. (95ml.)

332: Golly Bar wrapper, 1998. The Golly Bar, a vanilla ice cream on a stick, was introduced by HB in 1958. Forty years later it was still on HB's product list.

with unsympathetic character traits. The stories in which he appeared sometimes now had racist undertones and when society became generally more aware of racism in the early 1960s, toy manufacturers and publishers hastened to delete Golly from their catalogues.

In the 1980s, however, Golly became popular again, thanks to not children, but adults. Golly articles have become sought-after collectors' items. For a number of years there has been an International Golliwog Collectors Club with its own newsletter and manufacturers can see benefits in producing the Golly doll again. Over the years Robertson and HB, unruffled, have successfully continued with Golly, although HB's pack design has been gradually re-styled over the years.

¶ Before the advent of the 'Rollerbed' system, ice cream in most ice cream factories in Europe was frozen in hardening tunnels. When the chilled, but still not frozen ice cream came off the production line, it started a slow journey by conveyor belt through long, narrow tunnels in which the average temperature was -25°C. At the end of its journey the ice cream would be rock-hard and frozen solid. It was then packed and despatched to the coldstore.

In the Rollerbed system the ice cream, already packed in standard cartons, moves via the conveyor belt on to a broad bed of steel rollers, the Rollerbed. There are two such beds installed in the HB factory, each 100 metres long and comprising 550 rollers. Fifty cartons can be placed across the breadth of one roller. Every time that the conveyor belt has lined up 50 cartons at the beginning of the Rollerbed, the entire batch is automatically transferred from the belt onto the first roller of the bed. The previous row then moves on one place. A photocell ensures that the rollers only start to operate after a new row of fifty cartons has been placed on the bed. The rollers push the cartons forward until, row by row, the

ROLLERBED

SAVES SPACE / SAVES LABOR / REDUCES HARDENING TIME

UNLOAD AREA

PALLET STORAGE

333: In 1960 HB built a new ice cream facility. For freezing the ice cream a 'Rollerbed' was installed: a broad bed of steel rollers over which the ice cream, packed in cartons, is slowly pushed along. Blasts of ice-cold air from four freezers ensure that the contents of the cartons are frozen. In this way 6,000 cartons, each containing some 6.5 litres of ice cream, can be processed per hour. In 1997 the installation was still working well.

bed becomes entirely filled. In the 'Rollerbed' chamber an Arctic wind ensures that the cartons of ice cream gradually freeze. Four King freezers fitted with powerful fans continuously blow air at a temperature of -40°C over the cartons of ice cream as they move over the rollers. By the time the cartons have reached the end of the bed, they are

frozen and are then transported to the coldstore built beneath the Rollerbed. The coldstore is kept at the required temperature of -20°C using air from the Rollerbed chamber.

In this way a Rollerbed can process 6,000 cartons per hour, each containing approximately 6.5 litres of ice cream. More than 30 years after it was first installed, the system continues to function perfectly, the original King machines still blowing their blasts of Arctic air.

parties. By exporting to Britain, HB would be better able to utilise the capacity of its new factory. Exports would also attract subsidies and tax benefits. In return, supermarkets could count on a regular supply of good-quality ice cream at an attractive price.

• The Unilever study also established that joint ventures existed between Grace and the British company Lyons Maid which might lead to cooperation between the two in the area of ice cream. Lyons Maid was the main rival of Wall's, Unilever's ice cream business in Britain (see chapter 8).

• In the autumn of 1972 Unilever started talks with Grace about a possible purchase of HB. Unilever and Grace already knew each other from earlier meetings at the negotiating table, since in the previous year Grace had sold its Danish ice cream interests to Unilever.[40] However, the HB negotiations did not go easily, a major stumbling-block being the Urney chocolate factory. Grace had bought this Irish business in 1963 and had linked its accounting and management closely with those of HB. But Urney was unprofitable, so Grace would only sell HB to Unilever if Urney were included in the deal. Agreement was eventually reached in March 1973, with Unilever paying £5.2 million for the two companies.[41] Unilever sold Urney a couple of years later.

• It was not only HB's potential threat to the British market that prompted Unilever's purchase. With a market share of about 80%, a brand-new factory and some 10,000 sales outlets throughout the country, the Irish ice cream business was a healthy operation whose profit expectations exceeded even Unilever's high standards. In addition, the accession of the Irish Republic and the United Kingdom to the EEC in 1973 opened up new market opportunities for HB in Northern Ireland, with trade between North and South likely to become simpler since trade barriers would be removed. Membership of the EEC also meant Ireland would benefit from agricultural and export subsidies. These were introduced for milk and powdered milk and government support for investment increased.

• Another reason behind Unilever's move for HB was the fear that Grace might sell the company not to Unilever but to the American foods group Beatrice Foods,[42] a competitor that had already been active for several decades on the American and European ice cream market (see chapter 6).

• Unilever's acquisition of HB certainly did not mean the end of HB's own ice cream specialities. Successful local ice creams, such as Wibbly Wobbly Wonder, Brunch and Golly, still feature on pricecards. The Irish continue to buy the original vanilla brick, still packed in its cardboard carton, in large quantities and it tastes exactly as it did in 1952, the year when HB modified its recipe in line with the new regulations. But, alongside these local ice cream products, Irish consumers can also now enjoy a Magnum or a Solero - in the same way that they can go out for a meal in Dublin and choose between Japanese, Indian, Spanish or French cuisine - while their children surf the Internet as they lick a Golly Bar.

Licks, Sticks & Bricks

A WORLD HISTORY OF ICE CREAM

The Danish technological revolution

10

In 1917 a number of Danish confectioners united to form the Is-Konditor-Foreningen.[1] Since the end of the nineteenth century confectioners had been supplying Danes with ice cream. They fulfilled that role not always as independent producers, but certainly as sellers (see on box p. 334). As late as 1960, 150 of the 400 sales outlets of the Frisko ice cream factory in Copenhagen were confectionery bakers.[2]

• The huge popularity of nougat ice cream amongst Danish consumers also has its origins in this confectionery bakers' tradition. The same can be said of another ice cream based on a traditional product of the confectionery world and which remained a favourite in Denmark more than anywhere else in Europe: the 'Isbaade' (Ice Cream Boat). The name refers to the boat-shaped tray made from dough, into which the ice cream was put and then had chocolate sauce poured over it. Industrial ice cream manufacturers, too, marketed the Isbaade. In 1954, for example, one of Denmark's oldest ice cream companies, Hellerup Is, used posters to advertise its 'boat' ice cream in Copenhagen. They depicted burly sailors praising the product.[3] The Isbaade is still popular to this day.

• Industrial ice cream production really got under way in Denmark after 1925.

334: A fitter working in the Gram factory in Vojens in about 1950. Behind the man is an RIA mould table, standing on its side, with a diameter of over 2.5 metres.

As in many countries, the key factor underlying its development was a successful dairy industry which grew thanks to its close links with the industrialising economy of nineteenth century England. To meet increasing English demand for butter and pork, Danish farmers started to concentrate more and more on dairy cattle and pig farming. The emphasis in Danish agriculture had hitherto been on the cultivation of grain, but by around 1880 that situation had undergone a transformation. The introduction of a fast, continuous-operation centrifuge which enabled cream particles to be separated from milk – an invention of the Swede Gustav Laval – opened up new methods for the processing of milk. Agriculture expanded and dairy factories and slaughterhouses were established all over Denmark. As in Germany, and later also in Sweden, these businesses were cooperatives whose membership included both large and small farmers. By about 1890 one in every three Danish farmers sent his milk to a dairy cooperative and about one-third of the country's pork exports were processed in cooperative abattoirs.[4]

• Danish agriculture would never have been able to respond so successfully to developments were it not for important constitutional and social changes that had taken place. Some half a century earlier, in a Denmark that still had a distinctly feudal structure, there arose a people's emancipation movement in which liberal-minded large landowners also took part. A powerful motor behind this development was the adult education system which, fuelled by Danish Romantic nationalism, took shape in the years that followed 1844.[5] After the new constitution had been adopted in 1849, the changes were codified in a series of laws. Farm tenancies for life were abolished and during the 1850s a new group of independent farmers emerged. As a result of the further clearing and reclamation of the heathlands in Jutland, more and more land was made suitable for cultivation. Also important was the establishment in 1829 of

'The most beautiful woman of Skoubogade'

334

¶ In La Glace, the confectionery shop-cum-café at Skoubogade 5 in the heart of Copenhagen, it is good and crowded. Seated at small marble-topped tables that have gilded legs, customers sip their coffee and enjoy their cakes. In front of the large mirror behind the long counter the sales ladies dressed in white are as busy as bees. The copperwork of the counter, top gleams and the glass display cases sparkle. In the windows on either side of the shop door are decorative displays of gâteaux. The shop bell tinkles merrily as visitors walk in. What will they order this time? A piece of 'Sport-slagkage', baked to an 1891 recipe, or perhaps a wedge of the tempting 'Orthellolag-kage'? Not everyone comes to La Glace for its coffee or gâteaux. If the weather warms up a bit, people will order ice cream instead of cake. For the shop's ice cream, too, is famous in Copenhagen. Konditori La Glace has been held in high esteem in Copenhagen since 8 October 1870,[1] when the confectioner Nicolaus Henningsen, originally from Schleswig in Germany, opened for business. The following year, he married Anina Jørgensen. Dressed in a silk gown the young Danish woman stood behind the counter

making sure that the visitors at the tables were correctly served. Her charm and beauty contributed greatly to the success of La Glace. All Copenhagen called her 'the most beautiful woman of Skoubo-gade' and many came to eat ice cream or pastries simply to be near her.

The shop was rebuilt in 1896 by Thorval Schrøder, Anina's second husband. Before starting the rebuilding work, Schrøder visited Hamburg, Berlin, Paris and probably also Vienna, picking up ideas for furnishing and décor along the way. The original shop had been called Henningsen's Cellar after Anina's first husband, Nicolaus, who died in 1876. Now, twenty years later,

335: Konditori La Glace at Skoubogade 5 in the heart of Copenhagen. Since its establishment in 1870 the confectionery shop-cum-café has been famous both for its ice cream and for stories about Anina Jørgensen, 'the most beautiful woman of Skoubogade', who in the early years stood behind the counter of La Glace dressed in a silk gown.

its name was changed to La Glace, the French word for ice cream, reflecting the increasing popularity of ice cream among Copenhagen's citizens. The Danish association of ice cream-selling confectioners, founded in 1917, comprised 100 members.[2] About 65 of them were from Copenhagen. But La Glace was the only establishment that could boast a beauty in a silk dress behind the counter.

a Polytechnic College in Copenhagen. Generations of Danish engineers became profi-
cient in the construction principles of dairy
and ice cream machines at that institution.
• The cooperative basis of agriculture also
resulted in communal coldstores being set
up throughout Denmark, facilities which
later proved to be ideally suited to the distribution of ice cream.[6] A second major boost
to the Danish ice cream industry lay outside
the nation's borders – in the United States, to
which many Danes had emigrated towards
the end of the nineteenth century.

The US connection and Hellerup Is

• In 1913 the Danish-American Christian
Larsen published the book Dairy Technology.
Larsen was a professor at the Brookings
dairy institute in South Dakota, a thinly
populated, typical farming state in the
American Mid-West. In his book, Larsen
described in detail the latest developments
in the dairy sector and devoted much
attention to the production of ice cream.
Very soon after its publication in America,
the book was reviewed in the Danish dairy
industry trade magazine, Maelkertidende.[7]
This was characteristic of the close and
frequently personal connections that existed
in those days between representatives of the
Danish and American dairy industries. In this
case Larsen had sent a copy of his book to
his colleague Bernhard Bøggild in Odense.
• Denmark thus learned of the latest inventions and developments in the US dairy
sector more quickly than other countries in
the Europe of 1913. While elsewhere in
Europe ice cream was generally regarded as

something that you bought in summer from
Italian street or beach vendors, Danish dairy
manufacturers were receiving accurate
reports on the methods and techniques used
by dairy companies in the USA for the large-
scale production and sale of ice cream. 'Big,
modern factories are holding the reins there',
wrote Bøggild in his review of the book.
• One man who had experienced this development at close hand in America was Lauritz
Jensen, born in Sweden in 1881 and the
founder of Denmark's first ice cream factory,
Hellerup Is, in 1914. In 1906 Jensen had made
the acquaintance of a baker in Copenhagen
who had then just returned from Italy with
recipes for Italian fruit ice cream.[8] Inspired
by this, Jensen started an ice cream stall in
Copenhagen. Business was excellent,
enabling the enterprising Jensen, aged 26,
to travel to the United States in 1907 with the
aim of learning how to make factory ice
cream and earning enough money to start up
a factory of his own. In December 1912 he
was back in Denmark, with few dollars in his
pocket but much richer in terms of ice cream
experience.
• On 8 April 1914, with a starting capital of
1,000 Danish kroner, Jensen set up the
'Amerikansk Iskrem Fryseri A/S' in Hellerup,
near Copenhagen. The ice cream was manufactured in two small wooden, upright
freezers, powered by an electro-motor of one
horsepower. His customers were several
confectionery bakers in Copenhagen and
distribution took place using a sort of
motorised carrier tricycle.[9] The first season
was such a success that in 1915 he decided
to buy a modern American freezer with
which he could produce 200 litres of ice
cream in one hour.
• After the First World War Hellerup Is

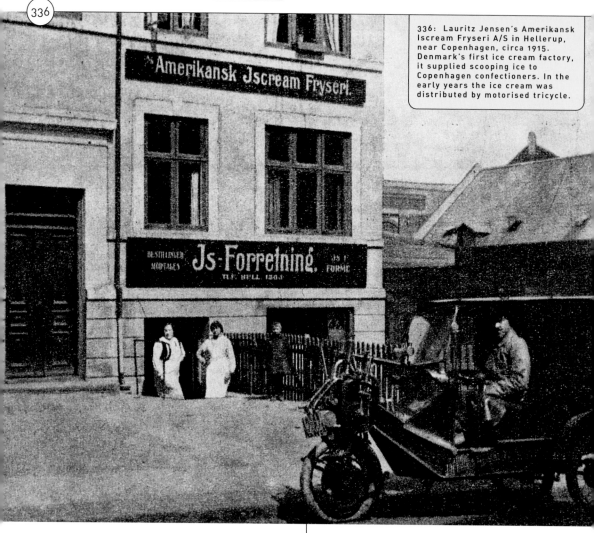

336: Lauritz Jensen's Amerikansk Iscream Fryseri A/S in Hellerup, near Copenhagen, circa 1915. Denmark's first ice cream factory, it supplied scooping ice to Copenhagen confectioners. In the early years the ice cream was distributed by motorised tricycle.

expanded rapidly. Another freezer was installed and a department was added for the production of ice that would cool the cabinets from which the confectioners sold the ice cream. Deliveries were no longer made by carrier tricycle but in three vans and by 1939 Hellerup Is had grown to be one of Copenhagen's biggest ice cream factories, with a workforce of 50 and twelve delivery vans.[10]

• The end of the First World War in 1918 saw Denmark, just like other European countries, plunge into an economic crisis which would last many years. In the meantime, contacts

'Ice cream, a new national dish'

with the US dairy industry were renewed and reinvigorated. Danish dairy trade journals published articles in which American ice cream consumption was held up as an example. 'In America everyone enjoys eating ice cream: men, women and children. Regardless of the weather, it is the dessert after every meal with meat, both at home and in restaurants and eating establishments, and indeed not only when it is warm', reported

337: Participants in the first ice cream maker's course in Denmark in 1926 standing in front of the Vesterbro dairy in Århus, where the course was held.

engineer J.F. Engberg in Maelker-tidende in May 1925.[11] He was speaking from experience, having lived for a while in Buffalo, North Dakota, 'where the winters are considerably colder than in Denmark', but where 'quite a big ice cream factory' operated the whole year round. Engberg had nothing but criticism for the ice cream in Denmark. 'The rubbish that is currently sold on street corners during warm weather is not real ice cream: the milk solids content is too low because often only skimmed milk is used and there is no thickening agent'. Things would improve, argued the engineer, if American production methods and recipes were adopted. That would certainly benefit the Danish dairy industry. 'Judging by the American situation, ice cream sales of some seventy million kroner per year should be

possible in Denmark', continued Engberg. Besides, the Danes certainly had the right sort of taste-buds for it. 'Nowhere in the world are the cookies as deli-cious, the chocolate as exquisite or the sweets as good as in Denmark. We really have a sweet tooth'. Ice cream would fit in very well with this predilection. 'It ought to be proclaimed a new national Danish dish!', enthused Engberg.

• A year later he commented in Maelker-tidende that within the Danish dairy industry 'there is growing interest for this new production area'.[12] But, he added, 'Most of those who are interested, however, drop their plans as soon as they realise how much a complete installation costs'. Engberg felt that it was only a matter of time before the investment would pay its way in the big cities

338: Hellerup Fløde Is, founded in 1914, was Denmark's oldest ice cream company. By 1939, Hellerup Is had become one of Copenhagen's biggest ice cream factories, with 50 personnel and twelve vans.

339: Advertisement by Hellerup Is to mark the ice cream factory's silver jubilee in 1939. The photo-collage shows the manufacture and selling of its extensive range of products. In the left foreground are thirteen ice moulds in a container of brine. Three telephonists are taking the orders of retailers. On the right is a production worker with a tray of ice lollies. The range is inspired by American products.

of Denmark. In this context he drew his readers' attention to a number of developments in neighbouring Germany. There, some 30 installations, distributed between all the big cities, were operating at the end of 1925 and ice cream manufacturers had set up their own trade association (see chapter 12).[13]

• Engberg's prediction soon became reality. The Danish economy began to recover from the post-war crisis, but the local dairy factories were having a lot of difficulty selling their relatively big quantities of cream during the summer months.[14] In 1926, the Vesterbro dairy factory in Århus was the first in Denmark to decide to commission a modern 'dairy ice cream installation'. The installation was manufactured by the Silkeborg machine factory, known until then only as a maker of dairy machines. It was this factory that took a step that was to prove decisive for the future development of the Danish ice cream industry. In August 1926 it organised a course in Århus on the production of ice cream 'in the American manner'. The course was set up together with the local association of dairy factories and was headed by the American 'dairy ice cream expert' M. Mortensen. This Danish-born professor of dairy technology was affiliated to a dairy research station in Ames, Iowa.[15] Mortensen gave a number of lectures and, with the aid of the new ice cream installation in the Vesterbro dairy factory, gave working demonstrations of the manufacture of various types of dairy ice cream. The course attracted widespread interest; some 50 directors of local dairies, margarine factories and the like took part. 'Here the basis was laid for the standard for dairy ice cream production in Denmark', concluded ice cream expert Oluf. S. Hansen more than twenty years later.[16]

• After the course the Silkeborg machine factory installed ice cream making plants all over the country. More than thirty such machines were in operation, in 1927 producing dairy ice cream with a fat content of between 12% and 16%, the levels customary at that time in the USA.[17] Engberg noted with satisfaction that 'we can now rightly speak of a Danish ice cream industry'.[18]

Premier Is and John M. Larsen

• By far the biggest and most modern ice cream business in those early years was Premier Is in the port of Esbjerg. Founded in 1868 and located on the west coast of Jutland, Esbjerg was of essential importance for exports of Danish dairy and meat products to England. Ice factories supplied large ice blocks for cooling these perishable goods, maintaining a sub-zero temperature in dockside coldstores and on ships.

• One of these ice factories in Esbjerg belonged to A/S De Forenede Isvaerker (The United Ice Works Ltd.), established in 1916 by the Danish-American John M. Larsen (see box on p. 340). The company increased its share capital in 1927 from 1,000,000 to 1,865,000 Danish kroner, using the new funds to set up a modern ice cream department, which started producing ice cream as the Premier Is company in August that year.[19] The far-sighted Larsen, who for many years had worked as an engineer in the US ice cream industry, made sure that his factory was equipped with the latest machines. Apart from modern freezers, Premier Is had two automatic filling and case packing machines and two Anderson

¶ Premier Is, the first modern ice cream company in Denmark, was founded in 1927 by Johannes Møller Larsen. Larsen was born in 1874 in the village of Bagterp in the far north of Jutland, not far from the city of Hjørring[1] where he attended a state school and took an education course as a dairy manufacturer. In 1892 he emigrated, as did so many of his fellow countrymen, to the New World. There he developed into a skilful engineer and introduced Danish dairy methods. He pioneered the manufacture of butter and pasteurised cream and had his own machine factory in Chicago for the production of refrigeration and ice-making machines. The products of Larsen Ice Machinery were sold throughout North America, from Canada to Texas.

But Larsen's talents went further than that. In 1907 the Falcon Engineering Co. in Chicago began marketing the Falcon De Luxe Gentleman's Roadster. Designed by Larsen, and costing $7,500, the car had a 120 hp engine and a top speed of 125 mph.

During the First World War Larsen advised the Allies on the preservation of foodstuffs while spending the years 1915-1917 in Denmark, which remained neutral. Ever one to spot an opportunity, Larsen noticed that the fishermen of West Jutland needed ice to preserve their fish, so he bought three Jutland-based factories which produced ice and founded A/S De Forenede Isvaerker (The United Ice Works Ltd.) in the port of Esbjerg. Big coldstores were built for storing fish and meat, which were cooled with refrigerating machines that he himself had supplied. In 1927 these were joined by the ice cream department of Premier Is and Larsen soon acquired the nickname the 'Ice Cream King of Denmark'.[2]

Larsen also continued his activities in America. In the years 1917-1918 he developed a passion for flying and in August 1919 the Danes would marvel at the exploits of Mr John Larsen, the 'flying engineer'. Their fellow countryman became the agent in the USA for the German-built Junker aircraft and in June 1925 Larsen was awarded a trophy in recognition of the first American mail flight flown non-stop from coast to coast.

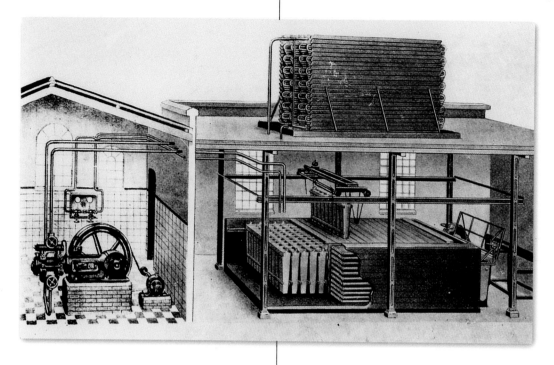

machines which produced ice creams of the Eskimo Pie type (vanilla blocks coated with chocolate). The Eskimo Pies were wrapped in silver paper and stored in one of the factory's three coldstores, each with a capacity of 200 tonnes of ice cream and cooled by enormous ammonia compressors.

341: Installation for the production of blocks of raw ice, taken from a Danish brochure of the 1920s. On the left is an ammonia freezer. In the room on the right stands a freezing installation for blocks of ice; it consists of long metal moulds filled with water and immersed in a container of brine. The ammonia freezer ensured that the brine had a temperature of around -18°C.

• Almost 90% of production consisted of packaged ice cream which was sold nationwide.[20] To do this, Premier Is set up what for those days was an exceptional distribution system. The ice cream was transported as far away as Copenhagen in railway wagons insulated with cork. The temperature in the wagons was kept below zero by brine that had been cooled to -13°c in the factory. Very soon Premier Is had its own coldstore depots in the cities of Copenhagen, Århus, Herning, Odense and Vejen. From the depots the ice cream was conveyed in special six-wheel Chevrolet trucks to restaurants, confectioners and shopkeepers. In 1929 Premier Is had 24 such trucks, which called on customers almost every day to top up the refrigerators with ice and salt and to deliver new ice cream.[21] The retailers were provided with free refrigerated cabinets on loan from Premier Is, but were only allowed to carry this one brand of ice cream in them. The contract was automatically extended each year unless sales figures were disappointing, in which case Premier had the right to remove the cabinet before the contract had run its full term.

• In 1928 the retailer profit margin was about 20%[22], too little for the liking of the association of ice cream confectionery bakers. In July 1928 the editors of the association's magazine, Is-Konditori-Tidende, advocated that the confectioners should have their own ice cream factory so that they could determine the prices and profit margins themselves. They did not want to end up in a situation like 'in the United States, where the ice cream factories are getting ever richer and the retailers can hardly keep their heads above water. We wish to remain spared from the Americanisation of the Danish business'.[23]

• Undisturbed by this, Larsen continued to build up his business. Initially his ice cream was sold under the name Premier Ice Cream, a clear reference to Larsen's American sources of inspiration. Use of the English language in this way was quite common in the early years of the European ice cream industry. For example, a Swiss dairy, the Verbandsmolkerei Zürich, advertised its ice cream using a poster that displayed the words 'ice cream' in big letters (see chapter 12). In 1938 Premier Is opened another ice cream factory in Glostrup, near Copenhagen, and two decades later the Danes had come to regard Premier Is as the only national ice cream brand.[24] But by then the Larsen family was no longer involved in the business and the company had different owners. The company was sold to its present owner, Nestlé, in 1996.

• Despite the worldwide recession and the economic crisis of the 1930s, the production of dairy ice cream in Denmark continued to grow steadily. In 1936 some 162 manufacturers – mostly dairy businesses with an ice cream department – produced ten million litres of ice cream per year, a tripling of the 1930 volume.[25] In 1927 they had set up their own trade organisation, the Iskremindustriens Sammenslutning, the Ice Cream Industry Association. The

association stimulated production and promoted the quality of ice cream by organising courses, lectures and meetings and via articles in its own periodical, Dansk Flødeis. The association also successfully urged the government to treat ice cream as a dairy product and not, as in Sweden, as sweets (see chapter 11).

• As well as Premier Is, a number of other ice cream factories were established in that period. In March 1927, for instance, the newly founded Dansk Ice-Cream Fabrik A/S in Copenhagen marketed ice creams under the name 'Stjevne (star) Ice Cream'. The company was housed in a former margarine factory, had modern machines and operated a separate business for distribution to hotels, restaurants, confectionery bakers and high-class sweet shops. Like Premier Is, the factory supplied retailers with wooden freezer cabinets on its own terms.[26] In 1926 the Frederiksberg Iskremfryseri had started operations to the north of Copenhagen, whilst in Frederikshavn, in the extreme north of Jutland, the local dairy had started an 'iskremfabrik' in 1927. In the same year ice cream factories were also set up in Rønbjerg and in Hesselager. Numerous other dairy businesses followed suit, but most of the ice cream was supplied by a few bigger companies. In 1937 fourteen of the 162 ice cream manufacturers accounted for 43% of total Danish ice cream production.[27]

• During the Second World War the growth in ice cream consumption was enormous: from six million litres in 1940 to eighteen million litres in 1944, an increase from 1.6 to 4.5 litres per capita.[28] Just as in Sweden, this was due in part to the

342: Advertisement from 1934 by the Danske Meieriers Faellesindkøb in Copenhagen, a wholesale business for flavourings and ingredients.

FREDERIKSHAVNS MÆLKEFORSYNING's
ISCREMFABRIK.

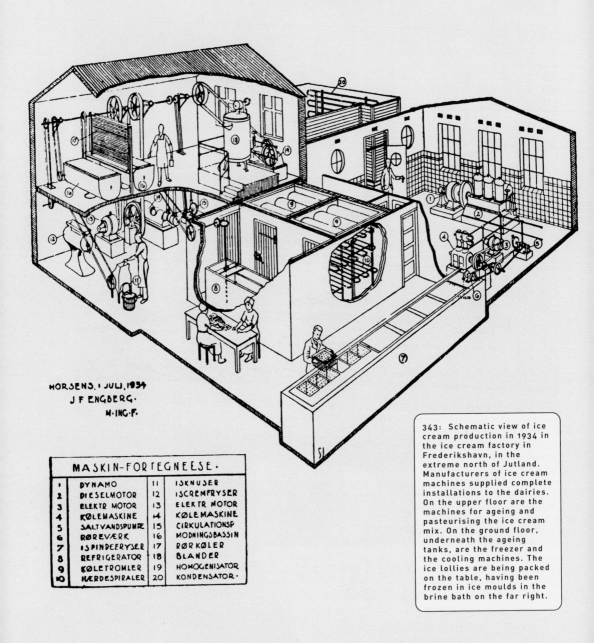

HORSENS, 1 JULI, 1934
J F ENGBERG.
M·ING·F.

MASKIN-FORTEGNEESE.

1	DYNAMO	11	ISKNUSER
2	DIESELMOTOR	12	ISCREMFRYSER
3	ELEKTR MOTOR	13	ELEKTR MOTOR
4	KØLEMASKINE	14	KØLEMASKINE
5	SALTVANDSPUMPE	15	CIRKULATIONSP
6	RØREVÆRK	16	MODNINGSBASSIN
7	ISPINDFRYSER	17	RØRKØLER
8	REFRIGERATOR	18	BLANDER
9	KØLETROMLER	19	HOMOGENISATOR
10	HÆRDESPIRALER	20	KONDENSATOR.

343: Schematic view of ice cream production in 1934 in the ice cream factory in Frederikshavn, in the extreme north of Jutland. Manufacturers of ice cream machines supplied complete installations to the dairies. On the upper floor are the machines for ageing and pasteurising the ice cream mix. On the ground floor, underneath the ageing tanks, are the freezer and the cooling machines. The ice lollies are being packed on the table, having been frozen in ice moulds in the brine bath on the far right.

Perspektivsnit for Hr. Glistrups Flødeisanlæg.

scarcity of other confectionery products and also to the fact that the raw materials needed to produce ice cream were still available. Characteristic of the situation was the closure by Frederiksberg Is of its dairy department in 1941 in order to concentrate on ice cream production.[29] In 1947 the Danes were even, for a while, Europe's biggest ice cream eaters, with a consumption of 24.3 million litres (about six litres per head). The most popular flavours were nougat and vanilla, accounting for 44% and 30% of total sales respectively.[30]

• The growth of Danish ice cream was attributable not least to the prominent position that Denmark had built up in developing modern techniques in the last two decades of the nineteenth century. Margarine manufacturers and farmers from the Dutch province of Friesland, for example, travelled to Denmark to study the 'Danish method' for the rapid cooling of butter and margarine that had been introduced in 1865.[31] This method and the rapid development of Gustav Laval's fast, continuous-operation centrifuge built the reputation of the Danish dairy industry.

• Nor was it only in dairy machinery that Danes took the lead; they were also well-versed in cooling technology. In 1895 Thomas Sabroe established a business in Århus for the manufacture of cooling installations. In the early years milk processing plants and dairy factories were the main customers. Together with his technical partner,

the engineer Carl Gottlieb, Sabroe then expanded the business, selling its machines additionally to chocolate manufacturers, shipping lines, fish processing plants, slaughterhouses and breweries. Confectionery bakers and ice cream factories were also supplied with specially designed installations and machines. In 1923, for instance,

BEDRE ISCREME - OG STØRRE FORTJENESTE

344: 'Better ice cream, more profit', a 1927 advertisement for electric refrigerators made by Frigidaire, part of the American company General Motors. The old cooling method using salt had become outdated. Electricity was reliable and could provide a constant temperature of -12°C to -15°C.

Sabroe advertised its 'iscremmaskiner' in the journal of the Danish bakers and confectioners.[32] In subsequent years Sabroe concentrated mainly on refrigeration technology.

• At the end of the 1920s more and more Danish machine manufacturers saw the opportunity to build machines for ice cream factories. Besides Sabroe and Silkeborg, other companies that entered the market included Phønix Mejerimaskinfabrik, A/S Atlas Maskinfabrik, Frederiksberg Metal-

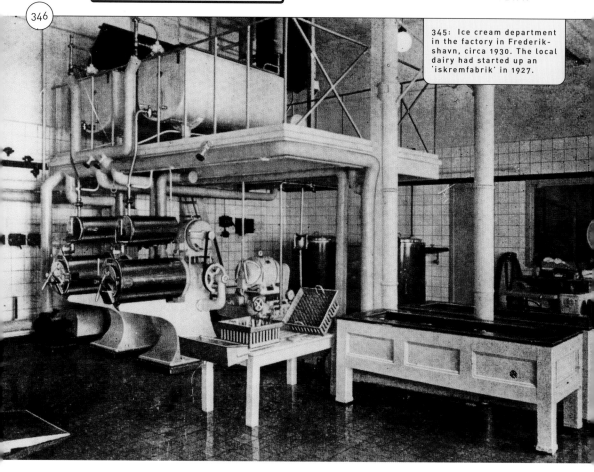

345: Ice cream department in the factory in Frederik-shavn, circa 1930. The local dairy had started up an 'iskremfabrik' in 1927.

FRIGORE elektrisk
Konservator og Fryser

Bliv uafhængig af Is og Salt og anskaf Dem det nyeste og fordelagtigste for enhver Forretning, der interesserer sig for Iskrem.

I Frigore Konservatoren opbevares Iskremen ved konstant Temperatur, og intet gaar til Spilde. Vi leverer Dem netop det, De har Brug for, hvad enten det er Konservatoren alene eller et komplet Fryseanlæg passende til Deres Behov.

Kom og se vore Maskiner, og lad os være Dem behjælpelig, hvor De er i Tvivl — eller forlang vort illustrerede Katalog tilsendt.

Bort fra det gamle System

MASKINKOMPAGNIET
NATIONAL A/S

ST. KONGENSGADE 40 · KØBENHAVN K. · TEF. C. 2183-2184

346: Advertisement for electrical refrigerators and ice machines from the machine factory National A/S in Copenhagen, 1931. Like Gram's machine factory, National supplied small ice machines and various formats of refrigerated cabinets to confectioners. The electric refrigerator meant the end of the cooling method using raw ice and salt.

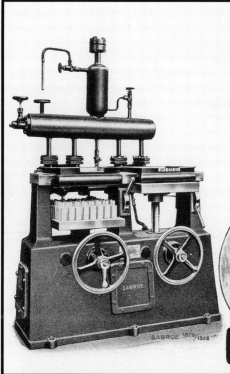

KENDER DE
SABROE-FRYSEREN?
FOR DIREKTE FORDAMPNING

HURTIGFRYSEREN FOR
DIREKTE FORDAMPNING
ER DEN NYESTE SABROE
KONSTRUKTION PAA
ISPINDE-OMRAADET –
FRYSER UDEN ANVEN
DELSE AF SALTVANDS
OPLØSNING.-

FORLANG VOR
NYE BROCHURE
OM HURTIGFRYS-
NING VED DIREKTE
FORDAMPNING. –

A/S THOMAS THS. SABROE & CO.

AARHUS   SDR. ALLÈ 41
         TLF 370
KØBENHAVN   BREDGADE 75
         CENTRAL 9842

SABROE

347: A cooling machine for ice lollies in an advertisement
by Thomas Sabroe & Co., circa 1936. Above the wheel on
the left is a tray of ice lollies. Thomas Sabroe established
his company manufacturing cooling installations in Århus
in 1895, suppling equipment and machines to a wide range
of businesses. Nowadays the Sabroe Group is one of the
world's biggest companies in its field.

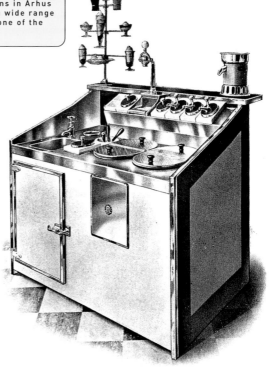

348: 'Baby fountain bar' by Gram dating
from 1935. The soda fountain bar is an
American method of selling ice cream that
was imitated in Europe. Gram produced the
bars in various formats and prices. The
luxury 'baby fountain' sold for 1,960 kroner.

Fornem og tiltalende
— naar Konsumenten
modtager den.

Laaget aabner selv,
naar Isen løftes opad!

— men mange foretrækker
at lade Isen blive i Æsken
og bruge Pinden som Ske.

Den kom— *og sejrede!*

og den vil sætte sit Præg
paa den danske Sommer,
— fordi den er praktisk,
hygiejnisk og tiltalende.

JYLLANDS PAPIR-VÆRK^{A/S}
TELF. 7878 - **AARHUS**

349: Advertisement by the packaging factory Jyllands Papir-Vaer A/S, Århus, 1935. This firm introduced a completely new way of eating ice cream, whereby the stick was used to scoop the ice cream out of the tub.

Machine manufacturer Gram

• In May 1901 Hans Gram started a small machine factory in Vojens, in the south of Jutland. His machine factory and installation business could supply all sorts of agricultural machinery, 'complete dairy installations' and 'windmills and wind turbines manufactured according to the mill theory of Mr La Tour'.[33] The Vojens location had been chosen with care by Hans Gram (1874-1929). Situated on a junction of provincial railway lines and in the middle of a rich agricultural and dairy farming district, Vojens was a good base for supplying the services he was to provide. Gram had attended technical courses and been an apprentice in a small machine factory in Ringkøbing. In 1907, after a few years spent running his factory in Vojens on his own, Hans asked his brother Åge to join him. As a graduate of the Higher Technical College in Copenhagen, and having worked for several years in Thomas Sabroe's cooling installations factory in Århus[34], Åge Gram brought with him a thorough knowledge of cooling techniques.

• This was the start of the business known as Brødrene Gram (Gram Brothers) and their combined talents served it well. Soon they were supplying cooling installations to dairy businesses; in 1920 they began making compressors; and in 1929 they won orders from Czechoslovakia and Poland.

• But it was in 1932 that Gram Brothers took a step that was to affect the way the ice

varefabrik, Dansk Mejerimaskinfabrik and Brødrene Gram A/S. The knowledge and ideas acquired over decades of dairy and cooling machine production, coupled with good contacts in the USA, provided fertile ground for innovation. Two of today's most prominent manufacturers of ice cream machines in the world, Gram and Høyer, have their roots in Denmark. Gram is still a fully independent Danish business, whilst Høyer forms part of the Swedish Tetra-Laval group.

cream industry was to develop not just in Denmark, but all over the world. The company discontinued production of dairy machines and instead turned its full attention to the development and manufacture of ice cream machines. Critical to this change in policy were the contacts with engineer Christian Morsbøl, director of the Copenhagen-based machine factory Maskinkompagniet National. Morsbøl had in fact initiated contact

350 & 351: Hans (1874-1929) and Åge Gram (1879-1957), founders of Gram's machine factories in Vojens, Denmark.

Gram produced small ice cream machines and various types of refrigerators. Equipment for what were known as soda fountain bars, a method of selling ice cream that had been introduced from the United States (see chapter 5), was also produced.[35] In 1936, as a result of payment difficulties, Maskinkompagniet National was absorbed by Gram.

• The 1932 change of policy was a great success. Though economies generally were stagnating, Gram's exports of continuous freezers, pasteurisers, homogenisers, compressors, storage tanks and ice cream moulds grew. In addition to the Scandinavian countries, Gram acquired customers in Germany, Poland, Italy, Greece, Palestine, Latin America and Africa.[36]

352: Advertisement for a two-stage ammonia compressor by Brødrene Gram A/S, Vojens, Denmark, 1937.

with the Gram brothers in 1929 with the aim of setting up a joint venture. He had also been to the USA, where he had familiarised himself with ice cream factories and had learnt all the ins and outs of producing ice cream the American way. Gram and Maskinkompagniet National now joined forces and were soon supplying complete ice cream installations to dairies in Denmark and, later on, Sweden too (see chapter 11). For confectionery bakers

In December 1934, for example, an ice cream factory equipped with machines supplied and installed by Gram was opened in Nairobi, capital of the then British colony of Kenya. The factory was even managed by Danes.[37]

B.G 1156/2

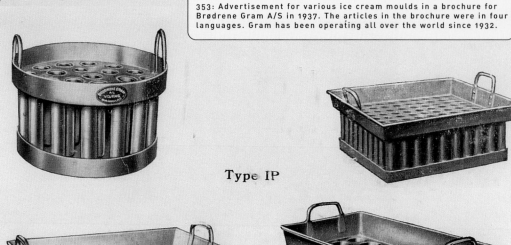

353: Advertisement for various ice cream moulds in a brochure for Brødrene Gram A/S in 1937. The articles in the brochure were in four languages. Gram has been operating all over the world since 1932.

Type IP

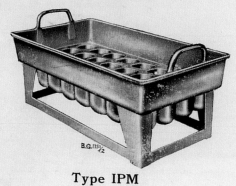

Type IPR

Type IPM

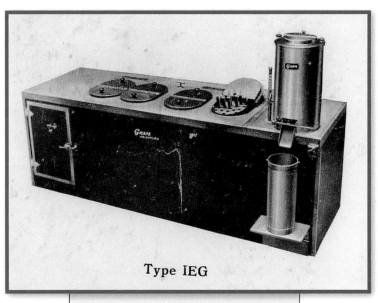

Type IEG

354: Gram ice cream machine, circa 1934. Ice cream machines like this one with cooled display trays were supplied to confectioners.

RIA, the rotating ice lolly automatic machine

• In those same years Gram was working on the development of a fully automatic, rotating ice lolly freezer that was to revolutionise the ice cream industry throughout the world. Until then production of ice creams on a stick had mainly been carried out manually. Metal trays with 24 or 48 moulds were filled by hand with ice cream or water-ice mixture. To freeze the ice cream, the trays were then placed in a bath filled with brine at about -13°C. When the ice cream was semi-frozen, the sticks were inserted by hand into the moulds. Finally, the trays were immersed in warm water so that the ice creams could be released from the moulds and coated with chocolate. Clearly, automation of this process – resulting in more efficient production, lower costs, higher profit margins and improved hygiene – would represent a real breakthrough.

• In March 1935 Gram applied to the Danish Royal Patent Board for a patent for a 'Fryseapparat til Frem-stilling af Spiseis, isaer Ispinde' – a freezing machine for the manufacture of ice cream, especially ice lollies. The patent was granted on 28 February 1936.[38] In the preceding years an entire team at Gram had worked hard on developing the machine, a project initiated by Åge Gram that was under the day-to-day leadership of

the talented young engineer Oluf Gudmund Høyer (1907-1982), assisted by another engineer, Mads Clausen.[39] Høyer was a nephew of Åge Gram and had studied at the Higher Technology College in Copenhagen. In 1933 he gained his engineer's diploma with honours and went to work for Gram. Thanks to donations from two industrial funds, Høyer was able to travel to the United States,[40] where between 1934 and 1935 he studied modern cooling techniques and the manufacture of ice cream in the Mid-West dairy belt of Wisconsin, South Dakota and Illinois. He also spent time in New York and Chicago, where he visited the big dairy and ice cream group Borden (see chapter 5). Borden had a patent for a method of production of ice lollies, which involved dividing up the ice cream blocks after the sticks had been inserted.[41]

• The prototype of the new ice lolly freezer developed by Høyer and his team was installed and tested in 1934 at the Rønbjerg Mejeri- og Flødeisfabrik in the north-west of Jutland.[42] In a brochure published by Gram at the time, the benefits of the machine are described as 'a bigger and more constant production,

355: Ice freezer, type FHM40, by Brødrene Gram A/S, circa 1934. The container held 40 litres of ice cream. The ice cream mix was fed via a pipeline to the drum-shaped container. The ice cream was rotated in the container and cooled to a very low temperature. With the aid of rotating scrapers fitted inside the container and by adding air, a creamy, ice-cold substance – ice cream – was produced.

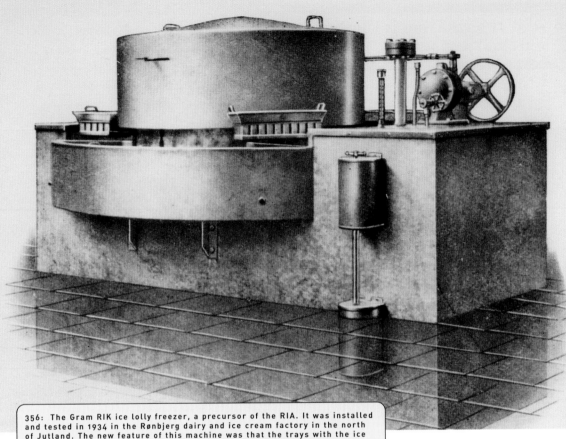

356: The Gram RIK ice lolly freezer, a precursor of the RIA. It was installed and tested in 1934 in the Rønbjerg dairy and ice cream factory in the north of Jutland. The new feature of this machine was that the trays with the ice moulds were no longer placed manually but automatically in a rotating tank of ice-cold brine (at a temperature of about -18°C). After they had been frozen, the trays were retrieved from the rotating tank by a lifting device and placed in a tank of hot water. The ice lollies were then removed from their moulds by hand. The filling of the moulds also still took place manually. A fully automatic version of the machine was first marketed in 1937.

less labour, no waste of brine, no waste of ice cream, employees do not need to touch the frozen moulds and the entire process is cleaner.'[43] At a major Danish dairy industry trade fair in Aalborg in 1935 the new Gram machine was the stand-out attraction. Its novel feature was that after the trays containing the ice cream moulds had been filled, they were then automatically frozen by being placed in a rotating tank containing brine. When the mix was semi-frozen, the sticks were inserted. Next, the trays were lifted out of the tank and immersed in a warm bath of water. The lollies were then removed from the moulds, were coated in chocolate and wrapped – all by hand.

A machine based on similar principles had been described the year before by Gram's competitor Silkeborg Maskinfabrik in Dansk Flødeis, the trade journal of the Danish ice cream manufacturers, but there was no mention of any actual installation.[44]

• In 1937 Gram introduced a much improved version of this machine, which performed all steps in the production process automatically.[45] The moulds of the 'Roterende Ispinde Automatic' machine or RIA, as it would henceforth be called, no longer consisted of loose trays, but of trays that were now arranged in three rows and fixed in a circular

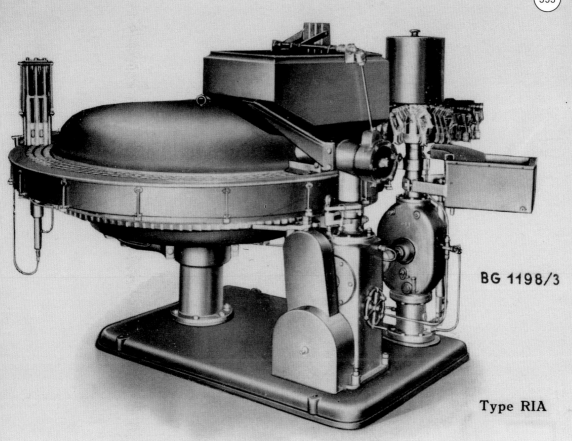

BG 1198/3

Type RIA

moulding table. The ice cream was dispensed automatically into the moulds, and after partial freezing the sticks were inserted into the ice cream by a specially designed machine installed above the mould table. The mould table rotated inside a sealed brine bath, freezing the ice cream and the sticks inside the mould. At the end of a full rotation of the mould table, the moulds were placed in hot water and a lifting device above the mould table gripped the ice creams by their sticks and lifted them out of the moulds. If required, the ice creams were dipped in warm chocolate before they were transported by a conveyor belt to the packaging machine. The RIA could

357: RIA-3, the automatic rotating ice lolly machine by Brødrene Gram A/S, Vojens, Denmark. This was a techno-logical breakthrough in the ice cream industry. The RIA-3 first came on the market in 1937.

make 3,000 ice creams per hour, almost two and a half times as many as could be made by hand.[46] • This revolution in ice cream production was reported in the Danish trade journal Nordisk Mejeri-Tidsskrift.[47] The later sales history of the Gram RIA machine showed that Danish pride was justified, although its success was initially impeded by the Second World War. During the wartime years, however, the machine was further developed in the neutral country of Sweden, at Gramkyl, a subsidiary of Gram which had been founded in 1943 (see chapter 11). As a result, Gram was able to present its latest model, the Gram RIA-3, as early as June 1945.[48]

358: Production hall of Gram in Vojens, in about 1951. After starting in 1901 as a factory producing agricultural machinery, Gram had expanded to become a business specialising in ice machines and refrigerators. Gram's ice freezers, pasteurisers, homogenisers, compressors, ice lolly machines, storage tanks and ice cream moulds are still sold around the world.

359: One of the first Gram RIA-3 machines in operation in 1948 at the firm of Bauman in Kalmar, Sweden. This model was fitted with a hydraulic transmission and had an output of 2,500 ice lollies per hour.

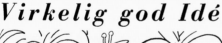

Virkelig god Idé

MAN BEDES IKKE FORURENE URSKOVEN MEN STIKKE PINDENE I NÆSEN.

STIK INGEN PIND!

EFTERLAD URSKOVEN I SAMME STAND SOM DE ØNSKER AT FOREFINDE DEM

URSKOVSDIREKTORATET

En Dansker agter at oprette en Forretning med Ispinde i det Indre af Afrika.

(Efter Politiken d. 16. Dec. 1934).

360: 'A really good idea!' reads the headline above this cartoon published in the Danish daily newspaper *Efter Politiken* on 16 December 1934. 'A Dane in a shop with ice lollies in the African interior' is the caption underneath. On the sign to the left of the ice cream stall are the words: 'Leave the jungle as you found it. Insert the sticks in your nose'. A sentiment we would today class racist would have been considered normal in those days.
The occasion of the advertisement was the opening of an ice cream factory in Nairobi, Kenya. The machines in the factory had been supplied and installed by the Danish company Gram and the factory was managed by Danes.

• Over the years the RIA technology was constantly improved and the machine's production capacity considerably enhanced. Post-war sales data show that the RIA freezer enjoyed success on an international scale. In the 1945-1965 period the machine was installed all over the world: in the United States, Russia, India, Israel, Iran, Australia, Cuba, Japan, Venezuela, Argentina, Yugoslavia, Czechoslovakia, Poland and in all West European countries.[49] Oluf Høyer, however, had long since parted company with Gram.

Høyer and the Rollo

• In 1939 major differences of opinion arose between Høyer and Åge Gram as to the RIA freezer's future development. Høyer felt that the moulding table should be driven mechanically. Gram preferred a hydraulic drive, which he thought would be more durable. Høyer wanted to place one big brine tank under the entire moulding table and use pumps and valves to transport the liquid refrigerant simultaneously in several directions. According to Høyer the resultant turbulent flow would cause the ice creams to be frozen more uniformly. Gram, however, still favoured the radial system in which the brine flowed out from the centre past the individual ice cream moulds. In other areas, too, their views diverged - a friction resolved in November 1939 when Høyer left his uncle's company and set himself up as an independent consultant.[50]

• During the Second World War Høyer began to entertain plans of establishing his own machine factory. Immediately after the end of the war he set off for Wisconsin in the United States to acquaint himself with the latest innovations in the ice cream industry there. On his return to Denmark Høyer redoubled his efforts to achieve his aim and on 2 January 1948 O.G. Høyers Maskinfabrik A/S opened its doors in Århus. His first big order – for the design of an ice cream factory in Casablanca, Morocco, for a Dane called Birk – got the new enterprise off to a flying start. Høyer supplied a complete ice cream installation, from ageing tanks[51] for the mix to machines for adding fruit[52]. The order provided work for seven men.[53]

• In the factory's initial period its production programme concentrated on the manufacture of storage tanks and continuous-operation freezers. Høyer had studied the principles of such freezers thoroughly during his two stays in the United States. The US company Cherry-Burrell was the main producer

361: Portrait, circa 1938, of the Danish engineer Oluf Gudmund Høyer (1907-1982). In the 1930s Høyer played a major role in the development of the Gram RIA. In 1948 he set up a factory of his own and turned his business into one of the world's foremost producers of ice cream machines. Today the Høyer company is part of the Swedish Tetra-Laval group.

of these machines, which had been invented by the American Vogt in the 1920s (see chapter 5). Høyer now worked with his engineers to develop their own type of continuous-operation freezers. Sales of these flourished. In the Netherlands Høyer sold his freezers in large numbers via Wortels Machinefabriek in the 1950-1956 period, but he also had customers for his products in other European countries.

• After 1953 the firm gained a foothold in the large neighbouring German market, due in large measure to the efforts of Adolf Miebach, its German agent. Høyer had met this clever and dynamic businessman during an annual trade fair in the Netherlands. That meeting signalled the beginning of a successful commercial collaboration which lasted for many years. Sales in Germany were decisive for the success of Høyer, since in its early years an estimated 60% of company production went to German customers.[54]

• If O.G. Høyers Maskinfabrik had limited itself to the production of storage tanks, filling machines and continuous-operation freezers, the business would never have gained the worldwide renown it eventually enjoyed. The key to Høyer's ultimate success was the development of his company's own make of fully automatic, rotating ice lolly freezer. In 1953 the ambitious Danish engineer applied for a patent for his Rollo machine, named after a Viking king.[55] The construction ideas that Høyer had not been able to realise with Gram before the war he had now incorporated in this new freezer. Gram contested Høyer's patent application, but to no avail. In 1956 the cantonal court in Århus rejected Gram's claims and three years later the court proceedings were definitively closed.

• Meanwhile, the first Rollo was operating in a dairy factory in the Swedish city of Karlstad. In 1954 Høyer had shown his design on paper to the factory's managing board. They were so enthusiastic about the Rollo that they immediately ordered one, making an advance payment of 55,000 Danish kroner, and in February 1956 it was installed in Karlstad. Another Rollo was sold soon after to a Japanese dairy company thanks to business contacts of Sabroe.[56] But Høyer's invention only became really successful in 1958, when the leading German ice cream company

Langnese ordered a number of Rollo machines for its new factory in Heppenheim (see chapter 12).[57]

• As with the RIA machines of Gram, the construction, technology and capacity of the Rollo was constantly being improved. The Rollo 20 from 1962, for instance, could turn out 10,000 ice creams per hour, but the Rollo 32, which appeared on the market in 1968, had a capacity of 30,000 ice creams per hour. In the 1960s O.G. Høyers Maskinfabrik started offering complete production lines, from continuous-operation freezers, filling machines, Rollo freezers and freezer tunnels to packing machines and conveyor belts. One of the complete production line installations was an ice cream factory in Iran in 1961. With the continuous upgrading of its production programme, Høyer was able to capitalise on the rising fortunes of the ice cream industry in the 1960s, especially in Europe where international companies like Unilever and Beatrice Foods were becoming more active in the ice cream market. Growth encouraged Høyer to expand, but the new factory he had begun to build had not been completed when O.G. Høyers Maskinfabrik was sold in July 1969 to the Swedish Alfa-Laval group.[58]

Innovations: cartoon and movie heroes

• The economic stagnation that followed the 1973 oil crisis accelerated the process of rationalisation and concentration in the ice cream industry. The steps taken by big ice cream companies in this period included the amalgamation of ice cream and frozen foods activities, the closure of factories and the introduction of more tailor-made production possibilities (see chapter 21). It was no longer sufficient for suppliers of ice cream machines to offer only standard products. Ice cream installations were increasingly customised, being costed, tested and commissioned in consultation with manufacturers. Factories had to operate with increasing flexibility so that they could respond to ever-changing market needs. Greater priority was given to reducing energy consumption and environmental impact. One result of the new-style production units was that operating personnel and maintenance engineers were trained by the machine manufacturers themselves.

• Both the Gram and Høyer companies responded to this development. Høyer, for instance, founded a separate company in 1980 to handle after-sales activities. Under the name Danice this company took care of the coordination of purchasing and delivery of all raw materials required in the production and distribution of ice cream, a service which was attractive to developing countries without good supplies or essential raw materials. Machine manufacturers had to meet ever higher demands because in each new season the ice cream producers wanted to introduce new types of ice cream on a stick with which to delight their public and confound their competitors. During the 1970s the ice cream industry started to look for machines which could consistently and efficiently produce ice creams on sticks that were more fully, and more ambitiously, shaped. Thus two-dimensional characters from the world of comic books and cartoon films, such as Mickey Mouse, Goofy, Tom and Jerry or Spiderman, now found themselves transformed into three-dimensional ice creams and lollies. This novelty market, which had first started

in the USA, became the driving force in the ice cream industry (see chapter 21). In England and Belgium Unilever developed a system of rubber moulds which were frozen on an American Vitaline freezer, largely due to the unswerving enthusiasm of an English marketeer, Doug Brennen, and his technical partner, John Pooler.

• In response, Gram and Høyer both developed 3D production processes using winged metal moulds, which when opened released the water-ice figures. The risk involved here was that brine could seep into the moulds. To prevent this Gram fitted the moulding table with double-walled moulds. Gram's first RIA machine to be specially designed for the production of three-dimensional ice cream figures was put on the market in 1977. In 1982 Høyer invented an entirely new system to solve the problem: instead of brine, air cooling was applied. This system, the Formline, made Høyer the worldwide leader in the field.

• Did this conquest by Gram and Høyer of the leading world positions in ice cream machine production also have its impact on the post-war development of the Danish ice cream industry? The availability of good machines certainly contributed to the fast growth of ice cream departments in dairy factories in the years before the Second World War. Moreover, compared to other European countries, Denmark was quick to achieve a high level of consumption. Even before the war Danish ice cream factories served as an example for Swedish dairy companies. In the same way that Dutch farmers and margarine manufacturers had familiarised themselves with Danish techniques for the manufacture of butter decades earlier, so in the years around 1930 the Swedes travelled to Copenhagen and Århus to find out more about the new produc-

tion methods for ice cream (see chapter 11).
• Danish ice cream manufacturers were also amongst the first to introduce shaped novelties. In the 1950s, for example, a bottle-shaped water-ice lolly was a children's favourite. In 1996 a version of this lolly was relaunched by Denmark's biggest ice cream company, Frisko.

Mergers and acquisitions: Frisko

• In 1959 the Kildegaard Fløde-Is business, founded by manufacturer Georg Jensen in 1942, merged with Frisko Fløde Is, which had existed since 1946.[59] Since the Second World War there had regularly been mergers between ice cream companies, starting at a regional level. In 1946, for instance, nine different ice cream companies in Århus and the surrounding area joined forces as Pyramide Is. A similar move took place on the island of Sjælland, where a number of companies merged to form Hellerup Is.
• In 1960 Unilever bought Frisko for nearly three million kroner.[60] At that time Frisko was active only in Copenhagen and its vicinity. With just under 400 retailers, Frisko held approximately 30% of the local market. Almost half of these customers were confectionery bakers and ordinary bakers,[61] as previously described. The year after its purchase of Frisko, Unilever acquired another ice cream company in Sjælland, the Helsingør-based Kronborg Is.[62]
• Unilever was not the only international company which was active in Denmark in the 1960s. In 1967 the American concern W.R. Grace bought Denmark's oldest ice cream company, Hellerup Is. Grace, a chemicals company which had been founded in 1854 and which was active throughout the world, expanded in the 1960s into foods and other consumer goods sectors. In 1964 Grace had purchased the Hughes Brothers ice cream company in Ireland (see chapter 9). In 1969 they acquired two further Danish ice cream companies, Pyramide Is and Hesselager Is. With a combined share of 35% Grace became Denmark's market leader in one fell swoop, much to the alarm of Frisko.[63] Grace gave the amalgamated companies the name of Sol-Is. The company did not last for long, however, since in April 1971 Grace sold Sol-Is to Unilever for $1,666,000.[64] This transaction made Frisko the biggest ice cream company in Denmark, with Premier Is in second place.
• The number of independent industrial ice cream manufacturers in Denmark had meanwhile decreased from 162 in the 1930s to 13 in 1971. In 1994 there were only eight left. However, the concentration drove consumption steadily up, from 35 million litres in 1971 to more than 52 million litres in 1994.[65]
• The capacity of the Frisko ice cream factories turned out to exceed the needs of the domestic market, so in 1983 the firm started producing three-dimensional ice creams for other countries, such as Italy and the UK. Exports of Viennetta ice cream gâteau followed. The first dedicated production line for Magnum was developed in 1988 by Frisko (see chapter 21).[66] By 1992 Frisko was producing 224 million Magnums, of which no fewer than 209 million were destined for export. This is indicative of Denmark's technological position in the world of ice cream and of the special place it occupies in the international ice cream market.

Licks, Sticks & Bricks

A WORLD HISTORY OF ICE CREAM

Sweden: Europe's ice cream champions

En glace och 3 théskedar!

'One ice cream and three teaspoons, please!', calls the visitor in a Stockholm Konditori to the girl behind the counter. He, his wife and daughter will savour the delicacy that is so expensive that the one ice cream is all they can afford. This scene is depicted on a Swedish engraving dating from around 1840 with the satirically intended text printed beneath it.[1] The location may well have been the Behrens confectionery shop, where the citizens of Stockholm went to eat ice cream from 1841 onwards.[2]

• Ice cream, or glass as the Swedes call it after the French word glace, was then already familiar to the nobility and the bourgeoisie. Ice cream became popular at the court of King Gustav III, who greatly admired the French. Shortly before he was crowned king in 1771, he received from King Louis XV of France a 586-piece service which included 56 ice cream cups and four ice cream pots (see chapter 3). The palace employed French chefs, whose bombes glacées were famous.

• Just under a century later, the court was no longer supplied with ice cream by French chefs but by Swedish confectioners. King Charles XV (1826-1872) ordered his ice cream from the Konditori of Carl Grafström.[3] In those days ice cream was still reserved for the upper strata of society. Only at the beginning of the twentieth century does ice cream make its appearance on the streets in summertime. As in most other European countries, it was introduced by Italians (see chapter 4), but also (unlike elsewhere) by Russians.[4] For a payment of 25 öre a day, ice cream vendors were allowed by Stockholm's City Council to sell 'scooping ice

362: Lithograph by Fritz Dardel, Stockholm, circa 1840. The text underneath the picture translates as 'One ice and three teaspoons'. In the nineteenth century ice cream was sold in Stockholm by confectionery bakers.

cream in cones on street corners from crates cooled with ice blocks and salt', notes the Swedish ice cream manufacturer Eric W. Hanner (1907-1987) in a unique report of 1938 about the early days of factory-made ice cream in Sweden. 'They dwelt and still dwell in filthy cellars', writes Hanner, 'and produce a type of ice cream which has a fat content of no more than around 1% to 6% and is manufactured not solely from dairy products, but also from coconut fat and whale oil, and later also from 'Vitin' cream. In other words, it is what we call margarine ice cream.'

• In a dairy country like Sweden this bordered on the criminal - especially for a man like Hanner. From the second half of the 1930s, his company produced ice cream made exclusively from pure dairy products, with a fat content of around 16%. In Swedish official ice cream regulations drawn up in 1952, the minimum fat level was set at 12%. The prominent position of the dairy industry in Sweden has made the Swedes Europe's biggest ice cream eaters. With a per capita consumption in 1996 of approximately 14.5 litres, they are surpassed only by the Americans (22.5) and the Australians (18.5).

• This dairy tradition was by no means the only factor driving Swedish consumption. If it had been, dairy countries such as Denmark and the Netherlands would also have become huge ice cream consuming nations. But in Sweden a unique combination of political, economic, demographic and culinary circumstances played its part. Because of its policy of neutrality, Sweden was not involved in the two World Wars, while its social policy meant that purchasing power was spread evenly across the population. In economic terms an exceptional level of industrial development, rooted in an ingenious use of vast natural resources, helped Sweden develop an affluent society more quickly than any other country in Europe. Moreover, its population is small in relation to the size of the country and fats play an important role in the rather plain Swedish diet because of the harsh climate. All these factors stimulated certain developments in ice cream in Sweden decades earlier than elsewhere in Europe. New manufacturing techniques; modernisation of distribution; business concentration; freezers in the home; the rise of packs of 'family ice cream', often sold by supermarkets – much of this was routine before other countries had even embarked on it. In fact, Sweden almost kept pace with the USA, the ice cream world's number one.

'Surreptitiously eating ice cream in a doorway'

• Sweden had not always been a dairy nation. Like Denmark (see chapter 10) it started to became one in the final quarter of the nineteenth century, as a result of fundamental changes in the world market. That was when the early mechanisation of US agriculture and the reduced cost of transport led to the bulk shipment of cheap American and Russian grain to European countries. Prices plummeted and soon many farming businesses in Europe plunged into a crisis that lasted until the end of the century.
• For Sweden, long one of the granaries of Europe, this had sweeping consequences. From being a grain exporter Sweden became a grain importing country, with 30% of Sweden's grain requirement met from abroad[5] by 1900. Recession in agriculture

precipitated in a drastic shift from arable to livestock farming. In particular, the number of cows and pigs increased substantially. Sweden turned into a dairy and meat nation, with milk cooperatives and small dairies springing up everywhere.
• In 1927, dairy manufacturers from all over Scandinavia held a conference in a small town called Ladelund on the German-Danish border, the sixth time that the conference had been held. One of the speakers was the Dane Oluf S. Hansen, a lecturer on dairy techniques. He gave a speech that was devoted to a new phenomenon in Scandinavia: the industrial production of ice cream. He observed that at that time ice cream was being made in this way in some 30 to 40 different places in Denmark. At the end of his talk Hansen described the Danish development as 'an ice glacier that had really started to move' and said he considered it likely that the glacier would soon reach 'the southern parts of Sweden, Norway and Finland'[6].
• Hansen's glacier had in fact already reached Sweden. As early as 1924 a family business named Premiärglass had begun supplying the delighted citizens of Malmö, which faces Copenhagen across the Sont, with industrially manufactured ice cream; and in 1925 the Hvilan (The Rest) dairy factory, also Malmö-based, had followed suit.[7]
• Up to the end of the 1920s no factory-made ice cream was on sale in Stockholm. Instead, people ate artisanal ice cream at the Mengarelli ice cream parlour or went to Pipers Glace, a shop on the Kungsholmen that is still there today. Ice cream was largely a Sunday treat, although an ice cream cone could be bought for ten öre at Gubben och Gumman in Humlegården.[8] Production

Det smakar härligt med.....

Uppklistra detta märke, i tele-fonkatalogen eller kokboken.

TILL DESSERT
RING
11 32 38
20 29 07

SÖNDAGAR
20 29 02

Nyco grädd·glace

Nyco grädd-glace

depended on the ice cream machines that were usually hand-operated and were cooled with ice and salt. This changed in 1928 when the first factory-made ice cream went on sale in Stockholm. The initiative came from chocolate manufac-turer Förenade Chokladfabrikerna A.B. Thule, which started up an ice cream making department shortly after the introduction of the Vogt ice cream freezer, an American invention which enabled continuous ice cream production (see chapter 5). The

363: 'It tastes delicious … Nyco dairy ice cream.' Adver-tisement from the early 1930s for the Nyco Glacefabrik, founded in about 1926. Nyco was probably the first ice cream factory in Stockholm.

company sold its chocolate mainly from kiosks, a distribu-tion channel that was now also used in the summer to sell ice cream.

• There was still no industrial production of ice cream on a large scale, however. Hotels and restaurants made their own ice cream, but very little was sold through shops.[9] Ice cream was eaten only during the summer and not much of it at that – probably less than half a litre per capita each year. And people still had to get used to eating ice

364: The premises of Förenade Chokladfabrikerna A.B. Thule in Stockholm in a photo dating from around 1972. This chocolate factory started producing ice cream in 1928. In 1942 Thule's ice cream operations became part of the newly established Glace Bolaget ice cream company.

cream in the street. 'It took many years before adults dared to eat an ice cream in public. They stood in doorways, surreptitiously licking an ice lolly', wrote Eric Hanner.[10]

• In 1930 Thule found itself facing a competitor in Fyris, an ice cream company from Uppsala. At the Stockholm summer exhibition Fyris launched a product that was new to Sweden:

365: Employees of Affa (United Dairy Ice Cream Factory Århus) in Kyrkheddinge, southern Sweden, pose behind a production table in 1935. The products are ice creams on sticks.

the American ice cream, Eskimo Pie, which had been invented in the USA in 1921 (see chapter 5). In 1930 it went on sale in Stockholm for 25 öre.[11] Fyris produced Eskimo Pie under licence from the American manufacturer of packing machines, Anderson Manufacturers Co. of New York. Fyris was unsuccessful, however, being affected by the Great Depression, and in 1933 the company went bankrupt.

Pioneers

• It was only in the second half of the 1930s that the Swedish ice cream industry started to expand. In that period various ice cream companies were set up in quick succession: they included Trollhätteglass, Igloo, Alaska, Affa, Ge-Ge and Mjölkcentralen. Many of these businesses were linked to dairy cooperatives. Just as in other countries with a sizeable milk production, the dairy factories were confronted with summer milk surpluses. The manufacture of ice cream, alongside that of cheese and butter, offered a solution, especially after 1932 when the farmers received higher prices for their milk. This price increase had been insisted on by the Swedish farmers' party, Bondeförbundet, as a condition for its participation in the government.[12]

• The dairy cooperatives now had more capital at their disposal, enabling them to invest in expensive ice cream machines. Leading businessmen in the Swedish dairy industry had in fact been exploring the possibility of ice cream production for some time. Oskar Persson was one such man. He ran a cooperative dairy factory in the town of Kyrkheddinge in the south of Sweden. In 1933 Persson visited various ice cream factories in Denmark. On returning to Sweden, he bought ice cream machines and sent an employee to Århus to learn the trade of ice cream maker. In 1934 the production of ice cream started in Kyrkheddinge. Persson named the company Affa, standing for Aarhus Förenade Flöde Aarhus (United Dairy Ice Cream Factory Aarhus), a clear reference to its Danish origin.[13] Affa produced ice cream on sticks – with success – and in 1936 ice cream production was transferred to an entirely new building.

• Another pioneer was Oscar Olsson from Trollhättan, near Göteborg. Olsson had started making ice cream, by hand, in a small basement here in 1927. Only in 1934 did 'Glass-Oscar' ('Ice Cream Oscar') install the first electric machines for blending the ice cream mix. Five years later, in 1939, he started using machines to produce ice cream.[14] This laid the basis for the Trollhätteglass company, which after the war gradually became the leading ice cream supplier for the Swedish west coast. Thanks to its beaches this area was a popular summer holiday destination and thus a lucrative sales proposition. When the company was bought by Unilever in 1962, it had a market share of 10.8% and was the third biggest ice cream producer in Sweden.[15]

• Another of the ice cream companies that was set up in the 1930s, Alaska Glace, had its roots not in the dairy industry, but in distribution. The company was established by A.B. Svenska Pressbyrån (The Swedish Press Bureau Ltd.), because of dissatisfaction about Thule's ice cream supplies to the kiosks in Stockholm. Pressbyrån, as holder of the licences for some 300 kiosks, had been buying ice cream from Thule for just under four years. In 1934, with sales on the increase, Pressbyrån decided to start up its own ice cream production using machines from the bankrupt stock of Fyris. Nor did Pressbyrån restrict itself to newspapers and ice cream; in 1938 it decided that toffee could be profitable too.[16]

The Mjölkcentralen

• Of all the developments in ice cream manufacture in the 1930s, the establishment in 1935 of an ice cream department in the Mjölkcentralen dairy operation situated in Stockholm turned out to be the most important by far. This formed the basis for what subsequently became Glace Bolaget (GB), now Sweden's biggest ice cream company.

• The Mjölkcentralen itself had been founded on 26 April 1915 in the Kronprinsen Hotel in the capital. On that day some 30 farmers from Stockholm and the surrounding area agreed to merge with the Stockholm Mjölkförsäljnings AB to form the cooperative dairy business known as Lantmännen Mjölkförsäljningsförening. As a result of the merger the supply, processing, distribution and sale of milk in Stockholm were all combined under one roof. From 1927 onwards the operation was known as simply Mjölkcentralen.[17]

• In 1925, Mjölkcentralen director K. Benzinger had put forward a plan to start making ice cream. He had just returned from the USA, where he had picked up all sorts of new ideas. His proposal did not come to fruition, but a few years later Eric Hanner, son of one of the other directors, was sent on a study trip to Denmark, Germany, Switzerland and the USA. His mission was to analyse new developments in the dairy sector. The intelligent and dynamic Hanner, then 21, had studied at the Bröderna Påhlmans business institute and had just completed the dairy course at Alnarps Mejeri-institut when he set off in 1929. He kept his eyes and ears wide open and noted down in a journal everything he learned about the dairy sector. Above all, he recorded facts and new developments relating to the manufacture and sale of ice cream. On his return from the USA in 1932, he too urged the managing board of the Mjölkcentralen to set up an 'ice cream dairy department'. But, as in 1925, they thought the time was not yet ripe.

• In October 1934 the idea was tabled once more. This time it was decided to work out the plans in detail, for which Hanner was given responsibility. As he had always been convinced of the opportunities in the industrial manufacture of ice cream, he tackled his assignment energetically. In 1938 he wrote the comprehensive report quoted earlier on the setting up of the ice cream department. His document is a most valu-

366: Eric Hanner (1907-1987) founded the ice cream department of the Mjölkcentralen dairy business in 1934. This was the precursor of Sweden's biggest ice cream company, Glace Bolaget. Hanner was the driving force behind Glace Bolaget for more than three decades.

able testimony, filled with details about factory layout, production, distribution, ice cream varieties, prices, wages, organisation, sales and advertising.[18]

First of all, Hanner travelled to Copenhagen, where he made a close study of the economic aspects of the ice cream business at the firm of Maelkeforsyningen.

On his return to Sweden he asked two Danish machine manufacturers, Phoenix and National, for price quotations for ice cream machines and started drawing up cost calculations. He chose Phoenix and on 25 October 1934 Hanner presented his plans to the management of the Mjölkcentralen. It agreed to invest 250,000 kronor in setting up an ice cream department.

• Work began immediately on construction of a production hall. Some urgency was required, as sales of ice cream were planned to start at the beginning of the new season in March 1935. The new factory was designed with two floors. On the top floor three compressors were installed. These cooling machines ensured a constant temperature of -25°C in the freezing room, which was insulated with two thick layers of cork and built directly beneath the cooling machines. Two pasteurisers and one homogeniser processed the milk on the ground floor. Two 'portion' freezers cooled the ice cream mix. These were modern installations for those days and were cooled not with brine, but with ammonia evaporators. In seven minutes they could produce 40 litres of ice cream.

The new factory was also equipped with a freezer for making ice cream lollies. Initially the ice cream was produced under the supervision of a Danish master ice cream maker[19] who taught the trade to Gösta Lilja, a foreman of the Mjölkcentralen. Lilja later became technical director of the ice cream department.

'Puck'

• The management of the Mjölkcentralen knew that to promote ice cream sales they needed an appealing symbol and a catchy name. Benzinger came up with a cheerful little harlequin figure whom he called Puck, a short and powerful name calling to mind both the character in Shakespeare's play A Midsummer Night's Dream but also ice hockey, a very popular sport in Sweden. Although Mjölkcentralen was absorbed by Glace Bolaget in 1942, the Puck figure was still in use in the 1980s, albeit for individual products such as the Choklad-puck and Stor-puck. This was because, in 1965, Glace Bolaget had invented a new corporate logo, a laughing clown wearing a bowler hat.[20]

• The first Puck ice cream went on sale on 23 March 1935. The launch, at a big exhibition, 'Vårt dagliga bröd' (Our daily bread), in Stockholm, was accompanied by an extensive advertising campaign. The campaign drew on Hanner's experiences in the USA. Posters, shop-signs, parasols, advertisements in daily papers and weekly magazines, gift articles such as badges and harlequin toy dolls and 150,000 brochures were aimed at ensuring that from then on Puck dairy ice cream would be eaten in the homes and on the streets of Stockholm. In the most well-to-do districts errand boys distributed 50,000 price lists door-to-door. In Stockholm men dressed in Puck costumes walked the streets, while cinemas screened a special promotional film showing how the ice cream was distributed. Every day, including Sundays, orders could be made by telephone, provided they had been placed before twelve noon. These orders were delivered to the customer's home on the same day, using six specially constructed delivery vans. In the vans the ice cream was cooled by means of solid carbon

367: The figure of Puck, reproduced from a report written by Eric Hanner in 1938 about the establishment of Mjölkcentralen's ice cream department in 1934. For many years from 1935, this jolly harlequin character appeared on Puck ice cream sold by Mjölkcentralen and later by Glace Bolaget.

dioxide ice supplied by the Svenska Kolsyreisfabriken. In 1935 the use of carbon dioxide ('dry') ice in Stockholm may have been five times more expensive than traditional cooling with ordinary ice and salt, but it did offer advantages: a saving on personnel costs, improved load-space utilisation and less wear-and-tear on the vans. The method was also more hygienic. Alaska Glace, a competitor which had already been in the market for a year, also used dry ice.

• Every day the drivers would call at the sales outlets on a fixed schedule, on a cash on delivery basis. The customers were kiosks, grocers, fruit shops and the many milk stores that were already customers of the Mjölkcentralen. The ice cream supplied to these customers consisted mostly of ice lollies wrapped in

368: This laughing clown became the new logo of Glace Bolaget in 1965.

aluminium foil and chocolate-coated vanilla ice creams on sticks. Attempts were made to sell packs of scooping ice cream to restaurants, hotels, cafeterias, bars and swimming-pools, but without much success. The Mjölkcentralen loaned freezer cabinets free of charge to kiosk proprietors, on condition that the cabinets would be used only for the sale of Puck ice cream, and undertook to provide advertising materials free of charge and to look after the freezing system in the cabinets. Agreements were laid down in an 'ice cream contract' that could be extended each year. If the sales results were disappointing, the Mjölkcentralen had the right to terminate the contract with immediate effect.[21] For street traders, the Mjölkcentralen provided smaller freezer boxes, which could be carried by a strap on the shoulder.

• Kiosks were by far the most important sales channel. Decorated with ice cream advertisements, kiosks are part and parcel of the Swedish street scene, and buying an ice cream from these outlets has become a collective childhood memory.[22] The kiosks were given the biggest freezer cabinets, capable of holding 70 litres of ice cream. Like the vans, the cabinets were cooled with carbon dioxide ice. Hanner had considered supplying electric refrigerators, as was done in Denmark; the expectation, however, was that most sales would take place via the kiosks and street vendors, who did not have electricity.

• The product range in the 1930s was simple: bulk scooping ice cream, dessert ice cream, ice cream in tubs, blocks of ice cream dipped in chocolate, round ice lollies and chocolate coated ice creams on sticks. Dessert ice cream was supplied to restaurants and hotels, but also direct to consumers at home. It took the form of a bombe glacée or a pyramid (see also chapter 3). The Mjölkcentralen started by selling only vanilla ice cream, but by about 1938 other flavours had been added: strawberry, blackcurrant, mocha, nougat, pistachio and, if the weather was really hot, refreshing lemon ice cream too.

369: 'If you please! Eight simple ways to decorate Puck ice cream'. Mjölkcentralen advertising brochure, 1935.

Till Er tjänst!

8 enkla sätt

att dekorera Puck-glass

MJÖLKCENTRALEN
Lantmännens Mjölkförsäljningsförening u. p. a.

Populära Puck-prylar tog Stockholm med storm.

371: Puck dairy ice cream being sold on the streets of Stockholm in 1936.

370: 1935 advertisement for Puck dairy ice cream.
The harlequin figure holds two ice creams on sticks. The long round shape of the ice creams was typical of Puck ices in those days.

372: Selling ice cream, 1936.
The street vendor carried a special cool-box hung by a shoulder strap.

'Brine hands' and piece-rate wages

• Apart from the use of a packaging machine, production was still largely manual. The trays with the ice cream moulds were frozen by placing them by hand in a brine bath and then taking them out again. Wearing gloves could not really prevent 'brine hands'. The sticks for the round ice lollies and for the square,

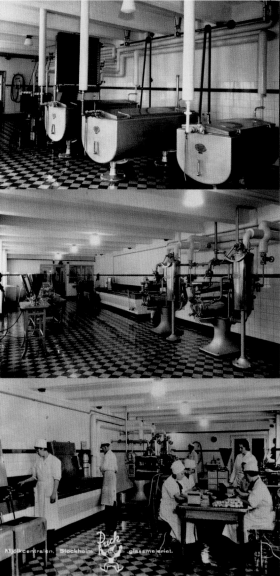

373: Production hall on the upper floor of Mjölk-centralen's new ice cream factory in Stockholm in 1935. The photo shows three tanks in which the ice cream mix could 'ripen'. Behind the last ripening tank is a pasteurising machine.

374: The production and packing area of Mjölkcen-tralen's new factory in Stockholm, 1935. In the right foreground are two Vogt continuous freezers.

375: Production of Puck ice cream in 1936 in Mjölkcentralen's ice cream department. On the left are the brine tanks and on the right women are busy packing ice creams on the production table.

chocolate-coated vanilla ice creams were pushed into the moulds by hand (see also chapter 4). Tubs of ice cream were also filled and sealed by hand; and up to 1939 the Eskimo Pie-type ice cream blocks were packed singly by hand. In the high season, work continued day and night. The day-shifts consisted of twelve to fourteen women; at night only men were employed. In addition to a fixed monthly wage the shift workers also received piece-rate wages: 0.03 öre for each ice cream they packed.

• In 1935, Thule, Alaska and Mjölkcentralen were faced with a new competitor for the Stockholm market, Igloo Glacefabrik A.B. Superba. Located in Märsta, approximately 40 kilometres north of Stockholm, the company advertised its dessert ice cream as 'based on an American recipe'.[23] The Mjölk-centralen had no alternative but to match the lower prices of the new entrant. Thus, despite its thorough preparations and its modern, American-style approach, the ice cream department of the Mjölkcen-tralen operated at a loss during its first four years. In February 1939 the accountants of the dairy company wanted to call it a day. Hanner managed to convince the management to continue for one more year. His forecast that the operation would be in profit within five years came true: that season the department recorded a profit of 63,000 kronor.[24]

Doing business in wartime

• On 9 April 1940 Germany invaded Norway and Denmark and the Germans warned the Swedes not to intervene or they would be occupied as well. As in the First World War, Sweden stayed neutral, but many things including some foodstuffs were rationed. Rationing did not include ice cream, but it did affect the ingredients for ice cream and the fat content had to be reduced from 20% to 4%. Furthermore, in 1942 the government introduced a luxury tax of 24% on ice cream, which put pressure on the profits of the country's 75 or so ice cream businesses.[25]

• These developments were the trigger for major rationalisation in the Swedish ice cream industry. The larger manufacturers joined forces in 1942 to establish the Sveriges Glassindustriers Riksförbund (Swedish Ice Cream Industry Association). A first wave of business concentrations took place, with companies merging both in the south of the country and in Stockholm. Early in 1942 Mjölkcentralen, Thule and Alaska Glace in Stockholm came together to form a new company, Glace Bolaget A.B., usually known as GB. Hanner became its director. Igloo had already been bought by Mjölkcentralen, which meant that Stockholm now only had one big ice cream supplier.

In 1943, Malmö Glass A.B. bought up all the significant regional ice cream manufacturers in the South: Premiär, Ambrix, Ge-Ge and Affa. From then on all the ice cream was called Ge-Ge, the abbreviation for Grädd-Glass (Dairy Ice Cream), and production was concentrated at the factory in Kyrkheddinge.[26]

376: In the 1930s, Mjölkcentralen supplied ice cream daily to consumers' homes using specially constructed delivery vans insulated with cork. The van was loaded through special hatches in the roof.

• During the Second World War, while elsewhere in Europe people were being killed and industries destroyed, Sweden carried on trading with both Britain and Germany[27] and economic development continued, albeit at a much slower pace than in the previous decade. The ice cream industry still looked to move forward. In June 1943, for example, GB ordered a packaging machine, complete with aluminium foil and wax paper, for 'glacepinnar' - ice cream on sticks - from a company in another neutral country, the Swiss firm S.I.G. (Schweizerische Industrie-Gesellschaft)[28]. Whether delivery took place is not confirmed, but plainly it was feasible.

• Ice cream industry trade was not however restricted to neutral countries. As well as a packaging machine, GB at this time was casting around for a machine to apply chocolate coating to its vanilla ice cream blocks. S.I.G. wrote back to GB saying it could not,[29] nor was Gram in occupied Denmark able to meet the enquiry. But in August 1943 the Swedish representative of the Dresden-based firm Johannes Kegel sent GB prospectuses of a chocolate-dipping machine, called the Kadema-Super, and assured GB that the machines could be delivered in various types and sizes. It is not known whether this led to an actual order and delivery,[30] but clearly the turmoil engulfing Europe was no obstacle, in principle at least, to trade between warring Germany and neutral Sweden.

• Ice cream was in high demand during these years because sweets, chocolate and other confectionery products were difficult to come by. GB's production figures for the months of April to September 1944 show how much its business was prospering. In those six months the factory produced over 9.3 million ice creams[31]. In the autumn of 1944 GB drew up plans to expand production capacity. The firm of Gramkyl in Göteborg was asked to submit a quota-

377: Ice cream sales at a Glace Bolaget kiosk, late 1940s. Kiosks remained the principal sales channel for ice cream in Sweden for many years.

tion for delivery of a compressor and a freezer tunnel. Gramkyl was the Swedish branch of the Danish machine manufacturer Gram. Because Sweden kept out of the war, it proved possible to develop the technology of ice cream machines further and in the south of the country a revolutionary Danish invention was greatly improved. This machine was a fully automatic, ice lolly freezer made by Gram. The first version of this machine had been put on the market in 1937 (see chapter 10); now it was further developed in the Swedish city of Kalmar at the Bauman ice cream company.[32] There they came up with the idea of driving the rotating freezing table not mechanically but hydraulically, a more reliable method.[33]

• Thanks to refinements like this devised in Kalmar, Gram was able to present a radically new ice cream machine to the world, known as the RIA-3, as early as July 1945.[34] The RIA-3 proved to be of crucial importance for the post-war development of the ice cream industry worldwide. Hundreds of millions of ice lollies are still produced each year using this type of ice cream machine.

378: The moulds for 'pyramid' dessert ice cream were still being filled by hand in the Glace Bolaget factory in about 1950.

Refrigerators and freezer cabinets

• After 1945 the Swedish economy, relatively unaffected by the war, grew rapidly. Big companies like ASEA, Ericsson, Svenska Kullager Fabriken (SKF), Electrolux, Astra, Volvo and SAAB expanded to become multinational businesses capturing leading positions in world markets. While other European countries were carrying out reconstruction programmes and preaching a policy of austerity, living standards in Sweden rose sharply.

• For the Swedish ice cream industry this prosperity signalled the start of a long period of growth. In the immediate post-war years two new ice cream businesses were established: Triumf Glass in Göteborg on the west coast (1946) and Gille-Glass in Stockholm (1947).[35] Gille-Glass was set up by the margarine manufacturer Nordiska Margarinfabriken. As a result of high butter surpluses shortly after the war, production restrictions were imposed on the margarine industry. For some years no margarine was allowed to be manufactured for several months each year, so Nordiska Margarin-fabriken saw the manufacture of ice cream as a way of keeping its personnel employed throughout the year.[36]

• Before the Second World War efforts had been made to induce the consumer to eat ice cream during the long winters, with GB, for example, selling packs of dessert ice cream varying in size from half a litre to two litres. They made little impact, taking a share of total annual sales of less than 10%. After 1945, however, the industry had much more success in stimulating winter consumption. More and more Swedish families could afford to buy durable goods like refrigerators and freezers, many of them from the highly-regarded national manufacturer, Electrolux, which had begun marketing modern electric refrigerators in 1925. By 1957, an estimated 100,000 Swedish households owned a freezer

379: Wooden refrigerator of Ge-Ge, around 1943. Ge-Ge ice cream was first marketed in the Malmö area in 1943, being stored by shops and kiosks in refrigerators like this one. The refrigerated boxes were supplied by Ge-Ge and were cooled with finely crushed natural ice and salt.

and a further 125,000 families had refrigerators with a freezer compartment. Some 13,000 freezer cabinets were installed in the retail trade.[37] A survey conducted in 1960 showed 82% of Swedes owning a refrigerator, 45% of these having a freezer storage facility.[38]

According to a 1970 study, 52% of all Swedish homes had freezers, ahead of Norway (49%) and Denmark (45%). In fourth place came Germany with only 20%.[39]

• For the ice cream industry in Sweden, a country (like Norway and Denmark) with short summers, this increasing penetration was of great importance, since freezers and refrigerators with a freezer compartment offered the consumer the possibility of keeping family packs of ice cream in the home throughout the year. By the 1950s GB was advertising more in the winter than in the summer. 'In the summer in fact', wrote Hanner in 1957, 'there is already a sort of free advertising thanks to our delivery vans with their bright colours and to the kiosks in their permanent locations. Higher sales in winter will give the business more backbone and provide a certain cover for the costs incurred in that period.'[40] Malmö-based Ge-Ge also pushed its winter sales under the headline 'Winter sales about to start', addressed to shopkeepers in its house journal in 1956. 'With the freezer cabinets that are in the shops it is no longer a technical problem to keep a stock of ice cream. Just like other frozen products – fish, meat, soup, vegetables – it should be accessible in the cabinets.'[41]

Distribution with isoflex and cork

• Slowly but surely, sales of ice cream for home consumption increased and Swedish ice cream companies became less dependent on the summer months. The emergence in the 1960s of supermarkets helped push Sweden to the top of Europe's ice cream eating league. In 1950 3.9 million litres of ice cream were produced; by 1965 that had risen to 50.4 million, an average annual growth rate of 17%. Per capita ice cream consumption in 1950 was less than 0.6 litres; in 1965 it was 6.8 litres. More than 56% of this was ice cream for home consumption, outstripping the 34% represented by impulse purchases outside the home, largely consisting of ice cream on a stick or in cones.[42] Back in 1947 the balance had been the other way: 17% dessert ice cream and 64% impulse.[43] In 1955 a half-litre pack of vanilla ice cream cost three kronor; by 1961 the consumer only had to pay two kronor for it, due largely to the efficiencies of large-scale automated production.

380: Glace Bolaget price list, circa 1955. Glace Bolaget was formed in 1942 by a merger of three ice cream companies: Mjölkcentralen, Thule and Alaska Glace. The harlequin figure, which had been the logo of Mjölkcentralen's Puck ice creams since 1935, was subsequently redesigned a number of times.

• Ice cream consumption could not have increased to such an extent had manufacturers not been able to make significant improvements in distribution. Cost-effective distribution of ice cream had always been difficult for its early manufacturers and achieving economies of scale demanded not only major investments in vehicles, cold-stores and freezer cabinets for shopkeepers, but the building from scratch and testing of many of the links in the distribution chain.

• For GB after the war, the distribution challenge grew in parallel with its expanding customer base. Ever greater distances had to be covered and ice cream had to be transported in trains and trucks to depots around the country. In a speech in September 1950 Hanner described some of the problems that GB was then facing in renewing its distribution system.[44] Following a study trip by Hanner to the US in 1949,

382: Glace Bolaget publicity photo from the second half of the 1950s. Two Danish stars of those days, actor Dirck Passer (left) and Sven Asmussen (right), violinist in the popular trio the Swe-Danes, eat an ice cream at a Glace Bolaget kiosk. The photo formed part of a campaign to stimulate ice cream consumption during the winter months.

the company had decided to build its own trucks and trailers for transporting ice cream. The walls and ceilings of the trucks were insulated with isoflex and the floors lined with 180mm of cork. The trucks were cooled by electric compressors to approximately -25°C. In practice, however, the insulation did not work as planned and the cooling units were damaged by the vibration of the trucks. The trucks were then fitted with galvanised coils which were frozen during loading using a calcium chloride

381: 'Become the most popular Daddy in Sweden - surprise them with Alaska!', runs this 1958 advertisement for GB's popular family ice cream. In the 1950s fathers, as undisputed heads of the family, had to be consulted before buying a luxury like ice cream. Similar advertisements ran in countries like Great Britain, the United States and Germany.

solution pumped from the factory through the coils at about -35°C. The trucks could then count on a temperature of about -23°C in their loading compartment lasting for twelve hours. Although Hanner had been satisfied with this system, he now announced that GB would be switching to a new system. The trucks would be cooled using 'the very latest refrigeration equipment' from the US, known as 'Dole plates'. In this method stainless steel plates were filled with a liquid refrigerant, were cooled in the factory and then placed in the trucks. This system spread throughout the world in the 1950s and 1960s, in trucks and also in small ice cream carts for street sales.

'Steaming' ice cream cakes

383: As they move along the conveyor belt, ice cream cakes are decorated with fruit and whipped cream in GB's factory in Flen, circa 1958.

¶ Traditionally, the Swedes ate ice cream cakes on festive occasions, at birthday parties, engagements, weddings and at Christmas, and the customary suppliers were confectioners. For decorated cakes in particular, this group of craftsmen seemed indispensable. Illustrative of the early growth in Sweden's prosperity was the fact that from 1947 onwards such ice cream cakes were ordered more and more frequently, at least in Stockholm and its surrounding area.[1] In 1956, therefore, GB decided to perfect its production line for the decoration of ice cream cakes in order to boost its ability to compete with the confectioners. From then on the undecorated cakes rolled along a conveyor belt past the female employees who, just as in a car assembly plant, each worked on one part of the decoration only. This method enabled labour costs to be halved and capacity doubled. The cakes cost nine kronor, which included home delivery and, according to a study in 1957, was 'considerably below the prices of the confectionery bakers'. The delicacies were wrapped in cellophane and delivered to the home in boxes which had double corrugated cardboard walls and were filled with carbon dioxide ice. When the box was opened, the carbon dioxide ice started to 'steam'. A 1995 consumer survey revealed that the memory of the 'steaming' ice cream cakes was still very much alive among older respondents from higher income brackets. The 'steam' heralded the final course of a festive dinner.[2]

384: Overall view of the production area in GB's new factory.

Drumstick

• Of course, production capacity and systems had also to be developed alongside those for distribution. Several ice cream companies, such as Ge-Ge in Kyrkheddinge, installed the new, fully automated ice lolly freezer manufactured by Gram; and in 1950 GB unveiled plans for a new factory in Stockholm. When the city authorities refused to approve the plans, GB turned to the site of an old dairy at Flen, some 120 kilometres south-west of Stockholm. Sweden's most modern ice cream factory was officially opened here in 1957. Two fully automated Gram RIA ice cream freezers, each with a capacity of 30,000 ice creams per hour, were installed. An S.I.G. machine from Switzerland could fill up to 6,000 two-litre cartons of ice cream per hour. These were frozen in a specially constructed, fourteen metre-long freezer tunnel equipped with six conveyor belts.

• A new feature was the almost fully auto-mated production of ice cream cones filled with ice cream, chocolate and nuts. Both the product type and the production

385: Ice moulds for GB's ice creams on a stick being filled by hand in the company's Flen factory.

method originated from the American firm Drumstick, which had been marketing the cones under that name in the US since 1936 (see also chapter 5). The filling of the cones and their wrapping in aluminium foil were both automated. By European standards of 1957, this large-scale industrial production of ice cream cones was completely new. Until then ice cream cones had been hand-filled in shops or kiosks from bulk containers. In 1959 manufactured ice cream cones were launched in Italy by Algida, under the name Cornetto. After many improve-ments in the keep-ability of the cone and quality of the ice cream, Cornetto was to become one of the world's greatest ice cream brands (see chapter 21).

¶ Question: 'Can I let my child, who is sick with a high temperature, eat ice cream?' Answer: 'Especially where children are concerned, I am pleased to prescribe that they eat ice cream in cases of sudden fever when they no longer even want to drink water'. So writes Dr Bertil Söderling in 1951 in his column 'The doctor gives advice' in the Swedish magazine Barn, a publication full of advice for parents.[1] 'Cold? Yes indeed, but that's what's nice about it', maintains Söderling, chief medical officer in the city of Borås, concluding: 'Is there any danger for the stomach? Why should there be? Surely, cream and sugar are not dangerous? Unfortunately we are faced with prejudices only too often.' Dr Söderling's opinion must have been music to the ears of Swedish ice cream manufacturers. For centuries it had been held that ice-cold food was not good for the stomach or throat (see also chapter 2), and now here was a high profile member of the medical profession advocating that feverish children be fed ice cream. Nor was Dr Söderling alone in his views. In 1952 he gained the support of the head of the children's

clinic in Uppsala hospital, Dr Lars Söderhjelm, who published a report in a medical magazine on his positive experiences with serving ice cream to sick children.[2]

386: Showcard for Glace Bolaget ice cream cakes, circa 1958. The gâteaux were wrapped in cellophane and delivered to the consumer at home in double-corrugated cardboard boxes cooled with dry ice (solid carbon dioxide). This ensured that the cakes stayed frozen for several hours.

As a rule, however, ice cream at that time was too fatty for ill people and its quality could not be trusted. It was also too expensive. This situation was remedied when GB started marketing a special diet ice cream for hospitals. It contained more proteins and considerably less fat (4% instead of 12%), a fact which enabled it

to retail at a price 25% below that of regular ice cream.[3] In 1955 the same medical magazine featured an article which reported that the diet ice cream had been successfully tested in various hospitals. The author pleaded for it to be used as hospital food and pointed out that the eating of ice cream was considered quite normal in hospitals in the USA.[4] His plea did not fall on deaf ears. Before long, Malmö ice cream manufacturer Ge-Ge proudly declared that ice cream was being served to 1,500 patients in the hospital in Lund. Ge-Ge simultaneously announced that, together with the hospital's Professor H. Malmros, it had developed a special type of ice cream for patients with a heart condition. This also attracted interest in England.[5]

The inference was clear: the image of ice cream was being boosted by the voice of authority. Eric Hanner, a director of the GB ice cream company in Stockholm, was able to note with satisfaction that 'publications against the consumption of ice cream have made a complete U-turn ... . Ice cream is useful for sore throats and high fevers.'[6]

Newcomers and mergers

• In 1960 one of the wettest summers for 300 years caused panic amongst Swedish ice cream manufacturers. After the summer of 1959, during which all records had been broken, most of them had geared up their capacity and stocks in anticipation of another good season. But now they were left with ice cream they could not sell. In August the beaches near Göteborg were deserted as holiday-makers left their summer houses and returned home early. Never before had the Swedish ice cream industry been so affected by the vicissitudes of the weather and the losses it suffered precipitated a second wave of business concentration.

• Rationalisation was accelerated by the growing strength of the supermarket chains. They started to negotiate ever higher discounts, which squeezed the profit margins on packs of 'family ice cream' in particular. Karlshamn Glass – the result of a merger between a dairy business started in 1910 and a margarine manufacturer from Norrköping – was set up in 1965 at Karlshamn on the Swedish south coast specifically with the aim of supplying ice cream to KF, a national chain of cooperative stores. The venture's success led to a new factory being opened in 1972 with an estimated ice cream capacity of 20 million litres.[45] In 1994 Karlshamn Glass was second behind market leader GB, with a share of some 16%.

• Another newcomer was Hemglass in Strängnäs, some 100 kilometres west of Stockholm. Founded in 1968, Hemglass supplied ice cream and frozen foods solely to consumers at home. In remote areas the ringing bell of Hemglass trucks was a welcome sound and the company experienced rapid expansion until 1972, when its sales seemed to have reached the formula's natural limit. In 1994 Hemglass had a market share of 10%.

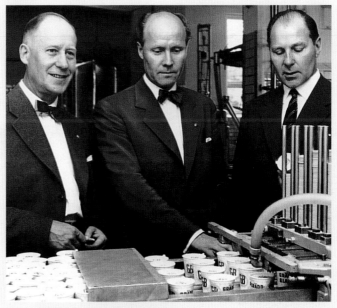

387: GB's management in the Flen ice cream factory, circa 1960. Eric Hanner (centre), Gösta Lilja (right) and Bernd Gohde watch ice cream tubs being filled automatically.

• The battle for the consumer's favour became increasingly hard-fought. Many small, locally operating ice cream firms threw in the towel or were bought up by big companies. In 1987 Gösta Lilja, GB's technical director, wrote in the company magazine that GB had taken over more than 50 smaller ice cream businesses in the period between 1937 and 1972.[46] One of them, Strand Glass in Piteå, on the Gulf of Bothnia in the far north of Sweden, joined GB in 1972.

• The first major consolidation in the market occurred in 1962, when Unilever bought Trollhätteglass for 4,963,000 kronor and amalgamated it with Gille-Glass,[47] which it had acquired in May 1960.[48] The merged company traded under the name Trollhätteglass, enjoying a market share of about 17.5%. GB remained market leader with a 21% share and Ge-Ge in Malmö was number three with 15%.[49]

388: Lakrits-puck, a vanilla ice cream dipped in liquorice water-ice, was launched with much success by Glace Bolaget in 1982. The ice is shaped like an ice hockey puck.

• One rationalisation led to another and a second concentration took place the following year. Five ice cream businesses, all affiliated to dairy cooperatives, joined GB in 1963: Arla Glass from Göteborg, Cupglass from Örebro, Freja from Gävle, Nordan from Luleå and Solglass from Karlstad. This megamerger was orchestrated by Eric Hanner. With Malmö Glass (Ge-Ge) also joining GB in 1966, the company now had nationwide distribution and a market share of more than 50%.

• In 1963 the government abolished the luxury tax on ice cream that had been introduced in 1942. Yet despite this relaxation, business concentrations and the introduction of numerous new ice creams backed by substantial advertising, Trollhätteglass

knaprig · annorlunda
"88"
Vaniljglass med
ischoklad
täckt med knapriga
krokantsmulor

TROLLHÄTTE Glass

389: 1965 Trollhätteglass advertisement for '88', a vanilla ice cream with a crunchy coating and filled with chocolate fudge. The recipe for '88' had originally been developed by the American Good Humor ice cream company. Since the early 1960s both Good Humor and Trollhätteglass had been owned by Unilever.

sustained losses year after year. The situation was so serious that in 1971 Unilever considered closing down or selling the company.[50] Negotiations with GB brought a solution. At the end of 1972 Trollhätteglass was transferred to GB, in return for which Unilever acquired a 30% minority interest in GB. Because of the losses at Trollhätteglass, the deal allowed GB to buy back the Unilever shareholding within five years. For whatever reason, that did not happen. Because of GB's good profitability, Unilever, although not usually comfortable in a minority position, prolonged the partnership in 1977; and in 1982 a know-how contract was concluded.[51] As a result GB was able to start marketing Unilever brands including Carte d'Or and Viennetta desserts (see chapter 21). Between 1983 and 1985,

100 million kronor was invested in new products and in modernising the ice cream factory in Flen.

• The pace of growth of the ice cream market had been slowing dramatically from an average of 17% in the 1950s and 1960s to as little as 2% in 1984. It seemed as if ice cream consumption in Sweden had hit its ceiling. In the first half of the 1980s per capita consumption fluctuated at around 13.8 litres.

• In 1983, Unilever was considering making an offer for the Arla dairy cooperative's 59.8% shareholding in GB.[52] Serious talks started at the beginning of 1984, but the difference in views about the value of the shares was so wide that it took until August 1985 before agreement was reached. Arla sold the greater part of its shares to Unilever, which thus became the owner of 90% of the shares in GB. The leading role played for more than half a century by dairy cooperatives in the Swedish ice cream industry was over.

• In the meantime, Sweden itself was changing rapidly. In 1990 commercial television was finally launched, the last country in Western Europe to do so. Discussions about seeking membership of the European Union were revived. In restaurants and shops the luxury ice

cream of Häagen Dazs and Mövenpick made its appearance and chocolate manufacturer Mars entered the ice cream market, developments which influenced the marketing of ice cream (see also chapter 21). In 1987, for example, responding to the entry of Mars, GB, in cooperation with the Swedish chocolate manufacturer Marabou, successfully launched a new ice cream, Daimstrut. Two years later Marabou was bought by Philip Morris.[53] As the name for a chocolate bar with crispy caramel, Daim had long been popular throughout Scandinavia. Cooperation between GB and Marabou had started the year before, with the marketing of Daimglass as family pack.[54] The arrival of Daimstrut meant that, 45 years after Förenade Chokladfabrikerna A.B. Thule, Alaska and the Mjölkcentralen had set up GB, a chocolate manufacturer again became involved in the production of ice cream. The event was indicative of the process that had taken place. Ice cream was no longer a luxury treat for a lucky few, but a mass-market product manufactured and sold by companies operating globally.

390: Advertisement for the new Daimstrut ice cream, first marketed by Glace Bolaget in 1987. Daim was a chocolate brand, licensed from the Swedish chocolate company Marabou.

391: GB choc-ice advertisement, 1963.

Licks, Sticks & Bricks

A WORLD HISTORY OF ICE CREAM

Germany: Goethe's passion lives on

12

392: Tinplate figure of an ice cream seller
from a Teatro Mundi, Germany, third quarter
of the nineteenth century. A Teatro Mundi
was a theatre of mechanical dolls, in which
the figures were moved by a continuous
rotating chain.

'One day our mother caused us great sorrow when she threw away the ice cream that was served to us at table, as it seemed impossible to her that a stomach could really tolerate ice cream', wrote Johann Wolfgang von Goethe (1749-1832) in his autobiographical work Dichtung und Wahrheit, describing something that he had experienced as a boy.[1] The incident did not prevent the poet from becoming an enthusiast, with a particular passion for raspberry ice cream.[2]

• Ice cream became popular in Germany and Austria in the second half of the eighteenth century. Since the end of the seventeenth century German-language cookery books had contained recipes for making ice cream (see chapter 3), but for a long time it remained a luxury product whose price was mainly governed by the cost of sugar, a commodity so expensive that only the affluent could afford sweet dishes like cake and ice cream. It was not until about 1780 that ice cream appeared on the menu of Vienna's coffee houses, becoming by the century's end an accepted part of middle-class life in both Germany and Austria.[3] The ice cream was prepared by confectioners, who strove to outdo each other by creating special bombes glacées. Devising new bombes glacées - or Eisbomben - went on to become all the rage in the nineteenth century, one of the most famous German confections being the 'Fürst Pückler' (see box on p. 392).

From Bismarck to the 'Wirtschaftswunder'

• Germany's history in the second half of the nineteenth century is dominated by the struggle to unify the nation. Otto von Bismarck achieved this in 1871, yet the 'Iron Chancellor' was no fan of ice cream, declaring it to be 'something wishy-washy and suited only for the ladies'.[4] He evidently managed to swallow his distaste during the negotiations in Rome in 1882 over what was to become the Triple Alliance (the treaty between Germany, Austro-Hungary and Italy), showing every sign of relishing an ice cream dessert that was served in the colours of the alliance partners.[5]

• Towards the end of the nineteenth century more and more Italian ice cream sellers and their colourful carts appeared on the streets of German and Austrian cities (see chapter 4). For northern Italians, southern Germany and Austria were close and had a comparable climate. From the south of Germany the Italians then spread throughout the whole of the country, returning to Italy during the winter months, as is still their custom today. In 1997 there were some 3,000 Italian ice cream parlours in Germany, with a market share of between 13% and 15%. When they return to Germany to re-open their parlours, people say: 'The Italians are back, spring has started'.[6]

• After the Second World War a devastated Germany was quickly rebuilt, including the factories of well-known ice cream firms such as Langnese, Jopa and Schöller. Before the war America was already serving as an example for the German ice cream market; after it that influence became even stronger. In the difficult post-war period ice cream manufacturers focused primarily on the US occupying forces in Germany. The GIs had grown up on ice cream and they also had the money to buy it.

• The post-war history of German ice cream, however, is chiefly the story of West Germany

The Fürst-Pückler-Eisbombe

¶ Germany's most famous ice cream confection is the Fürst-Pückler-Eisbombe [Prince Pückler's bombe glacée]. The eccentric Prince von Pückler-Muskau (1785-1871) was an artist, landscape gardener, travel writer, adventurer, ladies' man – and gourmet. His princely title is inseparably linked to the ice cream creation that bears his name: the three-flavoured Fürst Pückler ice. It consists of a base of strawberry ice cream, then a layer of vanilla, topped off with a layer of chocolate. The bombe is then 'studded' with cherries steeped in maraschino liqueur and topped with whipped cream. According to one of the historical records, it was the court confectioner Schulze who gave the Prince's name to the new ice cream confection. Naming a new ice cream creation after a well-known personality was very much the custom in those days. According to another version, the Prince himself thought up the recipe for the bombe glacée. When Prince von Pückler-Muskau asked his dinner guests what name he should give to his new creation, his friend Hardenberg spontaneously cried out: 'Fürst-Pückler-Eis!'[1] In their products and advertising modern-day ice manufacturers like Langnese and Schöller regularly recall the Prince's tricoloured ice cream. Advertisements in the 1950s and 1960s claim their vanilla-strawberry-chocolate ice cream is made in the genuine 'Fürst Pückler' manner.

and of the Wirtschaftswunder (economic miracle). East Germany lay trapped behind the Iron Curtain. When ice cream production began in Germany in 1925, there were about 23 ice cream manufacturers; by the 1960s rationalisation and re-organisation had left only a few producers in West Germany, the top three being Langnese, Jopa and Schöller. Average consumption at that time was 2.4 litres of ice cream per person per year.

Ice cream or a slice of pumpernickel bread & butter?

• As the twentieth century opened, it was no longer only the élite or even the wealthy middle classes who ate ice cream. Labourers, farmers and tradesmen did too, though usually only on red letter days like birthdays and weddings. One striking feature in those days was the contrast in ice cream's popularity between the north and the south of Germany. Ice cream spread first from Saxony to Holstein and Mecklenburg, where it soon replaced traditional desserts like cold custard and rice pudding. But in spite of the warmer climate of southern Germany and Austria, the presence of Italian ice cream sellers failed to tempt people away from their traditional desserts such as cakes and pastries. Ice cream only became really popular there in the 1920s and 1930s.[7]

• For both ice cream and entertainment, the place to be in the 1920s and 1930s was Berlin. The German capital acted like a magnet, attracting everything that was new and popular. It also had a public, both German and foreign, which was willing to buy ice cream. On 19 June 1931, for example, the New York Evening Post reported how

popular ice cream was becoming in Berlin. The prime rendezvous for young Germans was the 'soda fountain' near the Kurfürstendamm, Berlin's main shopping street, where you could eat ice cream and drink soda water.[8] As well as in Berlin, the ice cream industry was strong in Hamburg and Munich.

• In the 1920s Germany was still recovering from the First World War. Reparation payments to the Allies were high and there was galloping inflation. There was no money for investment on the scale required for ice cream machines. It was principally the dairy businesses that started making ice cream in the summer to use up their milk and cream surpluses. The Kiel-based Prussian Research Institute for Dairy Production, headed by Professor Berthold Lichtenberger, had started organising ice cream making courses in 1924. The first course was a great success, attracting more than 100 participants, mostly from the dairy industry in Northern Germany and Prussia.[9] Lichtenberger had been to the United States to learn the ice cream trade and, as the Americans had, he founded a trade journal for the German ice cream industry. The first issue of Zeitschrift für Rahmeis was published on 23 December 1924. A month later, it was retitled Zeitschrift für Eiskrem. 'Eiskrem' was derived from the English 'ice cream' and Lichtenberger considered it a more appropriate term for this young product.[10]

• A year after the first ice cream course, the Schlesien dairy ice cream factory in Breslau produced the first industrial ice cream in Germany. In Berlin the firm of Grönland followed suit and Ude started up ice cream production in Hamburg.[11] In October 1926 the restaurant owner Hinrich Friedrich Ude had

393: Street sale of ice cream, Berlin, 1901. The ice cream vendor is offering raspberry, vanilla, lemon and chocolate flavours in five or ten pfennig portions.

bought a small ice cream business from the trader Wilhelm Böhmke. The business was located at Schmidts Passage in the Altona district of Hamburg. Böhmke had started making ice cream in 'the American way' in that location in 1925, but after a year he was forced to sell the business to Ude for 68,500 Reichsmarks. The purchase price comprised not only the land, buildings and machines but also a lorry and ice cream moulds, including 30 'Fürst Pückler' moulds.[12] Machinery for the new ice cream factories came from America, but also from German and Danish manufacturers (see chapter 6). In 1925, the Lübeck firm of Wilh. G. Schröder advertised its ice cream machines in Zeitschrift für

Eiskrem. In Dresden the firm of Otto Hänsel produced similar machines. Another Dresden-based company was Pauer & Comp. A.G., which manufactured cardboard ice cream tubs that were 'fully airtight and watertight' and had a 'taste-free and odour-free impregnation'.[13] German ice cream companies also sought co-operation with manufacturers in neighbouring countries and joined with ice cream producers from Austria, Switzerland and the Netherlands in setting up the 'Verband mitteleuropäischer Eiskremfabrikanten' (Association of Central European Ice Cream Manufacturers) in 1925. The Association's symbol was the polar bear, the same animal as graced the cover of Zeitschrift für Eiskrem.

Eishändlerin
„Eis gefällig, Portion 5 ⟨?⟩"

Its objectives were to support its members in building their businesses and to convince the public that an ice cream was 'just as nutritious as a slice of pumpernickel bread with butter'.[14]

394: Sale of 'fruit & vanilla ice cream' in Germany, circa 1910. Under the copper lids in the enormous ice cream cart are four churns filled with ice cream.

• The public also had to be reassured that ice cream was being made in a hygienic manner, which meant that regulations and legislation were needed. In contrast to the Netherlands (see chapter 10), where the government had taken the lead in passing ice cream legislation in the 1920s, in Germany it was the ice cream industry itself that approached the government with a request for regulation. This did not happen until July 1933, by which time Adolf Hitler had seized political control. The new ice cream decree stipulated that ice cream had to contain at least 10% milk-fat. Fruit ice had to contain at least 20% fresh fruit or fruit pulp.[15]

• It was now up to the ice cream manufacturers to widen their consumer base and the American invention of ices on a stick – Eis am Stiel - proved most valuable for that purpose (see chapter 5). In 1935 the first ice creams on a stick went on sale in Berlin during the intervals of theatre shows, films, operas, revues and other forms of entertainment. The first firm in Germany to start the production of Eis am Stiel in 1935 was Ude in Hamburg, followed a few months later by Langnese and Warncke. Of these, it was Warncke which was particularly successful.

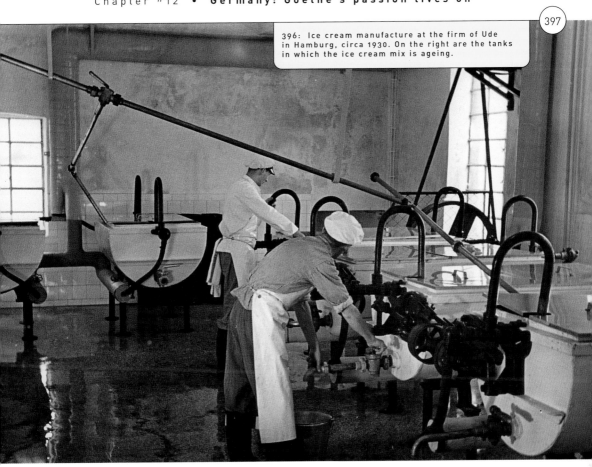

396: Ice cream manufacture at the firm of Ude in Hamburg, circa 1930. On the right are the tanks in which the ice cream mix is ageing.

395: Poster by Bernard Rosen for the Berlin-based ice cream manufacturer Grönland, circa 1927. Grönland, established in 1925, was Berlin's oldest ice cream firm. The Eskimo figure is a standard way around the world of symbolising the coldness of ice cream.

397: The founder of the Ude ice cream factory, Hinrich Friedrich Ude, with his wife, circa 1930. Ude started an ice cream factory in Hamburg's Altona district in 1926.

Warncke: from 'Schmalz' to ice cream

• Hans Warncke Sr. was the director of a margarine factory in Hamburg in the 1920s. He also had a wholesale trade in Schmalz, melted and resolidified lard usually spread on bread, and imported fats like palm oil and coconut fat. On 1 October 1933 he handed over the reins to his son, Hans Warncke Jr., who built a new factory for the production of both Schmalz and ice cream at the beginning of 1936. In the summer there was much less work for the Schmalz department, offering the chance to make ice cream. Before start-

ing construction of the factory, Warncke father and son went on an extensive fact-finding mission to Danish ice cream factories. In the end, however, they bought their machines from Bergendorfer Eisenwerk in Hamburg, which supplied ice cream equipment and freezing machines and claimed to be the world's largest manufacturer of machinery for the dairy industry.

398: Berliners try to escape the summer heat on one of the lakes surrounding their city, 1927. The ice cream man reaches them by boat.

As well as in Hamburg, Bergendorfer Eisenwerk had branches in Berlin, Breslau, Kiel, Munich, Vienna and Prague.

• Warncke began production in the spring of 1936, with a capacity of 3,000 ice creams on a stick per hour. The Olympic Games held in Berlin that year presented an excellent opportunity to sell pre-packed ice cream. The weather was fine and hundreds of thousands of people attended. Every night Warncke salesmen, their vans bursting with ice cream, drove from Hamburg to Berlin and took up station at every stadium entrance. From boxes slung from their shoulders and cooled with dry ice, the salesmen stood ready to tempt the public into buying ice creams. A vanilla ice cream on a stick cost ten pfennigs; one coated with chocolate cost twenty pfennigs.[16]

• In 1937 the 17-year-old Werner Warncke, nephew of Hans Jr., travelled to Hannover to sell ice cream to the Nepken chain of kiosks. These kiosks had an exclusive contract to sell Langnese products, so Werner journeyed on to Magdeburg, where he was able to conclude a deal with 25 kiosks to supply them with metal chests cooled with dry ice on condition that they would only sell Warncke ice creams. Distribution was then extended to Dessau, the home base of the Junkers aircraft factory, which employed a workforce of thousands. Warncke sold 5,000 ice creams a day there. Since Dessau is more than 350 kilometres from Hamburg, Warncke set up a coldstore in Magdeburg in 1938, but the outbreak of the Second World War brought Warncke's ice cream expansion to a halt.

The 'long nose' of Langnese

• In 1932 the Deutsche Margarine-Verkaufs-union (German Margarine Sales Union), a subsidiary of Unilever, was set up in Berlin. The German government was already imposing restrictions on the transfer of company profits out of the country, but after Hitler seized power in 1933 it became impossible. Unilever therefore invested the accumu-lated surpluses of the Deutsche Margarine-Verkaufsunion in a large-scale shipbuilding programme and in the purchase of several German businesses.[17]

• One of the businesses was the Langnese Eiskrem Gesellschaft, which Unilever bought for £50,000 in 1936 following an inspection by Wall's director Cecil Rodd. The owner, the merchant Karl Josef Seyfert, had acquired the right to use the Langnese name for ice cream from the Hamburg-based honey producer V.E.H. Langnese. Seyfert had start-ed his ice cream business in April 1935 in the Hamburg suburb of Wandsbek, but after a successful first season had got into difficul-ties because of restrictions imposed by the Nazi regime on the supply of raw materials. The agreement with Unilever therefore came at a very opportune moment for him.[18]

• Sales of Langnese ice cream had in fact already been transferred into third-party hands in the autumn of 1935. According to a notarial deed dated 18 October, Ilse and Erich Illgen, Helena and Richard Ehring and Franz Stoiber founded on that date the Langnese Eiskrem Vertriebsgesellschaft (Langnese Ice Cream Sales Company), with a starting capital of 20,000 marks[19]. The company's objectives were 'the sale of the products of the firm of V.E.H. Langnese in Hamburg, especially those of the ice cream factory department and the activities relating thereto'. When the new company's balance sheet was drawn up on 31 December 1935, it showed that the business had oper-ated at an initial loss of around 5,000 marks.[20]

399: Advertisement for Langnese 'Eis am Stiel', circa 1938. The name Langnese had long been known in Hamburg as the name of the A.H. Langnese biscuit-making firm, established in 1863. That firm's logo also depicted a girl with ponytails cocking a snook (or, as the Germans say, 'making a long nose'), but with both hands.

When Unilever bought the ice cream busi-ness in 1936 it had the firm registered in the Berlin commercial register under the name Langnese Eiskrem GmbH with the trading names 'Eis am Stiel V.E.H. Langnese', 'Lang-nese Eis am Stiel', 'Langnese Eiskrem' and 'Langnese Eis'.[21]

• There was some confusion regarding the Langnese trading name at that time. As well as the honey business V.E.H. Langnese,

400: Ice cream van selling Langnese 'Eis am Stiel', circa 1937. On the left is Max Schmeling. World boxing champion between 1930 and 1932, Schmeling was a very well-known personality in Germany.

there was also a Hamburg-based firm called A.H. Langnese, which had been producing biscuits since 1863 under the Langnese-Keks brand name. This firm's logo was very well-known in the Hamburg area: a girl with a ponytail cocking a snook or, as the Germans say, making a 'long nose' (Lang Nese) with both hands. Langnese ice cream was now being advertised using a picture of a boy making a 'long nose' with one hand and holding an ice cream on a stick in the other. A.H. Langnese objected to the use by another company of the Langnese brand name and on 5 January 1937 wrote to the legal authorities in Berlin, asking them to delete Langnese Eiskrem from the commercial register.[22] The precise details of the settlement are not clear from the few docu-

ments that have survived, but clearly A.H. Langnese's complaint did not succeed, for sales of 'Langnese Eis am Stiel' continued as normal.

• In 1936 Langnese sold some three million ices on a stick. Langnese also supplied ice cream in churns to bars and restaurants and in 1937 the firm employed 120 workers.[23] Among the company's very first promoters were the recent boxing world champion Max Schmeling and his actress wife Anni Ondran. Exploiting the glamour evoked by this popular man-and-wife team, Langnese had Schmeling drive through Hamburg in an ice cream van bearing the words 'Langnese Eis am Stiel' and the portraits of ordinary men and women eating ice cream on a stick. After all, ice cream from Langnese was 'Das Eis

für Jedermann' – the ice cream for everyone.
• Ice cream was still a seasonal product and its manufacturers looked for ways of expanding and supplementing their business during the winter. They found one in quick-frozen food. In 1932 Unilever had acquired a jam factory in Hannover-Wünsdorf. The production of jam was gradually discontinued in favour of frozen foods, a switch formalised in 1939 when Unilever set up the frozen foods company Solo Feinfrost, later re-named Iglo. The firm had its registered office in Berlin but its production facilities were located in the former jam factory. During the war more and more workers were withdrawn to serve in the armed forces and from 1940 the Hamburg ice cream factory was faced with an increasing scarcity of raw materials and tighter restrictions on production. There came a point where the firm could no longer pay its creditors and on 25 January 1943 the business was liquidated.[24]

Jopa's ice cream saloon

• In Bavaria the name Jopa stood for both ice cream and frozen foods. On 21 June 1933 the 25 year-old Josef Pankofer had opened the doors of his first ice cream saloon on Munich's Sonnenstrasse, christening his business using the first two letters of each of his names. Pankofer's starting capital consisted of 500 marks of his own and a couple of thousand marks he had borrowed from his uncle. The tables and chairs to furnish his saloon were provided by the Hanselmann dairy factory in exchange for the contract to supply him with milk and cream. The ice cream machine was installed on a hire-purchase basis by the firm of Stich & Co in return for a payment of ten Reichsmarks a day. On the first day he had 900 customers, on the second 2,000 and on the third day it was up to 3,000. Within three months Pankofer had repaid all those who had lent him money. The successful advance of the Jopa ice cream brand had begun.[25]

• Frozen foods, too, attracted Josef Pankofer's interest. He was one of the first people in Germany to trade in quick-frozen vegetables, meat and fish. In fact, prior to the Second World War this was Jopa's principal source of income. In 1934 Pankofer opened a second ice cream shop in the Thalkirchnerstrasse in Munich. In those days hundreds of thousands of jobless workers passed down this street on their way to the labour exchange to sign on. Even so, they could usually find 10 pfennigs to buy an ice cream and forget their plight for a moment.

• In 1935 Pankofer went on a trip to the south of France and Spain and in Barcelona saw an ice cream bar fitted out in the latest American fashion. On his return he rebuilt his ice cream saloon in the same style and called it 'Pankofers Eis-Salon'. Its centre-piece was the 'Ice Cream Soda Bar' made by the Chicago firm of Bastian & Blessing. In 1936 Pankofer sold his business in the Thalkirchnerstrasse, having decided that he wanted to start producing industrial ice cream. He kept the parlour in Sonnenstrasse whose profits supported his investment in a new ice cream factory at 131, Lindwurm-strasse. In its first year the factory turned out no fewer than one million portions of ice cream, Jopa being sold in almost all the bars, kiosks, restaurants, bathing resorts and health spas in Bavaria. Very soon

Pankofer's twenty delivery vans could not cope with the work, so he set up a series of coldstores. In 1942 the Jopa factory on the Lindwurmstrasse was destroyed during an Allied air raid. Pankofer's ice cream saloon on the Sonnenstrasse in Munich stayed open until 1943 when it, too, was hit by a bomb.[26]

• Jopa ice cream also helped to trigger the start of the Schöller ice cream empire. In 1935 Theo Schöller, then aged eighteen, had his first taste of 'Eis am Stiel' at a revue theatre in Berlin.[27] The next year Theo and his brother Karl took particular pleasure from their Jopa ice creams while watching a motor-car race near Munich. The brothers contacted Josef Pankofer and obtained a licence to make and sell Jopa ice cream in the region north of the Danube as far as the River Main. On 18 June 1937, Theo Schöller celebrated his birthday by pulling his first ice cream on a stick out of its ice cream mould in the small factory at 5, Martin Richterstrasse in Nuremberg. The brothers sold the ice cream in picture-houses, kiosks and restaurants. In 1938 they also embarked on the production of quick-frozen foods. After the outbreak of the Second World War ice cream production came to a stop, though the Schöllers' business did continue its line in frozen meat, vegetables and fruit.[28]

• In the first few years after the war raw materials for ice cream

401: Poster, 1952, for Jopa ice cream by the Swiss poster artist Herbert Leupin (born 1916). Jopa was an abbreviation based on the first two letters of the name and surname of Josef Pankofer, who founded the ice cream firm in Munich in 1935. Until the beginning of the 1960s Jopa was the biggest ice cream brand in southern Germany.

402: Schöller ice cream production, 1937.

production were either unobtainable or in extremely short supply, and ice cream was a rarity. The turning point came with the currency reform of 20 June 1948. The Lebensmittelmarken (food rationing coupons) were abolished, while the Reichsmark was devalued in the ratio of 1:10 and replaced by the Deutsche Mark. In addition, every German was given a Kopfgeld (a one-off grant per head) of 40 new marks. After a long period of hardship and deprivation the German consumer could at last afford to buy something again. Sugar rationing also came to an end.

• In 1949 buying ice cream was possible once more and the ice cream decree of 1933 regulating its content came back into force. In 1950 only 5.3% of German households possessed a refrigerator and per capita consumption was an insignificant 0.15 of a litre, about one large scoop of ice cream; but the economy in the Federal Republic was growing fast and ice cream consumption grew steadily, to over eight litres per head by the 1990s.

403: Eating an ice cream in the street in the Bavarian town of Fürth, circa 1949. In the first post-war years ice cream was hardly available in Germany. This changed In 1949 when sugar was again allowed to be used for production of ice cream.

Warncke and the acquisition of Ude

• After the war, companies such as Ude, Warncke, Langnese, Pankofer and Schöller had to start again from scratch. Hamburg was in the British occupation zone, where until 1948 the rationing of foodstuffs such as sugar prevented Hans Warncke from manufacturing ice cream. His nephew, Werner Warncke, therefore moved to Bremen and built a new ice cream factory there.

In Hamburg Warncke mainly produced ice cream in tubs and 'Eis am Stiel', whilst the Bremen factory manufactured not only ice creams on a stick but also a product called Kluten. This was a bar of vanilla ice cream with wafers covering one half, the other being wrapped in chocolate, which soon became an enormous success.

• Throughout the 1950s Warncke continued to expand, building ice cream factories in

Menninghüffen (1954) and Hannover (1959). To keep abreast of the latest developments, Werner Warncke travelled regularly to the United Kingdom and America. In 1964, on a visit to the firm of Breyers in New York, he saw a new method for cutting a one-litre block of ice cream. The machine sliced the block into ten equal portions. Then, in the blink of an eye, the machine inserted a piece of paper between each portion. Warncke now adopted this method, which met with great success.

• In 1968 Warncke Eiskrem constructed another large ice cream factory at Brundorf, near Bremen. This became the new centre of the Warncke ice cream empire; all other sites were closed down.

• In 1970 Germany's oldest ice cream firm, Ude, merged with Warncke. The union was prompted by the regeneration of Hamburg's Altona district, where the Ude factory was located. The factory was closed down and Ude faced the prospect of starting afresh elsewhere. Instead, Ude decided to tie the knot with Warncke, with which it had long-standing amicable ties.

• In 1972 Warncke took over the firm Wipa Eiskrem (established in 1927). By about 1988 Warncke was operating twenty depots in northern Germany and was exporting ice cream, for instance to Belgium.[29] In 1989, however, the company was bought by the French ice cream manufacturer Miko. Four years later one of the European Union's conditions for approval of Unilever's purchase of Miko in France was the disposal of Warncke in Germany, for monopoly reasons. Unilever duly sold Warncke to Nestlé in 1994 and the Warncke business name finally disappeared.

404 and 405: (above and top)
The 'Eissalon Panciera', an ice cream
saloon in Duisburg, circa 1955.

406: Advertisement for
ice cream sold by Panciera
in Duisburg, circa 1955.

Schöller: from licensee to ice cream giant

- Ultimately Schöller's ownership structure also changed, with the setting up in 1995 of Schöller Holding, a company in which the Südzucker Group, Europe's largest sugar refiner, held a 65% share.
- After the Second World War, Theo Schöller had been forced to reorganise the firm. His brother Karl left the family business, leaving Theo to handle things on his own. He set up his ice cream department in a new production room with a floor area of just 150 square metres. Ice cream production recommenced in September 1945 and Schöller's lucky break was the stationing of US occupying forces stationed around Nuremberg. The soldiers did not want to miss out on their beloved ice cream and Schöller was awarded the contract to keep them supplied. The firm expanded from this point and in 1958 bought a 'Rollo 29' automatic ice lolly machine from the Danish company Høyer. Schöller's was the second German company, after Langnese, to invest in a Rollo (see chapter 6) and the purchase represented a great step forward, for the Rollo had an output of 5,000–7,000 ices per hour.[30]
- Schöller's ice cream was meanwhile still being sold under the Jopa brand name under the licence acquired in 1937. In 1956 Jopa's production ran to 30 to 40 million portions of ice cream which were sold throughout Bavaria,[31] an increase of 400% over a period of 20 years. By 1959 the business, including Schöller, held a 23% share of the market, second behind Langnese's 50% share. In 1960 the licensing agreement with Jopa expired and Schöller began producing ice creams under its own name.[32] Schöller's other products, such as gingerbread, were already being sold all over the country under the trading name 'Allgemeine Lebensmittel-Betriebe Inh. Theo Schöller', so the Schöller brand name was already familiar to consumers throughout Germany.
- In 1960, its first ice cream season as an independent operator, Schöller was offering twelve different varieties, one of them being the Fürst Pückler recipe that combined strawberry, vanilla and chocolate.[33] In the 1960s expansion continued as new technologies were introduced including in 1964 the production of ice cream cones, following Langnese's runaway success with the Cornetto cone. Schöller's cone, Nucki, became one of the company's best-selling products.
- In 1967 a new Schöller factory came on stream in Nuremberg. This ultra-modern plant had a capacity of between 9,000 and 12,000 lollies per hour, while the tub-filling line could handle between 16,000 and 18,000 tubs of ice cream per hour. Schöller was now producing 125,000 litres of ice cream a day. By 1970 Schöller had a turnover of DM85.2 million and its workforce had swelled to 1,600 people.
- In 1971 the company opened a new cold-store and made the move into foreign markets. In Vienna the firm of Schöller Lebensmittel was established with its own production lines and sales outlets. Its promise was a 'fröhliche Eiszeit mit Schöller Eiskrem' [a happy ice-time with Schöller ice cream]. In the 1970s German children grew up with Schöller ice creams like the Biene Maja (Maja the Bee), Pinocchio and Wickie the Viking. Then, in 1974, the company entered into what would become a highly

successful joint venture with the Swiss Mövenpick group, whose first restaurant Ueli Prager had started back in 1948. From 1974 onwards Schöller's premium ice cream varieties were marketed under the Schöller-Mövenpick brand. Through this brand the business focused on a gourmet public willing to pay more for a better quality ice cream that came in many varieties, flavours and formats, from one-litre packs to cones. Gourmets enthused about the quality of this ice cream: 'every scoop is a world in itself'.[34] Today Mövenpick is a worldwide group with a chain of more than 200 luxury hotels and restaurants.[35]

• In 1978 Schöller acquired Südmilch Eiskrem und Tiefkühlkost GmbH & Co. Rationalisation of production from 1995 led to the closure of two ice cream factories, leaving three in Germany and one each in Belgium, Poland and Hungary. Even so, Schöller remained Germany's second biggest ice cream brand after Langnese, with a market share of 20.8%.[36]

Jopa's ice crystals

• Josef Pankofer and Theo Schöller went their own ways in 1960, but whereas Schöller opted to remain independent, Pankofer decided to co-operate with Nestlé's Findus group in Germany. Pankofer had by then built up a market share of 23%.

• Back in 1947 Pankofer had been supplied by the US army with the raw materials needed to make ice cream for its soldiers. In addition to ice cream, he began trading in frozen foods again. As before the war, this was an important part of his business.

In 1952 Pankofer acquired the Wagner ice cream factory in Stuttgart. He also made home deliveries. Orders could be placed by telephone, which students employed by Pankofer then executed. Jopa ice cream was successfully also sold in kiosks, too. In fact, for many Germans in the 1950s, especially those in the south of the country, the Jopa ice crystal logo was synonymous with ice cream.

• Pankofer was fully aware of the importance of marketing and branding his products. At a culinary trade fair in Munich in 1952 he introduced the Melba brand that had been specially designed for restaurants. The business flourished and in 1953 Jopa-Munich, Jopa-Nuremberg (Schöller) and Wagner-Stuttgart combined had some 4,500 sales outlets. In the same year Pankofer began exporting ice cream to southern Italy; and in Bari he launched the Lola brand which carried the same ice crystal logo as Jopa.

• In 1960, however, a turning point occurred. Schöller in Nuremberg carried on under its own name, while Jopa lost ground to Langnese, which was fast expanding its sales southwards through its new factory in Heppenheim. In the frozen foods trade competition intensified due to the arrival of foreign companies. Findus, Sweden's biggest frozen foods producer, took a majority shareholding in Jopa in 1960. In 1962 the Swiss company Nestlé acquired Findus International, leading to the creation of the Findus-Jopa brand. Jopa-Vienna was then established.

• Josef Pankofer died in 1963, but his firm continued until 1969 when Findus-Jopa and Langnese-Iglo merged. Langnese had become Germany's best-known ice cream brand and held a controlling 75% share in the

merged business. In 1970 the Jopa ice cream factory in Munich was closed and the Jopa ice cream brand disappeared from the stage.[37]

The Langnese Domino

• After the Second World War Langnese's property was sequestered by the British, and it was 1947 before the firm succeeded in getting its property back. On 17 August 1948 Langnese re-started production. Step by step volumes were increased and in 1950 construction began on a factory in Hannover specifically for the production of 'Eis am Stiel'. In those days the sticks were still inserted into the ice creams by hand, but in Hannover the ice creams were now packed using new SIG machines which had a capacity of 100,000 ices a day. The new factory became operational in 1952.

• For adults who considered an ice cream on a stick to be more of a product for children, a new wafer ice cream was developed. Called 'Happen', it adopted the Fürst Pückler combination of vanilla, chocolate and strawberry and permitted the respectable lady or gentleman on the tennis court to be seen eating an ice cream. Langnese also introduced the first family packs of ice cream.

407: Poster for Langnese, circa 1952. The picture was also reproduced on enamel advertising signs in various formats.

But in the early 1950s ice cream was still a luxury in Germany and Langnese lost money. Unilever even contemplated selling the company.

• In 1952 Unilever owned two ice cream companies: Langnese and Wall's in the United Kingdom, established in 1922. Wall's Ice Cream provided Langnese with support. Twice a year the Wall's board of directors – Messrs. Rodd, Stonestreet and Knowles – travelled from London to Hamburg for talks. It is fair to say that management in Hamburg did not always look forward to their arrival and came to view proposals made by the Wall's board with suspicion. For example, the British said that, to supplement sales of ice cream in the summer, Langnese should produce sausages in the winter, as Wall's was doing at that time. The subsequent 'Böcklunder Würstchen' venture was a complete flop. Stocks of unsold sausages in the storerooms at the Wandsbek ice cream factory were used in the soup served in the staff canteen. According to Helmuth Möller, the manager of Wandsbek at the time, the staff at least thought the soup tasty.[38]

408: Two of Langnese's best-sellers in the 1950s: Domino and an 'Eis am Stiel'.

• After the 1952 discussions with the Wall's board it was decided to produce two new ice creams: the Joker and the Domino. The Joker, a simple slice of ice cream without a stick, did not catch on; more successful was the Domino, a slice of vanilla ice cream with the bottom half held with wafers so that consumers could keep their hands clean. The top part of the ice cream was covered in chocolate.

RUNDSTIEL   **-,10**

KUNSTSPEISEEIS

EIS *am* **STIEL**   **-,20**

EINFACH-EISKREM

EIS - NEGER   **-,25**

EINFACH - EISKREM

EIS - HAPPEN   **-,30**

EISKREM

EIS - HOBBY   **-,45**

EISKREM

LANGNESE-EISKREM G.M.B.H. HAMBURG UND HANNOVER

410: The Langnese ice cream factory in Hamburg, circa 1960. The factory was located in Wandsbek, until the war an independent suburb of Hamburg.

409: Langnese ice cream price list, circa 1954.

411: Langnese ice cream van, circa 1954.

412: Lorry operated by the Viennese ice cream company Eskimo in 1927.

¶ 'Ober! Another Eskimo ice cream, please', calls a dapper gentleman. The waiter notes the order, hurries to the kitchen and scoops a portion of ice cream from a five-litre canister into a dish. He carries the dish of ice cream to the customer, who is sitting at a table, leisurely studying the front page of the Wiener Zeitung. The year is 1927 and we are in a typical 'Milchtrinkhalle' [milk bar] in the Prater, Vienna's main entertainment district. Between the two world wars Eskimo ice cream was the best-known Austrian ice cream brand. It still is: Eskimo is to Austria what Langnese is to Germany.

In the 1920s the Milchindustrie AG (Miag) was founded in Vienna. In its fresh milk shops and on the streets this dairy company began to sell ice cream under the Eskimo name. In 1927 Miag was already producing ices on sticks: Eskimo ice lollies.[1] In the 1940s Eskimo began a co-operation with frozen foods pioneer Hans Petter. His quick-frozen vegetables were sold in the shops under the 'Petter' brand and he also acted as general agent for the Swedish Findus company, which exported frozen fish to Austria. Also in the 1940s the Viennese dairy business Wimo began producing quick-frozen

vegetables. Wimo turned for its alliance to the Munich-based ice cream manufacturer Jopa. In 1957 Wimo launched its own ice cream on the Austrian market. Two years later Unilever conducted a survey of the Austrian ice cream market and its eye was caught by Miag, by now Austria's biggest ice cream producer with a market share of 80% and 3,500 sales outlets in prime locations throughout the country.[2] In 1960 Unilever bought Eskimo from Miag and placed its activities within a new frozen foods

and ice cream subsidiary: Delikat Feinkost. At the time the Austrian economy was flourishing and prospects for the ice cream and frozen foods market were excellent. Wimo, Eskimo's only competitor, was acquired in 1962 by the Munich-based firm of Jopa and its ice cream was sold under the Jopa brand name from then

413: Enjoying the summer under an Eskimo parasol in a Vienna park, 1963.

on.[3] Jopa itself had by then become part of the Nestlé group.

Although Schöller also started selling ice cream in Austria in 1971, Eskimo has remained the undisputed market leader right up to the present day. Today in

Vienna the consumer, perhaps now dressed slightly less formally, can still take a seat in a typical coffee house – where time seems to have stood still – peruse his newspaper and ask the Ober for another Eskimo ice cream.

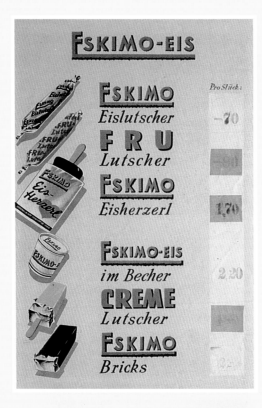

414: Eskimo price list, Vienna, early 1960s.

415: Poster for the Viennese ice cream business Tichy, from the campaign for the 1998 season.

416 and 417 : Posters for the Viennese ice cream business Tichy, 1992. The sugar confectionery baker Kurt Tichy had established the company in 1952. On the left, ice cream as a flying saucer. On the right, Tichy's Eismarillenknödel (apricot ice cream dumplings) which are renowned in the Austrian capital.

Domino became one of Langnese's best-sellers and was probably the model for Warncke's Kluten. By 1978 some 900 million had been sold, of which 700 million were manufactured in the Wandsbek factory.[39]

• Profits rose. Langnese expanded its ice cream production and in about 1953 moved south, starting to sell ice cream in Munich. Langnese had studied the latest ice cream machines of the Danish firm Gram (see chapter 6) and on installing them in Wandsbek in 1952 saw production soar. In 1956 22% more ice cream was made than in the previous year.[40] In 1957 Langnese achieved a turnover of DM28 million offering a range of seven impulse ice creams costing between 10 and 50 pfennigs. The Wandsbek factory was now too small and Langnese looked for a location for a new factory, in the centre of Germany so that both North and South could be supplied. That location was Heppenheim.

A new ice cream factory in Heppenheim

• In 1958 Langnese purchased a 100,000 square metre plot of land in Heppenheim. This wine-producing town, situated in the Bergstrasse area between the Rhine, Main and Neckar rivers and less than 30 kilometres from cities like Heidelberg and Darmstadt, was an ideal site for a new ice cream factory. Langnese gained the support of Heppenheim's mayor: in exchange for an investment of DM27 million and the promise of 600 new jobs, the burgomaster arranged for the town's infrastructure to be greatly improved. Langnese needed good supplies of water, roads had to be upgraded or re-routed and bridges had to be rebuilt. Langnese

loaned Heppenheim the necessary money. Work to the road network alone cost DM400,000.[41]

• On 1 March 1959 the coldstore came into operation. To produce the ice cream Langnese bought a number of Rollo 29 machines from the Danish firm Høyer. On 23 April 1960 production started, the first ice cream rolling off the conveyor belt at 10.30 a.m. The official inauguration of the factory took place on 31 August 1960. The factory in Heppenheim was then the most modern in continental Europe. Every day it used 25 to 30 tons of butter, 30 to 40 tons of sugar, 100 tons of concentrated skimmed milk and around 20 tons of strawberries in making 100 different types of ice cream. Annual production capacity was one million litres.[42] The old Langnese slogan from the 1930s – 'ice cream for everyone' – was more appropriate than ever.

• The underlying factors behind the growth in consumption were the regular introduction of ice cream novelties each season, ever improving distribution, the continuing spread of supermarkets and the market entry of new firms like Heimdienst, which from 1971 began supplying ice cream gâteaux to consumers at home. In 1965 per capita consumption in Germany was 2.4 litres, of which 1.4 litres was accounted for by factory-made ice cream. In 1968 there were only three ice cream manufacturers which operated beyond the borders of their own region: Langnese, Schöller and Jopa. Together they had 75% of the market, of which 50% was held by Langnese. But the ice cream market was heading for difficult times.

• At the end of the 1960s Germany's population was ageing fast, whereas ice cream was generally a young person's product. Ice cream manufacturers therefore increasingly

418: View of the new Langnese ice cream factory at Heppenheim, with the small wine-producing town in the background. The factory, built at a cost of DM27 million between 1958 and 1960, was then Europe's biggest and most modern. The budget included money loaned to the town for improvements in the infrastructure.

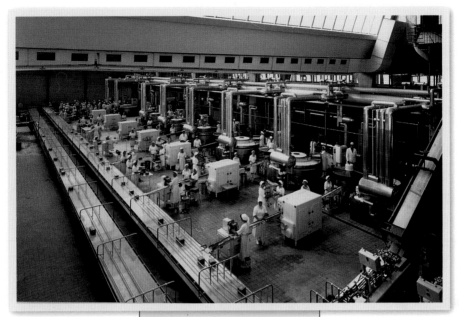

419: Overall view of a production hall in the new Langnese factory at Heppenheim, circa 1960.

420: Compressor room in the Langnese ice cream factory at Heppenheim, circa 1965.

421: Production line workers in the Langnese ice cream factory, Heppenheim, early 1960s.

targeted families, promoting ice cream as a dessert for eating at home in both summer and winter. Langnese serviced this family dessert market with products like Königsrolle and Royal, but the biggest profit was still to be made from the sale of impulse ice creams. To ensure that the impulse market did not lose its momentum, ice cream producers each year launched new products or revamped their 'classics'. One example is Nogger, a vanilla ice cream lolly with chocolate and biscuit that was introduced by Langnese in 1960. In the 1980s Nogger's positioning was as a big, 'tough guy' ice cream aimed at young adults: 'Nogger, zarter Schmelz mit Wumm!' [Nogger, a soft melt with oomph!], as it was described in an advertisement of the time.

• In the 1960s Langnese became the undisputed number one in Germany. But new players were still arriving, such as Heimdienst and Dr. August Oetker. The Oetker family business, founded in Berlin in 1896, traded in many types of goods but had greatest success in foods. In about 1959 Oetker bought the honey producer Langnese Bienenhonig from Karl Seyfert[43] and began manufacturing ice cream in Karlsruhe, where it subsequently built a new plant. The firm chiefly produced ice cream for the take-home sector and in 1996 it introduced an important new brand, Landliebe, based on country values. With a market share of 8%, Oetker was Germany's third biggest ice cream manufacturer in 1997, behind Langnese and Schöller.[44]

422: Production of Cornetto ice cream at Langnese's new factory at Heppenheim, early 1960s.

423: In about 1960 Langnese launched its 'Eiskrem Cocktail'. This tub of vanilla-strawberry ice cream was a copy of a product made by Wall's Ice Cream in the UK, where it had been selling successfully under the name Gaytime Tub since the early 1950s.

The ice cream agreement between Unilever and Nestlé

• On 1 January 1962 the sales organisations of the Unilever businesses Solo Feinfrost and Langnese were amalgamated to form the Langnese Verkaufsorganisation.[45] In 1963 Solo Feinfrost was renamed Iglo and the company subsequently traded under the Langnese-Iglo name. The market share of Langnese-Iglo at that point amounted to 50% for ice cream and 35% for frozen foods. Its biggest rival was Nestlé, whose recent acquisition of Findus-Jopa gave it market shares of 25% for frozen food products and 14% for ice cream.

424: Advertising leaflet for Dolomiti, a new mountain-shaped water-ice by Langnese, circa 1973. Langnese launched new ices on sticks each season, mostly aimed at children.

• At the end of 1969 a spectacular move took place in the German ice cream industry. Langnese-Iglo entered into a co-operation with its competitor Findus-Jopa, making the big ice cream rivals Unilever and Nestlé partners through their Langnese and Jopa brands. Unilever held 75% of the shares in the new business and Nestlé 25% (see also chapter 21). This situation continued until 1986, when the co-operation was terminated and Unilever became the sole owner of Langnese-Iglo.[46]

• In the period from 1975 to 1985 ice cream consumption in Germany grew from 4.8 to 6.8 litres per head. The German economy was prospering, influencing consumer spending patterns. Between 1987 and 1988, consumption of impulse ice cream rose by 6.1% to 90.7 million litres, whilst take-home ice cream and supplies to ice cream saloons, hospitals and other institutional caterers grew by 6.5% to 207.3 million litres. The more expensive 'premium ice cream', for hotels and restaurants as well as for consumption at home, also sold well. Langnese introduced brands such as Gino Ginelli (fourteen Italian ice cream varieties) and Sorbetteria di Ranieri (a range of nine luxury desserts); and the dessert ice cream Viennetta, launched by Walls in 1982 (see chapter 21), also met with great success on the German market.

• At the end of the 1980s Langnese, Schöller and Oetker found themselves faced by new competitors. In a blaze of publicity, American manufacturers such as Häagen Dazs and Mars entered the European ice cream scene. Mars had bought the American ice cream company Dove in September 1986. The Dove Bar was a superb large-format vanilla ice on a stick covered with a thick layer of real chocolate (see also chapter 6) which had opened up the market for luxury impulse products in the USA. Langnese

425: Poster for Langnese, late 1980s.

went all out to counter-attack its competitors and in 1988 was one of the first Unilever companies to launch Magnum ice creams. It proved to be unprecedentedly successful, ushering in a new era in ice cream history in Germany and throughout Europe.

¶ We alight from the train in Zürich. It is 1930 and mid-summer. Along the promenades beside the oh-so-clean waters of Lake Zürich the city's inhabitants are taking a stroll: the gentlemen in top hats, the ladies resplendent in elegant gowns, and the children in cheerful clothes. The month is July – and it's a scorcher! Girls dressed in long white coats move amongst the public. Their coats have a blue armband with the word 'Eis' on it, for these are ice cream sellers employed by the Verbandsmolkerei Zürich [Zürich Dairy Association]. From their shoulders a heavy, metal container hangs on a leather strap. For 50 centimes the citizens of Zürich can treat themselves to an ice cream brick of the Eskimo Pie type. And it is selling very well: last month the Verbandsmolkerei sold over 250,000 of this product, newly introduced from America. Few other refreshments are on sale, since in the Zürich of 1930 vendors of lemonade and beer are not yet seen on the streets. The ladies from the Verbandsmolkerei are therefore doing good trade. With luck they will sell between 20 and 25 Swiss francs' worth of ice cream today - and they get to keep 10% of that for themselves. A

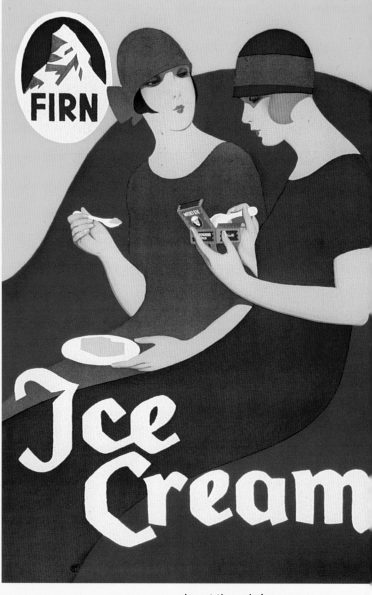

426: Poster for the Verbandsmolkerei Zürich (Zürich Dairy Association) by Carl Moos, circa 1926.

tidy income for those days! And what about the Verbandsmolkerei's ice cream factory? On a hot day like today, at full capacity, it is turning out almost 1,000 litres of ice cream. The Verbandsmolkerei is

almost the only ice cream producer in the Zürich area. Exclusive contracts with picture-houses, kiosk proprietors and shopkeepers provide the business with guaranteed sales. Once a week the ice cream is sent by van or by train to depots or direct to sales outlets in the outlying areas of Zürich. Since the start of ice cream production in 1926 output has almost doubled, climbing from 55,000 litres per annum to 100,000 litres in 1929. Sales in picture-houses in particular are progressing well. A cinema programme will be on four or five reels, so there are many intermissions for reel changes when ice cream will be on sale. The ice cream is sold from freezer boxes cooled with ice and salt, all supplied by the Verbandsmolkerei.

This sketch derives from a diary penned in 1930 by the Swedish ice cream pioneer Eric Hanner (see also chapter 11).[1] Thirty years later the Verbandsmolkereien, which had joined forces under the name Pierrot, were still a major force in the market with a share of 25%. Other ice cream businesses were Migros (26%), Frisco/Findus [Nestlé] (21%), Lusso (9%) and Alemagna (9%). Between 1962 and 1968 sales of factory-made ice cream doubled in Switzerland. At 3.5 litres per person per year, ice cream consumption equalled that of West Germany.

In 1969 Unilever Schweiz conducted a study of the Swiss ice cream market, leading to entry in 1970 under the Eldorado brand name. The ice cream was imported from the Vienna-based Unilever ice cream company, Eskimo Austria, because of the favourable import duties from Austria.

The target was to build a 6% market share within five years. In 1973 Unilever bought Gelbar, an ice cream manufacturer in the Geneva region, and by early 1974 Unilever was able to report its target achieved.[2] Success itself caused supply problems with Austria, so Unilever decided to convert an existing factory in Steffisburg, some 60 kilometres south of Bern, into an ice cream plant. The location was favourable, buildings and energy were available and there was no shortage of local manpower.[3] By December 1974 machinery had been installed and the ice cream plant was ready to commence production.

The acquisition of Lusso in 1981 brought a substantial expansion for Eldorado. The combined business was renamed Lusso-Eldorado and in its first year it recorded a turnover of 52 million francs. In 1995 a joint venture was formed with Pierrot, thus creating the Pierrot-Lusso ice cream business. In 1997 the new company held a 27% share of the market, just ahead of Migros (26%), making it market leader in the land of mountains, milk and chocolate.

Licks, Sticks & Bricks

A WORLD HISTORY OF ICE CREAM

Ice cream in the Low Countries: the ijscoman cometh

13

'Schep IJs, versch IJs!' ['Scooped ice cream, fresh ice cream!'] was the slogan that the Dutch Association of Ice Cream Makers used on a poster it offered to its members in 1933 at a cost of 60 cents. A map of the Netherlands was pictured on it, together with an ice cream wafer, tub and cup. At the bottom of the poster, which was also issued as an enamelled advertising sign, were the words 'Product van Nederlandsche arbeid' ['Product of Dutch labour'].[1] The Association wanted to convince consumers of two things: to buy their ice cream from Dutch ice cream salesmen and not from Italian ice cream sellers; and to leave the packed ice cream made by the newly emerging ice cream manufacturers well alone.

• The advertisement typified the situation in which ice cream production in the Netherlands found itself in the early 1930s. Ice cream, as elsewhere in Europe, was no longer eaten only by the well-to-do, but also by the working man (see chapter 4). Scooped ice cream made by artisans dominated the market and, although people ate on average less than one litre a year, the product was supplied by hundreds of ice cream vendors all over the country and only in the summer. Barely 50 years later there had been a complete transformation with ice cream being eaten all year round, on average some seven litres per head, and supplied in a wide range of varieties by a handful of large ice cream manufacturers.

• In the Netherlands and to a lesser extent in

427: Enamel advertising sign of the 'Nederlandsche Bond van consumptie-ijs-bereiders', 1933. This association of ice cream makers, founded in 1929, used the slogan 'Scooped ice cream, fresh ice cream!' and emphasised, in view of the competition from the growing numbers of Italian ice cream makers, that its products were the fruit of 'Dutch labour'.

Belgium – formerly referred to jointly as the Low Countries – ice cream had long remained a luxury item. In the nineteenth century it was exclusively a delicacy for the élite and was made according to French recipes that formed part of the culinary culture introduced into the Netherlands during the period of French rule (1806-1813). One of the first works published in Dutch and devoted to ice cream recipes appeared in 1807 under the title De Fransche Parfumeur.[2]

428: Sales of 'Vanilla and Chocolate Ice Cream', Rozengracht, Amsterdam, 1898. Photo by B.F. Eilers (1878-1951).

• Nonetheless, very little ice cream was eaten in the Netherlands for most of the nineteenth century. Towards the end of the century, however, this began to change. Growing numbers of confectioners and upmarket speciality shops now sold ice cream alongside their cakes, sweets, pastries and other delicacies.

• Confectionery bakers also began to sell ice cream from barrows in the streets. For a 'respectable' person, buying ice cream in the street was 'not done': it was something ordered from the confectioner to serve as a dessert at birthday parties and on feast days. In the early years street ice cream was therefore mainly bought by the working man and his children. There was hardly any variation in the product offerings and quality fluc-

429: Ice cream cart at Stad-
houderskade in Amsterdam,
1902. The cart is strategically
positioned opposite the
entrance to the Vondelpark.

tuated widely. Only after the Ice Cream Decree proclaimed by the government in 1929 did this change. Ice cream makers began paying greater attention to hygiene, quality and advertising and the image of the product slowly improved. Eating an ice cream outdoors on a summer's day became more popular and the first ice cream saloons also opened. During the Second World War ice cream became a much-loved treat, as until 1944 it was one of the few sweet products that could be bought without a rationing coupon.

• As well as confectionery bakers and street vendors, dairy cooperatives also manufactured ice cream in the Netherlands. Following the 1929 Ice Cream Decree they gradually started using their milk surpluses to make ice cream, in addition to the more traditional butter and cheese. Although more than 100 members attended the founding meeting of the Dutch Association of Ice Cream Manufacturers in 1949, ice cream remained a sideline activity for most of them until the late 1950s. The arrival of Unilever on the ice cream market in Belgium in 1956, and in the Netherlands three years later, brought increased competition. Dairy cooperatives amalgamated or closed down their ice cream production. Confectionery bakers stopped making ice cream and the number of artisanal ice cream makers fell sharply. Assisted by the advance of the refrigerator and the supermarket, industrially manufactured ice cream began to dominate the market and consumption, both in the home and on the street, increased by leaps and bounds.

The beginning: confectionery bakers and street vendors

• In the summer of 1889, on the seafront boulevard of the Dutch bathing resort of Scheveningen, an Italian called Lanza did good trade with his ice cream cart. This was where C.E. Simons, later known as 'Keesje de IJssiesman' [Keesje the Ices Man], began his career. Aged fifteen, he and a friend travelled to Scheveningen 'where Lanza the Italian could always use a couple of sturdy lads to sell his ice cream to the seaside visitors'. Keesje Simons spent one summer season selling for Lanza and then set up in business for himself in the Katendrecht district of Rotterdam.[3]

• In the Belgian city of Liège Italian ice cream sellers also appeared on the streets at the end of the nineteenth century. One of them was Antoine Marziale, the founder of the ice cream business today known as Mio. But street selling of ice cream was still relatively rare – if you wanted to buy ice cream in the Low Countries in about 1900, you had a better chance of obtaining it from a confectionery baker.

• Even so, not many bakery shops sold ice cream. Jantje van Leyden, the pseudonym of the author of Eten en drinken in Amsterdam (1898), mentions in his book only two shops in the capital where you could purchase ice cream. The first was 'the elegant and neatly furnished "confiserie" of the firm of Jolitems', from which you could order the 'most exquisitely prepared types of ices, such as vanilla, raspberry and fruit ice, sorbets or plombières (individual ice cream

bombs)'. The other was the recently opened saloon of Gerhard Dreihus, who as a 'pâtissier-glacier' sold ice cream and sorbets from his premises on the Kalverstraat.[4] A little later, in 1907, 'confiseur and cuisinier' W. Berkhoff opened a business 'with refreshment saloons' at 46, Leidsestraat. It was a fashionable shop in which the clientele could choose from as many as 52 different varieties of 'bombes glacées'. Among the chiefly French names for the ice cream dishes, one of the more unusual was the 'Bombe Uncle-Tum', so-called after Harriet Beecher Stowe's book Uncle Tom's Cabin (1852).[5]

WINKEL EN SALONS: LEIDSCHESTRAAT 46.

430: Shop and 'refreshment saloon' of W. Berkhoff at 46, Leidsestraat in Amsterdam, 1907. The delicacies served by 'confiseur cuisinier' Berkhoff comprised a wide selection of ice creams, including 52 different types of 'bombes glacées'.

• The de-luxe confectionery bakers mentioned by Van Leyden also organised street sales of ice cream by vendors with carts. The author describes one such ice cream cart trading under the name 'De Kleine Konkorent' [The Little Competitor]. This 'ambulant pâtissier-glacier supplied plombières of half white and red ice to the hot-faced Amsterdammers, and also sold what are known as 'ice tablets'.[6] Ice tablets were slices of ice cream that were served to the consumer on a piece of paper. Ice cream was also served in a small glass, as in Great Britain (see chapter 4). Ice cream cones and wafers were not yet available.

• The itinerant ice cream trade in the Netherlands was not confined to the big cities. In the early years of the new century ice cream makers could also be found in provincial towns such as Hoorn and Zwolle and in villages like Ammerzoden and Raalte. In 1903 the 11 year-old C. Doffer helped the ice cream man Japie Vorst to lug his churns from door to door during the annual week-long fair held in Hoorn.[7] In Zwolle the 12 year-old Hein de Jager stood behind an ice cream cart in 1907, selling ices for one cent a portion.[8] In the cellar of his father's confectionery bakery in Ammerzoden in 1915, J. de Wit made ice cream by hand in a small ice cream machine cooled with ice and salt. When the ice cream was so stiff that it could no longer be stirred, he knew that it was ready and the machine was carried upstairs. The ice cream was sold straight from the machine, after which it was a case of back downstairs and start again.[9]

IJscompagnieën (ice cream cooperatives)

• The number of confectionery bakers selling ice cream continued to grow in the first decades of the twentieth century. Here and there, lunch-rooms and café-restaurants in various cities had also started selling ice cream. In those years eleven businesses engaged in the ice cream trade were registered with the Amsterdam Chamber of Commerce. The oldest registration relates to

'IJssalon cafetaria Kruijswijk', established in 1910 at 81, Rijnstraat. In 1920 Bakkerij van Schaik started making ice cream at 61, Merwedeplein, followed in 1924 by Bakkerij Westerbos at 4, Hugo de Grootplein.

• During the First World War (1914-1918) many raw materials were rationed in the neutral Netherlands. Competition was fierce and prices were low. In some cities confectionery bakers started to join forces in what were known as 'ijscompagnieën' (ice cream cooperatives). Ingredients were bought jointly and the ice cream was manufactured in one central location, thereby reducing overheads and allowing ration allowances to be used more efficiently. The first ijscompagnie was established in Utrecht in 1916. It bore the name 'Utrechtse ijscompagnie der Ver-eenigde Banketbakkers van Utrecht en omstreken "De IJsbeer"'. ['The Polar Bear' Ice Cream Cooperative of United Confectionery Bakers in Utrecht and district]. Its members were not only confectionery bakers. For example, the famous Figi café-restaurant in Zeist was also a member. The objective of the public limited company 'De IJsbeer' was 'to manufacture and sell, both in bulk and on a small scale, vanilla and other types of ice cream that meet the highest standards of hygiene.'[10] According to address directories from those days, ijscompagnieën were also set up in Leeuwarden, Breda, Dordrecht, The Hague, Haarlem and Amsterdam. In popular parlance the ice cream seller quickly became known as the ijscoman, from whom you bought an ijsco – short for ijscompagnie. Until recently many Dutch people still used the word ijsco for an ice cream.

• The emphasis on hygiene in the objectives of ijscompagnie 'De IJsbeer' was not without reason. Generally speaking, hygiene was

pitifully poor. The tin boxes containing the ice cream were often only washed after mould had started to grow on them – and then only in cold water. Glassware too was simply rinsed off in cold water. Take-away ice cream was not always wrapped in clean paper, nor milk always pasteurised, which made it a breeding ground for bacteria and infectious diseases such as typhoid fever and dysentery, sometimes with fatal consequences. Moreover, ice cream was eaten using spoons made from lead, which were cheap to buy but poor in quality. The ice cream tasted of lead and occasionally resulted in poisoning.

• The introduction of the ice cream wafer brought some improvement. The wafer had

431: Picture postcard, Utrecht, 1918. Nurses in front of a cart selling 'dairy ice cream with vanilla'. The nurse on the left carries glasses on a tray. In Utrecht an ijscompagnie of confectionery bakers had existed since 1917. They had their ice cream manufactured in a central location and then sold it in their shops and from ice cream carts in the street.

first made its appearance in Venice in the second half of the nineteenth century, but its use only became widespread at the end of the century when biscuit factories began to include the product in their range. In 1898 the Italian Antonio Valvona had founded a factory in Manchester, England, one of the first specifically designed for the production of ice cream wafers. It was a great success and he exported his wafers to France, Belgium and Italy.[11]

• The wafer was slow to take off in the Netherlands, but by about 1910 they were plentiful and available in a wide choice of shapes. You could eat ice cream in wafers shaped like a tortoise, an egg, a butterfly, a fan, a sea-shell or a horseshoe. They also came with romantic inscriptions such as 'I love you', 'I expect you tonight' and 'You will marry this year'.[12]

• And yet it was not young lovers who bought the most ice cream on the streets in those early years. The biggest customers of the ijscoman were children. Women were amongst the clientele, but they did not eat ice cream in the street. They hid it under their aprons and only started on it when they were safely out of sight.[13]

Consumer Goods Act 1919: a standardisation

• Concern about hygiene did not relate to ice cream preparation alone. Production and selling conditions of other foodstuffs were also frequently poor. At the end of the nineteenth century some municipalities and provinces had already introduced bye-laws that enabled the inspection of foodstuffs. In 1898, for example, an Inspectorate for Consumer Goods was set up in Rotterdam. But supervision generally left much to be desired and standardisation was underdeveloped.

• When more and more surrogate products came into use during the First World War, calls for more detailed government legislation became louder. The legislation had to ensure that appropriate measures could be taken even in municipalities without a consumer goods inspectorate. A Consumer Goods Act was passed by Parliament and became effective on 19 September 1919. The Act had a twofold aim: to protect public health and to promote fair trading. It was a 'framework Act', on the basis of which all sorts of detailed measures could be enacted by means of a Royal Decree. Initially, the

Consumer Goods Act had few consequences for ice cream preparation. It was only after the more detailed General Decree of 1925 that it became possible to set more stringent requirements covering places of preparation.

• Backed by the new legislation, the foods inspectors set to work. In 1926 the Consumer Goods Inspectorate in Amsterdam reported that, of 414 locations employed for the preparation of ice cream, 58 were also used as living and sleeping quarters and in a number of cases typhus or dysentery bacilli were found to be present in the ice cream. The majority of complaints in the 1921-1929 period related to the use of non-boiled or insufficiently boiled milk.[14] The inspectors were given much wider powers to do their work after the introduction of the Ice Cream Decree of September 1929. This subjected ice cream production premises to a sort of licensing system. Henceforth ice cream had to comply with certain bacteriological requirements and each ice cream maker had to have a separate place of preparation.[15]

• For ice cream makers who had until then simply prepared their ice cream at home, the 1929 decree had far-reaching implications. They would have to invest in clean new workplaces and better equipment. This provided the impulse for the establishment, the day after the decree, of the 'Nederlandsche Bond van Consumptie-ijsbereiders' [Dutch Association of Ice Cream Makers]. This group attempted first to get the Ice Cream Decree temporarily suspended

432: Poster by Charles Verschuuren, circa 1922. The ice between wafers held by mother and child was manufactured by ijscompagnie De Amstel, one of the many cooperatives of confectionery bakers set up in Dutch cities from 1916 onwards. [The abbreviation of the word ijscompagnie – ijsco – was for a long time used as a generic word for an ice cream.

to allow its members more time to make the required changes to the way they made ice cream. It succeeded: the ice cream makers were given a year's respite. The Association then set up departments all over the country and soon had many dozens of members. Exhibitions, trade fairs and congresses were organised and the Association published its own journal, De Consumptie-ijsbereider, subsequently renamed De Conservator in 1936. From 1938 onwards trade fairs were regularly organised under the name Romijva (Room- en -Consumptie-ijsbereidersvakbeurs - Ice Cream Makers Exhibition). The exhibitions grew in size as more and more ice cream machine manufacturers and other suppliers presented their products.

• The Association launched a combined advertising campaign in 1933 using the slogan 'Scooped ice cream, Fresh ice cream!' and the text 'Product of Dutch labour'. In doing so, the Dutch artisans and ice cream makers were attempting to make a stand both against the emerging industrial ice cream manufacturers (who in January 1934 had formed their own association, NIJFA, with 34 members[16]) and, more than anything, against the growing number of Italian ice cream vendors. The Association did its utmost to prevent Italians setting up in business, while its chairman gave vent to his dislike for Italian ice cream makers in the form of a rhyme:

'Mocha, all the strangest flavours,
Grinning greens and yellows
Were brought into our fatherland
By those odd Italian fellows'.[17]

• In 1935 the Association convened a national protest meeting in Amsterdam's Bellevue Theatre. Hundreds of Dutch ice cream makers backed a petition to the government

asking that Italians no longer be allowed to practise the trade.[18] As a result, a statute was introduced making it almost impossible for foreigners to set up ice cream businesses. The municipal councils of Alkmaar, Breda and Zwolle all specifically prevented Italians from starting up an ice cream business; but in those Depression years Dutch tolerance towards foreign street vendors in general was at a very low ebb. Unemployed Chinese seafarers, for instance, who tried to earn a livelihood by selling home-baked peanut cookies, quickly found themselves confronted by irate Dutch street vendors.

Italian ice cream makers

• Italian ice cream makers reached the Netherlands much later than they did other European countries. In 1889, as mentioned, Lanza was active on the boulevard in Scheveningen. But he was an exception. Italian ice cream makers really only arrived in the Netherlands after 1927. Until the 1930s it was still fairly simple for them to obtain a hawker's licence to sell home-made ice cream from their carts, so the Dutch ice cream man's cream-coloured cart with its copper lids was joined by the brightly painted Italian ice cream cart.

• One of the first Italian ice cream sellers in the Netherlands was Guido De Lorenzo, who started selling ice cream in Breda in 1928. Later, the family moved to Utrecht, where two ice cream parlours still operate successfully under the De Lorenzo name. In the 1930s a number of Italian ice cream saloons were established in Amsterdam: 'Peppino' and 'Tofani' (both set up in 1933), 'Venetië' (1935) and 'Gamba '(1938).[19] In The Hague one of the many such establishments was the well-regarded Florencia saloon, while in Amsterdam there was the famous Koco saloon on Van Woustraat, which was run by E. Cahn and A. Kohn, Jewish immigrants from Germany. Koco would become known as a place where acts of resistance against the Germans were organised, until a raid on the shop on 19 February 1941 brought this to an end.[20]

• Italian ice cream caught on. People found it delicious and affordable. Sales increased and family members were brought to the Netherlands to help sell or prepare the product. Those who had earned enough money from street sales bought premises in which they could set up ice cream saloons. The use of mirrors on the walls, a light-coloured tiled floor and small tables with marble or Formica tops gave the ice cream saloons a bright and clean appearance. The saloons popularised new flavours like coffee and introduced new ice cream confections such as the cassata gâteau (see chapter 15).

• There were other influences than the Italians. After the Bijenkorf department store in Amsterdam had been rebuilt in 1926, visitors to the fourth floor could take their seats in a real soda fountain bar, the first in the Netherlands. Furnished in the American style, the bar served not only ice cream coupes, ice cream sodas, sorbets, parfaits and coffee, but also the store's own 'Bijko Speciale', a cup containing vanilla ice cream with pear, hazelnuts, whipped cream and hot chocolate sauce.[21]

• Despite the economic slump of the 1930s and the consequent decline in sales, ice cream had acquired a place of its own in the Netherlands, particularly as a result of the Ice Cream Decree, which had given rise to an enormous improvement in ice cream quality. In Amsterdam, the number of ice cream samples recorded as unfit for sale decreased steadily after 1933[22]. Not everyone was still willing to risk the social disgrace of eating an ijsco in the street, but the days when you rushed to hide in a doorway before eating your ice cream had passed. The song entitled 'Ik ben Sally met de roomijskar' [I am Sally with the ice-cream cart] – composed in around 1935 and sung by Louis Davids, a very popular Dutch singer – was on everyone's lips.

'Coupe Vesuvius' and soft-ice

• The first years of the Second World War saw an upsurge in ice cream sales in the Netherlands. While many products were rationed or unobtainable, ice cream remained available and since there were few other treats, it sold well. By 1943, however, many of the ingredients used in preparing ice cream had gone from the shelves and most ice cream saloons had closed their doors; and in 1944 the production of ice cream using cream and sugar was prohibited.

• After 1945 the Association of Dutch Ice Cream Makers, which had been disbanded by the Germans during the war, tried to pick up where it had left off. It was not a simple task. Sugar rationing only ended in 1948 and another year passed before sugar and cream were again allowed to be used in ice cream. A noteworthy event was the merger in 1951 between the 'non-denominational' Bond van Nederlandsche IJsbereiders [Association of Dutch Ice Cream Makers] and the Rooms-Katholieke Bond van Consumptie-ijsbereiders

en Patates-Frites bakkers 'St. Pancratius' [Roman Catholic Association of Ice Cream Makers and Potato Chip Friers 'St. Pancras']. The latter association promoted not only the interests of ice cream makers but also those of the proprietors of snackbars, a recent arrival from America. For many ice cream businesses fried potato chips [patates-frites] offered a solution to the low sales of winter months. The new merged organisation now operated under the name 'Unie van Consumptie-ijsbereiders en Patates-Frites bakkers'.

• Ice cream had become accepted in the Netherlands, but much more had to be done through better selling methods, collective

433: ERMI ice cream men in The Hague set out on the road, late 1930s. ERMI (Eerste Rotterdamsche Melk-inrichting) was a dairy business that had started producing factory-made ice cream in 1932. In 1971 ERMI and several other ice cream factories joined the IJsunie (Ice Cream Union).

advertising and special attractions. In 1951, for example, De Conservator described a new creation aimed at boosting ice cream sales in the winter. This 'coupe' was known as 'Vesuvius' and consisted of a ball of orange ice cream representing the volcanic lava flowing from Mount Vesuvius. The 'volcano' was finished off with a coating of whipped cream sprinkled with cocoa powder, on top of which sat a small metal cup containing a little rum. After this had been lit, the coupe was ready for serving.[23] In fact, save for a walnut shell in place of the metal cup, this 'new' concept had been referred to by John W. Miller in 1929 as having been around in New York since 1880.[24]

• In 1955 the Stichting Propaganda IJsver-bruik [Foundation for the Propagation of Ice Cream Consumption] – a joint initiative of manufacturers of wafers and makers of arti-sanal ice cream – spent 40,000 guilders on a collective advertising campaign in daily newspapers under the slogan 'Ice cream, too, is good for everyone and tastily refresh-ing'. As in the United States, ice cream was presented as being nutritious: it 'caresses the tongue and strengthens the body'.[25]

• Ice cream manufacturers were in fact picking up more and more ideas from America. In The Hague, for instance, in July 1949 the milk and ice cream company De Sierkan on Stationsweg opened a 'milkbar' furnished in the style of the American soda fountains. Four waitresses dressed in yellow and pale green uniforms served customers with coffee, tea, cakes, ice cream, lemonade and something totally new, a 'milkshake'.[26] As well as a cup of coffee for 22 cents, the visitor could also 'treat himself to delectable drinks, which are not only tasty but also have a high nutritional value. Our soda fountain manager with his wealth of American experi-ence will make you just the drink you like', announced the dairy company in an adver-tisement published the day before the open-ing.[27] The manager in question, Anthony Aalders, had learned the trade after the war at an American airbase in Bavaria.

• Another example of the US influence on the post-war history of ice cream in the Netherlands was the arrival in the spring of 1951 of an expert from Washington, C.W. England. At the request of nine Dutch dairy companies, he provided them with detailed advice on how to improve their ice cream production. The American trade journal The Ice Cream Review, which reported this news,

also stated that 90% to 95% of the factory-made ice cream in the Netherlands at that time consisted of vanilla ice cream on a stick, sometimes with a thin coating of chocolate. Packs of ice cream to take home were almost completely unknown. The jour-nal attributed this to the absence of refriger-ators in Dutch households.[28]

Factory-made ice cream, safe ice cream!

• Factory-produced ice cream only appeared on the market after the introduction of the Ice Cream Decree in 1929. Now that compli-ance with stricter regulations was enforced, dairies realised that it would be profitable to compete with artisanal ice cream makers. Furthermore, a new and more efficient ice cream freezing machine had just been devel-oped in the United States: the horizontal continuous ice cream freezer invented in 1927 by the American Clarence W. Vogt (see chapter 5). Machine manufacturer Cherry (later Cherry-Burrell) exported this new machine all over the world.

• In the Netherlands it was the co-operative dairies in the big cities which were the first to embark on the production of ice cream: the Amsterdamsche Melkinrichting (VAMI), the Rotterdamsche Melkinrichting (RMI) and the 's-Gravenhaagsche Melkinrichting 'De Sierkan' in The Hague. All three had been founded in the years 1878-79.

• The Amsterdamsche Melkinrichting had merged in 1917 with other dairies in the capi-tal and from that moment traded under the name of Vereenigde Amsterdamsche Melkin-richting [United Amsterdam Dairy], or VAMI for short. Later this organisation was joined

by many other dairies, including OVV in Amsterdam and Campina in Eindhoven. It is fair to say that VAMI pioneered factory-made ice cream in the Netherlands. In 1929, the year of the Ice Cream Decree, VAMI set up an ice cream department in its new dairy in Amsterdam's Overtoom district, where it installed one continuous freezer and several packaging machines.[29] The recipes and machines for making VAMI 'dairy cream ice' originated from the United States, now the mecca of the ice cream industry. On its packs, on posters and in advertisements VAMI emphasised that its ice cream was safe, meaning it was hygienically prepared, properly inspected and free from harmful bacteria. Hence the description of VAMI's new ice cream department published in the Nederlandsch Weekblad voor Zuivelbereiding en -handel in 1929: 'An automatically operating packaging machine ensures that dairy ice cream is packed in a hygienic manner.'[30]

• Other dairies such as RMI, De Sierkan and Campina followed VAMI's example. They distributed their ice cream through their milk shops, whose numbers had increased substantially in line with the population growth in the big cities. By about 1940, for example, RMI had 72 dairy shops in Rotterdam, while De Sierkan in The Hague had 78 outlets.[31]

• Until 1955 RMI was 50%-owned by Unilever. A subsidiary of the group, margarine producer N.V. Van den Bergh, had sold the milk business 'Koninklijke Confederatie' in 1923.

434: Poster for VAMI, circa 1937. VAMI was an Amsterdam dairy business which had been manufacturing ice cream 'in the American manner' in the Overtoom district since 1929. At the foot of the poster are the words 'safe, nutritious, delectable'. On its packs, too, VAMI emphasised that the ice cream was safe, hygienically prepared and properly inspected, with no risks of harmful bacteria as could occur in artisanally-made ice cream.

As payment it had received cash plus 50% of the shares in RMI.[32] In 1932 RMI commenced the production of factory-made ice cream under the ERMI brand name. In its Rotterdam dairy Dfl. 14,821 was spent on setting up a dairy ice cream department and Dfl. 18,891 on ice cream carts and vans during the 1930s.

• As well as in Rotterdam, RMI sold its ice cream via a subsidiary in The Hague. Premises on the Beestenmarkt were rented in 1932 for the distribution of ice cream and in Scheveningen beach tents were purchased to promote ice cream sales.[33] In the meantime, Unilever considered it desirable 'for one of the RMI gentlemen to visit London [to be] fully informed of the selling and production methods of Wall's'.[34] Wall's Ice Cream was a wholly-owned Unilever business and had been making ice cream since 1922 (see chapter 8).

• After the war RMI's dairy operations fared less well but, according to a report by the Unilever accountant in 1948, the company possessed 'a favourable money-maker in the form of ice cream'.[35] When the RMI board of directors – in need of a cash loan from its partner – proposed in 1951 that the company's ice cream department be hived off as an independent operation in which Unilever would have a majority shareholding, Unilever director Harold Hartog was not averse to the idea, having himself made the same suggestion to RMI in 1949. 'I still believe that ice cream has potential', he wrote on 30 July 1950 in an internal aide-mémoire about the negotiations with RMI. One month later, however, the idea was dropped, as the RMI board would not agree to Unilever having the casting vote in the management of the proposed new company.[36] By that time the poorly performing RMI dairy company no longer fitted within Unilever's activities and

¶ During the Second World War sales of ice cream went on as usual in the Netherlands. In the first years of the war they even experienced an upsurge, as ice cream was one of the few sweet foods that was not rationed. It was only in September 1944 that the preparation of ice with sugar and cream was banned. Just how common ice cream was in those early years of the war can be seen from the 1947 children's book Marja verkoopt ijsco's [Marja sells ice creams] by Riek Goudappel-Bos.[1] The story takes place during the occupation. Marja and her family go to see Mr Boomstra's ice cream shop. In front of the shop door is a van, which has come to deliver blocks of ice for cooling. Mr Boomstra is a milkman by trade, but now he has set up a shop to sell ice creams. His doors are due to open at 2 p.m. and a crowd is waiting eagerly in front of the shop. Then the great moment arrives: 'First Boomstra and his wife warmly welcomed the customers and then a neatly-dressed shop-girl brought the first glasses of ice

435: Cover of the children's book Marja verkoopt ijsco's [Marja sells ice creams] by Riek Goudappel-Bos, Haarlem, 1947.

cream. Oh, did that taste good!' Boomstra also owns a three-wheeled ice cream cart. Old Bram is allowed to drive it. Marja and her friends stand by as the cart is filled with ice cream. 'While the children watched closely, two blue-painted barrels were put into the cart. Inside the barrels, pieces of crushed ice surrounded the churns filled with the ice cream that the boys and girls were so fond of. Ting-a-ling! The cart set off on its way.'
Marja is the lucky one chosen to help Old Bram. They are off to Aalsmeer to sell ice cream during the sailing races. On their way there they often have to pull into the side to make way for cars driven by soldiers. The ice cream goes really well, especially once Marja starts selling. 'Up came a small boy: "One for five cents please, miss." "There you go", said Marja. "Isn't that a big 'un'", and she handed the beaming lad his tub in which she had stacked an extra high portion. What fun it was, first scooping the ice cream from the churn and into the tub, and then putting the money in the bag.' The ice cream quickly sells out and Marja and Old Bram set off home again. But then misfortune strikes. Marja hears a bang and: 'Oh! ...what had happened? A big German lorry stood at right-angles across the road. Bram's ice cream cart was lying upside down'. Bram has had a collision. The police soon arrive and the German driver admits it was his fault. After everyone has calmed down, Bram and Marja continue on their way, a sad ending to what had been a wonderful day.

437: Wrapper of a 'Sjokijs' product by Davino, circa 1950. A 'sjokijs' was a vanilla ice cream with a chocolate coating. Established in the early 1930s, Davino was an abbreviation of 'De Aangenaamste Versnapering in Nijmegen en Omstreken'.

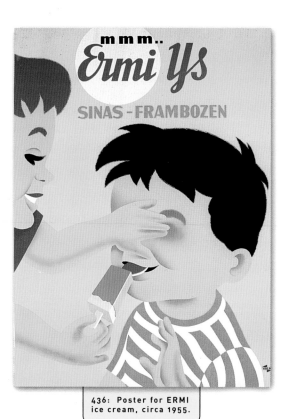

436: Poster for ERMI ice cream, circa 1955.

438: Selling ERMI ice cream, summer 1949. The girl wears a big ribbon in her hair, after the fashion of the time, and watches the boy in short trousers as he pays. The boy on the left is holding out his ice lolly. Will he shortly be sharing it with his friends next to him?

439: A clearance sale of fur coats at the Gamba ice cream parlour, 27-29 Regu-liersbreestraat, Amster-dam, January 1951. In the winter months the Italian ice cream parlours in Am-sterdam were often trans-formed into furriers' shops.

in 1954, after protracted negoti-ations, the group reached agreement with RMI on the sale of its shares. During the negoti-ations one suggestion made by the RMI board was that Unilever should now 'take over the entire ice cream business'; Unilever did not regard the idea as having potential.[37]

• Alongside the dairy companies, the choco-late and confectionery factory Jamin, estab-lished in Rotterdam in 1887, also began to manufacture ice cream and sell it as a side-line in its many shops.[38] Companies like Jamin, De Sierkan, VAMI and RMI sold ice cream not only in their own shops, but also on the streets. In contracts concluded with ice cream vendors, matters such as clothing,

starting times and other work-ing conditions were stipulated in detail. At Jamin the vendors had to 'set off on the road at the latest by 10 a.m. each day'. The company also provided the vendor with two uniforms each week, in return for which he had to pay 75 cents a week to cover laundry costs.[39] Vendors usually travelled on fixed routes and at fixed times and on warm summer evenings the ringing of the bells on their ice cream carts and the long drawn-out cry of 'IJs!' were familiar sounds in residential districts of the big cities.

• After the Second World War small fac-tories specialising in ice cream were also established, among them De Hoop in Onnen

440: Davino ice cream carts in front of the factory building in Nijmegen, late 1930s.

(Groningen), Het Provinciaal Room-IJsbedrijf 'De Friesche Koe' in Leeuwarden, Okay in Gilze, Sibema in Sittard, Hygiea in Roermond, Van Scheijndel in Arnhem and Davino in Nijmegen. In the 1950s none of these ice cream factories operated on a national scale, most working within a radius of 25-30 kilometres of their home town.[40] This aspect was reflected in the name of the Davino ice-cream brand. Davino was not the surname of some Italian ice cream maker, as people outside Nijmegen often thought, but the acronym of 'De Aangenaamste Versnapering in Nijmegen en Omgeving' [The Most Pleas-

ant Refreshment in the Nijmegen area].
• In 1949 the Nederlandse Vereniging van Consumptie-IJsfabrikanten [the Dutch Association of Ice Cream Manufacturers] was set up. When it was first founded, the NVC represented the interests of around 100 affiliated members. However, most of the small ice cream factories had difficulty in keeping their businesses afloat and many of them either discontinued their ice cream production or were taken over. By 1953 the NVC's membership had dropped to 64.[41] Mergers created bigger businesses which invested in new machines, delivery vans and

coldstores. 'These factories then seek a sales area outside the place where they are established, so that smaller manufacturers are sometimes forced to close down their business, since they do not have the cash capital to purchase good machines', noted NVC chairman P. Wiersma in 1953, commenting on the causes of the decline in his Association's membership.[42]

• Despite all this activity, the Netherlands in the mid-1950s was still not a country of ice cream lovers and ice cream makers were very dependent on the weather. One poor summer and everyone's sales plummeted. In 1956 a Unilever study of the feasibility of selling ice cream in the Netherlands concluded that it was not a commercial proposition. In the meantime, however, Unilever was testing the temperature in Belgium, where selling prices for ice cream were considerably higher than in the Netherlands.[43]

called the biscuits oublies. They were boat-shaped following a long tradition and made with shortcrust pastry. Later on, the Italians rolled this pastry into a cone which they filled with ice cream. The product caught on and soon the streets of Liège were enlivened by ice cream carts, depicting on their sides colourful views of Mount Vesuvius or the Bay of Naples. Almost all the Italian ice cream makers in Liège originated from the little mountain village of Atina, in the Frosinone region to the southeast of Rome.[44]

442: Female employees at the Mio ice cream factory in Liège busy with the production of vanilla ice creams on sticks, circa 1965.

• Business flourished and the ice cream carts became bigger and heavier. They were no longer hand-carts, but drawn by horses and often carrying gaslights so that selling could continue late into the evening. Around 1900, the Respentino, D'Inverno, Franchi and Marziale families who controlled the ice cream trade took up joint residence in premises in the Rue du Palais. They parked their carts in a big indoor courtyard, where the ice cream production was also located. In the winter they fetched ice from the frozen River Meuse, pulling the pieces of ice onto the banks with long poles, then wrapping them in

Ice cream in Belgium: 'white flavour' and 'dark flavour'

• In Belgium, too, ice cream owed its popularity to the Italian influence. In about 1875 many Italian emigrants settled in the industrial city of Liège. They worked in the local coal mines and tried to earn a little extra money by selling sweet confectionery and biscuits they made themselves. The inhabitants of the French-speaking city

straw and storing them in cellars. After the World Fair in Liège in 1900, they bought the first small ice cream machines and their sales began to grow. There was as yet little production variety: you could buy either 'white flavour' (vanilla) or 'dark flavour' (chocolate). At Christmas they offered roast chestnuts, but in the February run-up to Carnival ice cream carts came out onto the streets again.

• In the years 1911-13 the first Italian ice cream saloons opened their doors in Liège. In addition to ice cream they sold Italian wines and local alcoholic beverages such as the popular 'Pequet'. Not surprisingly, the saloons rapidly became popular: while Father downed a quick drink, Mother and children would tuck into ice cream.[45] During the First World War the ice cream business in Belgium virtually dried up as many Italians returned to their native land, only slowly reviving after hostilities ceased.

• In 1928 Antoine Marziale started his own ice cream business in Liège under the name Mio (Italian for 'my' or 'mine'). After the interruption of the Second World War, Mio expanded to become a flourishing ice cream manufacturer (see box on p. 448).

Cycle racing and ice cream

• As in the Netherlands, artisanally made ice cream dominated the Belgian market until the 1960s, though the post-war years witnessed the start of a concentration amongst ice cream manufacturers with Frisco, Pinguin, Every Day, Igel and Watty all amalgamating with Artic, which was set up in 1945. Today Artic – together with Ola,

Mio and IJsboerke – is one of Belgium's best-known ice cream brands.

• The founder of IJsboerke, Gustave ('Staf') Janssens, had begun hawking ice cream in the 1930s, at the age of fourteen. A policeman once described him as the IJsboerke [ice cream bumpkin], so when Staf started his own ice cream business shortly after the Second World War, that was the name he gave it. Gradually his company grew and in 1956 Staf bought his first refrigerated van, a motorised three-wheeler, from which he could sell his ice cream.[46] He devised his own sales formula: in summer his ice cream salesmen would call on retailers and householders twice a week, in winter just once a month. This approach, combined with the good quality of his pre-packed ice cream and relatively low prices, resulted in excellent sales. IJsboerke's advertising was also inspired. It was one of the first ice cream companies to sponsor a team of racing cyclists, enabling the business to cash in on the growth in the sport's popularity in Belgium.

• In 1968 the factory was extended and modernised and by 1975 IJsboerke held a 15% share of the market. In 1978 the company had 20 depots, operated a fleet of 130 vans to distribute its ice cream and was selling some 12 million litres of ice cream per annum.[47] IJsboerke ice cream was still delivered direct to consumers via refrigerated delivery vans and, from 1984, also through Belgium's leading grocery stores and supermarkets. In 1991 the company started exporting to Germany and France.

• The big industrial ice cream business in Belgium, Artic, had been set up by Max Willick. An ice cream man through and through, Willick started work at a young age in the Frisco ice cream factory, which had been founded in Brussels in 1933. In 1952, seven years after founding Artic, he entered into a partnership with J. Rahm, the owner of the Pinguin ice cream firm. The new combined business prospered and in 1957 Artic acquired Frisco, plus another Belgian ice cream company, Every Day.[48] In 1960 Artic began exporting ice creams to the Netherlands. France followed the next year and Germany in 1962. In that same year Willick also started a frozen foods business, with Bianca (quick-frozen vegetables) and Iceberg (quick-frozen fish).

• The year 1962 also saw Artic's acquisition of the Igel ice cream factory in Liège. Founded in 1935, Igel had done good business after the war as a supplier of ice cream to the US troops. Gradually the business had built up a wide base of regular customers in the on-premise trade, also selling through some 300 cinemas. The purchase of Igel by Artic – a mainly Flemish company – made sense, for it gave Artic a firmer foothold in Wallonia, the French-speaking part of Belgium. Unilever had been interested in Igel but had missed the boat, nor did its approaches to Willick over a period of many years about acquiring Artic lead to agreement.[49]

• Artic continued to expand and in 1975 it bought the Watty ice cream company, which owned a chain of snackbars and ice cream saloons. Artic's share of approximately 31% of the ice cream market was lower than in 1962 (58%), yet the business was still market leader.[50] In 1979 Artic became part of Beatrice Foods.[51] Today it is owned by Moraco Ltd. In the meantime Ola, an ice cream company set up by Unilever, had become one of Artic's biggest competitors.

Unilever ice cream in Belgium: Hola becomes Ola

• In 1955, Unilever decided to start producing ice cream in Belgium. Until then the group had only been active in ice cream in the UK and Germany. It has been impossible to trace the precise reasons why an ice cream operation was set up in Belgium.[52] However, a study that Unilever conducted in 1956 revealed that whereas in Belgium consumers paid an average of five francs for an ice cream (equivalent to 38 Dutch cents in 1956 money), in the Netherlands consumers paid just ten cents - a price level that would have made it very difficult for a newcomer to enter the Dutch market.[53]

• Unlike the situation in much of Europe, industrial ice cream in the UK was often made using vegetable fats such as coconut oil and palm kernel oil, ingredients which Unilever – then still predominantly a soaps, detergents and margarine business – understood well. Ice cream made with vegetable fat was considerably cheaper to produce than dairy ice cream. It seemed to Unilever that there would be possiblities in due course to sell ice cream according to the Wall's formula elsewhere in Europe (see chapter 8). Even though the legislation on dairy ice cream was strict in many European countries, there was still room for ice cream made with vegetable fats. In the Netherlands, for instance, a distinction was made in those years between dairy ice cream [roomijs] and ice cream [consumptie-ijs]. Dairy ice cream had to contain at least 12% milk-fat, while consumptie-ijs could be manufactured with vegetable fat, although it was not allowed to be described as dairy ice cream on the pack or in advertising.[54]

¶Antoine Marziale, from the small Italian mountain village of Arpino to the south-east of Rome, was one of Belgium's ice cream pioneers. Marziale came to Liège in 1895 and sold ice cream there from 1898 onwards. In 1900, together with a number of other Italian ice cream making families, he moved into a big house at 66, Rue du Palais. Trade developed so well that Marziale, now married to a Liège girl, decided in 1928 to set up his own ice cream business: Mio (Italian for 'mine'). Antoine had seven children, all of whom helped him in the ice cream business. In 1935 Marziale thought up an original way of making choco-late-coated ice cream. The ice cream was quick-frozen into blocks and then cut into small portions. These were then dipped in a warm chocolate sauce and hung up to dry by S-shaped hooks from the rim of a bicycle wheel! After that, the ice creams were packed and stored in a cork-insulated freezer cabinet that ran on methyl gas.[1] The product was marketed under the name Chocos Mio and was an instant hit. From the profits a lorry

was bought to go out on the road and sell ice cream. Antoine Marziale's death in 1939, and the outbreak of the Second World War, temporarily halted Mio's activities. But after the war, Antonie's sons Dominique and Cosme followed in their father's footsteps. In 1950 they decided to carry on their business, bought the very latest ice cream machines and began distributing Mio ice cream again, mainly by refrig-erated van and across Wallonia. Cinemas were impor-tant customers, but so too were the 'salles de spectacles' (meeting halls) often owned by political parties, and the Catholic community centres. Another important distribution channel was L'Union Co-opera-tive, a chain of co-op grocery shops.
In 1959 the first fully auto-mated, rotating ice lolly freezing machine was installed – a Rollo from Høyer – and production increased substan-tially. In 1964 a second Rollo was bought. At that time pro-duction only took place during the ice cream season and amounted to about one million litres a year[2].
From 1962 Cosme's sons also began to work in the business. Trade got better and better. Whereas in the pre-war days of Antoine Marziale the firm had

produced some 2,000 choc-ices a day, that figure had reached 100,000 in 1977.[3] Exports began – to Germany, France and the Netherlands. By the time Cosme died in 1978, Mio had become one of the biggest ice cream producers in Belgium. Mio France was set up in 1984 to promote exports there. French sales grew phenome-nally and Mio France began to make its presence felt in the French-speaking market over-seas, such as in French Guiana and Martinique. New dessert creations, such as an ice cream gâteau with Cointreau, also proved highly popular.
In 1992 Mio was acquired by the French Ortiz-Miko group, which since 1994 has formed part of Unilever. In 1997, how-ever, Mio was sold back by Unilever to the Marziale family.

443: Antoine Marziale, in front of his ice cream cart in Liège, circa 1910. Marziale went on to found Mio in 1928. After the war the business, then managed by his sons, expanded to become a very well-known ice cream brand, especially in the eastern part of Belgium.

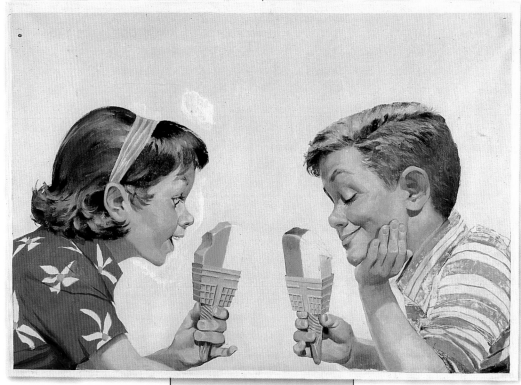

444: Painted advertisement for Ola
ice cream, oil on canvas, circa 1960.
This anonymous work reflects the
then popular realistic style of the
famous American advertising artist
Norman Rockwell (1894-1979).

• The view of the director of Unilever-Belgium, C.S. Pettit, also played a role in the proposal to begin an ice cream company there. Until that time the margarine and fats business Société Huilever was Unilever's main activity in Belgium. Pettit, however, was very impressed by the success of Wall's Ice Cream and felt that something similar could be achieved in Belgium.[55] Another consideration was the possibility offered by the Benelux customs union, formed in 1946, for the unrestricted export of ice cream to the Netherlands.

• Whatever the precise case, Ola S.A. was established on 3 February 1956 in Brussels, the name of the new company being derived from the Hola margarine brand which was already registered as a trademark.[56] That summer Ola started selling ice cream, which for the first few years was shipped in from Wall's Ice Cream in the UK via Ostend whilst a factory was being built in Baasrode alongside the Huilever margarine factory. By 1958 the ice cream factory had become operational with a production capacity of half a million litres; in 1981 its annual output had climbed to 40 million litres.[57] The recipes and production process were very similar to those of Wall's Ice Cream,[58] as were the distribution and selling methods (see chapter 8). Delivery vans transported the ice cream from coldstore to shopkeeper and also to the consumer. 'Listen out for the merry tune of the bells on the Ola delivery van. It will be coming past your house regularly', advertised the company in 1960.[59]

445: Ola ice cream being sold from cool-boxes on Ostend beach, circa 1958.

446: Ice cream sales on the Belgian coast, circa 1960.

447: 'Jolly tasty, Ola real dairy ice.' Advertisement for Ola in Belgium, circa 1960.

448: Sale of Ola dairy ice cream from a mobile freezer cooled with dry ice, circa 1960.

449: Production of ice lollies in the Ola ice cream factory in Baasrode, Belgium. Opened in 1958, this was the first ice cream factory to be built by Unilever in continental Europe. It was subsequently expanded several times, finally closing down in 1992,

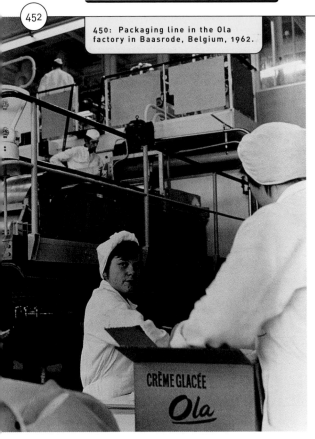

450: Packaging line in the Ola factory in Baasrode, Belgium, 1962.

451: Window poster for the 'Super Fruti Ananas' product by Ola, Belgium, circa 1960. For five Belgian francs you could enjoy a water-ice of 'thirst-quenching freshness', according to the French text.

452: Window poster for Ola dairy ice cream gâteau, Belgium, 1965.

453: 'Completely new. Ola, more than 8% butter and nothing but butter! Judge for yourself.' Advertisement for Ola ice cream in a sales manual for the retail trade in Belgium, circa 1958.

• Despite the modern production facilities and the wealth of experience of Wall's Ice Cream, for a long time Ola in Belgium operated at a loss. The system of distribution proved unsuitable for a small country like Belgium, in which turnover was low and competition intense. Ola's market share grew only slowly: in 1962 Ola held 17% of the ice cream market and Artic 58%.[60] The amalgamation of Iglo (frozen foods) and Ola (ice cream) in 1964 represented a substantial step on the road towards better performance. From the 1970s EEC subsidies on butter-fat, aimed at reducing the 'butter mountains' that had grown up as a result of the Common Agricultural Policy, provided a further fillip.

• The merger between its frozen foods and ice cream interests also represented Unilever's response to the combination of Bianca and Iceberg that Artic had initiated two years before. The frozen products – principally vegetables and fish – were imported via Unilever's Iglo company in the Netherlands, but it was a great many years before frozen food products caught on in Belgium. Freezer cabinets were at first only to be found in shops that sold fresh fish. Later, they came to be filled with vegetables and fish in the winter and, after considerable persuasion by the Ola salesman, with ice cream in the summer.[61]

454: Fruti 10-cent water-ices made by Vita, 1959.
The water-ices being enjoyed by the short-trousered lads with cropped hair still at that time had their sticks inserted at an angle. Vita was a frozen foods business that had been bought by Unilever in 1958. In 1960 its name was changed to Iglo. Some time later the Ola ice cream brand was added to the company and the business was renamed Iglo-Ola.

'What's ice-cold and sits on a stick?'

• The low prices chargeable for ice cream were not the only reason why Unilever did not enter the Dutch market. Another consideration was that sales of dessert ice cream would have stood little chance of success, as only 4% of Dutch homes owned an electric refrigerator. For dessert the Dutch ate the cheaper 'cream yoghurt'. As can be seen from the study carried out by Unilever in 1956, expenditure on this dairy yoghurt had increased considerably between 1951 and 1954, whereas Dutch consumer spending on ice cream had remained static for years. The greater part of the ice cream market was still in the hands of small, artisanal ice cream makers and keen competition existed between the many local ice cream factories.[62]

• Two years later, in 1958, a new study was conducted into the Dutch situation, at a time when Unilever had decided to focus more attention on the ice cream market worldwide (see chapter 21).[63] Unilever had owned the Birds Eye frozen foods company in the UK for many years and this second study made it clear that ice cream in the Netherlands would only be profitable if ice cream sales were combined with the sale of quick-frozen food products.

• Such was the background to Unilever's purchase of the Dutch frozen foods business Vita in 1958. Founded in the 1930s, Vita had a sales network of 8,500 freezer cabinets in shops throughout the Netherlands.[64] Ice cream was sold in about 20% of these outlets, supplied by depot operators who enjoyed a good degree of autonomy. Unilever maintained this system until sales volumes had become big enough for the company to take over the selling activities itself.

• By the following year, 1959, Unilever was already using the Vita network to sell Fruti water-ices in the Netherlands. Fruti was a ten-cent orange or raspberry ice lolly developed by Wall's in the UK. For any Dutchman asked in 1959 'What's ice-cold, tastes of orange or raspberry and sits on a stick?', there was only one answer: 'Fruti!'[65]

Further acquisitions in the Netherlands

• In 1960 Unilever bought the small, successful ice cream factory De Hoop in Onnen. In the following year De Hoop began producing Ola ice creams and within a few years the De Hoop brand name was phased out. At the same time the name Vita was changed to Iglo, which was more suitable for export purposes since the brand name could be protected more effectively abroad[66] (at about the same time Iglo was adopted by Unilever for frozen food use in Germany and Belgium). The frozen foods produced by Iglo in the Netherlands soon found their way to Belgium, while Ola ice cream produced in Baasrode made the reverse journey to freezer cabinets in Dutch shops. Unilever thus made optimal use of the possibilities

455: Series of posters for Ola ice creams, the Netherlands, 1962.

456: Poster for an 'Arizona Cup' product by Ola, the Netherlands, 1962. Ice cream with nuts and fruits: 'Resoundingly tasty!'

457: Poster for an Ola 'Napolitana' ice cream wafer, the Netherlands, 1962: 'A treat for 3, 3 flavours'.

offered by the Benelux trade agreements.

• In the meantime, the grocery chain Albert Heijn, which in 1947 had taken over VAMI, continued to sell VAMI ice cream in its shops throughout the country. Despite this, VAMI remained a loss-making business and in 1962 Albert Heijn sold the company to Unilever for 2.6 million guilders.[67]

• The acquisition of VAMI was the first in a series of purchases that would lead to Ola holding a market share of approximately 75% by 1996. In the 1960s, however, Ola was still struggling in the Netherlands and suffered continual losses. In 1962 the annual loss came to more than 1.6 million guilders[68] and in 1965 the discontinuation of ice cream activities was considered.[69] However, in the late 1960s prosperity increased and the Dutch began to eat ice cream more as a dessert at home. Ola introduced a half-litre family pack and advertised it widely, with great success. Between 1966 and 1969 sales of dessert ice cream rocketed, from 0.5 million litres to 1.9 million litres, and in 1969 – an exceptionally warm summer – Ola was finally able to report good financial results.[70]

• At the end of the 1970s Ola further improved its position by taking over De IJsunie. This company, set up in 1971 in response to the establishment of Iglo-Ola, was an affiliation of various dairy cooperatives from the very early days, such as De Sierkan, HORNA and RMI. Further expansion of Ola followed in 1985 with the purchase of Caraco, the brand name of IJsfabriek De Valk, which had started life as a confectionery bakery in 1937, and of the Nijmegen-based ice cream factory Davino.[71] From these acquisitions Ola gained access to an enormous increase in numbers of sales

originated from a merger between a number of dairies that operated under the name C.M. de Kempen in Eindhoven in the 1930s. In 1970 Campina bought Sibema of Sittard, a company founded in 1933. In 1995, however the ice cream activities of Campina in the south of the country also had to face competitive reality as they in turn were taken over by Nestlé, the giant Swiss foods group. The Campina name disappeared from the market as an ice cream brand, to be replaced by Motta-Nestlé.

• In most respects, the post-war history of ice cream in the Low Countries is a story of acquisitions and mergers. However, Italian ice cream makers also modernised. The days when they knew their recipes by heart, and prepared their product

outlets. In supermarkets, grocery stores, greengrocers, kiosks, filling stations, cinemas, swimming pools and sports canteens, consumers could not escape Ola ice cream, whose promotional flags, parasols and advertising boards were everywhere.

• Large-scale national competition was provided by Campina, a company which had

458: Postmen next to a Van Scheijndel ice cream cart, circa 1950. Van Scheijndel had started in 1935 as a confectionery baker in Arnhem and also sold ice cream he had made himself. In 1956 Van Scheijndel stopped baking and concentrated on ice cream. IJsfabriek Van Scheijndel still operates independently and remains well-known in the region.

more or less by guesswork, were long past. In 1972 they formed their own organisation – Ital – and nowadays Italian ice cream parlours can make use of computer programs that show them the most cost-effective possibilities for exploiting the mix of ingredients, prices, flavours and sales opportunities. Consumers in the Low Countries can still enjoy Italian ice cream prepared in the artisanal way, but they can also now treat themselves to ice cream from foreign companies that were unknown until recently, such as Schöller-Mövenpick, Häagen-Dazs and Ben & Jerry's. The delivery vans of the German company Heimeis are a familiar sight in Dutch cities and, as in other European countries, supermarket chains fill their freezer cabinets with their own private-label ice cream.

• There are still independent companies which have operated on a regional basis for years, such as IJsfabriek Van Scheijndel in Huissen and Het IJspaleis in the little village of Sprundel in Brabant Province. Van Scheijndel started in Arnhem in 1935 as a confectionery bakery which also sold dairy ice cream. In 1956 Van Scheijndel stopped making pastries and concentrated on ice cream; and in 1978 a new factory was opened in Huissen, south-west of Arnhem. The ice cream gâteaux of this family-owned business are much-famed and are now exported to Germany, Belgium and the UK.[72]

• Another story of considerable independent success is that of Den Hertog, based in Melissant on the island of Goeree-Overflakkee in Zuid-Holland Province. At the end of the 1970s Den Hertog, a milkman, started making his own ice cream and selling it. His foresight and hard work enabled him to build up a nationally respected ice cream company specialising in high-quality dessert ice cream. This luxury ice cream benefited from the growing Dutch interest in food an drink in the 1980s, and, almost without advertising, his ice cream found its way to consumers through supermarket freezer

18 Juni 1960.

Dimme, damme, dijn :
Ys moet Roomijs zijn !
't Lekkerst in de mond,
Voedzaam en gezond !
Dus op warme dagen
Altijd Roomijs vragen !

459: 'Dimme, damme, dijn: ijs moet roomijs zijn!' [Eenie, meenie, me, dairy ice cream it should be!]. Rhyme on a sticker for a girl's scrapbook, June 1960. Pictures like these were offered by the Dutch Dairy Bureau through the ladies' magazine Libelle.

cabinets and those of small greengrocers.

• Eventually, however, Den Hertog felt it was time to call it a day and sold his company to the foods group Bols Wessanen, which in turn sold the business to Unilever in 1995. The strength of the Den Hertog brand as a high-quality dessert ice cream was such that it is still successfully sold under that name and is marketed in novel flavour variants. Recently a Den Hertog impulse ice cream has also gone on sale – a simple, pure vanilla dairy ice cream on a stick, almost the same as the ice that signalled the birth of factory-made ice cream in the Netherlands.

Licks, Sticks & Bricks

A WORLD HISTORY OF ICE CREAM

Russia: a warm treat in a cold climate

460: Two men on a cart with a crate of ice cream near St. Petersburg, circa 1913. On the crate is the Russian word for ice cream, 'morozhenoye'

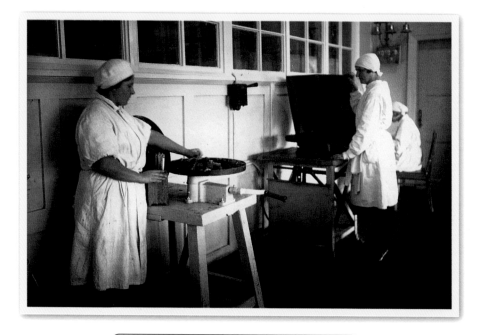

461: Manufacturing of ice creams similar to the Eskimo Pie ice cream in a Moscow factory, 1935.

'Mamma, what sweets are we going to have?', asks thirteen year-old Natasha Orlov during her birthday party in Leo Tolstoy's masterpiece War and Peace, published between 1866 and 1869. 'Ice cream, only you will not be allowed any,' replies Maria Dmitrievna, an older friend of her mother, teasingly. Natasha persists and almost shrieks: 'Maria Dmitrievna! What sort of ice-cream? I don't like ice-cream!' Still joking, the friend says: 'Carrot-ices.' But Natasha refuses to be fobbed off with this answer and eventually learns that it is to be pineapple ice for dessert.[1]

• Tolstoy's War and Peace is largely set in the year 1812. During his invasion of Russia that year Napoleon came up against an enemy much worse than the Russian army: the freezing cold of the Russian steppes. The French army, ravaged by cold and starved by the defending army's scorched earth tactics, was shattered. Trying to conquer such a country was nonsense, said the British Prime Minister Winston Churchill, when in 1941 Hitler tried to succeed where Napoleon had failed. How could you conquer a country whose people still ate ice cream in winters as bitterly cold as Russia's? [2]

• Ice cream first appeared at the Russian court in the time of Catherine the Great (1729-1796) (see chapter 3). In the nineteenth century the Russian nobility ate ice cream as a treat on feast days and name-days. Everyone in Russia was named after a saint and the name-day of that saint was celebrated like a birthday. Wealthy Russians ate ice cream in the café-restaurants of Moscow and St. Petersburg. In the years after 1840 the merchant Ivan Izler owned St. Petersburg's most popular café, on the Nevsky Prospekt. Izler, a Swiss, also sold ice cream

prepared in a machine he had developed himself. In September 1845 the periodical Severnaya Pchela [The Bee of the North] reported that the Ministry of Trade and Industry had received a patent application for an ice cream making machine. The application had been submitted by 'the merchant of the second guild, Ivan Izler.'[3] Izler was granted his patent (no. 307) on 16 November 1845,[4] two years after the American Nancy Johnson had invented the first ice cream machine in Philadelphia (see chapter 4). It is not known what Izler's ice cream machine looked like, since the patent has not been found.

• Until the October Revolution of 1917 ice cream was only produced on a small scale in Russia and was reserved for a select group of people in cities like Moscow and St. Petersburg. A popular ice cream was the Plombir, a creamy ice cream filled with pieces of fruit or nuts. The recipe was copied from the French plombière. The ordinary Russian bought his ice cream from ice cream carts, which had existed from the earliest pre-revolutionary days. Georg Johann Kohl, the Viennese author and frequent traveller through Russia, noted in an account of a journey in 1841 that in the summer ice cream was on sale in the streets of St. Petersburg, Moscow and Odessa. The ice cream sellers announced their wares with loud cries of 'Morozhenoye! Morozhenoye!' [Ice cream! Ice cream!].

• Although ice cream could be bought on the street, some thought it bad manners to eat it outdoors. In fact, one difference between a 'sophisticated' city like St. Petersburg and the more 'bourgeois' Odessa was the way people in Odessa ate ice cream – and smoked – in the streets. In St. Petersburg such behaviour was frowned upon.[5]

• The quality of the ice cream was very poor. Conditions were unhygienic. In 1898 the Peterburgsky Listok [The St. Petersburg Gazette] gave a description of what went on during the making of ice cream: 'The ice cream sellers form a united group of about forty men. They all live together in one house near Sennaya Square. In that same house there is also a "laboratory" which they claim is used to check on the quality of the ice cream. This "laboratory" is by no means a clean place. The actual ice cream preparation takes place in a dirty back garden in between cases filled with raw ice, herrings, sauerkraut and so on. The ice cream is made very quickly and all sorts of lemonade syrups of dubious appearance are added to it. Ice cream left unsold from the previous day is also added to the mix.'[6] For all that, conditions were little worse than those prevailing amongst London's Italian ice cream makers at the time (see chapter 4).

• After 1917, ice cream was generally unavailable in Russia until 1926 when Anasta Mikoyan, the Soviet Minister for Trade, opened the first ice cream factory in Moscow.[7] In that first year the Soviet Union's total production amounted to some 300 tons of ice cream. It was decided that ice cream had to be made affordable for every Russian and available throughout the year. During the 1930s ice cream factories were opened all over the Soviet Union, bearing names redolent of the impersonal jargon of the five-year plans: 'Refrigerator No. 2' and 'Cold Kombi-

462: Selling ice cream, July 1944. On the right is a barrel with ice.

nat' (kombinat is a kind of industrial complex). On 16 January 1936 Mikoyan gave a speech to the Central Executive Committee of the Communist Party in which he proclaimed: 'Formerly ice cream was eaten only on feast days. This must change! Ice cream must become a product that everyone can eat every day. Ice cream must be produced in the summer and the winter, both in the south and in the north of the Soviet Union!'[8] In practice, however, little of this objective was realised and then the Great Patriotic War, as the Russians call the Second World War, delayed any chance of progress.

• After the war, the Russians returned to the task. In the 1960s foreign visitors to Russia were astonished to see that everyone was eating ice cream, even in temperatures of twenty degrees below zero! For Russians ice cream was a snack to ward off the cold! Luxury foods were scarce in Russia in the 1960s and ice cream was cheap with a high fat content. A popular product was ice cream in blocks of 400 grams or more that were eaten at home, often with home-made fruit sauces poured over them. As this ice cream contained little air, it was solid and very fatty, being frequently likened to a pack of butter. Russian ice cream had, and still has, a typical fat content of between 13% and 15%.

• All ice cream factories in the Soviet Union produced the same ices, which were sold at the same prices. Ices were in fact not known by their name, such as Eskimo or Borodino,

but by their price: '10 kopeks' (Eskimo) or '28 kopeks' (Borodino).[9] This would only change with the introduction of new economic policies – perestroika – under President Gorbachov in 1985, when foreign firms began to appear on the Russian ice cream market for the first time. First to arrive were Polish and Finnish manufacturers. Small local Russian factories also started producing ice cream. Towards the end of the 1980s, with the old Soviet system falling apart, milk shortages arose and local ice cream production slowed dramatically. But after the collapse of the Soviet Union in 1991 a great deal changed. Local production, albeit hesitantly, started up again. Major foreign brands, such as Mars, Baskin-Robbins, Nestlé and Schöller, and

463: Ice cream gâteaux produced to mark the fiftieth anniversary of the Soviet Union in 1967.

Finnish brands like Valio and Ingman, found their way to Russian consumers.

• But the Russian market is difficult. In today's confusing times Russians often look back nostalgically to a period when everything seemed better and ice cream was tasty and filling. Nothwithstanding the initial successes of foreign ice cream brands such as Mars and Nestlé, Russians still prefer Russian ice cream, not least because it is cheaper. In the meantime Unilever, after much deliberation, decided in 1997 to begin its own ice cream company in Moscow, under the Algida name, in partnership with Ice Fili, Russia's biggest ice cream manufacturer. In May 1998 the first Algida ice creams were launched at a children's festival in Moscow's Kolomenskoye Park.

Licks, Sticks & Bricks

A WORLD HISTORY OF ICE CREAM

Italy: the 'dolce' in La Dolce Vita

'Un gelato al limon, gelato al limon, gelato al limon...', sings the smoky-voiced Italian singer and composer Paolo Conte in Gelato al limon, a popular song of the mid-1980s.[1] In Italy, a country where ice cream holds high status, a musical tribute to lemon ice cream raises no eyebrows. The origins of Italian ices lie in the South, in Naples and Sicily. Lemon-flavoured water-ice is the oldest local ice recipe (see chapter 2) and the combination of strawberry, vanilla and chocolate ice cream was invented in Naples. In the eighteenth century Italian ice cream makers travelled to other European countries,

464: Ice cream seller in Naples, 19th century, painted by Pellicia.

notably to France. By the second half of the nineteenth century Italian ice cream carts were plying their trade on the streets of most of Europe's capitals (see chapter 4).

• In the south Italian summer, water-ice was sold in the street as a refreshment against the heat rather than as a food, as ice cream would later become in Northern Europe. In the north of the country, ice cream was at first only sold as a sideline product in latterias (dairy shops), but by the end of the nineteenth century special ice cream parlours were to be found throughout the big cities of the region. Whereas in Northern Europe factory-made ice cream was already in evidence in the 1920s, the existence of thousands of small ice cream parlours offering local flavours, together with the restrictions imposed by Mussolini during the Second World War, delayed its appearance in Italy until the late

465: Lithograph by Gaetano Dura of a vendor of ices in Naples, circa 1850. As wafers and cones were only introduced later, sorbets sold in the streets were served in glasses.

1940s. The first ice cream manufacturer was Algida in 1947, followed by Motta in 1951, the two of them accounting for the greater part of the Italian ice cream market.

• For most consumers, however, Italian ice cream means artisanally produced ice cream. Outside Italy the word 'Italian' on an

Sorbettaro ambulante

ice cream cart or over an ice cream parlour is seen as a promise of fresh, high-quality ice cream. The same is true in the country itself: nowhere in the world is as much artisanal ice cream eaten. In terms of industrial ice cream consumption, Italy in the early 1990s occupied a low place in the

Acquajolo ambulante, e Venditore di forbetti puro ambulante.

466: One of the earliest-known pictures of the street sale of ice cream, Naples, circa 1817. The drawing is the work of Bartolomeo Pinelli (1781-1835). In front of the vendor on the right is a wooden barrel, inside which stands a pewter container with ice cream. The girl is tasting a sample from the long spoon that the vendor uses to scoop the ice cream out of the container.

rankings with about six litres per person per year. But if the consumption of artisanal ice cream (four litres) is added to this, Italy's annual per capita consumption of around ten litres pushes it up to third position in Europe, ahead of Germany, France and the UK.

• Good food and drink are an important part of the Italian lifestyle. Italians enjoy their food and are prepared to spend money on it. In 1992, for example, they spent twice as much money on food per head as the British.[2] Enjoying an ice cream in the 'gelateria' on a summer's evening with a group of friends is as commonplace there as a pint in the pub is for the British or the Irish. For an Italian there is 'nothing more pleasurable than to eat an ice cream in the street on a sunny June morning, when the air is still fresh and the heat is not yet causing the air to shimmer, when the city is on holiday and groups of young people walk through the streets and gather together at ice cream parlours; when you can sense the new season in the air, the longing to bring in the sunny summer at last and taste it in your mouth in the freshly delicate flavour of lemons and strawberries...'[3]

Southern Italy: from sorbet to granita

• Until 1870 Italy was still far from being one country. In the North the houses of Savoy and Hapsburg were dominant, in the central region the Pope held sway and in the South, the King of Spain. In 1860 Giuseppe Garibaldi began his march from Sicily towards Rome with his army of 'a thousand volunteers', providing the impetus for eventual unification. When Garibaldi captured the Sicilian capital of Palermo, the representatives of the Spanish king fled or hid in their palaces. Garibaldi is reputed to have said: 'Good-for-nothings I did not see; they stayed far away inside their palaces. They had had the windows hermetically sealed and were sitting eating sorbets, so cold that they robbed them of any further appetite.'[4] But once Garibaldi and his followers had driven out these 'sorbet eaters' and taken up residence themselves in the Royal Palace of Palermo, they too indulged in large quantities of ices. According to a follower of Garibaldi, Ippolito Nievo, they ate 'ices as big as beefsteaks',[5] preferably in the pistachio, lemon and cherry flavours that matched the colours of Savoy, which under premier Cavour[6] was leading the unification process.

• That the 'Spaniards' ate sorbet was not surprising, since sorbet originated in Naples and Sicily. In the south of Italy there was little dairy farming and milk long remained scarce. Ices provided relief from the summer's heat and in the eighteenth century were popular as an entremets during the lengthy meals eaten at the European courts. A sorbet refreshed the palate prior to the next course.

• Sorbets were also popular during entertainments. In the eighteenth century a visit to the opera was the principal form of entertainment for the upper classes and, as today, arias were the most popular parts of the opera. The aria di sorbetto ('sorbet aria') was one normally sung by the less distinguished singers, during which the audience could relax for a while and cool off by eating a sorbet. It has been claimed that the French author Stendhal (1783-1842) even went to the opera specially to sample the sorbets. Stendhal was a regular visitor to La Scala in Milan, where during the 'sorbet arias' he could choose from three textures: soft, semi-soft and hard. All three, so the story goes, were so delicious that Stendhal had to return evening after evening because he could not decide which he liked best.[7]

• Apart from the ordinary sorbet, Sicily also had an ice confection called the 'spongato'. This was a special sorbet that was enclosed in 'pan di spagna' (sponge-cake) which was soaked in rum. The 'spongato' was closely related to the 'pezzo duro' ('hard piece'), a flat, broad, cylindrical ice, usually prepared in individual portions. There was also the 'spumone', which is said to originate from the small Sicilian town of Acireale. This consists of two creams: on the outside a cream made from chocolate, vanilla or pistachio and on the inside a yellow cream made from whipped egg whites and sugar. The most famous Sicilian ice is the 'cassata'. The word cassata is derived from the Arab 'quasat' (a round bowl). The cassata was round in shape, covered with 'pan di Spagna' on the outside and had three concentric layers of vanilla ice cream, pistachio ice cream and whipped cream on the inside.[8]

• The spumone, cassata and spongato were,

however, only obtainable in the best cafés and restaurants, on account of the cost of their ingredients and their complicated preparation. The most popular ice in the south of Italy was 'granita', whose ease of preparation made it a cheap alternative to the sorbet. Granita is made from grainy, scraped ice, with fruit juice or coffee poured over it. Coffee granita is still a common sight at breakfast tables in the summer in central and southern Italy, sometimes topped with whipped cream and accompanied by a biscuit.

• For a long time ices were sold in southern Italy on the street and in cafés; then, in the nineteenth century, primitive ice cream carts pulled by donkeys also appeared. Later on, tricycle carts were introduced. These carts, decorated with images of saints, folklore figures or swans and other birds, travelled from village to village, the ice cream seller announcing his presence by loudly tooting a brass horn, the same type of horn as was used to indicate that a passenger train was about to depart.[9]

Northern Italy: from latteria to gelateria

• Compared with central and southern Italy, northern Italy was much more densely populated and also had much more industry, agriculture and cattle. In Piedmont and Lombardy an extensive dairy industry existed. In big cities like Milan, Turin, Bologna and Venice, ice cream had been on the menu of the aristocracy ever since the seventeenth century. However, even after the unification of Italy in 1871 ice cream was still not a product eaten by many people. Only on festive days like Carnival or at annual fairs did the ordinary public eat ice cream. As in other countries, hygiene was often conspicuous by its absence. 'They did not clean the pots and pans; that was seen as a waste of time', wrote the American trade journal The Ice Cream Review in 1923 in an article about ice cream making in Italy.[10]

• In the second half of the nineteenth century population numbers increased, but there was no work. The country as a whole had little industry and hundreds of thousands of Italians were forced to emigrate. Many emigrants made a living in their new countries selling ice cream (see chapter 4).

• Towards the end of the nineteenth century the dairy industry in northern Italy expanded. By about 1900, there were latterias in most big cities in northern Italy and they began to sell ice cream in summer. The introduction of cones and wafers stimulated sales, making it possible to eat an ice cream while strolling along the street. In the first years of the century the ice cream sold by the 'Latteria Milanese' in Bologna became renowned for its quality for two reasons. First, the butter sold in this shop came from Milan, the main industrial city in the North, whose strongly developing dairy industry made butter using new factory processes. Second, the ice cream sold by 'Latteria Milanese' was made 'in the Neapolitan manner'.

• The Neapolitan reference reminded the consumer that Naples was the cradle of ice cream. It was there that the product had originated in the sixteenth century (see chapter 2). In the 1920s Giovanni Cuccioli opened an ice cream parlour in Bologna under the name 'Vera Gelateria Napoletana' (Genuine Neapolitan Ice Cream Parlour); and in 1937, together with Augusto Negrini,

467: Giolitti, one of the oldest and most famous ice cream parlours in Rome city centre, circa 1920.

he set up the Pino ice cream parlour, which was to become the city's most famous ice cream parlour.[11] Another famous ice cream maker in Bologna, Enrico Giuseppe, had also learnt his trade in Naples. He was soon nicknamed 'the Neapolitan of Bologna', and his ice cream parlour was a popular haunt of the city's cultural elite.[12]

• It was not only in Bologna that ice cream parlours blossomed. In 1885 Pietro Pozzi, a cattle farmer from Lodi, opened a dairy shop in Milan. In his shop Pozzi sold not only milk and cheese, but also drinks such as lemon-flavoured granita. In 1895 he bought an ice cream machine which was operated by hand and cooled with ice and salt, creating Milan's first 'gelateria'. In the 1920s Giuseppe Pozzi took over his father's business and began to sell his ice cream through vendors who travelled with their carts from village to village.

• After the Second World War Carlo Pozzi, Giuseppe's son, in turn became the owner of the parlour. He established himself as one of Italy's first ice cream wholesalers, selling products to Milan's cafés and restaurants. The business flourished until the 1950s, when the first factory-made ice cream came on the market and competition became so strong that Pozzi discontinued supplies to third parties. However, his ice cream parlour

remained the largest and most famous in Milan and in the 1980s it was equipped with the very latest machines.[13]

• Since 1927 ice cream makers all over the world have been supplied with machines by the firm of Cattabriga in Bologna. When it started, this family-owned business manu-factured 200 ice cream machines a year, climbing, by the 1950s, to over 5,000 units.[14] Cattabriga stayed undisputed market leader

468: Poster by Cantini, 1954, advertising coffee ice on a stick by Soave, then an Algida ice cream brand.

until 1955, when it was overtaken by another Bologna machine manufacturer, Carpigiani. In 1946 the two Carpigiani brothers had begun producing a small-scale ice cream making machine of their own devising. The spatula in the machine scraped the ice off the inside wall by means of a helical motion. The ice was then blended with the mix of flavourings, which was in turn pushed upwards by the same helical motion.

• The ice cream machines of Carpigiani and Cattabriga are popular with artisanal ice cream makers all over the world since, unlike the closed American machines, they have a container which can be opened at the top. It is thus possible to add ingredients by hand to the ice cream during the freezing process – be they fruits or fruit juices, pieces of nut or biscuit, coffee or chocolate.[15]

Algida: the birth of industrial ice cream in Italy

• Until the Second World War small-scale artisanal ice cream makers had the market to themselves in Italy. Immediately after the war Italy was a poor country, with 51% of the population working in agriculture and

industrialisation only spreading slowly. With only 180,000 inhabitants Milan was the country's second-largest city after Rome. In 1950 the average annual income of a manual worker was 311,000 lire, there was still no television and an electric refrigerator cost 73,000 lire.[16] Nor did the Italians eat much ice cream in 1950: a mere 250 grams per annum per person.[17] An Italian would typically buy only a couple of ice cream cones each year at twenty lire apiece. In Italy as a whole there were some 3,000 ice cream parlours, of which 100 or so were in Milan.

• Against this background a Yugoslavian called Alfredo Wiesner began manufacturing ice cream in Rome in 1947. Before the war, Wiesner had been an architect in Zagreb where, after studying the ice cream business with MIAG in Vienna, he had built a small ice cream factory. In 1944 he had worked in Rome for the American Red Cross. In 1945 and 1946 American troops were stationed there; the American Red Cross ensured that the armed forces got their ice cream by operating its own production facilities, managed by Wiesner.[18] As an experiment Wiesner also sold the American ice cream to the Roman public – with enough success that he concluded that there was a market in Italy for industrial ice cream manufactured to an American recipe. He therefore made plans to sell the ice cream through small coffee bars and pastry confectioners.

• Many Italians thought that Wiesner was crazy. The owner of the famous Motta bakery in Milan, Angelo Motta, told Wiesner that his plan was insane and that he himself would never go into the ice cream business.[19] But Wiesner persevered and on 28 April 1947 he set up the ice cream firm Algida in Rome.[20] The business began operations with three employees and ice cream machines obtained from the American Red Cross. At first, Algida produced each day between 700 and 900 chocolate-coated vanilla ice creams on a stick, but by 1948 production had increased to 20,000 ice creams a day. In 1950, with the help of four Italian friends, Italo Barbiani, Giorgio Preger, E. Guadagnini and Dr. L. Boriello, Wiesner set up a new firm in Naples under the name Spica, the acronym of 'Società Partenopea Imbottigliamento Confezioni Alimenti' (Neapolitan company for canned and packaged foods).[21] The Spica factory in Naples gradually took over the activities of the Algida factory in Rome and, in the space of ten years, made Spica Italy's largest ice cream company, marketing its products under the Algida brand name.

Spica

• That Wiesner chose Naples as the site for Spica's factory was no coincidence.[22] After the Second World War the Italian government had drawn up an economic aid plan for the poorer southern part of Italy. Businesses investing in the South were granted financial incentives in the form of low-interest loans.[23] The Spica factory in Naples performed well, which left the small, outdated Algida factory in Rome surplus to requirements; it was closed in 1959 and its production facilities and offices were transferred to Naples. At the end of the 1950s Spica owned ice cream factories in Naples and Palermo, the Pontinia dairy company near Rome and around 100 depots. Spica was also the owner of Aifel, a manufacturer of refrigerators and freezers. Through these businesses Spica controlled the ice cream making process from start to finish. Pontinia supplied the milk and cream, the factories in Naples and Palermo manufactured the ice cream and Aifel supplied the freezer cabinets to bars and other sales outlets on condition that they stocked only Spica ices in the freezers.

469: Poster for the Fortunello ice cream sandwich product made by the Milan-based ice cream manufacturer Alemagna, circa 1953.

• In contrast to northern countries, little ice cream was eaten in the home. Spica's main products were therefore impulse ice creams: ice cream sandwiches, ices on sticks, in tubs and in cones. In 1960 between two and three million units rolled off the production lines each day.[24]

• In 1961 Spica had some 30,000 sales outlets, chiefly bars, most of them located in the central and southern parts of the country. The business had a market share of 31%. Apart from the premium brand Algida, Spica also marketed ice cream under the Soave and Seletti brands, which were well known in Rome and the surrounding area. Algida was made from real cream and Seletti from vegetable fat. Soave, also made from vegetable fat, was a more familiar name in Naples and southern Italy.[25] In 1961 Spica produced 13.1 million litres of ices; 80% of these were ices made from vegetable fat for the cheaper brands Soave and Seletti.[26]

• By then, however, Spica was far from being the only ice cream company in Italy. By 1960 there were some 50 other manufacturers, the largest being Motta, Eldorado, Alemagna and Chiavacci.[27] Eldorado had been established in 1952 in Milan and, in addition to its factory there (Eldorado Nord), it operated another in Naples (Eldorado Sud). Chiavacci was located in Turin, where about 30% of its sales in 1960 were achieved. Chiavacci

himself had started as a street vendor, but soon ice cream vans were driving round the streets of Turin bearing the inscription 'Chiavacci industria gelati Torino' (Chiavacci ice cream company Turin).[28] Alemagna had started out as a bakery in the 1920s in Milan and in the 1930s it was popular for the typical Milanese sweet bread, panettone. In the early 1950s Alemagna also began selling its own factory-made ice cream. Spica's most important competitor, however, was Motta.

470: Poster by Mengardi for Alemagna's Eskibon ice, circa 1953.

Motta: from Panettone to Mottarello

• In 1919 Angelo Motta (1890–1957) had opened a small bakery in Milan. In 1921 he changed both the recipe and shape of his panettone, making the dough more cake-like, putting more raisins in it and giving it a high, conical shape instead of a flat one. In this new shape, which resembled a turban, Motta's Panettone became a great success. By 1925 Motta was a familiar name in Milan and a new city-centre shop was opened on the Piazza del Duomo (Cathedral Square). This became a popular meeting place, not least because of the presence of attractive waitresses in colourful uniforms. In addition to panettone, Motta sold chocolate, cakes, jams and lemonade.

• As these products were mainly sold in the winter, Motta looked around for summer products. He found one in ice cream, and so in 1951 Angelo Motta – the same man who had poured scorn on Wiesner's plans – started up 'Gelati Motta' and became a competitor of Spica's. He had done his homework. With help from the Marshall aid plan a factory was built in Milan, after Motta had sent his best technicians to America to learn all about industrial ice cream production. On their return from America Motta's technicians were accompanied by American colleagues.[29] Several products were test-marketed and the Mottarello product, a chocolate-coated vanilla ice cream on a stick, and the dairy ice cream product Fiordilatte (flower of milk) were selected for production. The launch was a major and lasting success, thanks mainly to the modern, American image of the products. In the shops people asked not for a Mottarello, but for a 'Gelato Americano'.[30]

• In the mid-1950s Motta put a new ice cream product on the market: the Coppa del Nonno ('grandfather's cup'), a small tub of coffee ice cream in the shape of a cup. Like the Mottarello product, it quickly became established and, by the end of the 1950s, Motta had become the best-known ice cream brand in the north of Italy. The products were supported by what for those days

471: Poster by M. Rossi for Motta ices, circa 1951.

were large-scale advertising campaigns. Posters of the early 1960s depicted doctors, housewives and sportsmen recommending Motta ice cream as healthy and delicious.

Artisanal ice cream in the 1950s: healthy or unhealthy?

• In their advertising campaigns both Motta and Spica emphasised the hygienic way in which their ice cream was made. Hygiene was still a weakness of artisanal ice cream makers. In the 1950s the newspapers regularly contained reports of cases of food poisoning that were attributable to artisanal ice cream.[31]

• For this reason and to promote other common interests, the artisanal ice cream sector decided to form its own trade association. In 1953 the ice cream makers in Milan set up a profes-sional association: Alga (Associ-azione Latterie Gelaterie e Affini). The organisation focused its efforts on improving the reputation of artisanal ice cream.[32] Congresses were held and courses run in order to convince ice cream makers of the need for a professional approach to hygiene. Publications were issued to emphasise the need for pasteurisation and for the thorough clean-ing of equipment. Another

step was the establishment of a laboratory in which artisanal ice cream could be tested for the presence of bacteria. Affiliated ice cream makers could have their products analysed free-of-charge.

• These initiatives had the desired effect: by May 1954 the number of bacteria found in the artisanal ice cream tested had fallen below the threshold set by the Association of 200,000 per cc.[33] (Legal standards for ice cream production were not introduced in Italy until the 1970s.) Alga also gave the cause of

473: Ice cream seller in Rome, July 1957.

hygienic production a boost by advocating the use of modern ice-making machines, negotiating favourable terms with manufacturers like Carpigiani and Cattabriga.

• In 1956 Alga decided to start collective advertising. A promotional film was screened in Italian cinemas, claiming that artisanal ice cream was better-tasting and had a higher nutritional value than factory-made ice cream. Three years later, the first interna-tional trade fair for artisanal ice cream makers was held in the small town of

472: Poster for Motta ice, circa 1959. The poster was originally designed by Rossi in 1951. Eight years later the picture was still popular, but the woman's face was now depicted in more vivid colours and with the allure of a film star.

Longarone in northern Italy. The favourable publicity generated did wonders for the product's image and, over the years, the Longarone event expanded to become the world's leading exhibition for artisanal ice cream makers.[34]

• By 1959 ice cream consumption in Italy had climbed to two litres per person per annum. Of this, some 50% was industrial ice cream and 50% artisanal ice cream. During the 1960s and 1970s artisanal ice cream volume grew, although it declined as a proportion of the total market. The early 1990s saw its market share rising again, to an estimated 45%.[35]

'La dolce vita'

• The 1960s are known in Italy as the years of 'la dolce vita' (the sweet life), a tag borrowed from the Federico Fellini film title of 1959. After the difficult 1950s the economy began to flourish. Italians had more money to spend and took more holidays. What could be nicer than to sit on an Italian beach and enjoy an ice cream in the sunshine?

• The industrialised north of the country benefited most from the growth in prosperity. The South lagged behind, so the ice cream firms all differentiated their prices, reducing them in the South.[36]

• In 1961 Spica contacted Unilever. In view of the establishment of the EEC Spica foresaw a process of consolidation that would ultimately leave only a few international ice cream brands in Europe. 'They [...] want to play an active role in this development in order not to find themselves in a less favourable position from a competition point

of view at a certain moment', ran an internal Unilever memo from October of that year.[37] In the course of the discussions with Unilever, Wiesner pointed out that selling industrial ice cream in Italy was difficult because of the strong position held by the artisanal ice cream makers.[38] Against this, Unilever noted the growth rates in the market at that time, which were around 20% per annum,[39] and early in 1962 decided to buy 48% of the shares in Spica subject to the condition that the remaining 52% would be sold to Unilever in phases over a five-year period.[40] The purchase followed the recently formulated Unilever policy to extend its ice cream business (see chapter 21).

• The Unilever people were pleasantly surprised by the excellence of the Spica products during a visit to the Naples factory in May 1962. Whether ice cream or water-ice, the products were of a quality rarely found elsewhere in Europe.[41] One ice in particular attracted the visitors' attention. 'One of the successful lines is an ice cream in a cone made from pastry covered with chocolate and nuts', wrote J. Loopuyt in his report of the visit. 'The surprising thing is that the wafer remains crisp after lengthy storage. This is achieved because they dip the wafer in a mixture of oil, chocolate and sugar. The competition in Italy has not yet succeeded in imitating this; we have assured ourselves of that fact. The cornets are made in a bakery department in the factory'.[42] He was describing the now world-famous Cornetto ice cream cone, which Unilever launched in 1963 in Germany, France, Belgium and the Netherlands. The name was registered as a trademark in all countries and new packag-

474: Summer in the 1960s, 'la dolce vita' by the lake: sun, scooters, swimming, lazing around, playing ball and eating ices.

. . . una delizia per tutti !

creme per gelati

de nardo : *una marca in Italia ed all'estero nel campo della gelateria*

ing was designed.[43] The Cornetto cone, based on the Spica recipe, was first produced for these countries at the Belgian factory and later in other Unilever factories.

475: Sales brochure of Nardo, one of the oldest Italian manufacturers of ice cream cones and wafers, 1960.

• By 1964 Unilever owned 100% of Spica.[44] Traditionally, Spica had been most active in central and southern Italy. In the more densely populated and affluent North, strong competition was posed by Motta, Alemagna and Eldorado. In 1967 Unilever therefore acquired the Turin-based Eldorado, with its two well-equipped factories in Milan and Naples and a market share of 12%.[45]

• With Spica and Eldorado, Unilever now had a strong presence throughout Italy. After 1968 Spica's Algida house brand concentrated on the teenage and adult market, while Eldorado sold ices for children. The Eldorado logo, a smiling boy in a cowboy hat,

was in fact entirely appropriate to its target market and from 1967 could be regularly seen at peak viewing times in commercials broadcast on Italian television.[46]

• Ice creams were still mainly eaten in the summer.[47] In the winter, most artisanal ice cream parlours closed their doors. To counteract this seasonality, Unilever began – as it had done in Germany, Belgium, the Netherlands and the UK – to invest in the emerging frozen foods market. In succession it bought the frozen foods businesses Genepesca (fish), Invito (vegetables) and Findus (a frozen food brand owned in other countries by Nestlé). In 1968 the Unilever frozen foods and ice cream activities were amalgamated within a new company: Sages (Società Alimentari Gelato e Surgelato). The new head office of Sages was established in Rome in 1970.

Italgel versus Sages

• In the 1970s competition intensified. The American companies Grace and Beatrice Foods purchased the ice cream businesses Tanara (Parma) and Sanson (Verona) respectively. Motta and Alemagna entered into an alliance and in 1973 they sold their shares to the Italian state, which attempted to protect its domestic ice cream businesses against the strong foreign competition.

• Sages, too, tried to strengthen its market by taking over other businesses. Negotiations with the family-owned Sammontana business in Tuscany broke down in 1973. However, talks held in that same year with the ice cream firms Chiavacci (Turin) and Toseroni (with factories in Sardinia, Rome and Milan) were successful.[48] They became part of Sages, giving Unilever a share of over 40% of the industrial ice cream market.

• In 1975 Grace sold its shares in Tanara, which in the preceding years had bought a number of smaller ice cream factories, to the Italian state. The following year the state combined Motta, Alemagna and Tanara to form the new business Italgel, which held the number two position in the ice cream market with a share of over 32%[49] (and would in 1996 be bought by Nestlé). In the meantime, industrial ice cream consumption was growing: by the mid-1970s it had climbed to five litres per person per year.

• After the mergers of the 1970s, Italian ice cream manufacturers focused their energies on developing new ices for new market segments. Motta, for instance, launched the Maxibon ice cream sandwich in 1981 and in the early 1980s Sages put the Calippo brand on the market.

476: Advertising campaign for Motta ice cream, summer 1960. Ice cream is good for you, everyone eats it: young men and women, the housewife, the doctor, children, the sporting holidaymaker. The idea and execution of the campaign are typical of the advertising style of that period. Each of the target groups is tastefully pictured and the photograph has replaced pencil and brush.

478: Poster for Solero
ice cream, Rome, 1997.

to 40%, equating to some four litres per person per year.

• The ice cream manufacturers once more took up the challenge and hit back with their own versions of 'artisanal' ice. Motta was the first when it launched Antica Gelateria del Corso in 1981. The name and pack radiated a high quality hand-made image. In its advertising, too, the brand was praised as artisanal ice cream. It was highly successful, not only in Italy, but also in other countries. One year later, Sagit, as Sages had been renamed, marketed its own Sorbetteria di Ranieri.

The strategy worked: annual consumption of industrial ice cream climbed in the mid-1980s to almost seven litres per head.

• Meanwhile, the artisanal ice cream makers tried to regain market share. They set up the magazine Il Giornale dei Gelateri, organised new trade fairs and regulated prices. Their main marketing tool, however, was still their wide product range and continuous flavour innovation. It was easier for the artisanal ice cream makers to take the risk of introducing a new flavour on a small scale. Their higher prices did not deter consumers, who in the prosperous 1980s and 1990s were only too willing to pay more for a quality product that was available in thousands of attractive ice cream parlours all over the country – over 33,000 of them by 1990.[50] The artisanal market share grew in this period

479: Poster from Algida advertising campaign for Solero ices, summer 1997.

477: Poster for Motta ice cream bonbons, Rome, 1997.

• The launch of these sophisticated luxury brands is typical of the dynamic nature of Italy's ice cream history and the constant search by both artisanal and industrial companies for innovative, ever higher quality ice cream products with which to entertain and delight the consumer.

Licks, Sticks & Bricks
A WORLD HISTORY OF ICE CREAM

France:
ice cream
cuisine

In 1929 Paris, Lyon and Marseilles were the only French cities where you could buy ice cream at all times of the year, according to the American George Kent.[1] Even in chic bathing resorts like Biarritz, which attracted a fashion-conscious public all year round, there was, he said, no ice cream to be had in winter. Prior to 1929 ice cream production was totally in the hands of artisanal ice cream makers. If the French ate ice cream, it was as a dessert course after dinner, not as a snack between meals as in America. In the whole of Paris there was only one soda fountain bar that was worthy of the name, in La Coupole. Nor was there any ice cream advertising.

• Such was the picture Kent painted of the French market in The Ice Cream Journal. And yet, in 1929 the French were eating ten times as much ice cream as they had before the First World War. Even as Kent's article was being published in the United States, the first ice cream factory was established in France. Its founder, the Gervais dairy company, began selling ice cream for the first time in cinemas, where talking pictures were just being introduced. Seven years later the Ortiz family, who were ice cream street vendors, would start supplying ice cream to the cinemas in north-east France, later becoming the main competitor of Gervais in the French market. The Ortiz family came from Spain's Basque country, as did many of the other ice cream makers in France, the only country where the Spanish were able to rival the Italians in influencing the development of the ice cream market.

• Ice cream in 1929 was still made by the people who served it: owners of cafés, tea rooms and restaurants and confectionery bakers (see also chapter 4); by 1995 their share of the market had dropped to less than 15%. The domestic manufacturers, of which Gervais and Ortiz were by far the largest, were faced in the 1960s with competition from foreign groups, such as Motta from Italy, Nestlé from Switzerland and the Anglo-Dutch Unilever Group.

'Les Esquimaux de Gervais'

A la Renommée de la Bonne Glace

481: The splendidly decorated ice cream cart of Ortiz, circa 1920. The text on the awning translates as 'Renowned for Good Ice'.

• As in other countries, part of the French ice cream industry originated from the country's dairy industry. In 1850 a 20 year-old sales representative from Paris, Charles Gervais, set up a factory in Normandy to produce a new type of cream cheese.[2] Later on, the business started producing fresh cream, butter and ice cream. In 1929

Gervais pioneered the manufacture of ice cream for sale in restaurants, grocers' shops and cinemas. In 1931 a separate ice cream factory was established in Bobigny, a suburb of Paris. It had an output of 20,000 litres a day and its products included the 'Esquimau'[3], a chocolate-coated vanilla ice on a stick which was to become a renowned ice cream brand, much-loved in cinema intervals. In the 1950s it was the subject of a popular song:

'Quand le soir vient sur la ville
Je vais retrouver mon amour
Et dans l'ombre familière
Dans l'ombre claire d'un cinéma
Aussitôt que revient la lumière
Je sais alors qu'elle me dira:
Les voilà, les voilà, les voilà,
Les Esquimaux, les Esquimaux,
[..]
Les seuls, les vrais, les Esquimaux Gervais.'[4]

['When evening descends on town I'll meet my love again. And in the cosy darkness, in that bright darkness of the cinema, I know that when the lights are turned back on she'll say to me: "Look, there they are – the Eskimo ice creams, the only real Eskimo ice creams from Gervais" '].

• In 1960 Gervais placed its ice cream operations in a newly established company, France Glaces. Partners in the new company were Heudebert, La Société des Glacières de Paris and Nestlé. In 1967 Gervais merged with Danone, a company founded in Barcelona in 1919 which specialised in yoghurts and other desserts. In 1970 Gervais Danone increased its holding in France Glaces from 23% to 49%. In the following year France Glaces merged with Findus, which was wholly owned by Nestlé; Gervais Danone had a 35% participation in the new business, which became market leader with about a third of the industrial market for ice cream.[5]

• In 1973, after its merger with the foods group BSN (Groupe Boussois Souchon Neuvesel), Gervais Danone withdrew from ice cream manufacturing to concentrate on its core activities, selling its interests to Nestlé, which thus acquired ownership of the Glaces Gervais brand.[6]

A travelling ice cream vendor from the Basque country

• The successful French ice cream brand Ortiz-Miko was created by the Ortiz family, whose roots lie in the Cantabrian Mountains, south of Santander. In the tiny village of San Pedro del Romeral in the valley of the Rio Pas, the 'pasiego' Luis Ortiz was born in 1889.[7] Local people made their living from cattle farming and from the production and sale of biscuits and milk ice. The farmers' children were often sent to the Basque region of France where, depending on the season, they sold ice cream, roasted chestnuts or oublies in fashionable resorts like Biarritz or Saint Jean-de-Luz; they were called 'les marchands de plaisir' [traders in pleasure].[8]

• In 1905 Luis Ortiz, with his simple machines to make ice cream and oublies, moved first to the Basque region in France, then to the Côte d'Azur and, later on, much deeper into France. In 1911 he married Mercedes Josefa Martinez de la Maza in Nancy, in the north-east of the country. She had been born in the same region as Luis and also made ice cream.[9] Between 1913 and 1922 they had five sons – Louis, Jean, Vidal, André and Joseph –

482: Joseph Ortiz and his ice cream cart in Saint-Dizier town square, late 1930s.

who were to play an important role in the history of the French ice cream industry.

• On the outbreak of the First World War Luis moved to south-west France where he worked in the shipyards at Rochefort. In 1921, however, the family returned to the north-east and settled for good in Saint-Dizier. Luis, along with many other Spaniards, resumed his former occupation as an itinerant trader in ices, wafers, peanuts and sweet chestnuts.[10] He and his sons travelled the countryside around Saint-Dizier selling their wares. Each day they covered some 40 to 50 kilometres, at first on foot and by train and later by cycle. In about 1930 the Ortiz family began to modernise: they moved their production into a separate workplace; electrical ice cream making machines and freezer cabinets were installed; and they purchased motorised ice cream carts which enabled them to serve a much wider area. They also expanded their product range, making ices on a stick and Neapolitan ice cream gâteaux by hand.[11]

¶ The history of Ortiz-Miko is the tale of an extraordinary family business, of the success of a father and mother and their five sons.[1] A story of five lads with hardly any schooling who pushed hand-carts through the French countryside selling ice cream and sweet chestnuts, braving the wind and the rain and the hottest days of summer, and who went on to become directors of France's largest ice cream business. They achieved success through hard work, perseverance, family loyalty, thriftiness, a willingness to do anything and try anything and a clear view of the market opportunities. As immigrants they integrated so successfully in French society that the government wanted to see a French ice cream and frozen foods multinational created around their companies. From a modest, cottage industry rose an industrial group with factories and affiliates in France, Spain, Belgium and Germany.

From Santander to Saint-Dizier
As a fifteen year-old, the father Luis Ortiz (1889-1948) had left Santander in Spain's Basque country for France to sell ice cream in the summer and sweet chestnuts in the winter. In Nancy, in 1911, he married Mercedes, who originated from

483: Ortiz motorised ice cream cart, circa 1936.

the same region, had travelled the same route and made her living in the same way as he did. After their marriage Luis worked in a glass-blowing factory in Clichy to support his young family. Their sons Louis and Jean were born there, in 1913 and 1914 respectively, and through his itinerant trading Luis earned some extra money. With the onset of the First World War, the Ortiz family moved for safety to the town of Rochefort on the south-west coast of France, where Luis got a job in a shipyard. Vidal was born in Rochefort in 1918 and André in 1920. In October 1921 they returned to north-east France to settle for good in Saint-Dizier, where Joseph was born in 1922. There they began to sell ice cream, initially from hand-carts. As the sons grew up they started working in the business. Their parents were

not sufficiently versed in French, so the eldest son, Louis, was entrusted with the handling of complicated contacts from an early age. Gradually he was to become the informal leader of the clan. In about 1930 the Ortiz family modernised: they began production in a separate building from their living quarters, motorised the carts, brought in delivery bicycles and acquired electric ice cream making machines and freezers. From 1936, they focused their Freski brand on the growing cinema public and it was this trade which allowed them to survive the Second World War. When France was liberated by the Americans in 1944, they immediately saw a new market: US troops. When Luis died in 1949, it was Louis who built up a large and fruitful network of retailers across France. In 1946 he had founded an association of itinerant ice cream vendors, maintaining numerous useful contacts and fulfilling many posts on industry committees. The expansion of the family business was attributable more than anything to his organisational and social skills and to the fact that he was known as a man of his word: there was no need to put agreements with him down in writing.

After the purchase of a Danish machine for the manufacture of ices on sticks, which made possible an enormous increase in productivity, the business was in a position to 'go national'. The installation of the new machine in 1953 can be regarded as a turning point in the firm's history: from itinerant traders the Ortiz sons had now become industrialists.

Purchase of Délico

After Luis' death, mother Mercedes was the formal boss. All the finances were entrusted to her; she gave her sons only what they needed, say, to buy a suit. In 1964 – when Mercedes was about 80 years old – the family bought Délico from Unilever, a transaction which formed a second turning point

484: The factory tower of the old Miko ice cream factory in Saint-Dizier, circa 1968.

in the history of the family. The structure of the business was now brought up to date and the production and distribution operations began to pick up speed. The five brothers from now on received a salary based on their age, their seniority in the business and their responsibilities. Louis became president and managing director, Jean vice-president, Vidal technical director, André director of the Moselle district and Joseph director of manufacturing. However, certain characteristics of the family business remained unchanged: important decisions were taken by unanimous votes, a factor which delayed the eventual sale of the company. To finance the purchase of Délico the family mortgaged all their assets: equipment, factory, even their private homes. The brothers were not yet ready to give up

their independence and tolerate a corporate board of management above them. Even within this structure, however, the business in effect revolved around one man, Louis. Middle management in this family-owned business was not well developed.

The family had a good feel for publicity. Louis was an advocate of a clear house style; the choice of the name Miko was a good move; they very quickly understood the importance of cinema advertising and the sponsoring of sports events; and they had good taste in selecting their designers.

485: Miko sticker promoting ice cream sales in cinemas, early 1960s.

But then the brothers grew old and their health began to decline. When the pressure of the growing size of the business became too heavy a burden, the Ortiz family finally accepted the offer from Unilever which would guarantee the continuation of their lives' work.

Ice cream in the interval at the cinema

• Despite – or perhaps because of – the Depression, leisure pursuits like walking, cycle racing, football and boxing were on the increase; and in 1936 France introduced the 40-hour working week and paid holidays. Cinema attendance was also increasing following the invention of talking pictures, and provided a cheap and popular form of entertainment. Saint-Dizier, though it only had a population of 15,000, had five cinemas in front of which the five Ortiz brothers, who had no competitors in the town, positioned their carts and sold their ice cream, chestnuts and other goods. In 1936, they loaned a freezer cabinet to one cinema and soon afterwards extended the facility to its rivals. They went on to supply

various cinemas in the départements bordering the River Marne.[12]

• Early in the Second World War, Germany occupied the northern half of France. As a result the Ortiz clan lost their sales to the local French garrisons; they were not allowed to supply the German occupying forces and there was a general decline in sales. The brothers increasingly concentrated their sales effort on cinemas, to which – despite restrictions on the use of electricity and the doubling of admission prices – visits soared in Saint-Dizier as in the rest of the country. Cinema admissions in France leapt from 6 million in 1939 to 310 million in 1942 and 400 million in 1944, even though audiences had to put up with more and more inconvenience as the war dragged on: unheated auditoriums, no British or American films, censorship, ever higher taxes on the price of entry,[13]

486: Motorised ice cream cart with the 'exquisite ices' of Ortiz, mid-1930s.

487: Ice cream vendor in front of the 'Union' cinema in Forbach, near Saarbrücken, circa 1928. In 1936 Ortiz began making freezer cabinets available on loan to cinemas. On the right is a poster for the 1926 American film What Price Glory?, whose action takes place in France during the First World War.

488: From left to right: the three brothers Louis, Jean and Vidal Ortiz with their motorised ice cream carts, circa 1935.

489: Holiday-time at Les Sables d'Olonne on the Atlantic coast, 1937. With a good eye for business, the ice cream seller has parked next to the tents.

and a reduction in the number of cinemas as premises were requisitioned by the Germans or destroyed by the Resistance. Before and after the film, and in the intervals, cinema-goers liked to eat – and growing attendance figures meant more consumers of ice cream and chestnuts. The war thus allowed the eldest son, Louis, to expand his contacts with cinema operators in the east of France, which would prove extremely valuable in peacetime.[14]

• In September 1944 France was liberated by the Americans whose garrisons replaced those of the Germans in the north-east of France. The Ortiz family began to supply ice cream to the Americans, who wanted to eat ice cream every day, just like back home. They made ice creams in the flavours the Americans liked, such as chocolate, butterscotch and candied fruits, obtaining many of the ingredients from the Americans themselves.[15]

• In 1946 Louis set up an association of itinerant ice cream sellers which subsequently formed the basis of his national distribution network. He also began buying up small firms of ice cream makers, while many others became concessionaires for Ortiz ice cream and sold it alongside their own.[16] Meanwhile, cinema attendance figures continued to climb, reaching 424 million admissions in 1947.

Ortiz becomes Miko

• In 1950 Louis and Vidal travelled to the United States to visit the ultra-modern Breyers factory (see chapters 5 and 6) and the international trade fair for ice cream

making equipment in Atlantic City. There they saw and ordered a Gram RIA machine that could produce 4,000 ices on a stick per hour, which they finally installed in 1953.[17] Then, from a business contact in Nancy, they bought the rights to use a fine-sounding name for their vanilla/chocolate ice on a stick, a name they thought had a young and American ring to it: Miko.[18]

• In the 1950s cinema attendance figures declined to around 380 million a year, remaining stable at that level for a number of years. Of cinema-goers at that time, 45% were aged between 15 and 20 years old and went not with their family, but with their friends.[19] Miko's sales were highest among young people; and, as the children of the post-war 'baby boom' grew older, the volume in this segment also grew. 'Allez au cinéma, et dégustez Miko, le chocolat glace de qualité totale', ran one of the firm's advertising slogans ['Go to the cinema and taste Miko full quality chocolate ice cream'].

• In these years Ortiz-Miko expanded the geographical scope of its operations. From its home base in north-eastern France, it captured positions on the Côte d'Azur and round Bordeaux. Between 1950 and 1960 the family business developed from its origins as ice cream vendors into a fully fledged industry with 650 employees and 20 depots. Production output increased twentyfold.[20] Specific advertising films for use in cinemas were produced by Tonio Paccioni, a friend of the Ortiz family and himself a cinema operator. The storylines were based on cinema archetypes such as the Wild West, Supergirl or Pancho, the Mexican hero.[21]

490: Poster of the Confédération Nationale des Glaciers de France, designed by Reinoso, circa 1952. For many years this confederation of artisanal ice cream makers issued a new poster at the beginning of each ice cream season.

491: Miko ice lolly wrapper, 1958.

492: Miko poster, circa 1958. The ice floe with the blue, snow-capped letters 'Miko' had been the firm's logo since Ortiz first introduced the Miko brand name in 1951.

494: Poster showing the Miko ice cream sandwich Big Treat, circa 1955. The chocolate flavoured wafers were made by La Basquaise, one of France's oldest wafer and cone manufacturers, owned by the Gomez brothers, another Basque family and friends of the Ortiz.

493: Miko pack, late 1950s. The words 'La Grande Marque Française' emphasised the firm's French identity, as a counter to foreign competitors.

The firm and its ice cream were invariably present at the film festival in Cannes.[22]

• From the mid-1960s, with cinema attendance declining in the face of TV viewing in the home, Miko changed the thrust of its strategy from cinema products to family packs of ice cream sold through the emerging supermarkets.

Growing competition from abroad

• Before Unilever (1958), Nestlé (1960) and Motta (1962) entered the French ice cream market, no multinationals had been active there. Consumption in France was still low: half that of the Germans and one-third that of the Italians.[23] In 1961 a marketing war broke out between the international groups and Ortiz-Miko. Ortiz-Miko was able to stand its ground, as it had created a great deal of consumer loyalty over the years. It also appealed successfully to nationalist sentiment with ringing statements such as 'Foreign ice cream does not meet French tastes'. At the end of 1961 Miko had a supporting network of 15,000 retailers who were located at strategic points in or near markets, sports grounds, swimming baths, schools and beaches. France Glaces (Nestlé) had slightly fewer than that number, Motta

495: Poster dating from about 1958 showing the specialities on sale in an ice cream shop in Cano. The company name Miko was applied to the vanilla and chocolate stick, which consequently became known as 'a Miko'.

less than half and Délico (Unilever) only 2,000. In cinemas Miko had an even bigger lead.

• France Glaces now sought to copy Miko, offering thousands of freezer cabinets free to retailers, conditional on the exclusive sale of Nestlé ice creams. Motta and Délico promptly followed suit. Though this increased the number of sales outlets, consumption hardly budged; the market had reached saturation point.[24] In 1964 Miko acquired Délico. Unilever's loss-making operation had wanted to buy Miko, but Louis Ortiz persuaded Unilever that the reverse made more sense. The deal gave the Ortiz family ownership of an ultra-modern production plant and an enlarged distribution network, particularly in the regions around Tours, Toulouse and Lille.

• In the same period the structure of the business was modernised and Ortiz-Miko expanded further, with production growing from 4 million litres of ice cream in 1960 to 21 million in 1970. In the early 1970s the business had 1,100 employees, a turnover of FF160 million, a fleet of 600 refrigerated trucks, 80,000 square metres of production facilities, 100,000 cubic metres of cold storage space, 150 depots and 90,000 sales outlets. During the summer 15,000 litres of cream were processed each day, as well as 80,000 litres of milk, 20 tons of sugar, five tons of chocolate and ten tons of fruit.[25]

496: Jean Ortiz selling Miko ices in the mid-1950s from a special ice cream van.

Sponsorship and television advertising

• Marketing and advertising activities were also updated. Ortiz-Miko ice cream vans were already among the 'caravan' of advertisers and sponsors that followed the racing cyclists in the Tour de France. From 1971 Ortiz-Miko also became the sponsor of the yellow jersey that is awarded after each stage to the overall leader on the Tour. From 1962 onwards the world's most famous cycle race was broadcast live each day on television,[26] so that millions of TV viewers at home, in addition to the the millions of spectators lining the route, became familiar with the Miko name. In the second half of the 1970s Miko joined with bicycle manufacturer Mercier in co-sponsoring their own cycle racing team, attracting top stars like Raymond Poulidor, Sean Kelly and Joop Zoetemelk. This switch from cinema to sports events and TV mirrored the changes that were taking place in society. Between 1953 and 1971 the annual number of cinema-

497: Miko price board, 1962.

498: The proprietor of a confiserie in front of his shop in Bar-sur-Aube in 1962. On the shop front is an illuminated sign and the ice cream manufacturer's latest poster advertisement: 'Miko pour tous, tous pour Miko' ['Miko for everyone, everyone for Miko'].

499: Miko poster, circa 1960.

500: Following the Tour de France, Miko used to serve ice cream in the late 1960s from this futuristic van, constructed by Chausson of Reims.

goers fell from 420 million to 180 million, while ownership of TV sets climbed from 65,000 to 12 million. By 1965 the French citizen was spending an average of 25 hours a week watching television.[27]

• From 1970 the Ortiz family also began trading in frozen food products under the name Mikogel. In 1974, they bought the Vivagel frozen foods firm and by 1987 65% of their sales were accounted for by frozen foods, with ice cream sales of Miko, Frigécrème and Nouki – founded in the 1930s and in 1959 respectively and both acquired in 1984 – representing the balance.[28]

• In 1970 a Miko factory was opened in Spain. Operating as an independent venture,[29] it became one of the four biggest branded ice cream businesses in Spain and in 1984 it

held a market share of over 10% (see chapter 17). In 1975 Miko bought Stromboli, an ice cream brand that had been active for decades in and around Paris. This gave Ortiz-Miko a much larger share of the important Parisian ice cream market. In 1983 Ortiz-Miko successfully became a publicly listed company[30], although the majority of its shares remained in the hands of the family.

Frigécrème and Nouki

• In Nantes, the Decré family owned the ice cream company Frigécrème and a department store. From the 1930s Frigécrème supplied the store's restaurant until the ice cream factory and the store were destroyed in the war. In 1948 Michel Decré had paid a study visit to North America. In the United States he studied department store management techniques and in Canada he took part in a course in the production and marketing of ice cream. On his return, still only twenty years old, he decided to start up an ice cream business again.

• For the next 10-15 years his firm remained one of the many small French operations that supplied the local market. Then, in 1962, Frigécrème opened its first semi-industrial production facility to serve the whole region round Nantes (with sales in 1969 worth FF3 million). Two-thirds of the Frigécrème shares were held by the Decré family and one-third by the Colarena dairy co-operative. By 1975 Frigé-crème had over 10% of the national ice cream market through its 25,000 sales outlets.[31] Some 30% of the ice cream was sold outdoors, 23% to the retail trade and 47% to restaurants, including those in the now twelve department stores of the Decré family.[32]

• Half of the advertising budget was spent on point of sale materials; the other half was spent on advertising in cinemas, at sports events, on television and in magazines.[33] Like Ortiz-Miko, Frigécrème also sponsored a cycle racing team – in conjunction with

501: Poster for a refrigerator made by Faure, circa 1962.

Gitane – whose members included Joop Zoetemelk, Leo Duyndam, Gerard Vianen and Raymond Martin.[34]

• Nouki had been established in 1959 producing bakery products such as pastry dough and quick-frozen cakes, but also ice cream. Its factory and head office were located not far from Geneva.[35] In 1984, BSN, which had owned Frigécrème and Nouki for four years, held talks with both Unilever and Miko about the sale of these businesses, as ice cream no longer fitted its long-term strategy. Unilever had shown an interest in Frigécrème in 1976, but without outcome, partly because the French government of the time displayed a pre-ference for mergers between French businesses rather than see them pass into foreign hands. This remained true in 1984: the French government preferred Frigé-crème and Nouki to be bought by Miko rather than by Unilever.[36] So, with the support of state-owned banks and subsidies, Miko bought Frigécrème and Nouki, whose distribution network complemented Miko's. Ortiz-Miko, in pursuit of the French government's vision of a French multinational frozen food and ice cream company, entered the European market, buying the German company Warncke and in 1992 Mio in Belgium (see chapters 12 and 13).

CRÈMES GLACÉES *Délico si crémeuses!*

502: Poster for Délico ices, circa 1962.

Délico and Eldorado

• In 1958 Unilever purchased Gella, a Paris-based ice cream business, in the hope of capturing a substantial share of the French market. Gella chiefly sold its products in factory canteens, restaurants and cafés, producing 30 million litres of ice cream in 1958.[37] A new brand name, Délico, was introduced and a new ice cream factory was opened at Saint-Denis in 1961. However, the business was not a success[38], mainly because other ice cream brands had already established so many ties with strategically located concessionaires and depots that there was little space left for Unilever. Délico's sales remained confined principally to Paris and the Riviera,[39] and in 1965 Unilever sold the company to its competitor Miko.

• In 1971 Unilever tried a different approach. It imported ice cream from Belgium and sold it in the areas around Paris, Lille and Lyon, using the sales organisation and distribution network of the Unilever frozen foods company Iglo, which had started up a few years earlier. Unilever's ice cream sold under the name Ola in Belgium, the Netherlands and Portugal, but in France Ola was the name of a brand of condoms! Unilever therefore adopted the Eldorado name, derived from an Italian ice cream company that it had recently acquired[40] (see chapter 15).

• In the 1970s marketing efforts were concentrated on the fastest-growing segment of the market: take-home dessert ice cream sold in hypermarkets and supermarkets.[41] Eldorado ice cream was positioned as a supplement to Iglo's range of dessert products. In 1971 French consumption was just three litres per person per year and the competition from a wide range of local desserts, including fruits, cheeses and superb pâtisseries, was intense. The strong French culinary tradition guaranteed a preference for home brands; and Unilever's late entry on the French ice cream market meant that most retailers were already exclusive suppliers of another ice cream brand.

• Eldorado's market share therefore remained limited in the first few years: Ortiz-Miko brands dominated outdoor and cinema sales, whilst Gervais had the lion's share of the take-home sector. In 1974 Unilever tried, as it had done ten years earlier, to buy Miko and was again rebuffed by the Ortiz family. Of the total ice cream market in 1975, Miko and Gervais each held about one-third, followed at some distance by Frigécrème and Motta, each with 10% to 12%. Eldorado had a market share of less than 1%.[42] Moreover, Eldorado was seen as a supplier of speciality ice cream products rather than a complete range[43] and it was the most expensive supplier on the market.

503: 1985 poster for the 3-D Gervais water-ice product, Mickey.

By 1977 there had been little improvement[44] and in the impulse sector, then representing one-third of the market, Eldorado had failed to make any headway at all.[45]

Motta, Unilever and Carte d'Or

• In the second half of 1977, however, Unilever seized an opportunity to buy Motta, making Iglo-Eldorado the third largest ice cream manufacturer in France.[46] The Italian Motta company had built a new factory in 1962 in Argentan, in the heart of the dairy farming district of Normandy. Motta had imported ice cream from Italy, along with coffee, confectionery products, cream crackers, and marrons glacés, which were distributed through 55 concessionaires with their own depots. Motta's ice cream business lay mainly in two-and-a-half litre packs of ice cream and in the manufacturing of ice cream products for others, including supermarkets. In 1977 all national brands had more or less the same product ranges[47], the same flavours, the same quality levels and practically the same prices. Competition was limited to the area of promotions.[48] The outcome was a price war, leading to low profit margins and brand switching by consumers.

Carte d'Or: the quality of pureness

¶ Carte d'Or was first marketed in 1978, based on the propositions that the flavours were natural and unadulterated ('Le goût à état pur'); that it used a large proportion of pieces of real fruit or confectionery (sometimes as high as 35% by volume); and that the ingredients were of high quality ('La qualité qui fait la différence').

Since 1978, thirty-four flavours have been rolled out in France at a rate of two or three new flavours a year: apple, apricot, Armagnac plum, banana, blackcurrant, caramel, cherry, chestnut, coconut, coffee, dark chocolate, Grand Marnier, lemon, lime, lychee, mandarin, mango, melon, mint, nougat, nuts, orange, passion fruit, peach, pear, pineapple, pistachio, praline, raspberry, red grapefruit, rum-and-raisin, strawberry, vanilla, white chocolate. This achievement, masterminded by Motta's development department in Argentan, Normandy, was recognised in 1984 with the award of the Grand Prix de L'innovation des Industries Agro-alimentaires.[1]

The range encompasses both ice creams and sorbets. Sorbet reflects traditional French tastes – it contains no fat whatsoever. Sorbets are easily digestible, light and have a hint of 'nouvelle cuisine'. The pack design is sober but elegant, and everything in the design, such as the golden colour of the tubs, is aimed at creating a style that appeals to the connoisseur. Initially, the product was launched in the two-and-a-half-litre pack with an eye to the primary target group of restaurants, hotels and institutional caterers.

504: Pack of Carte d'Or ice cream, 1998.

The smaller pack sizes were introduced to meet the needs of a second target group, families. As there are so many flavours, it is possible to make new combinations all the time. Just three scoops and twenty flavours allow as many as 1,360 different combinations; four scoops and twenty flavours offer an amazing 8,855.[2] Although Carte d'Or ice cream is expensive, it has been outstandingly successful through a combination of sophisticated product innovation – often inspired by the regional cuisine of France – and effective marketing. From 1984 the brand was also rolled out in other countries.

In 1997 12% of the total ice cream sales in France were accounted for by Carte d'Or products, making the brand one of the stand-out successes of Unilever's ice cream activities.

PILPA AUX FRUITS DE LA PASSION. DU SOLEIL DANS LES GLACES.

505: A 1983 poster for Pilpa, a new children's ice with the flavour of passion fruit.

dessert sector, that all main competitors felt obliged to imitate the concept, albeit to rather less effect.[52] In 1994, after three decades of trying to buy Miko, Unilever's perseverance was rewarded when the Ortiz family at last agreed to sell.

• Compared with 1958, when Unilever first entered the French ice cream market, the situation in 1995 was dramatically different. With its Miko, Frigécrème and Motta brands, Unilever had captured one third of the market; Nestlé, with its Gervais brand, had declined to a share of just under 15%. Factory-produced ice cream had captured 85% of the market; artisanal ice cream makers now commanded only 15%. Of the 80% of the population who ate ice cream, 95% ate it at home, 52% in restaurants, 31% in the street and 8% during events. In the super-premium segment Häagen Dazs had appeared on the

• After Motta had been acquired by Unilever, it was decided that the business would raise its profile against the competition by making a new high-quality ice cream.[49] A small team was formed of Motta ice cream makers and creative marketing people who came up with a brand concept with the chic name Carte d'Or[50] (see box opposite).

• From the beginning the focus was on two distribution channels: restaurant proprietors on the one hand and supermarkets and hypermarkets on the other. Ice cream was now the fastest-growing part of the foods market – consumption would increase from 70 million litres in 1978 to 130 million litres in 1987[51] – and family packs represented its strongest growth segment. Carte d'Or ice cream became such a resounding success, commanding a 75% share of the premium

market. More and more French consumers were also eating ice cream in the winter. In 1995 per capita consumption of ice cream in France was almost seven litres,[53] having more than doubled in the previous 25 years to place French ice cream consumption more or less in line with the European average.

ROYAL CONE MIKO MIKORAMA
L'instant plaisir du 7ème Art

506: Much of Miko's advertising in the 1980s referred to memorable moments from cinema. This poster for the Royal Cone apes Clark Gable and Vivien Leigh in Victor Fleming's 1939 classic Gone with the Wind.

Licks, Sticks & Bricks

A WORLD HISTORY OF ICE CREAM

Spain:
'Por favor,
un Frigo!'

507: Badge with logo of
Frigo, Barcelona, late 1950s.

The cry: 'Por favor, un Frigo!' was often heard in bars in Barcelona or Madrid in the 1950s.[1] For many years Frigo was the only factory-made ice cream available in Spain. Founded in 1927, Frigo started producing ice cream in 1930 and became synonymous with ice cream in the eyes of consumers. After the Second World War more and more kiosks selling ice cream appeared on Spanish streets. They were the best possible sales outlets in the summer months, when virtually all the ice cream eating took place. Before the advent of factory-made ice cream, artisanal makers supplied their products to bars and, especially, push-carts. Water-ices were particularly popular, being refreshing and cheap.

• Spain was a poor country. The famous film director Luis Buñuel (1900-1983) wrote in his memoirs that in his village near Zaragoza the Middle Ages lasted right up until the start of the First World War.[2] In Spain the centuries-old institution of the church and the great landowners, for whom most Spaniards worked as labourers, maintained their power until well into the twentieth century. The little industry that existed was located mainly in and around Bilbao and Barcelona. The modernisation and expansion of industry only started, with American support, in the mid-1950s. Other ice cream manufacturers then emerged, the main ones being Camay, Marisa and Avidesa.

• Despite the climate, Spaniards were not great consumers of ice cream. In 1960 they ate at most one litre of ice cream a year each. With increased prosperity in the 1960s and 1970s, ice cream consumption did grow, reaching two litres per head in 1978, but it was the mid-1980s before consumption rose substantially. By 1995 Spaniards were eating five litres per person per year[3], but that still left Spain languishing near the bottom of the West European league table.

'Aloja de nieve'

• Ices had been known in Spain since the seventeenth century. In those days they were eaten mainly as a dessert, in one of two types: the cooled, non-frozen sorbetes and the frozen garrapiña (see chapter 3). Both were cooled with snow and salt. In Spain, incidentally, cooled drinks were, and still are, more popular than ices. Horchata, for example, is a typical Spanish summer drink made from the chufa, a small juicy ground-almond, or from ordinary almonds, sugar and water. Aloja is a centuries-old drink, a mixture of water, honey and herbs. These drinks, too, were cooled with snow; indeed, aloja was also known as aloja de nieve [snow-water].

• In the nineteenth century sorbetes, garrapiñas and cooled drinks were sold in horchatarias and in botillerias [bottle bars], establishments found in big cities like Madrid, Barcelona and Valencia. Ices were also eaten in the ordinary cafés. In a Madrid café, you could enjoy a refreshing leche merengada (ice made with milk, egg-white, cinnamon and sugar) while listening to the pianist or violinist, according to the Spanish author Benito Perez Galdos in Cánovas.[4] Most Spaniards, however, could not afford the café, horchataria or botilleria and had to make do with a water-ice made from snow drenched in fruit juice and pressed into a small mould, with a stick inserted in it.

This type of 'ice' remained on the market for a long time, even after the introduction of factory-made ice cream: you could still buy one on the street up until the 1950s.[5]

Rimblas y Rimblas: a family enters the ice cream business

• If there is one name that stands out in the history of Spanish industrial ice cream, it is that of the Rimblas y Rimblas family from Barcelona. At the end of the nineteenth century the parents of Juan and José Rimblas owned a sugar plantation in Holguin on the island of Cuba, until 1898 a Spanish territory.[6] Juan was educated as an engineer in Switzerland and Britain. In 1919 he was married in Barcelona and then returned to Cuba to learn the sugar business.

• Juan's brother, José, had studied law in Barcelona and was an importer of meat from Argentina, giving him knowledge of the cold storage business. On 18 July 1927 he was one of the founders of the firm 'Industrias Frigorificas y de la Alimentación S.A.'. With a starting capital of 500,000 pesetas and its head office in Barcelona, the company had as its objectives 'the installation and operation of public coldstores, the manufacture of cooling ice and all sorts of refrigerated products in general, the buying and selling of foodstuffs and the operation of farms and industries in which raw materials are produced for agriculture and cattle farming, as well as all other legitimate trading activities'.[7] In the following year, on 16 November 1928, the firm was renamed 'Industrias Frigorificas S.A.'. The authorised capital was increased to two million pesetas and the company's objectives were now limited to 'the installation and operation of public coldstores, the production of cooling ice and of all refrigerated products in general'.[8] The cooling ice was also used for the cold storage of Jose's Argentinian meat.

• Following the 1929 stock market crash, the Cuban sugar industry collapsed and Juan Rimblas decided to concentrate instead on ice cream. He sent his family back to Barcelona, before himself going to New York where, in the space of a few months, he learnt the trade of ice cream making.[9] He returned to Barcelona in 1930 and at 312, Cortés Catalanes, he started up an ice cream business, helped by his brother José and other family members and using machines imported from America. The financier of the business was Juan's brother-in-law, Joaquin Sopena Domper, a Barcelona publisher. In the first year around one million litres of ice cream bricks were produced.

508: The Granja Frigo ice cream parlour on Madrid's Plaza de Canalesas, early 1950s.

• The business flourished and in 1932 moved into larger premises in Casanovas Street.[10] The freezers were installed in the central section, while another room housed four or five machines that were used to cut the blocks of ice cream into small portions.[11] Helados Frigo was delivered three or four times a day to numerous of the city's restaurants and bars.[12]

• To safeguard their supply of milk, Industrias Frigorificas established the Sindicat de Vaquers Rurals S.A. in 1933. This was a cattle farmers' cooperative, which was contracted to supply Frigo with milk. The cooperative was also headquartered in Casanovas Street.

Civil War – then expansion

• Barcelona and Bilbao excepted, 1930s Spain was predominantly agrarian, with over half the population making their livelihood from farming. The economic crisis of the 1930s triggered strikes, riots and street fighting. In the ensuing Spanish Civil War, José's coldstores in Barcelona were shelled. After three years of heavy fighting the war ended on 1 April 1939 with General Franco's accession to power.

• The Rimblas family had to rebuild their companies. In the next three years, the Sindicat de Vaquers Rurals S.A. changed its name several times until, on 8 February 1942, it was rechristened Productos Frigo S.A.[13] Productos Frigo, together with Industrias Frigorificas S.A., formed the basis for the Frigo group. Industrias Frigorificas produced the ice cream and dairy products, while Productos Frigo handled the sales side of the business, looking for agents to sell its products in other cities. In the course of the 1940s, Frigo set up a network of franchises. These were independent operations, but in many cases strong family ties and friendships played a major role. Frigo Madrid, for instance, was formed on 25 January 1941 by Don Joaquin Sopena Domper, who had financed the original Frigo ice cream factory back in 1930.[14]

509: Madrid, circa 1950. Thirty ice cream sellers with their push-carts stand in front of the Helados Ilsa ice cream factory with company management.

• In 1945 Industrias Mallorquinas de la Alimentación 'Frigo' was set up in Palma de Mallorca, to produce chocolate, biscuits and ice cream under the Frigo brand. In the following year Frutos Españoles 'Fesa' was founded in Valencia. Apart from producing canned and candied fruit, this business also supplied Industrias Frigorificas with fresh fruit for its ice cream. In the 1940s this led to establishments operating under the Frigo name in Madrid, Valencia, Seville, Alicante, Mallorca and Las Palmas (Gran Canaria). All these businesses were licensed by Industrias Frigorificas to use the Frigo brand, which thus became known throughout Spain. Their reputation was further reinforced by Frigo's own ice cream parlours. The first of a total of five, employing dozens of people, was opened in 1943. The most famous was Granja Frigo on Madrid's Plaza de Canalesas.[15]

Frigo during the 1940s

• The Frigo product range was already extensive in the late 1940s and 1950s. Apart from cream cakes, chocolate and sweets, the Barcelona factory produced 'polos', lemon or orange water-ices on a stick. In addition, Frigo was well known for its ice cream gâteaux, ice cream between wafers and coffee ice. Very popular was Esquimal (Eskimo), an ice cream on a stick. Another much-loved product in those days was Dos en Uno (Two in One), an orange-flavoured ice bonbon coated with a layer of chocolate and packed in its own sachet.

• At Casanovas Street there was a continual movement of Frigo trucks, bringing in milk, butter, strawberries, pineapples and

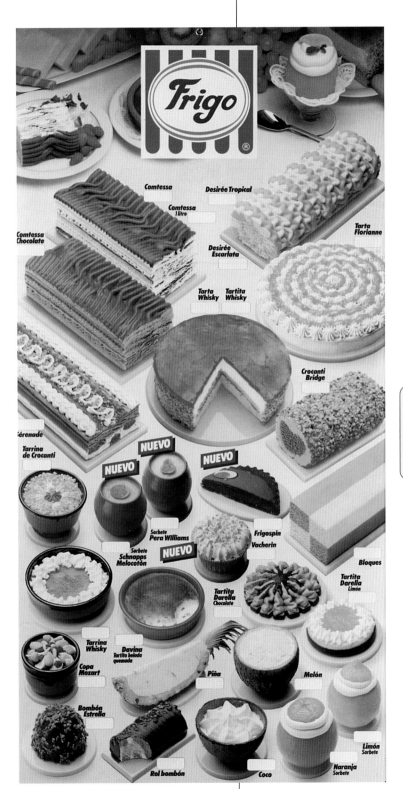

Comtessa

Desirée Tropical

Comtessa
1 litro

Comtessa
Chocolate

Tarta
Florianne

Desirée
Escarlata

Tarta
Whisky

Tartita
Whisky

Crocanti
Bridge

Sérenade

Tarrina
de Crocanti

NUEVO

NUEVO

NUEVO

Sorbete
Pera Williams

Frigospin
Vacherin

Sorbete
Schnapps
Melocotón

NUEVO

Bloques

Tartita
Darella
Chocolate

Tartita
Darella
Limón

Tarrina
Whisky

Davina
Tartita helada
quemada

Copa
Mozart

Piña

Melón

Bombón
Estrella

Limón
Sorbete

Rol bombón

Coco

Naranja
Sorbete

510: 1994 price
card showing
Frigo ice cream
gâteaux and ices
for restaurants
and hotels.
Centre, the
'Tarta Whisky'.

cherries and departing with finished products. Once the ingredients had been unloaded, female Frigo employees like Marina Lahoz Serrano and Maria Guilleme Arellano handled their processing. 'Baskets full of strawberries arrived all at the same time', they explained in a 1986 interview.[16] 'The required quantity of sugar was added and the whole mass was boiled until it had the right consistency'. The moulds for the ice lollies made from lemon juice and orange juice had to be filled by hand. They were cooled in tanks filled with brine and as they cooled down, the sticks too were inserted by hand. 'That was an unpleasant job, as we were constantly bothered by the icy-cold vapours rising up from the tanks.'

• In 1946 the female employees at Frigo worked for a weekly wage of between 35 and 48 pesetas. The hourly wage was 0.90 pesetas on the dayshift and 1.10 pesetas at night. A normal working day was from 7 a.m. until 3 p.m., but could sometimes last until 9 or 10 p.m. and work also had to be done on Saturdays and Sundays. During peak production times the women often did not leave work until midnight. The cleaning of the fruit baskets was a task in itself, carried out by women who were paid 2.50 pesetas for each basket.[17] Members of the Rimblas family could also be found on the factory floor until late in the evening. Juan Rimblas' wife was in charge of the production department, supervising the cleaning, approving the ice cream mix and making final adjustments to the flavour.[18]

The 1950s: competition

• During the 1950s, Spain under General Franco slowly emerged from its isolation. In 1947 Franco had proclaimed the country a kingdom and nominated Don Juan de Bourbon to accede to the Spanish throne after Franco's death (which turned out to be not until 1975).

• In 1952 Spain was admitted to UNESCO and in 1955 it became a member of the United Nations. In 1953 an agreement on economic and military co-operation was signed with the United States. There were already strong American influences in the Frigo product range of those days. Water-ices, so popular in Spain, were sold by Frigo under the brand name Popeye, based on the popular American cartoon character. Popeye ices were sold from 1952 onwards in various flavours, such as orange, mint, lemon, vanilla, chocolate and coconut. In July 1962, 150,000 Popeye ices were produced every day.[19] Other popular Frigo ices in that period were the Frigolin and the Negrito, small cylindrical ices wrapped in a sort of silver foil. The former was a vanilla ice cream coated in chocolate; the latter consisted of chocolate ice cream.[20]

• In the 1950s the Frigo group comprised four firms: Industrias Frigorificas (Barcelona), Productos Frigo (Barcelona), Industrias Mallorquinas de la Alimentación (Palma de Mallorca) and Ilsa Frigo (Madrid). Ilsa Frigo had been created in 1951 by the merger of Frigo Madrid with Industria Lacteas (Ilsa).[21] One of Ilsa Frigo's directors was the attorney Manuel Gubern Puig; he had been on the Frigo board since the company's formation in 1927, and went on to become President of Productos Frigo in 1958. Dozens of depots with cold storage facilities were built in this period all over the country.

• During the 1950s other ice cream companies were established. One of them was Marisa, a foods business founded in Barcelona in 1944, producing buñuelos (sweet sticks) and turrones (cakes) and later ice cream, which it sold mainly in Catalonia. In 1959 Marisa had a market share of 6%.[22] Another company, Derivados Lacteos, marketed its products under the Helados Camy brand. Like Frigo, Camy distributed its ice cream products nationwide, becoming Frigo's main competitor.

Camy

• Camy, originally spelt Camay, had also been founded by members of the Rimblas family. In 1959 Juan Rimblas, founder of the first Frigo ice cream factory in Barcelona, died. His two sons, Juan José and Juan (called 'Johnny' because of the time he had spent in America) also worked in the firm. Juan José Rimblas Rey was managing director of Ilsa Frigo (Madrid). His brother travelled to the United States again in 1953, where he studied the production of ice cream gâteaux. In about 1954 Frigo began marketing 'Tarta Whisky', a product that has remained a best seller to this day and has also been included in the ranges offered by other manufacturers.

• After their father's death the brothers sold their 40% holding in Frigo and in 1955 set up a new business in Madrid: Derivados Lacteos

(Camy).[23] Its immediate success was attributable in part to co-operation with another ice cream business, Fridox. Fridox had been set up in 1940 by an Italian, Arturo Degli, who had run a bakery in Padua, Italy. In 1939 he began making ice cream in San Sebastian,[24] moving in 1940 to Madrid to produce ice cream under the trading name Productos Fridox, selling direct to the public from vans. When the co-operation with Camy started in 1955, he expanded his factory.[25] In 1956 'Johnny' Rimblas left Madrid to settle in America for good.[26]

• By 1959 Camy had a 15% share of the market for industrial ice cream, some way behind that of Frigo.[27] So Spain's two largest ice cream firms, Frigo and Camy, were both headed by members of the Rimblas y Rimblas family.

'Frigo is an ice cream, but not all ice creams are Frigo'

• After the difficult 1950s the economy began to grow and incomes increased, reflected in growing sales of ice cream. The value of the market climbed between 1960 and 1969 from 15 million to 50 million pesetas. Per capita ice cream consumption rose from 1 litre to 1.6 litres over the same period.[28] And yet ice cream was still considered a luxury. Three-quarters of all ices were eaten outside the home in granjas (milk bars), coffee bars, snackbars or in the street, while the rest was eaten as the final course of a meal, mainly in restaurants.[29] Household consumption was virtually zero.

• Camy ice cream was now considered to be the best,

512: Women buying an ice from a Camy kiosk in Madrid, second half of the 1960s.

according to a market survey in 1960 when eight out of ten respondents cited Camy as their preferred brand.[30] That was partly due to publicity, since Camy was the first ice cream manufacturer to broadcast commercials on Spanish television and radio.[31]

• Frigo advertised under the slogan 'Frigo es un helado pero...no todos los helados son Frigo' (Frigo is an ice cream, but not all ice creams are Frigo). This was the theme of posters and signboards in and around the sales outlets, since Frigo at that time did not invest in other media.

• In 1960 there were between 6,000 and 8,000 kiosks in Spain.[32] Spanish ice cream manufacturers, as elsewhere in Europe, supplied freezer cabinets, free of charge to the kiosks, which were delivered from depots all around the country. Everywhere white vans could be seen with the words 'Helados Camy' or 'Helados Frigo' painted on the side. Business was very seasonal – the kiosks were open only from June to October.

The 1960s: takeovers and new firms

• In the 1960s the development of the Spanish ice cream industry picked up speed. In 1961 Nestlé acquired 60% of the shares in Camy, followed by a further 38% in 1965.[33] In 1962 a new ice cream company was established by the Beretta family, Italians who had become naturalised Spanish citizens. Their 800 square metre factory in Madrid was equipped with American Clark freezers, Italian ice cream machines and a Danish Gram RIA ice lolly machine. Beretta mainly focused on the market for more expensive

premium ice creams; its speciality was cassata, which it sold under the brand name Ondina.[34]

• The Berettas were not the only Italian family to make ice cream in Spain. During the Civil War an Italian division had fought on Franco's side. After the war, many Italians remained in Spain, a number of them starting small ice cream businesses and gaining good reputations. The Marisa ice cream business in Barcelona built on this with its slogan 'Mama mia, che gelati!' [Mama mia, what ices!].[35] In 1967 Marisa was taken over by the American company Beatrice Foods (see chapter 6).[36]

• Besides the Italians, the ice cream makers from the ancient port of Valencia were also famous.[37] In 1965 Luis Suñer de Avidesa began producing industrial ice cream there. He already owned a citrus fruit export business, a printing works and an operation for farming and selling frozen chickens. Ice cream provided a good income for the summer months, when sales of frozen chickens declined. The factory was located in Alcira, a small village near Valencia, and produced mainly water-ice.[38] His

513: Children with Camy ices, second half of the 1960s.

good contacts with shopkeepers enabled Avidesa's ice cream department to grow very rapidly and by 1969 it enjoyed a market share of 20%, making it Spain's third-largest producer after Camy and Frigo. Avidesa's factory was well located for Spain's principal ice cream markets: Valencia, Barcelona, Madrid and Seville, the three latter cities being almost equidistant from Alcira.[39]

• In 1969, alongside the four major ice cream manufacturers Camy (25%), Frigo (20%), Avidesa (20%) and Marisa (20%), there were an estimated thousand or so artisanal ice

cream makers from whom the Spaniards could buy and enjoy, say, a 'Helado de Mantecado', the classic Spanish ice cream made with milk, cream, egg-yolk, sugar and grated lemon peel.[40]

Unilever buys Frigo

• An attempt by Frigo to join up with Unilever in 1963 fell through. Unilever felt the Spanish ice cream market to be unattractive, as ice cream sales were still low.[41] Later in the 1960s, however, rising domestic ownership of refrigerators, coupled with the production hygiene requirements laid down by the 1965 Code Alimentar [Food Standards Code], stimulated the group's interest. By tradition, Spaniards were enthusiastic eaters of desserts, but ice cream still hardly featured on the menu. Cheese, fruit, pastries and cakes were their favourite final courses. Unilever therefore wanted to promote ice cream desserts for eating in the home and at the end of the 1960s the group was looking for ways to enter the market.[42]

• The idea of setting up its own Spanish factory was rejected.[43] Experience in France had shown how difficult it was to develop a profitable ice cream operation in an established market (see chapter 16). Unilever then looked into the possibility of taking over an existing ice cream business. The main candidates were Frigo and Avidesa. Frigo's problems included its antiquated factories and its old-fashioned style of operation but, against that, it was Spain's longest-established and best-known ice cream brand. It also had its own yoghurt factory, which was of interest to Unilever. Avidesa did have modern manufacturing facilities, but its combination of ice cream and chicken products was less attractive.[44] In the early 1970s Unilever therefore re-opened negotiations with Frigo, buying the business in 1973.[45]

• The two global ice cream players, Unilever and Nestlé, were now squaring up to each other in Spain. Could the Rimblas y Rimblas family, the founder of both Spanish operations, ever have dreamt that this would happen?

• After acquiring Frigo, Unilever re-organised the group, closing various factories. Ultimately, only the Barcelona factory, which had been modernised, remained open. Personnel numbers were cut back from 1,100 in 1973 to some 600 in 1979. The Unilever ice cream logo was adopted; packaging was brought up to date. Frigo began to sponsor sports such as cycle racing, equestrian events, tennis tournaments, the Costa Brava Rally and the Olympic Games.[46] During the 1992 Olympics Frigo launched the Cobi ice cream, named after and resembling the official mascot of the event. The business regularly invited groups of visitors to look round its factory in Barcelona and, until its closure in 1992, its Madrid factory. The visiting public

514: Impulse price card for Frigo from the 1992 season, the year Barcelona hosted the Olympic Games. Frigo was one of the sponsors.

varied from doctors, teachers and children to soldiers.[47]

• The introduction of novelty ices was also tackled energetically. In 1989 Frac, a vanilla ice cream on a stick with a thick coating of pure dark chocolate, was launched, following the lead from Italy in 1988. The modified Spanish foods legislation stipulated that only pure chocolate could be used and Spaniards' preference is for plain, unsweetened chocolate.

territory by taking over other ice cream producers, purchasing Avidesa in 1995 and also the Spanish operation of Miko, the French company (see chapter 16). (The Miko business in Spain had been in existence since the second half of the 1970s and operated independently). The acquisitions meant a tremendous increase in the number of Camy sales outlets. In 1997 it had a network of some 230,000 of them: kiosks, bars, confectionery bakers' shops, restaurants, institu-

• An interesting novelty was the Boomy water-ice product that made its debut in 1991.
It comprised three small fruit water-ices – in the shape of a strawberry, a lemon and an orange – on a stick. The product was moulded in very much the same way as the ice moulds used in the nineteenth century to make small ices in the form of fruits (see chapter 4). In 1995 Frigo's price lists were offering a total of some 35 different types of ice, many of them highly imaginative. Spain, like other Mediterranean countries, has a high percentage of ice cream sales in the impulse area.

• And so Frigo once more gained market leadership in the 1990s. Camy (now part of Nestlé) made every effort to regain lost

515: Frigo's Boomy water-ice product from 1991. The concept recalled the moulded fruit ices of the early nineteenth century.

tions – in addition to sales through an estimated 30,000 supermarkets.[48]

• Novelties had given the ice cream market in Spain a new vigour, as they had in other countries. And although there had been a wave of mergers and acquisitions among industrial manufacturers, the Spanish consumer could still opt to buy from one of the remaining 3,000 or so makers of artisanal ice cream. But today, if a Spaniard buys a newspaper from a street kiosk, or is in a bar and says 'Por favor, un Frigo', then it's still clear to everyone that he is asking for an ice cream.

Licks, Sticks & Bricks

A WORLD HISTORY OF ICE CREAM

Latin America: overseas influences, local ingredients

18

In 1927 the American export specialist J. Estes asked in The Ice Cream Trade Journal: 'What is the foreign market?' He went on to identify opportunities particularly in the Latin American countries, which were relatively close to the US and had a climate conducive to ice cream eating. 'It is interesting to note that there is no ice cream industry in Latin America such as we understand it [...]. There, nevertheless, is an annual consumption of about one billion ice cream cones.'[1] Many Central and South American countries had traditionally made use of ice to produce chilled drinks and water ices. The Aztecs in Mexico, for instance, used snow from volcanoes to cool their food and drink as long ago as the fifteenth century. Snow from the Andes Mountains in Peru and Colombia was also used for cooling.

• In the sixteenth century the Spanish conquistadores introduced sorbets and other ice-cold drinks. As in Spain, for a long time helado meant water-ices. After centuries of Spanish and Portuguese influence, however, the late nineteenth and early twentieth century brought immigrants, chiefly from Italy, who introduced the Latin American countries to new customs, including the making and selling of ice cream. In those countries with a dairy tradition, such as Argentina and Uruguay, ice cream quickly became popular. To this day many of the ice cream companies in the region still bear Italian names.

516: A Caiapo Indian from the Amazon basin eats a water ice during a pause in negotiations with the Brazilian government in 1988.

• For many years ice cream was produced on a small scale using simple equipment. However, the advent of American ice cream machines led to the establishment of the first ice cream factories in the 1930s.

In the 1950s American companies with ice cream divisions, such as Borden and Beatrice Foods, took their know-how into the Latin American market. They were followed by Nestlé and Unilever in the 1970s and 1980s. By the second half of the 1990s, however, the American businesses had disappeared from the scene and the two European multinationals were left to lead the ice cream markets in this vast continent.

'Snow post' in Mexico

• Mexico has one of Latin America's oldest ice cultures. It owes its origins to the permanently snow-capped peaks of the Popocatepetl and Ixtaccihuatl volcanoes to the southeast of Mexico City. Tradition has it that the Aztecs were already using ice to cool their food and drink in the fifteenth century.[2] When the Spaniards conquered Mexico in 1519, they were already familiar from their own country with the use of snow and ice to cool drinks (see chapter 17). The conquistadores introduced to Mexico the habit of mixing snow with sugar[3] and themselves became acquainted with chocolate and vanilla. Just before the Spanish commander Hernando Cortez entered the Aztec capital Tenochtitlan, he is said to have been offered a warm chocolate drink by the emperor Montezuma II. Cortez was apparently so taken with the drink that, after he had completed his conquest of Mexico, he had cocoa trees planted and sent cocoa beans back home for the Spanish court to sample. King Charles V, however, thought the drink bitter and so experimented with adding sugar, almonds and even chilli to it.

517 : Anonymous painting of a 'botilleros',
a stall selling fresh water and ices in Mexico,
in the second half of the nineteenth century.

• From about 1585 onwards chocolate began its advance, first in Spain, then in France, Italy and the rest of Europe.[4] The Mexicans themselves made the chocolate taste less bitter by adding vanilla, which is native to Mexico. During the seventeenth century vanilla also became known in Europe, where it was increasingly used to flavour drinks and, later, ice cream.[5]

• Mexico is even warmer than Spain, so snow was scarce and much sought-after. The trade in snow in the seventeenth and eighteenth centuries was controlled by the Spanish. The transport of snow was known as the 'snow post', since it was delivered to the home, just like letters. People living in the foothills climbed up the mountains in the cool of the night with donkeys to fetch snow and glacier ice. After paying tolls at the city gates the caravans made their deliveries to merchants who then supplied snow and ice to their customers.[6] In 1620 Leonardo Leanos, a Spaniard living in Mexico City, was the first to receive a government licence to sell ice for cooling, a centralised monopoly that was to remain in place for two centuries. Paying for licences made the ice expensive, so it was mainly wealthier people who had access to it. Consequently, a black market emerged. If the illegal makers and sellers were caught, they had to pay hefty fines and forfeit their donkeys and equipment.[7]

• In the second half of the seventeenth century mantecado, ice cream made from milk, eggs, butter, beaten egg white and lemon, was introduced to Mexico by the Spanish.[8] Local fruit, such as the guava, was also used as an ingredient. The custom also developed of finishing copious meals with a sorbet. There is a record of sorbets being served at the end of a dinner in 1702 for the archbishop Juan de Ortega.[9]

Neverias and cañutos

• Mexico gained its independence from Spain in September 1821. Two years later the monopoly on ice was abolished and within a few years the number of ice cream producers increased and prices fell. In Mexico City, Durango, Veracruz and other cities neverias (ice cream shops) were opened and ice cream was also sold in the streets by men known as neveros, who introduced the cañuto, a precursor of the ice lolly, made by pushing ice mix into a hollow sugar-cane stem and then freezing it.

• The travelling ice seller became a familiar figure in Mexico, carrying a bucket of ice on his head and in his right hand a small pail containing spoons and dishes for dispensing his wares. His loud cries would punctuate every open-air festival, market and bullfight. Lime and guava ices

518: Ice cream making in Mexico around 1900.

519: Ice cream stall in Mexico,
early twentieth century.

were particularly popular and, according to
the vendors, the best medicine for an upset
stomach.[10]

• By the mid-nineteenth century the Mexicans, like the Spanish and the French,
could increasingly eat their ices in coffee
shops, where hygienic conditions were
significantly better.

Helados **or** glaces:
French influence in Mexico

• The 1855-1860 civil war in Mexico was
followed by the French intervention of 1861-
1867. The French presence influenced the
cuisine of the upper classes and brought new

ice cream combinations to Mexico, such as
the vanilla, strawberry and mocha flavours
that go to make up Neapolitan ice cream.
New techniques were also introduced and ice
cream making in Mexico City soon reached
the same standard as in European cities. In
1865 Archduke Maximilian of Austria, who
had been persuaded by Napoleon III to
become governor of Mexico in 1864, was
served vanilla and strawberry ice cream.[11]
In September 1865 Maximilian granted the
French Mexican Julián Hourcadé the exclusive right to import Carré freezers into
Mexico. These machines operated on ammonia gas, a process invented by the French
engineer Edouard Carré (see chapter 4).
In 1866 Hourcadé, in partnership with the

520: Seller of cold lemonades in action in Mexico City. As well as bottles of concentrated lemonade syrups, there is a block of cooling ice on his wheelbarrow. Date unknown.

Frenchman Louis Binel, set up a firm with two machines to produce ice in Mexico City under the name 'Compaòia Privilegiada para Fabricar Hielo'; they had a starting capital of 60,000 pesos.[12]

• In 1867 Mexican insurgents ended this brief period of French rule and Maximilian was executed by a firing squad. The ice factory came into the hands of the Mexican Manuel Mùgica. The new government of Benito Juarez granted Mùgica the exclusive right to sell ice, which he retained for twenty years.[13] It was not until about 1890 that the import of American ice machines patented in 1872 by Charles B. Lee was permitted. Around the turn of the century Mexico City had five factories producing ice and restaurants, bars and hotels could be assured of a constant supply. The travelling neveros continued about their business, selling natural ice from the mountains which had been stored in special cellars in which the night temperature dropped below zero even in summer.

'The Mexican miracle'

• In the early twentieth century Mexico experienced a series of uprisings and revolutions, entering calmer waters around 1920. The process of industrialisation then got under way, and while much of the world was convulsed by the Second World War, Mexico experienced an unprecedented period of economic growth which became known as 'el milagro mexicano' (the Mexican miracle).[14] Many North American and European companies invested in Mexico: most of its ice cream businesses were set up in the 1930s and 1940s, some of them still occupy-

ing important positions to this day.

• In 1935, the first sizeable ice cream factory, ISCA, was established in Monterrey in northern Mexico by Lino Landeros Hernández, with his partners Cantú and Silva. Hernandez, who had learnt industrial ice cream making techniques in the United States, bought out his partners in 1935 and renamed his firm Lyla. In the west of the country, the Helados Regia business was founded in Guadalajara in 1940 by the Martinez brothers. Regia ice cream was reputed to be the best in the province of Jalisco, in which Guadalajara was situated.[15] Regia shops were also opened on a franchise basis in other cities, including Mexico City, Aguascalientes, Durango, León, Monterrey, the US cities of Los Angeles and San Diego – and even in Panama. One of the Martinez brothers, Pedro, also opened his own ice cream shop, Koldy, in Acapulco.

• In the 1940s Pedro Mendoza began the ice cream firm Regia y Ray's in Mexico City, exploiting the public's familiarity with the Regia brand name. Other ice cream producers in Mexico City at that time included Shamrock and Chantilly. Most of the firms sold their products from ice cream carts, the largest of them operating a fleet of 50 vehicles[16]. The Michoacán region to the west of Mexico City was also known for its ice cream production. This was particularly true of the city of Tocumbo, where businesses had names such as 'The Flower of Michoacán' or 'The Lady of Tocumbo'. These ice cream makers ultimately transferred their activities to Mexico City and in 1970 some 35% of the ice cream shops in Mexico City were in fact owned by ice cream makers from Tocumbo.[17]

• The largest and most important firm in Mexico City, however, was Helados Holanda.

521: Ice cream cart in Mexico City, early twentieth century.

522: Mexican girl with ice lolly in the 1920s.

523: Street sales of ices in Mexico in the 1920s.

524: Holanda's first ice cream freezer in operation in Mexico City in 1949.

Helados Holanda also produced cream, cheese and ice.

• In 1954 the factory moved to bigger premises in Clavijero Street. A production area of 1,500 square metres was fitted with modern machines made by the American manufacturer Vitaline, enabling more than 3,000 litres of ice cream to be produced each day. In 1956 the Alatorre family sold the business to Borden, the major American dairy and ice cream group (see chapter 6), which made substantial investments in the business. In 1958 the nephews of the founders of Holanda bought back the rights to the Holanda ice cream brand from Borden, only to sell them ten years later to another US company, the multinational Beatrice Foods. By 1969, Holanda ice cream was being produced at a rate of 2,000 litres of ice cream per hour and 150,000 ice cream bars per day. Two years later it was on sale throughout Mexico via a franchising system and Holanda became the country's leading ice cream firm.

• In 1992 Unilever studied the possibility of purchasing Helados Holanda,[19] concluding negotiations in 1997. The purchase eventually included Helados Bing which, along with Bambino and Danesa, had been one of Mexico's biggest ice cream operations since the 1960s.

This business had been set up in 1939 by the Alatorre family with an initial capital of 25,000 pesos. Holanda's logo consisted of a Dutch windmill, tulips and a Dutch girl wearing a traditional cap.[18] The firm had only a couple of ice cream machines and much of its production was still done by hand. Nevertheless, its ice cream caught on and within ten years Holanda had three ice cream shops in Mexico City, as well as a new ice cream factory on Revillaguigedo Street. The ice cream was available in hazelnut, chocolate, vanilla and strawberry flavours, and was both supplied to restaurants and sold direct to consumers in the street, through Holanda shops and in cinemas. The Balmori cinema was one of the first customers in this market segment in 1954. Besides making ice cream,

Helados Bing, Bambino and Danesa

• Helados Bing had been set up in Guadalajara in 1965 by the American Adolf R. Horn. His firm's name was a shortened version of Bingham, his wife's maiden name. Horn's

525: Seller of Popy ice cream in Mexico in the 1960s.

premium ice cream was aimed at the more affluent Mexicans. Between 1970 and 1982 Helados Bing opened fifteen parlours in Guadalajara, Puerto Vallarta and Mexico City; and a new factory with a daily capacity of 5,000 litres of ice cream also came on stream. But these investments overstretched the finances of the business and in May 1983 Horn sold his company to the Mexican investment group Quan. This group considerably expanded the number of parlours and by 1988 there were 120 Bing outlets in 40 Mexican cities. In that year the Quan group also acquired the Helados Holanda ice cream firm from Beatrice Foods. The company now controlled 40% of the Mexican ice cream market.[20]

• Quan's main competitor was Nestlé, which in 1969 had bought the Bambino ice cream company from Mario Rodriguez, the founder of the company in the early 1960s. Though active in frozen foods in Mexico since 1965, from 1974 onwards Nestlé concentrated fully on ice cream.[21]

• Danesa had begun operations in 1935 in the Jalisco region as a dairy business. From 1972 it produced ice cream in Guadalajara and Mexico City under the 'Danesa 33' brand and was the first Mexican ice cream company to start advertising regularly on radio, television and in the press. In 1988 Nestlé bought Danesa, which gave it a 40% share of the ice cream market, equal to that of the Quan group.[22]

• In the 1980s the economic crisis in Mexico hit the dairy industry hard. Many smaller ice cream firms went to the wall; it was the large businesses that had investments abroad that survived. Yet, despite the reces-

526-529 : Price cards from the 1950s of the ice cream manufacturer Holanda in Mexico City.

530: Holanda ice cream van in Mexico City, circa 1970.

531: Ice cream stall in Mexico,
late 1980s. The ice cream was kept
cool in barrels of ice and salt.

sion, ice cream consumption actually increased. In 1979, 60 million litres of ice cream were sold and in 1985, 90 million. Given the size of Mexico's population, however, this figure is still very low by international standards, representing a per capita consumption of just over one litre per year.[23]

Guatemala and Panama

• In Guatemala, the firm of Fabrica de los Productos Helados 'Lys' was using American machines in 1927 to manufacture the 'Raqueta Helada'. This hugely popular ice lolly was made from real fruit juices, mixed with milk or water and vanilla and available in vanilla, strawberry, lemon, lime, orange, pineapple, coconut and milk, chocolate and milk, strawberry and milk, and banana and milk flavours. Two thousand of these ices were sold each day, rising to 4,000 on Sundays. They were distributed by road and rail[24] and sold from ice cream carts in the street.

• In Panama, ice cream making had been started by Americans. The construction of the Panama Canal, begun in 1907, involved 5,000 American workers and 40,000 from Panama and other countries. The project created the perfect captive market for ice cream, making consumption in the Canal Zone in those years as high as in the United States itself. Each American construction worker ate ice cream three times a day. In 1911 The Ice Cream Trade Journal wrote that in Panama 'the flavors are changed from four to six times a week' and, in order to meet the high demand, a special factory was built in Panama City.[25]

532: Helados Tio Rico ice cream being sold on the beach near Caracas, Venezuela, 1998.

• After the opening of the Canal in 1920, demand for ice cream remained high, so the Panama Railroad Co. built another cream factory in the 1930s at Mount Hope and by about 1937 its ice cream was on sale throughout the Canal Zone. As in North America, vanilla was the most popular flavour, followed by chocolate, strawberry, cherry and walnut. Most of the ice cream was made using powdered milk.[26]

Colombia and Venezuela

• In Colombia the ice cream firm La Fuente de Soda was set up in 1941 in Antioquia near the city of Medellín by a group of Colombian businessmen headed by Bernardo Cock and Gonzalo Vélez. The name was derived from the soda fountain that had been introduced from North America, from where the company's ice cream machines also came. In Medellín itself La Fuente opened a coffee shop-cum-ice cream parlour close to Bolivar Park and next door to the Union Club. In the first few years the ice cream was made by 'a dark-skinned fat Jamaican' who also created his own recipes.[27]

• In the 1950s the company moved to a new factory site and started producing ice cream on a larger scale. The ice cream was, and still is, sold from small, low ice cream carts known as tilenes, which are fitted with an insulated compartment and pushed by hand. The carts are equipped with a row of bells whose tinkling sound is recognised by everyone.

• The business grew and the firm's logo, a boy eating ice cream on top of an ellipse bordering the name of La Fuente ice cream,

533: Selling Nestlé's Savory ice creams in Cochabamba, Bolivia, 1998.

became well known. In the 1970s La Fuente opened branches throughout Colombia, completing its national coverage in 1991 with a branch in the capital, Bogotá. By then La Fuente had become market leader and in 1994 the firm entered into a joint venture with Unilever, handing over full control three years later.

• In neighbouring Venezuela the US company Borden, together with Diego Cisneros, set up the ice cream business Helados Club in 1952. Located on Avenida Francisco de Miranda in the Chacao district of Caracas, the firm grew to become the country's biggest ice cream operation. In 1978 co-founder Cisneros acquired full ownership of Helados Club and changed the firm's name to Helados Tio Rico. Branches were established in Barcelona, Maracay, Valencia, Barquisimeto and Mara-

caibo and, as in Colombia, the ice cream was sold from small carts in the street. At the end of the 1970s there were some 5,000 such carts and a national network of distributors ensured that Tio Rico ice cream was available everywhere. In 1995 Helados Tio Rico was sold to Unilever.

Brazil: 'the painful cold of pineapple ice cream'

• On 6 August 1834 the North American vessel Madagascar, carrying a cargo of 217 tons of ice, arrived in the Brazilian port of Rio de Janeiro. Several days later Deroche and Lorenzo Fallas, two traders, bought the load for use in the production of water-ices. By 23 August they were selling fruit-flavoured ices to the inhabitants of Rio. Fallas sold them in his shop on the Lago do Paço, where he also sold blocks of natural ice which were used in homes and restaurants to chill foods in summer temperatures that could reach 40°C. Deroche sold his in his baker's shop at 175, Rua do Ouvidor.

• A year later the Italian Luigi Bassini began selling ice cream in his coffee house, Circulo do Commércio. On 30 December 1835 the Jornal do Commércio reported that 'between the hours of ten in the morning and ten at night, from the very first day of the year, you could go to Bassini's coffee shop and buy ice blocks, iced coffee, Italian ice cream, et cetera, of a quality equal to that obtainable in the best ice cream parlours of Naples.'

• During the nineteenth century ice cream appeared in all Brazil's major cities: Salvador, Rio de Janeiro, Recife, São Paulo, Curitiba and Porto Alegre. On 4 January 1878 the newspaper A Provincia de São Paulo published an advertisement with the text 'Ices – ices at 15.00 hours all days, Rua Direita 44'.[28] Emperor Dom Pedro II (who ruled from 1840 to 1889) and his wife were ice cream aficionados and regularly visited the ice cream parlour of Antonio Francione, another maker of Italian ices in Rio de Janeiro. The Emperor's particular favourite as a flavour was pitanga (pitanga is a small, slightly sour-tasting local fruit).[29]

• Blocks of natural ice brought in by sea were shipped miles into the interior. In about 1880 a wealthy fazendeiro (farmer) from Lorena shipped in ice from Norway for the marriage of his daughter. After being unloaded in Rio de Janeiro, the ice was carried on the backs of slaves to Lorena, 200 kilometres inland and 600 metres above sea level.[30]

• Ice cream gradually became more popular. The Brazilian author and poet Carlos Drummond de Andrade (1902-1987) gives a description in one of his short stories of a visit by two boys to the cinema. The story is set in 1916 in a small Brazilian town whose cinema is next door to a coffee shop offering 'Delicious Pineapple Ice Cream'. The boys, aged eleven and thirteen, have never eaten ice cream in their lives. They know what pineapple tastes like and the combination with ice cream fires their imaginations. But it turns out to be a huge disappointment, as one of the chastened boys explains: 'The ice cream was horrible, so painfully cold that it shut out every trace of pineapple taste. It brought tears to my eyes'.[31]

• Until well into the twentieth century ice cream production in Brazil was a small-scale, artisanal business. The quality of the ice cream varied greatly from shop to shop. Ice cream was sold in small ice cream saloons known as sorveterias, which remain a lively and important part of ice cream culture in Brazil today.

'Que Bom' becomes Kibon

• On 24 July 1941 the American Ulysses Harkson was among those who founded a limited company in Rio de Janeiro called Cia U.S. Harkson do Brasil Industrias Alimenticias.[32] Harkson had been selling ice cream for the American business Henningsen in Shanghai (see chapter 19). War between China and Japan in 1937 caused the Shanghai market to collapse, so Harkson instructed his right-hand man, John Lutey, to look for somewhere else where he could set up his

534: Kibon ice cream truck in Rio de Janeiro in 1943.
For fuel the truck used coal instead of petrol.

535: The American John Kent Lutey, director of the Kibon
ice cream factory in Rio de Janeiro, Brazil (1948).

own business. Lutey travelled all over the world and, after meeting a manager of Coca-Cola in Rio de Janeiro, he came up with a proposal for an ice cream factory in Brazil. Lutey became one of the shareholders in the new firm and was appointed chairman. In 1942 the company bought the small Rio ice cream company called Gato Preto [Black Cat]. After some rebuilding work, ice cream production started on the company's first birthday, 24 July 1942, though not without problems. Brazil was not involved in the Second World War, but sugar was rationed and there were shortages of petrol, milk powder and qualified personnel.

• The Ayer advertising agency was commissioned to think up a company name. The result was Kibon, derived from the Portuguese 'Que bom!' ['That's good!']. The first impulse products were the Eskibon (a combination of Eskimo and Kibon) and, priced at one cruzeiro, the Chicabon ('Chica' meaning 'girl', from the short form of Francisca). Cylindrical ice lollies were sold under the name Sorvex. Kibon's products sold well, particularly during Rio's famous carnival when ice cream sellers carrying boxes of ices on their head walked amongst the revellers. Kibon also sold ices from its own purpose-built ice cream carts and through grocers. In 1943 a second ice cream factory, in São Paulo, was bought and rebuilt and after the Second World

536: 1947 poster for the Chicabon product, Kibon's first ice cream in 1942. Chica is an abbreviation of the girl's name Francisca.

War depots were set up all over the country. A special truck was developed by General Motors for the transport of ice cream.

• In 1946 construction started on a brand new factory in Rio de Janeiro state. Kibon launched new ices on the market and began to advertise: the Brazilian model Eleonora Fuchs was used to endorse Chicabon ices on the posters for 1947. Kibon also started supplying special freezer cabinets to confectioners and grocers who sold its products.[33] During the 1950s Kibon began to work with other businesses, such as Gina, which supplied the sticks for Kibon ices; and in 1956 Kibon introduced telephone ordering and delivery of ice cream gâteaux direct to consumers' homes.

• In 1957 one of the world's biggest importers of Brazilian coffee, the General Foods Corporation of North America, bought a majority stake in Kibon. When founder Harkson withdrew from the business three years later, the company's name was changed to Kibon Industrias Alimenticias S.A. John Lutey, now President and CEO, stepped down in 1962.

• Meanwhile, Kibon was growing steadily and in 1963 branches opened in the north of the country, in Recife and in Salvador. Two years later, the business began publishing its own house journal, Kibonoticias. From 1967 American Vitaline freezers meant the ice lollies no longer had to be packed by hand.[34]

537: Kibon ice cream sellers pictured with their carts at the factory in Rio de Janeiro in the 1950s.

538: Row of Kibon ice cream vans in Rio de Janeiro in 1966, with the famous Sugar Loaf Mountain in the background.

539: Clockwise from above, packs of Eskibon ices dating from 1962, 1966 and 1970.

540: From top row, left to right, packs of Chicabon ice lollies from 1955, 1962, 1966 [2x] and 1975.

• The Brazilian consumer was now eating 0.9 litres of ices per person per year, rising to 1.5 litres in the cities.[35] In 1971 Kibon held a 45% share of the Brazilian ice cream market, the remainder being served by small businesses, confectioners and sorveterias. Kibon concentrated its sales efforts in the South, where the biggest cities were located and where consumption was higher. To serve the North a separate company, Sorvane, was set up in 1976[36] - at just the time Brazil's economy was running into problems. Although the ice cream business was performing well, the expansion into other areas, which had been encouraged by General Foods, was unsuccessful. In the 1981-1982 period, Kibon suffered a loss of 30%, chiefly on its 'dry' products such as 'Ping Pong' chewing gum.[37] Two million fruit ices per day were being produced in Rio and São Paulo, however, and Kibon's market share climbed.

• In 1985 General Foods was taken over by the American company Philip Morris. Meanwhile, the European companies Unilever and Nestlé had also entered the Brazilian ice cream market.

Nestlé and Unilever enter the Brazilian ice cream market

• As the largest country in South America, Brazil offered a promising market for Nestlé and Unilever. In 1972 it had a population of 98 million, 58% of whom lived in the cities.[38] Nestlé had been active in Brazil since 1969 under the name Companhia Industrial de Commercial Brasileira de Productos Alimentares. In 1972 this company launched the Yopa choc ice,[39] based on the name of the German firm Jopa which Nestlé had

bought in 1962 (see chapter 12). Unilever's Lever business had operated in Brazil since 1929, selling soap and washing powders. In 1960 Lever merged with Gessy so that, when in 1971 Gessy Lever began marketing margarine under the Doriana name, Unilever entered the foods business. Its next step was to enter Brazil's ice cream market.

• After Kibon (with a market share of 76%), the three largest ice cream firms in the early 1970s were Alnasa (11%), Maquary (7%) and Sanbra (2%).[40] Sanbra had only been founded in 1971 by Bunge & Born, a large, well-known grain shipment business. The factory was located in Rio de Janeiro and its products were sold under the Rico brand and priced at the same level as of Kibon's.[41]

• Maquary was a family business in the north-east of Brazil and was owned by Tavares de Mello, originally producers of tropical fruit. In 1969 Maquary opened an ice cream factory in Recife, where it mainly produced fruit ices.[42]

• The third small company was Alnasa with its Gelato brand. Founded in 1970 by three Brazilian former employees of Kibon,[43] Alnasa was headquartered in São Paulo and sold mainly children's products there and in Brasilia and Porto Alegre[44]. Unilever acquired Alnasa in 1973, but Kibon's pre-eminent position led to mounting losses at the company. In 1985 Unilever failed to persuade General Foods to part with Kibon for $65 million;[45] so in 1990, in an attempt to eliminate the losses suffered by both their subsidiaries, Unilever and Nestlé surprised the outside world by setting up a joint venture. However, within a few years two events took place. Nestlé announced that ice cream production would become one of its core activities and at the end of 1993 Unilever

541: Aerial view of the Kibon ice cream factory in Rio de Janeiro, 1985.

acquired the Breyers ice cream company in the USA from Philip Morris.[46]

• Unilever now sold its share in Alnasa to Nestlé and began negotiations once more for the acquisition of Kibon. In November 1997 Unilever finally succeeded in securing its target. Success came with a hefty price tag, however – Kibon's new American owner, Philip Morris, received in return the huge sum of $930 million, nearly 15 times the Unilever bid twelve years previously. But with 170 million inhabitants, Brazil had the potential to become an enormous market and to increase the per capita ice cream consumption far beyond the 1997 level of 2.2 litres per year.[47]

Italian cassata on the Argentinian dining table

• Like Brazil, Argentina has a long history of immigration. The Spaniards were the first Europeans to land, but the largest influx arrived between 1875 and 1930 in the form of more than six million Europeans, most of whom were Italians.[48] Many of the new-comers from Britain, and also from North America, possessed technical skills and brought machines with them.

• Argentina is a rich agrarian country with large herds of cattle, so its ice cream is made with dairy fat. Water-ice was originally

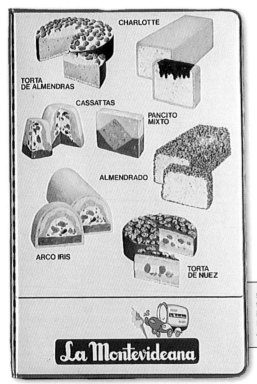

543: Sticker for La Montevideana ice cream, Buenos Aires, 1970s.

542: Price list of the Argentinian ice cream business La Montevideana, Argentina, 1970s.

544: Interior of a Freddo ice cream parlour in Buenos Aires, 1998. Freddo is one of the leading ice cream companies in Argentina with 37 ice cream parlours in the country's main cities.

available only in the summer and was eaten on the beach. It was again principally the Italians who began making ice cream, introducing cassata, for example, to the Argentinian dining table.[49]

• In 1925 Pablo Saint started an ice cream factory in Buenos Aires under the name Saint Hermanos. Saint had studied ice cream making in North America and equipped his factory with American and, later, Danish machines. The brand name he chose was Laponia (Spanish for Lapland). Laponia produced the American Eskimo Pie ices under licence, but also made cassata[50] and the Cremino, a chocolate-coated ice cream on a stick, which could be bought in every street corner kiosk in Buenos Aires.

• In the city of Rosario, in-land from Buenos Aires, the ice cream firm Monthelado had been set up in the 1960s by a family from Uruguay. On Rosario's two main boulevards they opened ice cream parlours, La Uruguaya and La Montevideana, and in 1973 built a new factory in Villa Gobernador Gálvez. Twenty years later, in 1993, Monthelado was acquired by Philip Morris, which also owned Kibon in Brazil.[51] With a market share of 12.8% La Montevideana was, and still is, number two in the ice cream market behind leader Nestlé with its brand Frigor.

• Today the Argentinians eat 3.2 litres of ice cream per person per year,[52] much of it in the numerous Italian-style ice cream

parlours that can be found all over the country. After Brazil, Argentina is the second largest ice cream market in South America and, having been briefly active in the mid-1970s, Unilever returned to Argentina through its purchase of La Montevideana from Philip Morris in October 1997.

Uruguay and Peru: 'dulce de leche' and lucuma ice cream

• Around 1900 many Spaniards and Italians emigrated to Uruguay, taking their ice cream traditions with them and disseminating them throughout the country. Like Argentina, Uruguay was a dairy nation and ice cream was chiefly made with milk and cream. The biggest ice cream producer today is Conaprole, which started life as a dairy cooperative in 1934 and began producing ice cream in 1936. Its 'dulce de leche' ice cream, made with condensed milk, is a national delicacy.

• Unilever entered the market in 1994 and began selling its Magnum, Cornetto and Calippo products under the Bresler house brand. In 1996 Unilever acquired the then number two in Uruguay's ice cream market, Gebetto.[53]

• Peru, too, was traditionally a dairy farming nation. As early as the 1930s cookery books containing ice cream recipes were published there. Milk formed the basis

545: Newspaper advertisement for a coffee house in Montevideo, Uruguay, in the 1920s. The shop is also alerting readers to the fact that ice cream is available there throughout the year.

Dressed in a white uniform, Pedro D'Onofrio walked the streets of Lima with his ice cream cart, announcing his arrival by blowing a copper horn, as was the custom in his native Italy.

• Sales went well and D'Onofrio hired people to sell ice cream from his growing number of carts. In 1908 he bought a machine to make ice, which signalled the start of his firm's mechanisation. In about 1910 he produced his first mechanically manufactured ice cream under the name 'Imperial' and from 1934 D'Onofrio's production was fully mechanised. The business expanded to become Peru's largest industrial ice cream manufacturer, with a

for many of the recipes, for instance for the 'dulce de leche'.[54] Another popular variety in Peru is prepared with the tropical fruit lucuma.

• In 1897 the Italian family D'Onofrio arrived in the capital, Lima. Pedro D'Onofrio came from Caserta, a small village north of Naples. The inhabitants of Lima were accustomed to quenching their thirst in summer with snow from the Andes mixed with fruit juice. D'Onofrio fetched snow from the mountains and began to make special 'ice cream shakes', which he sold from a cart that he called 'The Founder'.

547: Portrait of Pedro d'Onofrio, the Italian ice cream maker who arrived in Lima in 1897.
In about 1910 he bought his first ice cream machine. Today d'Onofrio is Peru's biggest ice cream manufacturer.

market share of 85% in 1997.[55] In April of that year, exactly 100 years after it was founded, D'Onofrio was acquired by Nestlé.

• A year earlier, Unilever had bought into the long-established business Industrias Pacocha, with which it had worked during the 1960s. Industrias Pacocha had been founded on 24 January 1929 by Juan Tidow and the Grunther family as a firm trading in oil, chemicals and margarine.[56] Following Unilever's acquisition of Pacocha's ice cream activities in 1996, the products were marketed under the Bresler house brand, which had been used for many years by Unilever in Chile and, latterly, in Uruguay. However, Unilever withdrew from Peru in 1998 following Nestlé's acquisition of D'Onofrio.

Chilean Chocolitos

• In Chile, Italians were again the first to start industrial ice cream production. In 1959 the Simonetti family set up the firm Savory, using American freezers. The first ice cream they put on the market was the Chocolito, a chocolate-coated ice on a stick that still sells well today. Other successful ices from these pioneering days were the Cremino, the Lolly Pop and the Cassata Brick. In 1966 the family sold the business to Nestlé. Three years earlier the business had found itself facing a new competitor, Bresler.

• Chileans proved to be avid ice cream eaters, consuming 20 million litres in 1970; four million litres of this was produced by artisanal ice cream makers, often of Italian origin. Consumption worked out at three litres per head per annum, comparable to countries such as Italy and Austria. Savory was market leader with 57%, followed by Bresler with 23%, Chamonix with 10% and Hayskrim with 6%.[57] All these firms were based in or near Santiago.

• To compete more effectively with Savory (Nestlé), Bresler expanded its factory in Matt Vial in 1980 and installed new ice cream machines from Italy. Despite this, the business ended up in difficulties and in 1985 Bresler was sold to Citroën. In 1986 Nestlé purchased Chamonix, which boosted its market share even further. Bresler was sold from one business to another, ending up by being acquired by Unilever in 1993. At the same time Unilever bought the small ice cream firm of Panda and thus entered into competition with Nestlé in the Chilean market.

• In a short space of time a sea-change had occurred in the Latin American ice cream market. All the North American ice cream manufacturers – Borden, Beatrice Foods, General Foods – which had since the 1950s followed the advice given by J. Estes back in 1927 had disappeared from the Latin American stage. Their place had been taken by the European companies Nestlé and Unilever. The series of acquisitions that Unilever made in the second half of the 1990s in Latin America helped the group achieve a better balance in ice cream markets worldwide. A product like the Lucuma Magnum, made with tropical fruit, showed the company responding to regional tastes and traditions moulded by ancient native customs, centuries of Spanish influences, North American entrepreneurs, Italian ice cream makers and characteristic local ingredients.

Licks, Sticks & Bricks

A WORLD HISTORY OF ICE CREAM

Asia: a flavour

of the exotic

548: Ice cellar in Ch'angnyôn, located in Kyônsang province in the south of South Korea. The ice cellar was built in 1742 during the Yongjo's government (1724-1776), but ice cellars had been in existence on the Korean peninsula ever since the sixth century.

549: Pack of Asian Delight ice cream, 1998. This ice cream was specially developed by local Unilever marketeers for the Asian market. The recipe uses coconut milk and the product is available in various Asian fruit flavours: durian, taro, mango and ruammitre. The picture shows the flavours taro and ruammitre.

'Steam non-sticky rice meal until cooked. Using a stick the length of a thighbone, make it into a round cake. Cut it into small, pearl-shaped pieces. Place it in honey-water and cool it with ice before eating', instructs a mid-nineteenth century Korean recipe for the dish known as sudan. The natural ice for use in this recipe undoubtedly came from one of the many ice cellars that had been in use on the Korean peninsula ever since the sixth century.[1] For centuries it was the custom in Korea and China to harvest ice in winter and store it in specially constructed cellars located along river banks. In other Asian countries, such as India, the ice was harvested at night time in the desert (see chapter 2).

• Despite the availability of natural ice, the eating of ice cream in Asian countries only began in the twentieth century. By contrast with Europe and North America, milk products have only come to feature on the Asian menu relatively recently. Dairy farming and its consequent dietary traditions have historically been little known in Asia, which is one of the reasons why ice cream has been slow to penetrate the culinary culture of its nations. Perhaps as a result, people in general exhibit a higher degree of lactose intolerance in Asia than in Europe – another reason for the lower consumption of dairy products.

• Other inhibiting factors have been the enormous distances over which the distribution has to take place and a much later industrialisation. The freezing installations – so indispensable for ice cream making and which in Europe and the United States were on hand from about 1870 – came to Asian countries only much later. The same goes for electricity and modern freezers and refrigerators. Cultural and religious differences have also made their influence felt. In many Asian countries ice cream is still seen as something that can cause colds, sore throats or stomach upsets. That the unhygienic conditions under which foods like ice cream were long produced are more likely to have been to blame for this than the product itself is a realisation that is only now gradually emerging.

• Today Asia has the fastest growing ice cream markets in the world. Ice cream production in China stood at 845 million litres in 1997.[2] In second place in volume terms came South Korea, whose three big ice cream manufacturers (Lotte, Haitai and Bingrea) helped entice the nation's consumers to lick their way through some 208 million litres in 1997.[3] Nonetheless, the three billion people living in the Asian countries (excluding Japan)[4] included in a 1998 study had an annual per capita consumption of just 0.6 litres of ice cream against an equivalent figure for the United States of 19.3 litres.

• Asian countries show similarities not only in their dramatic increase in ice cream consumption, but also in their exotic recipes, using all kinds of local ingredients, and in their reintroduction of traditional means of distribution such as ice cream carts. And yet each of them has a different ice cream history. In China, for example, contrary to what most people think, ice cream was only introduced in the 1920s.

'The nuttiest man in China'

• The birthplace of China's modern ice cream industry is Shanghai, where an enterprising American businessman started to import and produce ice cream in the 1920s. When in 1924 Paul Crawley gave up his cinema businesses in the Far East and instead began importing ice cream into Shanghai, people thought he was mad and named him 'the nuttiest man in China'.[5] Conventional wisdom had it that the Chinese did not like ice-cold food. For refreshment they drank tea, so how could Crawley hope to succeed? The Shanghai of those days was a lively, cosmopolitan seaport with many hotels, theatres and cinemas and long, hot summers. As a cinema operator himself, Crawley knew how many ices were sold in American movie-houses. 'I had looked the field over carefully', explained Crawley in 1926, 'and I was convinced that if the Chinese could be induced to use cigarettes universally they could be taught also to like ice cream.'[6]

• Crawley began with a trial batch of 45 litres of ice cream, imported in November 1924 by ship from Seattle. The impact was dramatic. In his first year Crawley sold more than 40,000 litres of ice cream in Shanghai under the Velvet brand name – and an additional 167,000 dozen Eskimo Pie products. In February 1926 alone, Crawley shipped a launch stock of 10,000 one-litre blocks of vanilla ice cream and 35,000 dozen chocolate vanilla ices ('Arctic Bar') to China on board the President Madison. From then on, most of the ships that steamed from Seattle to Shanghai carried at least 2,000 blocks of vanilla ice cream in a special storage hold.[7]

• Crawley's success persuaded another American company, Henningsen Produce Co., to enter the ice cream market in China as well. Henningsen was at that time the world's biggest producer of dried eggs, with exports to Germany and Great Britain as well as to Shanghai. Dried eggs are a seasonal product and their peak production occurs in the winter months. To make use of its spare capacity in the summer, the company decided to produce ice cream and, later on, chocolate. In 1926 Henningsen built an ice cream factory in Shanghai and marketed its products under the trade name Hazelwood Ice Cream.[8]

• This factory, which also produced margarine, was managed by the American John Kent Lutey. Henningsen's son-in-law, the extravagantly named Ulysses Sverin Harkson, was its president and managing director.[9] As a result of the Sino-Japanese War which broke out on 7 July 1937, Henningsen lost all its cattle in China and closed down as an ice cream manufacturer.[10] Meanwhile, Harkson had asked Lutey to look out for alternative locations. Lutey travelled all over the world and, after a meeting with a Coca-Cola manager in Rio de Janeiro, returned with the proposal to set up an ice cream operation in Brazil (see chapter 18).[11]

• Besides Crawley and Henningsen, several other companies were active in ice cream in Shanghai. Tai Kan, founded in 1914, produced biscuits, canned foodstuffs, ice cream and soft drinks. Tai Kan's chocolate ice cream cakes and blocks of vanilla ice cream were very popular and won awards for their quality. Other ice cream companies in Shanghai in the 1920s were Yi Min, a foods business, and Hai Ning, founded in 1927 by a Shanghai-born American businessman and the first to market ice creams on sticks there. A British company, probably Geddes Trading & Dairy Farm Co., also produced ice cream in Shanghai.[12]

• According to a 1934 report by C.E. Tatlow, a Unilever manager who had just visited China, there was only one ice cream factory in Shanghai that had the potential to distribute on a significant scale, and that was

550: View of the Henningsen ice
cream factory in Hazelwood Park,
Shanghai, early 1930s.

551: Employees of the Henningsen
ice cream factory in Shanghai, 1935.

Henningsen. Tatlow, however, was not impressed by the quality of its ice cream. 'Shanghai management has been informed that Henningsens use Purico instead of butter in their ice cream, which may account for the poor quality of their product', he wrote in his report.[13] Purico was presumably a brand name for a vegetable fat.

• Tatlow's visit to China was part of a mission that took him to a number of countries to research whether they would be worthwhile locations for Unilever to start up ice cream operations. This followed the recommendation made in September 1932 by the Special Committee, the group's governing body, that 'in view of the excellent results obtained by Messrs. Wall's in this trade (Unilever's ice cream manufacturer in Great Britain, see chapter 8), we should consider the possibility of introducing it [ice cream] to other countries'.[14] Since Henningsen held a monopoly position, Tatlow felt that a newcomer in Shanghai would have to undercut it on price while investing a considerable amount of money in advertising, 'as the Chinese palate does not seem to be sufficiently educated yet in the matter of foreign foods'. From this it may be inferred that ice cream was still perceived in China as a foreign product. Tatlow concluded: 'The proposition to enter the ice cream trade does not appear attractive.'[15]

• This assessment was revised, however, following the withdrawal of Henningsen as an ice cream manufacturer from Shanghai after 1937. On 22 June 1939 Unilever's Special Committee approved a plan to buy a factory in Shanghai to produce milk from milk powder and to manufacture ice cream. The outbreak of the Second World War prevented the implementation of this plan.[16]

Ice cream in Communist China

• After the Second World War, China's political landscape underwent fundamental change. In 1949 the Communist Party took power and nationalised foreign companies. These included the British firm Geddes Trading & Dairy Farm Co., which continued in 1950 under the name Korde Dairy and specialised in the production of sterilised milk, milk powder, malted milk, condensed milk, yoghurt and ice cream. A bakery business, Lao Dachang, originally French-owned, was also nationalised in 1949 and started producing ice cream in addition to its cakes and confectionery products.

• However, ice cream for a long time remained a marginal product in China. In 1951 there were only two ice cream factories in the whole country, together turning out just 169 tons of ice cream a year. In four other factories a further 2,340 dozen ice lollies were produced. But in the second half of the 1980s the Chinese economy began to show substantial growth. An indication of this can be seen in the increase in the number of refrigerators produced for household use. Whereas only 28,000 refrigerators left the factory gates in 1978, in 1985 14.5 million did so.[17] By 1997 69% of homes in urban areas possessed a refrigerator (against 36% in rural areas).[18] Ice cream manufacturing likewise expanded and in 1984 came the first imports of modern Gram and Høyer machines from Denmark for the production of ice lollies. In the absence of a refrigerator at home, many Chinese like to eat their ice cream in

552: Wall's ice cream on sale on the Great Wall of China, circa 1996.

¶ Between 1857 and 1859 the Austrian frigate Novara circumnavigated the globe. During this voyage the vessel called at the British colony of Ceylon, now Sri Lanka. In 1864, one of the crew members, Karl von Scherzer, published an account of the voyage in which he wrote about his visit to Ceylon's capital, Colombo. 'During our peregrinations through the streets of what they call the fort, it was in Catham Street, the most popular part of Colombo with the most important and most elegant shops, where we saw a confectioner offering ice for sale, a surprising sight in a city so close to the Equator that displays only little luxury in other respects.'[1]

The ice cream was shipped in from Boston in the United States via the Cape of Good Hope. The confectioner sold an estimated 1,000 pounds of water-ice and ice cream by weight each day at a time when eight pounds of ice cost one English shilling. 'One cannot but be seized by a feeling of admiration for the enterprising Yankee people, who transport even such a liquid and perishable article as ice cream [...] over thousands of miles [...] and are still able to sell it at a profit,' wrote von Scherzer. Ice cream was evidently available very early on in Sri Lanka. By 1863 the Ceylon Cold Stores business had started producing ice cream under the name Elephant House. In 1932 came the purchase of the dairy business Ceylon Creameries Ltd. and a more widespread distribution of fresh milk and ice cream got under way. One hundred and fifty years after its establishment, Elephant House ice cream is still enormously popular with the Sri Lankan people and the company has for some time been broadening its base by producing soft drinks as well.

Since 1991 Ceylon Cold Stores has been owned by John Keells Holdings.[2] Elephant House now mainly sells take-home packs of ice cream through supermarkets. Most of the impulse ice creams for sale in the streets today are supplied by Wall's Sri Lanka. Unilever opened a new ice cream factory in Baduragoda in 1997. As in other Asian countries, the company chose a moment when the income of the population had increased sufficiently to permit good sales prospects with adequate profit margins.[3] But Unilever's interest in the ice cream potential of Sri Lanka goes back at least as far as March 1960, when Jamie van den Berg, the Unilever world-wide foods co-ordinator, had looked into the possibility of acquiring two of the country's small ice-cream businesses, Plaidona and Alerics, without result.[4]

the street, a need which industrially produced and pre-packaged ice lollies fulfil. However, standards of hygiene can leave much to be desired: in the early 1990s, for example, the ice lolly wrappers were still being collected up after sale and re-used.[19]

• A characteristic feature of ice cream production in China is the use of milk powder in the South, whilst fresh milk is more widely available in the north of the country. In 1997, for instance, China's most important ice cream producing region, the southern province of Guangdong, contained only three farms that produced milk, compared with the 4,000 or so dairy businesses operating in the North.[20]

• In contrast to hot cuisine, ice cream recipes in China reveal hardly any regional differences, mainly copying Western examples. This was the logical consequence of the fact that ice cream was introduced into China from abroad through Shanghai, from where know-how spread outwards across the country. For many years ice cream remained a luxury, before new economic policies in the 1980s encouraged the establishment of more and more joint ventures with foreign companies, including ice cream firms. The first to partner China in this sector was Cathay Pacific, based in Hong Kong, manufacturing ice cream under the name Meadow Gold.

• Unilever entered the market in 1992. In a joint venture with Chinese partners it opened a new ice cream factory in Beijing in 1994, followed by a second factory in Shanghai. Imports of ice cream produced by foreign businesses, such as Nestlé, Häagen-Dazs, Baskin-Robbins and Dairy Queen, also increased, as ice cream came to be eaten in growing volumes, mainly in the urban areas of Guangdong province, Shanghai and Beijing. Today more than 100 ice cream companies operate in China, the biggest being the fully Chinese-owned Meiyile company in Guangdong. This is a significant step up from the two factories operating in 1951; and even though per capita consumption in China was estimated in 1997 to be only 0.7 litres, 845 million litres of ice cream were nonetheless sold,[21] at some of the lowest prices in the world.

Ice cream in India, 1955

• In contrast to China, its neighbour India – another vast country, with a population of 962 million in 1996 – did have a history of cold cuisine. In cities in the north of India kulfi has long been a traditional dish. Kulfi is thick, sweet and cold and made from buffalo's milk which has been boiled repeatedly. After the milk has been sufficiently reduced in this way, it is sweetened and then cooled or frozen in a barrel filled with ice and salt. Vendors carry with them small weighing scales and keep the kulfi wrapped in moist, white cloths; it is then sold by weight and served on the leaves of trees and shrubs. Kulfi is also widely available in restaurants; today almost every restaurant freezer contains kulfi that has been made on the premises.

• Before the Second World War the consumption of ice cream in India was chiefly limited to the households of the local aristocracy and of British colonials. The ice cream was prepared by the household staff. After the war, other population groups began eating ice cream, for example in restaurants. 'The eating of ice creams in restaurants is

MILK. ICE. CREAM.

553 : Picture postcard dating from 1930 showing a milk and ice cream vendor in India. At the back of the ox-drawn cart is a container with ice cream.

pushed to the extreme – big or small, no meal is complete without a good choice of ice creams', wrote the French ice cream maker M. Mortier in 1955 in a report on his experiences in India. Mortier published his findings in the French trade journal Le Glacier.[22] He noted however that only a tiny minority in India could afford to eat ice cream in restaurants. Others ate ice lollies that they bought for a few rupees in the street or at the cinema. These were water-ices, which occasionally contained a little milk, but were quite often just finely pounded ice to which some lemonade had been added.

• In terms of hygiene, the situation was still poor in 1955. Milk went uninspected, with prospective buyers commonly tasting the milk by scooping it from the buckets in the palm of their hand. After licking their fingers, they would move on to another bucket, being no more scrupulous about hygiene than the early producers in Europe. In 95% of all cases, wrote Mortier, the ice cream was stirred by hand and packed by women and children 'whose bodily cleanliness is extremely dubious.'[23] Children pooled their money until they had enough to buy an ice cream, which they then took turns to lick.

• Ice cream, as Mortier observed, was almost exclusively sold in the cities. In rural areas, where 90% of the Indian population still lived, ice cream was seldom available. At a time when famine was rife and the average lifespan was 24 years, perhaps that was not so surprising.

Iqbal Ghai, 'the maharajah of ice cream'

• The selling of ice cream in restaurants started in New Delhi and Bombay. Major contributions to this were made by the related Ghai and Lamba families from the Punjab. In the 1940s they had opened a snackbar in New Delhi. They discovered that American soldiers stationed in New Delhi were desperate for somewhere to buy ice cream. Under the leadership of Iqbal Ghai, who was later nicknamed 'the maharajah of ice cream' in India, and Pishori Lal Lamba, the production and sale of ice cream began in small quantities.[24] The families sold it not only to the GIs, but also to the increasing number of Indians who came to eat at their restaurant.

• The business was a great success and in 1954 members of the Ghai family travelled to London to learn about the industrial production of ice cream. They visited the agent for the American ice cream machine manufacturer Cherry-Burrell and at his suggestion called on a small South London ice cream factory in which Cherry-Burrell machines were installed.[25] This factory was owned by the Bertorelli family, who had been producing ice cream there since 1948, mainly for restaurants. The visitors were enthusiastic about what they saw and placed an order for Cherry-Burrell ice cream freezing machines. However, after the machines had been installed in New Delhi in 1955 and the Ghais wanted to commence production, they encountered a number of technical problems. They contacted Bertorelli's and asked whether someone from the London ice cream business could come and help them. That was how Remo Bertorelli ended up in New Delhi. A native of New York, Remo ran the factory in London. He travelled to India and, with the help of his engineer David Wild, succeeded in getting the machines in New Delhi to work. The family was delighted and asked Bertorelli to stay on and help with the construction of an ice cream factory in Bombay. This was opened in 1956, followed by an additional factory in Calcutta. Bertorelli continued to provide the Ghai family with advice for a great many years. In 1958 he even journeyed to Lahore in Pakistan, where he set up yet another ice cream factory, this time for a Pakistani owner.

• The factories of the Ghai and Lamba families marketed their ice creams under the Kwality Ices trade name. Because they were owned by various members of the two families, the factories largely operated independently as they expanded and spread throughout India. Initially, their ice cream mainly reached consumers via the street vendors who toured the streets with cooled ice cream carts. Later on, Kwality Ices also began supplying ice cream to small grocery stores and similar outlets, whose proprietors bought their own freezer cabinets in which they stored all sorts of other articles. Unlike in most other countries, restaurants were significant customers for Kwality ice cream, including the chain of restaurants that the Ghai family had built under the names Gaylord and Kwality.

• The Ghai family achieved success outside India too. Kwality ice cream was exported to Dubai and Jeddah; Gaylord opened branches in London, Chicago and Japan.[26] Thanks to these exports, Kwality Ices obtained foreign currency, which enabled the business to invest both in licences and in modern ice cream making machines imported from abroad.

554: Eating kulfi on the promenade in Bombay. A traditional Indian delicacy, kulfi is a cold confection made from buffalo's milk which has been repeatedly boiled to condense it.

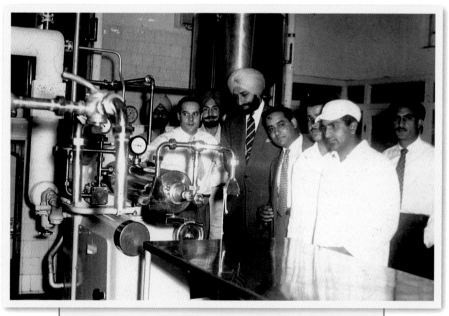

555: The Maharajah of Patiala (centre, with turban) is shown round Kwality Ices' new factory in Bombay by Remo Bertorelli (to the Maharajah's left) in about 1956. Bertorelli, an ice cream maker from London, was an adviser to Kwality Ices for many years.

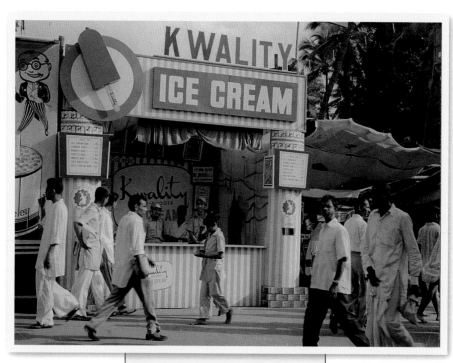

556: Kwality ice cream stall, circa 1958.

557: Ice cream makers in the Kwality factory in Bombay dip ices in chocolate sauce, after which the ices are transported to the packing table (circa 1958).

558: Kwality ice cream cart in New Delhi in 1957. Standing next to the cart are two daughters of Remo Bertorelli. The ice cream carts are cooled using eutectic plates which have been frozen in a refrigerant liquid in the ice cream factory. The plates were claimed to maintain a temperature of -20°C for about 24 hours.

As a result, Kwality Ices was able to undertake the industrial production of ice cream cones in 1978. At first the nuts were applied on the ice cream cones by hand, as were the lids. This involved three shifts of 100 workers each.

559: Movie-goers at the entrance to the Metro Cinema in New Delhi, 1957. A visit to the cinema was a night out for which people dressed up in their best clothes. In 1957 Kwality Ices convinced the cinema management that it would be advantageous to sell ice cream as well as soft drinks during the interval. After a successful trial, Kwality Ices acquired a contract to sell ice cream in cinemas throughout India.

• Apart from Kwality Ices, numerous other companies supplied ice cream, such as Volga ice, Joy ice made by Jawa and ice cream from the Vadilal family business.[27] But Kwality Ices was the biggest ice cream producer. Major sales opportunities for ice cream in India were (and still are) cinemas, weddings and other festivities, such as the opening of new business premises or railway stations.

Going to the movies is extremely popular in India and a great deal of ice cream is sold during the lengthy intervals. A wedding in India is a very important event for which the guest list sometimes runs into thousands. Religion and tradition dictate that all wedding guests must be given a meal, and ice cream frequently forms the final course.

• Unlike in China, ice cream recipes developed in India linked to regional culinary traditions, for example ice cream with saffron, a Kashmiri speciality,[28] or mango ice cream, as eaten in the areas round Malabar and Madras where mangos are plentiful.

560: Sale of ice and lemonades in Pakistan from a traditional ice cart. The cart contains an insulated container filled with blocks of ice.

Mango ice lollies and ice cream bars were already featuring in the Kwality product range in 1957, whereas in the West it took much longer for this flavour to gain acceptance. Ice cream made from coconut milk is also typical of the Indian market, serving as a substitute for buffalo's milk, which is taboo for the strictly orthodox Hindustani.

• Despite this link between ice cream and culinary culture, the level of consumption in India remains low, the 117 million litres of ice cream eaten in 1997 amounting to less than that consumed in that same year in the Netherlands,[29] a country of just 16 million people. This can be attributed in part to the low income of the mass of the population, but it also reflects an often negative attitude towards the product itself. As in a number of other countries in the Far and Middle East, many people in India look upon ice cream as something that causes colds and throat infections.[30] Similarly, the belief that too much cold in your stomach cannot be good for the body is still widely held. The idea that ice cream is a cause of disease has a certain logic to it wherever the circumstances of its preparation are unhygienic. It is a view, moreover, that has been around for centuries. Indeed, the founding father of medicine, Hippocrates (circa 460-377 B.C.), writes that the eating of cold substances such as snow and natural ice is 'harmful to the chest, and provokes coughing, discharges of blood and catarrhs.'[31]

561: Indian boy enjoying an ice, 1998.

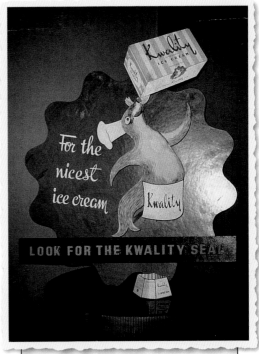

562: Advertisement for Kwality Ices, circa 1957. As its logo the Indian ice cream company used a seal wearing a chef's hat.

563: Employees of the Kwality factory in Bombay busy filling cartons with ice cream. The semi-frozen ice cream is pumped directly from the machines into the cartons. Strawberry sauce is added to the ice cream from a pipe. After they have been filled, the cartons are frozen in a special freezing room.

• Notwithstanding these cultural and economic barriers, ice cream consumption in India has in fact been growing rapidly in recent years: from 62 million litres in 1993 to 117 million in 1997. One year after the acquisition of Kwality ice cream by Unilever in 1995, consumption in India had increased by 29%, the steepest rate of growth the country had yet seen.[32]

564: Various typical Asian fruits and the ices made from them. Clockwise, from bottom: sweetcorn, black bean, pandan green noodles (cendol), durian, preserved plums, jackfruit, mango and yam.

Malaysia and Singapore

• After the Second World War Unilever began making small-scale exports of ice cream from Great Britain to Malaysia and Singapore, until in 1959 the group decided to start producing ice cream in a joint venture with the Singaporean ice cream business Cold Storage. Cold Storage owned three small ice cream factories; Unilever obtained 51% of the shares in the joint venture.[33] Until the 1950s the business had been slow-moving, but in 1965 Singapore became an independent country and its economy began to boom. Disposable incomes increased and the ice cream activities of Wall's Singapore, as Unilever's ice cream company had been re-named, started to flourish. The company was streamlined and made more efficient by closing down the ice cream production unit and transferring the distribution activities to a concessionaire which sourced its ice cream from the Unilever factory in Kuala Lumpur, capital of neighbouring Malaysia, and at a later stage also from the Unilever ice cream factory in Indonesia. In 1962 Unilever set up a new ice cream operation in partnership with the Fitz-patrick supermarket chain in Kuala Lumpur. Much later, in 1979, Wall's-Fitz-patrick Co. Ltd. came fully into Unilever ownership. Ice cream sales in Malaysia thereafter made steady, if slow, progress.

565: 'Ice rolls' from Kuala Lumpur, Malaysia, in various flavours. From left: cendol in coconut water, sweetcorn, milo, sour plums, black bean and orange.

566: Series of photos showing the making of cendol pandan green noodles in the streets of Kuala Lumpur, Malaysia, 1998. The ice is first shaved off the block and then the various fruits (or fruit juices) are added to it.

567: Thai youngsters enjoy an ice sitting in a tuk tuk.

Ice cream sells like hotdogs in Thailand

• In 1965, two years after the start-up of the Kuala Lumpur factory, Unilever's Overseas Committee – the body which at that time steered the group's operations outside Europe and North America – decided to investigate the viability of starting up an ice cream business in Bangkok.[34] Thailand was a country in which water-ices – usually a form of granita – had been eaten ever since the 1930s. Hawkers plied the streets with carts filled with blocks of raw ice. With a metal blade, they scraped off ice, put it in a cup and poured on the customer's choice from the many syrups they carried on their carts.

• Coconut milk is even more popular in Thailand than in India. It is used in all sorts of desserts and in ice cream, making coconut milk ice cream as ubiquitous as vanilla ice cream is in the West. A favourite way to eat coconut ice cream involves scooping it into a bread roll, just as you would with a hotdog. The coconut ice cream may contain pieces of breadfruit, taro or sweetcorn and the snack is completed by adding some condensed milk and a sprinkling of roasted peanuts.[35]

• It was only after the Second World War that the Thais were able to sample dairy ice cream prepared in the Western manner. This was produced by the American dairy company Foremost, which had set up an ice cream factory in Bangkok to serve the US army units on leave in Thailand. For decades Foremost was the country's leading ice cream manufacturer. After the Americans withdrew from South-East Asia in the mid-1970s, Foremost was sold in 1984 to the Dutch dairy business Frico Domo. Unilever maintained a watching brief until 1987 when it decided to build a 'greenfield' ice cream operation in Thailand to take Foremost head-on. The group had been active in Thailand since 1908, firstly with imports of soap, then through the local production of soap and other personal care products. Competition from Japan then prompted Unilever to seek possibilities for expanding its activity base in Thailand. Thai eating habits ruled out margarine, while the dominant position held by Foremost made entering the ice cream market appear unattractive.[36]

• Unilever's decision to go into battle was supported by a new approach to ice cream production. For a number of years the company's engineering departments and laboratories had been researching the development of a simple, flexible ice cream factory which required lower levels of investment than a traditional operation. The principles of this plan had been discussed in the Overseas Committee as far back as in 1982.[37] The concept was tailored to countries with developing economies. Its starting point was a stripped-down operation, focusing initially on the production of ice lollies in a few flavours and on ice creams on a stick, with or without a chocolate coating, with fast changeover times from product to product. The capital outlay on machines and plant and on their installation was not allowed to exceed £500,000.[38] If it proved successful, an ice cream factory set up according to the principles of 'Project Icicle' could expand its

production lines flexibly and cost-efficiently.
• It was on this basis that Unilever built its first Asian ice cream plant in Thailand in 1987-1988. The operation was a great success and was followed in 1992 by the purchase of Foremost's factory. Wall's – the brand name that Unilever uses for its ice cream sales in Thailand – became the country's leading ice cream company with a market share of 65%.

Indonesia and Vietnam: durian ice cream and 'car-em'

• In Indonesia ice cream was a rarity prior to the Second World War. Dutch colonials ate it in restaurants in the big cities, such as Pico-bello in Jakarta. Picobello had been making its own ice cream since 1938; thirty-five years later it was also supplying ice cream to other restaurants and to a dozen or so shops.[39] Here and there water-ices were sold in the streets, while the few mentions of ice cream recipes made in cookery books destined for Dutch colonies also relate to water-ice, sweetened with sugar and local fruit.
• In fact, there was only a little more ice cream to be had after Indonesia gained its independence in 1949. Home-made water-ices were sold on the streets and sometimes, as in India and Thailand, ices made with coconut milk were on sale. A much-loved local flavour was durian, a spiny, oval-shaped, greenish-yellow fruit common in the region. The use of nuts and spices such as coriander, ketoembar and cloves was, and still is, a popular way of flavouring ice cream.
• By around the end of the 1960s, however, ice cream producers in Singapore, such as Wall's (Fitzpatrick's Food Supplies) and Cold

568: Ice cream sold in a bread roll on the streets of Ho Chi Minh City, 1994.

Storage, were starting small-scale exports of ice cream to Jakarta. There, the product was mainly sold via the freezer cabinets of the newly emerging phenomenon of the super-market. Cold Storage had already built up a sizeable ice cream business in the Philip-pines, giving it a market share of 82% in 1972.[40] In 1968 the Australian ice cream com-pany Streets was another to begin exporting ice cream to Indonesia (see chapter 7).

• In 1971 a sea-change occurred in the Indonesian ice cream market when local entrepreneurs Greyhound, Flipper, Ye Ye and Ex Combi all acquired licences to start ice cream factories in Jakarta. By 1972 Grey-hound had become the largest, producing some 110,000 litres of ice cream per annum, followed by Flipper with 76,000 litres. Pico-bello production had so far expanded as to put it in third place with 37,000 litres.[41] Ye Ye used Japanese ice cream machines and ice cream mix from Morinaga Milk Industries Ltd. in Tokyo and produced its own ice cream cones. Shortly afterwards several other companies entered the market: they included Indomilk as well as Peters of Australia (see chapter 7). Other newcomers were Campina Indonesia (currently called PT

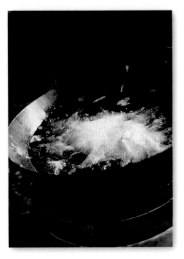

569: Series of photos showing the preparation of deep-fried ice cream in an ice cream business in Kuala Lumpur, Malaysia, 1998.

Ultrajaya), owned by the Indonesian Sabana dairy business, and Cold Storage of Singapore, which began producing ice cream in Indonesia under the Diamond trade name.

• A quarter of a century later, in 1997, Campina, Diamond and Peters had all expanded to become national ice cream businesses, but were overtaken by PT Unilever Indonesia. After many years of research and numerous reports – Unilever had conducted a preliminary study of the Indonesian ice cream market in 1970 – the group gave its approval in 1990 for the start-up of a greenfield ice cream operation under the name of Wall's in Indonesia similar to that in Thailand. Two years later, in February 1992, a brand-new ice cream production facility was opened in the Jababeka industrial estate, 40 kilometres east of Jakarta. In 1997, its ice cream having been made available first in Jakarta and then throughout the archipelago, Wall's achieved market leadership with a production volume (in 1996) of around 20 million litres of ice cream.

570: Wooden ice cream stall in Ho Chi Minh City, 1994.

• As in Indonesia, ice cream was not an established consumer product in Vietnam. It was introduced by the French and in the early 1950s it was possible to buy 'car-em' – 'cream on a stick' – on the streets of Saigon. These hand-made ice creams were flavoured with sugar and typical local fruits such as guava, lychee or durian.[42] The itinerant vendors stored them in small square boxes, which were filled with salt and ice, closed by a lid at the top and fitted with four small wheels. In those days Saigon had an ice cream factory producing the chocolate-coated ice creams on sticks, along with ice lollies, mainly for sale to cinema-goers.[43]

• The long war between North and South prevented the further development of ice cream culture until relatively recently. Various ice cream enterprises were then established and in 1995 the Vietnamese government gave Unilever permission to build a new ice cream factory on a site 35 kilometres north-west of Ho Chi Minh City (formerly Saigon). After the site had been cleared of landmines, the factory was constructed and the sale of Wall's ice cream began in 1997.

• In preparing for its new ice cream operation in Vietnam, Unilever's experience in Thailand, China and Indonesia proved invaluable. Like other non-Asian companies, Unilever increasingly focuses on meeting local market needs. To complement its international brand favourites, Unilever's marketing departments – largely staffed and led by local experts – tailor their products to Asian tastes. These include the Asian Delight range of ice creams, based on coconut milk and available in flavours such as taro, durian and mango.

Licks, Sticks & Bricks

A WORLD HISTORY OF ICE CREAM

Japan:

tradition meets

high tech

20

'Although the Japanese people are educated year by year to the use of ice cream as a staple food, still there is a large amount of prejudice against its use as a hot-weather food', wrote Toshihide Matsui in 1926 in an article about the emerging ice cream industry in Japan. 'In time', continued Matsui, 'with constant advertising, this prejudice will change to the idea that temperature has little to do with appetite for foods. As this thought is popularly developed, the construction of large ice cream plants, producing the whole year round, will be a natural development in Japan, meeting the changing ideas of the people'.[1]

• His prediction has been proved correct. In 1997, with 823 million litres of industrially manufactured ice cream, Japan held third place in the league table of world production behind the United States and China. A number of factors have contributed to this: Japan's vigorous industrialisation; the fast and successful development of dairy farming in the north of the country; early and intensive contacts with the American ice cream industry; the devising of ice cream recipes attuned to the nation's tastes; the introduction of modern food regulations; a high standard of product innovation; and the widespread prosperity achieved in the 1960s.

• There were ice cellars in Japan as early as the fourth century. They took the form of pits three metres deep in which ice harvested from ponds in the winter was stored. The pits were lined at the bottom with reeds and, when full, were covered with grass.[2] The Engishiki, a fifty-volume book of laws that was completed in the year 927, decreed that over a period of six months in every

571: Japanese cherry blossom ice cream gâteau, circa 1996. The first blossoming of the cherry trees heralds the start of a festive period in Japan.

year between one and three horseloads of ice blocks had to be supplied to the court. Each load comprised eight big blocks of ice and, if converted to today's measurements, the requisite supply equates to more than 75,000 kilos of ice per year.[3]

• As in China, Korea and Europe (see chapter 2), the ice was used by the élite for the cooling of foods and drinks. In about the year 1000 the courtier Sei Shonagon described in her famous book Makura no Soshi (Diary for next to the pillow) how she rasped ice into a metal bowl and then poured over it either honey or amazura, a sweet juice pressed from ivy and then reduced by boiling.[4]

• There was still no mention of ice cream being prepared in Japan. No indications have so far been found that people in Japan were familiar with the process of artificial freezing with ice and salt that had been developed in Europe in the sixteenth century (see chapter 2). It was only after 1853, when American warships under the command of Commodore Matthew Perry had forced the Tennô (or the Mikado, as foreigners used to refer to the Japanese Emperor) to open up Japan to trade with the West, that the Japanese became acquainted with ice cream. First to enjoy a taste were the members of a delegation who travelled to the United States in 1860 to sign a trade treaty between the two countries. After their ship, the Kanrin-maru, had arrived off San Francisco Bay, they transferred to an American frigate. On board the Japanese were treated to a festive meal and to 'something uncommonly tasty that is called aisukurin', records the shipboard journal kept by one of the delegation's members, Tosei Yanagawa. 'They colour the water-ice, put it in a mould and serve it. The taste is very sweet. When you put it in your

572: Members of the Japanese delegation who journeyed to the United States in 1860 to sign a trade treaty between the two countries. There, the Japanese first became acquainted with 'something uncommonly tasty that is called aisukurin', records the journal kept by one of the delegation's members.

mouth, it melts immediately. It really tastes delicious'.[5] Aisukurin was of course a phonetic rendition of ice cream. The term was used in Japan for many decades, but went out of fashion after the Second World War. Nowadays the term ice cream is used.

1873: ice cream for the Emperor of Japan

• Another member of the same delegation, the nobleman Fusazo Machida, a vassal of the last shogun, Tokugawa, was very impressed by the experience. He soon paid a second visit to the New World, where he studied the production methods for various items including matches, soap, rivets and ice cream. In 1868, when the shogunate came to an end, Machida had to look for different work.[6] With energy and vision he launched himself into all sorts of activities. He started producing matches, was active in shipbuilding and in 1869 he was the first person in Japan to open a shop that sold ices.

• His shop was situated on Basha Street in the seaport of Yokohama. At first, hardly anyone patronised it apart from foreigners on shore leave. Most Japanese stayed away; they thought ices much too dear. One portion of ice cost two 'bun', a sum in those days about equal to half the monthly wage of a female worker.[7] In April 1870 Machida gave the venture another try. He timed the

明治二年

馬車道之景

re-opening to coincide with
the beginning of a festival of
Iseyama Kodai Jingu (the
Iseyama Kodai Shrine). It
proved to be a smart move, as
the festival public now eagerly
bought his ices, which he
served in bowls made of bamboo, porcelain
or earthenware. Fusazo earned a great deal
of money and his success quickly led to
other enterprising Japanese in Yokohama
opening shops selling ices.

• Machida and his imitators, however, sold
only water-ice. Since Japan still had scarcely
any dairies, milk for ice cream was not
available. Dairy products were virtually non-
existent on a Japanese menu dominated by
rice, fish and vegetables. Under the new
Meiji regime (1868-1912), however, Japan

573: View of Basha Street,
Yokohama, 1869. The
second house from the left
is the shop of Fusazo
Machida, who was the first
to start an ice cream business in Japan. Outside,
next to a small red square
flag, is a vertical white
pennant with the words 'ice
cream' in Japanese writing.

began to modernise at a fast
pace. The seat of government
was moved from Kyoto in the
middle of the country to Tokyo in
the North where, in districts
such as Ginza, new stone buildings were constructed based on
Western models. Electric lighting was
installed in Tokyo after 1880. The Emperor
dressed in Western-style clothes and
encouraged the modernisation of his country
in many ways. In June 1873 he visited Japan's
first experimental agricultural station in
Aoyama, where, reported the Hochi Shimbun
daily newspaper, he was offered lychees
with ice cream. The lychees came from
greenhouses and the ice cream had been
made by Matsuzo Dejima, an imperial court
official who worked at the experimental

574: Woodcut showing the American ex-president, Ulysses S. Grant arriving on a visit to Japan in July 1879. Escorted by soldiers, Grant travels in a carriage under a triumphal arch formed by the Japanese and American flags. At the reception given for Grant, the Japanese hosts served Western delicacies such as ice cream and cake.

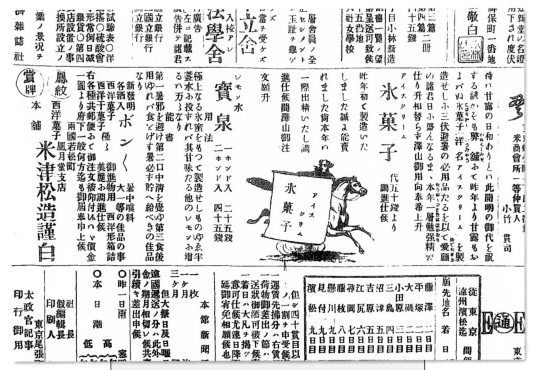

575: Advertisement published in the *Tokyo Nichinichi Shimbun* newspaper of 24 July 1879 by the Fugetsudo ice cream parlour. 'Since last year in our shop we have been making absolutely delicious korigashi (the Western name is ice cream). If you want to escape from the heat, we can definitely recommend it'.

site and had learnt how to make ice cream on a farm during a nine-year spell in the United States.[8]

• Ten years later, in 1883, 590 cows could be found grazing in the Tokyo area and producing some 600,000 litres of milk. Another ten years later, 1,797 cows provided almost 2.5 million litres[9] and it became possible to serve ice cream in Tokyo. So costly was this delicacy, however, it was only served at receptions given by members of Tokyo's high society seeking to impress their guests. For example, in July 1879 the welcome party for the visiting American ex-president, General Ulysses Grant (1822-1885), was held in the recently renovated and now ultra-modern Shintomi-za theatre, which boasted gas lighting on stage and in the auditorium. Proprietor Kanya Morita pulled out all the stops, serving Western specialities such as ice cream and cakes.[10] To show that Japan could emulate Europe and America, a hall was built in Tokyo in 1883 specifically for the reception of foreign dignitaries. In this splendid Rokumeikan a constant stream of bazaars, garden parties and balls were organised in European style and here, too, ice cream was served as a symbol of modernity.

• As Tokyo continued to modernise, increasing numbers of restaurants were established. In 1875 the Kaishindo saloon began selling ice cream and the Hakodateya teahouse also put ice cream on its menu. On 24 July 1879 readers of the Tokyo Nichinichi Shimbun daily newspaper were able to read the following advertisement by the Fugetsudo ice cream saloon: 'Since last year in our shop we have been making absolutely delicious korigashi (the Western

name is ice cream). If you want to escape from the heat, we can definitely recommend it. Every day more and more esteemed customers like you come to buy ice cream from us.'[11] Equally famous was the ice cream, based on a French recipe, sold by the Shiseido shop, which opened in 1900 in the Ginza shopping district. Following the American lead, it even installed a handsome soda fountain (see chapter 4).

• Making ice cream by hand in small ice cream machines imported from the USA was a time-consuming and laborious job. For ice, makers were often still reliant on the stocks available in ice cellars, although factories were being set up at around that time for the

576: Kaishindo tea-saloon and confectionery bakery, Tokyo, circa 1900. Kaishindo first sold ice cream in 1875.

production of ice blocks. The first modern freezing installation was imported from Germany in 1873.[12] However, the ice produced by these machines was used primarily for preserving fish. Ice cream continued to be a luxury item sold in restaurants for between 15 and 25 sen per portion, a price that was beyond the reach of most Japanese.[13]

• The position was different with kaki-gori, a kind of water-ice. This was made by shaving ice from a block and pouring sweet syrups over it, just as had been done in earlier times at the imperial court and as later became common practice in other Asian countries (see chapter 19). Already in the third quarter of the nineteenth century water-ice was sold during the summer months in tents, which had straw awnings and cheerfully coloured pennants and were part and parcel of the Tokyo street scene. Customers could go there to buy kaki-gori with syrups in lemon, strawberry, melon and red bean flavours.[14] In 1964, the Akagi dairy company launched 'Akagi Shigure' ('Akagi's Cold Rain') an industrially manufactured, 'shaved' ice; it was an overnight success and has since acquired a permanent place on the Japanese ice cream market.[15]

• More and more factories were built for the production of blocks of ice. By 1923 the Nitty Ice Manufacturing Co. alone was operating some 160 factories throughout the country,[16] supplying ice to restaurants and to private individuals who used it both for preserving foodstuffs and for the preparation of ices.

577: Shiseido Parlour, Tokyo, circa 1966. Opened in 1900 in the elegant Ginza shopping district, this establishment was famous for its ice cream, prepared according to a French recipe.

• In 1904 the first book containing ice cream recipes was published in Tokyo: Shokudoraku (Gourmandism), written by Gensai Murakami. Ice cream also found its way into Japanese literature. One of Japan's most famous authors of the Meiji period, Soseki Natsume (1876-1916), regularly mentions ice cream in his writing. In his 1914 novel Kokoro (Feelings), the lady of the house asks the maid to clear the table and serve ice cream and water-ice (korigashi), remarking to her guest: 'This is home-made'.[17]

1920: the start of the Japanese ice cream industry

• The first ice cream factory in Japan was founded in 1920 in Tokyo by Fuji Ice.[18] At first business was slow. 'Since people do not know that ice cream can be supplied from a large manufacturer, every drugstore, restaurant, department store etc. is making its own ice cream, using the primitive tub freezer, and also very well-to-do people are making their own ice cream, with much difficulty', observed one of the founding fathers of Japan's modern ice cream industry, S. Okimoto, in the American trade journal The Ice Cream Review in 1924.[19] Nevertheless, he also noted that an

578: Pack for Snow ice cream in bricks, 1933.

579: Female employees of the Snow ice cream and dairy company stacking tubs of ice cream in the Nagoya factory, 1936. A rotary filling machine can be seen in the background.

580: Containers of ice cream destined for restaurants and tea-houses are loaded into a lorry at Snow's Utashima ice cream factory.

581: Sales leaflet for Snow ice cream, 1938.

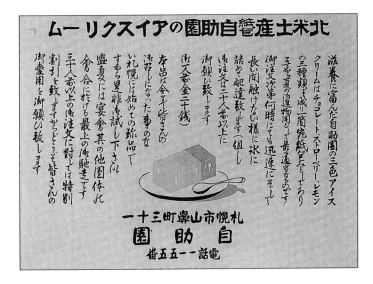

582: Advertisement for Jijoen ice cream from Sapporo on Hokkaido island, 1920s. In 1923 Jijoen was the first to market ice cream bricks combining lemon, strawberry, chocolate and in place of vanilla, popular elsewhere in the world, lemon flavours.

ice cream industry was beginning to develop and that demand for ice cream was increasing year by year. Okimoto was therefore convinced 'that this industry will grow in this country to be as great as in the USA in the near future.'[20]

• Okimoto himself had set up a modern ice cream factory in Tokyo in 1921. The machines were American and the factory formed part of Kyokuto Rennyu, a dairy business specialising in the production of condensed milk. In 1924 Okimoto built another ice cream factory in Osaka, this time solely for the production of ice cream. Later on, the ice cream factories became part of Meiji Nyugyo, today one of Japan's biggest dairy and ice cream companies.

• Industrial production took place on American lines. Bricks of ice cream of various flavours, packed in cartons, formed the bulk of production, followed by ice lollies from 1928 onwards. But unlike in Europe and the United States, lemon ice cream, and not vanilla, was the most popular flavour, so ice cream bricks in Japan combined lemon with the chocolate and strawberry. This type of ice cream was first manufactured by Jijoen, a factory that was set up in 1923 in Sapporo on the northern island of Hokkaido, Japan's main dairy

583: Direct selling of Snow products at an exhibition in Otaru on Hokkaido, Japan's northernmost island, 1936. On the building are the words 'butter, cheese, ice cream'. The signboard on the right reads: 'Snow Brand – Ice-cream'.

region, where an American-style agricultural college had been established as long ago as 1876. In 1928 another dairy business, Yoki-jiroshi (Snow Brand Dairy Products), also started producing ice cream in Sapporo. Like Meiji, the company is today one of the leading businesses in the Japanese dairy industry.

• As well as in bricks, ice cream was marketed in cardboard tubs. Snow Brand pioneered this format in 1935 – some ten years after the launch of Dixie-cups, the most successful ice cream tub in the United States (see chapter 5). Around the same time, a packaging industry – essential for the distribution of ice cream – was developing in Japan. Whereas in 1922 Japan was still reliant on imports for a product like cellophane, by 1930 it was producing the very latest packaging material itself: aluminium foil, still a much-used product in the ice cream industry.[21] The Toppan Printing Co., established in 1900, invented many new techniques, including its 1938 process for printing on plastic films. In a country with a deep-rooted culture of presentation, packaging assumed great importance. Another innovation, this time facilitating the distribution of ice cream, was the establishment in 1929 of a dry

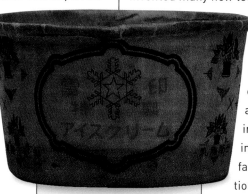

584: Cardboard tub for Snow ice cream, 1941, capacity 80 ml.

ice factory in Tokyo. As in Europe and the United States, dry ice was used to keep ice cream cold during transport.

• Alongside these developments in packaging and distribution, ice cream formulations tailored to Japanese tastes began to emerge, such as ices flavoured with green tea (matcha), rice cake with ice cream (sakura-mochi) and ices with ginger or sesame seed. Another favourite, deep-fried ice cream, is made by wrapping a frozen ball of ice cream in a layer of dough and then frying it briefly in hot fat; and when ogura ice cream using a purée of sweet beans first came on the market in 1921, it was an immediate hit and has remained so to this day.[22]

Post-war modernisation of the Japanese ice cream

• In 1941 Japan's attack on the American naval base at Pearl Harbor plunged the nation into the Second World War. As almost all means of production for dairy products were requisitioned by the Japanese army, there was no possibility of producing ice cream until some time after the war. The first post-war ice product in Japan was ice candy, created in about 1948. It was a simple ice made from water, sugar and lemonade that was frozen in a tin tube. Half-way through the freezing process a bamboo stick was inserted. The product was made in elementary freezers installed at the front of shops.

• Rationing of milk and cream remained in force in those early post-war years, so ice cream was eaten in Japan only by American army units, who manufactured their own ice cream using powder imported from America.[23] Relief for the Japanese arrived in the 1950s when the first soft ice cream machines, also imported from the USA, appeared in Tokyo. Soft-ice could be quickly prepared using ice cream powder, which was cheap and easily obtainable now that the Japanese dairy industry was again allowed to supply it. Soft-ice soon became a big seller, its popularity only declining in the second half of the 1950s as a result of competition from the ice cream industry, which had re-started operations, and because of hygiene problems with the soft-ice machines that came to light when the supervision of food products was intensified. Modern regulations based on the Foodstuffs Hygiene Act[24] now covered the production and composition of 'milk and dairy products', a category which also embraced ice cream.

• Apart from ice cream manufacturers like Meiji and Snow, familiar names from pre-war times, there were newcomers to the Japanese ice cream market, such as Kyodo, Napoli, Glico and Morinaga. Napoli had been founded in 1953 by Vittorio Tortolano, a member of a Neapolitan family of ice cream makers.

585: Ice cream being sold on the street from a 'moving shop', as it says on the awning of the ice cream cart, 1949.

586: Street sales of ice candies by bicycle in 1948. In the initial post-war years an ice candy was almost the only ice available in Japan. It was a simple water-ice made in a tin tube. The ices are in the freezer box at the back of the vendor's bike. The pennant on the box says 'ice candy'. The girl is also selling ices from the small box she carries in front of her.

587: Freezer box, made from walnut, for the storage of ice candies, 1948. The ice cream vendor carried the box on the back of his bicycle.

Tortolano enjoyed great success, especially with his ice cream cakes which he supplied to restaurants, tea-houses, hotels, night-clubs and airline companies. Some of his creations, such as the wedding cakes he produced, weighed in at more than 120 kilos. His Fuji ice cream gâteau, shaped like the mountain and covered with chocolate and marzi-pan, was famous.[25]

• Napoli was later taken over by Mori-naga, the most widely known of all the ice cream oper-ations set up after the war. Established in 1899 as a producer of confectionery products, biscuits, chocolate and caramel, Morinaga had since 1917 also been producing condensed milk and other dairy products. After the Second World War the dairy activities were split off and two companies traded under the Morinaga name: a dairy products manufacturer and a business that made biscuits, chocolate and other confectionery products. In 1954 the Morinaga dairy business began producing soft-ice and, shortly afterwards, regular ice cream. Since then the business has expanded to become a foods group with activities in many countries and sales in 1996 of $3.7 billion.[26]

• A characteristic feature of the modernisa-tion of the Japanese ice cream industry in the second half of the 1950s was the early, large-scale purchase of very latest, fully automated rotating ice lolly freezing machine, RIA, from

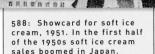

588: Showcard for soft ice cream, 1951. In the first half of the 1950s soft ice cream sales boomed in Japan.

the Danish machine manufacturer Gram (see chapter 10). Between 1955 and 1959 no fewer than 26 Gram RIA machines were installed in Japanese ice cream factories. In terms of machine numbers, Japan held second position in the world, behind only the USA (approaching 50 machines) and well ahead of third-placed Australia.[27] In other countries with a bigger industrial production of ice cream, such as Great Britain and Germany, the modernisation of plant only really got under way at the end of the 1950s.

• The Gram RIA machine's early popularity in Japan can be ascribed to the tremendous possibili-ties that the machine offered for mass-producing a product that was ideally suit-ed to the Japanese ice cream market at that time: the simple water-ice on a stick. It was a cheap, clean and refreshing product which could be supplied in many flavours. It matched the needs of Japanese consumers perfectly, since they regarded ice cream mainly as refreshment, rather than as food, as did consumers in the USA or Europe. The popularity of water-ice had long been pronounced in Japan and, against the trend elsewhere, remains the case today. In 1972, for example, the share of water-ices in industrial ice cream production was 35%; in 1996, it had fallen only slightly to 31%.[28]

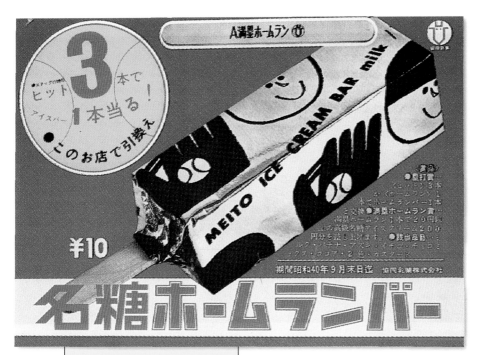

590: Publicity material for the Homerun Bar by Meito, circa 1960. The campaign promised that one out of every three ice creams had a stick with the word 'Hit!' on it. The winning stick entitled its owner to claim a free ice cream. The campaign was an enormous success with children.

591: Sorbet made with Blue Curaçao, circa 1996.

589: Japanese children enjoy a tub of Snow ice cream, early 1960s.

• The Japanese also have a preference for impulse ices, reflected in the very high market share of ice lollies, cones, sandwiches and tubs. In 1996 the share of impulse single products stood at 57%, rising to 88% when including 'multipack' ice creams – several impulse ice creams contained in one pack. By contrast, ice cream in packs of a litre or more which is kept in the freezer for consumption at home, as is customary in Europe, Australia and the United States, has yet to capture Japanese hearts, having a market share of only 5% in 1996, a year in which the Japanese consumed a total of 900 million litres of ice cream, equivalent to 7.1 litres per head.[29]

592: Poster for Snow ice cream, 1954.

569 million litres, with a sales value of 20 and 80 million yen respectively. Prices rose too: in 1960 an ice cream still cost only 5 yen on average; ten years later it cost 30 yen.[30]

• The ice cream industry stimulated growth in consumption by borrowing a market strategy from the United States that involved continuously introducing new ice cream flavours and new varieties (for a description of this development in the United States, see chapter 6).

The Gram RIA machines, the machines made by Høyer and those made by the American business Vitaline offered plenty of scope for introducing innovative stick products; and in 1960, just one year after Algida had launched the first Cornetto ice cream in Italy (see chapter 15), Japanese consumers were also able to sample this mass-produced ice cream cone.[31] Innovation transfer was a two-way street: another novelty was the 'push-up' ice, a tapering, cylinder shaped water-ice, packed in a cardboard tube, that is pushed up by squeezing the bottom of the tube. This was invented in Japan and spotted by a Unilever manager from Italy, Gianni Moretti, who took samples of the packaging back to Italy in 1979 and adapted it. Marketed under the Calippo brand name, this is one of Unilever's most successful ices.

Breakthrough in the market: prosperity and innovations

• The breakthrough in ice cream consumption in Japan came in the early 1960s. It coincided with growth in disposable income and in the nation's overall prosperity, a development symbolised by the 1964 Olympic Games held in Tokyo. In 1959 Japan's gross national product had been 12.9 trillion yen; ten years later its GNP had reached 59.7 trillion yen. Over that same period the annual production of industrial ice cream went up from 190 to

593: Publicity material for the Homerun Bar by Meito, depicting Shigeo Nagashima, a popular baseball player at the time (circa 1960).

594: Election of Miss Ice Cream 1984. Based on the American example, the contest was organised for the first time in 1981 by Japan's association of ice cream manufacturers.

• Another example of Japanese innovation was the manufacture of many types of 'mini' ice creams. In the early 1950s ice cream manufacturers in Japan made small ices out of necessity, hoping to maximise sales to a public that was still far from affluent.[32] Later, in the 1970s, necessity became the mother of innovation when a stream of new ideas was needed to induce children in particular to buy the very latest ice cream novelties each season. Innovative ice cream varieties were introduced for adults too, such as enclosed wafers filled with ice cream or two mini ice cream balls, in coconut and green tea flavours, on a cocktail stick.

• By 1966 Japanese ice cream manufacturers had joined forces to form an industry association. Apart from promoting their interests by lobbying the government, the association also tried to stimulate ice cream consumption. From 1981 onwards, for instance, an annual Miss Ice Cream contest was organised, following the United States' example. An annual National Ice Cream Day was also instituted.

• All over the world, public holidays, festivals and anniversaries are an appropriate time to eat ice cream. During parties in Japan it is quite customary for a guest to bring along an ice cream cake or to present his host with a gift voucher to buy ice cream. In Japan such feast days and public holidays are based on a mixture of Japanese and American traditions. Apart from birthdays, weddings, New Year's Day and Christmas, people in Japan also celebrate the first appearance of cherry blossom, the Festival of the Dolls and Children's Day. The doll festival or 'Girls' Day' is on 3 March. Dolls are displayed in the house and sometimes a coloured ice cream cake is eaten, based on the recipe for the traditional rice cake dish, mochi. On 5 May comes the children's day, or 'Boys' Day', when ice cream is served in the shape of a carp. The carp in Japan is a symbol of strength, that of a fish swimming against the current. American feast days such as Valentine's Day and Halloween are also celebrated in Japan, with ice cream cakes in the form of a heart and a hollowed-out pumpkin mask.

• Even more significant factors driving ice cream consumption were the improved distribution structure and the growing sophistication of automated manufacturing processes. Japan was one of the early pioneers of computer-controlled production. Morinaga, for example, constructed a new ice cream and milk plant in 1969 in which the supply of the ice cream mix to the production lines was controlled by a digital 'on-line' computer system.[33] Besides providing labour savings and greater accuracy, this system allowed the business to operate more flexibly, a major benefit when increasingly novel ice creams needed to be rolled out in double-quick time.

Ice cream in small shops and vending machines

• The first freezers with transparent lids had been installed in Japanese shops by around 1960, earlier than in Europe. This made it easier for consumers to see the ice creams and more likely that they would buy one.[34] In Japan ice cream is distributed via a myriad of small sales outlets supplied from big, centrally located coldstores or smaller sub-depots. Unlike in Europe, the freezer cabinets are mostly provided not by the ice cream manufacturers, but by wholesalers. In 1995 some 1,100 wholesalers were supplying ice cream to 212,000 outlets, mainly sweet shops and bakeries. Another typically Japanese distribution method is the automatic vending machine. Although mainly used for soft drinks and beer, as many as 25,000 ice cream vending machines were in operation in 1995 (in addition to more than 2.5 million machines for vending soft drinks and beer).[35]

• In Japan's retail trade culture, small shops were traditionally protected by the government. This situation worked to the advantage of the wholesale distributors and made it virtually impossible (and certainly unprofitable) for ice cream manufacturers to supply retailers direct via a costly, nationwide network of coldstores. In 1972, Japanese wholesalers were still not facing significant competition from supermarkets. Ninety per cent of ice cream sales went through small shops.[36] This was a very different position from that in Europe and even further removed from that in the United States, where supermarkets in large shopping malls were already pointing the way to the future. Twenty-five years later, in 1997, small shops and the somewhat bigger neighbourhood and convenience stores still represented the most important sales channels, accounting for 27.5% and 29.5% of total sales respectively. The share of supermarkets and department stores, however, had grown to 32%.[37]

• Remarkably enough, this shift in distribution structure has not so far led to the supermarket chains offering their own, more cheaply priced ice cream brands. Take-home packs of ice cream, which are the basis of own brand production in Europe and the USA, are a much less developed sector in Japan, while Japanese supermarket chains have to date preferred to market ice creams that have been produced exclusively for them but are still sold under the manufacturer's own brand. The retail trade is thus using the manufacturer's ice cream brand as an umbrella name for its own 'exclusive' products.[38]

• When foreign ice cream producers first attempted to gain a foothold in the Japanese

595: Strawberry ice cream served in the form of flowers, circa 1996.

major player in the wine, liqueur, distilled beverage and mineral water sector. The high-quality, but very expensive ice cream of Häagen Dazs struck a chord with the increasingly affluent Japanese consumers, with their continuing penchant for Western brands. Sometimes the product was adapted to meet local tastes: in Tokyo today, for example, Häagen Dazs sells an ice cream with a sauce prepared from sweet satsuma potatoes. Häagen Dazs ice cream also benefited from the growth of ice cream parlours in the big cities and reached a market share of 9.3% in 1997. That put the company in fifth place in the ice cream market that year, behind the market leader Meiji (13.7%), Morinaga (13.4%), Glico (13.0%) and Lotte (9.8%).[39]

• Foreign appeal is also a popular basis for advertising messages in Japan. French fashions and culinary traditions are particularly favoured. In 1983, a TV commercial for Eskimo ice cream, the brand name used by Morinaga, showed three young women praising an ice cream in Japanese.

596: Advertisement for Morinaga ice cream, circa 1997.

However, the pay-off line of their eulogy was in French: 'Cent pour cent Europe!'[40] – a good example of how the Japanese ice cream industry and its national market have been, and still are, open to foreign influences.

market in the 1970s and 1980s, in most cases they did so in co-operation with a Japanese ice cream manufacturer. One of the first was Borden, a respected name in the American ice cream and dairy industry. It entered into a joint venture with Meiji in 1971 and shortly afterwards Lady Borden premium ice cream was available in the freezer display cabinets. The USA ice cream companies Dairy Queen and Baskin & Robbins, both specialists in setting up chains of parlours on a franchise basis (see chapter 6), followed suit in November 1973. After many years of market study Unilever entered into a co-operation agreement with Morinaga in 1979 covering marketing and technical know-how; but in the late 1980s the alliance was terminated and eventually Borden pulled out of the Japanese market.

• Häagen Dazs had more success entering the Japanese ice cream market in 1984 after embarking on a joint venture with Suntory, a

Licks, Sticks & Bricks

A WORLD HISTORY OF ICE CREAM

Modern times:
the coming of the
multinationals

Unilever has played a major part in shaping modern ice cream history. In 1922 the British company T. Wall's & Sons Ltd. set up an ice cream department and, on the creation of Unilever in 1930, Wall's became part of the new group. Despite the Depression Wall's ice cream achieved good profits, delighting the Unilever board. On the basis of the 'excellent results obtained by Messrs. Wall's in this trade', the Special Committee, the group's senior executive body, decided in September 1932 to investigate whether Unilever ought to start producing ice cream in countries outside the UK too.[1] The managements of the Unilever businesses in Continental Europe would be asked to send people to study the Wall's business so that they could draw up recommendations.

• It is clear that Unilever, today the world's largest ice cream producer, identified the opportunities for selling factory-made ice cream at a very early stage. The group also looked beyond the European ice cream market. In 1934 the Unilever manager C.E. Tatlow studied the viability of setting up an ice cream factory in Shanghai. In the light of the market situation, he advised against it (see chapter 20); but the withdrawal from China in 1939 of the major competitor, Henningsen, changed matters and the Special Committee approved the purchase of a factory there. The plan was to make milk and ice cream from milk powder,[2] but the Second World War intervened.

> 597: Ice cream sales in Nigeria, early 1960s. In 1952 Unilever had set up a small, simply-equipped ice cream factory in the town of Sapele which sold ice cream under the Wall's name.

• In 1936, meanwhile, Unilever had bought the Langnese ice cream business in Germany (see chapter 12). Although the underlying considerations for this purchase and for the China decision were not based on a conscious strategy of entering the ice cream business worldwide, they were – with hindsight – important steps for the future of Unilever's ice cream activities, providing a platform from which it was able to expand its ice cream activities in future years.

1958: a turning point

• It was not however until the early 1950s that Unilever took further initiatives in the international ice cream market. Some of these took place in British colonies, or ex-colonies, where the company already had a strong position; others in Western Europe.

• In 1952, for example, in the town of Sapele in Nigeria a small ice cream factory was installed next to West African Cold Storage, a Unilever business that produced meat, sausages and pies.[3] Ice cream was also exported to countries like Cyprus, Malta and Singapore and in 1957 a decision was taken to set up an ice cream factory in South Africa at Boksburg, just outside Johannesburg.[4]

• A market survey conducted in Belgium in 1954 described the prospects there as 'fairly promising'.[5] A year later Unilever began selling ice cream in Belgium under the Ola brand name (see chapter 13) and preparations were started for construction of an ice cream factory in Baasrode. Similarly, in 1955 Unilever's world foods coordinator, J.P. ('Jamie') Van den Bergh, asked the management in Austria to conduct a study into the potential for starting an ice cream business there.[6]

¶ Turkey has a centuries-old tradition of drinking serbet – sweet drinks cooled by snow or ice. From the early days of the Ottoman Empire in the thirteenth century ice was harvested on the high plains of Anatolia and stored in ice cellars. By the seventeenth century the karci (snow traders) were an important professional group in Istanbul.[1] The snow was transported by mules from Anatolia to other districts, where it was mixed with condensed grape juice.

However, despite the availability of snow and ice, ice cream itself was not eaten in Turkey at a particularly early date, probably not until the seventeenth century. Turkey has its own typical ice cream called dondurma, made with goat's milk, sugar and salep, a substance obtained from the tubers of wild orchids. As with kulfi in India, the mixture is boiled until reduced to the right consistency, then it is cooled, whipped for a long time and frozen. Dondurma is by then so thick that it can be sus-

598: Sale of ices in about 1920 in the Ottoman Empire. The ice was eaten on the spot from small cups which were then handed back.

599: Ice cream cart in Istanbul, 1960s.

pended from a hook; and the traditional way of eating it is with a knife and fork, served on a tin-plated copper plate and accompanied by baklava, a honey cake made from puff pastry and pistachio nuts.

There is no set recipe for making dondurma. Knowledge of the recipe and ingredients, and of the time the milk has to be boiled and whipped, is passed down by word of mouth from one generation to the next. Mado, an ice cream manufacturer in Maras in south-east Turkey, claims to have been making its very popular dondurma now for four generations. People are proud of its Turkish origins and take pleasure in the way it is served: men dressed in traditional clothes fetch the dondurma from a freezer compartment, hang it from a hook and cut portions off with a large knife.

Until recently most ice cream in Turkey was made artisanally and only sold between May and September.

The first factory-made ice cream came from

600: Maker of traditional Turkish 'dondurma' at work, circa 1997.
The ice cream is so chewy that you can hang it from a hook.
This consistency is achieved by adding salep (a substance obtained from
the dry tubers of wild orchids).

is not known. Later, in 1968, Atatürk Orman Çiftligi (Atatürk's Forestry Farm), founded in Ankara in 1923, began producing ice cream. Sold in tubs, the product had a tremendous reputation in Ankara, but was virtually unknown elsewhere. In the second half of the 1960s the Alaska ice cream business was also set up, selling its products mainly through cinemas.[3]

Large-scale ice cream consumption in Turkey only started relatively recently, with the establishment in 1985 of the fully Turkish-owned ice cream factory, Panda.

In the years that followed, the Panda brand spread across the country, until in 1990 Panda found itself facing competition from Algida, a Unilever subsidiary. Consumption at that time was still less than half a litre per head – well below the level in other countries – mainly because Turkish consumers believed that ice cream caused sore throats. Algida therefore initiated a successful campaign to educate consumers as to the nutritional value and safety of industrially produced ice cream, resulting in a doubling of consumption per head by 1998 – and market leadership for Algida.

Istanbul, where there were two factories operating in 1954. One was Pinguin, established in 1950, whose ice lollies sold well on the beaches and in cinemas;[2] the name of the other

601: Ice cream being manufactured at Boksburg, just outside Johannesburg, circa 1965. The factory had been opened by Unilever in 1957.

The study showed that the market conditions in Austria were not favourable: there was a ban on street sales of ices and a 10% tax on ice cream; while cinemas offered no sales openings, there being no intervals during film shows.[7] Opportunity beckoned in Australia, however, where a well-developed ice cream market existed and where sales, as in the United States, were being channelled less through small shops and increasingly through the rapidly emerging supermarkets.

• In 1957 six European countries – Germany, France, Italy, the Netherlands, Belgium and Luxembourg – signed the Treaty of Rome establishing the European Economic Community (EEC), which came into being on 1 January 1958. One of the central objectives of the EEC was to abolish customs duties between its member states; later efforts would focus on the harmonisation of tax systems, labour legislation, transport and consumer goods legislation, especially in the area of foods. For multinational companies like Unilever the establishment of the EEC was an important step which the group supported right from the start. 'We welcome the institution of the European

Economic Community for the part it seems about to play in raising the standards of living in the member countries', wrote the Special Committee in its 1958 annual report.[8]

• Unilever had been preparing itself for the EEC. Twelve months before its institution, a group headed by board member A.W. Caron was commissioned to review Unilever's foods business.[9] At that time the group was active in a variety of food categories: fish, meat products, chicken, fruit and vegetables, dairy products, cereals, sugar confectionery, tea, frozen foods, soup, mayonnaise, salad dressing and ice cream.[10] The question was: which of these would be worth developing further over the long term?

• In October 1958 the group recommended that the ice cream, soup, meat products, chicken and frozen foods categories should be expanded. Regarding ice cream it said: 'We strongly recommend expansion into other European and Overseas countries.'[11] According to the study group, the results of Wall's and Langnese in the preceding years had been most satisfactory. In 1957 Wall's had achieved a 22% return on capital employed; at Langnese that figure was 12%. The report warned that new ice cream businesses would operate at a loss in the first few years, largely because of the high initial costs of coldstores, depots, special lorries and freezer cabinets. As soon as a certain level of turnover had been reached, the picture would be transformed. 'Through its high gross margin ice cream then becomes a very profitable product.'[12]

• The study group had also investigated changes to the organisation which it felt were necessary for the future development of the sector. To realise the recommended expansion, the world foods coordinator would need the support of groups of industry experts who would coordinate activities in the various countries.[13]

• In September 1958 the Special Committee agreed to sanction the expansion of ice cream activities, but specified that first the existing ice cream businesses in the United Kingdom, Germany and Belgium needed to be consolidated. After that, a gradual start could be made on gaining a share of the market in other countries, if necessary through acquisition.[14]

• The 1958 decision represented a turning point in the history of Unilever's ice cream activities. A major new ice cream factory was now to be built for Langnese in Heppenheim, Germany. The first phase alone required an investment of over DM13.5 million. A year later came the decision to construct a new factory for Wall's in Gloucester, which involved a capital outlay of £4.38 million.[15] A start was then made on purchasing ice cream businesses throughout the world (see box on p. 614). As a result, by the early 1970s Unilever was represented in ice cream in virtually all West European countries, as well as in other countries including the United States, Australia and Singapore.

Ice cream conferences and an international logo

• In addition to expanding its ice cream activities, Unilever also overhauled the structure of its organisation. Although not in complete accordance with the study group's proposals, the main recommendation – the establishment of international product coordination groups – was implemented.

This was necessitated not only by the growth of the market and the complexity of Unilever's activities, but also by the emergence of supranational organisations like the EEC which called for a strengthening of international coordination within Unilever. Six 'Coordinations' were set up: from 1962 ice cream, together with frozen foods, meat products, fish and soup, became part of what was known as Foods II Coordination.[16]

• The first coordinated approach to ice cream had in fact begun well before the study group's report was published. In May 1958 the technical directors of Langnese, Wall's and Ola held their first conference. Initially, two to three such meetings were held each year. The subjects discussed ranged widely from recipes, ingredients, ice cream moulds, cold storage and the keeping properties of ice creams to the pros and cons of various types of freezers, electricity consumption and packaging methods. Some subjects, such as freezers and ingredients, were frequent agenda items.[17]

• Conferences were not confined to discussion of technical matters. In October 1961 a first meeting was held in Rotterdam between the full managements of the ten Unilever ice cream companies. This first ice cream conference was chaired by A.W. Caron,

by then a member of European Continental Management. Other participants were J.P. Van den Bergh and members of Unilever's central departments for marketing, packaging and engineering. During the conference Van den Bergh emphasised the importance of regularly putting novelty ices on the market.[18] The possibility of introducing a common logo was also discussed for the first time.

602: Entrance to the Olá Portuguese ice cream factory, 1968. Unilever had bought the factory in Lisbon in 1958 and changed its name from Esquimeau.

The recently acquired Austrian ice cream company Eskimo was already using the same logo as Langnese: a rectangle of red and white stripes enclosing a central oval in which the name of the company was written. The chairman of Unilever's Austrian ice cream business, L.R. Montijn, reported that a common approach offered major benefits in the purchase of packaging materials and in German-language advertisements that were understood in both Germany and in Austria. The logo which appeared on packs, freezer cabinets and advertising materials was easily recognised by German tourists in Austria and this stimulated sales.[19]

603 + 604: Old and new logos of Unilever's ice cream businesses. The red and white, vertical stripe design was introduced in 1961, to be replaced in 1997 by the red and yellow heart on a white background.

• In 1963 Unilever began introducing an international logo for its ice cream, using a design not very different from the logo already being used by Langnese and Eskimo. It was not implemented everywhere: Wall's Ice Cream, Sagit in Italy, Frisko in Denmark and GB in Sweden, for instance, retained their own logo. The international logo remained in use for more than 30 years, before being replaced in 1997 by a heart shape in swirls of red and yellow against a white background.

• After 1961 an international ice cream conference was organised almost every year; and during the 1970s these conferences were extended to three days and were attended by marketing and technical specialists representing all Unilever ice cream businesses. Annual international meetings were also held involving the chairmen of the ice cream companies. Both events provided an invaluable forum for discussing product development, for promoting the harmonisation of policy and for mapping out future strategies.

605: Sagit Algida ice cream factory in Caivano, just north of Naples, circa 1995.

Unilever and Nestlé

• Successful products from one Unilever ice cream company were often adopted by others. One of Unilever's outstanding successes has been the Cornetto cone, an ice cream that was first marketed in 1959 by the Italian company Sagit (see box on p. 614). And yet the expansion of the group's ice cream activities did not always meet with success.

In France the Délico business suffered ongoing losses and in 1965 it was sold to rival Miko. The Ola company in the Netherlands also suffered substantial losses in its first few years, whilst Good Humor in the US struggled for a long time to break even (see chapters 13 and 6).

• The most profitable companies were Wall's Ice Cream in the UK, Sagit in Italy and Langnese in Germany. In Germany Langnese-Iglo was embroiled in fierce competition with Findus/Jopa, the frozen foods and ice cream subsidiary of the Swiss multinational Nestlé. Langnese-Iglo was badly hit by the aggressive discounting that Findus/Jopa offered on its frozen food products. Findus/Jopa halved the prices of all its ice cream products during the winter months.[20] On the other hand, Nestlé's position was also precarious, as Findus/Jopa had long been incurring losses of around DM10 million annually.[21] From the early 1960s the boards of both companies had had regular contact. It was therefore no great surprise when the chairman of Unilever's Foods II Coordination,

Forty years of Unilever and ice cream

1. Ice cream businesses acquired

Before 1959 Unilever acquired Langnese in Germany (1936) and United Dairies in the UK.

1959
Austria: Eskimo
Australia: McNiven Bros.
France: Gella
Portugal: Esquimeau
1960
Australia: Streets
Denmark: Frisko
Singapore: Cold Storage
1961
Australia: Sennitt
Denmark: Kronburg Is
The Netherlands: De Hoop
Sweden: Gille-Glass
USA: Good Humor
1962
Canada: Good Humor
Italy: Spica
The Netherlands: VAMI
Sweden: Trollhätteglass
1967
Italy: Eldorado
1971
Denmark: Sol Is
1973
Brazil: Alnasa
Ireland: Hughes Brothers
Switzerland: Gelbar
1974
Italy: Chiavacci and Toseroni
Spain: Frigo
1977
France: Motta
1978
Australia: Amscol

1981
Argentina: Laponia
1983
Switzerland: Lusso
1985
The Netherlands: Davino, Caraco
Sweden: Glace Bolaget
1989
USA: Gold Bond, Popsicle
1992
Canada: Dickie Dee, Popsicle
Thailand: Foremost
USA: Klondike
1993
Belgium: Mio
Canada: Beatrice, Natrel
Chile: Bresler, Panda
France: Miko
India: Kwality Ices
USA: Breyers
1994
Colombia: Helados La Fuente
Venezuela: Helados Tio Rico
1995
Belgium: Mio
France: Miko
Israel: Strauss (49%)
The Netherlands: Den Hertog
1997
Argentina: Monthelado
Brazil: Kibon
Mexico: Helados Holanda

2. Unilever 'greenfield' ice cream operations

Greenfield operations before 1987 were Ola (Belgium, 1955), Wall's Nigeria (1954), Wall's South Africa (1957), Ola (Netherlands, 1960).

1988
Greece: Algida
1989
Thailand: Wall's
1990
Turkey: Algida
1991
Hungary: Algida
1992
Czech Republic: Algida
Indonesia: Wall's
1993
India: Kwality Wall's
1994
Bahrain: Wall's
China: Wall's
Pakistan: Wall's
Saudi Arabia: Wall's
1996
El Salvador: Wall's
Guatemala: Wall's
1997
Sri Lanka: Wall's
Vietnam: Wall's
1998
Russia: Algida

Gerrit Klijnstra, reached agreement with Nestlé chairman Pierre Liotard-Vogt in October 1969 that the two companies' respective ice cream and frozen foods activities in Germany, Austria and Italy would be brought together within a joint holding company, with effect from 1 January 1970. Unilever had 75% of the shares in the new company and Nestlé 25%. Later, this 25% interest was also acquired by Unilever in Germany and Austria.
• This deal was of great strategic importance to Unilever.[22] For more than two decades there was no competition from Nestlé in the three countries. It was 23 years before the Swiss group entered the Italian market through its 1993 purchase of Italgel and its Motta ice cream brand; while in 1994 its acquisition of the Warncke ice cream business brought about its return to the German market (see chapter 12). These moves reflected Nestlé's new policy, adopted in about 1990, of expanding its own ice cream activities. In 1960 Nestlé had only one ice cream factory, in France.[23] The 1962 Jopa acquisition was later sold. It was not until 1977 that Nestlé bought Camy in Spain (see chapter 17). In 1988 Nestlé entered the American ice cream market by purchasing the Carnation dairy and ice cream company (see chapter 6). From then on, its expansion was rapid. Between 1990 and 1997 Nestlé took control of some 20 ice cream businesses worldwide, as well as establishing several new ice cream operations of its own. In consequence, the group became the world's number two ice cream producer after Unilever.
• Following the agreement with Nestlé in 1969, Unilever decided that its presence in the markets of Europe, the United States and Australia should be followed up by entry into the Latin American ice cream market.

In 1973 the Alnasa ice cream business in Brazil was bought and in 1981 the group acquired a share in Laponia, an Argentinian ice cream firm. Neither initiative lived up to expectations. In Brazil, competition from Kibon (with a market share of around 76%) was severe (see chapter 18) and it proved very difficult for Unilever to achieve profitability. After many years of losses, the group eventually sold its interest in Alnasa in 1990. By this time, it had pulled out of Argentina, South Africa, New Zealand and Canada.
• Because of these failures, the members of Unilever's Overseas Committee – responsible for operations outside Europe and the US – were wary when they received proposals from the ice cream group for setting up a greenfield ice cream operation in Thailand. In the end, however, the plans were approved and in 1989 Unilever's first new ice cream factory in Asia was opened near Bangkok, with great success (see chapter 19).

The changing trade

• In Western Europe during the 1970s the market for take-home ice cream underwent considerable change owing to the growth of powerful supermarket chains, which had begun to sell their own-label brands. Manufacturers of branded ice cream found it increasingly difficult to maintain market share. In France, this difficulty was demonstrated by the price and quality differentials of the one-litre packs of ice cream of the various manufacturers, which had become increasingly narrow. The year 1978 saw the introduction of a new premium dessert ice cream under the name Carte d'Or (The golden menu).

¶ When employees of Unilever paid a visit to the Spica ice cream factory in Naples in May 1962, there was one product that particularly caught their eye. 'One of their successful lines is an ice cream in a cone made from pastry and covered with chocolate and pieces of nut', wrote the engineer J. Loopuyt in a report on the visit. 'The surprising thing is that the wafer remains crispy even after lengthier storage. This is achieved because they dip the dough in a mixture of oil, chocolate and sugar. The competitors in Italy have not yet succeeded in imitating this; we have assured ourselves of that fact. The cornets are made in a bakery department in the factory.'[1] What Loopuyt was describing was the Cornetto, now known the world over and for many decades the flagship product of Unilever's ice cream businesses. But in 1962 all that was still in the future. Unilever had just bought 48% of the shares in Spica (it acquired full ownership in 1964) and the advance of the Cornetto product had not yet begun. The Cornetto ice cream's origin can be traced to the summer of 1959, when Spica commenced production using a couple of second-hand machines and 'with scarcely any technical know-how of the specific keeping problems relating to this product'.[2] At that time Spica had two house brands: the more expensive, more up-market Algida and the cheaper Soave. The Soave ice creams were made with vegetable fat; Algida ice cream was prepared with cream and milk. The first Cornetto ice creams were put on the market under the Soave brand name and were sold for

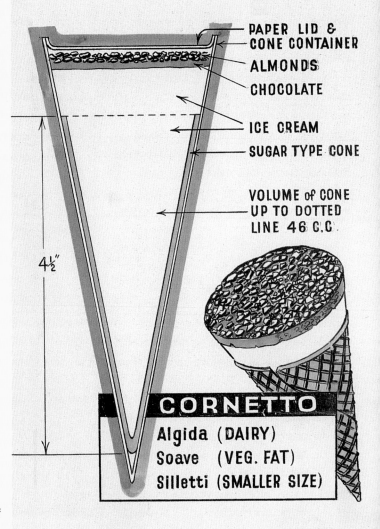

PAPER LID & CONE CONTAINER
ALMONDS
CHOCOLATE
ICE CREAM
SUGAR TYPE CONE
VOLUME of CONE UP TO DOTTED LINE 46 C.C

4½"

CORNETTO
Algida (DAIRY)
Soave (VEG. FAT)
Silletti (SMALLER SIZE)

606: Drawing of the first Cornetto from a 1963 Unilever technical report. In those days the Cornetto contained 46 cc of ice cream up to the rim of the cone, plus 6 gms of chocolate, 3 gms of almonds and 3 gms of cone crumbs. Today it is 125 cc by total volume.

100 lire. They were not advertised. The reason for launching the ice cream under the Soave brand was that Spica wanted first to find out how well the cone would keep. If that proved to be a disappointment, then the Algida brand's reputation

for quality would not be compromised.[3] At the beginning of 1960, however, it became clear that the Cornetto brand was destined to be a big hit. The name was registered as a trademark and Spica invested in new machines obtained from the American company Big Drum, which specialised in machinery of this type (see also chapter 5).

In 1962 Spica decided to sell the Cornetto product under its Algida house brand. Although the more expensive mix of cream and milk was used from that moment on, the price remained the same, meaning margins for retailers were lower. However, the product was now supported by a substantial advertising spend. The Algida Cornetto proved a great favourite with consumers: in the autumn of 1962 the volume of Cornetto ice cream sold already represented 19% of Spica's total sales.[4]

Unilever immediately took steps to replicate this success elsewhere in the world. In September 1962 Spica in Naples hosted a conference of Unilever ice cream directors and the decision was taken to launch the Cornetto brand in other countries. This happened in Belgium, the Netherlands and Germany in 1963; the United Kingdom followed in 1964.

Before the roll-out, however, some problems still needed resolving. In the spring of 1963 Unilever engineers made an extensive study of all aspects of the production process in the Naples factory: the composition of the dough, the type of machines in use, the packaging, the costs and the keeping properties of the cones. Keepability was of especial importance and had been substantially improved by spraying the inside surface of the cone with a mixture of coconut oil and chocolate. This insulating coating served to prevent the ice cream from coming into contact with the cone and softening it; according to a 1963 report, Spica claimed that this technique kept the ice creams fresh for three weeks.[5] In practice, however, that was not always the case, a flaw that was to undermine the launch of the Cornetto brand in the UK. The stock turnover rate for ice cream was much lower in the UK than in Italy and because of the product's relatively short keeping time, it proved difficult to sell there. Technical people from Unilever's ice cream companies and research centres studied this problem intensively for many years. As time went by, they succeeded in radically improving the production process, the packaging and the storage methods. As a result, the product will today keep for at least 30, and in some countries over 40 days. Although much of the success of the Cornetto brand can be attributed to these improvements, its profitability has also depended on other factors, such as sophisticated marketing and effective distribution. Several flavour variants were put on the market and a wider variety of toppings was introduced. New formats were launched under brand names such as Super Cornetto and Giant Cone. In most Unilever ice cream companies the Cornetto brand today stands proudly at the top of the price list for impulse ice creams.

607: Cornetto Classic.

The concept behind this range was that the taste had to be pure and unadulterated ('Le goût à l'état pur') (see box story, chapter 16). Available in more than 30 flavours, Carte d'Or was outstandingly successful.

• Across the English Channel, the problem was similar, but the solution entirely different. A team at Gloucester were working on ice cream versions of various classic desserts. One version, in which they patiently sprayed chocolate between thin layers of ice cream, created what would become the ice cream dessert sensation of the 1980s and the brand which did more to improve ice cream profitability for Unilever than any other to date. Viennetta ice cream gâteau, launched in the UK in 1982 (see box on p. 618), proved to be a outstanding performer.

609: Calippo, first marketed in 1982.

search for the appropriate products and at the beginning of the 1980s the business developed a new variant of the Nogger product, a large-sized vanilla ice cream with a coating of chocolate. As a response to the new market situation, however, it was unspectacular.

• In that same period a revolution was taking place in the American ice cream market. In 1984 Dove, a small company in Chicago, launched a generously sized vanilla ice cream enveloped in a thick layer of pure chocolate. It retailed for the hefty price of $1 and it caught on. Even more successful was a similar ice cream that was launched on the market just under two years later by Häagen Dazs (see chapter 6). Both these high-quality impulse ice creams were a successful response to the changes that were taking place in the market.

The adult 'baby boomers' had developed a taste for 'affordable luxury' and the new premium ice creams met that need.

A market had arisen consisting of young, high-earning adults who had grown up with ices on a stick and who now had money to spare for a quality ice cream.

The changing consumer

• During the 1970s, a significant change in European demographics had major consequences for the ice cream industry. Birth rates were in decline, while the number of older people was growing. The population, in other words, was 'greying' – and nowhere was that trend felt more keenly than in Germany. For ice cream manufacturers like Langnese this demographic shift had far-reaching repercussions, as the lucrative market for impulse ices had become static. The message was clear: more new and appealing ices had to be introduced for adults. Langnese diligently began to

608: Advertisement for the Spider-Man children's ice. New technology made it possible to produce popular comic strip creations in the shape of an ice cream. The superhero Spider-Man was created in 1962 by Stan Lee (script) and Steve Ditko (art) for Marvel Universe.

Mars enters the ice cream market

• The 1986 purchase by the confectionery giant Mars Ltd. of the producer of the highly successful Dove bar heralded a radical shift in the global ice cream market.

¶ In December 1980 Kevin Hillman, Product Development Manager at Wall's Ice Cream, gave his wife a cookery book for Christmas. A few weeks later, as he was looking through it one evening, his attention was caught by an illustration of the time-honoured French recipe for

to travel between the dream and its realisation. Not one of the world's ice cream machines was capable of producing anything that would come close to Kevin Hillman's idea. The development team at Wall's set to work. In the Wall's factory complex in Gloucester a small trial plant was built and the experimenting started.

an artisanal product, the fourth, eighth and topmost layers were applied in distinctive waves[2] for which protection had been obtained as a trademark. The Dutch Court of Appeal in The Hague described the characteristic wavy pattern as the 'Frans Hals' collar, a reference to the sartorial style of the local dignitaries portrayed in the seventeenth

millefeuille **cake.**[1]
Hillman suddenly saw not a 'thousand thin leaves' of puff pastry filled with cream and jam, but a cake consisting of

610: Pack of a Viennetta ice cream gâteau. Viennetta first came on the market in 1982.

layers of ice cream alternated with strata of chocolate. His flash of inspiration was to result in one of the major innovations in the modern ice cream industry: the Viennetta ice cream gâteau.
But there was still a long road

A suitable size for the gâteau, it was decided, would be 600 cc and it should consist of twelve layers of vanilla ice cream, about three millimetres thick, interleaved with paper-thin layers of chocolate. To make the overall appearance that of

century paintings of the well-known Dutch painter.[3]
A decisive factor in developing the right production technology was the construction of nozzles of the correct dimensions to create the unique interleaving. The ice cream mix was

extruded through thin nozzles onto a polystyrene tray carried by a conveyor belt. Twelve such nozzles were spaced alongside each other, one for each layer of ice cream. The wavy layers were formed by several of the nozzles extruding at a slightly higher speed, thereby creating a corrugated profile in those layers. In between the nozzles spray jets applied to each layer of ice cream a wafer-thin layer of chocolate sufficient to achieve the unique crackling texture. This was the key to the ultimate quality of the Viennetta product.[4]

After the topmost layer of chocolate had been applied by the final spray jet and the product had been sliced into gâteau-sized pieces, these were transported into the freezer tunnel. When the gâteaux emerged from the tunnel, they were then wrapped and boxed. This technique was based on successful packaging methods already being applied by Unilever's Langnese ice cream business in Germany.[5] A patent application was submitted for the technology, the product design was registered as unique and in 1982 the first Viennetta products went on the UK market as a Christmas speciality. Sales expectations were modest – two million portions, or around one million litres of ice cream – but the product met with a wildly enthusiastic reception and was continued as a year-round brand.

In 1983 Viennetta was introduced in Germany. In that year some 20 million Viennettas were sold in Belgium and Germany combined.

Competitors tried in vain to copy the 'piece of lace', as the Belgian Unilever ice cream company Ola described the gâteau in an advertisement, and Unilever fought dozens of legal battles to protect its intellectual properties. Viennetta's success proved no flash in the pan. It was rolled out around the world, becoming a major success in most markets. New flavours were introduced and the manufacturing technology was further refined. Viennetta developed into an international brand that captured a key position in the market for dessert ice cream.[6]

The financially strong, family-owned Mars business immediately set about tackling things in a big way. To serve the European market the company built an ultra-modern ice cream plant in Steinburg near Strasbourg and, after two years of preparations, an ice cream based on the Mars Bar was rolled out simultaneously in sixteen countries in 1989. The new product was sold through

611: La Sorbetteria di Ranieri, introduced in 1986.

supermarkets, vending machines, shops and filling stations, where Mars installed its own freezer cabinets.

• The introduction was an extraordinary success. According to some reports, the business acquired an 18% share of the Western European impulse ice cream market within seven months.[24] Mars had thus instantly put itself on the world map of ice cream producers. This success was due to a combination of factors. In the first place, it was a new type of high-quality ice cream which initially could not be matched by similar products from competitors. In addition, there was enormous public awareness of Mars brand names and the company

possessed great international expertise in the marketing of impulse products and in staging successful advertising campaigns. Mars was thus able to command premium prices in the impulse sector. Its strategy was not based on a wide portfolio of impulse ices and take-home packs of ice cream geared to local market needs, as was the case with Unilever. Mars did the same thing with ice cream as it had long done with its 'sweet' snacks: it concentrated on a limited number of top products and gave them maximum promotion as individual brands.

• As a leading buyer of cocoa, Mars also had the advantage of being able to negotiate good prices on the world market. Not only did the volume of cocoa it bought now increase, but its purchases were also spread more evenly: in summer the cocoa was mainly used in ice creams and in winter in Mars Bars and the like. On top of that there were economies of scale to be exploited in Europe, following the evolution of the EEC into the European Union. Lastly, there was the tight organisation of the closed family business, characterised from the outset by strong central management.

• Mars Ltd. had originated from a sweets factory that had been set up in 1923 by Frank C. Mars in the US state of Minnesota. He had great success with a new product, Milky Way, a sweet aerated bar enveloped in milk chocolate. In the early 1930s Forrest E. Mars, the founder's son, went to the UK where he set up a subsidiary company and introduced the Mars Bar, the product which formed the basis for the further expansion of the business. After the Second World War Mars set up additional factories in Belgium, the Netherlands and Germany. With the help of much advertising and high-quality marketing, the business grew into one of the world's biggest confectionery manufacturers, with an estimated turnover in 1996 of $13 billion.[25]

• After its ice cream début in 1989, Mars expanded its range each year. It took good care to ensure that each target group – young and older children, young and older adults – were able to choose from products that fitted their needs. In developing new products the concept of the first Mars ice cream was elaborated further by seeking links with other popular chocolate bars. For instance, an ice cream cone was marketed with a topping of M & M's and a vanilla ice cream with chocolate and coconut was introduced under the Bounty name.

Magnum – a star is born

• The threat posed to both Unilever and Nestlé by the European entry of Mars was sufficiently worrying to warrant action. Unilever set up one of its first international strategic working groups to develop a response and, if possible, turn the challenge to advantage. Mars' entry depended upon two factors – leveraging its strong chocolate brands by presenting ice cream versions of them; and its use of real chocolate. A Unilever working group drew up an innovation programme and a range of ice cream products, also using real chocolate, was introduced that included Sky, with an aerated chocolate centre, and Winner, a bar with peanuts, caramel and a chocolate enrobing. Both these products

were launched widely throughout Europe, but without lasting success. Two companies, Wall's in the UK and GB in Sweden, entered into licensing agreements with chocolate manufacturers Cadbury and Marabou respectively to produce ice cream versions of brands such as the Cadbury's Dairy Milk bar, Crunchie, Cadbury's Caramel and, in Sweden, the Daim bar and Daim cone.

• But the brand which swept the board in terms of instant and massive public acclaim came not from the chocolate confectionery category, but was inspired by the Dove and Häagen Dazs bar products in the USA. Success, as the saying goes, has many fathers. It was certainly true of Magnum ice cream, which was launched in several countries in different versions before the formula was perfected. Magnum ice cream was first launched by Wall's UK and Ola Belgium in 1987; both ice cream and couverture were conventional. In 1988, Sagit in Italy launched a product, somewhat closer

612: Magnum Classic, which first went on sale in 1989.

to the eventual version, using high quality real chocolate, dairy vanilla ice cream and even packaged in a box, like the Dove and Häagen Dazs ice cream products in the US. Sagit called the product not Magnum, but Frac (Italian for a dinner jacket or tuxedo). None of these products was very successful.

• In Germany, meanwhile, the Langnese impulse marketing group, headed by Gino Coronato, was working on a premium version of its highly successful brand, Nogger.

After a series of iterative tests, the new pro-duct emerged – a thick, rounded, oval slice of ice cream, of very high quality, dipped in pure Belgian chocolate and presented on the paddle-shaped stick used by Häagen Dazs. The chocolate even came from the same supplier as Häagen Dazs' – Callebaut, then a subsidiary of Jacob Suchard. Hans Eggerst-edt, Unilever's Frozen Products Coordinator, had agreed the choco-late development project personally with Klaus Jacob. The development team was led by Gert Debevere of Ola in Belgium and Gordon Hall at Langnese and initially six chocolate couverture recipes were developed by Callebaut for Unilever's exclusive use.

• The brand name Magnum, originally used by Wall's for a strawberry ice cream 30 years before[26], was proposed in Germany as a alterna-tive to Nogger. Consumer research suggested that the name Nogger would lower quality expec-tations[27]. The positive and negative associations of Magnum ice cream were thoroughly debated: the echoes of size, opulence and luxury from the champagne connection versus the resonances from the gun, the TV detective series – and the fact that in the US the name was already in use for a brand of condom. The decision was

613: Magnum Clas-sic, which first went on sale in 1989.

made to proceed with the name Magnum and the chocolate working group initiated a worldwide trademark search, which luckily – and perhaps surprisingly – threw up few problems.

• In the meantime, process development progressed in Denmark, led by Mogens Vigh Larsen, the technical director of Unilever's subsidiairy Frisko. The blocks of vanilla ice cream were extruded onto a conveyor belt, had their sticks inserted, were dipped in a choco-late bath and were then packed and frozen. The right temperatures for ice cream and choco-late mix, the precise duration for dipping the ice cream in the choco-late, all had to be calcu-lated and tested.

• At the end of 1988 Lang-nese's marketing director, Leo Lakke, gave the starting signal for production of the new ice cream. In January 1989 it was marketed under the name Magnum at a price of DM2, which for Europe in those days was an unprecedentedly high price. Never-theless, the planned stocks were sold out within six weeks, encouraged by glorious weather, and demand for the new ice cream kept on growing throughout the year. Magnum products helped Langnese to a record profit for 1989. Ironically, it was the Mars threat that had triggered one of Unilever's greatest ice cream successes.

That day in autumn 1945, the cheese seller on the market in Tel Aviv had done a good day's trade, but his takings were still not enough to pay his supplier in cash. The supplier was Strauss Ltd., a small dairy company from Nahariya, a coastal town in the north of Israel. Hilda Strauss, who came to collect the money, noticed that the cheese trader had an old ice cream machine standing in a corner. The deal was soon done. Hilda rented a small truck and arrived home with an ice cream machine instead of money. With this spontaneous act she laid the basis for what was to become Israel's leading ice cream business.[1]

Hilda Strauss and her husband, Richard, had fled Germany in 1936 and travelled to the Promised Land. After a while the couple settled in Nahariya and started a farming business there. Unlike the farmers in the neighbourhood, they decided not only to grow cereal crops and vegetables but also to go in for dairy products. They built a barn, bought a

614: The Strauss ice cream factory in Nahariya, Israel, about 1955.

couple of cows and began producing milk and cheese. Little by little they built up their business, competing with the country's largest dairy company, Tnuvna, a cooperative that had been set up in 1927. Before Hilda arrived home with her ice cream making machine in 1945, she had already tried to persuade her husband to make ice cream from the milk surpluses in the summer, as the Americans did. But he would hear nothing of it.

615: Manufacturing ice cream cones at Strauss in the 1960s.

Now, however, he was faced with a fait accompli. Hilda set to work and soon the Strausses were selling ice cream to Nahariya's coffee shops. The enterprise was a success and some time later Strauss ice cream was also on sale in Haifa through a concessionaire. In the meantime Richard, too, had become convinced of the opportunities that ice cream offered and he decided to buy a bigger, modern ice cream machine.

Other ice cream manufacturers in Israel made similar investments in the early 1950s. In August 1953, the firm of Matokar Ltd. opened a modern ice cream factory in Tel Aviv equipped with American machines and soon its ice lollies, Kartiv (Hebrew for 'cold and good') and Cosatta, were known throughout Israel.[2] The best-known name in ice lollies was Artik, an ice cream factory which had been set up by Belgian immigrants and which had concluded a know-how agreement with Max Willick's Artic ice cream business in their home country

(see chapter 13). In the sub-tropical climate of Israel, sales of Artik's water-ices were fast and furious. Another success-ful ice cream company was Whitman Ice Cream Ltd. And if you wanted to enjoy an ice cream in Jerusalem, the place to be was the Kapulsky coffee shop of Fridle and Bracha Feldman.[3] In the 1950s Mr and Mrs Strauss went to visit family in New York and again it was Hilda who took the initiative to

616: Strauss ice cream
shop in Nahariya, about 1955.

modernise the business further. Accompanied by her American cousin, she shopped around and bought a batch of second-hand ice moulds for the manufacture of ice lollies. From that time on, Strauss was a player in the ice lollies market.

In 1962 the Strauss ice cream department moved to a new location in Akko. Production still involved much manual work. The moulds for the ice lollies, for instance, were put in the brine baths by hand, baths whose temperature was approximately -15°C. It was only during the 1970s that the first fully automatic, rotating ice lolly machine was installed. By that time Strauss had expanded to become a large, national dairy and ice cream company and a new generation, Michael and Raya Strauss, had taken over the helm. More than 70% of the turnover was still achieved from sales of dairy products: milk, yoghurt and soft cheeses. Later, the company also opened a department for special salads and took a stake in a coffee business. In 1978 Strauss bought its competitor Whitman and became the country's biggest ice cream manufacturer. The factory was modernised and over the years more and more new products were put on the market.

The Israelis have proved to be enthusiastic ice cream eaters. At 8.5 litres per capita in 1997, they stood high in the ranking of ice cream consuming nations. More than five litres of this figure is represented by impulse ices, making Israel the world leader for impulse consumption, well ahead of the 3.8 litres eaten by the Swedes. At the end of 1993 Unilever began talks with Michael Strauss about the possible acquisition of his company's ice cream activities. Two years later they reached agreement: the ice cream division was split off from the other activities and Unilever became the owner of 49% of Strauss Ice Cream Ltd.

'Me and my Magnum'

• The Århus factory was operating at full stretch, but was scarcely able to keep up with demand. In 1992 Frisko produced 224 million Magnum ice creams, of which 209 million were for export. By that time Magnum ice cream had been introduced in almost all Western European countries and in Australia and was also now being produced in factories in Baasrode (Belgium), Heppenheim (Germany) and Sydney. The results were spectacular. Between 1989 and 1993 sales climbed from just under 20 million to some 240 million a year.[28] This was reminiscent of the early 1920s when America fell under the spell of the first industrially produced ice novelties – the Eskimo Pie, Popsicle and Good Humor Ice Cream Sucker (see chapter 5).

617:
Pack of Magnum After Dinner ice creams. This type of product is aimed at stimulating ice cream sales during the winter.

• In its early years, Magnum ice cream had more or less sold itself, but, if its success was to be prolonged, good advertising was needed to turn Magnum into a powerful international brand. Again, success came after some experimentation. Campaigns were developed in Denmark and Germany, which were partially successful, but it was not until 1993 that a campaign devised by Barry Day, creative consultant with the Lintas Worldwide advertising agency, in association with Michael Bronsten, the Unilever ice cream advertising specialist, and Klaus Rabbel, Langnese's new marketing director, that Magnum took off. The secret of the campaign lay in its free-and-easy expression of the hedonistic, individual feelings of pleasure that eating a Magnum was said to induce.

• In 1991 Faith Popcorn, the American trend guru, published her Popcorn Report, in which she defined as a key nineties trend the all-too-human wish for immediate and intense gratification. This 'indulgence of the senses' was itself connected to a powerful desire for value for money,[29] while a third trend, noted Popcorn, was a desire to return to naturalness and simplicity. Magnum ice cream, made from pure ingredients and good value for money, fitted the bill perfectly. The 'Me and my Magnum' campaign formed the basis for a series of sophisticated TV commercials in which men and women described how they enjoyed their Magnum ice cream: 'It's like ordering the biggest lobster', 'jumping on a cloud', 'sliding between silk sheets' or 'buying black lingerie'.[30] These were real statements from consumers, mostly spoken by the consumers themselves.[31] A Magnum ice cream was, as Barry Day put it, 'a licence to indulge'.[32]

• Identical commercials and advertising material were produced for nearly all countries. Although the films were re-shot for some markets using local actors, the concept was identical. Only for important cultural reasons did the campaign vary. Thus for Western countries posters showed a young woman biting into a Magnum ice cream. For the Islamic world a woman was shown taking a Magnum ice cream out of its wrapper, as the consumption of products is not permitted in advertisements.[33]

• The campaign proved highly effective. During the period when the TV commercial was screened in Sweden, for example, the share of Magnum ice cream in GB's sales market increased from about 20% to almost 50%.[34] Within Unilever the success of the Magnum product meant a substantial reinforcement of the ice cream product group's position and a major contribution to the growing profits of the various ice cream companies. Breaking all the rules, Unilever's most expensive impulse ice cream had become by far its biggest selling brand, with worldwide sales in 1995 of over $1 billion.

Unilever's ice cream activities are given star status

• In the 1989-1992 period the Unilever Group undertook another review of its portfolio of businesses. The outcome of this review was that some businesses, including shipping and chemicals, were disposed of, enabling Unilever to focus on its core activities. The ice cream category emerged as one of seven 'starred' categories 'with clear opportunity for profitable leadership worldwide'.[35] Organisation was reviewed and 'Innovation Centres' were set up for the various product categories (take-home ice cream, impulse ices for children and younger people, impulse ices for adults). International Brand Managers were appointed to handle the global brands such as Viennetta and Magnum.

• Considerable investments were also made in new manufacturing facilities and in the purchase of strategic ice cream businesses. In 1993 the prominent Breyers brand was acquired in the United States (see chapter 6). In 1995 Kwality Ices in India became 51% Unilever-owned and a 49% stake was taken in Strauss Ice Cream Ltd. in Israel (see box on p. 623). In the same year the French market leader, Miko, a company that Unilever had long been seeking to buy, was also acquired (see chapter 16).

• There was a series of takeovers in Latin American countries, too, the highlight being the 1997 acquisition of the Brazilian ice cream company Kibon (see chapter 19); and during the same period new ice cream factories were built in Vietnam, China, Saudi Arabia, India, Pakistan, Venezuela, Sri Lanka and Indonesia.

• In the space of 40 years Unilever's ice cream activities had experienced a meteoric development. Back in 1957 ice cream sales had represented a mere 2% of the group's total turnover of £738 million.[36] In 1996 the ice cream product group together with beverages (mainly tea sold through Lipton International Ltd.) achieved a combined turnover of £4.7 billion, or around 14% of a total turnover of £33.5 billion.[37] And that meant that Unilever, more than 60 years after the Special Committee's expansion proposal in 1932, was the clear leader in the world ice cream market, with sales in over 90 countries across six continents.

Licks, Sticks & Bricks

A WORLD HISTORY OF ICE CREAM

The evolution of ice cream: a summary

"PUNCH" (SUMMER NUMBER), MAY 25, 1936

STOP ME AND BUY ONE

The Story of Frozen James.

What a charming boy was James !
Good at lessons, good at games,
Courteous to aunts and others,
Patient with his younger brothers . . .
Yet this almost perfect lad
One unholy passion had :
He would think and talk and dream
All day long about ice-cream.

In the middle of the morning
First would come the tinkled warning ;
Out he'd rush and gobble up
"Block" and "cornet," "brick" and "cup."
Then between his lunch and tea
He'd dispose of two or three,
And before the day was done
Cram in yet another one.
Foolish child ! This chilly diet
Caused his parents much disquiet.
"James," they said with bated breath,
"Mark our words—you'll freeze to death."

Parents' warnings (some have found)
Aren't so silly as they sound.
James, ignoring their advice,
One fine day was turned to ice.
What a lamentable plight !
Half was pink and half was white,
While, where fingers should have been,
Icicles were plainly seen.
"Will the wretched boy expire ?
Quickly—we must light a fire !
Henry, fetch some sticks and straw !"
Just in time his parents saw
James at last begin to thaw.

Now once more he's safe and warm,
Quite restored to human form ;
But somehow he doesn't seem
Half so partial to ice-cream.   JAN

The history of ice cream is one of centuries of evolution during which it developed from a luxury for the few into a treat for the masses. Unlike television, the vacuum cleaner or margarine, ice cream does not have an inventor or a clear date of birth. And yet if it is defined as a frozen product that can be prepared independently of the climate, its beginnings can be traced to when Renaissance scholars mastered the process of freezing. They discovered that, if they placed a pewter jug containing a mixture of water, sugar and fruit juice in a container filled with finely crushed ice and salt, its contents could be frozen into water-ice. Not long after that, the mix was enriched with cream and eggs... and ice cream was born.

• Ice cream is thus not a delicacy that was enjoyed by the emperor Nero, nor is it an invention brought back by Marco Polo from China in about 1295.[1] It is the result of a lengthy process that was triggered by man's need for cooling refreshment in warm climes, a process that was speeded up by the emergence of modern science during the Renaissance in northern Italy. It was the outcome of a prolonged period of experimentation. The publications by the Italian scholar Zimara in 1530 and by the Spanish physician Blas Villafranca in 1550 mark the end of this experimental phase of the freezing process.

• That techniques were now available for making ice cream was not in itself a guarantee of its future success. The achievements of the sixteenth century were just the beginning of a popularisation that was to take hundreds of years. In the seventeenth century Europe was still getting to know ice cream, as it was cocoa, coffee and tea.[2] Unlike those beverages, however, ices were

619: Picture postcard, UK, circa 1900. By now eating ice cream was so popular that it became the subject of a whole range of humorous picture postcards.

– except in Mexico – unknown on other continents at that time. Its introduction in Europe was chiefly the work of a small group of entrepreneurs, notably the French chef Audiger who had learnt how to make water-ices in Naples. Thanks to Audiger's perseverance, the French court of Louis XIV had its first taste of water-ice in about 1662. With the French court setting the pace in matters of taste and fashion in Europe, ices became familiar to a small but growing group of devotees, principally the nobility and members of the haute bourgeoisie. They were wealthy enough to construct ice cellars to store the winter harvest of natural ice and to afford costly ingredients like sugar. And if they preferred to eat out, they could go and enjoy sorbetto in one of the many coffee houses that were emerging in Europe.[3]

618: The story of 'Frozen James', a poem published in Punch, May 1936. James ate so much ice cream that he froze and his parents had to thaw him out over a fire.

• Ices in the seventeenth century were mainly water-ices. According to their charter of 1676, the 250 members of the Parisian guild of limonadiers and marchands d'eau de vie sold glaces de fruits et de fleurs (ices of fruits and flowers), but not crèmes glacées, as ice creams are called in France. The first French recipes for ices published in 1692 describe only the preparation of water-ices. Another booklet, published in the same year in Naples, does however include ice recipes employing milk and cream; and during the first half of the eighteenth century growing numbers of cookery books containing ice recipes were published in France and Great Britain (and sometimes translated into German), thus helping to popularise the eating of ices.

620: Card advertising an ice cream machine made by American Machine Co., Philadelphia.

Ices become accepted

• Reliable data on consumption are not available, but it seems fair to say that, mid-way through the eighteenth century, ices became accepted in France ('acceptance' being here defined as the stage at which around 10% of the population use a product[4]). There are a number of significant pieces of evidence to support this belief. The inclusion of a treatise on ices in the Encyclopédie of Diderot and d'Alembert in 1754 is one such indication. Another is that in the same period the Sèvres porcelain factory began producing ice cream cups and special coolers for ice cream as part of extensive dessert services. Pottery and china factories throughout Europe followed the example of Sèvres. This widespread and high volume production of tableware shows how a dessert culture in which ices played a prominent role developed amongst the élite throughout Europe – from St. Petersburg to Parma and from Paris to Copenhagen – in the second half of the eighteenth century. Further support is offered by the advent of ice moulds which, according to illustrations in Le Cannaméliste in 1751, were then widely available. Sources to corroborate this are few and far between, but include the letter that Lady Mary Wortley Montagu sent in 1716 from Vienna to friends in England with the news that ices were eaten in that city in both summer and winter.

• The introduction and acceptance of ices took place not only in Europe but, in an important parallel development, in the Spanish colony of Mexico. The Spaniards brought their knowledge of the freezing process to Mexico City, where snow and ice were brought down from the peaks of nearby volcanoes, as they had been from their own Sierra Nevada and elsewhere in Europe since ancient times. When crushed and mixed with salt, they supplied the desired freezing medium. At an early date, therefore, water-ice, and possibly also the ice cream mantecado, became known in Mexico City. However, the taxes levied on snow were to hamper the spread of ice cream in Mexico until their abolition following the country's winning of independence in 1821.

From acceptance to habit

• For the thirteen year-old Natasha Orlov in Tolstoy's novel War and Peace (1866) ice cream was still a rare treat. And even though the traveller through Russia, Georg Johann Kohl, noted in 1841 that the streets of St. Petersburg, Moscow and Odessa were filled with ice cream sellers in the summer, ice cream long remained that special treat, and not only in Russia.

• In cities like London, Paris, New York and Philadelphia, however, the situation was different. There, the number of suppliers of ice cream grew apace during the nineteenth century, spurred on by the arrival of Italian immigrants. Censuses show that during the last quarter of the century there was an enormous increase in street sales of ice cream, indicating the start of the 'adoption' stage in Europe and the United States. Ice cream carts became a familiar sight on the streets of all the major cities.

• New machines and technical advances speeded up the process of popularisation, particularly in the USA. An important milestone was the invention of the first ice cream making machine by the American Nancy Johnson in 1843. Subsequently numerous machines, both large and small, were devised that brought improvements in production and distribution: for example, the steam-powered machine harvesting ice from the lakes of North America (see ill. on p. 111). Other nineteenth century breakthroughs included condensed milk, milk powder and artificial flavourings such as vanillin, the vanilla substitute.

• Railways facilitated the transport in bulk of ingredients like milk and sugar over great

On the Sands at Blackpool.   Here you are Two flavers A'Penny.

621: Picture postcard of Blackpool, UK, circa 1905. Tens of thousands from the industrial cities of Liverpool and Manchester enjoyed the beach and an ice cream in the summer. Blackpool is still Britain's premier seaside resort.

distances. Sugar came from refineries, now powered by steam. The shipping of ice harvested in North America or Norway to European ports, or further afield to cities like Rio de Janeiro or Bombay, became a huge trade. Ice cream imported from Boston was on sale in Colombo in 1858.

• After about 1870 freezers that operated on ammonia also came into service, which meant that blocks of ice could be produced industrially. Ice cream makers increasingly made use of ice manufactured in this way and became less and less dependent on ice harvests.

• Thirty years later, ammonia compressors were adopted for the first time in ice cream freezing machines. Instead of using ice and salt to freeze the ice cream mix, brine, cooled by the compressors, circulated around containers holding the mix. This new freezing technique was the beginning of a much more efficient method of production. Refinements to this type of freezer followed one another in quick succession, notably the development of the continuous freezer by the American Clarence Vogt in 1927. From 1899 onwards, the homogeniser brought a great improvement in the quality of ice cream, making it possible to replace fresh cream with ingredients like milk powder or condensed milk that were less susceptible to spoilage.

622: Picture postcard, UK, circa 1905.

The birth of an ice cream industry

• The first ice cream factories, set up in the second half of the nineteenth century in the United States, signalled the start of rapid growth in that country's ice cream industry. The formation of trade associations from 1900 onwards in various American states speeded up the professionalisation of the still young ice cream sector. Serious attention was devoted to hygiene, which had long been the Achilles' heel of ice cream making. A growing understanding of how bacteria develop in ice cream and the development of new types of machines considerably improved the hygienic quality of ice cream, a key factor in the gaining of mass acceptance. Pasteurisation of milk was made mandatory state by state. Industrial quality standards were introduced, courses on ice cream making were organised and, for the first time, data about the production and consumption of ice cream were systematically compiled. This data illuminates the progress of the popularisation of ice cream: between 1906 and 1920 production in the United States grew from some 200 million litres to 560 million litres, an average annual growth rate of 12.8%. Part of this growth can be ascribed to the industrial production of ice cream cones and wafers, which started in the same period. Cones and wafers made it easier to sell ice cream in the street and brought an end to the unhygienic use of ice glasses.

• In the early 1920s the first novel types of ices, branded Eskimo Pie, and products on sticks branded Good Humor Sucker and

Popsicle, were introduced first in America and subsequently in Europe, bringing about a revolution in ice cream consumption.

The Eskimo Pie and the Good Humor Sucker combined the two most popular ingredients – chocolate and vanilla ice cream – in a single aluminium foil pack. This flavour combination was decisive for their success, while their pre-packaging, making them easier to handle than scooped cones, widened the availability of ice cream significantly, as well as providing reassurance on hygiene. 'Packaged ice cream is safe ice cream' was the slogan of the manufacturers of these new products.

• Distribution saw further dramatic improvements with the advent of dry ice and electrical refrigerators. New mass-communication media such as film and radio extended the reach of ice cream advertising. New outlets appeared, too. For pre-packaged ices the intervals in cinema shows were ideal sales opportunities and, as a result of growing car ownership, roadside restaurants mushroomed. More and more people had leisure time and took holidays. Ice cream began to form part of the everyday eating culture in the United States, whose ice cream industry became the example for the rest of the world. It was no longer 'Italian ice cream' but 'American ice cream' that was leading the way. Australia

A Chilly Silence.

623: Picture postcard, UK, circa 1900. The ice cream cart is fitted with curtains against the sun.

headed the following pack, having set up an ice cream industry prior to the First World War through the endeavour of pioneers such as J.P. Sennitt and Frederick Peters. In most countries industrialisation hastened the introduction of regulations for hygienic production methods. Since the reputation of vendors of artisanally made ice cream had long been poor on this score, manufacturers almost universally emphasised the 'clean' hygienic image of factory-made ice cream, often having their street sellers wear white uniforms implying a medical cleanliness.

• In Europe industrial production only commenced in the 1920s; at its forefront were dairy nations such as Great Britain, Ireland, Denmark and Germany, followed by Sweden, the Netherlands, Belgium, Austria, France and Spain. Energetic entrepreneurs with a vision of the future laid the foundations for a thriving European ice cream industry. They included Lauritz Jensen (Hellerup Is - Denmark), John M. Larsen (Premier Is - Denmark), the Hughes brothers (HB - Ireland), Cecil Rodd (Wall's Ice Cream - United Kingdom), Joseph Lyons (Lyons Maid - United Kingdom), Eric Hanner (Glace Bolaget - Sweden), Antoine Marziale (Mio - Belgium), Charles Gervais (Gervais - France), Louis Ortiz (Miko - France), Juan Rimblas (Frigo - Spain), Hinrich Ude (Germany), Hans Warncke

(Germany), Josef Pankofer (Germany) and Theo Schöller (Germany). Most of these had undertaken trips to America to visit the burgeoning ice cream industry there.

IT'S LOVELY HERE AT SUNSET.

624: Picture post-card, UK, circa 1900. As well as a term for ice cream, 'Hokey Pokey' had come to mean making love.

• Conspicuous by its absence from this list is any major name from Italy. Political circumstances – Mussolini's Fascist regime imposed restrictions on the production of ice cream – and the mass presence of arti-sanal ice cream makers put a brake on the establishment of ice cream factories. It was only after the Second World War that Alfred Wiesner and Angelo Motta were able to build up the companies of Spica Algida and Motta respectively. Wiesner did so by buying ice cream machines from the American Red Cross in Rome; Motta used funds made available under the Marshall Plan. The Ital-ians made up for lost time, however: in 1997, with a per capita consumption of 9.1 litres, they were amongst the biggest ice cream eaters in the world, after the Americans, Australians and Swedes. The Italians are also the world's second-highest spenders on ice cream, which accounts for 3.5% of their total spending on foods, just behind the Swedes with 3.6%.[5] Not that they have

dispensed with their traditions: approximate-ly 45% of the ice cream eaten in Italy is still supplied by artisanal ice cream makers.[6] Sorbets and water-ices remain more important in the Southern Euro-pean countries and Japan, where ice cream is regarded more as a refreshment product than a dairy-based food, which is how it is seen in Northern Europe and the USA.

• It is no coincidence that most European ice cream factories had their roots in the dairy industry. Apart from being used to make cheese and butter, milk surpluses were also used for ice cream in the summer. A second reason for these companies to set up ice cream factories was that for foods businesses whose products were mainly sold in the winter, ice cream ensured that they had work in the summer months as well. This was true of the Swedish chocolate factory A.B. Thule, the British sausage company T. Walls & Sons Ltd. and Motta, whose ice cream activities comple-mented the famous panettone cake it chiefly produced in the winter months.

• Nor was it only in 1920s Europe that an ice cream industry was established. In Shanghai and Manila ice cream factories based on the US model were also set up – not by local businessmen, but on American initiative. The ice cream only reached a small group of consumers, however, since, unlike in Europe, there was no local tradition of ice cream. Industrialisation in Asian countries was in its infancy and tradition stood in the way of the development of an ice cream culture. Milk, for example, occupied only a very small place in the daily diet as compared with Europe and the United States. In the rest of Asia ice cream making was all but non-existent – with one important exception.

• In Japan, too, ice cream factories using American machines were set up at the beginning of the 1920s. The circumstances, however, were very different from those in the rest of Asia. Unlike the Philippines, Indonesia, Vietnam and India, Japan had never been subjected to Western colonisation. The country had started rapidly to modernise of its own accord during the Meiji period (1868-1912), so that towards the end of the nineteenth century it already had a flourishing dairy industry and ice cream soon moved into its 'introductory' stage. And in the 1920s it was Japanese entrepreneurs, not Americans, who set up ice cream factories. They were able to sell their ice cream via an extensive, centuries-old trading network

THAT'S STOPPED YER, SO COME ON, LET'S HAVE ONE, BEFORE I GIVE THEE ONE!

STOP ME AND HAVE ONE

625: Picture postcard, UK, circa 1930.

comprising hundreds of thousands of small sales outlets. This latter characteristic was essential for the popularisation of ice cream in Japan and enabled it to achieve general acceptance much more quickly here than in the rest of Asia.

Ice cream in the modern era

• The mass production of ice cream; its bulk distribution by road, rail, ship and air (this last from as early as 1927 in both the USA and Australia) to ever more numerous sales outlets equipped with freezer cabinets; the growing use of advertising support - all these elements of what we now call the 'marketing mix' were coming together to make ice cream indispensable to the consumer. The growing use of radio, cinema and particularly television advertising with its intrusive power announced new products or new flavours for the coming season. Children clamouring for an ice cream on a summer's day, or wanting ice cream for dessert, became commonplace. Ice cream was no longer an exceptional and costly treat, but an affordable, everyday item. The process of assimilation was complete.[7]

• After the Second World War it was Sweden that set the pace in Europe - a country which, like the United States and Australia, experienced an enormous and immediate upswing in peacetime affluence. Domestic refrigerators and the emergence of supermarkets accelerated the assimilation of ice cream into popular culture, with large family packs of ice cream slipping easily from the supermarket freezer cabinet into the home freezer compartment in the refrigerator. America, Australia and Sweden are still amongst the most affluent nations, and have maintained their status as the pace-setters: in 1997 the inhabitants of these three countries ate the most ice cream in the world, with a per capita consumption of 20.4, 18.5 and 15.8 litres respectively.[8]

• In terms of ice cream production, the automation of the manufacture of ice-lollies on all continents was one of the most important events in post-war ice cream history. This revolution was made possible by the fully automated, rotating ice-lolly machine developed by the Danish machine manufacturer Gram in 1936. From the 1960s onwards the use of ever more sophisticated computers also brought automation to other areas, such as packaging, storage, distribution and accounting.

• Modern systems of production, the continuous development and introduction of new ices and the distribution infrastructure for frozen products all required substantial investment. Only large-scale production and sale warranted such financial risks. This triggered a process of business concentration in Europe, beginning around 1960. Fewer and fewer manufacturers produced more and more ice cream. This process had already started well before 1939 in the United States, where it mainly manifested itself in concentration in the dairy sector, which for a long time was the biggest supplier of ice cream to the American market. The growing competition from the emerging supermarket chains with their own-label brands and aggressive pricing policies now lent renewed impetus to rationalisation among ice cream manufacturers in the United States, Australia and Europe.

• Although supermarkets became the most important sales channel for take-home ice cream, the market also expanded because manufacturers and distributors began installing electrical freezer cabinets for impulse purchases in hundreds of thousands of small sales outlets. These outlets ranged from beachside huts, swimming pools, amusement parks, factory canteens and video rental shops to grocers, greengrocers, filling stations, garden centres, cafeterias, bars, theatres, cinemas, corner shops and kiosks. Just about anywhere, in fact, where the impulse to have an ice cream might result in a sale and a satisfied customer – hence the adoption in many countries of the word 'impulse' to represent pre-packaged, single portion ice cream products. The supermarket and the freezer cabinet have seen the ice cream man with his cart or van decline in numbers, at least in America, Australia and Western Europe, and the characteristic sound of his bell or musical jingle is less often heard. The street vendor has retreated to Eastern Europe, Asia and Latin America.

" Yes, the swankpot, he told me he was manager of a big transport company."

626: Picture postcard, UK, circa 1935.

• In Europe the establishment of the European Economic Community in 1957, and subsequently of the Single European Market, encouraged international foods manufacturers such as Unilever, Nestlé, Grace and Beatrice Foods to start up or expand their European ice cream activities. Much later, their example was followed by Pillsbury, the owner of Häagen Dazs, and by Mars. The most successful ice cream company in Europe, however, has been Unilever, and it has used its success on one continent as the launch-pad for securing market leadership in most other parts of the world mid-way through the 1990s. In the same period, Nestlé has also used its European base to expand globally.

• Häagen Dazs, Ben & Jerry's, Mars and the American parlour chains Baskin & Robbins and Dairy Queen have also entered the world ice cream market. Figures for consumption levels in the various continents demonstrate how the combined efforts of these businesses have popularised ice cream throughout the world. Between 1993 and 1997 ice cream sales in Asia more than doubled from 827 million litres to 1,813 million litres, as did annual per capita consumption. Growth in Latin America, the Middle East and Eastern Europe, albeit less spectacular, has also been substantial.[9]

The lasting success of ice cream

• The popularity of ice cream is partly based on its seemingly limitless range of flavours and presentations, from ices prepared with local fruits such as lucuma or durian, or with drinks such as armagnac, rum and whisky, to refreshing sorbets and richly filled cassatas. This versatility not only stimulates the fantasies of chefs de cuisine and specialist product developers in the industry, it also enables an effective response to the consumer's wish for choice. In his 1913 novel Combray, Marcel Proust describes this

WHEN FATHER HAS A CORNET WE ALL JOIN THE BAND!
(THE KIDS ARE HAVING THE TIME OF THEIR LIVES)
AT HASTINGS

627: Picture postcard, UK, circa 1930.

desire for variety as follows: 'Mamma was asking [...] whether M. Swann had had a second helping of the coffee-and-pistachio ice. "I thought it rather so-so", she was saying. "Next time we shall have to try another flavour."'[10]

• In terms of shape and presentation there are not many food products in the world that can be eaten in the shape of an asparagus, Puss-in-Boots, the bust of Napoleon, a company logo, a space rocket or Count Dracula. Human ingenuity is continually creating new and highly imaginative ice cream variants. More than anything, it is this characteristic that makes ice cream so amenable to constant innovation and adaptation, the keys to lasting success for any product in any sector of industry.

Licks, Sticks & Bricks

A WORLD HISTORY OF ICE CREAM

Notes

Bibliography

Indexes

Picture credits

Colophon

Notes

Abbreviations:
CA = Central Archives Rotterdam
HAR = Historical Archives Unilever Rotterdam
HAL = Historical Archives Unilever London

Chapter 1 Ice cream memories: an introduction

1 Exceptions to this are two recent publications, viz. the introduction to the recipes book Ices. A definitive guide, London 1996, by Robin Weir and Caroline Liddell, and the study Harvest of the Cold Months, London 1994, by Elizabeth David.

Chapter 2 From ice-water to water-ice

1 Sylvia P. Beaumon, The ice-houses of Britain, London 1990, p. 7. See also R.J. Forbes, Studies in Ancient Technology, Vol. VI, Leiden 1966, pp. 108-109; Xavier de Planhol, L'eau de neige, Paris 1995, pp. 155-156.
2 More details can be found in particular in Xavier de Planhol, L'eau de neige, Paris 1995. In his extensive study Planhol describes the discovery of ice cellars in numerous locations. See also A.W. Reinink and J.G. Vermeulen, IJskelders. Koeltechnieken van weleer, Nieuwkoop 1989; Sylvia P. Beaumon, The ice-houses of Britain, London 1990; Monica Ellis, Ice and icehouses through the ages. With a Gazetteer for Hampshire, Southampton 1982.
3 Arthur Waley, The Book of Songs, London 1937, p. 167.
4 Research on Ice-cream Development in China, Walls Beijing, April 1998, p. 2. The verse originates from Poetry of the South and was written between 475 B.C. and 221 B.C.
5 Rudolf Plank, Handbuch der Kältetechnik, Vol. I, Berlin 1954, p. 1.
6 Athenaeus, Deipnosophistae, III, 124. Athenaeus of Naucrites lived in the third century A.D. and in his work he quotes from the narrative of Protagorides, whose works have not survived.
7 Xavier de Planhol, L'eau de neige, Paris 1995.
8 Theocritus, Idylls, XI, 48.
9 Athenaeus, Deipnosophistae, III, 125c and 124b.
10 Forbes, 1966, p. 116.
11 Athenaeus, Deipnosophistae, III, 124c. Athenaeus quotes from the lost History of Alexander, written by Chares of Mytilene.
12 Seneca, Epistulae Morales, LXXVIII, 23.
13 Martial, Epigrammata, XIV, 103-104.
14 Seneca, Naturales Quaestiones, IVB 13, pp. 5-8.
15 Pliny the Elder, Naturalis Historia, XXXI 23.40.
16 For this book the Dutch classical scholar Elvira van Eeten carried out specially commissioned research in 1997 into all Greek and Roman sources relating to the use of snow and ice in antiquity.
17 Pliny the Younger, Epistulae, I, 15.
18 Apicius, De Re Coquinaria, IV, 1.2.
19 Ulrich Hellmann, Künstliche Kälte. Die Geschichte der Kühlung im Haushalt, Berlin 1990, p. 34.
20 Charles K. Wilkinson, 'Water, ice and glass' in The Metropolitan Museum of Art Bulletin, January 1943, vol. 1, no. 5, pp. 181-182.
21 Ibid.
22 Ibid., p.175.
23 Elizabeth David, Harvest of the Cold Months. A Social History of Ice and Ices, London 1994, pp. 249-250.
24 Rudolf Plank, Handbuch der Kältetechnik, Vol. I, Berlin 1954, p. 3.
25 Ibid.
26 The letter by Bernier is quoted in Emy's L'Art de Bien Faire les Glaces d'Office, Paris 1754, p. 11.

27 The Arabic text uses the expression 'tagmid al-ma'. Literally, this means 'freezing of water'. 'Tagmid' is based on the root gmd and means not only freezing but also making hard, hence the possible alternative translation 'making water into ice'. Information courtesy of Dr J.J. Witkamp, curator of the Oriental Collections of the University Library of Leiden, E-mail, 11.05.1998.
28 Ibn Abi Usaybi'a, Kitab Uyan al-Anba fi Tabqat al-Atibba, ed. August Müller, Cairo 1882/Königsberg 1884, pp. 82-83. Dr J.J. Witkamp kindly found the relevant passage in the text and translated it for me. Letter from J.J. Witkamp dated 11.03.1998. See also Fuat Segin, Geschichte des Arabischen Schrifttums, vol. III, Leiden 1970, p. 335. Segin states that Ibn Bakhtawayh was the son of a doctor and wrote his text in circa 1029.
29 Information courtesy of Dr J.J. Witkamp, e-mail 11.05.1998. Dr Witkamp's interpretation is based on an analysis contained in Walter Hinz, Islamische Maße und Gewichte, Leiden 1955, pp. 1-8. Dr Witkamp points out that there is no scientific clarity about the exact weight of a mithqâl. There are differences depending on place and time and many contradictory sources exist.
30 Lucie Bolens, Les sorbets Andalous (XIe-XIIIe siècles) ou conjurer la nostalgie par la douceur, Montreal 1992, p. 259. The author does not give an Arabic title for the work she discovered, but refers to it as the 'Livre des sorbets'.
31 Radu Stern (ed.), À manger des yeux. L'esthétique de la nourriture, Boudry-Neuchâtel 1988, p. 34.
32 Menon, La Science du Maître d'Hôtel Confiseur, Paris 1750. On pp. 163-164 Menon gives a recipe for rose-water ice. Recipes for the same type of ice were also published by Audiger (1692), Massialot (1692) and Emy (1768).
33 Frances Wood, Did Marco Polo go to China?, London 1995.
34 Ibid., p. 105.
35 Information courtesy of the British Sinologist Dr Frances Wood, head of the Oriental Collections of the British Library in London. As part of the research work for her publication Did Marco Polo go to China?, Dr Wood studied almost all travel reports and Western sources about China dated up to the sixteenth century. To corroborate the assertion that Marco Polo ate ice cream in China and was given ice cream recipes to bring back with him, modern-day Chinese sources refer to an article published in 1940 in a Japanese periodical: Japanese New Therapeutics, 15 April 1940. In this article the claim is made, unfortunately with no mention of any source, that the founder of the Yuan dynasty, Hu Bilie (1271-1368), gave Marco Polo ice (cream) recipes to take back home.
36 Edward H. Shaffer in Food in Chinese culture, ed. K.C. Chang, New York 1974, pp. 105-106.
37 Ibid., p. 126.
38 Caroline Liddell & Robin Weir, Ices. The definitive guide, London 1995, pp. 10-11.
39 Joseph Needham, Science and Civilisation in China, vol. V, part 3, Cambridge 1976, pp. 225-226.
40 Jean Jacques Dortous de Mairan, Dissertation sur la Glace, ou explication physique de la formation de la Glace et de ses divers Phénomènes, Bordeaux 1716.
41 Elizabeth David, p. 67.
42 Ibid., p. 67.
43 Ibid., pp. 70-71.
44 Ibid., p. 71.
45 Argenide. Eine historisch-politischer Roman. Aus dem Lateinischen Johann Barklay's neu übersetzt vom Verfasser der grauen Mappe, Berlin 1794, vol. II, book 9, chapter 6, pp. 521-525. See also Elizabeth David, 1994, pp. 55-57.

46 Elizabeth David, 1994, pp. 58-60.
47 P. Barra, L'usage de la glace, de la neige et du froid, Lyons 1676, p. 42.
48 D'Emery, Recueil de Curiositez Rares et Nouvelles, Paris 1674. However, Elizabeth David is of the opinion that this book was not the work of D'Emery. (See: Elizabeth David, p. 39, n. 41).

Box: A brief vocabulary of ice cream
1 Caroline Liddell & Robin Weir, Ices. The definitive guide, London 1995, p. 31. In their book the authors give an excellent list of definitions of a whole range of ice cream expressions.
2 The London Gazette, no. 2283, from Monday 17 September to Thursday 20 September, 1688. With acknowledgments to Robin Weir who kindly made his copy available for me to study. See also W.S. Stallings Jr, 'Ice cream and water ices in 17th and 18th century England', in Petits Propos Culinaires, no. 3, supplement, November 1979, p. 2.

Box: How can you make ice with salt?
1 Ibn Abi Usaybi'a, Kitab Uyan al-Anba fi Tabqat al-Atibba, ed. August Müller, Cairo 1882/Königsberg 1884, pp. 82-83.
2 Marco Antonio Zimara, Problemata Aristoteles, Padua 1530.

Box: Did Marco Polo bring back ice cream from China?
1 The first to do this on the basis of scientific arguments was the German Sinologist Herbert Franke in his article 'Sino-western relations under the Mongol Empire', in Journal of the Royal Asiatic Society Hong Kong Branch, 6, Hong Kong, 1966.
2 Frances Wood, Did Marco Polo go to China?, London 1995. Dr Wood, head of the Chinese Collections department at the British Library, provided invaluable assistance by supplying me with wide-ranging information relating to the scientific debate about the report of Marco Polo's travels.

Box: The ice cream legend of Catherine de' Medici
1 G.F. Young, The Medici, New York 1933, pp. 395-396.
2 Pellegrino Artusi, De wetenschap in de keuken en de kunst om goed te eten, Amsterdam 1997, 3rd edition, p. 440.
3 Barbara Ketcham Wheaton, Savoring the Past: the French kitchen and table from 1300 to 1789. New York 1996, p. 46. See also Elizabeth David, Harvest of the Cold Months. The social history of ice and ices, London 1994, pp. 41-49; Jacqueline Boucher, Société et mentalités autour Henri III, Lille 1977.
4 R.J. Knecht, Catherine de' Medici, London and New York 1998, pp. 17-59.
5 Claude-Gilbert Dubois [ed.], L'Isle des Hermaphrodites, Paris 1996, p. 108; p. 146.
6 Barbara Ketcham Wheaton, op.cit. (Dutch edition, p. 66-67)
7 An example of this can be found in the book by the prominent French culinary historian Maguelonne Toussaint-Samat, Histoire naturelle et morale de la nourriture, Paris 1987. In the English edition, History of Food, Oxford 1996, p. 750, she writes, without giving a reference: 'François I's daughter-in-law, Catherine de Medici, brought the fashion for sorbets to France'. Another example is the publication: James Trager, The Food Chronology, New York 1995, p. 91.
8 Le Journal des Confiseurs, Paris 1893, p. 62.

Chapter 3 Ices for kings, emperors and admirals

1 André Félibien, Les Divertissements de Versailles donnez par le roy à toute sa cour au retour de la conqueste de la Franche-Comté en l'année M.DC.LXXIV, Paris 1676, pp. 8-9.

2 Elizabeth David, 'A Midsummer Night's Dream?', in Petits Propos Culinaires, No. 5, May 1980, p. 59.

3 N. Audiger, La maison reglée et l'art de diriger la maison d'un grand seigneur et d'autres, tant à la ville qu'à la campagne ... avec la véritable méthode de faire toutes sortes d'essence, d'eaux et de liqueurs, fortes et refraîssantes à la mode d'Italie, Paris 1692.

4 Elizabeth David, Harvest of the Cold Months. The social history of ice and ices, London 1994, pp. 90-93.

5 Audiger, La maison réglée, Paris 1692, pp. 227-231.

6 Xavier de Planhol, L'eau de neige, Paris 1995, p. 180.

7 François Massialot, Nouvelles instructions pour les confitures, les liqueurs, et les fruits. Avec la manière de bien ordonner un dessert, & tout le reste qui est du devoir des maîtres d'Hôtels, sommeliers, confiseurs, & autres officiers de bouche, Paris 1698, 2nd edition, pp. 244-249.

8 W.S. Stallings Jr, 'Ice cream and water ices in 17th and 18th century England', in Petits Propos Culinaires, No. 3, Supplement, November 1979, p. 25.

9 Barbara Ketcham Wheaton, Savoring the past. The French kitchen and table from 1300 to 1789, New York 1996, p. 165.

10 K. Hantschmann, Nymphenburger Porzellan 1797 bis 1847. Geschichte, Modelle, Dekore, Munich/Berlin 1996, model 100 (ice pail), pp. 102-103.

11 Catherine Arminjon and Nicole Blondel, Inventaire général des monuments et des richesses artistiques de la France. Principe d'analyse scientifique vocabulaire des objets civils domestiques, Paris 1984, p. 110.

12 D. Collard-Moniotte, Catalogue des faïences de Moustiers, Paris 1988, p. 67, cat. no. 28, tot. h 17.5 x b 28.5 x d 21.5 cm, Musée National de Céramique, Sèvres, stock no. MNC 4779.

13 Sources of information about Sèvres include: exhibition catalogue Sèvres 1951, Les Grandes Services de Sèvres, Paris 1951 (Musée National de Céramique, Sèvres); P. Verlet, Sèvres, Le XVIIIe siècle, Paris 1953; S. Eriksen, Le porcellane francesi a Palazzo Pitti/French Porcelain in Palazzo Pitti, Florence 1973; exhibition catalogue Paris 1977, Porcelaines de Vincennes. Les origines de Paris 1977 (Grand Palais, Paris); M. Brunet & T. Préaud, Sèvres, des origines à nos jours, Paris/Freibourg 1978; S. Eriksen & G. de Bellaigue, Sèvres porcelain: Vincennes and Sèvres 1740-1800, London 1987; exhibition catalogue Paris 1993, Versailles et les tables Royales en Europe XVIIème - XIXème siècles, Paris 1993.

14 Gustav Weiz, Het porseleinboek. De geschiedenis van stijlen en technieken. Met uitvoerig merkenregister, Baarn 1965, p. 114.

15 Heidemarie Prell, Vom Gipfelschnee ... zur fröhlichen Eiszeit. Siegeszug der faszinierenden Köstlichkeit Speiseeis. Vom Genuss- zum Nahrungsmittel. Nuremberg 1987, p. 22.

16 W.S. Stallings Jr, 'Ice cream and water ices in 17th and 18th century England', in Petits Propos Culinaires, No. 3, Supplement, November 1979, p. 3.

17 H. Coutts, 'French drawing reveals more of the ice pail's history', in Country Life, 21 October 1993. Leeds Pottery and Pattern Books, collection of Victoria and Albert Museum, London.

18 The plateau à glace à ornament, the plateau de tasses à glace bouret and the plateau de tasses à glace triangle.

19 Caroline Liddell and Robin Weir, Ices: The definitive guide. London 1995, 2nd edition, p. 12.

20 For the illustrations see Encyclopédie ou Dictionnaire raisonné, des sciences, des arts et des métiers. Recueil de Planches

sur les sciences, vol. III under confiseur, Paris 1754; for the treatise on the preparation of ice see Encyclopédie.. vol. VII, Paris 1754, under glace, pp. 682-686.

21 The London Gazette, No. 2283, from Monday September 17 to Thursday September 20, 1688. With thanks to Robin Weir, who kindly made his copy available to me. See also W.S. Stallings Jr, 'Ice cream and water ices in 17th and 18th century England' in Petits Propos Culinaires, No. 3, Supplement, November 1979, p. 2.

22 See S. Eriksen, Le porcellane francesi a Palazzo Pitti/French Porcelain in Palazzo Pitti, Florence 1973; p. 75, no. 37. h. 20 cm. stock no. A.c.e. 1911, nn 845-847. Eriksen quotes from a 1760 invoice sent by Testard to the court of Parma for the 434 pieces of Sèvres porcelain supplied that year (to be found in Parma State Archive, Compuristeria e borbonica, Tesoreria en la Corte de Paris y Corresponsales, 1095). In view of the Sèvres date-letters (O, P, Q = 1767, 1768, 1769) on the ice pails, these must have been supplementary items that were produced later.

23 Guy Chaussin-Nogarey, La vie quotidienne des français sous Louis XV, p. 71. Here the author quotes the typesetter and prolific writer Nicolas Restif de la Bretonne (1734-1806), who records that in 1755 he had a weekly wage of 15 livres. Even though that wage had certainly increased by the time Catherine the Great ordered her service (1776), the price of the service was still in the region of 400 times the annual wage of a skilled craftsman such as a typesetter.

24 The main literary sources used for this paragraph are: exhibition catalogue Sèvres 1951, Les Grands Services de Sèvres, Paris 1951 (Musée National de Céramique, Sèvres), pp. 36-37; R. Savill, The Wallace Collection. Catalogue of Sèvres porcelain, London 1988, 3 vols., pp. 762-782; exhibition catalogue Paris 1993, Versailles et les tables Royales en Europe XVIIème - XIXème siècles, Paris 1993 (Versailles). See also exhibition catalogue 1996 (ed. John Vrieze), Catharina, de keizerin en de kunsten. Uit de schatkamers van de Hermitage, Zwolle 1997. The album with design drawings of the service is in the collection of the Bibliothèque Nationale, Paris, Cabinet des Estampes, L f. 8 pet.-fol., rés.

25 Michael Piljaev, [Remarkable Cranks and Eccentric Persons], St. Petersburg 1898.

26 Leonid Vyskochkov, ['Eskimo Pie: The History of Ice Cream in Russia'] in [Russia and the World Food Market], 1995, No. 4.

27 Quoted by S.G. Dettweiler, George Washington's Chinaware, New York 1982, pp. 119-120.

28 Ann Cooper Funderburg, Chocolate, Strawberry and Vanilla. A History of American Ice Cream, Bowling Green 1995, pp. 6-7.

29 Ibid., p. 3.

30 With thanks to Jay Boehm, Research Assistant, Thomas Jefferson Foundation, Inc., Charlottesville, Virginia, USA. Mr Boehm kindly sent me a copy of the full recipe in Jefferson's own handwriting. Letter dated 30.03.1998.

31 The manuscript is stored in the Archives Nationales, Paris, K.506, no. 21.

32 In 1811 the greater part of the service was bought for £1,973 4s 8d by the future George IV. It is still in the possession of Britain's royal family and is kept at Windsor Castle.

33 Simon Schama, Burgers, Een kroniek van de Franse Revolutie, Amsterdam 1989, p. 672.

34 The information about ice pails produced after the French Revolution is derived from: exhibition catalogue Sèvres 1951, Les Grands Services de Sèvres, Paris 1951 (Musée National de Céramique, Sèvres), pp. 57-58; exhibition catalogue Besançon 1957, Les Grands Services de Sèvres. Les Manufactures et Ateliers d'Art de l'Etat:

Imprimerie nationale, Monnaies et Médailles, Sèvres..., Besançon 1957, pp. 96-98, fig. XVIII plates and an ice pail, to be found at the Ministère des Affaires Etrangères]; exhibition catalogue Sèvres 1975, Porcelaines de Sèvres au XIXe siècle, Paris 1995 (Musée National de Céramique, Sèvres), pp. 15-16. Collection Musée National de Céramique, Sèvres plates only].

35 The author's research did not reveal any ice pails or ice cream cups made by Chelsea.

36 Caroline Liddell and Robin Weir, Ices. The definitive guide. London 1995, 2nd edition, p. 10.

37 W.S. Stallings Jr, 'Ice cream and water ices in 17th and 18th century England', in Petits Propos Culinaires, No. 3, Supplement, November 1979, p. 2.

38 Elizabeth David, 'Fromages glacés and iced creams', in Petits Propos Culinaires, No. 2, August 1979, pp. 23-27. Granville is also spelt as Grenville and even Grinville. At the time of David's publication Grace Granville's recipe book was in the keeping of the Herb Society, London. The recipe was marked with the letters Wth.all. A similar abbreviation, W:hall, was used in those days by Joyce Evelyn in his diary as shorthand for Whitehall.

39 W.S. Stallings Jr, 'Ice cream and water ices in 17th and 18th century England', in Petits Propos Culinaires, No. 3, Supplement, 1979, p. 3.

40 Ibid., p. 4.

41 The design is illustrated in R. Reilly, Wedgwood pottery & porcelain. Collectors' guides, vol. 1, p. 329.

42 As from 1780 the service was used on 24 June of each year to commemorate the victory over the Turks at Chesme in the Aegean Sea, which was the reason why the name of the palace was changed. For more details see exhibition catalogue Catharina, de keizerin en de kunsten. Uit de schatkamers van de Hermitage, Zwolle 1996, p. 205.

43 The remainder of the service (767 objects) is today in the collection of the Hermitage Museum in Leningrad. Important literary sources consulted are: H. Young, The Genius of Wedgwood, London 1995; M. Raeburn, L.N. Voronikhina and A. Nurnberg, The Green Frog Service, London 1995; G.C. Williamson, The Imperial Russian Dinner Service, London 1909, a book that was issued to mark the 150th anniversary of the Wedgwood factory.

44 Quoted in a letter from the English ceramics specialist G.A. Godden to researcher S.A.M. Braat, dated 02.10.1997.

45 The pattern book and an introduction to it can be found in L. White, Spode. A history of the family. Factory and wares from 1733 to 1833, London 1970, pp. 90-115. The illustrations have been classified by the author according to shape, with a mention of the original name for each shape.

46 B.L. Grandjean, Flora Danica Stellet/The Flora Danica service, Copenhagen 1973 edition, p. 70. fig. 73. In the factory's archives the ice bells are referred to not only as 'Isfad med Klok' (ice barrel with bell) but also as 'Fad til is med Klokke' (barrel for ice with bell) and as 'Flaskeskjul med tillhørende Iskumme' (bottle cooler with accompanying ice bowl). On the basis of the latter name it has been suggested that the ice bells were intended as a decorative bottle cooler. However, the service already contained 56 bottle coolers. The manufacture of the ice bells is extremely complex and costly. It therefore seems very unlikely that they were intended to fulfil such a commonplace function. Besides, because of its limited height, the basket can hardly hold a bottle of wine. My assumption concerning the presentation of bombes glacées is shared by Stinn Nottelman, curator of the collection of Royal Copenhagen. Mr Nottelman was kind

enough to exchange detailed thoughts with me about the ice bell in April 1997 in Copenhagen.
47 Vibeke Woldbye (ed.), Flowers into art. Floral motifs in European painting and decorative arts, The Hague 1991, p. 100. The book that Bayer had been working on was Beata ruris otia fungis Danicis impensa by Theodor Holmskiold.
48 Ibid., p. 83.
49 O.V. Krog, 'Usages et objets de table à la cour du Danemark', p. 175, in exhibition catalogue Paris 1993, Versailles et les tables Royales en Europe XVIIème-XIXème siècles, Paris 1993. The full menu for the meal can be found in H.V.F. Winstone, Royal Copenhagen, London 1984, p. 49.
50 Günter Wiegelmann, 'Speiseeis in volkstümlichen Festmahlzeiten' in Deutsche Lebensmittel-Rundschau, vol. 60, July 1964, no. 7, p. 201. The author quotes instructions for the preparation of water-ice given in the anonymous publication Schatzkammer Rarer und Neuer Curiositäten in den allerwunderbaresten Würkungen der Natur und Kunst, Hamburg 1689, p. 176.
51 For the information about porcelain from Berlin the following sources were used: E. Köllmann, Berliner Porzellan 1763-1963, Braunschweig 1966 (2 vols.); G. Schade, Berliner Porzellan: Zur Kunst und Kulturgeschichte der Berliner Porzellanmanufakturen im 18. und 19. Jahrhundert, Leipzig 1979; E. Köllmann & M. Jarschow, Berliner Porzellan, Munich 1987 (2 vols.); exhibition catalogue Hamburg 1993, Berliner Porzellan des 18. Jahrhunderts aus eigenen Beständen, Hamburg 1993 (Museum für Kunst und Gewerbe, Hamburg).
52 Quoted by: E. Köllmann, 'Die Porzellanservice des Hertogs von Wellington' in Keramos, No. 10, 1960, p. 97, note 6.
53 E. Köllmann, 'Die Porzellanservice des Hertogs von Wellington' in Keramos, No. 10, 1960, pp. 81-97.
54 C. Truman, The Sèvres Egyptian dinner service, Tunbridge Wells 1982; and E. Köllmann, 'Die Porzellanservice des Hertogs von Wellington' in Keramos, No. 10, 1960, pp. 81-97.
55 H. Reber, Hoechster Porzellan aus drei Jahrhunderten. Ausstellung zur Aspekten der Kunst-, Wirtschafts- und Sozialgeschichte, Hohenberg an der Eger 1988, p. 161, circa 1771, height 28.2 cm, collection Residenz Museum Munich; C. Fritsche and G.K. Stasch, Hochfürstlich Fuldische Porzellanmanufaktur 1764-1789, Fulda 1994, p. 193, No. 115, circa 1770, collection Vonderau-Museum, Fulda; E.J. Hürkey, Frankenthaler Porzellan aus den Sammlungen der Stadt Frankenthal und des Frankenthaler Altertumsvereins, 1990, p. 69, catalogue no. 35, circa 1775-1785. This porcelain was exported to Italy, see: L. Buccino Grimaldi and R. Cariello, Le porcellane europee nel Museo Correale in Sorrento. Cava dei terreni, 1978, no. 11, fig. CXLIII, collection Museo Correale in Sorrento; H. Scherf, Thüringer Porzellan unter besonderer Berücksichtigung der Erzeugnisse des 18. und frühen 19. Jahrhunderts, Leipzig 1989, no. 61, collection City of Gotha Museums, Schloßmuseum.
56 K. Hantschmann, Nymphenburger Porzellan 1797 bis 1847. Geschichte, Modelle, Dekore, Munich/Berlin 1996, model 100 (ice pail), model 101 (saucer), pp. 102-103 and catalogue 034, pp. 231-236, height 39 cm.
57 Maria Pilar Martin Galilea, Helados, sorbetes y otras delicias, Madrid 1996, pp. 18-21.
58 Ibid., p. 21.
59 A. Carola-Perotti, Le porcellane dei Borbone di Napoli. Capodimonte e real fabbrica ferdinandea 1743-1806, Naples 1986, pp. 397 ff. and colour plate LXVI, collection Enzo Catello, Naples.
60 Exhibition catalogue Sèvres 1951, Les Grands Services de Sèvres, Paris 1951

(Musée National de Céramique, Sèvres), pp. 58-59. The dishes were known as 'patelles à glace'.

Box: Coffee and ice at Le Procope and 'the unfortunate Neapolitan'
1 René de Lespinasse, Histoire générale de Paris. Les métiers de Paris. Collection de documents publiée sous les auspices de l'édité parisienne. Paris, vol. 1, p. 75.
2 Elizabeth David, Harvest of the Cold Months. The social history of ice and ices, London 1994, pp. 111-113.
3 M. Dubuisson, 'L'Art du Distillateur et marchand de liqueurs, considerées comme aliments médicamenteux', Paris 1770, vol. 2, p. 272.
4 Pim Reinders and Thera Wijsenbeek, Koffie in Nederland. Vier eeuwen cultuurgeschiedenis, Zutphen 1994, pp. 44-45. [The approximate translation of Au..DChoc..Caffe Italien & Glaces is: Chocolate drinks. Italian Coffee & Ices].
5 Ibid., p. 43. The original (rhyming) Dutch text on the sign-board that was found in Breda reads:
'Hier verkoopt men Koffie en Sukelade, Serbette, Thee en Limonade, Gezuiverde Huy en goe Tabak. Komt in en proeft het met gemak'.

Box: What's in a name: ice pail, glacière, Kühlgefäss, gelatiere...
1 D. Buten & J.P. Claney, 18th century Wedgwod. A guide for collectors and connoisseurs, London 1980, p. 46, (MS-9655-11). This MS number refers to the unpublished Wedgwood correspondence and factory records, which are now housed in the University of Keele in Staffordshire.

Box: The first cookery books with ice recipes
1 Most of this information about the first cookery books with ice recipes is derived from Elizabeth David, The Harvest of the Cold Months. The social history of ice and ices, London 1994, pp. 129-135 and pp. 141-253.
2 Günter Wiegelmann, 'Speiseeis in volkstümlichen Festmahlzeiten', in Deutsche Lebensmittel-Rundschau, vol. 60, July 1964, no. 7, p. 201, note 3.
3 Emy, L'Art de Bien Faire les Glaces d'Office, Paris 1768, pp. 76-78.
4 René Antoine de Réaumur, Sur les différentes degrés de froid que l'on peut produire en mêlant de la glace avec différents sels ... Histoire et Mémoires de l'Académie des Sciences, Paris 1734, pp. 178-179.
5 For example, in a letter to the editors of the American trade journal Ice Cream Review, published in the March 1923 issue, a representative of Italian ice cream vendors in England wrote as follows about the use of machines for freezing ice: 'But taken in all, the old fashioned Italian tub and zinc freezer or container, turned by hand, with a stick to beat and scrape the ice cream, is still the most used, at least by the Italians of the poorer type'. Ice Cream Review, March 1923, p. 86.

Box: 1766: a Prince of Orange eats 'ice of diverse sorts' in Zwolle
1 This information is drawn from Joh. Theunisz., 'De receptie van Zijne Hoogheid Stadhouder Willem V in Zwolle op 30 augustus 1766', in Verslagen en mededeelingen van Overijsselsch Regt en Geschiedenis, Zwolle 1939 (55), pp. 87-108.

Chapter 4 **Ices from the dining-table to the street**
1 Walter Artelt, 'Die deutsche Kochbuchliteratur des 19. Jahrhunderts', in Ernährung und Ernährungslehre im 19. Jahrhundert, Göttingen 1976, p. 360.
2 Giles MacDonogh, A palate in revolution. Grimod de La Reynière and the 'Almanach

des Gourmands', London/New York 1987, p. 115.
3 Almanach des Gourmand`s, I, Paris 1803, p. 183.
4 Ibid.
5 Jean Garrigues, Miko. Le goût de l'entracte, Paris 1992, p. 17.
6 Almanach des Gourmands, I, Paris 1803, p. 163.
7 Georges Bernier, Antonin Carême 1783-1833. La sensualité gourmande en Europe, Paris 1989, p. 93.
8 With acknowledgments to Robin Weir, London. The relevant card is in his collection.
9 Elizabeth David, Harvest of the Cold Months, London 1994, pp. 310-311.
10 Elizabeth David 1994, p. 322.
11 G.A. Jarrin, The Italian Confectioner or Complete Economy of Desserts, London 1829, p. 110.
12 Elizabeth David 1994, p. 352.
13 Ibid., pp. 327-328.
14 D.V. Proctor [ed.], Ice Carrying Trade at sea, London 1981, pp. 1-8.
15 Henry Hall, The Ice Industry of the United States. Brief sketch of its history, no place, no year prior to 1882], p. 1.
16 D.V. Proctor [ed.], Ice Carrying Trade at sea, London 1981, p. 36.
17 Elizabeth David 1994, pp. 346-347.
18 Henry Hall, no year, p. 20.
19 Ibid., 5.
20 Robin Weir et al., Mrs Marshall. The Greatest Victorian Ice Cream Maker, Otley 1998, pp. 5-7.
21 A.B. Marshall, Fancy Ices, London 1894, p. 135.
22 A.B. Marshall, Ices Plain and Fancy. The Book of Ices, Introduction and annotations by Barbara Ketcham Wheaton, no place [New York] 1976, p. XVII.
23 Robin Weir et al., Mrs Marshall. The Greatest Victorian Ice Cream Maker, Otley 1998, p. 8.
24 Jean Garrigues 1992, p. 17.
25 New York, London and Vienna were the cities in which this process began. In London Carlo Gatti started selling ice cream in the streets in 1850. In Vienna Antonio Tomea Bareta was granted a licence to sell ice cream in 1865. In Lima Pedro D'Onofrio began his ice cream activities in 1897; they still exist under that name to this day. In Liège the pioneer was Antoine Marziale (1898). He later founded the Mio ice cream factory. In the Dutch bathing resort of Scheveningen the Italian Lanza was active in 1889. In the summer of 1896 Giuseppe Cervi was the man behind the sale of ice cream in the streets of Dublin.
26 Information courtesy of Leena Arkio-Laine, director of the Helsinki City Museum, 26.05.1998.
27 Terri Colpi, The Italian factor. The Italian community in Great Britain, London 1991, p. 18.
28 Brian Reynolds, Casalattico and the Italian Community in Ireland, Dublin 1993, pp. 27-29. In chapter 1 of his book Reynolds looks at Italian migration in general and uses a series of mainly British studies as his basis.
29 1959-1989. Trent' anni di storia internazionale del gelato, Longarone 1990, p. 30.
30 Helmut Schwarz et al., Unter Nul. Kunsteis, Kälte und Kultur, Munich 1991, p. 293.
31 Ibid.
32 Sponza, Italian Immigrants in Nineteenth-Century Britain. Realities and Images, Leicester 1988, p. 94. Sponza is quoting from the second (1861) edition of Mayhew's book.
33 Felicity Kinross, Coffee and ices. The story of Carlo Gatti in London, London, no year [?], pp. 12-13. Most of the information about Gatti is derived from this publication.
34 Peter Barber and Peter Jaconelli,

Continental Tastes. Ticinese emigrants and their Café-Restaurants in Britain 1847-1987, London 1997, p. 14.
35 Ibid., pp. 14-19.
36 Sponza 1988, p. 97.
37 Sponza 1988, p. 54. Sponza gives a summary of the ten-yearly British census for the 1861-1911 period. Using that as a basis I have calculated the percentages of occupations registered.
38 The Confectioner's Union, July 15, 1896, p. 755.
39 The Confectioner's Union, September 15, 1893, p. 593.
40 Sponza 1988, p. 100.
41 Ice and cold storage, September 1925, London, p. 251.
42 The Confectioner's Union, London, August 1893, p. 527. The recipe is for a plain ice cream without flavourings such as raspberry or vanilla.
43 Ralph Selitzer, The dairy industry in America, New York 1976, p. 30.
44 Anne Cooper Funderburg, Chocolate, Strawberry and Vanilla. History of American Ice Cream, Bowling Green 1995, p. 72.
45 Funderburg 1995, p. 73.
46 The National Cookery Book, New York 1876.
47 United States Patent Office, Patent No. 3254, Sept. 9, 1843. Until a few years ago it was assumed that Johnson had not been granted a patent for her machine and that W.G. Young was the first to receive a patent for such a machine in 1848 (see, for example, Paul Dickson, The Great American Ice Cream Book, New York 1972, and Ralph Selitzer, The dairy industry in America, New York 1976, p. 31). However, the American ice cream expert Ed Marks (Lancaster, Ph.) succeeded in tracking down the patent on Johnson's machine. See also Funderburg 1995, p. 34.
48 Elizabeth David 1994, p. 174; p. 341 and p. 173.
49 Giacomo Perini, Der Schweizerzuckerbäcker, Weimar 1858, 2nd edition, pp. 181-183.
50 Patricia M. Tice, Ice Cream for All, Rochester 1990, p. 19.
51 Mary Anne Hinnes, Gordon Marshall, William Woys Weaver, The Larder Invaded. Reflections on Three Centuries of Philadelphia Food and Drink, Philadelphia 1987, pp. 33-34.
52 Funderburg 1995, p. 63.
53 Susan Williams, Savor Suppers and Fashionable Feasts. Dining in Victorian America, New York 1985, pp. 176-177.
54 Charles Ranhofer, The epicurean. A complete treatise of analytical and practical studies of the culinary art, including table and wine service and a selection of interesting bills of fare of Delmonico's from 1862 to 1894, making a Franco-American culinary encyclopedia, New York 1971. Photomechanical reprint of the New York 1893 edition), p. 1007.
55 Williams 1985, pp. 86-87.
56 Funderburg 1995, p. 87.
57 Funderburg 1995, pp. 100-101.
58 Robin Weir, One Leg of a Pair of Drawers. The American Soda Fountain Lingo, London 1994, pp. 7-11.
59 De Sylva, Brown and Henderson Inc. When I'm Sippin' a Soda with Susie, 1932, De Vincent Collection, Box 541 B, Archive of the Museum of American History, Washington.

Box: An ice cream for an opera singer
1 Agnes G. Murphy, Melba. A Biography, New York 1909, p. 82.
2 Auguste Escoffier, Souvenirs inédits, 75 ans au service de l'art culinaire, Marseille 1985, pp. 125-126.
3 Caroline Liddell & Robin Weir, Ices. The Definitive Guide, London 1994, p. 51.
4 Escoffier 1985, p. 126.

Box: About cooling machines and refrigerators
1 Roger Thévenot, A History of Refrigeration throughout the world, Paris 1979, pp. 43-44.
2 Ibid., p. 72.
3 Brochure Gesellschaft für Linde's Eismaschinen A.G., Wiesbaden 1900. Dossier Von Linde, archive Deutsches Museum, Munich.
4 Hans J. Teuteberg, 'Geschichte der Kühl- und Gefriertechnik und ihre Einfluss auf die Ernährung seit dem 19. Jahrhundert', in Ernährungsforschung, 1993, vol. 38, p. 140.

Box: 'Give us a licker, Jack'
1 The Daily Telegraph, July 27th 1918.
2 Caroline Liddell & Robin Weir, Ices. The definitive guide, London 1995, p. 20.
3 Ibid.

Box: Ice cream moulds: from Abraham Lincoln to Puss-in-Boots
1 A complete catalog of Metal Molds for Ice Cream and Display Models, Eppelsheimer & Co., New York, no year [circa 1940], p. 3.
2 Duvall Sollers, Those magnificent ice cream moulds, no year, no place, p. 8.
3 Ice Cream Moulds for Every Occasion, Krauss & Co., New York, no year [circa 1946], p. 2.
4 Information courtesy of Bill Stallings, Portland, Oregon, USA. The figures are derived from research work carried out by Sid Stallings, Bill's father.
5 Catalogue of A. Cadot, Paris, no year [circa 1895], no. 1028 and no. 1125; catalogue of Letang Fils, Paris 1933, no. 1852, p. 403.
6 Duvall G. Sollers & John P. Gauder, Pewter Ice Cream Moulds, no place, no year.
7 Ibid., p. 3.

Chapter 5 **How ice cream became an American favourite**
1 Nellie McClung, My sex is ice cream: the Marilyn Monroe poems: including In Her Own Writ, a selection of original poetry by Marilyn Monroe/Nellie McClung, [no place], 1996.
2 'What The Industry Thought And Did Just Ten and Twenty Years Ago', in The Ice Cream Trade Journal, October 1929.
3 Ibid.
4 'Population Shifts Producing Geographical Changes in Ice Cream Production', in The Ice Cream Review, May 1952.
5 Herman LeRoy Collins and Wilfred Jordan, Philadelphia, a story of progress, Vol. III, Philadelphia 1941, pp. 91-92.
6 Lorin Blodget Collins, The industries of Philadelphia as shown by the Manufacturing Census, Philadelphia 1877.
7 M.T. Fussell, 'Beginning of the wholesale ice cream business', in The Ice Cream Trade Journal, January 1905, p. 7.
8 Ibid., p. 8.
9 Invoice dated 06.03.1865 in Warshaw Collection, Refrigeration, Box 1, 'Fussell Ice Cream Folder', National Museum of American History Archives Center.
10 The Ice Cream Trade Journal, May 1951, p. 188.
11 Historical and Commercial Philadelphia, Second Edition, New York 1892, p. 225.
12 'An Index to Persons Naturalized in Philadelphia, Pennsylvania', V.1. no. WO/115FR/1977, Historical Society of Pennsylvania, Philadelphia.
13 The American Way. A History of the Breyer Ice Cream Company 1866-1946, no place, no year 1946]. The booklet was published by the company to commemorate the eightieth anniversary of the business.
14 Compressed Air, April-May 1997, pp. 8-13.
15 The Ice Cream Trade Journal, January 1905, pp. 11-14.

16 Ralph Selitzer, The Dairy Industry in America, New York 1976, p. 236.
17 The Ice Cream Trade Journal, May 1951, pp. 64-66, p. 195.
18 The Ice Cream Review, July 1921, p. 4.
19 The Ice Cream Trade Journal, May 1907, p. 12.
20 The American Way. A History of the Breyer Ice Cream Company 1866-1946, [no place, no year 1946].
21 The Modern Plant, Breyers Ice Cream Company, Philadelphia, no year [circa 1915], p. 15. Good Humor-Breyers archive, Green Bay, inv. no. 85.0087.
22 Ralph Selitzer 1976, p. 157.
23 Ibid., p. 159.
24 The Ice Cream Review, February 1923, pp. 100-102.
25 Advertisement circa 1920, Good Humor-Breyers archives, Green Bay, USA.
26 The Ice Cream Trade Journal, April 1924; The Ice Cream Review, June 1951, p. 46, pp. 76-80; The Ice Cream Trade Journal, May 1951; The Ice Cream Trade Journal, July 1955, pp. 40-41.
27 The Ice Cream Trade Journal, June 1955, p. 62.
28 Scientific American, July 1898, p. 74.
29 The Ice Cream Trade Journal, September 1910, p. 19.
30 The Ice Cream Trade Journal, January 1905, p. 22.
31 The Ice Cream Trade Journal, July 1911, p. 33.
32 Ann Cooper Funderburg, Chocolate, Strawberry and Vanilla. A history of American Ice Cream, Bowling Green 1995, p. 125 and The Ice Cream Trade Journal, July 1918, p. 27.
33 It is difficult to obtain reliable figures for this period. The US Department of Agriculture only started its annual reporting on ice cream production in 1925. The Ice Cream Trade Journal, September 1911, p. 36, gives figures for 1906 and 1911 of 55 million US gallons (= more than 207 million litres) and 100 million gallons respectively. The May 1952 edition of The Ice Cream Review contains an overview that lists the 1920 figure at 148,298,000 gallons (= more than 560 million litres).
34 J.S. Nelson, 'The ice cream cabinet and the dealer', in The Ice Cream Trade Journal, July 1916, pp. 26-27.
35 The Ice Cream Trade Journal, June 1955, p. 59.
36 The Ice Cream Trade Journal, June 1955, p. 224.
37 The Ice Cream Trade Journal, August 1919, p. 31.
38 'O! My It's Eskimo Pie', words and music by Dale Wimbrow, 1939. National Museum of American History Archives Center, Washington. In 1930 Wimbrow wrote another Eskimo Pie song for an Eskimo Pie on a stick. Eskimo Pie Collection, box 553.
39 Ralph Selitzer 1976, p. 263.
40 Ibid.
41 Ibid., p. 275.
42 Sara Beigel, Draft Inventory. The Eskimo Pie Collection, National Museum of American History Archives Center, Washington 1996.
43 The Ice Cream Review, September 1924, p. 148.
44 The Eskimo Pie Handbook, Season 1925-1926. General Information. Manufacturing Suggestions. Selling Plans. Eskimo Pie Corporation, no place, no year [1925], p. 11. National Museum of American History Archives Center, Washington, Eskimo Pie Collection, box 553.
45 The Ice Cream Review, June 1922, p. 8.
46 The Ice Cream Trade Journal, March 1928, and The Ice Cream Trade Journal, April 1928, p. 74.
47 The Ice Cream Trade Journal, May 1927, p. 64.
48 The Ice Cream Review, July 1937, pp. 28-29. The average running cost of this refrig-

eration method, which had been developed at the University of Leiden in the Netherlands, was twenty cents a day.
49 The Ice Cream Trade Journal, July 1930, pp. 33-34.
50 Sunshine, vol. VI, no. 4, February 6th, 1926. Sunshine was a weekly newsletter issued by the Joe Lowe Co. in New York, Good Humor-Breyers archives, Green Bay, USA.
51 Brochure Joe Lowe Co., 1939, Good Humor-Breyers archives, Green Bay, USA.
52 Ralph Selitzer 1976, p. 266.
53 Ice Cream Field, March 1931, pp. 46-47.
54 'That Good Humor Man', in Westchester Life, May 1952 pp. 12-13, p. 22.
55 Ralph Selitzer 1976, p. 266.
56 The Ice Cream Review, May 1952.
57 Wayne Smith, Ice Cream Dippers, Walkersville 1986, pp. 55-64.
58 The Ice Cream Trade Journal, June 1955, p. 223.
59 The Ice Cream Trade Journal, October 1930; Ann Cooper Funderburg 1995, p. 133.
60 Ralph Selitzer 1976, p. 270.
61 Ann Cooper Funderburg 1995, p. 138.
62 The Ice Cream Trade Journal, April 1933, pp. 25-30.
63 The Ice Cream Trade Journal, June 1955, p. 132.
64 Official Guide Book of the New York World's Fair, New York 1939, pp. 107-108.

Box: Dolly Madison: the 'First Lady' of ice cream
1   Amy La Follette Jensen, The White House and its thirty-five families, New York 1970, p. 23.
2   The collection of the Library of Congress contains six children's books about Dolly Madison, published between 1966 and 1991.
3   Elizabeth Lippincott Dean, Dolly Madison, the nation's hostess, Boston 1928.
4   'Our Industry's Debt to Dolly', in The Ice Cream Review, October 1925, p. XVI.
5   Ralph Selitzer, The Dairy Industry in America, New York 1976, p. 29. Selitzer gives no source for his claim that Jackson worked as a chef for Dolly Madison.
6   Ann Cooper Funderburg, Chocolate, Strawberry and Vanilla. A History of American Ice Cream, Bowling Green 1995, p. 14.

Box: 'The biggest little thing in the ice cream business'
1   L.J. Schumaker, 'How the Rising Generation Learns to Eat Ice Cream', in The Ice Cream Trade Journal, January 1920, p. 60.
2   The Ice Cream Trade Journal, May 1928, p. 78.
3   The Ice Cream Trade Journal, November 1929, p. 46.
4   Ann Cooper Funderburg, Chocolate, Strawberry and Vanilla. A History of American Ice Cream, Bowling Green 1995, pp. 117-121. In her book Funderburg gives seven different versions of the origins of the ice cream cone.
5   Ralph Selitzer, The dairy industry in America, New York 1976, p. 243.
6   Caroline Liddell & Robin Weir, Ices. The definitive guide, London 1995, p. 181.

Chapter 6 Ice cream in post-war America
1   The Ice Cream Review, July 1943, pp. 52-53.
2   The Ice Cream Trade Journal, December 1944, p. 28 and p. 70.
3   The Ice Cream Review, May 1952.
4   The Ice Cream Review, May 1952, and Dairy Field, February 1983, p. 44.
5   The Ice Cream Trade Journal, June 1955, p. 132 and p. 134. In 1936 the American ice cream industry produced 248 million gallons of ice cream and 5 million gallons of sherbet ice. The figures for 1944 were 446 and 48.7 million gallons respectively.
6   The Ice Cream Trade Journal, December 1944, p. 56. See also The Ice Cream Review,

January 1944, p. 18 and pp. 58-59.
7   Ibid., p. 232.
8   Ibid., p. 231.
9   The Ice Cream Review, June 1945, p. 50.
10 Folder issued by Ben Hur Manufacturers Co. in Warshaw Collection, box 1, National Museum of American Archives Center, Washington.
11 The Ice Cream Trade Journal, November 1952, p. 48.
12 The Ice Cream Trade Journal, January 1957, pp. 12-16 and p. 116.
13 For the 1938 and 1952 figures see: The Ice Cream Trade Journal, July 1953, p. 40 and p. 42; for the 1981 figure see: Dairy Field, February 1983, p. 41.
14 The Ice Cream Trade Journal, April 1962, p. 67 and pp. 212-222.
15 Ibid., p. 34.
16 The Ice Cream Trade Journal, May 1960, pp. 38-40 and p. 58.
17 The Borden Eagle, January-February 1930, p. 18.
18 A History of Borden, Columbus 1992, p. 4.
19 The Ice Cream Trade Journal, July 1957, p. 122.
20 The Ice Cream Trade Journal, April 1954, p. 20.
21 The Ice Cream Trade Journal, July 1957, p. 122.
22 A History of Borden, Columbus 1992, p. 8.
23 List of delivered ice bar freezers types RIA-4 and RIA-5-6-7, 03.07.1965, Gram archives, Vojens, Denmark.
24 The Frozen Novelties Market, Find/SVP, New York 1987, ch. III, p. 12.
25 Ibid., pp. 26-27.
26 John D. Weaver, Carnation. The first 75 Years 1899-1974, Los Angeles 1974, pp. 11-12.
27 Ibid., pp. 70-71.
28 Ibid., p. 240.
29 Ann Cooper Funderburg 1995, p. 160.
30 Neil R. Gazel, Beatrice. From Buildup through Breakup, Urbana and Chicago 1990, p. 4.
31 Miriam C. Larsen, The Midas Touch, Denison 1977, p. 51.
32 The Ice Cream Review, January 1932, p. 70 and Miriam C. Larsen 1977, p. 91. See also Miriam C. Larsen 1977, pp. 61-63.
33 Neil R. Gazel 1990, p. 20.
34 Ibid., p. 66.
35 The Cone with the Curl on Top. Celebrating Fifty Years, 1940-1990, Minneapolis 1990, p. 23.
36 Ibid., p. 30.
37 Ice Cream. A world survey, Euromonitor International, London 1998, pp. 311-314.
38 The Ice Cream World of Baskin-Robbins, New York 1975, p. 171.
39 Baskin-Robbins Ice Cream Co. A short profile, E & S Department, Unilever, 1976. HAR: AHK-2050.
40 The Ice Cream World of Baskin-Robbins, New York 1975, p. 173.
41 'Belgium' in American Trade Review, December 1974.
42 Ice Cream. A world survey, Euromonitor International, London 1998, pp. 215-221.
43 Steve Sherman, The Häagen-Dazs Book of Ice Cream, New York 1992, p. 12.
44 Ibid., p. 12.
45 Ibid., p. 18.
46 Ibid., p. 28.
47 Dairy Field, March 1980, pp. 45-47.
48 Dairy Foods, April 1987, p. 45.
49 Ice Cream. A world survey, London 1998, pp. 234-235.
50 Dairy Foods, December 1986, p. 31.
51 Between 1954 and 1964 at least 56 Gram RIAs were installed. See List of delivered ice bar freezers types RIA-4 and RIA-5-6-7, Gram archives, 03.07.1965, Vojens, Denmark.
52 BonBon's History, Nestlé 1998.
53 Dairy Field, September 1981.
54 The Frozen Novelties Market, Find/SVP, 1987, pp. III-19.
55 Ellyn E. Spragins, 'Passing the Hat...

Again', in Inc. Magazine, September 1990, p. 135. See also Internet: www.inc.com.
56 Ibid., p. III-12.
57 The Ice Cream Trade Journal, November 1963, pp. 14-18.
58 Unilever Ice Cream in The United States of America. A Position Paper, Good Humor Corp., 19.08.1984, HAR: ICG-32.
59 The Frozen Novelties Market, Find/SVP, New York 1987, p. III-5.
60 The Ice Cream Review, November 1963, p. 22.
61 Dairy Field, January 1983, p. 34.
62 Euromonitor 1998, p. 315.
63 Dreyer's History in the making, Dreyer's Inc., Oakland 1997, p. 2.
64 Ibid., p. 3.
65 Dairy Foods, June 1988, p. 43.
66 Ibid., p. 8.
67 Dairy Foods, April 1987, p. 30.
68 The Ice Cream Review, January 1951, p. 54.
69 The Ice Cream Trade Journal, March 1952, p. 28 and p. 58; and The Ice Cream Review, April 1957, p. 53 and pp. 87-89.

Box: Ben & Jerry's, Vermont's Finest
1   Fred Lager, Ben & Jerry's: The Inside Scoop, New York 1994, pp. 140-142.
2   Ice cream. A world survey, Euromonitor International, London 1998, pp. 283-286.
3   Fred Lager 1994, p. 117.

Chapter 7 Australia: 'health, strength and happiness'
1   Carol Odell, Ice-creams, sorbets and frozen delights, Melbourne 1984, pp. 17-18.
2   Ibid., p. 20.
3   W.R. Lang, James Harrison, pioneering genius, Newtown, Victoria, 1982.
4   Ibid., p. 20.
5   John Rickard, Australia. A Cultural History, London and New York 1996, second edition, pp. 181-185.
6   'The Soda Fountain in Australia' in Sweets Magazine, August 1928, reprinted in: The Ice Creamer, Issue 32, October 1987, pp. 5-6.
7   Rickard 1996, pp. 191-193.
8   Undated and untitled one-page document from the Streets archive, HAR: ICG, box 43, folder 2. All facts about the early period of J.P. Sennitt & Son Ltd. are taken from this document.
9   'Peters Ice Cream History to February 1996', Nestlé archives. See also 'The History of Peters Ice Cream' in Heritage Australia, November 1995, p. 35.
10 The Ice Cream Trade Journal, September 1911, p. 32.
11 Odell 1984, p. 20.
12 The Ice Cream Trade Journal, August 1927, pp. 59-60.
13 'Peters Ice Cream History to February 1996', Nestlé archives.
14 Ibid.
15 'The Soda Fountain in Australia' in Sweets Magazine, August 1928, reprinted in The Ice Creamer, Issue 32, October 1987, pp. 5-6.
16 The photo collection of the State Library of New South Wales, Sydney, contains a number of such photos.
17 Interview by Pim Reinders with Arthur Woodburry and Bill Philips, Sydney, 20.10.1997. Arthur Woodburry started working for Lynam's in about 1938.
18 Ibid.
19 'Edwin Street, O.B.E.', a biography compiled by M.W. Allen, 05.07.1984. Edwin's parents, James and Delia Street, were immigrants from Staffordshire in the United Kingdom. Edwin was the youngest of ten children, eight boys and two girls.
20 Telephone interview with Daniel Street's son Ronald, Sydney, 21.10.1997. After the Second World War Ron Street was a member of the Streets board of directors until 1961. The Australian and New Zealand Army Corps (ANZAC) was formed in 1915. Ultimately the corps numbered around

417,000 men; 330,000 of them travelled to Europe and took part in the war. Of these, 59,000 were killed and 174,000 wounded, many in the ill-fated Gallipoli campaigns. See Rickard 1996, p.120.
21 'The Young Man With The Starspangled Ice Cream Cart' in Financial Review, [Sydney], 04.04.1957.
22 Copy of the deed of foundation of The Illawara Delicacies Company, 13.12.1923.
23 Telephone interview with Ronald Street, Sydney, 21.10.1997.
24 Ibid. See also Carol Odell, Ice-creams, sorbets and frozen delights, Melbourne 1984, p. 22.
25 Financial Review, 04.04.1957.
26 'Hello, Boys & Girls', speech by Daisy Street 1986].
27 'Memorandum and articles of Streets Ice Cream Proprietary Limited', Sydney, 06.08.1974.
28 Letter to Mr. Oscar V. Jeffree from Reginald R. Merrett and Edwin Street, board of directors, 12.08.1936. Oscar V. Jeffree was the contractor who built the factory. The letter is an appendix to a letter from Wayne J. Thompson to Streets Ice Cream Ltd., 20.06.1985. Wayne J. Thompson is a grandson of Oscar V. Jeffree. The information about the ice cream machines derives from an interview by Pim Reinders with John Karlik, Sydney, 17.10.1997.
29 Twenty-Fifth Anniversary of Amscol. A Short History of Progress Extracted from Annual Reports, Adelaide 1947. HAR: ICG, box 43, folder 2.
30 Ibid.
31 Ibid.
32 'Amscol Turnover', Adelaide 1959].
33 The Ice Cream Review, March 1955, p. 138.
34 The figures for Amscol are taken from 'Amscol Turnover', Adelaide [1959]; those for Streets from '25th Annual Report. Notice of meeting and balance sheet 1959, Streets Ice Cream Limited', Sydney 1959, p. 10.
35 'Shifting ice cream in big licks' in The Unilever Australia Reporter, December 1960.
36 Interview by Pim Reinders with Arthur Woodburry and Bill Philips, Sydney, 20.10.1997. According to former Streets employee Don Scott, Heart was already on the market in 1946 [interview by Pim Reinders with Don Scott, 16.10.1997].
37 Telephone interview by Pim Reinders with Ronald Street, Sydney, 21.10.1997. During that conversation Ronald Street said that the name Paddle Pop had been thought up by him in Australia. In an interview with Tom Lutsey, the founder of Gold Bond, Lutsey said he had already referred to his ice lollies as 'Paddle Pops' in 1939, but it was not clear whether he also sold his ices under that name.
38 'Memorandum Overseas Committee to the Special Committee. Australia: Ice Cream', 01.02.1960, HAL. Unilever Historical Archive, London.
39 McNiven Bros. Ltd. Metropolitan Price List, Camperdown [circa 1959].
40 'Drinking Straws made by the million at McNiven's, Adelaide' in The Unilever Australia Reporter, May 1961, p. 11.
41 Ibid
42 'Peters Ice Cream History to February 1996', Nestlé archives.
43 'Memorandum Overseas Committee to the Special Committee. Australia: Ice Cream', 01.02.1960, HAL. Unilever Historical Archive, London.
44 The Sun, [Sydney], 19.11.1962. Ices of the Gaytime type proved to be very successful. In 1982 they still had a market share of 4.4% within the meanwhile much-expanded range of Streets impulse ices. In the 1997-1998 season Gaytime still featured on the price list, selling for $1.50; in 1966 it had retailed for 10 cents.
45 Debbie Hill, The Australian Ice Cream

and Frozen Confections Industry. Market Structure and the Demand Model, Canberra 1985, p. 7 and p. 1.
46 'Minutes Special Committee', 24.01.1975, HAR: AHK-225. H.1542. Unilever Historical Archive, London.
47 Ibid.
48 'Peters Ice Cream History to February 1996', Nestlé archives. See also 'The History of Peters Ice Cream' in Heritage Australia, November 1995, pp. 35-37.
49 Sydney Morning Herald, 10.09.1981.
50 'Streets to close Notting Hill site', Streets press release, 08.08.1991.
51 'Streets to build $70 million factory', Streets press release, 19.03.1996.

Box: The Paddle Pop Lion
1 Telephone interview by Pim Reinders with Ronald Street, Sydney, 21.10.1997.
2 'How to unlock Paddle's Greatest Potential', Streets report, 06.07.1992.
3 'The Paddle Pop Brand Positioning Statement', Streets, Sydney, 1992-1993.
4 The information about Max the Dog derives from a telephone interview by Pim Reinders with Paul Jay, 13.10.1998, who was marketing manager at Olá in the mid-1970s.

Chapter 8 United Kingdom: 'Stop me and buy one!'
1 Le Glacier, Paris 1960, pp. 75-82. The Selfridges soda fountain was not the first of its kind to be seen in the United Kingdom, having been one of the innovations displayed at the Crystal Palace Exhibition in the summer of 1900.
2 Charles Wilson, The history of Unilever: a study in economic growth and social change, Vol I, page 274.
3 Charles Forte, Forte. The autobiography of Charles Forte, London 1986, pp. 22-23.
4 Ibid., pp. 33-36.
5 Letter from T. Wall & Sons Ltd. to shopkeepers, 21.06.1922, in Store ledger T. Wall & Sons Ltd., HAL.
6 G.A. Stonestreet, Company History, no place, no year [circa 1969], p. 2; unpublished manuscript about the history of T. Wall & Sons Ltd., HAL, Port Sunlight, MWL 17.
7 Ibid., p. 3.
8 Ibid., pp. 4-5.
9 'The story of Wall's' in Progress, Unilever's international magazine, Autumn 1948, p. 6.
10 Wall's Magazine, Spring 1962, p. 4.
11 A personal sales talk, May 1933, T. Wall & Sons Ltd., HAR: ICG box 7, folder 5.
12 G.A. Stonestreet circa 1969], p. 5 and 'The story of Wall's' in Progress, Autumn 1948, p. 6.
13 Ibid., pp. 6-7.
14 'Board Minutes T. Wall & Sons Ltd.', pp. 98-99, HAL, Port Sunlight, MWL 1/2/1.
15 G.A. Stonestreet [circa 1969], p. 4; and John Burnett, Plenty & Want. A social history of food in England. From 1815 to the present day, London 1989, 3rd edition, p. 122.
16 'Minutes Managing Directors Conference Lever', 19.08.1925, HAL.
17 Ibid., p. 14.
18 G.A. Stonestreet [circa 1969], p. 21.
19 Wall's Magazine, Spring 1957, Vol. 10, No. 1, p. 20.
20 G.A. Stonestreet [circa 1969], p. 22.
21 Ibid., p. 23.
22 Ibid., pp. 17-18.
23 'Minutes Managing Directors Conference', 20.02.1936, HAL.
24 Stonestreet [circa 1969], p. 25.
25 'Managing Directors Conferences Unilever: Wall's Ice Cream', 26.07.1934, HAL: BB 45.
26 'Wall's Ice Cream Product History File No. 5', Lintas Ltd., London, [1945], HAL, Port Sunlight, LL 47.
27 Ibid.
28 Evening Standard, May 1949.
29 Ice Cream and Water Ices. A report on

the Supply in the United Kingdom of Ice Cream and Water Ices, HMSO, London 1979, p. 55, paragraph 147.
30 D.J. Richardson, 'J. Lyons and Co. Ltd.: caterers and food manufacturers 1894-1939', pp. 164-165, in Derek Oddy and Derek Miller, The Making of the British Diet, London 1976.
31 Ibid., p. 165.
32 Ibid., p. 167.
33 Ice Cream and Water Ices, London 1979, p. 54, paragraph 143.
34 Oddy and Miller, London 1976, p. 169.
35 G.A. Stonestreet [circa 1969], p. 43.
36 'Cold Comfort. Change from Hokey Pokey to Modern Ices', in The Times, 22.04.1957.
37 G.A. Stonestreet [circa 1969], p. 24.
38 'Wall's Ice Cream Product History File no. 5', Lintas Ltd., London, [1945], HAL, Port Sunlight, LL 47.
39 'Minutes Unilever Special Committee Meetings, re General Matters', 17.04.1940, HAL.
40 'Minutes Unilever Special Committee Meetings, re General Matters', 09.10.1940, HAL.
41 'Minutes Managing Directors Conference. T. Walls & Sons Ltd.', 19.11.1942, HAL, BB.27 (11].
42 Wall's Magazine, Spring 1962, p. 4.
43 Ibid., p. 45.
44 'Minutes Managing Directors Conferences Unilever Food Companies', 30.11.1944, HAL: BB 27 (11].
45 G.A. Stonestreet [circa 1969], p. 48.
46 Ibid. See also 'Minutes of the meeting of the Unilever Special Committee with the UK Co-ordination Director on UK Food Matters', 31.10.1960, No. M.320, p. 16, HAL.
47 G.A. Stonestreet [circa 1969], p. 48.
48 'Ice Cream and the Dairy Farmer', press release by Link Information Services Ltd. (LIS), 14.04.1959, Information Desk, Unilever House, London. LIS was a PR bureau that worked for Wall's in that period.
49 'Minutes of the meeting of the Unilever Special Committee with the UK Co-ordination Director on UK Food Matters', 31.10.1960, No. M.320, p. 16, HAL.
50 Burnett 1989, p. 283.
51 Yearbook Ice Cream Alliance, London 1951, p. 9.
52 G.A. Stonestreet [circa 1969], p. 49.
53 'Minutes Unilever Special Committee Meetings, re General Matters', 23.10.1947 and 11.02.1948, HAL.
54 Len Sharpe, The Lintas story, London 1964, pp. 89-90.
55 'Ice Cream Sales in Winter Times', in Cold Storage and Produce Review, February 21, 1924, p. 58. In a letter to the editor of this trade journal an 'observer' working in the cold storage industry wrote: '[The] argument that ice cream can only be eaten when the weather is hot seems to me to be just as foolish as it would be to say that one would not drink hot tea or coffee except when the weather was cold'. He went on to describe how on a trip to a London theatre he had seen the programme girls sell an estimated two hundred Lyons ices during the interval at one shilling each, bringing in a total revenue of £10. And, with foresight, the letter-writer then asked: 'How much more would the demand grow if a number of firms were selling and advertising ice cream?'
56 Ibid., pp. 91-92.
57 'Wall's Ice Cream 1947', Guard Books Wall's, HAL.
58 'Minutes Unilever Special Committee re UK Food Executive', 09.04.1953, HAL. Sales in February 1953 amounted to £363,772; in February 1952 they were £478,501.
59 'Minutes of the meeting of the Unilever Special Committee with the UK Co-ordination Director on UK Food Matters', 31.10.1960, No. M.320, p. 2, HAL.
60 'Wall's Ice Cream. Account History: 1955', Guard Books Wall's, HAL.

61 'Minutes Directors Conference',
14.02.1958, HAL.
62 'Cold Comfort. Change from Hokey Pokey
to Modern Ices', in The Times, 22.04.1957.
63 '5,000 M Ice Cream this year?', article in
The Financial Times, 28.07.1958.
64 'Minutes of the meeting of the Unilever
Special Committee with the UK Co-ordination Director on UK Food Matters',
31.10.1960, No. M.320, p. 5, HAL.
65 The Wall's Report 1978, p. 13, Information
Desk, Unilever House, London.
66 Ibid., p. 21.
67 Author's interview with Don Angel,
London 14.11.1996. Don Angel was the
Chairman of Birds Eye Wall's at the time the
decision was made. A similar computer-
controlled system to that at Gloucester was
later installed as part of the upgrading of
two other Unilever ice cream factories: the
Langnese factory at Heppenheim and the
Streets factory at Minto, near Sydney.
68 Charles Wilson, Unilever 1945-1965.
Challenge and Response in the Post-War
Industrial Revolution, London 1968,
pp. 195-196.
69 'List of delivered ice bar freezers types
RIA-4 and RIA-5-6-7', 13.05.1965, Archives
Gram, Vojens, Denmark.
70 Wall's Magazine, Autumn 1954, Volume 5,
Number 3, p. 5.
71 'Minutes Unilever Special Committee
Meetings with the Food Executive',
06.11.1952, HAL.
72 'Unilever Special Committee Meetings
with the Food Executive', 26.02.1947, HAL.
73 The House of Wall's, London [1950], HAL
Port Sunlight, MD/AL/22/4. 23/1.
74 'Minutes Unilever Special Committee re
UK Committee', 19.11.1965, HAR: AHK-1734.
75 'Minutes of the meeting of the Unilever
Special Committee with the UK Co-ordination Director on UK Food Matters',
31.10.1960, No. M.320, p. 12, HAL.
76 Wilson, London 1968, p. 41.
77 Ice Cream and Water Ices. A report on
the Supply in the United Kingdom of Ice
Cream and Water Ices, HMSO, London 1979,
p. 54, paragraph 144.
78 Lyons Maid. Ice Cream of the 70s,
London [no year].
79 'Minutes Unilever Special Committee',
11.10.1963, HAR: AHK-1743.
80 Forte, 1986, p. 104.
81 'Minutes Unilever Special Committee re
UK Committee', 19.11.1965, HAR: AHK-1743.
82 Ice Cream and Water Ices. A report on
the Supply in the United Kingdom of Ice
Cream and Water Ices, HMSO, London 1979,
p. 55, paragraph 147.
83 'Minutes Special Committee re Food
Executive', 10.03.1955, HAL.
84 Interview by Pim Reinders with Hugo
Mossel, Brussels, 15.01.1997.
85 The Wall's report 1978, p. 14, Information
Desk, Unilever House, London.
86 'Demand for Ice Cream in the UK', Foods
II/III Section Economics & Statistical
Department, Unilever, July 1970, HAR: AHK
1933-902523.
87 Author's Interview with John
Pooler, Gloucester, 20.11.1996.
88 The Wall's report 1981, p. 19, Information
Desk, Unilever House, London.
89 The Wall's report 1980, p. 17, Information
Desk, Unilever House, London.
90 Wilson, London 1968, p. 171.
91 The Wall's report 1981, p. 1, Information
Desk, Unilever House, London.
92 The Wall's report 1987, p. 11, Information
Desk, Unilever House, London.
93 S. Jones, J. Lyons & Co. A Company
Study, E & S Department, Unilever House,
London, January 1975, HAR: AHK-2009.
94 Forte, London 1986, pp. 164-165.
95 Ice Cream. A report on the supply in the
UK of ice cream for immediate
consumption, HMSO, London 1994, pp. 3-4.
The ice cream activities were continued
under the name Lyons Maid by Glacier

Foods Ltd.; from 1978 Glacier Foods was a
subsidiary of Allied-Lyons PLC, the company that was formed after the purchase of
Lyons by Allied Breweries Ltd.
96 UK Take Home ice cream, July 1986, ICH
32-902523. The percentages refer to the
value not the volume of the market share.
97 Wall's Ice Cream – Marketing Strategy,
January 1984, HAR: ICG 32-902523.
98 Ice Cream, HMSO, London 1994, p. 21.
99 Ibid., p. 20.

Box: The trikes that went to war
1 Wall's Magazine, Spring 1960, Volume 13,
No. 1, p. 15.

Chapter 9 Ireland: 'a brick after mass'

1 John Ardagh, Ireland and the Irish.
Portrait of a Changing Society, London,
1994, p. 28.
2 Evening Press, 06.11.1969. In 1962 94% of
HB's production consisted of vanilla ice
cream.
3 Report on a meeting between representatives of Unilever and W.R. Grace & Co.,
Paris, 23.10.1972, HAR, AHK 1891 - 901410.
4 Press release, HB Ice Cream Limited,
Dublin, 1968.
5 Xavier de Planhol, L'eau de neige, Paris,
1995, p. 181.
6 W.S. Stallings, Jr., 'Ice cream and water
ices in 17th and 18th century England',
Petits Propos Culinaires 3, supplement,
London, 1979, p. 2.
7 John Dubray (1682), James De Bord
(1686), Francis Guerrin (1696), in Database
of Freeman's Role of the City of Dublin,
Dublin Heritage Group, Dublin. Information
courtesy of Fiona Brennan, Assistant
Manager Dublin Heritage Group; letter
dated 29.07.1997.
8 Sylvia P. Beamon, The ice houses of
Britain, London, 1990, p. 21; Elizabeth David,
Harvest of the Cold Months, London, 1994.
9 Information courtesy of Robin Weir,
London, 06.06.1997. The invoice is in his
collection.
10 More pricks than kicks in A Samuel
Beckett Reader, Ed. John Calder, 1983,
pp. 48-49.
11 Brian Reynolds, Casalattico and the
Italian Community in Ireland, Dublin, 1993,
pp. 49 and 53.
12 Reynolds, op. cit., pp. 48-53 and 56-57.
The percentage of 46% for ice cream sellers is calculated from figures that Reynolds
gives in table 2.5 on p. 56.
13 Una Powder, Terra Straniera. The story
of the Italians in Ireland, Dublin, 1988, p. 70.
14 Thom's Directory, Dublin, 1900, mentions
four ice-making factories.
15 Thom's Directory, Dublin, 1927.
16 Author's Interview with Bernadetto
Cervi, Dublin, 25.06.1997.
17 Another such expansion occurred in
Liège, Belgium, where Marziale's ice
cream saloon established in the 1930s led
to the formation of the Mio ice cream
company after the Second World War; (see
chapter 13].
18 List of delivered and ordered ice bar
freezers type RIA-4 and RIA-5-6-7,
03.07.1965. Gram Archives, Vojens,
Denmark.
19 M. Black, W.R. Grace and Co. and the UK
Ice Cream Market, Economical & Statistical
Department, Unilever House, London, Aug.
1970; HAR: AHK 1933 - 902523.
20 Irish Times, 30.10.1924.
21 Terence Brown, Ireland. A Social and
Cultural History 1922-1985, London, 1985,
p. 15.
22 Pat Doyle, Louis P.F. Smith, Milk to
Market, Dublin, 1989, p. 30.
23 Irish Times, 01.07.1968.
24 Author's Interview with W.W. Hughes,
Dublin, 24.06.1997.
25 Memo by W.W. Hughes, Dublin,
01.01.1997.

26 Author's Interview with Bernadetto
Cervi, Dublin, 25.06.1997.
27 Hughes News, Dublin, December 1966,
p. 21. See also memo by W.W. Hughes,
Dublin, 01.07.1997; HAR: ICP - box 12, folder
7. The eternal quest for ice cream producers is to sell in the winter as well as in the
summer.
28 Memo by W.W. Hughes, Dublin,
01.06.1997; HAR: ICP - box 12, folder 7.
29 Ibid.
30 Hughes News, December 1959, p. 5;
HAR: ICP - box 12, folder 7.
31 Memo by W.W. Hughes, Dublin,
01.01.1997; HAR: ICP - box 12, folder 7.
32 Hughes News, Dublin, December 1960,
p. 10; HAR: ICP-box 12, folder 7.
33 Hughes News, Dublin, December 1959,
p. 5; HAR: ICP-box 12, folder 7.
34 Ardagh, op. cit., pp. 28-31.
35 Ardagh, op. cit., p. 31.
36 Pat Doyle, Louis P.F. Smith, Milk to
Market, Dublin, 1989, pp. 96-98. The authors
argue that from an economic point of view
there was no room for another dairy factory
in the sparsely populated Ireland of 1947.
37 Press release HB Ice Cream Limited,
Dublin, 1968. The total figure of 88,000 is an
aggregation of the capacities per machine
listed in this press release.
38 The Irish Press, 07.07.1968. The newspaper's article about the new factory was
headed 'Plans envisaged for further expansion in both national and international
markets'.
39 M. Black, W.R. Grace and Co., and UK Ice
Cream Market, Unilever House, London,
Aug. 1970; HAR: AHK 1933 - 902523.
40 Special Committee, 21.05.1971 X904,
HAR, AHK 1872.
41 Special Committee, 30.03.1973 II.185,
HAR, AHK 2225.
42 HB Ice Cream and Urney Chocolate in
Ireland. Memo for the Special Committee,
10.01.1973; HAR: AHK 2009 - 901410.

Box: The life story of 'Golly'
1 Juliet Savage, 'A Brief History of the
Golliwog' in International Golliwog Collectors Club Newsletter, No. 4, Woodstock,
USA, undated.
2 Jim Cullen, The Art of Democracy. A
Concise History of Popular Culture in the
United States, New York, 1996, pp. 65-69.
3 Westminster Gazette, 28.05.1907.

Chapter 10 The Danish technological revolution

1 Oluf S. Hansen, Fremstilling af Flødeis,
Copenhagen 1949, p. 20.
2 Ice Cream – Denmark, Memorandum to
the Special Committee, 02.06.1960, HAL -
Archive Special Committee, 6198.
3 Film to mark the fortieth anniversary of
Hellerup Is, Copenhagen 1954. Video edition
in HAR - VID - 4. 'Isbaade' products were
still being sold in Denmark in 1997.
4 Onno-Frank van Bekkum and Gert van
Dijk (ed.), Agricultural Co-operatives in the
European Union. Trends and Issues on the
Eve of the 21st Century, 1997, p. 41.
5 Stewart Oakley, The story of Denmark,
London 1972, pp. 171-174.
6 Interview with Moj Vieh Larsen,
23.04.1997, Århus.
7 Bernhard Bøggild, 'Dairy Technology' in
Maelkertidende, 1913, pp. 441-445.
8 Is-Konditori-Tidende, Vol. 6, No. 4, April
1939, p. 3.
9 Ibid.
10 Ibid.
11 J.F. Engberg, 'Maelkens Industrialiser-
ing' in Maelkertidende, 1925, pp. 319-323.
12 J.F. Engberg, 'Lidt om Ice Cream' in
Maelkertidende, 1926, pp. 424-427.
13 Ibid.
14 Oluf S. Hansen, Fremstilling af Flødeis,
Copenhagen 1949, p. 6.
15 Dansk Flødeis, Vol. 1, No. 1, January
1934, p. 2.

16 Ibid.
17 Oluf S. Hansen, 'Ise-Creme Fabrikatio-
nen' in Maelkertidende, 1927, pp. 665-677.
18 J.F. Engberg, 'Den danske Ice Cream
Industri' in Maelkertidende, 1927, pp. 991-
997.
19 Is-Konditori-Tidende, Vol. 5, No. 6, June
1928, p. 3.
20 'Danish Company Plans Distribution of
Ice Cream on National Scale' in The Ice
Cream Trade Journal, February 1929,
pp. 43-45 and 68.
21 J.F. Engberg, 'Den danske Ice Cream
Industri' in Maelkertidende, 1927,
pp. 991-997.
22 Is-Konditori-Tidende, Vol. 5, No. 7, July
1928, pp. 7-8.
23 Ibid.
24 Ice Cream – Denmark, Memorandum to
the Special Committee, 02.06.1960, HAL
Archive Special Committee, 6198.
25 Oluf S. Hansen, Fremstilling af Flødeis,
Copenhagen 1949, pp. 25-27.
26 Is-Konditori-Tidende, Vol. 4, No. 3,
March 1927, pp. 2-3.
27 Ibid.
28 Ibid.
29 60 års erfaring med iskager, article
published to celebrate the sixtieth anniversary of Frederiksborg Is, 1989.
30 Ibid.
31 Geschiedenis van de techniek in Nederland. Deel 1. Techniek en modernisering van
landbouw en voeding. De wording van een
moderne samenleving 1800-1890, Zutphen
1992, p. 109, pp. 158-159, p. 255.
32 Dansk Bager- og Konditor-Tidende,
Vol. 31, August 1923, p. 151.
33 Brødrene Gram A/S 1901-1951, Vojens
1951, p. 10.
34 Ibid.
35 Maskiner for Iskrem Fabrikation.
Brødrene Gram Vojens, circa 1936, p. 30,
Archives Brødrene Gram, Vojens.
36 Refrigram, Vol. 1, No. 1, July 1945, p. 7,
Archives Brødrene Gram, Vojens.
37 Dansk Flødeis, Vol. 2, No. 1, January
1935, p. 8.
38 Den Kongelige Patentkommission,
Copenhagen, Patent No. 51380.
39 Interview with Sørn Gram, Vojens,
21.04.1997.
40 Author's Interview with Carl Høyer,
Århus, 23.04.1997. Telefax from Carl Høyer,
16.02.1998.
41 Author's Interview with Sørn Gram,
Vojens, 21.04.1997.
42 Bødil Frederiksen, O.G. Høyer Maskinfabrik A/S 1948-1985, Århus 1985, p. 21.
43 Maskiner for Iskrem Fabrikation.
Brødrene Gram A/S, Vojens, circa 1935,
p. 22. Archives Brødrene Gram, Vojens.
44 Dansk Flødeis, Vol. 1, No. 9, September
1934, pp 69-71.
45 Den Kongelige Patentkommission,
Copenhagen, Patent No. 54707.
46 Bødil Frederiksen, O.G. Høyer Maskinfabrik A/S 1948-1985, Århus 1985, p. 16.
Capacity for manual production of ice
creams on sticks was 1,300 ice creams
per hour.
47 'Automatisk Ispindefryser' in Nordisk
Mejeri-Tidsskrift, 1937, p. 83.
48 Refrigram, Vol. 1, No. 1, July 1945,
Archives Brødrene Gram, Vojens.
49 List of delivered and ordered ice bar
freezers types RIA-4 and RIA-6, Vojens,
09.1958, Archives Brødrene Gram, Vojens.
Also List of delivered and ordered ice bar
freezers types RIA-4 and RIA-5-6-7, Vojens
13.07.1965, Archives Brødrene Gram,
Vojens.
50 Bødil Frederiksen, O.G. Høyer Maskinfabrik A/S 1948-1985, Århus 1985, p. 16.
51 These are tanks where the ice cream
mix is left for a time to "age" before
processing.
52 Fruit feeders introduce fruit and other
additions to the mix, with minimal damage,
and in prescribed amounts.

53 Ibid. p.18.
54 Author's Interview with Carl Høyer,
23.04.1997.
55 Bødil Frederiksen, O.G. Høyer Maskinfabrik A/S 1948-1985, Århus 1985, p. 20.
56 Ibid. p. 25.
57 Ibid. p. 25.
58 Ibid. p. 39. Since 1991 Alfa-Laval-Høyer
has formed part of the Swedish company
Tetra Pak, the world's biggest supplier of
packaging systems for liquid foods.
59 Den nye Frisko Is i Skovlunde, an article
published to mark the opening of a new
Frisko factory in Skovlunde near Copenhagen at the beginning of 1968.
60 Purchase contract Frisko, 15.07.1960,
HAR: AHK-1584.
61 Ice Cream – Denmark, Memorandum to
the Special Committee, 02.06.1960, HAL-
Archive Special Committee, 6198.
62 Letter from S.J. van den Bergh to Group
Management, Unilever NV, Rotterdam,
20.06.1961, HAR: AHK-1584.
63 Acquisitions west of Storebaelt,
09.10.1969, HAR: AHK-1766-8102523.
64 Memo 31.12.1972, HAR: AHK-1890.
65 Salgsudviklingen for konsumis i de
nordiske lande, 21.12.1995, Iskremindustriens Sammenslutning, (The Danish Ice
Cream Association), Copenhagen.
66 Author's Interview with Mogens Vigh-
Larsen, 23.04.1997, Århus. Mogens Vigh-
Larsen was the technical director of Frisko.

**Box: 'The most beautiful woman
of Skoubogade'**
1 Conditoriet La Glace. 125 år med kager i
København, 1995.
2 Dansk Flødeis, Vol. 1, No. 1, January 1934,
p. 8.

**Box: John Larsen, 'flying engineer and
ice cream king'**
1 'Larsens is og biler' in Bilhistorisk
Tidsskrift, No. 123, Copenhagen 1996,
pp. 8-11.
2 Is-Konditori-Tidende, Vol. 5, June 1928,
No. 6, p. 3.

Chapter 11 Sweden: Europe's ice cream champions

1 Ernst Nathorst-Böös, 'Glace' in Utdrag
ur Gastronmisk Kalender 1969, p. 95.
2 Mats Wickman, Glassboken. Ett stycke
glasshistoria, Stockholm, 1992, pp. 17-18.
3 Ibid. In 1859 Carl Grafström published a
23-page booklet of new ice cream recipes
and other desserts. Carl J. Grafström,
Åtskilliga nya sorter glass och söta
mellanrätter. (Entremêts sucrés). Några ord
om glass, Stockholm, 1859.
4 Eric W. Hanner, Mjölkcentralen Glassavdelning, 28.10.1938, GB archives, Stockholm. According to Hanner's report the
following ice cream parlours existed in
Stockholm in 1928: Cipriani, Pelligrini, D.
Jaconelli, R. Jaconelli, Glacefabriken Polar
owned by the Russian Korpoff, Puelli &
Jaconelli, A. Sneltorp, Nyco Glacefabrik.
5 Franklin D. Scott, Sweden, The Nation's
History, 5th enlarged edition, 1988, p. 444.
6 'Is-Crème-Fabrikationen' in Maelkertidende, Odense, 1927, pp. 665-677.
7 '50 viktiga år i den svenska glassens
historia' in Glaciären, Vol. 14, No. 5,
December 1984. Glaciären is the personnel
magazine of the GB ice cream company,
Stockholm.
8 Ernst Nathorst-Böös, 'Glace' in Utdrag
ur Gastronomisk Kalender, Årg. 9, 1969,
pp. 96-97.
9 'The Ice Cream Industry in Continental
Europe' in The Ice Cream Trade Journal,
July 1929, p. 40.
10 Interview with Eric Hanner in Glaciären,
June 1982.
11 'Eric Hanner: Jag var med när vi fick
sova i fabriken'. Interview in Glaciären, No.
3, June 1982, GB archives, Stockholm.
12 Franklin D. Scott, Sweden, The Nation's

History, 5th enlarged edition, 1988,
pp. 486-487.
13 '50 viktiga år i den svenska glassens
historia' in Glaciären, Vol. 14, No. 5,
December 1984.
14 'Sveriges största glassföretag går
samman' in Glaciären, 1973.
15 Report on Trollhätteglass, 02.04.1962,
HAR, AHK 1584 - 8301410.
16 Eric W. Hanner, Mjölkcentralen Glassavdelning, 28.10.1938, GB archives, Stockholm.
17 Stina Gottliebson, Arla 75 år 1915-1990,
Stockholm, 1990, pp. 4-7.
18 Eric W. Hanner, Mjölkcentralen Glassavdelning, 28.10.1938, GB archives, Stockholm. Most of the information about the
initial years of ice cream production by the
Mjölkcentralen originates from this
document.
19 'Pionjärerna' in Glaciären, 1972.
20 'Det här är Glace-Bolagets 40-åriga
historia' in Glaciären, Vol. 12, 3 June 1982,
p. 8, GB archives, Stockholm.
21 Mjölkcentralen, Glasskontrakt, 1930s.
An example of such a contract, without a
precise date, can be found in Eric W.
Hanner, Mjölkcentralen Glassavdelning,
28.10.1938, GB archives, Stockholm.
22 Ice Cream. Triggers & Barriers to
Consumption. National Dossier: Sweden,
May 1995, p. 29, URL - UK.
23 Folder Igloo Dessertglace en nyhet!
contained in Eric W. Hanner, Mjölkcentralen
Glassavdelning, 28.10.1938, GB archives,
Stockholm.
24 'Eric Hanner: Jag var med när vi fick
sova i fabriken'. Interview in Glaciären, No.
3, June 1982, GB archives, Stockholm.
25 Odd Sjetne, Report on the Ice Cream
Industry in the Four Nordic Countries, given
at the Sixth European Ice Cream Conference, Stockholm, 01.06.1972 - 02.06.1972,
HAR: AHK 1933 - 02523.
26 '50 viktiga år i den svenska glassens
historia' in Glaciären, Vol. 14, No. 5,
December 1984.
27 Franklin D. Scott, Sweden, The Nation's
History, 5th enlarged edition, 1988, p. 507.
28 Letter from Schweizerische Industrie-
Gesellschaft to A.B. Glace-Bolaget, Stockholm, 26.06.1943; GB archives, Stockholm.
29 Letter from A/B Bröderna Sjunnesson to
A.B. Glace-Bolaget, Stockholm, 13.07.1943;
GB archives, Stockholm. Bröderna Sjunnesson was the Swedish representative of
Schweizerische Industrie-Gesellschaft.
30 Letter from Ingeniör R. Pehrsson to A.B.
Glace-Bolaget, Stockholm, 10.08.1943, GB
archives, Stockholm.
31 Över utredning av div. kyltekniska frågor
vid Glace-Bolaget A.B., Stockholm,
11.09.1944, GB archives, Stockholm, p. 2.
This document gives an exact specification
of the monthly production of both round and
square ice cream on sticks in the April to
September period. The combined total
output of both types was 9,326,545 units.
In 1950 the total production amounted to 13
million units. See lecture by Eric Hanner,
Distribution av iskrem, 15.09.1950, GB
archives, Stockholm.
32 Author's interview with Sørn Gram in
Vojens, 21.04.1997.
33 Odd Sjetne, Report on the Ice Cream
Industry in the Four Nordic Countries,
presented at the Sixth European Ice Cream
Conference, Stockholm, 01.06.1972 -
02.06.1972, HAR: AHK 1933 - 02523.
34 Refrigram, Volume 1, July 1945, No. 1,
pp. 4-6 and 11.
35 Gille-Glass AB - General Information,
HAR: AHK 1584 - 8301410.
36 Ibid.
37 The estimate originates from the
Djupfrysningsbyrån ("Deep-Freeze
Bureau") in Stockholm; op. cit. in Eric
Hanner, Dessertis, 1957, GB archives,
Stockholm.
38 Report on the Gille-Glace operation to

date and plan for the future, 1961, Appendix 3, HAR: AHK - 1602.
39 Report on the Ice Cream Industry in the Four Nordic Countries, Stockholm, 1972, HAR: AHK 1933 - 02523.
40 Eric Hanner, Dessertis, 1957, GB archives, Stockholm.
41 Glass Nytt, No. 2, 1956, GB archives, Stockholm. Glass Nytt was the company magazine of Trollhätteglass.
42 Swedish Ice Cream Consumption 1960-1995 in litres per capita, 08.02.1996, GB archives, Stockholm.
43 Lecture by Eric Hanner, Distribution av iskrem, 15.09.150, GB archives, Stockholm.
44 Ibid.
45 Letter from Dansk Unilever, 21.03.1969. HAR: AHK-1890-83014.
46 Gösta Lilja 'Många ljusa minnen av Eric Hanner' in: Glaciären, No. 2, Vol. 16, 1987, pp. 8-9, GB archives, Stockholm.
47 Sweden - Ice Cream / Acquisition Trollhätteglass AB, memo from Legal Department to Mr Sidney van den Bergh, 14.09.1962, HAL: Archive Special Committee, 6817.
48 Minutes Special Committee, 10.04.1961, HAR: AHK 1581.
49 Sweden - Ice Cream / Acquisition Trollhätteglass AB, memo from Legal Department to Mr Sidney van den Bergh, 14.09.1962, HAL: Archive Special Committee, 6817.
50 Minutes Meeting Special Committee, 03.09.1971, HAR: AHK-1872.
51 Know-how agreement with Glace Bolaget, Sweden. Note from Frozen Products Co-ordination to the Special Committee, 08.11.1982, HAR: AHK 2590.
52 J.P. Erbé, Notes on visit to Glace Bolaget, Stockholm, 19th August, 1983, 12.09.1983, CA 8314.10 and Proposal to acquire the remaining 64% shareholding in Glace Bolaget, Sweden, 21.02.1984, CA 8301410.
53 In 1994 Philip Morris acquired the Swiss chocolate company Jacobs Suchard, which in turn owns Freia Marabou (Norway). Freia Marabou is the owner of Marabou Sweden. See Sweden's Food Market, Agriculture Affairs Office of the Foreign Agricultural Service/USDA, Stockholm, 15.07.1994, p. 8.
54 GB Annual Estimate 1987, 13.11.1986, HAR: AHK 2590.

Box: 'Steaming' ice cream cakes
1 Eric Hanner, Dessertis, 1957, GB archives.
2 Ice Cream. Triggers & Barriers to Consumption. National Dossier: Sweden, May 1995, p. 29, URL - UK.

Box: Ice cream, good for the sick!
1 'Doktorn ger råd' in Barn, No. 3, 1951.
2 Lars Söderhjelm, Svenska Läkartidningen, No. 43, op. cit. Sten Gullberg, 'Dietglass som näringsämne vid febersjukdomar' in Svenska Läkartidningen, No. 12, 1955.
3 Sten Gullberg, 'Dietglass som näringsämne vid febersjukdomar' in Svenska Läkartidningen, No. 12, 1955.
4 Ibid.
5 Glass-Nytt, No. 2, 1956.
6 Speech by Eric Hanner at a meeting of the Svenska Mejeritekniska Föreningen, 1955, GB archives, Stockholm.

Chapter 12 **Germany: Goethe's passion lives on**
1 Johann Wolfgang von Goethe, Verdichting en waarheid, Baarn 1995, p. 85. The English text quoted here is a translation by Alan Hemingway.
2 Heidemarie Prell, Vom Gipfelschnee ... zur fröhlichen Eiszeit, Nuremberg 1987, p. 31.
3 Deutsche Lebensmittel-Rundschau, July 1964, p. 201.
4 Felice Fava, 1953-1983. Trent'anni di

gelato all'Italiana, Milan 1983, p 19.
5 Ibid.
6 C. Tüllmann, 'Kunststück Verführung kann man studieren: Büffeln in der Eisschule', in Frankfurter Allgemeine Zeitung, 18.06.1997.
7 Unter Null: Kunsteis, Kälte und Kultur, Munich 1991, pp. 293-298.
8 The Ice Cream Trade Journal, July 1931.
9 Zeitschrift für Rahmeis, Hildesheim, 23.12.1924.
10 B. Lichtenberger, 'Where the Ice Cream Industry is New', in The Ice Cream Trade Journal, March 1924, p. 49.
11 C. Reinke-Kunze, Die Packeiswaffel. Von Gletschern, Schnee und Speiseeis, Basel 1996, p. 217.
12 Notarial deed, 09.10.1926, HAR: ICT, Box 42, Folder 5.
13 Zeitschrift für Eiskrem, 15.01.1926, p. 12.
14 H. Prell 1987, p. 73.
15 C. Reinke-Kunze, 1996, p. 218.
16 Author's Interview with Werner Warncke by Pim Reinders, Bremen, 08.09.1997.
17 Charles Wilson, The History of Unilever, Volume II, London 1954, pp. 370-371.
18 Möller 1992, p. 49.
19 Deed of formation of 'Langnese-Eiskrem-Vertriebsgesellschaft mit beschränkter Haftung', Berlin, 18.10.1935, Hamburg State archives, pp. 3-5.
20 'Gewinn- und Verlustrechnung am 31. Dezember 1935', pp. 1-5, Langnese archives, Hamburg.
21 Beglaubigte Abschrift aus dem Handelsregister Abteilung B, no. 49718, Berlin, 30.10.1936, Hamburg State archives.
22 Letter from A.H. Langnese Ww & Co. Keksfabrik to the Amtsgericht Berlin, Abtlg, Handelsregister, Hamburg, 05.01.1937, pp. 49-51, Hamburg State archives.
23 Wir sind 25 Jahre jung!, no year, no place Hamburg 1960]. 25th anniversary publication by Langnese Eiskrem, p. 6.
24 Anzeigen-Rechnung nr. [...] für das Amtsgericht Hamburg, Abteilung Handelsregister, in Hamburger Tageblatt, Hamburg, 25.01.1943, Hamburg State archives.
25 M. Pankofer, 'Die Jopa Story', in TK-Report, no. 4/66, 1966, pp. 12-13.
26 Ibid., pp. 14-18.
27 H. Prell, 1987, p.75, Nuremberg 1987, p. 16.
28 Ibid., p. 78.
29 Brochure Die Warncke Eiskrem KG, Bremen, no year circa 1988].
30 H. Prell 1987, p. 80.
31 M. Pankofer, 'Die Jopa Story', 1966, pp.11-18.
32 H. Prell 1987, p.83.
33 Ibid., p. 83.
34 Ibid., p. 101.
35 Schöller Nederland, 'Grande Finale', Twello, circa 1993, p. 9.
36 Letter from Susanne Kaiser, Schöller Pressestelle, 26.11.98.
37 M. Pankofer, 'Die Jopa Story', 1966, pp. 11-18.
38 H. Möller, Die Geschichte des Werkes Wandsbek der Langnese-Iglo GmbH von der Gründung 1935 bis 1978, Hamburg 1992, p. 20. Unpublished manuscript.
39 Ibid. pp. 4-21.
40 Ibid., p. 30.
41 'In Richtung Süden', pp. 1-5, Hamburg [1957], HAR: ICT box 35, folder 4.
42 Ibid., p. 12.
43 'Suggested purchase of Langnese Honey - Hamburg', Hamburg, 15.12.1958, pp. 2-10, HAR: AHK-1890.
44 Ice Cream. A World Survey, Euromonitor, London 1989, p. 298.
45 'Zusammenarbeit von Langnese und Solo', HAR: AHK-1600-1715162.
46 H. Prell 1987, p. 86.

Box: The Fürst-Pückler-Eisbombe
1 Heidemarie Prell, Vom Gipfelschnee ... zur fröhlichen Eiszeit, Nuremberg 1987, pp. 40-41.

Box: An Eskimo in Austria
1 C. Wolkenstein, Die Marke Eskimo, graduation thesis, Institut für Werbung und Marktforschung, Vienna, June 1997, p. 19.
2 'Minutes of meeting of the Special Committee held at Unilever House', No. X.394, London, 02.10.1959, no. 131. HAR: AHK-5906.
3 C. Wolkenstein 1997, pp. 19-20.

Box: The Swiss Eldorado
1 Eric W. Hanner, Mjölkcentralen Glassavdelning, 28.10.1938, archives GB, Stockholm.
2 J.H.W. Prudon, 'Eldorado Switzerland', CP 1973/4, 15.01.1974, pp. 1-2, HAR-AHK.
3 Food & Drinks Co-ordination, 'Note for the Special Committee', Rotterdam 11.01.1974, pp. 3-4, HAR: AHK-6025.

Chapter 13 **Ice cream in the Low Countries: the ijscoman cometh**
1 De Conservator, vol. 13 (1949), no. 17, p. 12.
2 J.J Machet and J.G. Klett, De Fransche Parfumeur, leerende het bereiden van alle soorten van room of crèmes, ys, en alle bij de toilette gebruikt wordende poeders, pommade, blanketsel, waschwater, tandpoeder, tinctuur, opiaat, mondwater, enz., Amsterdam 1807.
3 De Conservator, vol. 13 (1949), no. 17, p. 15.
4 Jantje van Leiden, Eten en drinken in Amsterdam, Amsterdam 1898., p. 18 and pp. 78-80, Amsterdam Municipal Archives, inv. no. V 491.
5 Brochure W. Berkhoff, Amsterdam 1907, p. 20, Municipal Archives Amsterdam, inv. no. N 38.03.002, no. 7.
6 Jantje van Leiden, Eten en drinken in Amsterdam, Amsterdam 1898., p. 18 and pp. 78-80, Amsterdam Municipal Archives, inv. no. V 491.
7 'Collega C. Doffer doet 50 jaar in ijs', in De Conservator, vol. 17 (1953), p. 125.
8 'Twee en veertig jaar in het ijs', in De Conservator, vol. 13 (1949), no. 12, p. 14.
9 'Collega J. de Wit vertelt over zijn leven als ijsbereider', in De Conservator, vol. 21 (1957), pp. 456 and 457.
10 Rijksarchief Utrecht, dossier 976 RA Utrecht.
11 E.T., 'De geschiedenis van de wafel', in De Conservator, vol. 18 (1954), no. 23, p. 260.
12 'Een beetje humor en wat romantiek bij de ijsverkoop', in De Conservator, vol. 14 (1950), no. 1], pp. 10-11.
13 'Twee en veertig jaar in het ijs', in De Conservator, vol. 13 (1949), no. 12, p. 14.
14 Jaarverslagen Keuringsdienst van Waren Annual Reports of Consumer Products Inspectorate], Amsterdam, 1921-1929.
15 Consumptie-ijsbesluit 1929 Ice Cream Decree 1929], Staatsblad, 1929, no. 321.
16 Archives Nederlandse Vereniging van Consumptie-IJsfabrikanten, Zoetermeer, appendix to agenda item 4 of the board meeting of 06.11.1953.
17 Jos van der Lans and Herman Vuijsje, Lage landen, Hoge sprongen. Nederland in beweging 1898/1998, Wormer 1998, p. 74. ['Mocca, alle vreemde smaken / Groen en geel wat tegenlacht / Hebben de Italiaansche snaken / In ons Vaderland gebracht.']
18 De Consumptie-ijsbereider, (1935), no. 1, 15.10.1935.
19 Archives Amsterdam Chamber of Commerce, inv. nos. 17139, 67261, 28396, 48149, 187607, 223267, 46526, 67388, 277993.
20 Haagse Courant, 17.03.1997.
21 Ileen Montijn, 't Gonst. 125 jaar Bijenkorf, Amsterdam 1995, p. 129.
22 S.H. van Dullemen, Regelgeving en consumptie-ijs, paper prepared for the post-graduate study group 'Cultuurgeschiedenis van het ijs in Nederland', University of

Amsterdam 1997, p. 27. HAR: ICT box 046, folder 4.
23 'Bevorder de verkoop van ijs in de winter', De Conservator, 15, 1951, p. 304.
24 The Ice Cream Trade Journal, April 1929.
25 Letter from F.P. Schutter, director of Stichting Propaganda IJsverbruik, The Hague, to Nederlandse Vereniging van Consumptie-IJsfabrikanten, 02.11.1955, with enclosures. Archives Nederlandse Vereniging van Consumptie-IJsfabrikanten, Zoetermeer, box 9.
26 The Ice Cream Review, January 1950, p. 48 and pp. 82-84.
27 Haagsche Courant, 06.07.1949.
28 The Ice Cream Review, October 1951, pp. 50-51 and p. 112.
29 Nederlandsch Weekblad voor Zuivelbereiding en -handel, 09.04.1929, second section.
30 Ibid.
31 P. van Lakerveld, 'RMI en De Sierkan, bloei en ondergang van twee melkinrichtingen', in NEHA-jaarboek, vol. 57, Amsterdam 1994, p. 420.
32 Letter from N.V. Van den Bergh's Fabrieken to The Board of Distributors, Ltd., London, 01.06.1923, HAR-112-1089.40.
33 N.V. Melkinrichting der Vereenigde Zuivelbereiders Den Haag, Rapport betreffende de periode 01.01. t/m 02.07.1932, Rotterdam 12.10.1932, HAR: SEC-14-281.1. For details of capital expenditure in the RMI's ice cream department, see: Vaste Activa R.M.I. per ulto 1939, HAR: 116-0432.3. The cost of purchasing the beach tents amounted to Fl. 4,812.58 according to a list of the fixed assets of the RMI subsidiary, the 'Residentie Melk Inrichting', as at 31 December 1939, HAR: 116-0432.3.
34 Abstract Continental Committee 20.09.1932, HAR: HIS 1091.1.
35 Accountant Nederland. Voorlopige notities omtrent RM.-groep, 28.09.1948, p. 5, HAR: 116-0432.3.
36 2e Aide-Mémoire, RMI, 30.07.1951 and 3e Aide-Mémoire, RMI, 23.08.1951, HAR 141-0457.1.
37 Letter from Dr. J.F. van Moorsel to F.J. Tempel, 30.10.1953, HAR: 141-0457.1.
38 Roomijs/consumptie-ijs Holland, Rotterdam 1956, HAR, HA 121, 250113, p. 6.
39 Afschrift uitspraak Centrale Raad van Beroep inzake ijsventers in dienst van N.V. C. Jamin te Rotterdam, 23.01.1952, archives Nederlandse Vereniging van Consumptie-IJsfabrikanten, Zoetermeer.
40 Roomijs/consumptie-ijs Holland, Rotterdam 1956, HAR, HA 121, 250113, p. 6.
41 Archives Nederlandse Vereniging van Consumptie-IJsfabrikanten, Zoetermeer, board meeting, 06.11.1953, appendix to agenda item 4.
42 Ibid.
43 Roomijs/consumptie-ijs Holland, HAR, archive no. HA 121, p. 6.
44 Raffael Gentile, Le Pudici Italiane dei Liegesi, Liège 1986, pp. 122-130.
45 Ibid.
46 'IJsboerke', in Le Maître Glacier Belge, Liste de prix, 1991.
47 IJsboerke, 1978, archives Unilever Rotterdam, CA: 014.10 – 201410.
48 R. Battelier, 'Artic Frisco Every Day', in Le Glacier, Paris 1950.
49 Letter from H.A. Bicker Caarten to G.E. Graham, 05.11.1962, HAR-AHK 1584; Minutes Special Committee 14.11.1962, No. T/II.12 HAL; letter from S.J. v.d. Bergh to M. Willick, 23.07.1963, HAR: AHK-1584; memo 22.08.1979, CA: 01210.
50 Rapport ARTIC, 07.10.1976, Iglo-Ola S.A., Brussels, archives Unilever Rotterdam, CA: 014.10.
51 Discussion with Beatrice Foods, 22.08.1979, archives Unilever Rottedram, CA: 014.10.
52 Despite intensive searches, reports on this matter, such as 'S.A. Ola - Ice cream planning for Belgium' written by R.M.

Griffiths, the first director of Ola Belgium, in 1956, could not be traced, nor was any further Unilever insight provided by a study of the minutes and appendices for meetings of the Special Committee during that period.
53 Roomijs/consumptie-ijs Holland, HAR, archive no. HA 121.
54 Ibid.
55 Author's Interview with Jef Vierstraeten, Knokke, 15.01.1997. Vierstraeten began his career with Unilever in 1951 as an engineer at Huilever in Baasrode, where he helped to construct the first Ola ice cream factory in 1956.
56 Letter from P. Gillain to C. Heyning, 20.01.1956, HAR: AHK-2085. Minutes Special Committee, 12.01.1956, T.33, HAL.
57 Projet de scenario pour l'audiovisuel historique Iglo-Ola, 28.01.1981, Iglo-Ola, HAR, ICG box 026, folder 4.
58 Ibid.
59 Advertisement for Ola, 1960, HAR: ICG box 026, folder 4.
60 HAR, CA: 014.10, België 1975, p. 6.
61 Author's Interview with Hugo Mossel, Brussels, 15.01.1997. Hugo Mossel was chaiman of Iglo-Ola and supervised the merger between Iglo and Ola in 1964.
62 Roomijs/consumptie-ijs Holland, HAR, archive no. HA 121.
63 Food Study Group Report 1957-1958, HAR-AHK, report no. 3109.B66.
64 Op Eigen Terrein, no. 18, (1960), pp. 387-391, HAR.
65 Op Eigen Terrein, no. 11, (1959), p. 183, HAR.
66 Op Eigen Terrein, no. 9, (1960), p. 187, HAR.
67 J.L. de Jager, Arm en rijk kunnen bij mij hun inkopen doen: de geschiedenis van Albert Heijn en Koninklijke Ahold, Baarn 1995, p. 174.
68 HAR, CAA 1496.
69 Ola, 22.10.1965, HAR, AHK-1734.
70 Archives Unilever Rotterdam, CAA 1631, 1975.
71 HAR, NUB 1122, 1985.
72 Josephine Woldring (ed.), 60 jaar IJsfabriek Van Scheijndel, Apeldoorn 1995, p. 57.

Box: Marja sells ice creams in wartime
1 Riek Goudappel-Bos, Marja verkoopt IJsco's, Haarlem 1947.

Box: Marziale and Mio
1 Author's interview with Robert Marziale, Liège, 12.03.1997. Robert Marziale is a grandson of Mio's founder Antoine and was director of Mio in 1997.
2 Le Glacier, Paris 1962, pp. 37-40.
3 Scope Liège, vol. 4, no. 3, March 1977, pp. 118-119.

Chapter 14 **Russia: a warm treat in a cold climate**

1 Leo Tolstoy, War and Peace, translated by Rosemary Edmonds, Penguin Classics, London 1982, pp. 73-74.
2 L. Vyskochkov, 'Eskimo Pie. History of Ice-Cream in Russia', in Russia and the World Food Market, no. 4, 1995.
3 Severnaya Pchela, no. 196, 01.09.1845.
4 G. Dezent, [Ice-Cream], Moscow 1972, p. 10.
5 L. Vyskochkov, 1995.
6 Peterburgsky Listok, 09.05.1898.
7 Cram International, Visibility/House Branding. The Essence of Ice Cream in Russia, 2.10.1997, p. 9, ICCT, Unilever House Rotterdam.
8 A. Mikoyan, [Food Industry in the USSR], Moscow 1939, p. 80.
9 Cram International, Visibility/House Branding. The Essence of Ice Cream in Russia, 2.10.1997, p. 10, ICCT, Unilever House Rotterdam.

Chapter 15 **Italy: the 'dolce' in La Dolce Vita**

1 F. Portinari, Voglia di Gelato, Milan 1987, p. 95.
2 Lorna Tee Consultancy, Barriers & Triggers to the consumption of ice-cream, Kent 1996, pp. 16-17.
3 Portinari 1987, p. 6.
4 Ibid., p. 92.
5 Ibid., p. 92.
6 Felice Favia, Trent'anni di gelato all'italiana 1953-1983, Milan 1983, p. 13.
7 Portinari 1987, p. 92.
8 Ibid., p. 49.
9 Ibid., p. 19.
10 'Ice Cream in Italy a National Asset', in The Ice Cream Review, June 1923, p. 26.
11 G. Roversi, PINO Cinquant'anni di Gelato, Bologna 1987, p. 19.
12 G.E. Grifoni, Trattato di Gelateria, Milan 1911, pp. 6-7.
13 Felice Favia 1983, pp. 66-68.
14 Author's interview with Cattabriga's Mr Diana, Bologna, 02.07.1997.
15 Ibid.
16 Felice Favia 1983, pp. 22-23.
17 Ibid.
18 'Topics of the speeches of Mr. Wiesner and Mr. Preger to the Unilever International Congress', p. 2, HAR: AHK-1678.
19 'Spica-Naples', Milan 13.10.1961, p. 1, HAR: AHK-1581.
20 Ibid.
21 Ibid.
22 SAGIT, Rome 1993, p. 1.
23 'Spica-Italy', Rotterdam 30.10.1961, p. 2, HAR: AHK-1584, and 'Ice Cream Italy', 21.02.1962, p. 2, HAR: AHK-1581.
24 'Spica-Naples', Milan 13.10.1961, HAR: AHK-1601-502523.
25 'Spica-Naples', Milan 13.10.1961, pp. 3-4, HAR: AHK-1581.
26 'Ice Cream Italy', 21.02.1962, HAL: Special Committee 6665, Appendix II.
27 'Spica-Naples', Milan 13.10.1961, p. 4, HAR: AHK-1581.
28 Ir. J. Maarschalk, 'Studie van consumptieijs, verkoop en distributie in Turijn op 3 juli 1962', 502523, July 1962, p. 1, HAR: AHK-1581.
29 Felice Favia 1983, p. 26.
30 G.F., 'Visite à Motta', in: Le Glacier 1959, pp. 121-126.
31 Felice Favia 1983, p. 26.
32 Ibid., p. 27.
33 Ibid., p. 28.
34 G. De Vecchi et al., Trent'anni di Mostra Internazionale del Gelato 1959-1989, Longarone 1990, p. 64.
35 Author's interview with L.G. Coronato, Sagit, Rome, 14.09.1996.
36 'Spica-Italië', 17.06.1968, p. 3, HAR: AHK-1766.
37 'Spica Italy', 20.10.1961, HAR: AHK-1584.
38 Ir. J. Loopuyt, 'Korte samenvatting van de gesprekken bij Spica in Napels op 17 en 18 mei 1962', Rotterdam, 28.05.1962, p. 1, HAR: AHK-1581.
39 Minutes Special Committee Meeting, re Rotterdam Group, 03.11.1961, supporting document 6560, HAL.
40 T. Drion, 'Ice Cream Italy', Rotterdam, 21.03.1962, HAR: AHK-6668.
41 Loopuyt 1962, p. 2.
42 Ibid.
43 A.L.A. van Unen, Cornetto Algida, Rotterdam, 10.01.1963, pp. 1-2, HAR: AHK-1581.
44 Letter from G. Hoekman and Mr J.H. Fransen van de Putte to De Nederlandsche Bank, Rotterdam, 02.05.1967, p. 2, HAR: AHK-1749.
45 Ibid.
46 'Projection Program Eldorado Wednesday 05.07.1967', HAR: AHK-1749.
47 'Minutes of meeting of the Special Committee held at S.p.A. SAGES, Rome, on 3rd, 4th & 5th June, 1974, with European Regional Management, No. X.972(a), 12.09.1974, p. 2, HAR: AHK-2225.

48 'Acquisition of Toseroni, an Ice Cream Business in Italy', Rotterdam, 29.05.1974, pp. 1-3, HAR: AHK-6162.
49 'Tanara', in L'Espresso, 27.04.1975, HAR: AHK-2044.
50 De Vecchi et al. 1990, p. 94.

Chapter 16 **France: Ice cream cuisine**
1 George Kent, 'Somewhere in France there is an industrial opportunity' in The Ice Cream Trade Journal, vol. 36, no. 2, January 1929.
2 Cathérine de Narbonne and Françoise Geoffroy, Chroniques des années fraîcheur. Gervais et Danone, Levallons-Perret 1997, p. 6.
3 Ibid., p. 27.
4 Ibid., p. 27.
5 Ibid., p. 27.
6 Ibid., p. 27 and p. 71.
7 Jean Garrigues, Miko. Le goût de l'entracte, Paris 1992, p. 10. 'Pasiego' is the Spanish term for a highlander of Valle del Pas.
8 Ibid., p. 20.
9 Ibid., p. 21.
10 Ibid., pp. 22-25.
11 Ibid., p. 33.
12 Ibid,. pp. 41-42.
13 Ibid., p. 43.
14 Ibid., p. 45.
15 Ibid., p. 50.
16 Ibid., p. 60.
17 Ibid., p. 52.
18 Ibid., p. 55.
19 Ibid., p. 63.
20 Ibid., p. 62.
21 Ibid., pp. 78-79.
22 Ibid., p. 83.
23 Ibid., pp. 89-90.
24 Ibid., p. 92.
25 Ibid., pp. 94-98.
26 Jean Nelissen, De bijbel van de Tour de France. De fabelachtige geschiedenis van de grootste wielerkoers ter wereld, Amsterdam 1998, p. 333.
27 Garrigues 1992, pp. 107-109.
28 Le nouvel économiste, 20.2.1987, p. 45.
29 Garrigues 1992, p. 112.
30 Le Glacier, September (?) 1984, p. 5.
31 Lehart Inc., 'Frigécrème, Société cremière Nantaise SA, St. Herblain', February 1975, pp. 1-3. Ca / Acquisitions / Frigécrème / Nouki / folder 1.
32 Ibid., p. 5.
33 Ibid., p. 10.
34 Le Glacier, 1973, p. 26.
35 'Note to Unilever Special Committee' from Frozen Products Co-ordination, 19.2.1985, p. 2 [no signature].
36 Letter from Unilever's Kees Huig to J.P. Erbé, 17.07.1984 [no signature].
37 'Minutes Unilever Special Committee Meetings, Rotterdam Group', 22.12.1958, HAL.
38 'France Ice-cream', 19.03.1963 [no signature].
39 'Unilever Special Committee', 25.03.1963, HAR: AHK-1580.
40 Interview by Pim Reinders with Kees Huig, The Hague, 02.05.1997.
41 'Ice Cream meeting Eldorado', Welwyn, 14th-15th July 1976, p. 1.
42 Ibid., p. 4.
43 Ibid., pp. 10 ff.
44 Patrick Morlet, International Ice Cream Meeting, Vlaardingen, 4th-5th August 1977. Glaces Eldorado, p. 18.
45 Ibid., p. 21.
46 Le Matin, 6 July 1977, p. 5.
47 Philippe Chapon in cooperation with Josseline Rigot, Le livre d'or de la glace, [Paris] 1998. Photos by Philippe Houzé, [p. 1].
48 Interview by Pim Reinders with Kees Huig, The Hague, 02.05.1997.
49 Chapon and Rigot 1998, [p. 1].
50 I.M.S. no. 21 Carte d'Or Case, Part 2. 12-

14 Oct. 1987., HAR, ICT, Box 10.
51 Ibid.
52 Ibid.
53 Figures derived from 'Le marché de la glace en France', a report dated 07.07.1997 by the Confédération Nationale des Glaciers de France [no signature].

Box: The Ortiz clan: from Basque farmer to French multinational
1 The facts on which this story is based are derived from: Jean Garrigues, Miko, Le goût de l'entracte, Paris 1992, and from Le glacier français, September, 1984.

Box: Carte d'Or: the quality of pureness
1 Philippe Chapon in cooperation with Josseline Rigot, Le livre d'or de la glace, [Paris] 1978, introduction.
2 I.M.S. no. 21. Carte d'Or Case, Parts 1 and 2. 12-14 October 1987, passim. The remainder of the text is also based on this. HAR, ICT, Box 10.

Chapter 17 **Spain: 'Por favor, un Frigo!'**
1 'Productos Frigo', Barcelona, 11.09.1962, p. 2, HAR: AHK-1765.
2 Luis Buñuel, Mijn laatste snik. Discrete Herinneringen, Amsterdam 1983, p. 13.
3 Helados. Alimento y placer todo el año, Asociación Española de Fabricantes de Helados, Mallorca 1996], p. 4.
4 Maria Pilar Martín Galilea, Helados, sorbetes y otras delicias, Madrid 1996, pp. 21-22.
5 Author's interview with Luis Fernando Garcia Duran, Frigo, Barcelona, September 1997. See also A. Deval, La Industria de los Helados, Barcelona 1948, p. 7.
6 Author's interview with Juan José Rimblas Rey, Madrid, September 1997.
7 Jorge Bordas, La historia de Frigo, p. 1.
8 Ibid.
9 Author's interview with Juan José Rimblas Rey, Madrid, September 1997.
10 'Hablamos con'. Marina Lahoz Serrano y Maria Guilleme Arellano', in Frigo revista trimestral, no. 2, June 1986, p. 6.
11 Ibid.
12 Ibid.
13 Letter from H.A. Bicker Caarten of Foods Committee to Mr C.H.C. Sunderman, 16.10.1961, p. 20, HAR: AHK-1601/4102523.
14 Archivo General de Protocolos de Madrid, Frigo Madrid, 25.01.1941, p. 2.
15 Author's interview with Juan José Rimblas Rey, Madrid, September 1997.
16 'Hablamos con'. Marina Lahoz Serrano y Maria Guilleme Arellano', in Frigo revista trimestral, no. 2, June 1986, p. 6.
17 Ibid., p. 7.
18 Ibid., p. 7.
19 'Productos Frigo', Barcelona, 11.09.1962, p. 2, HAR: AHK-1765.
20 Productos Frigo S.A., May 1952, Frigo Madrid.
21 Letter from H.A. Bicker Caarten of Foods Committee to Mr C.H.C. Sunderman, 16.10.1961, p. 2 HAR: AHK-1601/4102523.
22 Ibid., p. 2.
23 Author's interview with Juan José Rimblas Rey, Madrid, September 1997, and letter from H.A. Bicker Caarten of Foods Committee to Mr C.H.C. Sunderman, 16.10.1961, p. 14, HAR: AHK-1601/4102523.
24 Letter from H.A. Bicker Caarten of Foods Committee to Mr C.H.C. Sunderman, 16.10.1961, p. 15, HAR: AHK-1601/4102523.
25 Ibid., p. 15.
26 Author's interview with Juan José Rimblas Rey, Madrid, September 1997.
27 Ibid.
28 'Ice Cream Prospects in Spain', 02.09.1970, p. 1, HAR: AHK-1933/4102523.
29 Letter from H.A. Bicker Caarten of Foods Committee to Mr C.H.C. Sunderman, 16.10.1961, p. 1, HAR: AHK-1601/4102523.
30 'Spain Ice Cream', 02.10.1961, p. 8, HAR: AHK-1601.

31 Ibid., p. 8.
32 Ibid., p. 5.
33 'Ice Cream Prospects in Spain', 02.09.1970, p. 1, HAR: AHK-1933/4102523.
34 C.H.C. Sunderman, 'Proposal for the acquisition of the Spanish ice cream company Beretta S.A., Madrid', 11.12.1967, p. 4, HAR: AHK-1765-4102572.
35 'Spain Ice Cream', 02.10.1961, p. 9, HAR: AHK-1601.
36 'Request to open exploratory discussions on the possibility of acquisition of the Spanish ice cream group Frigo, Barcelona', Rotterdam, 17.07.1968, p. 1, HAR: AHK-1765.
37 'Ice Cream Study Spain', 21.09.1970, p. 5, HAR: AHK-1933/4102523.
38 C.H.C. Sunderman, 'Proposal for the acquisition of the Spanish ice cream company Beretta S.A., Madrid', 11.12.1967, p. 3, HAR: AHK-1765-4102572.
39 'Ice Cream Prospects in Spain', 02.09.1970, p. 3, HAR: AHK-1933/4102523.
40 'Ice Cream Prospects in Spain', 02.09.1970, p. 2, HAR: AHK-1933/4102523; for the recipe for Helado de Mantecado, see A. Deval, La Industria de los Helados, Barcelona 1948, p. 38.
41 Ibid., p. 4.
42 'Ice Cream Study Spain', 21.09.1970, p. 10, HAR: AHK-1933/4102523 and 'Ice Cream Prospects in Spain', 02.09.1970, pp. 1-4, HAR: AHK-1933/4102523.
43 'Spain Ice Cream', Foods II, 18.07.1968, p. 2, HAR: AHK-1735.
44 Ibid., p. 2.
45 'Minutes of meetings of the Unilever Special Committee held at Unilever España, Madrid, and Elida Gibbs, Talavera, on 26th/27th/28th November, 1979, with European Regional Management', no. X.1036, p. 1, HAR: AHK-2330.
46 'José Serratosa Puig', in Frigo Entrevista, no. 6, July 1987, p. 11.
47 Ibid., p. 11.
48 Answer to questionnaire Reinders Cultural History Projects, Short history of the Company, Nestlé, April 1998, HAR: ICT box 20, folder 7.

Chapter 18 **Latin America: overseas influences, local ingredients**
1 J. Estes, 'What is the foreign market?' in The Ice Cream Trade Journal, June 1927, p. 61.
2 M.G. de la Vara, Historia del Helado en México, Mexico 1989, p. 18.
3 Ibid., p. 14.
4 Sophie D. Coe and Michael D. Coe, The True History of Chocolate, London 1996, pp. 129-150.
5 M.G. de la Vara, Historia del Helado en México, Mexico 1989, p. 22.
6 Ibid., p. 20.
7 Ibid., p. 33.
8 Ibid., p. 20.
9 Ibid., p. 25.
10 Ibid., p. 41.
11 Ibid., p. 52.
12 Ibid., pp. 54-58.
13 Ibid., p. 58.
14 Ibid., p. 86.
15 Ibid., p. 90.
16 Ibid., p. 87.
17 Ibid., p. 96.
18 Ibid., pp. 112-115.
19 'Project Pedro', Mexico/Pedro 1992, proposal, 4th draft, HAR-AHK: 961320 (PEDR) 7900.
20 M.G. de la Vara, 1989, pp. 118-120.
21 Ibid., pp. 116-117.
22 Ibid., pp. 121-122.
23 Ibid., p. 108.
24 'Ice Cream Topics' in Ice and Cold Storage, August 1927, p. 215.
25 'Ice Cream in Panama' in The Ice Cream Trade Journal, April 1911, p. 52.
26 'Panama Railroad Operates Modern Ice Cream Plant in the Canal Zone' in The Ice Cream Review, June 1937, p. 26.

27 'La Fuente 50 Aòos' in Mi Fuente, No. 30, July 1991, p. 3.
28 Project 50 years of Kibon, Icone historisch onderzoek, Rio de Janeiro, [1992], p. 3.
29 Ibid., p. 3.
30 Xavier de Planhol, L'eau de neige, Paris 1995, p. 203.
31 Carlos Drummond de Andrade, 'Het ijsje', in Verhalen van een nieuweling, Amsterdam 1987, pp. 22-33.
32 Project 50 years of Kibon, [1992], p. 3.
33 Ibid., pp. 5-7.
34 Ibid., pp. 8-10.
35 'Preliminary report on the Brazilian Ice Cream Market', 17.09.1971, p. 1, in Industrias Gessy Lever, Ice Cream in Brazil, 27.09.1971, HAR-AHK: 1933.
36 Project 50 jaar Kibon, p. 11.
37 Ibid., p. 11.
38 'Brief for Brazilian Ice Cream Study', 11.01.1972, p. 2 (II), HAR-AHK: 1933-91502523.
39 'IJs op straat en thuis', 1972, p. 1, HAR-AHK: 1892.
40 'Extracts from the report The Brazilian Ice Cream Market', February 1972, p. 1, HAR-AHK: 1892.
41 Ibid., p. 28.
42 Ibid., p. 29.
43 Ibid., p. 2.
44 Ibid., p. 1.
45 Remmelt Otten, 'Braziliaanse zomer voor Unilever', in NRC Handelsblad, 04.02.1996.
46 Ibid.
47 'Unilever completes Purchase of Brazilian Ice Cream Business', url:http://www.businesswire.com, New York, 31.10.1997.
48 'Censydiam, Extracts of Market Research', January 1998, p. 20.
49 Ibid., p. 36.
50 'They're First in Argentina' in The Ice Cream Trade Journal, August 1926, pp. 45-46.
51 'Monthelado's History', fax message from Diego Montanara to Jean Callanan, Buenos Aires, 05.01.1998.
52 'Monthelado Ice Cream Market', Buenos Aires, 10.02.1998, p. 1.
53 'Uruguay Questionnaire Unilever Ice Cream History Project', 08.10.1997, pp. 1-2.
54 Manual de Cocina Criolla y Extranjera Dulces y Helados, Lima, circa 1930, p. 56.
55 Letter from Raul Marcenaro to Nestec Ltd., addressed to Mr Andrew T. Bradley, Nestlé, Geneva, 31.03.1998, pp. 1-2.
56 'Questionnaire Unilever Ice Cream History Project', Peru, 29.12.1997.
57 'Ice Cream Opportunities in Chile', Report on a visit 23rd February-6th March 1970 by J.J. Algra and B.F.P. Bona, p. 2, HAR: AHK 1933-91802523.

Chapter 19 **Asia: a flavour of the exotic**

1 Francis Macouin, 'Les glacières de pierre du Yongnam' in Culture Coréenne, no. 38, Paris 1994, p. 21. For the recipe see p. 22.
2 Unilever Beijing, e-mail 16.12.98.
3 Ice cream. A world survey, Euromonitor International, London 1998, p. 27.
4 Ibid., p. 22. The Asian countries covered by the study included: Indonesia, Malaysia, the Philippines, Singapore, South Korea, Taiwan, Thailand, China, Hong Kong, India, Vietnam, Bangladesh, Bhutan, Myanmar, Nepal, Sri Lanka and Pakistan.
5 'Teaching the Chinese to like Ice Cream' in Literary Digest, May 15, 1926.
6 Ibid.
7 Ibid.
8 Ice and Cold Storage, June 1926, p. 168.
9 Project 50 years of Kibon, Rio de Janeiro [1992], p. 4.
10 Mr. J.L. Heyworth's report on visit to China and Japan, January-February 1940, p. 31. HAR:DIR 18, folder 325.1.
11 Project 50 years of Kibon, Rio de Janeiro [1992], p. 4.
12 Research on Ice-cream Development in

China, Beijing, April 1998, pp. 11-12. Heyworth's Chinese study lists all the businesses mentioned here. For the British company it indicates the name Korde Dairy, but comments that the name is not correct because the English name is not given in the relevant source material. The firm of Geddes Trading & Dairy Farm was operating in Shanghai at that time. Its products included margarine, as did Henningsen's. (See Mr. J.L. Heyworth's report on visit to China and Japan, January-February 1940, p. 31. HAR:DIR 18, folder 325.1).
13 Mr. C.E. Tatlow's report of 1934, China – Ice Cream, Black Book no. BB 46, HAL. Black Book refers to the bundled documents that were selected by the staff of Charles Wilson for his book The History of Unilever, 1984 photomechanical reprint].
14 Minutes Special Committee, General Matters, 07-08.09.1932, no. E.87, HAL.
15 Ibid.
16 Minutes Special Committee, 22.06.1939, HAL.
17 Research on Ice-cream Development in China, Beijing, April 1998, p. 14.
18 Gallup survey, 1997.
19 Interview with Kees van der Graaf, 19.09.1996. In 1993 Van der Graaf handled the preparations for the establishment of Unilever's ice cream factory in Beijing.
20 John Rutledge, China Fancies Tasty Ice Cream, Foreign Agricultural Service, Guangzhou 1997, p. 1.
21 Unilever Beijing e-mail 16.12.98.
22 Le Glacier, Paris 1956, p. 32.
23 Ibid., pp. 65-66. 'dont la propreté corporelle est extrêmement douteuse'].
24 Ralph Pomeroy, The Ice Cream Connection, New York 1975, pp. 256-257.
25 Author's interview with Remo Bertorelli, London, 22.12.1997.
26 The Ice Cream Connection, p. 254, and interview with Remo Bertorelli, London, 22.12.1997.
27 Society, March 1983, p. 63.
28 Author's interview with Remo Bertorelli, London, 22.12.1997.
29 Ice cream. A world survey, Euromonitor International, London 1998, p. 46, table 3.4.
30 Ice Creams Barriers & Triggers in India, Bangalore 1996.
31 Hippocrates, Aër VIII 9-11. Aph. V 24.
32 Ice cream. A world survey, Euromonitor International, London 1998, p. 46, table 3.4.
33 Minutes Special Committee, 11.08.1959, HAL.
34 Minutes of meeting Overseas Committee/ Foods I + II Co-ordination, 07.04.1965, HAR: AHK-1736-0125.
35 Author's interview with Jan Dijkstra, 28.02.1997. Dijkstra worked in the ice cream industry in Thailand in the 1980s, first for Frico Domo and later for Unilever.
36 Minutes Overseas Committee, 19.12.1972, HAR: AHK 1492.
37 Minutes of meeting between Overseas Committee and Frozen Foods Co-ordination, 04.11.1982, HAR: AHK 2591-0125 OSC.
38 Memo R.J. Smith to Mr. C.J.A. Tieremans, 16.10.1985, HAR-ICG-33.
39 Ice cream – Indonesia, 17.02.1972, p. 6, HAR: AHK 1602-93102523.
40 Ice cream expansion, Foods II Co-ordination, London, 29.02.1972, HAR: AHK 1933-02523.
41 Ice cream – Indonesia, 17.02.1972, p. 6, HAR: AHK 1602-93102523.
42 Le Glacier, Paris 1954, pp. 27-29.
43 Ibid., p. 29.

Box: 1858: Yankee ice in Colombo

1 Karl von Scherzer, Reise der Oesterreichischen Fregatte Novara um die Erde in den Jahren 1857, 1958, 1859, Vienna 1864, p. 284.
2 Asantha Sirimanne, 'Cold war over ice cream' in Business, 22.06.1997
3 Ibid.
4 Visit to two local Ice Cream Manufacturers in Ceylon – 10.03.1960. HAL.

Chapter 20 **Japan: tradition meets high tech**

1 Toshihide Matsui, 'Ice Cream. Anew in Old Japan' in The Ice Cream Trade Journal, May 1926, p. 59.
2 Several Japanese books were used as sources for this chapter. The principal ones are [Ice Cream Book of the Japanese Association of Ice Cream Manufacturers], 1986, and [Ice Cream Book] published by Morinaga, Tokyo 1986. Extracts from these books were translated in two phases in March-May 1998 by Karin van Veldhuizen-Wanrooij and compiled in the form of two documents entitled 'Vertaling Japans Fase 1' and 'Vertaling Japans Fase 2' [Translation from Japanese, Phase 1 and Translation from Japanese, Phase 2]. References to the Japanese sources quoted relate to the page numbers in these translations. Translation from Japanese, Phase 2, Rotterdam 1998, p. 2.
3 Ibid., p. 2. One "horseload" of eight ice blocks was approximately equal to 216 litres. In the first and the last month of the six-month harvest period one such load was delivered each day. For those first and last months together, therefore, that meant a total of 60 deliveries. In the second and the penultimate months two deliveries per day were made, making a total of 120 trips. In the two middle months three horseloads came to the court each day: 180 deliveries. In total: 360 loads of 216 litres = 77,760 litres.
4 Ibid., p. 3.
5 Ibid., p. 4.
6 Ibid., p. 7.
7 Ibid., p. 7.
8 Ibid., p. 10.
9 Toshihide Matsui, 'Ice Cream. Anew in Old Japan' in The Ice Cream Trade Journal, May 1926, p. 58. The figures in the original article have been converted here into litres. In the article itself the figures are expressed in Japanese units [koku]. One koku, according to the article, is 47.6 gallons. One American gallon is equal to 3.785 litres. The 1883 production was 3,336.483 koku of milk; in 1893 it was 13,817.119 koku.
10 Translation from Japanese, Phase 2, p. 12.
11 Ibid., p. 32.
12 H. Ch. Gödeke, The World of Ice Cream. A report on Japan, Hamburg 1998, p. 17.
13 Translation from Japanese, Phase 1, p. 15.
14 Translation from Japanese, Phase 2, p. 22.
15 Translation from Japanese, Phase 1, p. 23.
16 'Japs Inspect American Ice and Ice Cream Industries' in Ice Cream Review, June 1923, p. 28.
17 Translation from Japanese, Phase 2, p. 30.
18 Translation from Japanese, Phase 1, p. 17.
19 S. Okimoto, 'The Dairy Industry of the Orient. Japan's Ice Cream Industry' in The Ice Cream Review, July 1924, p. 30.
20 Ibid., p. 30.
21 H. Ch. Gödeke, The World of Ice Cream. A report on Japan, Hamburg 1998, p. 16 and 26a.
22 Translation from Japanese, Phase 2, p. 21.
23 H. Ch. Gödeke, The World of Ice Cream. A report on Japan, Hamburg 1998, p. 15.
24 Translation from Japanese, Phase 2, p. 17.
25 'Naples au pays du Mikado' in Le Glacier, Paris 1954.
26 Brochure, Morinaga ... making a commitment to high quality foods, Tokyo, October 1985; Morinaga Annual Report 1996, Tokyo, October 1997; and H. Ch. Gödeke, The World of Ice Cream. A report on Japan, Hamburg 1998, p. 27.

27 List of delivered and ordered ice bar freezers types RIA 4 and RIA-6, Vojens, 09.1958, Archives Brødrene Gram, Vojens; and List of delivered and ordered ice bar freezers types RIA 4 and RIA-5-6-7, Vojens, 13.07.1965, Archives Brødrene Gram, Vojens.

28 For the 1972 figure see Katsuto Okada, The Ice Cream Industry in Japan, Tokyo 1972, p. 3, HAR: AHK-1933. For 1996, see H. Ch. Gödeke, The World of Ice Cream. A report on Japan, Hamburg 1998, p. 19.

29 H. Ch. Gödeke, The World of Ice Cream. A report on Japan, Hamburg 1998, p. 21. This figure is for both industrial and artisanal ice cream.

30 Katsuto Okada, The Ice Cream Industry in Japan, Tokyo 1972, p. 3 and p. 5, HAR: AHK-1933. In 1972 Okada was Managing Director of Morinaga Milk Industry Co. Ltd. and reported during the Sixth European Ice Cream Conference in Stockholm on developments in the Japanese ice cream industry.

31 Ibid., p. 2.

32 Ibid., p. 2.

33 Ibid., p. 13.

34 Translation from Japanese. Phase 1, p. 22.

35 H. Ch. Gödeke, The World of Ice Cream. A report on Japan, Hamburg 1998, p. 24.

36 'Ice cream venture in Japan', Hamburg/ Gloucester, 24.01.1972, HAR: AHK-1602, p. 11.

37 Gödeke 1998, p. 17.

38 Ibid., pp. 24-25.

39 Ibid., pp. 22-23.

40 Videotape 83/04/760 FP, Video Archives Unilever Corporate Centre, London.

Chapter 21 Modern times: the coming of the multinationals

1 'Minutes Special Committee Meetings, re General Matters', 07-08.09.1932, No. E.87, HAL.

2 'Minutes Special Committee', 22.06.1939, HAL.

3 Charles Wilson, Unilever 1945-1965. Challenge and Response in the Post-War Industrial Revolution, London 1968, p. 220.

4 'Minutes Overseas Committee', 07.06.1957, HAL.

5 'Minutes Special Committee Meetings Rotterdam Group', 29.10.1954, HAL.

6 'Minutes Special Committee re Food Matters Outside UK', 08.06.1955, HAL.

7 'Minutes Special Committee re Food Matters Outside UK', 11.10.1956, HAL.

8 Wilson 1968, p. 8.

9 'Minutes Special Committee', 17.01.1957, HAL.

10 'Food Study Group Report 1957-1958', London 1958, pp. 12-13, HAR: AHK-3109-2882.

11 Ibid., p. 46.

12 Ibid., p. 39.

13 Ibid., pp. 47-49.

14 'Minutes Special Committee re Food Matters Outside UK', 17.09.1958, HAL.

15 'Minutes Special Committee Meetings with Food Executive', 09.03.1959, HAL.

16 Wilson 1968, p. 41.

17 'Minutes Technical Conferences Ice Cream', 1958-1963, HAR: AHK

18 'Minutes of the International Ice Cream Meeting held in Rotterdam on 27th October 1961', p. 4, HAR: AHK-1678.

19 Ibid., p. 10.

20 'Memo Iglo/Tiefkühlgruppe to Mr. C.F. Sedcole', 19.06.1969, HAR: AHK-2096.

21 'Memo from Harold A. Hartog to G.D.A. Klijnstra', 12.05.1969, HAR: AHK-2096.

22 Author's interviews with H.F. van den Hoven, Johan Erbé and R.M. van der Meulen. Van den Hoven was Klijnstra's successor as Foods Coordinator and later became a member of the Special Committee. Erbé was also Coordinator in the 1970s and early 1980s and was later appointed to Unilever's Special Committee, while R.M.

van der Meulen as a member of the Coordination team. These three men were closely involved in the 1969 agreement with Nestlé and in interview underlined its strategic importance.

23 Jean Heer, Nestlé 125 Years 1866-1991, Vevey 1991, p. 254.

24 Ice Cream. A World Survey, Euromonitor Plc, 1998, London, p. 240.

25 Ibid., p. 240.

26 In 1957 showcards for the Wall's strawberry Magnum were distributed via sales depots.

27 'Magnum – Eine Marke erobert die Welt', Langnese, Hamburg 1997.

28 Ibid.

29 'Magnum presentation', Jean Callanan, 16.10.1996.

30 Ibid.

31 'Magnum Advertising Campaign Guidelines. Updated May '96', Lintas 1996.

32 Unilever Magazine, 1995, number 96, p. 15.

33 Ibid., p. 76.

34 'Magnum presentation', Jean Callanan, 16.10.1996. The commercial was screened in the months of June, July and September.

35 'Setting Corporate Growth Priorities', June 1993, ICT.

36 'Food Study Group Report 1957-1958', London 1958, p. 12, HAR: AHK-3109-2882.

37 Unilever Annual Review 1996, p. 27 and p. 50.

Box: Turkey: from serbet to dondurma

1 Xavier de Planhol, 1995, pp. 82-83.

2 'Les glaces dans la Turquie moderne' in Le glacier, 1954, p. 72.

3 The essence of ice cream. Turkey. Qualitative Research Report, Cram International, May 1995, Unilever Archives, Rotterdam – 702915.

Box: Cornetto: the success of an ice cream cone

1 Ir. J. Loopuyt, 'Korte samenvatting van de gesprekken bij Spica in Napels op 17 en 18 mei 1962', Rotterdam, 28.05.1962, p. 1, HAR: AHK-1581.

2 2nd International Ice Cream Meeting, Naples, September 1962, p. 2-iv, HAR: ICT, Box 22.

3 Ibid., p. 2-iv.

4 Ibid., p. 2-v. Spica's sales in those days mainly consisted of impulse ices.

5 B.M. Doouss, Cornetto Production – Italy, London 1963, p. 66. HAR: AHK: 170-doss. 487.

Box: Viennetta, 'a piece of lacework'

1 Interview by the author with Kevin Hillman, Rotterdam, 28 May 1998.

2 'Mille Feuilles. A Technical Progress Report', Gloucester, December 1981, p. 1.

3 Court of Appeal, The Hague, 4 June 1998, nr. 96/896.

4 Mille Feuilles, p. 6.

5 'Minutes of the Viennetta Workshop', 16.09.1987, Colworth House, p. 2, ICG-56-02523.

6 'Viennetta Meeting', 19.12.1986, ICG-56.

Box: The Strauss saga. The creation of a dairy and ice cream empire in Israel

1 The information about Strauss is largely based on the two-page document 'Strauss – a story of an industry and a family' by Iris Beck, Strauss Ice Cream Ltd., 05.07.1998.

2 The Ice Cream Trade Journal, February 1954, pp. 28-29 and p. 66.

3 Feldmans' Ice Cream started life in the Kapulsky coffee shop in Jerusalem in 1948. Fifty years later the family-owned business was producing an extensive range of ices under the Felco name in a modern ice cream factory in Rehovot. Source: www.doryanet. co.il/feldman.

Chapter 22 The evolution of ice cream: a summary

1 The underlying source references for the information in this chapter are generally given in previous chapters. Only where this does not apply has a separate reference source been included.

2 The framework for this chapter is based on the system applied by H. Baudet in his book Een vertrouwde wereld. 100 jaar innovatie in Nederland, Amsterdam 1984, pp. 143-151. Baudet distinguishes five stages in the innovation process. Briefly, these are: (1) the invention or development of a product; (2) its introduction on a limited scale; (3) its acceptance by a small but growing group of consumers; (4) its adoption, whereby the product becomes popularised on a wide scale and exchanges its novelty for familiarity; (5) the assimilation stage, in which the consumer can no longer do without the product.
My thanks go to Dr Thera Wijsenbeek of the Department of Socio-Economic History at the University of Amsterdam. She suggested the use of the above-mentioned innovation theory as a guiding principle for the research into the history of ice cream in the Netherlands. Students of Dr Wijsenbeek conducted that research work during the 1996-1997 academic year.

3 Pim Reinders and Thera Wijsenbeek, Koffie in Nederland, Vier eeuwen cultuurgeschiedenis, Zutphen 1994.

4 Baudet 1984, p. 143.

5 Ice Cream: A World Survey, Euromonitor, London 1998, pp. 37-38.

6 Ice Cream: A World Survey, 1998, p. 35. In Europe Italy is followed by Belgium, Germany and France. In these countries artisanal ice cream makers had a market share of 15%, 15% and 13% respectively in 1997. In global terms only China and Russia were ahead of Italy, with market shares of 46% and 68%. The percentages given here relate to sales by volume, not by value.

7 Assimilation is the term used by Baudet (1984) to describe this situation, i.e. the final stage in an innovation process (pp.143-141).

8 Ice Cream: A World Survey, 1998, p. 31.

9 Ice Cream: A World Survey, 1998, p. 16 and p. 22. In this report the following countries are classed as forming part of Asia: Indonesia, Malaysia, the Philippines, Singapore, South Korea, Taiwan, Thailand, China, Hong Kong, India, Vietnam, Bangladesh, Bhutan, Myanmar (Burma), Nepal, Sri Lanka and Pakistan.

10 Marcel Proust, À la recherche du temps perdu. Du côté de chez Swann. Combray [In Search of Lost Time, Volume I, Swann's Way. Combray], translated by C.K. Scott Moncrieff & Terence Kilmartin, revised by D.J. Enright, Vintage Books, London 1996, p. 38.

Bibliography

General
Journals
- Le Glacier, Paris 1948-1984
- The Ice Cream Trade Journal, 1906-1964
- The Ice Cream Review, 1916-1963

Books
- Arbuckle, W.S, Ice Cream, Connecticut, 1986
- David, Elizabeth, Harvest of the Cold Months. The social history of ice and ices, London 1994.
- Liddell, Caroline and Weir, Robin, Ices. The definitive guide, London 1995
- Planhol, Xavier de, L' eau de neige, Paris 1995
- Pomeroy, Ralph, The ice cream connection, New York 1975

Chapter 2 **From ice-water to water-ice**
Books
- Barra, Pierre, L'usage de la glace, de la neige et de l'eau, Lyon 1676
- Beaumon, Sylvia P., The ice-houses of Britain, London 1990
- Bolens, Lucie, Les sorbets Andalous (XIe - XIIIe siècles) ou conjurer la nostalgie par la doucer, Montréal 1992
- Boucher, Jacqueline, Société et mentalités autour Henri III, Lille 1977
- Dortous de Mairan, Jean Jacques, Dissertation sur la Glace, ou explication physique de la formation de la Glace et de ses divers Phénomènes, Bordeaux 1716
- Dubois, Claude-Gilbert [ed.], L'Isle des Hermaphrodites, Paris 1996
- Dubuisson, M., L'Art du Distillateur et marchand de liqueurs, considerées comme aliments médicamenteaux, Paris 1770, volume II
- Ellis, Monica, Ice and icehouses through the ages. With a Gazetteer for Hampshire, Southampton 1982
- Emery, D', Recueil de Curiositez Rares et Nouvelles, Paris 1674
- Emy, L'Art de Bien faire les Glaces d'Office, Paris, 1754
- Forbes, R.J., Studies in Ancient Technology, Vol. VI., Leiden 1966
- Hellmann, Ullrich, Künstliche Kälte. Die Geschichte der Kühlung im Haushalt, Berlin 1990
- Hinz, Walther, Islamische Masse und Gewichte, Leiden 1955
- Knecht, R.J., Catherine de' Medici, London and New York 1998
- Lespinasse, René de, Histoire générale de Paris. Les métiers de Paris. Collection de documents publiés sous les auspices de l'édité parisienne. Paris, volume I
- Menon, La Science du Maître d'Hôtel Confiseur, Paris, 1750
- Needham, Joseph, Science and Civilisation in China, Vol. V., Part 3, Cambridge 1976
- Réaumur, René-Antoine de, Sur les différents degrés de froid que l'on peut produire en mêlant de la glace avec différents sels...Histoire et Mémoires de l'Académie des Sciences, Paris,1734
- Reinders, Pim and Wijsenbeek, Thera, Koffie in Nederland. Vier eeuwen cultuurgeschiedenis, Zutphen 1994
- Reinink, A.W. and Vermeulen, J.G., IJskelders. Koeltechnieken van weleer, Nieuwkoop 1989
- Research on Ice-cream Development in China, Beijin, April 1998 [unpublished survey of Wall's China]
- Plank, Rudolf, Handbuch der Kältetechnik, Bd.I, Berlin 1954
- Stern, Radu [ed.], À manger des yeux. L'esthétique de la nourriture, Boudry-Neuchâtel 1988
- Waley, Arthur,The Book of Songs, London 1937
- Barbara Ketcham Wheaton, Savouring the past. French cuisine 1300 to 1789, 1988
- Wilkinson, Charles K., 'Water, ice, and glass' in The Metropolitan Museum of Art Bulletin
- Usaybi'a, Ibn Abi, Kitab Uyan al-Anba fi Tabqat al-Atibba, ed. August Müller, Cairo 1882 / Königsberg 1884
- Wood, Frances, Did Marco Polo go to China?, London 1995
- Young, G.F.,The Medici, New York 1933
- Zimara, Marco Antonio Problemata Aristoteles, Padua 1530

Chapter 3 **Ices for kings, emperors and admirals**
Journals
- Petits Propos Culinaires

Books
- Encyclopédie ou Dictionnaire raissonné, des sciences, des arts et des métiers. Recueil de Planches sur les sciences, volume III section confiseur, Paris 1754
- Audiger, N., La maison reglée et l'art de diriger la maison d'un grand seigneur et d'autres, tant à la ville qu' à la campagne.. avec la véritable méthode de faire toutes sortes d'essence, d'eaux et de liqueurs, fortes et refraîssantes à la mode d'Italie, Paris 1692
- Chaussin-Nogarey, Guy, La vie quotidienne des français sous Louis XV, Paris, 1994
- Félibien, André, Les Divertissements de Versaulines donnez par le roy à toute sa cour au retour de la conqueste de la Franche Comté en l'année M.DC.LXXIV, Paris 1676.
- Massialot, François, Nouvelles instructions pour les confitures, les liqueurs, et les fruits. Avec la manière de bien ordonner un dessert, & tout le reste qui est du devoir des maître d'Hotels, sommeliers, confiseurs, & autres officiers de bouche, Paris 1698, 2 ed.
- Prell, Heidemarie, Vom Gipfelschnee...zur frölichen Eiszeit. Siegeszug der faszinierenden Köstlichkeit Speiseeis. Vom Genuss- zum Nahrungsmittel, Neurenberg 1987
- Theunisz.,Joh.,'De receptie van Zijne Hoogheid Stadhouder Willem V in Zwolle op 30 augustus 1766', in Verslagen en mededeelingen van Overijsselsch Regt en Geschiedenis, Zwolle 1939 [55]
- Vié, Gérard and Noël, Marie-France, À la table des rois, Paris, 1993

Books about ceramics
- Arminjon, Catherine and Blondel, Nicole, Inventaire général des monuments et des richesses artistiques de la France. Principe d'analyse scientifique vocabulaire objets civils domestiques, Paris 1984
- Buten, D. and Claney, J.P., 18th century Wedgwood. A guide for collectors and connoisseurs, London 1980
- Brunet, M. and Préaud, T., Sèvres, Des origines à nos jours, Paris, Freibourg, 1978
- Buccino Grimaldi, L. and Cariello, R., Le porcellane europee nel Museo Correale in Sorrento. Cava dei terreni, 1978
- Carola-Perotti, A., Le porcellane dei Borbone di Napoli. Capodimonte e real fabbrica ferdinandea 1743-1806, Naples 1986
- Collard-Moniotte, D., Catalogue des faïences de Moustiers, Paris, 1988
- Dettweiler, S.G. , George Washington's Chinaware, New York 1982
- Eriksen, S. , Le porcellane francesi a Palazzo Pitti/French Porcelain in Palazzo Pitti, Florence, 1973
- Eriksen, S. and Bellaigue, G. de, Sèvres porcelain: Vincennes and Sèvres 1740-1800, London 1987
- Fritsche, C. and Stasch, G.K., Hochfürstlich Fuldische Porzellainmanufaktur 1764-1789
- Godden, G., Godden's guide to English porcelain, London 1978
- Godden, G.A., Chamberlain-Worcester porcelain 1788-1852, London 1982
- Grandjean, B.L, Kongelig Dansk Porcelain 1775-1884, Kopenhagen 1962
- Grandjean, B.L., Flora Danica Stellet/The Flora Danica service, Kopenhagen ed.1973
- Hantschmann, K. Nymphenburger Porzellan 1797 bis 1847. Geschichte, Modelle, Dekore, München/Berlin 1996
- Hürkey, E.J., Frankenthaler Porzellan aus den Sammlungen der Stadt Frankenthal und den Frankenthaler Altertumsvereins, 1990
- Köllmann, E., Berliner Porzellan 1763-1963, Braunschweig 1966 (2 volumes)
- Köllmann, E. and Jarchow, M., Berliner Porzellan, München 1987 (2 volumes)
- Raeburn, M., Voronikhina, L.N. and Nurnberg, A., The Green Frog Service, London 1995
- Reber, H., Hoechster Porzellan aus drei Jahrhunderten. Ausstellung zur Aspekten der Kunst-, Wirtschafts- und Sozialgeschichte, Hohenberg an der Eger 1988
- Reilly, R., Wedgwood pottery & porcelain. Collectors' guides, Volume I
- Savill, R., The Wallace Collection. Catalogue of Sèvres porcelain, London 1988 (3 volumes)
- Sandon, H., Flight and Barr Worcester Porcelain 1783-1840, Woodbridge 1978
- Schade, G. Berliner Porzellan: Zur Kunst und Kulturgeschichte der Berliner Porzellanmanufakturen im 18. und 19. Jahrhundert, Leipzig 1979
- Scherf, H. Thüringer Porzellan unter besonderer Berücksichtigung der Erzeugnisse des 18. und frühen 19. Jahrhunderts, Leipzig 1980
- Truman, C., The Sèvres Egyptian dinner service, Tunbridge Wells 1982
- Verlet, P., Sèvres, Le XVIIIe siècle, Paris 1953
- Weiz, Gustav, Het porseleinboek. De geschiedenis van stijlen en technieken. Met uitvoerig merkenregister, Baarn 1965
- Whiter, L., Spode. A history of the family. Factory and wares from 1733 to 1833, London 1970
- Williamson, G.C., The Imperial Russian Dinner Service, London 1909
- Winstone, H.V.F., Royal Copenhagen, London 1984
- Young, H., The Genius of Wedgwood, London 1995

Catalogues of ceramics exhibitions
- cat. Sèvres 1951, Les Grands Services de Sèvres, Paris 1951
- cat. Besançon 1957, Les Grand Services de Sèvres. Les Manufactures et Ateliers d'Art de l'Etat: Imprimerie nationale, Monnaies et Médailles, Sèvres, Besançon, 1957
- cat. Paris 1977, Porcelaines de Vincennes. Les origins de Sèvres, Paris 1977
- cat. Paris 1993, Versailles et les tables Royales en Europe XVIIème - XIXème siècles, Paris 1993
- cat. Hamburg 1993, Berliner Porzellan des 18. Jahrhunderts aus eigenen Beständen, Hamburg 1993
- cat Sèvres 1975, Porcelaines de Sèvres au XIXe siècle, Paris 1995
- cat. 1996 (ed. John Vrieze), Catherina, de keizerin en de kunsten. Uit de schatkamers van de Hermitage, Zwolle 1997

Chapter 4 **Ices from the dining-table to the street**
Journals
- Le Journal des confiseurs, Paris, 1890-1902
- Almanach des Gourmands, Paris, 1803-1811
- Confectioner's Union, London 1893
- Ice and cold storage, London 1920-1928

Books
- Artlett, Walter, 'Die deutsche Kochbuchliteratur des 19. Jahrhunderts', in Ernährung und Ernährungslehre in 19. Jahrhunderts, Göttingen 1976
- Barber, Peter and Jacomelli, Peter, Continental Taste. Ticinese emigrants and their Café-Restaurants in Britain 1847-1987, London 1997
- Bernier, Georges, Antonin Carème 1783-1833. La sensualité gourmande en Europe, Paris 1989

- Catalogue of A. Cadot, Paris [circa 1895]
- Catalogue of Letang Fils, Paris 1933
- Cooper Funderburg, Ann, Chocolate, Strawberry and Vanilla. A History of American Ice Cream, Bowling Green 1995
- A complete catalog of Metal Molds for Ice Cream and Display Models, Eppelsheimer & Co., New York, [ca. 1940]
- Dickson, Paul, The Great American Ice Cream Book, New York 1972
- MacDonogh, Giles, A palate in revolution. Grimod de La Reynière and the Almanach des Gourmands, London / New York 1987
- Escoffier, Auguste, Souvenirs inédits, 75 ans au service de l'art culinaire, Marseille 1985
- Garrigues, Jean, Miko. Le goût de l'entracte, Paris 1992
- Hall, Henry, The Ice Industry of the United States. Brief sketch of its history [before 1882]
- Hinnes, Mary Anne; Marshall, Gordon; Woys Weaver, William, The Larder Invaded. Reflections on Three Centuries of Philadelphia Food and Drink, Philadelphia 1987
- Ice Cream Moulds for Every Occasion, Krauss & Co., New York [ca. 1946]
- Jarrin, G.A, The Italian Confectioner or Complete Economy of Desserts, London 1829
- Kinross, Felicity, Coffee and ices. The story of Carlo Gatti in London, London, 1991
- Marshall, A.B., Fancy Ices, London 1894
- Marshall, A.B., Ices Plain and Fancy. The Book of Ices, Introduction and annotations by Barbara Ketcham Wheaton, z.pl. [New York] 1976
- Murphy, Agnes G., Melba. A Biography, New York 1909
- National Cookery Book, The, New York 1876
- Perini, Giacomo, Der Schweizerzuckerbäcker, Weimar 1858
- Ranhofer, Charles, The epicurean. A complete treatise of analytical and practical studies on the culinary art, including table and wine service, ... and a selection of interesting bills of fare of Delmonico's from 1862 to 1894, making a Franco-American culinary encyclopedia, New York 1971. [Fotomech. reprint. of the New York 1893 edition]
- Proctor, D.V. [ed.], Ice Carrying Trade at sea, London 1981
- Teuteberg, Hans. J., 'Geschichte der Kühl-und Gefriertechnik und Ihre Einfluss auf die Ernährung in Deutschland seit dem 19. Jahrhundert', in Ernährungsforschung, 1993, dl. 38
- Thévenot, Roger, A History of Refrigeration throughout the world, Paris 1979
- Sollers, Duvall, Those magnificent ice cream moulds, no place, no year
- Sollers, Duvall G. and Gauder, John P., Pewter Ice Cream Moulds, no place, no year
- Schwarz, Helmut, a.o, Unter Nul. Kunsteis, Kälte und Kultur, München 1991
- Sponza, L., Italian Immigrants in Nineteenth-century Britain. Realities and Images, Leicester 1988
- Weir, Robin, a.o, Mrs Marshall. The Greatest Victorian Ice Cream Maker , Otley 1998
- Weir, Robin, One Leg of a pair of drawers. The American Soda Fountain Lingo, London 1994
- Wiegelmann, Günter, 'Speiseeis in volktümlichen Festmahlzeiten' in Deutsche Lebensmittel-Rundschau, 60 jrg. Juli 1964, nr.7
- Williams, Susan, Savor Suppers and Fashionable Feasts. Dining in Victorian America, New York 1985

Chapter 5 **How ice cream became an American favourite**
Journals
- The Ice Cream Trade Journal, 1906-1964
- The Ice Cream Review, 1916-1963
- Ice Cream Field, 1930-1967

- Ice Cream Field and Trade Journal, 1967-1979
- Scientific American, 1879-1905
- Sunshine, weekly newsletter of Joe Lowe Co. in New York., 1924-1926

Books and reports
- The American Way. A History of the Breyer Ice Cream Company 1866-1946 [1946]
- Cooper Funderburg, Ann, Chocolate, Strawberry and Vanilla. A History of American Ice Cream, Bowling Green 1995
- Selitzer, Ralp, The dairy industry in America, New York 1976
- Smith, Wayne, Ice Cream Dippers, Walkersville 1986
- Tice, Patricia M., Ice Cream for All, Rochester 1990

Chapter 6 **Ice cream in post-war America**
Journals
- The Borden Eagle, January-February 1930
- Dairy Field, 1979-1991
- Dairy Field Today, 1990-1991
- Dairy and Ice Cream Field, 1969-1979
- Dairy Foods, 1986

Books and reports
- The Cone with the Curl on Top. Celebrating Fifty Years, 1940-1990, International Dairy Queen Inc., Minneapolis 1990
- Dreyer's History in the making, Dreyer's Inc., Oakland 1997
- Gazel, Neil R., Beatrice. From Buildup through Breakup, Urbana and Chicago 1990
- A History of Borden, Columbus 1992
- The Ice Cream World of Baskin-Robbins, New York 1975
- Lager, Fred, Ben & Jerry's: The Inside Scoop, New York 1994
- Larsen, Miriam C., The Midas Touch, Denison 1977
- The Frozen Novelties Market, Find/SVP, The Information Clearinghouse Inc., New York 1987
- Sherman, Steve, The Häagen-Dazs Book of Ice Cream, New York 1992
- Weaver, John D., Carnation. The First 75 Years 1899-1974, Los Angeles 1974

Chapter 7 **Australia: 'health, strength and happiness'**
Books and reports
- Hill, Debbie, The Australian Ice Cream and Frozen Confections Industry. Market Structure and the Demand Model, Canberra 1985
- Lang, W.R., James Harrison, pioneering genius, Newtown, Victoria, 1982
- Odell, Carol, Ice-creams, sorbets and frozen delights, Melbourne 1984
- 'The History of Peters Ice Cream' in: Heritage Australia, November 1995

Chapter 8 **United Kingdom: 'Stop me and buy one!'**
Journals
- Cold Storage and Produce Review, London
- Yearbooks Ice Cream Alliance, London 1951-1957
- Wall's Magazine, London 1948-1962
- The Wall's Reports, 1975-1988

Books and reports
- John Burnett, Plenty & Want. A social history of food in England. From 1815 to the present day, London 1989, 3rd.edition
- Ice Cream and Water Ices. A report on the Supply in the United Kingdom of Ice Cream and Water Ices, HMSO, London 1979
- Ice Cream. A report on the supply in the U.K. of ice cream for immediate consumption, HMSO, London 1994
- Forte, Charles, Forte. The autobiography of Charles Forte, London 1986
- Oddy, Derek and Miller, Derek, The Making of the British diet, London 1976
- Richardson, D.J., 'J. Lyons and Co. Ltd. : caterers and food manufacturers 1894-1939', pp. 164-165, in Sharpe, Len, The Lintas story, London 1964

Chapter 9 **Ireland: 'a brick after mass'**
Journals
- Hughes News, Dublin 1959-1966

Books and reports
- Reynolds, Brian, Casalattico and the Italian Community in Ireland, Dublin, 1993
- Power, Una, Terra Straniera. The Story of the Italians in Ireland, Dublin, 1988
- Doyle, Pat and Smith, Louis P.F, Milk to Market, Dublin 1989

Chapter 10 **The Danish technological revolution**
Journals
- Is-Konditori-Tidende, 1923-1940
- Dansk Flødeis, 1936-1940
- Dansk Bager-og Konditor-Tidende, 1917-1923
- Nordisk Mejeri-Tidsskrift, 1936
- Refrigram, Vojens 1945

Books and reports
- Frederiksen, Bødil, O.G. Høyer Maskinfabrik A/S 1948-1925, Århus, 1985. Unpublished thesis.
- Brødene Gram A/S 1901-1951, Vojens, 1951
- Hansen, Oluf S., Fremstilling af Flødeis, Copenhagen, 1949
- Salgsudviklingen for konsumis i de nordiske lande, 21.12.1995, Iskremindustriens Sammenslutning, (The Danish Ice Cream Association), Kopenhagen.

Chapter 11 **Sweden: Europe's ice cream champions**
Journals
- Glaciären, 1970-1984

Books
- Ernst Nathorst-Böös 'Glace', in Utdrag u Gastronomisk Kalender ,1969
- Stina Gottliebson, Arla 75 år 1915-1990, Stockholm, 1990
- Mats Wickman, Glassboken. Ett stycke glasshistoria, Stockholm, 1992

Chapter 12 **Germany: Goethe's passion lives on**
Journals
- Zeitschrift für Rahmeis, Hildesheim 1924
- Zeitschrift für Eiskrem, Hildesheim 1925-1926

Books and reports
- H. Prell, Von Gipfelschnee...zur fröhlichen Eiszeit, Nürnberg 1987
- C. Reinke-Kunze, Die PackElSwaffel. Von Gletschern, Schnee und Speiseeis. Basel 1996
- Unter Null: Kunsteis, Kälte und Kultur, München 1991
- Wir sind 25 Jahre jung! [Hamburg 1960]. Jubileebook of Langnese Eiskrem
- C. Wolkenstein, Die Marke Eskimo, graduation thesis, Institut für Werbung und Marktforschung, Vienna, June 1997

Chapter 13 **Ice cream in the Low Countries: the ijscoman cometh**
Journals
- De Conservator, 1949-1957

Books and reports
- Annual Reports of Consumer Products Inspectorate, Amsterdam 1921-1929
- Gentile, Raffael, La Pudici Italiane dei Liegesi, Liège 1986
- Jantje van Leyden, Eten en drinken in Amsterdam, Amsterdam 1898
- Machet, J.J., and Klett, J.G., De Fransche Parfumeur, leerende het bereiden van alle soorten van room of crèmes, ys, en alle bij de toilette gebruikt wordende poeders, pommade, blanketsel, waschwater, tandpoeder, tinctuur, opiaat, mondwater, enz., Amsterdam 1807
- Woldring, Josephine, (ed.), 60 jaar IJsfabriek Van Scheijndl, Apeldoorn 1995

Chapter 14 **Russia: a warm treat in a cold climate**
- G. Dezebt [Ice Cream], Moscow 1972

- A. Mikoyan [Food Industry in the USSR], Moscow 1939

Chapter 15 **Italy, the 'dolce' in La Dolce Vita**
- Favia, Felice, Trent'anni di gelato all'italiana 1953-1983, Milan 1983
- Portinari, Folco, Voglia di Gelato, Milan 1987
- Roversi, G., PINO Cinquant'anni di Gelato, Bologna 1987
- Vecchi, G. de, e.a., Trent'anni di Mostra Internazionale del Gelato 1959-1989, Longarone 1990

Chapter 16 **France: ice cream cuisine**
Journals
- Le Glacier, Paris 1948-1984
Books
- Chapon, Philippe and Rigot, Josseline, Le livre d'or de la glace, [Paris] 1998.
- Garrigues, Jean, Miko. Le goût de l'entracte, Paris 1992
- Narbonne, Cathérine de and Geoffroy, Françoise, Chroniques des années fraîcheur. Gervais et Danone, Levallons-Perret 1987

Chapter 17 **Spain: 'Por favor, un Frigo!'**
- Deval, A., La Industria de los Helados, Barcelona 1948
- Helados. Alimento y placer todo el año, Asociación Española de Fabricantes de Helados, Mallorca [1996]
- Pilar Martín Galilea, Maria, Helados, sorbetes y otras delicias, Madrid 1996

Chapter 18 **Latin America: overseas influences, local ingredients**
- Vara, M.G. de la, Historia del Helado en México, Mexico City 1989
- Project Kibon 50 years, Icone, Rio de Janeiro [1990]

Chapter 19 **Asia: a flavour of the exotic**
- Macouin, Francis, Les glacières de pierre du Yongnam', in Culture Coréenne, no.38, Paris 1994
- Research on Ice-cream Development in China, Beijing, April 1998 [unpublished survey of Wall's China]

Chapter 20 **Japan: tradition meets high tech**
- [Ice cream book of the Japanese Association of Ice Cream Manufacturers] Tokyo 1986
- Nakamura, H., [Ice cream book], published by Meiji, Tokyo 1986

Chapter 21 **Modern times: the coming of the multinationals**
- Heer, Jean, Nestlé 125 Years 1866-1991, Vevey 1991
- Unilever Annual Reports
- Wilson, Charles, Unilever 1945-1965. Challenge and Response in the Post-War Industrial Revolution, London 1968

Chapter 22 **The evolution of ice cream: a summary**
- Baudet, H., Een vertrouwde wereld. 100 jaar innovatie in Nederland, Amsterdam 1984

Notes, Bibliography, Indexes, Picture credits and Colophon

665

Tang dynasty, 36
Tatchell, T.W., 249
Tatlow, C.E., 560, 605
Testard, 60
Theobald, Earl of Carlingford, 314
Theocritus, 25
Thompson, Emery, 169, 275
Thompson, W.B., 249
Tidow, Juan, 555
Tiffany, 139, 141-143, 5
Tissain, 70
Tolstoy, Leo, 461
Tortolano, Vittorio, 591
Tortoni, 102
Tudor, Frederick, 109
Tuscany, Duke of, 91
Ude, Hinrich Friedrich, 393, 397
Uncle Sam, 147, 149, 207
Upton, Bertha, 326
Upton, Florence, 326-327
Valera, Éamon de, 324
Valvona, Antonio, 274, 431
Vélez, Gonzalo, 543
Verlaine, Paul, 50
Vestey, Edmund, 282
Vianen, Gerard, 507
Vigh-Larsen, Mogens, 622
Villafranca, Blas, 36-37, 631
Vogt, Clarence, 160, 197, 437, 634
Voltaire, 50, 62, 84
Vorst, Japie, 430
Wagner, Richard, 110
Walker, E., 169
Wall, Thomas, 274-276
Wanli, Yang, 36
Warncke Jr., Hans, 398
Warncke Sr., Hans, 398
Warncke, Werner, 17, 398, 404
Washington, George, 64-65
Wellington, Duke of, 88
Wiersma, P., 445
Wiesner, Alfredo, 473
Wild, David, 567
Wilhelm I, German Kaiser, 104, 106
William IV, Stadholder, 73
William V, Stadholder, 87
Willick, Max, 446, 624
Wimbrow, Dale, 181
Wit, J. de, 430
Wood, Frances, 17, 35
Woolworth, F.W., 319
Wortley Montagu, Mary, 55, 632
Yanagawa, Tosei, 583
Zhou dynasty, 24, 36
Zimara, Marco Antonio, 36
Zoetemelk, Joop, 503, 507

Index by institutional names

Adventures of Two Dutch Dolls and a Golliwogg, The, 324, 326
A & P, 21, 33, 52, 57, 62, 84, 179, 197, 248-249, 256, 261, 324-325, 440, 446, 520, 609-610, 617
A.B. Svenska Pressbyrån, 367
Abbotts Dairy, 174
Across the Table, 120
Adelaide Gallery, 126
Adelaide Milk Supply Co-operative Limited (Amscol), 256-257
Adventures of Popsicle Pete, 187
Affa, 366-367, 375
Aifel, 474
Akagi, 588
Alaska Ice, 367, 374, 378, 381, 607
Albert Heijn, 455
Alemagna, 423, 474, 476, 482-483
Alfa-Laval, 357
Alga (Associazione Latterie Gelaterie e Affini), 479
Algida, 195, 212, 288, 383, 463, 467, 473-474, 482, 487, 596, 607, 611-612, 614-615, 636
Allgemeine Lebensmittel-Betriebe Inh. Theo Schöller, 406
Allied Breweries, 225, 308
Allied Lyons, 225, 308
Allied-Domecq, 225
Almanach des Gourmands, 99, 101-102
Alnarps Mejeriinstitut, 368
Alnasa, 550-551, 612-613
Ambrix, 375
American Civil War, 116
American Declaration of Independence, 65, 169
American Eagle, 147
Lake Wenham Ice Company, 113
American Red Cross, 473-474, 636
Amerikansk Iskrem Fryseri A/S, 335
Amsterdamsche Melkinrichting, 437
Anderson Manufacturers Co., 182, 194, 236, 366
Antica Gelateria del Corso, 487
Arctic Bar, 560
Aerated Bread Company (ABC), 277
Argenis, 37
Arla Glass, 386
Art de la cuisine au XIXe siècle, L', 103
Art du Distillateur, L', 50
Artic, 212, 220, 446-447, 453, 624
ASEA, 377
Asian Delight, 558, 579
Associated British Cinemas (ABC), 292
Associated Confectioners of New York, 163
Astra, 377
Atatürk Orman Çiftligi, 607
Atlas Maskinfabrik, A/S, 345
Australian and New Zealand Army Corps (ANZAC), 255
Australian United Foods, 267
Avidesa, 515, 525, 527
Avis Rent-A-Car, 221
Ayer, 547
Bailey's Orginal Irish Cream, 233
Baked Alaska, 141
Bakkerij van Schaik, 430
Bakkerij Westerbos, 430
Bambino, 538-539
Barn, 384, 623
Baskin-Robbins, 208, 222-225, 239, 242, 463, 565
Bastian & Blessing, 401
Bauman, 355, 376
Beatle Nut, 224
Beatrice Creamery Co., 201, 207, 220
Beatrice Foods Co., 219
Beauchamp Bros., 256
Behrens, 363
Bell of Liberty, 147, 149
Bellevue Theatre, Amsterdam, 434
Ben & Jerry's, 6, 209, 231, 234-235, 242, 309, 457, 639
Benhill, 325
Bergendorfer Eisenwerk, 398
Bertorelli, 304
Bianca, 447, 453

Biene Maja, 406
Big Drum, 615
Bijenkorf, 435
'Bijko Speciale', 435
Bingrea, 559
Birds Eye, 307, 453
Birds Eye Wall's, 307
Blizzard, 223
Blue Bell, 208, 242-243
Blue Ribbon, 264
Bodley manuscript, 35
Bols Wessanen, 457
Bombe Uncle-Tum, 429
BonBon Company, 236
Bondeförbundet, 366
Book of Ices, 48, 84, 115, 588
Book of Songs, 24
Book of sorbets, 33, 115
Book of the Kings, 28
Boomy, 527
Borden Co. 163, 201-202, 208, 215-217, 219-221, 231, 239, 243, 351, 531, 538, 544, 555, 600
Borden Condensed Milk Company, 216
Borodino, 462-463
Bounty, 621
Bresler, 208, 231, 553, 555, 612
Breyers, 148, 166-167, 169-171, 174, 201, 203, 208, 220-221, 231, 233, 239, 241-242, 404, 498, 551, 612, 627
Breyers All Natural Brand, 241
Brieve e Nuovo Modo da farsi ogni sorte di Sorbette con facilità, 58
Grand Metropolitan Group, 233
British Oxygen Co., 278
Browns Velvet Ice Cream Co., 174
Brunch, 329
Bunge & Born, 550
Burger King, 233
Cadbury, 621
Cadbury's Caramel, 621
Cadot, 148
Café Zoppi, 103
Calippo, 483, 553, 596, 617
Callebaut, 233, 622
Camay, 515, 521
Campina (The Netherlands), 439, 456,
Campina Indonesia, 577
Camy, 521, 523, 525, 527, 613
Cannaméliste, Le, 59, 146, 151, 632
Cannes Advertising Film Festival, 306
Cánovas, 515
Capodimonte porcelain factory, 90
Caraco, 455, 612
Carlton Hotel, London, 110
Carnation, 201, 208, 219-220, 231, 236, 613
Carpigiani, 473, 479
Carte d'Or, 7, 386, 509-511, 613, 617
Carvel, 208
Cathay Pacific, 565
Cattabriga, 473, 479
Central Executive Committee of the Communist Party, 462
Ceylon Cold Stores, 564
Chamberlain, 70
Chelsea, 70, 196
Cherry Berry Swirls, 239
Cherry-Burrell, 197, 255-256, 356, 437, 567
Chesmensky Palace, 80
Chiavacci, 474, 476, 483, 612
Chicabon, 547, 549
Children's Day, 233, 598, 637
Chipwich, 236, 239
Chiquita, 239
Choco Taco, 240
Chocolate Eclairs, 239
Chocos Mio, 449
Cia U.S Harkson do Brasil Industrias Alimenticias, 545
Circulo do Commércio, 545
Ciro, 231
Citroën, 555
Clabir International Co., 241
Clarke Foods, 308-309
Cobi, 526
Coca-Cola, 239-240, 247, 560
Code Alimentar, 525
Colarena, 507
Cold Kombinat, 462
Cold Storage, 573, 576-577, 579, 605, 612

Picture credits

Colophon

Author: Pim Reinders,
The Hague, The Netherlands
Editor: Paul Jay, Cheltenham,
United Kingdom
Translation: Alan Hemingway,
Rotterdam, The Netherlands
Photo-research: Pim Reinders,
The Hague, The Netherlands
Photo organisation: Mariëtte van der
Elburg, Rotterdam, The Netherlands
Design: Mulder & van Meurs,
Amsterdam, The Netherlands
Printer: Snoeck Ducaju & Zoon,
Gent, Belgium
Lithographs: Snoeck Ducaju & Zoon,
Gent, Belgium
Binding: Troost Internationale
Boekbinderij, Turnhout, Belgium

ISBN 90.6496.162.X

628: The Good Humor Man was such a well-known figure that he featured as the main character in an issue from the famous series of Little Golden Books (New York, 1962).